Prehistoric Metal Artefacts from Italy (3500–720BC) in the British Museum

Anna Maria Bietti Sestieri and
Ellen Macnamara

with a scientific report by
Duncan Hook

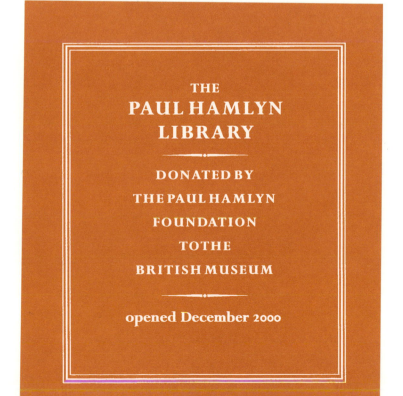

We dedicate this Catalogue to all the members of staff of the British Museum and of the British Museum Press, who have helped us so much in its preparation.

British Museum Research Publication Number 159

Publishers

The British Museum
Great Russell Street
London WC1B 3DG

Series Editor

Dr Josephine Turquet
Assistant Editor: Liesl Schapker

Distributors

The British Museum Press
46 Bloomsbury Street
London WC1B 3QQ

Prehistoric Metal Artefacts from Italy (3500–720BC) in the British Museum
Anna Maria Bietti Sestieri and Ellen Macnamara
with a scientific report by Duncan Hook
Front cover: short sword with ivory pommel, Final Bronze Age–Early Iron Age transition, cat. 226

ISBN 13: 978 086159 159 6
ISSN 1747-3640

Note: the British Museum Occasional Papers series is now entitled British Museum Research Publications. The OP series runs from 1 to 150, and the RP series, keeping the same ISBN preliminary numbers, begins at number 151; however the ISSN for the RP series has changed.

For a complete catalogue of the full range of OPs and RPs see the series website: www/the britishmuseum.ac.uk/researchpublications or write to:
Customer Services,
British Museum Press
38 Russell Square
London WC1B 3QQ
email: customerserivces@britishmuseum.co.uk

Printed and bound in the UK by 4-Print

Contents

Introduction

The original conception of this catalogue arose during the 1980s, when the Department of Greek and Roman Antiquities was beginning to plan the organization of a new gallery, to be entitled 'Italy before the Roman Empire'. In 1982, the British Museum invited scholars of all nations to come and study the early Italian collections within the Museum and to contribute to the Sixth British Museum Classical Colloquium. Anna Maria Bietti Sestieri was among the scholars who came from Italy; she researched the collections held by both the Department of Greek and Roman Antiquities and the Department of Prehistoric and Romano-British Antiquities and contributed an article entitled 'Italian swords and fibulae of the late Bronze and early Iron Ages' to the resulting colloquium publication, *Italian Iron Age Artefacts in the British Museum*, 1986, edited by Judith Swaddling. At the same time, Ellen Macnamara was familiarising herself with the collections as a consultant assisting Judith Swaddling with the preparation for the new permanent exhibition on 'Italy before the Roman Empire'. Thus both authors of the present catalogue recognized the number of Copper Age, Bronze Age and Early Iron Age objects of copper alloy of Italian origin in the collections of the British Museum, the vast majority of which were unpublished and forming a very considerable addition to the material already known to scholars. So, during the 1990s, having received permission from the Keepers of both Departments involved, the authors resolved to write this catalogue.

Over past years no general policy of demarcation, either by provenance, date or type, has existed concerning the Italian bronze objects held respectively in the Departments of Greek and Roman Antiquities (GR) and Prehistoric and Romano-British Antiquities (PRB), although a number of transfers between these Departments has taken place and all objects said to be from Greece are now in GR. Here it should be noted that, after the division of the general Department of Antiquities in 1866, GR became known by the name which it has to this day. In 1866, the Department of British and Medieval Antiquities was also formed and in 1969 this Department was divided, in part forming PRB. This Department is now incorporated into that of Prehistory and Europe but the PRB registration numbering is retained in this catalogue.

The authors, therefore, diligently searched the galleries and reserve collections of the GR and PRB Departments for all the copper or copper alloy objects which in their opinion were of Italian origin and to be dated before the end of the Italian Early Iron Age or towards the end of the 8th century BC, when the use of iron was becoming increasingly common for many forms. Many of the bronze objects were difficult to date with any precision and some, possibly of later date, have been included in this catalogue, as their form is known before the end of our period. Examples of several of the types of bronze object treated in this volume, but of somewhat later date, are well represented in the collections of the British Museum, but these objects must await a further catalogue.

The authors decided to omit from this catalogue the Sardinian bronze objects discussed in 1983 by Francesca Serra Ridgway in 'Nuraghic Bronzes in the British Museum' and those treated in 1984 by Ellen Macnamara, David Ridgway and Francesca Serra Ridgway in *The Bronze Hoard from S.Maria in Paulis, Sardinia* (see **Bibliography**). They have, however, included all the objects described by Bietti Sestieri in her article in *Italian Iron Age Artefacts* of 1986, mentioned above. With occasional exceptions, bronze needles, tweezers and fish-hooks have been omitted, as they so often are undatable. Some objects, mainly of bronze but including another material, glass, a precious metal or amber, have been included in this catalogue.

The authors agreed to order the catalogue under the major chronological periods, that is the Copper Age, followed by the Early, Middle, Recent and Final Bronze Age and Early Iron Age, the latter divided into two phases, Early Iron Age, Early, and Early Iron Age, Late (see **Chronology** below). The catalogue finishes with a short section on unclassified objects. Within these periods, the objects are ordered under their classification: for example axes, fibulae or swords, sometimes with an introduction to their form (see **Classification** below). The exceptions to this rule are, firstly, objects originally closely linked together, like the swords with their sheaths and the spearheads with their spear-butts, and, secondly, groups of objects probably once associated together in a hoard or grave group; the latter are listed in their groupings at the end of the text of the relevant period. The origin of the forms is not discussed. Each object has been given a catalogue number, which appears in the text and on the plates. All the objects are illustrated: those with a provenance or with decoration have been drawn and the others have been photographed. Unless otherwise noted on the plates, all objects are illustrated at half-scale.

Over 100 of objects were investigated in the Department of Scientific Research (now the Department of Conservation, Documentation and Science). These were selected by the authors in order to obtain significant information on chemical composition, alloys, technology and relative chronology of the artefacts, and to determine whether ancient smiths used differing alloys for the various parts of an object, for example the blade of a halberd as opposed to its associated rivets. We wanted to establish during which period of the Bronze Age, perhaps in the Middle or Recent Bronze Age, Italian bronze smiths achieved a constant ratio between copper and tin in the alloy. We wished to test the probability of the association between objects, which we believed once formed part of a hoard or grave group and we sought information concerning the methods of manufacture of some of the objects. Finally, we wished to demonstrate the genuine antiquity, or the lack of it, of parts of some objects in the collections and even of some of the objects themselves. The results of these investigations are set out by Duncan Hook in his report and summarized in the catalogue: all his analyses are mentioned under the individual entries of the objects, together with a reference to those previously carried out by Paul Craddock (see Craddock 1986).

Under each catalogue entry, after the registration number and collection or other source, all recorded provenances of the objects are stated as in the registration books with some corrections of the spelling of place names and their modern equivalents. When no provenance is given, either in the text or in the Plate captions, this is not known. We should add here that, when the provenances given in the registration books may be checked against current knowledge of bronze typologies relevant to the various Italian regions, these provenances carry conviction. The authors agreed to use Italian place names with some exceptions, when the name is so familiar in English that it seemed pedantic to use the Italian form: thus we have used Rome and Apulia. Elsewhere, we have used place names as they appear in the registration books, so we have written Corneto, followed by its modern form of Tarquinia in brackets. We have used modern Italian boundaries for the regions and it should be noted here that these do not always coincide with ancient borders; for example modern Lazio is considerably larger than ancient Latium, reaching north across the Tiber into territory which was once ancient Etruria. The catalogue numbers of all the objects with provenances in Italy mentioned in the text are to be found on the **maps**.

We include some notes on major collectors and collections (see **Collectors and Collections** below). We give separate concordances of the catalogue numbers in this volume with the registration number of PRB (**Concordance A**), those of GR (**Concordance B**) and with the numbering of H.B.Walters, *Catalogue of the Bronzes in the British Museum*, 1899 (**Concordance C**) (see **pp.333–336** below). The **Typological Table** (**pp. 337–342**) sets out in running order the catalogue number, the relevant Plate number, registration number and their types, as described in the catalogue (see below). The **Index of Types** gives a descriptive list of all the objects in the British Museum collection in alphabetical order, from Adzes, winged, to Vessel and lid, with their relevant catalogue number (see **pp.343** below). An **Index** of place names of the provenances or alleged provenance of objects given in the registration books is also included (see **pp.345–346** below).

The authors have used Arabic numerals in all references to figures and plates of published works with the exception of those books in which the numbering of the plates is differentiated by the use of both Roman and Arabic numerals in the same volume; in these cases we have followed the published form of the plate numbering. These books are: Montelius 1895–1910, Series A in Roman numerals, Series B in Arabic numerals; Johannowsky 1983; and *Pithekoussai* 1993.

The authors have tried to keep the use of abbreviations to a minimum, citing in full all titles of books, articles, journals and other works in the Bibliography, with the exception of *PBF* for the volumes of *Prähistorische Bronzefunde*. This abbreviation is also included in the text. The abbreviations PRB and GR have been mentioned above. We also use CA for the Copper Age, EBA for the early Bronze Age, MBA for the Middle Bronze Age, RBA for the Recent Bronze Age, FBA for the Final Bronze Age, and EIA for the Early Iron Age.

Acknowledgements

The authors acknowledge with gratitude the ever helpful encouragement and assistance they have received from so many of the staff of the British Museum. We owe our thanks to Brian Cook and Dyfri Williams, successively Keeper of GR, and to Ian Longworth, Timothy Potter and Caroline Malone, in turn Keeper of PRB, and also to Leslie Webster, Keeper of the Department of Prehistory and Europe.

We wish to record our deep appreciation of Judith Swaddling, Head of the Italian Collections of GR, who has given us so much support over the years, and also of Stuart Needham, the Curator of the Bronze Age collections in PRB. Other members of staff and the Museum Assistants of both Departments have helped us in every way; they include Donald Bailey, Lloyd Gallimore, Kim Overend, Clare Pickersgill, Neil Adams, Ray Waters, Anthony Spence, Pam Young, Keith Lowe, Renee Pfister,Tim Chamberlain, Marion Vian and Kate Down. P.H. Nichols was responsible for the excellent photographs of the GR collection and Sandra Marshall for those of PRB. The drawn illustrations of GR objects were by Anna Maria Bietti Sestieri, Susan Bird, Candida Lonsdale and Kate Morton and those of the PRB collection were by Anna Maria Bietti Sestieri and Nick Griffiths with Karen Hughes. We would like to record our gratitude to Yasmeen Al-Hamar and Cindy Forest-Young for their assistance in making up the plates for this catalogue and especially to Kate Morton for her immense help in providing and organizing the illustrations. We wish to thank them all for their expertise and care.

We also wish to thank Sheridan Bowman, Keeper of the Department of Conservation, Documentation and Science, her successor as Keeper, David Saunders, and Paul Craddock of the same department, as well as Duncan Hook for his close co-operation and contribution to this volume.

We wish to thank Judith Toms for her help in setting up our computer programme, Fiona Campbell for her invaluable help in many ways, especially in checking and emending the text, John Wilkins for his able assistance in solving many of the problems with our computers and Fulvia Lo Schiavo for her kind permission to read her forthcoming *PBF* volume on the fibulae of southern Italy before its publication. Finally we are grateful to Mark Pearce for reading the manuscript and for his helpful comments and suggestions, and to Josephine Turquet, series Editor for the British Museum Research Publications, who saw the volume through to publication.

Notes on the Collectors and their Collections

For general histories of the British Museum and its collections, see Miller 1973 and Wilson 2002. Here, there follow brief notes on some of the major collectors and collections which are represented in this catalogue.

Miss M.H.M. Auldjo was niece of John Auldjo, a famous mountaineer and geologist, who lived in Naples during the early 19th century and who amassed a collection of antiquities. Miss Auldjo lived in Naples for a short time and also formed a collection of antiquities, largely from Campania, which she bequeathed to the British Museum in 1859.

The Avebury Collection was acquired by Sir John Lubbock (1834–1913), who was created Lord Avebury in 1900. A banker by profession, he also served as a Member of Parliament, President of the Society of Antiquaries and a Trustee of the British Museum. He was a very distinguished man of science, antiquarian and author; he conducted excavations at Hallstatt in Austria and visited Italy, including Naples. At his death, his collection of antiquities passed to his son, the second Lord Avebury, who presented them to the British Museum in 1916.

The Blacas Collection was formed by two successive Ducs de Blacas. The elder was French Ambassador at Rome and Naples during the early 19th century and his son added to the collection after the death of his father. He directed that, after his death, the entire collection should be sold and it was bought by the British Museum in 1866.

Carlo Campanari was a member of the Campanari family of Tuscania, who excavated widely in southern Etruria during the early 19th century. They acquired a large collection of Etruscan antiquities, which they exhibited in a museum at Tuscania. In 1838 Carlo Campanari brought an exhibition of Etruscan and other Italian objects to London. Subsequently many of these objects were bought by the British Museum. There were further purchases from Campanari during the following years.

Alessandro Castellani (1823–83) was the eldest son of Fortunato Castellani, a jeweller and dealer in antiquities in Rome, who founded a school where young goldsmiths could learn the methods and styles of antiquity. Alessandro was exiled from the Papal states in 1860 and opened a branch of the family business in Paris; later he transferred his commercial and antiquarian activities to Naples.

The Reverend Greville J. Chester (1830–1892) was a clergyman, who served in several English parishes until 1865 when ill health caused him to retire. Subsequently he spent many winters abroad, travelling widely in southern Europe, Egypt, Palestine and Syria. A man of wide interests and knowledge, during his travels he acquired many antiquities and was held in great respect both by local dealers and by other contemporary collectors, archaeologists and museum curators. On his return to England, he would sell or present his antiquities to museums, including the British Museum, the Victoria & Albert Museum, London, the Ashmolean Museum, Oxford, and the Fitzwilliam Museum, Cambridge, as well as to the Reverend William Greenwell (see Seidman 2007).

Henry Christy (1810–1865) was a wealthy banker who traveled widely and collected ethnographic material as well as prehistoric artefacts. He bequeathed his collection to trustees, one of whom was Sir Augustus W. Franks, who were empowered to present it to a permanent institution. He also left a fund to the trustees so that the collection might be further augmented. The Christy Trustees presented the collection to the British Museum in 1865 and subsequently used the Christy Fund to purchase and donate further objects.

Sir Augustus W. Franks (1826–1897) was appointed an Assistant in the Department of Antiquities of the British Museum in 1851 with the principal charge to build up the British collections. In 1866 he became the first Keeper of the new Department of British and Medieval Antiquities and served until he retired in 1896. A scholar of international reputation, Franks travelled widely in Britain and Europe, visiting Italy in 1857: he was present at many international conferences and visited many exhibitions, private and public collections and museums, often acquiring objects both for the British Museum and his own private collection. A wealthy man, in all he donated some 7,000 objects to the Museum, which covered a great diversity of material; most of the objects he gave to his own Department but he also made donations to the Departments of Coins and Medals, Egyptian Antiquities and Greek and Roman Antiquities. Franks was knighted in 1894. For further information on the life and work of Sir Augustus Franks, see Caygill and Cherry (eds) 1997.

The Reverend William Greenwell (1820–1918) was a noted antiquarian of the late 19th century. He was a Canon of Durham Cathedral from 1854 to 1907 and excavated widely in the north of England and also collected British antiquities. He presented his collection of pottery and flints to the British Museum in 1897. He also acquired a large collection of bronze objects from Europe and beyond, both by gift and by purchase; he sold this collection to the American banker and philanthropist, J.Pierpont Morgan (1837–1913), who presented it to the British Museum in 1909. Greenwell's manuscript notes with careful descriptions of the bronze objects in his collection, often recording their provenances and associations, together with his sources, are in PRB and are followed in this catalogue.

Sir William Hamilton (1730–1803), collector of fine art, vulcanologist and connoisseur of antiquities, was appointed Envoy Extraordinary or British Minister to the Court of Naples in 1764, a post he fulfilled for some 36 years until 1800. In Naples, he immediately started to collect Greek vases and other antiquities, which he acquired mainly from Neapolitan collectors and antique dealers but also sometimes from current excavations or on his travels in southern Italy. In 1772 he was in England and his collection was bought by the British Museum;

subsquently Sir William donated some objects to the Museum. In 1778, the so-called Baron d'Hancarville wrote a manuscript description of the objects exhibited in the Museum, including some not from the Hamilton collection. The Register of GR for 1772, probably written towards the end of the 19th century, was based on d'Hancarville's description, though by this time some of the objects had lost their Hamilton connection and must be among those 'Found unregistered' in 1975. Thus the complete inventory of the 1772 Hamilton collection lacks clarity but from the internal evidence of the early bronze objects, it may be said that those registered under the Hamilton collection of 1772 are mainly of Early Iron Age date and from Campania. For further information on Sir William Hamilton and his collections, see Fothergill 1969, Jenkins and Sloan (eds.) 1996 and Burn (ed.) 1997.

Richard Payne Knight (1751–1824) was a wealthy connoisseur, who during the later 18th and early 19th centuries assembled a large collection of antiquities, which he acquired from dealers in Italy and from other contemporary collectors. He often concentrated upon objects of bronze. He travelled in Italy, was a friend of Charles Townley and a friend and correspondent of Sir William Hamilton, in 1793 buying over 100 bronze objects from him. Knight's manuscript inventory of his collection is preserved in GR and his numbering was used when, in 1973, his collection was registered under the year 1824. In this registration, Knight's Arabic chapter headings were transposed to Roman numerals, followed by his numbering within each chapter, and thus do not indicate the month and day of registration, plus item number within their entry, as GR registration numbers normally do. Unfortunately, Knight seldom recorded details concerning small bronze objects within his collection, such as fibulae or bracelets, but these must have come from sources similar to those of the Hamilton collection.

The Meyrick Collection was formed by Sir Samuel R. Meyrick (1783–1848), a lawyer and antiquary. The collection was chiefly composed of arms and armour, upon which Sir Samuel was a leading authority, and of medieval works of art. Sir Samuel bequeathed his collection to his cousin, then Captain A.W.H. Meyrick; much of the collection was exhibited in the South Kensington Museum (now the Victoria & Albert Museum) between 1866 and 1871. Part of the collection was sold in 1871 and in 1878, Major General A.W.H. Meyrick presented many of the remaining objects to the British Museum.

General A.H. Lane Fox Pitt Rivers (1827–1900) was a soldier and a renowned archaeologist of the late 19th century, who amassed great ethnographical and archaeological collections. In 1880, he inherited the Pitt Rivers estate in Dorset; he became a wealthy man and changed his name from Lane Fox to Pitt Rivers in honour of his benefactor. In 1884, he gave his first collection to the University of Oxford, withholding some objects, which he exhibited in a private Museum at Farnham, together with new purchases and objects from his own excavations in Dorset. The Museum at Farnham remained open until 1966 but subsequently its contents were sold, some being bought by the British Museum.

The Honourable Sir William Temple (1788–1856), brother of the Third Viscount Palmerston, was British Minister at Naples from 1833 to 1855. He formed a large collection of antiquities from southern Italy, which is recorded in the manuscript of R. Gargiulo, now in the archives of GR. Gargiulo noted the provenance of many of the objects but none of their associations. At his death, Sir William bequeathed his collection to the British Museum.

Charles Townley (1737–1805) is chiefly remembered as a wealthy and knowledgeable collector of marble classical sculpture, which he mainly acquired in Rome and its neighbourhood during the later 18th century. A friend of Sir William Hamilton, he traveled in Italy, visiting Naples, Sicily and Apulia. He bequeathed his collections to his family who subsequently sold them to the British Museum; his collection of marble sculpture was bought in 1805 and his 'second collection' in 1814, which included the bronze objects described in this catalogue and which Townley probably acquired from sources similar to those of the Hamilton collection. Though no complete contemporary inventory of the bronze objects of the 'second collection' exists, some were recorded in a manuscript inventory of the second Townley collection and given serial numbering. In 1971, an attempt was made to complete the GR Register of the collection, using the contemporary serial numbering, where extant, and adding objects known to have been included in the collection. For further information on the Townley collections see Cook 1985; Jenkins and Sloan 1996; Hill 2001.

Sir Henry Wellcome (1853–1936) started to assemble his vast collection at the beginning of the 20th century, intending it to form the basis for a Museum of Mankind. He employed agents to buy objects from dealers in Britain and abroad; these agents often recorded the dealers name and place of purchase, together with the provenance of the object, as provided by the dealer. At Sir Henry's death, the Trustees of the Wellcome Foundation abandoned the project for a Museum of Mankind and dispersed the collections, said to include over half a million objects. The British Museum received donations from the Wellcome Trustees, the first in 1966 and another in 1982; all those in PRB are registered under 1964.12-1 followed by their current numbering (in this catalogue, we have included in brackets after this the former PRB numbering) and those in GR were included in the registrations for the years 1975 and 1982. The inventory numbering of the whole Wellcome Collection is hard to follow, since it had four numerical sequences, two sets with A or accesssion numbers and others with registration or R numbers or R-year numbers. In this catalogue, the Wellcome accession number is recorded, when available; sometimes further Wellcome numbers are also noted.

Classification

The 800-plus copper and bronze Italian objects in the Departments of Greek and Roman Antiquities, and Prehistory and Europe, of the British Museum constitute a unique sample, comprising a large percentage of the groups, categories and types of artefacts at present known, dating from the Copper Age to the Early Iron Age. In good agreement with the chronological trend of the Italian metal industry, the number of metal objects as well as the variety of functional groups (tools, ornaments and weapons), and of categories and types within each group, grows fairly systematically with time, though EBA pieces are more numerous than MBA ones. Moreover, this sample includes a few entirely new types, and several groups of associated artefacts from single hoards and burials.

Information on the provenance has been preserved for 289 pieces, i.e. 34.5% of the total of 837.

Provenances of the BM metal artefacts by present Italian regions and European countries

	CA	EBA	MBA	RBA	FBA	EIA, ea.	EIA, late	Unclass.
Friuli V. Giulia							1	
Veneto			1	4			1	
Lombardy	1	1	2		5			1
Val d'Aosta								1
Liguria							1	
Emilia Romagna		1		2		2	3	
Marche				1				
Umbria	4	8	1	1	4	2	8	2
Tuscany		1		1	3	2	10	
Lazio	1	4	3	1	3	14	10	2
Abruzzo	1	1	2	2	5	8	2	
Campania	4	4	1	1	6	23	18	2
Apulia	1				1	8	5	
Basilicata				2	1	4	2	
Calabria					2	2	5	
Sicily		5	1	1?	7	4	1	
Sardinia					1			
UK				4	1	2	8	
France					1		2	
Germany						1		
Switzerland						1		
Slovakia							1	
Austria				1	1	1	2	
Hungary							2	
Slovenia							1	
Croatia			1					
Serbia						1		
Albania				1				
Greece		1		1	2	3	3	

N.B. General indications of provenance (e.g. 'Magna Graecia', 165; 'Etruria', 270, 528) are not included in the table.

Some of the high number of pieces for which the only information now available is 'Found unregistered' may have originally been linked to provenances which were either not passed on to the British Museum, or which have been lost because there is insufficient means of identifying the pieces with earlier brief inventory entries.

As is shown by the table above, some regions of northern Italy, Friuli Venezia Giulia, Val d'Aosta and Liguria, as well as Marche in central Italy and Sardinia, are only represented by single pieces. Six to ten pieces are recorded from each of Lombardy and Emilia Romagna (northern Italy), Basilicata and Calabria (southern Italy). The main concentration of provenanced pieces is in Campania, with a total of 59, and there are also relatively high numbers from Lazio, 38, Umbria, 30, Abruzzo, 21, Tuscany, 17, all in central Italy, and from Apulia, 15, and Sicily, 19, in the south.

However, this distribution over the present Italian territory depends mainly on the overall trends in the activity of both British collectors and Italian antique dealers between the end of the 18th and the early decades of the 20th century, as is shown in detail in the section relative to the BM collections. Quite probably, the relatively high number of pieces from Campania depends basically on Sir William Hamilton's early collecting activity in this region, and on the fact that 19th-century collectors, such as R. Payne Knight, bought parts of his collection.

However, it is useful to remember that the great majority of provenanced pieces belongs to categories and types that correspond rather precisely to the local (regional) repertoires. Obviously this can be considered as an indication of the reliability of the provenances that have been recorded.

A few pieces, 42 in all, also come from other European countries, including England, France, Germany, Slovakia, Switzerland, Austria, Hungary, Slovenia, Croatia, Serbia, Albania and Greece.

As far as the sample's documentary relevance is concerned, although some Italian regions are scarcely represented, others, such as, mainly, Campania, have a significant number of types not previously documented. Another important point is the occurrence of a number of groups of associated artefacts, for many of which the provenance is also registered. These include at least six hoards or parts of hoards, dating from the CA to EIA, late, and several groups of ornaments and weapons from burials, mostly of EIA date.

Most of the bronzes which constitute the British Museum's collection of early Italian antiquities were not finds from systematic excavations, and were probably gathered with the intention of sale to collectors. Several pieces are indeed of outstanding quality and state of preservation: see for example the short sword with ivory pommel and hilt-plates, **cat. 226**, the group of weapons from Cassino, **cat. 457–459**, and the two oversize parade spearheads from Bomarzo, **cat. 799–800**.

In other words, the sample provides a valuable illustration of the development of the Italian metal industry, as well as contributing several important additions to its knowledge. In order to make these two features easily perceptible, we decided to present all the artefacts in classified form, either in relation to the current typological conventions, or according to our own, and to organize the catalogue by chronological sections.

As is well known, the Italian metal industry has been intensely studied and classified in the last decades. Chrono-typological classifications represent the most frequent approach in this field of research, whereas compositional and provenance analyses, and technical-functional studies have been carried out rather sporadically.

A relatively high percentage of the BM pieces can be classified according to the *Prähistorische Bronzefunde* (hereafter *PBF*) Italian series, which includes the following groups: horse-bits (*PBF* XVI. 1, 1969, by F-W. von Hase); swords and sword-sheaths (*PBF* IV. 1, 1970, by V. Bianco Peroni); pins (*PBF* XIII. 2, 1975, by G.L. Carancini); knives (*PBF* VII. 2, 1976, by V. Bianco Peroni); fibulae from northern Italy (*PBF* XIV. 5, 1976, by P. von Eles Masi); razors (*PBF* VIII. 2, 1979, by V. Bianco Peroni); FBA and EIA axes (*PBF* IX. 12, 1984, by G.L. Carancini); daggers and halberds (*PBF* VI. 10, 1994, by V. Bianco Peroni); armour plates (*PBF* III. 3, 2000, by G. Tomedi); miscellaneous objects (*PBF* XX. 1, 1974, edited by H. Müller-Karpe). The volume devoted to the south Italian and Sicilian fibulae, by F. Lo Schiavo, is due to appear shortly (*PBF* XIV, forthcoming).

However, several groups of objects which are more or less widely represented in the BM sample, e.g. spearheads, CA, EBA, MBA, RBA and the majority of FBA axes, tools, personal ornaments, bracelets, and the fibulae from central Italy have only been classified in very general works (for example, Carancini and Peroni 1999) and in regional or contextual studies. Among the regional classifications which have been used in our catalogue, it is worth mentioning the works by R.M. Albanese Procelli on Sicily (Albanese Procelli 1993), by G.L. Carancini on central and southern Italy (Carancini 1991–92, 1993, 1999), and by R. De Marinis on the early metallurgy of northern Italy (De Marinis 1992, 1998). As regards contextual studies, recent complete editions of IA cemeteries, that have been especially useful for the typological definition and relative chronology of some important groups of bronzes, such as fibulae and weapons, are quoted in the bibliography by site name and year of publication. These are Veii Quattro Fontanili, published by many authors in *Notizie Scavi* between the years 1963 and 1976, and the relative chronology by J. Toms published in 1986 (*Quattro Fontanili* 1963, 1965, 1967, 1970, 1972, 1975, 1976, 1986); the cemeteries of Pontecagnano, by B. D'Agostino and P. Gastaldi (*Pontecagnano* 1988), S. De Natale (*Pontecagnano* 1992) and T. Cinquantaquattro (*Pontecagnano* 2001); the study of the Latial cemetery of Osteria dell'Osa by A.M. Bietti Sestieri (*Osteria dell'Osa* 1992); the Greek cemetery of ancient Ischia, by G. Buchner and D. Ridgway (*Pithekoussai* 1993), and the new study by M. Pacciarelli of the cemetery of Torre Galli, Calabria, which had been originally published by Paolo Orsi (*Torre Galli* 1999). Specific references to these complexes are given among the typological and chronological parallels in the individual catalogue entries.

Based on a sample of 20 pieces from the collection of the Ashmolean Museum, a study of the main technological and typological features of Italian Early Iron Age fibulae has been published recently by J. Toms (Toms 2000).

An early series of analyses of metal artefacts from Italian CA burials was carried out within the research programme of the Arbeitsgemeinschaft für Metallurgie des Altertums in Stuttgart (Otto and Witter 1952; Junghans, Sangmeister and Schröder 1960). The analyses resulting from this work have been reconsidered by G. Barker in his paper on the CA and BA metal artefacts in the Pigorini Museum in Rome (Barker 1971), which includes new analyses by E. Slater, of the Department of Metallurgy and Materials Science, Cambridge University.

A number of Italian and Sardinian bronzes in the BM collections, including some pieces described in this catalogue, have been analysed by P. Craddock (1986).

Recently, a new consistent series of analyses, both destructive and non-destructive (XRF), has been carried out, especially in the context of regional studies or of research concerning single archaeological complexes. Some of these works have appeared in the proceedings of specific conferences: see for example Antonacci Sanpaolo 1992, Piola Caselli and Piana Agostinetti 1996.

As regards regional studies, a significant sample of the north Italian MBA and RBA bronze artefacts has been analyzed by metallographic and AAS techniques on the occasion of the *Terramare* exhibition, held in Modena in 1997 (Garagnani, Imbeni and Martini 1997). The most complete programme of analyses on a regional scale has been carried out in Sardinia by F. Lo Schiavo and other scholars (Lo Schiavo 1996, 1997; Lo Schiavo, ed., forthcoming; Giardino and Lo Schiavo, forthcoming).

Recently published studies include XRF and non-destructive metallographic analyses of the metal artefacts of the CA south Italian Gaudo culture (Giardino 2000); the most significant result is the comparatively frequent use of arsenical copper, whereas in contemporary Rinaldone contexts of central Italy the great majority of artefacts is made of pure copper. Bietti Sestieri *et al.* 2003 is a preliminary report of a programme of XRF analyses of different classes of artefact from the hoard of San Francesco, Bologna, Emilia Romagna.

Another interesting work (Caneva, Giardino and Guida 2003) is a comparative evaluation of the results of different analytical techniques (XRF, SEM and ICP) applied to the artefacts from the Sicilian IA hoard of Polizzello.

Some recent works, usually also on a regional or supra-regional scale, are concerned with the collection and systematization of existing analyses. Among them are the research studies by R. De Marinis on the earliest metallurgy of northern Italy (De Marinis 1992, 1998). The most recent paper by this author (De Marinis 2005), relative to the CA and EBA metal industry of northern Italy, is a detailed study of the chronological significance of variation in chemical composition throughout this period. The analyses indicate that CA artefacts were all made from pure copper, except for halberds and daggers, which are of arsenical copper; the earliest EBA pieces (EBA IA) are also pure copper, or, more frequently, copper with high values of As, Sb, Ag and Ni. The copper-tin alloy appeared during EBA IB, and a stable proportion of the two main components (copper with 8–10% tin) became fully established from EBA II onwards.

Other works in this group include a study by M. Pearce (1998) on the relevance of chemical analyses of CA and BA metal artefacts to a thorough understanding of prehistoric technology and artefacts function, and two works on the EBA of Tuscany (De Marinis 2001, and Giardino 2001); also, an overview of the BA metallurgy of Sicily (Albanese Procelli 2003), and the wide-ranging research by C. Giardino on the metallurgy of Italy and the west Mediterranean, 14th–8th century BC (Giardino 1995).

Technical and functional studies, usually in connection with experimental reproductions and use of bronze artefacts, constitute another field of research which has been developed recently: see for example Bellintani and Moser 2003. Fibulae are one of the most frequent subjects of these studies. Recent works comprise a technical study on Italian LBA and EIA fibulae (Le Fèvre-Lehöerff 1999), an experimental study on LBA–EIA fibulae and swords from Abruzzo (Bietti Sestieri, Formigli and Pacini 2003), a technological and typological study of FBA and EIA Sicilian bronzes, especially fibulae, from the cemetery of Madonna del Piano, and from the Modica hoard (Lo Schiavo, Albanese Procelli, and Giumlia-Mair 2002), and a collection of papers entirely devoted to the study of fibulae (Formigli 2003); see especially the general remarks by F. Lo Schiavo relative to south Italian and Sicilian fibulae (Lo Schiavo 2003), and the paper by A. Giumlia-Mair on the fibulae and pins of the east-Alpine area (Giumlia-Mair 2003).

Overall, the chrono-typological, technical and experimental studies carried out in the last decades provide a very sound basis for our study and classification of the British Museum artefacts, whereas comprehensive programmes of analyses are still lacking. For this reason, the *c.* 100 artefacts that have been analyzed by Duncan Hook, of the British Museum's Department of Conservation, Documentation and Science, and that are published in this catalogue, represent a significant contribution to our study, as well as to the general knowledge of the Italian metal industry from the CA to the EIA.

In order to give this catalogue a coherent structure, each of the main groups of artefacts, which as a rule has been further subdivided into more specific categories or subgroups, is arranged by types identified by running numbers. For every type, the corresponding type or types in the *PBF* series or in a few other main classifications has been indicated.

The following pages set out the classification headings and are followed by a brief discussion of the classifications. The artefacts have been divided into groups, categories or sub-groups, and types; within each category or sub-group, the types (some of which encompass a few already defined types that are sufficiently close in shape and chronology) are arranged in chronological sequence.

Sections 1–11 comprise all the objects which have been individually classified by groups, categories/sub-groups, and types, in the order in which they appear in each chronological range. Of the last two sections, 12 is devoted to a brief examination of those objects which are indicated to have been originally associated by the following criteria: chronological coherence, common provenance, continuous registration numbers, similar chemical composition, similar patina. Although these objects have been classified according to the general typology, they appear in the catalogue at the end of each chronological section, so as to emphasize their association. The majority of CA and BA pieces in this section were apparently part of hoards, whereas EIA ones probably come mainly or exclusively from burials. Section 13 comprises a small number of relatively rare or single pieces, all of EIA, late or later date, that are described but not formally classified by categories and types.

For the specific typological parallels, chronology and bibliography of each piece see the individual catalogue entries. For the **Typological Table** see pp.337–342, and for the **Index of Types**, pp.343–344.

Section 1
Group: Axes
CATEGORIES:
– Flat (**Axes types 1–5**)
– Flanged (**Axes types 6–18**)
– With contiguous wings (**Axes types 19–25**)
– With medial and medial-butt wings (**Axes types 26–33**)
– With butt wings (**Axes types 34–43**)
– Shaft-hole (**Axes types 44–52**)
– Socketed (**Axes types 53–62**)
– Lugged (**Axes type 63**)
– With lozenge lateral profile (**Axes types 64–65**)
– Lugged 'trunnion' axes (**Axes type 66**)
– Tanged (**Axes type 67**)
– With lateral loop (**Axes type 68**)
– Sardinian double axes (**Axes types 69–70**)

Section 2
Group: Tools
SUB-GROUPS:
– Needles (**Needles type 1**)
– Chisels (**Chisels types 1–4**)
– Winged adzes (**Winged adzes type 1**)
– Sicilian socketed tools (**Sicilian socketed tools types 1–2**)
– Hammers (**Hammers type 1**)
– Sickles (**Sickles type 1**)
– Spindles (**Spindles type 1–2**)

Section 3
Group: Knives
CATEGORIES:
– Tanged (**Knives types 1–7**)
– Socketed (**Knives type 8**)
– With separately cast rectangular handle (**Knives type 9**)

Section 4
Group: Razors
CATEGORIES:
– Symmetrical (**Razors types 1–9**)
– Lunate (**Razors types 10–16**)

Section 5
Group: Ornaments
SUB-GROUPS:
– Pins (**Pins types 1–9**)
– Embossed sheet bronze discs (**Sheet disc type 1**)
– Hair rings (**Hair rings type 1**)
– Pendants (**Pendants types 1–12**)
– Belt clasp ring
– Torques (**Torques types 1–2**)

Section 6
Group: Fibulae
CATEGORIES:
– Derived from the violin-bow series (**Fibulae types 1–2**)
– Arch (**Fibulae types 3–13**)
– Composite arch (**Fibulae types 14–15**)
– Arch with disc foot (**Fibulae types 16–18**)
– Leech-boat-lozenge (**Fibulae types 19–30**)

– Arch with foliate bow (**Fibulae types 31–34**)
– Composite arch with disc foot (**Fibulae type 35**)
– With disc foot and bow formed of graduated bronze discs (**Fibulae types 36–37**)
– One-piece serpentine (**Fibulae types 38–41**)
– Two-piece serpentine (**Fibulae types 42–45**)
– Serpentine with two coils and elongated catch-plate (**Fibulae types 46–49**)
– Drago (**Fibulae types 50–51**)
– Spectacle (**Fibulae types 52–55**)
– Four-spiral (**Fibulae types 56–58**)

Section 7
Group: Bracelets
CATEGORIES:
– Spiral (**Bracelets types 1–2**)
– Ribbon (**Bracelets type 3**)
– Coiled wire (**Bracelets type 4**)
– Coiled rod (**Bracelets types 5–9**)
– Annular (**Bracelets type 10**)
– Penannular (**Bracelets type 11**)
– D-shaped (**Bracelets type 12**)
– Hollow (**Bracelets type 13**)

Section 8
Group: Halberds and Daggers
Halberds 1–2
DAGGERS, CATEGORIES:
– With socketed hilt (**Daggers type 1**)
– With cast hilt riveted to the blade (**Daggers types 2–5**)
– Triangular (**Daggers type 6**)
– Tanged (**Daggers type 7**)
– With triangular tang (**Daggers types 8–9**)
– With flanged hilt (Peschiera daggers) (**Daggers types 10–12**)

Section 9
Group: Swords and Sword sheaths
CATEGORIES:
– BA short (**Swords types 1–2**)
– Flanged (**Swords types 3–5**)
– T-hilt (**Swords types 6–10**)
– Tanged short swords with shoulder cap (**Swords type 11**)
– Antennae (**Swords type 12**)
– Sword sheaths (**Sword sheaths types 1–4**)

Section 10
Group: Spearheads/Javelins and Spear-butts
SPEARHEADS, CATEGORIES:
– With conical socket and elongated symmetrical blade (**Spearheads types 1–17**)
SPEAR-BUTTS, CATEGORIES:
– Conical, with pointed or flat tip (**Spear-butts types 1–5**)

Section 11
Group: Arrowheads
CATEGORIES:
– Socketed (**Arrowheads types 1–3**)

Section 12
Groups of associated artefacts

CA:

1 – Two flat axes and an axe blade, **cat. 15–17** from Terni, Umbria.

EBA:

1 – Group of five flat and flanged axes, **cat. 47–51** from Agrigento, Sicily.

2 – Group of eight flanged axes, **cat. 52–59** from Terni, Umbria, probably from a hoard.

3 – Two daggers, **cat. 60–61**, probably from central Italy.

MBA:

1 – Two flanged axes, **cat. 82–83** from Lodi (Milan), Lombardy; part of a hoard.

2 – Two winged axes, **cat. 84–85** from Nemi (Rome), Lazio; part of a hoard.

FBA:

1 – Group of three winged axes and a tanged knife, **cat. 241–244** from near Lake Como, Lombardy; probably part of a hoard.

EIA, EARLY:

1 – Two fibulae, **cat. 443** and **444**, probably from a tomb.

2 – Two fibulae, **cat. 445** and **446**, probably from a tomb.

3 – Two bracelets, **cat. 447** and **448**, found at Bologna, Emilia Romagna, probably in a tomb.

4 – Two bracelets, **cat. 449** and **450**, probably from a tomb.

5 – A javelin-head and a spearhead, **cat. 451** and **452**, found at Sulmona (L'Aquila), Abruzzo, probably in a tomb.

6 – Two spearheads, **cat. 453** and **454**, found at Bari, Apulia, probably in a tomb.

7 – Two spearheads, **cat. 455** and **456**, found at Arezzo, Tuscany, probably in a tomb.

8 – Group of a sword and two spearheads, **cat. 457–459**, found at Cassino (Frosinone), Lazio, probably in a tomb.

EIA, LATE:

1 – Pair of fibulae, **cat. 784** and **785**, probably from a tomb.

2 – Pair of bracelets, **cat. 786** and **787**, probably from a tomb.

3 – Pair of bracelets, **cat. 788** and **789**, probably from a tomb.

4 – Group of five bracelet-weights, **cat. 790–794**.

5 – Pair of bracelets, **cat. 795** and **796**, probably from a tomb.

6 – Pair of bracelets, **cat. 797** and **798**, probably from a tomb.

7 – Two spearheads, **cat. 799** and **800**, part of a group, from a tomb at Bomarzo (Viterbo), Lazio.

Section 13
Miscellaneous artefacts

Section 1 – Axes

Besides forming the most substantial group of metal artefacts in the British Museum's early Italian collection (212 pieces), axes provide some of the most significant new data on the Italian metal ages. The study of these pieces was supported by a consistent number of analyses of the metal and alloys, but could be based on *PBF* classification for only one section of the sample, i.e. the axes of all groups and categories dating mainly from the EIA (see G.L. Carancini, *PBF* IX.12, 1984).

Flat, flanged and winged axes

The first category, **flat axes**, includes a total of 16 pieces which belong mainly, although not exclusively, to the CA. Metal analyses have been essential to the separation between copper and bronze pieces, which presumably implies a specific chronological significance, not always identifiable on purely typological grounds. A valuable feature of this sample is the relatively high number of pieces for which a provenance is indicated.

The main recent research on CA Italian metal artefacts, including the analyses of several pieces, has been carried out by R. De Marinis (1992, 1998), mainly on north Italian material, and recently on Tuscany (De Marinis 2001). Carancini's 1993 and 1999 works are a typological assessment of the CA metal industry in the Tyrrhenian regions, while the main study on Sicily is the 1993 book by R.M. Albanese Procelli. It may be interesting to remark that the CA types circulating on the whole territory of mainland Italy are relatively homogeneous.

Axes types 1, 2, and **3**, all plain shapes with flat surfaces, comprise some well identified CA types; the analyses of many pieces in this group indicate consistently that they are made of pure copper. **Axes type 1: cat. 1**, from Naples, Campania, is the most archaic in shape, since it is rather close to some types of Neolithic stone axe with narrow upper end, which were first described by G.A. Colini (Colini 1898, pl. 15.4); parallels are known mainly from Lombardy and Emilia. **Axes type 2**: the only example in the collections (**cat. 2**, from Naples), is a large and heavy tool with good parallels both in northern and central Italy (De Marinis, type Bocca Lorenza; Carancini, type Bibbona), probably dating from an early phase of the period. **Axes type 3**: (**cat. 15** and **16**, a group of pieces from Terni, Umbria, that also includes **cat. 17**, unclassified: see **Section 12**), are small tools with close analogies in central and northern Italy, especially De Marinis' type Cumarola.

Axes type 4: cat. 3, 4, from Abruzzo; **cat. 5** from Corneto (Tarquinia, Viterbo), Lazio, **cat. 6**, from Ruvo (Bari), Apulia; **cat. 7** from Capua (Caserta), Campania, is a group of heavy copper tools (average weight 500g) characterized by slightly dished faces, that in some of the pieces are marked by a slight step running parallel to the edges; this seems to be a technological feature meant to improve the effectiveness of the hafting. The closest parallel is Carancini's type Poggio Aquilone, which is dated by this author to an advanced phase of the CA. The inclusion in this type of **cat. 5**, which is considerably smaller than the other pieces, is based on its general shape and on its close similarity to a piece from tomb 62 of the cemetery of Remedello (Brescia), Lombardy.

The following type, **Axes type 5a** and **5b**, is constituted by a group of small and medium-sized tools, relatively thin in section, with flat faces and flaring blade, apparently a late feature. **Type 5a** includes two pieces, **cat. 8** and **9**, presumably from mainland Italy, close to Carancini's types Orvieto and Città di Castello, possibly CA; **Type 5b**, three axes, **cat. 47–49** from a group found at Agrigento (Sicily), are all bronze, and belong to local types dating from the EBA to the LBA (Albanese Procelli 1993).

Unclassified pieces in this group include the copper axe blade from Terni, **cat. 17** and an unprovenanced miniature flat axe(?), **cat. 13**.

Flanged axes are the next category; these constitute one of the main markers of the European and Italian EBA, as well as of the earliest part of the MBA. Two technological and formal features which are specific to the great majority of flanged axes are still found in a decreasing number of axes of MBA and LBA date: the continuous profile, which implies that the blade is not separated from the haft by a distinct element; and the extension of the wings over at least two-thirds of its total length, so that the blade usually is very short. These two features characterize the category of **axes with contiguous wings**, which is well represented in the BM sample.

A general classification of Italian BA axes, that will also be the mainframe of the next *PBF* volume, has been published by Carancini and Peroni (1999); this has been widely used in this catalogue, although other works have also been considered.

Overall, the basic principle of Carancini and Peroni's classification is the formal evolution shown by the different types of axes, while relatively little attention is paid to functional features and to technical and technological change. However, it should be mentioned that formal change in this kind of artefact corresponds, in a more or less direct way, to the adoption of technical and functional innovation. Another implication of Carancini and Peroni's formal typology is that it generates a sequence that bears little or no reference to specific contexts, local features, and the possible co-existence of what were formerly thought to be later chronological shapes and types: the relative chronology which is built directly upon a series of formally defined types should be considered as an ideal sequence, rather than as an actual temporal development. We have consistently tried to point out these limitations, although it is quite clear that they can hardly be avoided in a catalogue of objects which were collected at random in the course of more than two centuries.

Axes type 6 includes two slightly flanged axes, **cat. 18** from Rome, and **cat. 50** from the Agrigento group above; the type is well known in Sicily throughout the BA, and the occurrence of a formally similar piece in Lazio might be casual. **Axes type 7: cat. 51**, also from the Agrigento group; **cat. 19** from Brescia, Lombardy; **cat. 20** from Naples, correspond to the simplest types of flanged axes identified by Carancini and Peroni in their first horizon of EBA hoards. **Axes type 8: cat. 21, 22** from near Naples; **cat. 23** and **24**, also comparable to types in the first horizon, is more regular in shape and with a central notch or a slight indentation of the butt.

Axes type 9 is constituted by an exceedingly large and heavy flanged axe, **cat. 25**, also comparable to the earliest types in the EBA series. A totally identical piece from Campania (type Salerno) is published by Carancini 1993. **Axes type 10: cat. 26, 27** from Capua (Caserta), Campania, **cat. 28–30** from Tarquinia (Viterbo), Lazio, and **cat. 31**, are a group of axes with a central

notch to the butt and relatively developed flanges; parallels can be found both in the second and third horizons of the EBA hoards.

Axes types 11, 12 and **13** differ significantly from the earliest BA types, and can all be connected to the third and fourth EBA horizons. The former two types are characterized by wide faceted flanges with concave profile, apparently an important improvement in the efficiency of the hafting, and by a more or less sharply distinct butt with central notch. **Axes type 11: cat. 32** from Anagni (Frosinone), Lazio, **cat. 33** from Bazzano, Emilia Romagna, and **cat. 34. Axes type 12**: this type includes an axe from the Greenwell collection, **cat. 35**, which was recorded as found at Athens; **cat. 36–38** from Alba (L'Aquila), Abruzzo, and a group of eight axes, **cat. 52–59**, all probably part of a hoard found at Terni, Umbria, and almost identical in size, composition (Cu-Sn proportion in the alloy, and trace elements), and patina. **Axes type 13** includes two large pieces, **cat. 39** and **40** from Bagni di Lucca, Tuscany, with markedly concave sides and a central notch to the butt.

The parallels for the formal and technical characteristics of **Axes types 14–18**, the most recent group of flanged axes in the BM collections, can be found in some MBA hoards and complexes, especially from the north-western regions of Italy: the hoards of Lodi (end of the EBA and MBA, early) and Cascina Ranza (MBA, early), both in Lombardy, and the lake settlement of Avigliana, in Piedmont, dating from MBA, middle (Carancini and Peroni 1999, pls. 6, 9.1–14 and 15–18). As is well known, several MBA and LBA bronzes from this part of Italy show a strong connection to the adjacent European regions north-west of the Alpine range: south-eastern France and Switzerland.

Axes type 14: two pieces, **cat. 62** and **63**, are still close in general shape to the most common EBA flanged types, although the width and overall profile of the flanges probably indicate an early MBA date. **Axes type 15**: two flanged axes with distinct blade **cat. 64** and **65** with close parallels in the hoard of Cascina Ranza (Milan), Lombardy.

Axes types 16 and **17**: two slightly different types of flanged axes with rounded blade, each represented by a single piece, **cat. 82** and **83**; both were probably part of a bronze hoard found in the area of Lodi (Milan), Lombardy. Close parallels can be found in the hoard of Cascina Ranza, as well as in some axe types which are specific to the regions north-west of the Alps (France and Switzerland, see *PBF* IX. 4).

Axes type 18, probably the most recent type in this category, comprises a flanged-winged axe with straight butt and distinct blade, **cat. 66**, from Terni, Umbria, close to some of the pieces from the lake settlement of Avigliana, in Piedmont.

The category of **Axes with contiguous wings** includes **types 19** to **25**, dating mainly from the MBA.

Axes type 19: cat. 67 and **68** corresponds to Carancini and Peroni type Sezze, early MBA, a group of elongated tools with almost parallel sides and a short flaring blade. **Axes type 20**, very close to **Axes type 19** in general shape, is a Sardinian type (type Orosei), also present in Sicily. However, given the persisting difficulties as regards the dating of the Sardinian bronze-hoards and bronzes, especially the earliest ones, an attribution of these axes to the MBA should be considered as tentative. The type includes **cat. 69, 70**, and possibly **cat. 71**, from Nola (Naples), Campania.

The seven pieces classified as **Axes type 21** are rather homogeneous as regards the overall shape, that is flaring toward the blade, with slightly convex sides and wings widening in the central part; however, there is a certain degree of variability between **cat. 72** and **cat. 75**, two elongated tools, apparently rather close to **Axes type 19**: and **cat. 84**, with a wide flaring profile and heavily hammered wings, both of which probably are late features in the MBA series. Arranged in this hypothetical evolutionary sequence, **Axes type 21** comprise **cat. 72**, from Abruzzo, **cat. 73–76** from Poli (Rome), Lazio; **cat. 84** and **85**, probably from a hoard found at Nemi (Rome), Lazio. It is interesting that, besides being apparently linked in a close typological sequence, both **Axes types 19** and **21** are among the very few types of this date that seem to be specific to the central Tyrrhenian zone south of the Tiber, i.e. Lazio and the adjacent interior area.

Axes type 22: **cat. 77**, a single piece with straight butt and flaring blade from Palermo, Sicily, is at home among the axes of MBA, middle phase, from northern and central Italy; no close published parallels are known in Sicily. **Axes type 23** and **Axes type 24** belong to a different typological series, found mainly in the central and eastern regions of northern Italy, especially in Terramare contexts; the majority of the pieces are characterized by a rather long butt, usually ending in an indentation or with a central notch; moreover, there is a clearly identifiable development of blades both in length and width, accompanied by a parallel decrease of the wings. These changes appear in **Axes type 23**: **cat. 78**, with narrow wings and wide trapezoidal blade; the best parallels are to be found in some types of axes which are specific to the Terramare and Palafitte region. A date in the middle phase of the MBA can be based on its similarity to axes from the hoard of Rocca di Badolo, Emilia Romagna, and to an axe from the lake settlement of Fiavé (Trento), Trentino Alto Adige, phase VI. **Axes type 24**: **cat. 86**, with a long butt and a very short blade, also belongs to a Terramare type, probably of RBA date.

Axes type 25, the only FBA type in this category, is very close to Carancini and Peroni's type Silea, dating from an intermediate phase of the period. The only piece, **cat. 241** is one of a small group of four FBA objects, **cat. 241–244**, a hoard or part of a hoard from around Lake Como, Lombardy.

The following category, **winged axes with medial and medial-butt wings**, reflects the generalised adoption of an important technological innovation: the sharp distinction between haft and blade. This feature had already appeared in some axe types dating from the end of the EBA and the MBA (see **Axes types 15** and **18**), although it was never widely adopted. This category appeared probably in northern Italy in an advanced phase of the MBA (see Terramare 1997, fig. 232.61–63). **Axes type 26**: **cat. 87**, a relatively small artefact with wide wings and thin blade, possibly a weapon, is rather close to these early pieces. However, the main technological implication, i.e. the availability of a longer, and presumably more efficient blade, that was especially needed for the large heavy tools, was only achieved in the RBA. The technological evolution of these axes includes a gradual increase in overall length and curvature of the wings, as well as in blade thickness; also a moderate decrease in butt height and width and the gradual appearance of slight lateral protrusions marking the distinction between haft

and blade can be observed on these axes. **Axes type 27**: **cat. 88**, **89** and **Axes type 28**: **cat. 90** found at Foxcote, (England); **cat. 91** from Pozzuoli (Naples), Campania, **cat. 92** from Talamone, in the Tuscan Maremma, may be seen as an ideal RBA sequence, at least as regards the formal development of both wings and butt. It is interesting to note that the latter three pieces, all heavy tools, are extremely close both in shape and in weight (755–774g); the implication might be the existence and wide circulation of detailed technological know-how and models.

Axes type 29: **cat. 134** from Perugia, Umbria, **cat. 135** from the Marsica, Abruzzo, **cat. 136** from Canino (Vulci, Viterbo), Lazio, and **cat. 137** from near Naples, Campania; **cat. 138–141**, and the variant **142**, represent the subsequent development of this series, which can be dated to the earliest phase of the FBA. These axes are characterized by the continuing decrease in butt height and, mainly, by the smoothing of the blade, which is consistently oval or elliptical in section. This feature is found also on shaft-hole axes dating from the same period (see **cat. 161**), and should bear a specific significance. It is possible that the absence of angular edges allowed a deeper impact of the blade, especially if the axe was used as a weapon. Also an aesthetic factor might be implied, since the smooth surface clearly adds a special elegance and refinement to both winged and shaft-hole axes, many of which are finely decorated (cf. Bietti Sestieri 1973, figs. 11.1, 3, 4; 15.3-5; Jurgeit 1999, no. 221). The nine axes in this type range from a few large, heavy tools (**cat. 134, 139, 142**, weighing between 630 and 850g) and a majority of smaller pieces, probably weapons. **Cat. 135** has a fine pointillé decoration on the blade. The fact that small pieces of precisely this type circulated widely throughout Europe, from northern Germany (a decorated axe from Osternienburg, Anhalt; Bietti Sestieri 1997: 392, fig.7.d) to Greece (the mould from the House of the Oil Merchant at Mycenae; Bietti Sestieri 1973, fig. 15.2) indicates that they were highly valued prestige objects.

Axes type 30, the immediate successor to **Axes type 29**, dating from a relatively early phase of the FBA, is characterized by the markedly concave sides of the blade. It comprises a number of small elegant pieces which were apparently manufactured in central Italy (Tuscany, Umbria, Marche, Romagna: sporadic pieces, and hoards of Poggio Berni and Casalecchio) and in the northern Po plain, especially Veneto (settlement of Frattesina), and circulated in eastern Europe (Austria and the Balkans); they were probably prestige objects, meant as accompanying gifts along the main trade routes in this area of Europe (Bietti Sestieri 1997), which reached as far as mainland Greece, as is indicated by the provenance of the typologically earliest piece, **cat. 143**. The other two, **cat. 242** and **243**, are slightly later and belong to the FBA hoard from Lake Como, Lombardy.

Axes type 31 is represented by a single piece, **cat. 144**, that belongs to a contemporary type (type Teor) also found in north-eastern Italy and in the adjacent area of the Balkans.

Axes types 32 and **33**, both comprise single pieces, from the River Ticino, Lombardy (**cat. 145**, a massive tool with narrow trapezoidal butt, also found north of the Alps) and from the Tyrol (**cat. 146**, a wide, heavy winged axe in Alpine style); although formally close to more elegant contemporary types such as **Axes types 34** and **36**, these two types are very local in character, and overall quite different from the Italian FBA metal production.

The following category, **Winged axes with butt wings**, marks the FBA–EIA transition and the EIA. A small group of axes, mostly unprovenanced, illustrates the main types to be found in the central Italian bronze hoards dating from the final phase of the FBA (hoards of Gabbro, Pariana and Limone) and the FBA–EIA transition (Campese, Goluzzo, Piediluco-Contigliano, S. Marinella). These are **Axes type 34: cat. 148–151**, and the variant **152**, with wide trapezoidal blade, a feature especially found in the bronze hoards of Gabbro and Limone(Livorno), Tuscany, dating from FBA, late; **Axes type 35: cat. 153**, a specialized type of later FBA date, probably a heavy working tool, and **Axes type 36: cat. 154–156** from Terni (Umbria), all close to the Piediluco-Contigliano group.

The following winged axe types are of full EIA date. The majority of the provenanced pieces comes from the Villanovan regions of central and northern Italy (Tuscany and Emilia Romagna), the most important areas of the Italian metal industry in this period. It is interesting to note that a relatively large number of BM Italian axes in this group was found in different parts of Europe, including France, Hungary, Greece and Britain. The reliability of these provenances is supported by the fact that EIA Italian axes from many European countries have been published in the *PBF* series; this is a further indication of the wide international circulation of Villanovan metal and metal artefacts.

The earliest group, which, however, is generally dated to the second phase of the EIA, includes **Axes type 37** (**cat. 460** from Fiesole (Florence) Tuscany; **cat. 461** from Tarascon, France; **cat. 462–464**), and **Axes type 38** (**cat. 465**, and the variant **cat. 466**, both from Tuscany; **cat. 467** from Olympia, Greece; and **cat. 468**). These are all winged axes of regular shape and accurate making, with wide wings, marked shoulders and wide trapezoidal blade, (see *PBF* types Grottazzolina v. A, San Francesco, Bambolo, Cignano, Benacci var. A).

The bulk of the pieces belongs to the two types (San Francesco and Ardea) which are more widely represented in the most important Italian bronze hoard, found in the early years of last century near the church of San Francesco, Bologna, Emilia Romagna (Zannoni 1907). The hoard included over 14,000 pieces, mainly of EIA date, and was probably buried early in the 7th century BC. Another relatively important contemporary hoard was found in 1963 at Ardea, south of Rome. It is worth noting that the majority of the EIA axes in the BM collection belong to the the the two types which are most widely represented in the archaeological record in Italy. **Axes type 39** corresponds to type San Francesco, an elegant artefact of regular proportions, with upturned shoulders and wide trapezoidal blade, probably a weapon. It includes **cat. 469** from Tuscany, **cat. 470** and **471** from Emilia Romagna, **cat. 472** from Hungary, and **cat. 473–478**, unprovenanced. **Axes type 40**, type Ardea, is a considerably less refined, stout artefact; its wide range of formal variation is particularly remarkable if compared to the regularity of the San Francesco type, and probably indicates its main function as a widely-adopted working tool. It includes **cat. 479** from Sarzana, Liguria; **cat. 480** from 'Alba della Massa', probably Massa d'Albe (Aquila), Abruzzo, and **cat. 481** from Naples, **cat. 482** from France, **cat. 483** from England, and five unprovenanced pieces, **cat. 484–488**.

Axes type 41: cat. 489 and **490**, *PBF* type Marsiliana

d'Albegna, characterized by wide sloping shoulders, is also found in the hoards of San Francesco and Ardea, although in relatively smaller proportion.

Axes type 42, type Roselle, is a slightly later type found in the San Francesco hoard, dating to the EIA-Orientalizing transition (late 8th–early 7th century BC); it comprises **cat. 491** from Lake Trasimeno, Umbria, and **cat. 492**.

Finally, **Axes type 43** is a rare type of axe with faceted wings, type Mazzone, EIA, early; the only piece is **cat. 245**, from Rome.

Shaft-hole axes

The earliest pieces in this group, **Axes type 44**, belong to a distinctive type with markedly concave sides and central nervature on the haft, which is found in Sicily and the Aeolian islands in local Thapsos-Milazzese contexts of MBA–RBA date (Albanese Procelli 1993, type R8A). The technical innovation in the hafting of these axes is believed to have been brought to Sicily from the eastern Mediterranean. One of the three pieces, **cat. 93** is from Sicily, the second, **cat. 94**, is unprovenanced, while **cat. 95**, an axe rather close, though not identical to the former two, was found near Bournemouth, Dorset, England.

Axes types 45 and **46** are heavy massive tools with continuous lateral profile, and belong to RBA–FBA types found both in Sicily-Aeolian islands and in southern-central Italy. **Axes type 45** corresponds to *PBF* type Cuma: **cat. 96–98** from Potenza (Basilicata), probably RBA; close to this type are **cat. 157** from Castrovillari, Calabria, and **cat. 158** from Paternò, Sicily, probably FBA. Two axes from Abruzzo, **cat. 159, 160** are classified as **Axes type 46**, which corresponds to *PBF* type Menaforno, also dated to the FBA.

Except for a few pieces of late EIA date, all the subsequent shaft-hole axes belong to south Italian types. The main area for the development of this series of artefacts throughout the FBA and the beginning of the IA was Apulia, which was strongly connected to Basilicata, Calabria, eastern Sicily and Campania. A limited number of shaft-hole axes of southern type is known also from central Italy and from the coastal Adriatic regions of the Balkan peninsula.

Axes type 47 comprises a group of seven pieces with angular butt and distinct blade, which constitute an evolutionary FBA series. The earliest one, **cat. 161**, has a distinctive rounded blade section also found on contemporary winged axes (see **Axes type 29**); along with **cat. 162** from Cuma (Naples), Campania, it corresponds to *PBF* type Zinzulusa var. B (FBA early–middle). **Cat. 163** from Bovino (Apulia), **cat. 164** from Pozzuoli (Naples), **cat. 165** from 'Magna Graecia' (= southern Italy) and **cat. 167**, can be attributed to *PBF* type with pentagonal profile to haft (FBA, late); **cat. 166** from Lake Trasimeno (Umbria), is close to *PBF* type San Francesco var. B, same date.

Axes types 48 and **49**, close to *PBF* types Chiusi var. A, Soleto var. B and Cerchiara, show some FBA features, such as the angular butt, hammered in some of the pieces, and wide trapezoidal blade slightly separated from the haft. **Axes type 48: cat. 168** from Populonia (Livorno), Tuscany, **cat. 169** from Corinth (Greece), **cat. 170** and **171**. **Axes type 49: cat. 172** from Mineo (Catania), Sicily, **cat. 173, 174** from Naples, and **175**. **Axes type 50: cat. 246**, a wide tool with hammered butt from Mineo (Sicily), with no close parallels, can be associated to this group; it might be dated to FBA, late, or possibly, to EIA, early. This period is also represented by **Axes type 51**, with continuous profile and straight edges, close to *PBF* type Manduria; the type comprises **cat. 247, 248** from Capua (Caserta), Campania, and **cat. 249** from Calabria. **Axes type 52: cat. 493**, a decorated piece with asymmetrical haft, close to *PBF* type Doss Trento, dates from an advanced phase of the EIA.

Socketed axes
Socketed axes with continuous profile appeared for the first time in central and northern Italy in the RBA, probably in connection with the flourishing of the Palafitte-Terramare metal industry: see **Axes type 53**, *PBF* type Casinalbo, **cat. 99** from Bologna, Emilia Romagna, and **cat. 100** from near Ancona, Marche. However no subsequent development of this class is documented in these regions of the central and northern Adriatic area. Probably not earlier than the FBA–EIA transition, a new autonomous series developed in Apulia, especially in the Salento peninsula, which was systematically connected to the Balkan coast opposite. **Axes type 54**, a single decorated piece with raised double collar, **cat. 250**, belongs to one of the earliest types in this series, *PBF* type Manduria var. H. **Axes type 55: cat. 494**, with no close parallels, and **Axes type 56: cat. 251** from Terni, Umbria, and **cat. 495**, is close to *PBF* types Manduria var. C (EIA, early) and Ripatransone (EIA, late), both plain types with oval socket, also connected to the Apulian series.

The last three types in this group, **Axes type 57**, with lateral lugs, **Axes type 58**, with lateral loops, and **Axes type 59**, with slightly marked shoulders, belong mainly to the San Francesco-Ardea metal industry, centered in Villanovan Emilia Romagna and Tuscany and dating from the late phase of the EIA (see **Axes types 39** and **40**). **Axes type 57**: close to *PBF* type Cortona, **cat. 496** from Fondi, Lazio, and **cat. 497**. **Axes type 58**: *PBF* types Città della Pieve and Ardea var. A, **cat. 498** from Bari, Apulia, **cat. 499** from Verona, Veneto, **cat. 500** from Naples, and **cat. 501**. **Axes type 59: cat. 502** from Grosseto (Tuscany).

Socketed axes with separate blade
These pieces also are of EIA date, although it is possible to divide them into two main groups, which differ in style as well as in chronology. The earliest one, **Axes type 60**, probably dating from the beginning of the EIA and later, corresponds to *PBF* type Cuma, which is loosely distributed in central and southern Italy and is characterized by a conical socket inserted at the centre of a thin flat blade. **Cat. 252** from Perugia, Umbria; **cat. 253** from near Rome, Lazio, and **cat. 254** can be dated to EIA, early; **cat. 503** and **504** are probably slightly later.

Axes types 61 and **62** both comprise slightly different variants of the *PBF* socketed axes type San Francesco; their main features, which show their strong formal and functional connection to the winged axes from the San Francesco-Ardea metallurgical tradition (see **Axes type 39**), comprise the wide trapezoidal blade and protruding shoulders, often combined with geometric decoration. **Axes type 61: cat. 505** from Talamone (Grosseto), Tuscany; **cat. 506** from Orvieto, Umbria; **cat. 507** and **508**. **Axes type 62: cat. 509–513**.

A few other axe types, all relatively rare in the Italian archaeological record, are each represented by no more than one or two pieces.

Lugged axes
Axes type 63 (type Terni, Carancini 1993): a single CA axe with thick blade and pointed lugs, **cat. 10** from Pozzuoli (Naples).

Axes with lozenge lateral profile
Axes type 64 (type Terni, Carancini 1993): heavy tools of late CA date, known from central and southern Italy, mainly from Gaudo contexts, **cat. 11** from Terni, Umbria.

Axes type 65 (type Mirabella Eclano, Carancini 1993): heavy tools with elongated butt and raised and hammered concave edges to the blade, probably CA, late, **cat. 12.**

Lugged ('trunnion') axes
Axes type 66: cat. 176 from Enna, Sicily: this type belongs to a widely diffused class of FBA date, found in Sicily, Sardinia, central Italy, the Iberian peninsula and France (Giardino 1995).

Tanged axes
Axes type 67: cat. 177 from the Marsica, Abruzzo; this is a FBA–EIA type found mainly in southern Italy.

Axes with one lateral loop
Axes type 68: cat. 178 from Castro Giovanni (= Enna), Sicily: a 'western' FBA type, found in Sicily, and the Iberian peninsula (Giardino 1995).

Sardinian double axes
Axes type 69: double axe with parallel or converging cutting edges: **cat. 179, 180**; **Axes type 70**, axe-adze **cat. 181** from Cagliari, Sardinia; these are specific Sardinian types, both of late FBA or EIA date (Giardino 1995).

Unclassified axes
Two axe-blades, **cat. 823** from Naples, and **cat. 824**.

Section 2 – Tools
Tools make up a small and mixed collection dating from the RBA to EIA, late.

Needles
Needles type 1: two pieces, **cat. 101** and **102**, both from Peschiera (Verona), Veneto, made from thin wire with bent eye, a specific north Italian RBA type.

Chisels
Chisels type 1: rod chisels without stop ridge. **Cat. 103** is of square section, only slightly narrowing at the tang. Parallels for this basic shape are known in RBA Terramare context of northern Italy. **Cat. 104** is more elaborate, with section square at tang and circular in the central portion. The type is rather standardized, and is known from RBA–FBA bronze-hoards in central and southern Italy: Gualdo Tadino, in Umbria and Surbo in Apulia.

Chisels type 2: cat. 182, thick rod of square section with marked stop ridge; this is a type usually found in bronze hoards dating from FBA, late, and FBA–EIA transition.

Chisels type 3: cat. 514, and **Chisels type 4: cat. 515** from near Naples, both are socketed tools with EIA, late, parallels in Campania (cemeteries of Pontecagnano) and in the hoard of San Francesco (Bologna, Emilia Romagna).

Winged adzes

Winged adzes type 1: this is a previously unknown type, consisting of a hafting section identical to those of RBA–FBA winged axes, and of a narrow blade set transversely to the haft. Based on the decreasing height of the butt, the three pieces can be dated to the RBA (**cat. 105** from Potenza, Basilicata) and to FBA, early, **cat. 183** and **184**, possibly from Tuscany.

Sicilian socketed tools

A very specific group of blunt tools, known from the Sicilian FBA hoards of Niscemi and Noto Antica, consisting of a conical or angular socket with bulging upper edge and wide openings on each face. A function as plough-heads seems likely.

Sicilian socketed tools type 1: cat. 185, straight; **Sicilian socketed tools type 2: cat. 186**, L-shaped, from Syracuse (Sicily). Both types can be dated to FBA, middle.

Hammers

This category of tools is represented by a single type, **Hammers type 1**, which includes a piece, **cat. 187**, possibly from Florence (Tuscany). This is a massive FBA tool with parallels in bronze hoards from southern Italy, such as Mottola (Taranto, Apulia).

Sickles

This category, too, is represented by one type, **Sickles type 1**, including a single piece, **cat. 188**, which belongs to the most common type found in Italian bronze hoards of FBA middle and late date.

Spindles

The two types in this category correspond to the most common types found especially in Villanovan cemeteries both in central and southern Italy, from EIA, early, and are quite similar in basic shape (a straight rod with discs set upon the shaft). **Spindles type 1: cat. 255**, is made from a thick rod with three discs; **Spindles type 2: cat. 256**, is of thin rod with two discs only.

Unclassified tools

This group includes a wide trapezoidal blunt blade of pure copper, possibly of CA date, **cat. 825**, and two chisel blade tips, **cat. 826, 827** from Terni, Umbria.

Section 3 – Knives

The small BM sample includes 13 pieces, dating from the FBA to EIA, late; except for two pieces, **cat. 193** and **194**, they correspond to well identified *PBF* VII.2 types.

Tanged knives. The specific technical feature of this wide category, spanning the FBA and EIA, is the hafting system: the blade ends in a tang, which may be flat, either plain or flanged, or a narrow rod of rectangular section. The handle, usually of organic matter, encapsulated the tang, or was riveted to it.

Knives type 1: cat. 189–191; 244, from a bronze hoard found near Lake Como (Lombardy), and **Knives type 2: cat. 192**, belong to a group of tanged tools with slightly serpentine blade mainly from north Italian FBA contexts, especially *PBF* VII.2 types Bismantova and Iseo.

Knives type 3: cat. 193 from Regalbuto (Enna), Sicily, a tanged and flanged piece with markedly serpentine blade, is comparable for its general features to the FBA north Italian type Fontanella, although no precise Sicilian parallels are available.

A provenance from Sicily is also possible for **Knives type 4: cat. 194**, with curved blade and tang ending in a ring, that is close to FBA pieces from the Sicilian cemetery of Cassibile (Turco 2000).

The two types of EIA, early, date belong to the same general category with the FBA types above. **Knives type 5: cat. 257**, with serpentine blade and tang, is close to *PBF* type Piediluco; **Knives type 6: cat. 258**, tanged with continuous profile, belongs to the south Italian type Spezzano Calabro.

EIA, late, pieces, include a tanged type, **Knives type 7: cat. 516**, with flat tang, close to *PBF* central Italian type Leprignano.

The other types of EIA, late, date belong to two different categories, based on the hafting system.

Socketed knives. Knives type 8: cat. 517 from Castiglione del Lago (Perugia), Umbria, with narrow cylindrical socket attached to the end of the blade, and close to *PBF* type Morlungo, which is found mainly in northern Italy.

Knives with separately cast rectangular handle. This is a specifically Latial and Campanian group dating from EIA, late, and the Orientalizing period. Given their technical complexity, as well as their consistently large size and the frequent occurrence of incised decoration, these were probably ceremonial tools. **Knives type 9: cat. 518**, and **519** from Palestrina (Rome). See *PBF* type Caracupa.

Section 4 – Razors

The 32 pieces belong to two general categories: symmetrical (i.e. with two symmetrical cutting edges), and lunate (with a single convex cutting edge and a concave back). Symmetrical razors are known from the MBA, although no pieces of this date are included in the BM sample. From the FBA, the two categories run in chronologically parallel series. The great majority of the BM pieces belongs to types defined in *PBF* VIII.2.

Symmetrical razors include the earliest specimens in this group, dating from the RBA or the FBA: **Razors type 1**, a narrow tool with a wide triangular tang: **cat. 106, 107** found in Suffolk, England, **cat. 108**, and **109** from Abruzzo. The type is comparable to the Sicilian type Pantalica defined by Giardino 1995. **Razors type 2: cat. 110–112**, with a narrow tang, is more similar to south Italian pieces (e.g. *PBF* VIII.2, 64, from Tropea, Calabria, type Pertosa). **Razors type 3: cat. 195**, characterized by a wide blade cast in one piece with the suspension loop, belongs to a common FBA type (*PBF* type Pianello). **Razors type 4: cat. 196, 197**, *PBF* type Terni, marks the FBA–EIA transition. The attached handle ending in a ring of twisted wire is found also on the earliest EIA types in this category, **Razors type 5** (**cat. 259** and **260**, the former found at Athens, cf. *PBF* type Capua), and **Razors type 6** (**cat. 261**, also from Athens, **cat. 262**, and **263**; they correspond to *PBF* type Savena). **Razors type 7** (**cat. 264**, cf. *PBF* miniature razors with two cutting edges) is a miniature reproduction of an actual symmetrical razor; it probably comes from ancient Lazio, where the miniaturization of grave goods was a common feature of FBA and EIA cremation graves.

Razors type 8: cat. 265, belongs to a specific south Italian EIA group (*PBF* types Cairano and Amendolara); **Razors type**

9: **cat. 520**, with blade and handle cast in one piece, is comparable to *PBF* type Suessula, dating from EIA, late.

Lunate razors: the earliest lunate razors are characterized by the mild curvature of both cutting edge and back, a feature reminiscent of the FBA type Fontanella; they include **Razors type 10: cat. 266**, *PBF* type Tarquinia, and **Razors type 11: cat. 267–269**, a miniature piece from Rome; cf. *PBF* types Vulci and Tarquinia). Both can be dated to the earliest phase of the EIA. **Razors type 12 (cat. 270** from Etruria), with a more marked blade curvature, had the handle originally riveted to the blade, a rare feature for lunate razors. It is identical to *PBF* type Sirolo-Numana var. B, EIA early and late. Also **Razors type 13: cat. 271**, belongs to a well identified EIA type, *PBF* type Fermo, with an angular spur surmounted by a knob and a decoration of hatched meander elements along the upper edge.

The last three types date from the late phase of the EIA and are characterized by the pronounced curve of both cutting edge and back. These include **Razors type 14 (cat. 521** from Chiusi, Tuscany, **cat. 522, 523**), similar to *PBF* type Grotta Gramiccia var.A; **Razors type 15 (cat. 524**, also from Chiusi), close to *PBF* type Valle La Fata both in shape and decoration; and **Razors type 16 (cat. 525–528**, from Etruria), similar to *PBF* type Benacci.

Section 5 – Ornaments

This is a mixed group, which comprises different sub-groups of ornaments dating from the RBA to EIA, late.

The sample includes a total of 36 pieces: 9 pins, 1 small bronze disc, 1 hair-ring, 21 pendants, 3 torques, 1 belt clasp ring. Owing to the limited typological variation within each group of ornaments, some of which are represented by single pieces, they have not been divided by categories, but only by general sub-groups and by types.

Pins. From the EBA, pins were an important accessory to fabric clothes, both as a decoration and, mainly, as a functional device for fastening cloaks or mantles. During the RBA and FBA the functional role of pins became progressively more important than their decorative element, as is indicated by their usually small, barely discernible heads. In these periods they were first the functional precedents, and then the alternative to fibulae, especially in northern Italy: the bronze pin was securely fastened to the cloth by a thin string of leather or by thread, as is indicated by the relatively high number of pins which were curved in order to fasten the cloth more efficiently in this way. In the IA, the use of pins marks a significant difference in fashion between the northern regions and the rest of Italy: in the north elaborate pins were the most popular ornament and dress fastener in use, just as were serpentine fibulae with disc foot in the Tyrrhenian regions of central and southern Italy (see for example Pincelli and Morigi Govi 1975, 570 and fig. 77.1-8, for the use of pins in male burials in the EIA cemetery of San Vitale, Bologna; see below for serpentine fibulae in male burials from Lazio and Campania).

The BM sample for this group of ornaments is made up of a few pieces, mainly of RBA and FBA date; all correspond to *PBF* XII.2 types.

Pins types 1 to 4, all represented by a single piece (**cat. 113–116**), belong to some of the most common north Italian types of RBA date, which are found mainly in Terramare contexts.

The same applies to the three FBA pieces, **Pins type 5: cat. 198**, **Pins type 6: cat. 199**, and **Pins type 7: cat. 200**, close to *PBF* types Sarteano, Fontanella, and 'a capocchia di chiodo', and found in FBA Protovillanovan contexts from both central and northern Italy.

Pins type 8: cat. 272, and **Pins type 9: cat. 529**, from Florence, belong to the wide group of pins in the shape of a spoked wheel; both are found in EIA cemeteries from central and northern Italy, although **Pins type 9** (*PBF* type Vetulonia) is later, and dates from EIA, late, and the Orientalizing period.

Embossed sheet bronze discs. These relatively rare artefacts probably were used to perform different functions in Italian and Sicilian contexts of FBA and EIA date, such as the cemeteries of Lipari, Piazza Monfalcone, FBA, and Molino della Badia-Madonna del Piano (Catania, Sicily), FBA–EIA. **Sheet disc type 1** includes a single piece, **cat. 201**, from the Marsica (L'Aquila), Abruzzo. The general decorative style of the disc, although also known in EIA contexts, might indicate a FBA date.

Hair rings. This is one of the most common ornaments found especially in IA female graves over the whole Italian territory, with some precedents dating from the FBA. The basic shape is a spiral ring of varying diameter, usually made from thin double wire, and with ondulating ends.

Hair rings type 1: cat. 273, is close to EIA, early, types from Villanovan, Latial and south Italian fossa-grave cemeteries, as for example Osteria dell'Osa and Pontecagnano.

Pendants. This group comprises a variety of pendants of different shapes and types, probably all of IA date. Except for **type 1** and possibly the unclassified saltaleone **cat. 275**, all the other pendants are of EIA late or later date.

Pendants type 1: cat. 274, from Ruvo (Bari), Apulia, is a spectacle, or two-spiral, pendant with suspension loop.

The general shape was already known in the BA, but the parallels from southern Italy can be dated to the FBA–EIA transition (cemetery of Carinaro, Caserta, Campania) and to the EIA (cemeteries of Pontecagnano and Capua).

Pendants or Ornaments unclassified, cat. 275, a cylindrical ornament of coiled bronze wire (so-called 'saltaleone'), is an ubiquitous find from EIA and later graves especially in central and southern Italy.

Pendants type 2: cat. 530 from Gela (Sicily), a miniature shaft-hole axe, belongs to a category of ornaments which is specific to Sicily from the FBA. The circular hole of this piece might indicate a date in EIA, late.

The next two types, both of solid bronze, **Pendants type 3: cat. 531**, a small pointed globe, and **Pendants type 4: cat. 532**, a composite ornament formed by a decorated tube with smaller pendants suspended, are quite common in EIA, late, cemeteries from central and southern Italy, as for example Veii Quattro Fontanili.

Pendants type 5: cat. 533, 534 from Torre Annunziata (Naples) and the variant **535**, **Pendants type 6: cat. 536**, and **Pendants type 7: cat. 537–539**, all belong to a different metallurgical tradition; the main feature is a globe with a pair of opposed birds' heads attached. They are specific to southern Italy, especially to regions and contexts with strong Balkan connections: Campania (cemeteries of Suessula, Capua, and of the Oliveto-Cairano group) and Apulia, and they all date from EIA, late, and later. See *PBF* XI. 2, for parallels from Serbia and Thessaly.

A small group of pendants in the form of animals includes **Pendants type 8: cat. 540**, a small horse with incised decoration, and **Pendants type 9: cat. 541** and **542**, in the form of a bird. Similar ornaments appear in Italian EIA, late and later contexts from Villanovan Etruria and Campania, and are also found in the cemetery of Ischia and in Greece (see *PBF* XI. 2 for bird pendants).

The next group, **Pendants type 10: cat. 543**, **Pendants type 11: cat. 544, 545** from Ruvo (Bari), Apulia, and **cat. 546**, are more or less complex types of bullae, a circular bivalve ornament that was quite popular in central and southern Italy from EIA, late, to the Orientalizing and later periods.

The two stylized horse-birds, **cat. 547** and **548**, which make up **Pendants type 12** are very close in shape and general style to a type of horse-bit of EIA, late, and Orientalizing date, also found in Etruria and southern Italy (see *PBF* XVI.1); they were probably part of the decoration of horse trappings.

Belt clasp ring. **Cat. 549**, a small ring of thick wire with incised decoration, is the only representative of this sub-group, with parallels in EIA, late, graves from ancient Lazio and Etruria.

Torques. This group comprises two rather similar types of open collars, both made from rod of circular section with coiled ends. **Torques type 1: cat. 276** and **277** from Cuma (Naples), of thin rod of circular or square section, is close to pieces from FBA and EIA, early, contexts from southern and central Italy, for example the FBA cemetery of Castellace (Calabria), and the EIA cemeteries of Torre Mordillo, also in Calabria, Rome Esquilino and Osteria dell'Osa. **Torques type 2: cat. 550**, made from thick circular rod, is close to EIA, late, collars from Campania (Capua, Calitri) and Calabria (Francavilla Marittima).

Section 6 – Fibulae

Italian fibulae have been the subject of several classification works, as part of both regional studies and the analysis of individual cemeteries; moreover, they have been systematically classified by three major specific corpora: the classic book by Sundwall (1943), and two volumes of the *Prähistorische Bronzefunde* series. The first, by Patrizia von Eles, was published in 1975 and is devoted to the fibulae from northern Italy (*PBF* XIV.5); the second, by Fulvia Lo Schiavo, is on the fibulae from southern Italy and Sicily and is due to be published shortly (*PBF* XIV, forthcoming).

Overall, these ornaments are among the best known and studied of Italian protohistory; close parallels for many types that have been defined for the present catalogue can be found in published contexts.

The group as represented in the BM collections consists of 181 pieces, dating from the FBA to the EIA, late. For 40 of these a provenance has been recorded: there is a comparatively low percentage of pieces from Campania (9, *c.* 5%), 14 from other Italian regions, of which 7 are from near Rome, 1 each from Serbia, Greece, Hungary, France, Germany and Czechoslovakia, 3 from Austria and 8 from England.

The majority of the unprovenanced pieces belongs to south Italian, especially Campanian types.

Seventeen pieces are of FBA date, while all the others are divided between the early and late phases of the EIA. The great majority, or perhaps the totality of them probably were part of sets of grave goods. This is indicated by their generally good

state of preservation, as well as by the occurrence of a few pairs of associated identical pieces, probably from female burials, where they were often worn symmetrically on the shoulders or on the chest to fasten a cloak or a mantle.

The first category, **fibulae derived from the violin bow series** includes two types.

Fibulae type 1: cat. 202, a transitional shape between violin bow and stilted fibulae with two knobs, is the only representative of the initial phase of the FBA. **Fibulae type 2** is a late version of the violin bow type; **cat. 203**, with two coils, is a Campanian and Sicilian type and an early predecessor of the EIA 'Sicilian' fibulae (see here **Fibulae types 46–48**), while **cat. 204** (close to **Fibulae type 2**), a large fibula of similar shape with multiple coils, is a unique piece, with possible EIA parallels in Umbria (Terni) and Lazio (Rome).

Arch fibulae form a consistent group of types, mainly of EIA, early, date. They were one of the most popular functional ornaments from a late phase of the FBA to the EIA, and throughout the Italian peninsula and Sicily. Especially during the EIA, they were mainly worn by women. Although the basic shape is extremely simple, there is a wide range of variation in all its main features, depending both on regional-local fashion and on chronology. These include the relative thickness of the bow, its section and general profile, the proportions of symmetrical catch-plates, and the different varieties of discs attached to some types, as well as a wide range of incised and plastic decorations. As a rule, it is possible to identify rather precise regional parallels for the unprovenanced pieces in this category.

Fibulae types 3 and **4** (**cat. 205** and **206**) are two versions of the FBA arch fibula with two knobs: the first one is relatively standard both in shape and size, while the second belongs to a well-known group of very large pieces from southern Italy (Calabria and Basilicata).

Fibulae type 5 (**cat. 207** and probably **cat. 208**) with stilted and slightly thickened bow, is a FBA type which is very close to EIA fibulae from Lazio to Calabria. **Fibulae type 6: cat. 209**, is an arch fibula with straight ends to the bow and a distinctive incised decoration, found in FBA–EIA cemeteries of eastern Sicily and Calabria.

Fibulae type 7 is one of the most common types found in female graves, especially inhumations of EIA, early, date, in Lazio, Campania and southern Italy. **Cat. 278** from the Blacas collection, could be a transitional FBA–EIA piece from Lazio. **Cat. 279**, from Belgrade, former Yugoslavia, and **cat. 280** have an incised and plastic decoration especially found in EIA, early female inhumations from Lazio, Campania and Calabria. The slightly asymmetrical arch of these four pieces is probably reminiscent of FBA stilted arch fibulae. The other three, **cat. 281, 282** (possibly from Zürich, Switzerland) and **283**, are common pieces possibly of slightly later date, as indicated by the more regular curvature of the arch.

Some features of both **Fibulae type 8: cat. 284, 285** and **Fibulae type 9: cat. 286–288**, such as the wide symmetrical catch-plate and the patterns of the incised and plastic decorations, indicate a provenance from Campania, with parallels especially at Cuma. The thickened arch is specific to EIA, early, fibulae, although these Campanian shapes and decorations probably continued in the subsequent phase.

Fibulae type 10: cat. 289–292, with bow thickened and

lowered, mark the transition between the early and late phase of the EIA, and are found especially in Villanovan contexts of central and southern Italy. This also applies to the relative chronology of **Fibulae type 11**, with thickened bow lowered in the central part, and **Fibulae type 12**, with thickened leech bow. The former (**cat. 293–295** from Germany, **cat. 296**, and **297** said to be from England) is found especially in Villanovan cemeteries of both central and southern Italy, and in Lazio. The second type includes four pieces with a standard decoration of encircling lines and chevrons, that is well known from EIA, early, contexts of Etruria, Lazio and Campania (**type 12a, cat. 298** perhaps from England, **cat. 299** from Steiermark, Austria, **cat. 300**, and **301**), while the wide oblique engravings on the arch of **cat. 551** (**type 12b**) probably indicate a slightly later date.

Fibulae type 13: cat. 302, belongs to an exclusive Campanian type, especially found at Cuma, and probably of transitional date.

The next category, **composite arch fibulae**, includes two types characterized by the arch of thin wire threaded with glass beads. **Fibulae type 14: cat. 303**, a small fibula with high bow and wire coiled at both ends, is a distinctive Villanovan type, spanning the EIA and the subsequent period. **Fibulae type 15: cat. 552**, is a specific type of leech fibula with the bow concealed by a large glass bead, found especially in the Villanovan cemetery of Verucchio, in Emilia Romagna, and dating from the EIA, late and later.

Fibulae type 16: cat. 210, is the earliest type in the category of **arch fibulae with disc foot**; it is closely related to a group of FBA fibulae from central Italy with thin arch with multiple coils (see for example Peroni *et al.* 1980, pl. XXIIIC).

Fibulae type 17 includes a group of nine pieces (**cat. 304–308** from near Rome, **cat. 309–311** also from near Rome, and **cat. 312**) with thickened arch and spiral disc of hammered bronze sheet. This is a specific Villanovan type of EIA, early, date, worn mainly by women, which is also found in relatively small numbers in Latial and south Italian fossa-grave contexts, as for example Osteria dell'Osa and Torre Galli. **Fibulae type 18: cat. 313** from near Rome, is closely related to the former type, except for the arch, which was probably covered by graduated amber or bone beads.

Although they constitute a formal development of arch types, the category of **leech, boat and lozenge fibulae** belongs entirely to the late phase of the EIA, with some types continuing into the Orientalizing period. The introduction of these types brought some significant innovations in the making of fibulae: first, the body of the fibula was modelled by casting, and its shape was largely unmodified by further hammering; then leech fibulae were cast hollow over a core of clay; and finally there was the introduction of the boat fibula, with open lower bow. Moreover, the complex incised decoration of these types was mainly obtained by the lost-wax technique. These widespread technical innovations also favoured a higher degree of homogeneity among the productions of local and regional workshops.

Fibulae type 19 is characterized by some features which are specific to the earlier, thickened arch types: solid arch and symmetrical or very slightly elongated catch-plate. Another early trait, the encircling decoration, appears only in some of these pieces. **Cat. 553–555** from Slovakia, and **cat. 556** from Orvieto, Umbria, have the standard early decoration for this type of fibulae, which is found in southern Etruria, Lazio and Campania: rows of bands with an incised herringbone pattern, separated by plain ones. The other three pieces **cat. 557, 558** from Steiermark, Austria, and **cat. 559** show some later decorative patterns such as deeply incised oblique lines and concentric circles .

Fibulae type 20, another type with solid leech bow, includes two pieces **cat. 560**, and **561** from York, England, probably made in northern Italy, as is indicated by the incised meander pattern on the upper side of the bow. A similar provenance is also likely for **Fibulae type 21: cat. 562** and **563** from Semlin, Hungary, with lowered leech bow decorated with parallel grooves. The lowered and flattened arch of **Fibulae type 22: cat. 564**, is specific to an advanced moment of EIA, late. **Fibulae type 23** marks the beginning of the casting of leech fibulae over a clay core; the decoration of these pieces spans from the bands of herringbone pattern seen on early leech fibulae, **cat. 565**, to bands of concentric circles, **cat. 566** from the Tyrol, Austria; **cat. 567**, from Reculver, Kent, England, and **cat. 568** from Perugia, Umbria, hatched triangles, **cat. 569, 571**, and meander patterns, **cat. 570**, the latter probably a north Italian feature.

Fibulae type 24, expanded hollow leech, **cat. 572**, and **573**, is a transitional type between the leech and boat shapes, also as regards the increasingly complex patterns of the decoration, and the elongated catch-plate. The standard boat type, with lower face wide open and elongated/long catch-plate is represented by **Fibulae type 25: cat. 574** from Box, Wiltshire, England, **cat. 575** from Orvieto, Umbria, **cat. 576, 577, 578** from near Taunton, Somerset, England, **cat. 579**, and **580** possibly from Dorset, England. A north Italian variant of this shape is represented by **Fibulae type 26: cat. 581**, a hollow lozenge fibula with elongated catch-plate and an incised decoration of longitudinal lines.

Along with the main steps of the chrono-typological evolution of this category of fibulae as represented by **types 19–21**, and **23–26**, there is another, relatively late series of types (**Fibulae types 27–30**) all characterized by the association of a solid leech or lozenge bow and an elongated or long catch-plate. This difference in technical and typological development probably depends on the fact that since, with few exceptions, the fibulae in the latter series are of relatively small size, it would have been difficult or impossible in this case to adopt the technique of the casting over a clay core.

Fibulae type 27: cat. 582–584; 585 from Athens, and **Fibulae type 28: cat. 586–588,** and the variants **cat. 589–591,** are two rather close types with elongated catch-plate and incised decoration including longitudinal bands on the upper body; the main difference is represented by the slight lateral expansions of the arch of **type 28**, which makes it closer to the later lozenge types. It is interesting to note that **cat. 585**, the only large piece in this group, was probably made by the clay core technique, as is indicated by an opening on its upper face. The closest parallels for both types are in Campania, especially the cemeteries of Capua, Suessula and Pontecagnano, while **cat. 590** and **591** are close to types from Veii.

Fibulae type 29 (four decorated pieces, **cat. 592–595,** and two plain ones, **cat. 596** and **597**) is a group of small solid lozenge fibulae with elongated catch-plate; the decorated pieces are common Campanian types, mainly from Capua, while the plain version is widely diffused in Italian contexts of the end of the EIA. **Fibulae type 30**, small solid leech or lozenge fibulae with elongated catch-plate, decorated by three plastic birds' heads, probably is a Campanian type that is also found in Villanovan cemeteries of southern Etruria. The type is represented by two slightly different varieties, **Fibulae type 30a: cat. 598** and **type 30b: cat. 599–602**.

The category of **arch fibulae with foliate bow** is perhaps best included with the next type in this classification, along with some more common shapes.

Fibulae type 31 is a relatively modest representative of the outburst of flamboyant parade fibulae that appeared at the end of the EIA in northern Campania, especially in the cemeteries of Capua and Suessula.

The basic shape is an arch fibula with large symmetrical catch-plate, with bow formed by two flat bands, and rows of aquatic birds attached to the arch and originally also suspended from its outer edge. The pair in the BM sample, **cat. 784** and **785**, probably come from the same tomb. A unique feature of this pair is that the two fibulae are symmetrical, i.e. in one of them the foot opens on the left, and in the other on the right side of the front face, so that these very special ornaments look identical.

Parallels in EIA, early, contexts of Sicily and Campania can be found for **Fibulae type 32: cat. 314**, a small foliate type with a distinctive incised zigzag decoration. **Fibulae type 33** (**cat. 315** and **316**, both found near Rome) is a more common, central Italian type of foliate fibula with disc foot, also of EIA, early date. A later version of this basic shape is represented by **Fibulae type 34: cat. 603**, from Gorizia (Friuli Venezia Giulia), formerly Görz, Austria: this is a large parade fibula with close parallels in Abruzzo, probably an Adriatic type also found in Umbria (Terni).

Composite arch fibulae with disc foot, the bow made of thin wire of square section covered by groups of bronze discs and amber beads (**Fibulae type 35**) are only represented by a pair, **cat. 443** and **444**, probably from an important female burial dating from EIA, early.

Fibulae with disc foot and thickened or leech bow formed of graduated bronze discs are a technically complex product of the Villanovan metal industry, with parallels in Campania in the cemetery of Pontecagnano; **Fibulae type 36**, the thickened arch version, **cat. 317**, and **Fibulae type 37**, with leech bow, **cat. 318** from Ruvo (Bari), Apulia, and the pair **cat. 445–446**, both date from EIA, early.

The earliest types in the wide category of **one-piece serpentine fibulae**, usually with spiral disc, appeared in Italy in a late phase of the FBA and continued during EIA, early. They are widely distributed in the southern and central regions of Italy, and are found both in Villanovan and in fossa-grave contexts. The early version, with straight pin, is represented in the BM sample by two types: **Fibulae type 38**, with disc of spiral wire, dating from FBA, late, and the FBA–EIA transition (**cat. 211** from France; **cat. 212–215**, possibly from Dorset), and **Fibulae type 39**, with spiral disc of hammered sheet, mainly of EIA, early date (**cat. 216**, still with some FBA features, **cat. 319–322**).

A small fibula of Protovillanovan tradition, with loops on the arch and spiral-wire disc foot (**Fibulae type 40: cat. 323**,

from near Rome) can be dated to the initial phase of EIA, early, e.g. in the cemetery of Pontecagnano (Salerno), Campania.

The most popular types of serpentine fibulae which are found throughout EIA, early, are those with curved pin; an early version, **Fibulae type 41a: cat. 324**, with plastic decoration, has parallels mainly in central Italy (the Piediluco hoard and the Latial cemetery of Castel Gandolfo, in the Alban Hills). The slightly later version, **Fibulae type 41b: cat. 325**, with incised decoration, is the most common fibula type used by men in Villanovan Etruria, Lazio and the Villanovan groups of Campania (see for example *Osteria dell'Osa* 1992, 372–373, pl. 38, types 40a, 40b, 40c; *Pontecagnano* 1988, 52–53, pl.18 and fig. I.12, 21: types 32B4, 32B4a, 32B5, 32B6).

Two-piece serpentine fibulae make up another important category spanning the FBA–EIA transition and EIA, early. **Fibulae type 42: cat. 217, 218**, the earliest type in this group, characterized by the straight pin and plastic decoration of the bow, is a well-known product of the Piediluco-Contigliano metallurgical tradition, which probably originated in Etruria, and distributed its models and artefacts over the whole territory of the Italian peninsula. The other two types, **Fibulae type 43: cat. 326**, and **Fibulae type 44: cat. 327**, from Nola (Naples), both specifically Campanian, can be dated to an advanced moment of the local EIA, early, and probably continued in the following phase; this also applies to **Fibulae type 45: cat. 328**, with parallels in the Adriatic regions of Italy. Three unclassified pieces, **cat. 348** from the Marsica, Abruzzo, **cat. 349**, and **350** belong to fibulae in this category.

Serpentine fibulae with two coils and elongated catch-plate (so-called Sicilian fibulae) are apparently an elaboration from FBA types which took place between FBA, late, and the FBA–EIA transition (see for example Giardino 1995, 240, fig. 120.C.1, 2, from Molino della Badia and Modica, Sicily). They are a basically Sicilian and south Italian group, which in its earliest phase is found as far north as ancient Lazio. The basic shape of the Sicilian fibula was also adopted in the Villanovan cemeteries of Campania and of southern Etruria in an advanced moment of EIA, early.

The EIA, early, pieces are characterized by a markedly limited degree of formal variation and by a basic decoration of incised chevrons.

Fibulae type 46: cat. 329–331, the earliest type in this group, are characterized by the circular section of both bow and coils. **Fibulae type 47**, a slightly later type, with a higher proportion of relatively large pieces (**cat. 332–336**), have rectangular section to the coils, while for **Fibulae type 48: cat. 337–339**, both bow and coils are quadrangular in section. **Fibulae type 49** comprises a single piece, **cat. 340**, a small fibula with a foliate expansion substituting the back coil, with parallels from both southern Italy and Lazio.

Drago fibulae represent the formal development of the former group, dating from EIA, late, and later. The main typological features which characterize this group are the bow forming an elbow instead of a coil above the long catch-plate, the symmetrical protrusions decorating the bow, and the pin with double upper end. The types, with slight variations, include **Fibulae type 50: cat. 604**, **type 51a: cat. 605**, and **type 51b: cat. 606–608**.

The next categories all belong to a metallurgical tradition which was radically different from the Italian ones (both arch and serpentine fibulae), and was probably introduced to Italy from the Balkan regions at the end of the FBA. The basic shape is the spectacle fibula, made from two joined flat spirals of bronze wire, with the relatively early four-spiral variants. These fibulae are rather popular in southern Italy, especially during EIA, late. In northern Campania, especially Capua and Suessula, these fibulae developed into spectacular oversize ornaments, decorated by plastic figurines representing both humans and animals, also present in the BM Italian collection.

Spectacle fibulae. Formally, the earlier type in this category is **Fibulae type 52**, with pin and hook springing from the centre of the spirals, which are joined at the centre by a figure-of-eight loop. This type includes **cat. 341**, from Paestum (Salerno), Campania, **cat. 342–344**, all probably dating from EIA, early.

Fibulae type 53a: **cat. 609**, and **type 53b**: **cat. 610** and **611**, are later large spectacle types, with backing-plate of violin-bow shape and figure-of-eight loop; the backing plate may be with or without coiled spring. **Fibulae type 54**: **cat. 612**, also dating from EIA, late, is a large spectacle fibula without figure-of-eight loop; the spirals are supported by a violin-bow backing plate without spring and by perpendicular bronze bands. **Fibulae type 55**: **cat. 613** from Ruvo (Bari), Apulia, **cat. 614, 615**, includes large damaged spectacle fibulae with central figure-of-eight loop, conical or hemispherical cap at the centre of each spiral, and violin-bow backing plate, mostly missing. **Cat. 616, 617** from Naples, **cat. 618**; three pieces, **cat. 619–621** from Torre Annunziata (Naples), and **cat. 622**, might belong to this type. Another damaged piece, **cat. 623** from Ruvo (Bari), Apulia, might belong to **Fibulae types 54** or **55**.

Four-spiral fibulae: **Fibulae type 56** includes relatively large pieces (**cat. 624–626** from Caserta, Campania) with a small bronze disc attached to the centre of the spirals and pin and hook springing from the centre of two opposing spirals; it is close to the *PBF* types Incoronata and Amendolara, of EIA, late, date.

Fibulae type 57, a small four-spiral type with central disc- or diamond-shaped plate, violin bow backing plate with spring, and supporting bronze bands is close to *PBF* type Torano, EIA, early. **Cat. 345**, and **346** from Santa Maria Maggiore di Capua (Caserta), Campania, belong to this type, while **cat. 347**, two spirals from a four-spiral fibula, might belong to **Fibulae types 56** or **57**.

Fibulae type 58: this type of four-spiral fibula of EIA late date is well known from Suessula and other Campanian sites. The type's main features are the four-spiral bow with a horned bird figurine attached at the center, and the violin-bow backing plate. Of the two BM pieces, **cat. 627** includes the backing plate and horned bird figurine, **cat. 628** the bird only.

Cat. 629–631 from 'the Maremma, near Veii' (Rome), Lazio, **cat. 632–634** are spirals, possibly from large spectacle fibulae of **types 54** or **55**.

Section 7 – Bracelets

Although it constitutes a relatively frequent component of Italian Bronze and Iron Age contexts, the group of bronze artefacts which goes under the label of bracelets is not among those that have been given particular attention by specialists. However, as we shall see, it is not without interest. As regards the present sample, which includes a total of 134 pieces, all

dating from the EIA or later, at least two significant features can be highlighted: first, there is a rather consistent group of pieces belonging to a specific archaeological component of the Campanian Iron Age, the so-called Oliveto-Cairano culture; and, second, a relatively significant percentage of pieces made from coiled bronze rod, especially those classified as **Bracelets types 5**, **6**, **8**, and perhaps **7** and **9a**, probably are bracelet-shaped weights (see below).

Based on a number of differences in technique and/or aesthetic value, these bracelets can be divided into several categories: spiral, ribbon, coiled wire, coiled rod, annular, penannular, D-shaped, hollow. Spiral and ribbon bracelets are among the earliest in this group, with some FBA precedents, and also continuing in EIA, late; all the other categories are found mainly in context dating from EIA late, and later.

Spiral bracelets: **Bracelets type 1**, a pair from Bologna, **cat. 447–448**, and another pair unprovenanced, **cat. 449–450**, are made from thick wire of plano-convex section with coiled ends. This type is usually found in pairs especially in Villanovan cemeteries, as part of the funerary set of young girls. **Bracelets type 2a**: **cat. 351–354**, and **Bracelets type 2c**: **cat. 635** from Armento (Potenza, Basilicata), formed by several coils of thin wire of even or decreasing diameter, usually with flattened coiled ends, are south Italian female ornaments, found in fossa-grave, Oliveto-Cairano and Villanovan contexts. **Bracelets type 2b**: **cat. 355** from Cuma (Naples), Campania, and **type 2d**: **cat. 636**, rod of triangular section, (probably slightly later), with ends forming one or two flat spirals, are close to pieces from Villanovan cemeteries in northern, central and southern Italy (Bologna, Veii Quattro Fontanili, Pontecagnano).

Ribbon bracelets: the types in this small group of coiled ribbon bracelets with spiral or coiled ends are probably of south Italian origin. **Bracelets type 3a**: **cat. 356** from Armento (Potenza), Basilicata, made from flat decorated ribbon with spiral ends), and **type 3b**: **cat. 357**, ribbon with central ridge with flat coiled ends, can be compared to EIA, early pieces from Calabria and eastern Sicily (cemeteries of Torre Galli and Molino della Badia); **Bracelets type 3a variant**, **cat. 637** probably is a later version of **type 3a**.

Coiled wire bracelets: **Bracelets type 4**, the only type in this category, consist of a group of remarkably standardized coiled double-wire bracelets with ends wrapped together, **cat. 638–643**, probably **cat. 644** from Armento (Potenza), Basilicata, and the two pairs **cat. 786–787** from Palestrina (Rome), and **cat. 788–789**. This is a specific Campanian, Oliveto-Cairano type, as is the group of D-shaped pieces labelled as **Bracelets types 12a-d** (see below): all are of EIA, late, or later date.

Coiled rod bracelets: as already noted, rather than personal ornaments, **Bracelets type 5** quite probably should be identified as weights. The type includes nine unprovenanced pieces; **cat. 645–648**, entered the BM at different times and as part of distinct lots, as is indicated by both registration data and marked differences in patina. The other five pieces (**cat. 790–794**), all identical in shape, colour, patina and general state of preservation, probably were found together, and should be considered as a group, although no information on their provenance has been recorded.

They are all made from relatively thick rod of rounded or

roughly square section, with ends narrowing and overlapping. Although extremely simple, the shape is clearly identifiable. Their weights all seem to refer to a unit of approximately 19.5g.

Cat.	Weight	Relation to the unit of 19.5g			
645	10g	19.5	x ½	=	9.75
646	62g	19.5	x 3	=	58.5
648	77g	19.5	x 4	=	78
647	138g	19.5	x 7	=	136.5
790	78g	19.5	x 4	=	78
791	118g	19.5	x 6	=	117
792	162g	19.5	x 8	=	156
793	197g	19.5	x 10	=	195
794	215g	19.5	x 11	=	214.5

The approximation is rather close, especially as regards the five pieces that were probably found together.

The parallels, mainly in Campania and in Etruria, indicate an EIA, late, or later date.

An interesting point relative to this and to the other types of bracelet-weights (**Bracelets types 6, 8,** perhaps **7** and **9a**) is whether or not they are related to the early Greek (or Phoenician) presence in Campania.

Bracelets type 5 variant, cat. 649, apparently is a real bracelet made from thin rod, that is close to **type 5** in general shape. It probably belongs to a group of plain bracelets usually found in male burials, especially in Villanovan contexts.

Bracelets type 6: cat. 650–652, made from thick circular rod, with overlapping ends decorated with groups of parallel grooves, are also quite likely to be weights, although the identification of a common weight unit apparently is more difficult. Similar pieces are rather common at Pithekoussai, in LGI-II graves.

Cat.	Weight
650	567g
652	112g
651	70g

Bracelets type 7: cat. 653 and **654,** with a ring and a bulla and ring suspended to the rod, are similar to **type 6,** although both size and weight might indicate their use as real bracelets.

Bracelets type 8, cat. 655 and **656,** made from thick rod in two coils, and also with parallels at Pithekoussai, may definitely be identified as weights, both from the amount of metal used for their making, and from the small diameter of cat. 655 (5.2cm).

Cat.	Weight
655	140g
656	462g

Bracelets type 9, coiled rod with molded ends, comes in two varieties: **type 9a,** plain (**cat. 657–660**) and **type 9b,** with incised decoration (**cat. 661**). This is mainly a late Villanovan type, found both in Campania and Etruria.

Annular bracelets: Bracelets types 10a: cat. 662–666, and **10b, cat. 667,** are plain circular bracelets made from bronze wire, with parallels in Villanovan II and Latial III contexts.

Penannular bracelets: Bracelets type 11: cat. 668, 669, plain or incised rod with ends touching, probably a Campanian

type of EIA, late, date, found in fossa-grave and Oliveto-Cairano contexts.

D-shaped bracelets: this category is specific to the Oliveto-Cairano culture; the two main types, **Bracelets types 12a** and 12b, both comprise several pieces, whose most notable characteristic is a high degree of standardization in shape as well as in decoration. The same feature has been noted relative to **Bracelets type 4,** that also belong to the Oliveto-Cairano repertoire. This group of artefacts in the BM collection, almost all unfortunately found unregistered, might come from an unknown cemetery of this culture, which is confined to inner Campania, provinces of Salerno and Avellino, along the Sele and Ofanto valleys. The chronology of this category of bracelets, as known in the cemeteries of Cairano, Calitri, Oliveto Citra, and Bisaccia, ranges from EIA, late, to the Orientalizing and archaic periods.

Bracelets type 12a: 54 pieces, **cat. 670–723,** all made from plain thin bronze rod with open ends; **cat. 724, type 12a variant,** is of plain thick rod with plano-convex section.

Bracelets type 12b: 13 pieces, **cat. 725–737,** made from thick bronze rod of circular or plano-convex section, with ends open and touching; the outer surface is covered by parallel incised lines. A provenance from Tarquinia (Viterbo), Lazio, is recorded for **cat. 726.**

The other two types, both consisting of a single piece, are similar in general shape, and may be tentatively attributed to the Oliveto-Cairano group, although no precise parallels are known: **Bracelets type 12c: cat. 738,** is a flat bronze ribbon with incised *tremolo* decoration, while **Bracelets type 12d: cat. 739,** is made from a thicker ribbon with separate ends of narrow cylindrical form.

Hollow bracelets: the pieces in this category are made from hammered bronze sheet, bent to form a hollow bracelet, either coiled or with open ends; they are of EIA, late, or Orientalizing date, with parallels in Etruria, Lazio and Campania. **Bracelets type 13a: cat. 740,** and a pair probably from a tomb, **cat. 795–796,** is coiled, with moulded overlapping ends; **Bracelets type 13b: cat. 741,** is also coiled, with plain ends. **Type 13c,** a pair, **cat. 797–798,** and **type 13d: cat. 742** from Locri (Reggio Calabria), are penannular, of plano-convex section; the latter has a rich incised decoration, with close parallels in the cemetery of Veii, Quattro Fontanili.

Unclassified bracelets: part of two coiled wire bracelets, probably of EIA date, **cat. 828** from Sesto Calende (Varese), Lombardy, and **cat. 829.**

Section 8 – Daggers and halberds

Two halberds and 17 daggers, dating from the EBA to the RBA, make up the BM sample. Most of the types correspond to the *PBF* VI.10 classification.

Halberds

This relatively rare type of weapon, characterized by a slightly asymmetrical triangular blade, was in use from the CA, and apparently went out of use after the EBA. **Halberds type 1,** a single piece, **cat. 14,** from Calvatone (Cremona), Lombardy, made from arsenical copper, belongs to a distictive type with large triangular blade and central rib. *PBF* pieces classified as type Calvatone come mainly from contexts of the CA Rinaldone culture, in central Italy; this piece is the only one from northern Italy. The use of arsenical copper can be considered as a confirmation of its CA date.

Halberds type 2: cat. 41 from Frosinone, Lazio, belongs to a group probably of EBA, late, date, distributed in central and southern Italy (see *PBF* type Cotronei).

Daggers

The earliest BM pieces in this group of metal artefacts, which also appeared in Italy from the CA, can be dated to the EBA.

The sample includes seven pieces of EBA date, divided into five types, that show a general correspondence with some EBA types classified in *PBF* VI.10. However, the parallels are not absolutely precise, and the combination of formal and decorative features does not seem to correspond to a linear chronological development. All the pieces are decorated prestige weapons, that were probably selected from their contexts by both finders and collectors as the most valuable pieces. **Cat. 60** and **61** were found together.

Daggers with socketed hilt

Daggers type 1: cat. 42, is a superb weapon originally *c.* 50cm long, with triangular blade and socketed hilt for a composite handle. It is close to *PBF* types Ripatransone var. B (for the socketed handle) and Montemerano (for the blade with converging nervatures).

Daggers with cast hilt riveted to the blade

Daggers type 2: cat. 43 and 60, and Daggers type 3: cat. 61, are close to *PBF* types Cetona var. B, with a rich incised decoration, and Montemerano var. B, with nervatures on the blade. **Daggers type 4: cat. 44**, a small plain piece, is comparable to type Loreto Aprutino var. B, and **Daggers type 5: cat. 45** and **46** from Torre Annunziata (Naples), Campania, both with a central rib, are close to *PBF* type Parco dei Monaci.

MBA and RBA daggers are more standardized, and usually belong to specific north Italian types found in Palafitte-Terramare contexts.

Each of the two MBA pieces is representative of a specific category. **Daggers type 6: cat. 79** from Magliano (L'Aquila), Abruzzo, is an elongated **triangular dagger** that belongs to *PBF* type Monte Castellaccio, and **Daggers type 7: cat. 80** from Peschiera (Verona), Veneto, 26cm long, is a compromise between a well-known type of **tanged dagger** with thick diamond section (e.g. *PBF* VI. 10, no. 1119) and a short sword.

The majority of RBA daggers correspond to common Terramare types; for some of them a possible use as domestic tools, the predecessors of knives, is indicated especially by their small size (weight 23–37g, length *c.* 12–14cm). This is probably the case with the category of daggers with triangular tang: **Daggers type 8: cat. 117**, and **118** from Bologna, Emilia Romagna, with open triangular tang, close to *PBF* types Torre Castelluccia var. C and Campegine, and **Daggers type 9: cat. 119** from Teramo, Abruzzo, also with triangular tang, and close to *PBF* type Glisente.

The pieces in the category of **daggers with flanged hilt**, usually called Peschiera daggers, are all of larger size (average weight *c.* 60g, except for **cat. 124**, 97g; length *c.* 18 –25cm), and with a more efficient hafting. A function as proper weapons seems therefore more likely. This group, probably originating from the Peschiera-Terramare metal industry, is widely distributed in Europe and the Aegean (see for example *Terramare* 1997, fig. 343), as is confirmed by the provenances of some of the BM pieces. **Daggers type 10: cat. 120** from Peschiera (Verona), Veneto, has a tapering flanged hilt terminating in a suspension ring; a *PBF* parallel is type Toscanella var.C. **Daggers type 11: cat. 121** from Steiermark, Austria, **cat. 122** from Peschiera, and **cat. 123** from Sussex, England, belong to types Bertarina and Verona.

A specific type of Peschiera dagger, which is found in Greece as well as in Italian contexts with Aegean connections, is represented by **Daggers type 12: cat. 124**, with blade widening towards the lower part, and ivory or bone hilt-plates extant, from Naxos, Greece, *PBF* type Pertosa var. A.

Section 9 – Swords and sword sheaths

The majority of the 41 pieces corresponds to the types defined by Bianco Peroni in *PBF* IV.1. The BM sample is largely representative of Italian bronze swords of LBA and EIA date. It includes a few MBA–RBA short swords (**Swords types 1** and **2**); a few flanged weapons (**Swords types 3** and **4**) of the Naue II group, widely distributed in Europe and the Aegean; a transitional FBA–EIA flanged type (**Swords type 5**); a chronologically significant series of the EIA, so-called Italic T-hilt swords (**Swords types 6** to **10**); a late EIA type of tanged short sword (**Swords type 11**), and two early antennae swords (**Swords type 12**). The swords are often associated with their sheaths.

The division between long and short swords, not always coinciding with overall typological differences, can be placed around a length of *c.* 45cm, which obviously does not include the full height of the pommel.

BA short swords

This rather heterogeneous category includes the short MBA sword from the Island of Cres, Croatia, with plain trapezoidal blade base (**cat. 81, Swords type 1**), and the single unprovenanced piece classified as **Swords type 2: cat. 125**, apparently a short version of some of the earliest (RBA) tanged and flanged swords known in Italy.

Flanged swords

Swords type 3: cat. 126, from Scutari, Albania, a plain flanged long sword, is close to *PBF* type Treviso, an early type in this series.

Swords type 4, an Italian type with close parallels in central Europe (Erbenheim type) and in Greece, corresponds to *PBF* type Allerona (RBA–FBA); the piece from Frosinone, Lazio, **cat. 127**, is one of the finest long swords of this type known in Italy, while the short sword from Bisignano (Cosenza), Calabria, **cat. 219**, probably is a local version of the type, which might be either of FBA, late, or of EIA date, as is indicated by its reduced length and by the incised decoration on the blade.

Swords type 5, consisting of six pieces, **cat. 220** from Naples, Campania; **cat. 221** with its sheath **cat. 222**; **223, 224** from near Perugia (Umbria), **cat. 225**, and **226**, close to the type, correspond to *PBF* type Contigliano, a group of flanged swords characterized by a wide range of variability; this type, dating from the FBA–EIA transition, marks the earliest appearance of the Italian EIA short swords. However, while the latter are characterized by a cast T-hilt which was originally covered with plates of organic matter, the hilt of the Contigliano type swords was surmounted by a pommel entirely made of organic material, as is shown by the magnificent sword **cat. 226**, with ivory pommel, hilt and shoulder plates.

The fragment of sheath **cat. 222**, associated with the sword **cat. 221**, probably belongs to the *PBF* type Torre Galli (**Sheaths type 1**), also dating from the end of the FBA or the initial phase of the EIA.

T-hilt swords

Swords types 6 and **7** illustrate the FBA–EIA transition in southern Italy. **Swords type 6**, a solid cast T-hilt from Armento (Potenza), Basilicata, **cat. 227**, is very close typologically to the Torre Galli-Modica and to the Contigliano swords, and its pointillé decoration has good parallels in other categories of Italian FBA bronzes. The latter type, **Swords type 7**, comprises a single specimen of T-hilt short sword, **cat. 358**, from Naples, Campania, of a type known both from the EIA cemetery of Torre Galli, in Calabria, and from the FBA–EIA hoard of Modica, in Sicily; its sheath, **cat. 359**, belongs to **Sheaths type 1**.

T-hilt short swords and sheaths dating from the earliest phase of the EIA form the largest category in this sample. The nine swords correspond to two *PBF* types rather close in shape and chronology. **Swords type 8a**, close to type Cuma, includes **cat. 457**, part of a group of weapons found at Cassino (Frosinone), Lazio; **cat. 360, 361** from Naples, **cat. 362** from Ruvo (Bari), Apulia, **cat. 363** from Naples, **cat. 364, 365** from Armento (Potenza), Basilicata, with its sheath **cat. 366, Sheaths type 3**. **Swords type 8b**, (*PBF* type Pontecagnano) comprises **cat. 369**, and **367**, associated with its sheath, **cat. 368, Sheaths type 2**, which also corresponds to the *PBF* sheaths type Pontecagnano. **Cat. 373** is another sheath of the same type.

Flanged T-hilt short swords dating from EIA, late, correspond to three *PBF* types: **Swords type 9a: cat. 743** from Locri (Reggio Calabria), is close to type Terni; it is associated with its sheath, **cat. 744, Sheaths type 3**.

Swords type 9b, close to type Vulci, includes **cat. 745**, and **746**, an Italian sword found at Sticna, Slovenia, still in its sheath, **unclassified**. **Cat. 747**, from Naples, is also classified as **Sheaths type 3**.

Swords type 10, *PBF* type Ardea, a very short weapon ending in a narrow carp's tongue, is the most recent of the T-hilt EIA types in the sample; the only piece, **cat. 748**, is associated with the sheath **cat. 749, Sheaths type 4**.

Tanged swords with shoulder cap

Cat. 750, from Acerra (Naples), Campania, **Swords type 11**, belongs to a different and much less popular category, with short carp's tongue blade and a long and narrow tang; a cast bronze shoulder cap covers the junction of blade and tang, and the hilt and pommel, now disappeared, were of organic matter. The corresponding *PBF* pieces belong to a small group from Etruria and Lazio, dating from the final phase of the EIA.

Antennae swords

The two pieces in this category, **cat. 370**, and **371**, with the remains of its sheath, **cat. 372, unclassified**, grouped in **Swords type 12**, correspond to *PBF* types Tarquinia and Fermo, both EIA, early, continuing into the advanced phase.

Unclassified swords

The sample includes two pieces: **cat. 830**, another antennae sword, probably a fake, as is indicated by its unusual technical and typological features as well as by the composition of its alloy, and **cat. 831**, possibly a BA sword point.

Sword sheaths: the pieces in this group are all made of hammered bronze sheet joining on the back side, usually decorated on the front with vertical nervatures and incised geometric patterns. The lower terminals, which are riveted to the bronze sheet or joined to it by casting, end with a solid bronze globe or with discs in the later pieces: see for the experimental reproduction of a sword sheath Bietti Sestieri *et al*. 2003. In general, only the outer, metal part of these objects is preserved. From a few well-preserved pieces, e.g. the sword **cat. 746** from Sticna, we know that the sheath's inner lining was made of wood. In some pieces (see **cat. 359, Sheaths type 1**), the decoration on the front ends some centimetres below the rim; this is an indication that the upper end of the sheath was covered by a strip of organic matter, usually leather, which served the purpose of joining the outer metal part to the wooden lining, as well as of attaching some bronze suspension rings. The upper section of the sheath could be covered with an ivory plate decorated with discs (two swords from Torre Galli) or with a bronze terminal bearing different kinds of decorations (e.g. *PBF* IV.1, nos. 347, 259a).

Several sheaths from our sample were associated with their swords, and belong to chronologically matching types. **Cat. 359** and probably **222** belong to **Sheaths type 1**, *PBF* type Torre Galli, EIA, early, and are associated with swords **cat. 358** and **221** (**Swords types 7** and **5** respectively).

Cat. 368 and **373, Sheaths type 2**, correspond to *PBF* type Pontecagnano, also of EIA early date; **cat. 368** is associated with the sword **cat. 367, Swords type 8b**. The lower part of a sheath, **cat. 372**, associated with the antennae sword **cat. 371**, is generally close to **Sheaths type 2**.

Cat. 366, 744, and **747** are classified as **Sheaths type 3** (cf. *PBF* type Guardia Vomano, EIA early and later): **cat. 366** goes with sword **cat. 365, Swords type 8a**; **cat. 744** with **743, Swords type 9a**. **Cat. 749**, a short sheath ending in a narrow carp's tongue with discs terminal (**Sheaths type 4**, cf. *PBF* type Narce, EIA late) is associated with sword **cat. 748, Swords type 10**.

It was not possible to classify the sheath associated with sword **cat. 746** (**Swords type 9b**).

Section 10 – Spearheads/javelins and spear-butts

The 130 plus pieces in this group, mainly spearheads with the addition of a few spear-butts, constitute a substantial section of the BM Italian bronzes. However, due to the highly functional characteristics of this class of offensive weapons in the Italian metallurgical tradition, which from the MBA consist of a conical socket and elongated symmetrical blade, the range of typological variability is limited.

Among the few pieces which can be attributed to the FBA, an especially interesting one is **cat. 228**, registered as found in the River Tiber near Rome, probably following the widespread European BA tradition of offering weapons to the waters of lakes and rivers.

Apparently, the majority of the spearheads belong to EIA south Italian types, with a concentration between the end of period I and period II, early, as documented in the southern Villanovan cemeteries, especially Pontecagnano. It is important to remember that throughout EIA I the practice of including real functional weapons in men's funerary sets was specific to inhumation burials; in particular, weapons are exceedingly rare in early Villanovan contexts, where cremation is almost exclusive, and were often broken before being placed in the grave. We can therefore assume that the great majority of weapons dating from EIA I are more likely to come from inhumation burials, which were specific to the so-called fossa-grave culture of Campania, possibly southern Lazio, and Calabria (e.g. the cemetery of Torre Galli), as well as to the inhuming communities of Abruzzo, Apulia and Sicily. The most interesting group of EIA spearheads is represented by the large decorated pieces classified as **Spearheads types 4** and **5**, possibly the distinctive weapons of military/political chiefs.

In general terms, bronze weapons were rather rare after the beginning of EIA II, when the use of iron became quite common. However, some bronze weapons, especially a group of oversize spearheads and spear-butts of very accurate manufacture, clearly ceremonial in scope, are known from contexts dating from the final phase of the EIA (phase IIC in the usual relative chronology of Villanovan complexes) as well as from the subsequent Orientalizing period. Besides being of bronze, these weapons conform to the EIA tradition also as regards their formal features. The BM sample includes some pieces which belong to this group: the two huge spearheads from Bomarzo, **cat. 799** and **800**, and the large spearhead and butt bought from Castellani, **cat. 765** and **766**.

Several pieces in this group have provenances, including two pieces from Olympia, Greece, **cat. 395** and **764**; **cat. 458** and **459** were found at Cassino (Frosinone, Lazio) along with a sword, **cat. 457**, while **cat. 453** and **454** were found together at Bari (Apulia) and were part of funerary sets, as were two more pairs, **cat. 451–452** from Sulmona (L'Aquila), Abruzzo and **cat. 455–456** from Arezzo, Tuscany.

Spearheads/javelins

Spearheads type 1, a FBA type found in north Italian and trans-Alpine contexts, consists only of a spearhead from the River Tiber at Rome, **cat. 228**. **Spearheads types 2** and **3**, both plain types of spearheads/javelins, with wide conical socket and foliate blade, can be dated between the FBA and the EIA: **cat. 229–232** (**Spearheads type 2**), and **cat. 233** from Pozzuoli (Naples), Campania; **cat. 234–236** from Rome, (**Spearheads type 3**) and the variant **cat. 237** have parallels in FBA bronze-hoards as Monte Primo (Marche) and Poggio Berni (Romagna) (*PBF* IV.1, pl.78B.8; *PBF* VII.2, pl.67.10,11,12), while an EIA date is more likely for **cat. 374–376** from Capua (Caserta), Campania; **cat. 451** and **452** from Sulmona (L'Aquila), Abruzzo; **cat. 377–383** and **751** (**Spearheads type 2**); **cat. 384, 385, 752** (**Spearheads type 3**), and two variants, **cat. 386** and **753**.

Spearheads type 4 is one of the most interesting types of the whole collection: it consists of large weapons with foliate blade and faceted upper socket, characterized by a rich incised decoration, which in some of the largest pieces creates the approximation of a human face. Apparently, these are prestige weapons, as is indicated by the association of **cat. 458** with another spear and a sword; the human face probably is meant to add a magic or supernatural power to the spear. **Cat. 389**, possibly a variant of the type from a cremation burial, is a miniature spear with an incised decoration clearly reminiscent of the full size pieces. Apparently, the earliest pieces are those in which the figurative purpose is clearly identifiable: **cat. 458**, from Cassino (Frosinone), Lazio; **cat. 387**, from Bari, Apulia, and **cat. 388**, along with the miniature spear **cat. 389**. **Cat. 390** and **391** can be compared to a spearhead with some figurative elements from Pontecagnano, tomb 180, dating from phase IA or IB of this cemetery. The other pieces, **cat. 754, 755** from Bari, Apulia, **cat. 756** from Naples, **cat. 757**, and the variant **cat. 758**, all of which bear some decorative elements that are clearly reminiscent of the earliest image, can be compared to a number of pieces from south Italian cemeteries dating to EIA, late.

Spearheads type 5: **cat. 392, 393**, from Capua (Caserta), Campania, **cat. 394** from Popoli (Pescara), Abruzzo; **cat. 395** from Olympia, Greece; **cat. 396, 459** from Cassino (Frosinone), Lazio, is an early type that is apparently specific to southern Italy and characterized by the faceted upper socket. **Spearheads type 6** with faceted socket, **cat. 397** from Naples, **cat. 453** and **454**, both from Bari (Apulia), the variant **cat. 398** from Bovino (Foggia), Apulia, associated with its spear-butt, **cat. 399**, is a popular EIA type, which was in use from the beginnings of the period; the two larger pieces, **cat. 759** and the variant **760**, probably are the most recent in this group.

Spearheads type 7: **cat. 761–763** from Arezzo (Tuscany); **cat. 764** from Olympia, Greece, **cat. 765** with its spear-butt **cat. 766** (**Spear-butts type 5**), can possibly be dated to the advanced phase of the EIA, since **cat. 765** and **766** are almost identical to the spear and spear-butt from the Warrior grave of Tarquinia (Kilian 1977b, fig.7.5, 6), of late Villanovan or Orientalizing date. **Spearheads type 8** (**cat. 400–402** from Capua (Caserta), Campania, and **cat. 403** from Naples) of general EIA date, is characterized by the narrow elongated shape of both blade and socket.

Spearheads type 9: **cat. 404** probably from the Marsica, in Abruzzo, and **cat. 405** from Cuma (Naples), Campania, is a well-characterized type of javelin with angular foliate blade decorated by two nervatures. No precise parallels have been found, although an EIA date is likely.

Spearheads type 10 (**cat. 406** from Cuma, **cat. 407** from Calabria, **cat. 408** from the Marsica, Abruzzo, **cat. 409, 410, 411, 413** and **412**, variant), and **Spearheads type 11**: **cat. 414, 415** from Pozzuoli (Naples), **cat. 416** found near Metaponto (Matera), Basilicata, **cat. 417** from near Naples, **cat. 418** from Capua (Caserta), Campania, **cat. 419** from Marsica, **cat. 420** and **cat. 421**, are plain EIA types of spearheads/javelins with rounded profile to the blade, which is narrower in **type 11**.

Spearheads type 12: **cat. 767–770** from Capua (Caserta), Campania, is a prestige weapon of accurate making, including some very large parade pieces. It can be dated to EIA, late (see *Quattro Fontanili* 1975, fig. 51.7, tomb A-B 11–12, phase IIB). **Spearheads/javelins type 13**, with flame-shaped blade, **cat.**

422 from Abruzzo, **cat. 423** from Agrigento, Sicily, **cat. 424** from near Naples, **cat. 425, 426** from Naples, **cat. 427–432** and 455 from Arezzo (Tuscany), associated with **cat. 456**, and **Spearheads type 14** with flame-shaped blade (**cat. 456** from Arezzo, Tuscany, **cat. 433, 434**) have parallels in EIA contexts spanning both the early and late phases.

Spearheads type 15: cat. 799 and **800**, part of a group from Bomarzo (Viterbo), Lazio, **cat. 771, 772** probably associated with spear-butt **cat. 773** (**Spear-butts type 4**), **cat. 774–777** from Capua (Caserta), Campania, comprises some very large, probably ceremonial spearheads, the two from Bomarzo nearly 1m in length, with flame-shaped blade and faceted socket. The shape of these pieces indicates a late phase of the EIA, although especially the largest ones are likely to be later versions of traditional models. See for another large parade spear of similar size (L. *c.* 50cm), **cat. 765, Spearheads type 7**.

Spearheads type 16, also with flame-shaped blade, **cat. 435** from Capua (Caserta), Campania, **cat. 436, 437** from Viterbo, Lazio, and **cat. 438** from Mineo (Catania), Sicily, associated with spear-butt **cat. 439**, can be compared to pieces of both early and late EIA date. **Cat. 435** belongs to the Piediluco-Contigliano metal industry, which originated in southern Etruria and Umbria in coincidence with the FBA–EIA transition and circulated widely over peninsular Italy.

Spearheads type 17: cat. 238, from S. Maria di Licodia, near Paternò (Catania), Sicily, is a specific Sicilian type with narrow straight blade, of FBA to EIA date.

Unclassified spearheads include a few fragments and unidentified pieces: **cat. 832** from Rome, part of a javelin-head covered by thick incrustations, **cat. 833**, perhaps part of a miniature spearhead, **cat. 834** from Perugia, Umbria, a broken spearhead point probably re-used as an arrowhead, and **cat. 835** from Val d'Aosta, a conical socket.

Spear-butts

Like the spearheads, spear-butts are basically functional artefacts with little formal variation. Therefore, the division into types may be simply the result of functional convergence, as is probably the case with the simplest shapes, especially type 1, while those of more accurate manufacture, apparently part of prestige or parade weapons, are proper types depending on specific models. An EIA, late, date is probable for most of the pieces, although types 4 and 5 also include some earlier ones.

Spear-butts type 1: cat. 778 from Calabria, **cat. 779** from the Marsica (L'Aquila), Abruzzo, **cat. 780** from Bolsena (Viterbo), Lazio: plain conical form with lower end more or less sharply pointed.

Spear-butts type 2: cat. 781 from Calabria, is characterized by its flaring, flat lower end. The last three types, **Spear-butts types 3, 4** and **5**, all are accurately manufactured, with outer surface faceted (*see* **Spear-butts type 3: cat. 782** from Orvieto, Umbria, and **cat. 783**), and with plastic or incised decoration below the opening: **Spear-butts type 4: cat. 440, 773** probably associated with spearhead **cat. 772**; **Spear-butts type 5: cat. 399** from Bovino (Foggia), Apulia, associated with spearhead **cat. 398**; **439** from Mineo (Catania), Sicily, with spearhead **cat. 438**; **766**, probably associated with the spearhead **cat. 765**.

Cat. 239, unclassified, with two lateral prongs, could be an unusual type of spear-butt; however, the closest parallel, a piece from the FBA Sicilian hoard of Niscemi, is identified as a spit point.

Section 11 – Arrowheads

Owing to the obvious fact that they are often the result of sporadic finds, and to the basic formal homogeneity of both solid and socketed pieces, the relative chronology of bronze arrowheads can only be considered as an approximation. Bronze arrowheads probably replaced the traditional flint ones as late as the RBA, although socketed javelins/spearheads were already in use from the MBA (see for example *Terramare* 1997, fig. 223.14, 15).

The BM sample amounts to a total of 11 pieces.

Socketed arrowheads are the only category in this group of weapons which has been divided into types.

Arrowheads type 1: cat. 128, 129 from Lake Trasimeno (Umbria), and the variants **cat. 130, 131**, all are rather close to the most popular RBA Terramare type, with triangular blade with pointed ends.

Arrowheads type 2: cat. 132, 133, with elongated winged ends, could be dated to the RBA or later.

A FBA and EIA, early, date is also possible for **Arrowheads type 3: cat. 240**, similar to **Spearheads type 2**, FBA, **cat. 441** and **442**, which are rather close to **Spearheads types 10** and **11**, both EIA, early.

Unclassified arrowheads: two solid cast pieces of uncertain chronology, **cat. 836** from Tarquinia (Viterbo), Lazio, and **cat. 837** from Cuma (Naples), Campania.

Section 12 – Groups of associated artefacts

The identification of a significant number of groups of associated artefacts, many of which are of known provenance, is an important contribution by the present catalogue to our knowledge of the Italian CA, BA and EIA.

Three CA pieces from Terni, Umbria, flat axes **cat. 15** and **16**, both **Axes type 3**, and an **unclassified** axe blade, **cat. 17**, all pure copper, make up the earliest group in the BM sample. They might be a small hoard, or part of a larger one.

The EBA sample includes three significant groups. The first one is formed by five axes from Agrigento (Sicily): three flat axes, **cat. 47–49, Axes type 5b**, and two with slight flanges, **cat. 50, Axes type 6**, and **cat. 51, Axes type 7**. The provenance from Sicily is confirmed by the fact that, unlike the Italian mainland pieces, which are usually made from pure or arsenical copper, the flat axes are a copper-tin alloy; moreover, the two flanged axes belong to specifically Sicilian types.

The second group comprises eight identical flanged axes, **cat. 52–59, Axes type 12**, all probably found together at Terni (Umbria) in the early decades of the 20th century. The axes weigh between 420 and 484g, and are quite similar as regards both chemical composition and patina. They were probably part of an important hoard from Umbria, in central Italy, which confirms the wide circulation of this type of flanged axe, dating from a rather late phase of the period, which is also found in southern Italy, Campania and Molise.

The third EBA group is formed by **cat. 60, Daggers type 2**, and **cat. 61, Daggers type 3**, both central Italian types with hilt riveted to the blade, dating from the middle phase of the period. They were found together, probably in central Italy, as part of a hoard or a set in an important burial; this is indicated by their consecutive registration numbers as well as by the similarity in chemical composition and patina; moreover theblade of **cat. 60** was originally tinned, so as to give them the appearance of silver.

The two groups of MBA date are part of already known bronze hoards. **Cat. 82**, **Axes type 16**, and **cat. 83**, **Axes type 17**, are early MBA types of flanged axes with rounded blade, found mainly in north-west Italy and in the adjacent regions of France and Switzerland. They belong to a hoard found in the 19th century near Lodi (Milan), Lombardy, which had been partly dispersed by its owner (De Marinis 1975).

The two axes with contiguous wings, **cat. 84** and **85**, both **Axes type 21**, from Nemi (Rome), Lazio, are the only surviving pieces from another hoard which originally included a total of nine or ten similar axes. These belong to a category of MBA heavy working tools, probably slightly later than the two from Lodi, and specific to central Italy between Lazio and Abruzzo.

No groups are included, or have been identified, among the RBA bronzes.

The only FBA group, probably part of a larger context from the area of Lake Como, Lombardy, includes four pieces: a relatively rare type of axe with contiguous wings, **cat. 241**, **Axes type 25**, two winged axes with slightly protruding shoulders and concave sides to the blade, **cat. 242** and **243**, both close to **Axes type 30**, and a small tanged knife with serpentine blade, **cat. 244**, **Knives type 1**. It is interesting to note that the composition of the four pieces in this group is characterized by a considerable similarity as regards the occurrence of trace elements, especially the relatively high percentages of elements such as antimony and cobalt; this apparently indicates that the objects belong to the same workshop, or at least to a specifically local metal industry, and confirms their original association.

The great majority of the groups is to be found in the two EIA samples, which from a quantitative point of view are also considerably more important than all the earlier ones. Apparently, they are mainly from burials, and were part of sets of grave-goods, formed especially of personal ornaments and weapons.

The EIA, early, sample includes four pairs of ornaments, probably from female burials: **cat. 443** and **444**, composite arch fibulae (**Fibulae type 35**) with disc foot and the arch threaded with bronze discs and amber beads. These are early sophisticated products of Villanovan craftsmanship, with parallels in the Campanian cemetery of Pontecagnano. **Cat. 445** and **446**, **Fibulae type 37**, a pair of leech fibulae with disc foot and the arch covered by graduated bronze discs, probably slightly later than the former pair, belong to the same metallurgical tradition. Two pairs of small spiral bracelets with coiled ends, all **Bracelets type 1**, include **cat. 447** and **448**, from Bologna, Emilia Romagna, and another pair unprovenanced, **cat. 449** and **450**. These bracelets, usually worn on the upper arm, are a relatively common ornament of very young girls that is found in EIA cemeteries throughout Italy.

There are also four groups of weapons, all probably from male burials. Three of these consist of pairs of spear or javelin-heads of relatively small size. **Cat. 451** and **452**, both **Spearheads type 2**, are from Sulmona (L'Aquila), Abruzzo;

cat. 453 and **454**, **Spearheads type 6**, from Bari, Apulia; **cat. 455**, **Spearheads type 13**, and **cat. 456**, **Spearheads type 14** from Arezzo, Tuscany. During EIA, early, real weapons are relatively common in the funerary sets of inhumed males, while they are absent or extremely rare in early Villanovan cremation cemeteries. Their occurrence in EIA, early, graves in Abruzzo and Apulia, where inhumation was the usual funerary ritual in this phase, is therefore quite likely; the provenance of the third pair from Etruria possibly indicates their association with an inhumation burial of relatively late date within the EIA.

The fourth, and most interesting group of weapons consists of a T-hilt sword and two spearheads from Cassino (Frosinone), Lazio. The sword, **cat. 457**, **Swords type 8a**, belongs to one of the earliest EIA types (*PBF* IV.1 type Cuma), and provides the main ground for the group's relative chronology. The largest of the two spearheads, **cat. 458**, **Spearheads type 4**, is the most important piece in this group, both for its outstanding proportions (L. 37cm) and technical quality, which qualify it as an indicator of prestige and status, and for its incised decoration, a rare example of figurative representation consisting of a human face surmounted by a complex headdress. The other spearhead, **cat. 459**, **Spearheads type 5**, is a relatively large weapon (L. 29cm) of accurate manufacture. Quite probably, this group was found in a male inhumation burial. The sword is a rather rare weapon as compared with spears and javelins, that as a rule were given to all the able-bodied male members of EIA communities. Its presence indicates that the owner held an important social role in his group. The large spearhead, whose decoration may represent a supernatural being, is an extremely rare item, and probably a further indication of the social relevance of its owner. It is interesting to note that the three weapons, as well as the decoration of the spearhead, all are specifically south Italian features. This group from southern Lazio is a significant indication of the close cultural and ideological relationships linking Lazio to the southern Tyrrhenian regions of Italy.

Seven groups can be dated to EIA, late. Six, at least, of these may be rather safely identified as parts of funerary sets. A pair of identical fibulae, **cat. 784** and **785**, **Fibulae type 31**, make up the first group: these belong to a rare type with flat arch with two rows of aquatic birds attached, almost certainly a product of the rich metal industry which characterized northern Campania during this period, and is known mainly from the cemeteries of Suessula and Capua.

The next two groups are two pairs of bracelets made from coiled wire, **cat. 786–787**, from Palestrina (Rome), Lazio, and **cat. 788–789**, unprovenanced, all **Bracelets type 4**, a type specific to the Campanian group of Oliveto-Cairano (see above). The *c.* 70 pieces belonging to the distinctive metal production of this group, found unregistered among the BM Italian collections, seem to indicate that a lot of material from an unknown cemetery of the Oliveto-Cairano group entered the BM at some time. It is not surprising, therefore, that the only pieces of Oliveto-Cairano type for which a provenance is indicated are those that did not belong to the main lot: the pair from Palestrina and another piece already mentioned, **cat. 726**, **Bracelets type 12b** from Tarquinia.

The most interesting group in the EIA, late, sample is the one which has been described in the typological section (pp.19–20). It consists of five bracelets of thick coiled rod, **cat. 790–794**, all **Bracelets type 5**, very close in shape, with the same patina, and apparently all belonging to a weight system based on a unit or sub-unit of 19.5g; a provenance from Campania is rather likely. This group might be part of a funerary set, since coiled rod bracelets, probably weights, appear frequently in Campanian cemeteries, especially at Ischia (Pithekoussai) and Cuma. Another possibility is that this small group of weights was lost or intentionally buried by a craftsman or merchant.

Two other pairs of bracelets, **cat. 795–796**, **Bracelets type 13a**, and **cat. 797–798**, **Bracelets type 13c**, both types of hollow sheet-bronze ornaments, were almost certainly found in burials.

Another rather spectacular pair of grave offerings is represented by two oversize decorated spearheads, **cat. 799–800**, **Spearheads type 15**, *c.* 1m in length, which were found with several other identical pieces in an Orientalizing burial at Bomarzo (Viterbo), Lazio. As already noted, these two spearheads are representative of a development in the use and function of spears which took place in Etruria in the Orientalizing period: traditional EIA types were reproduced in huge proportions, and, rather than as functional weapons, were clearly meant as parade and prestige indicators, which accompanied their owner in the grave.

Section 13 – Miscellaneous objects

This small group includes 22 bronze objects, some of which are 19th-century pastiches made from parts of different ancient bronzes held together by means of modern metal plaques and wire.

All the original pieces date from EIA, late, or later.

Cat. 801 and **802** are horse-bits with articulated mouth pieces, outer loops and rings; both can be attributed to types classified in *PBF* XVI, 1, with parallels especially at Veii, Quattro Fontanili.

The openwork disc **cat. 803**, probably part of a horse harness, with human figure and birds at centre, is very similar to a type of openwork handle for bronze cups which is found in several Villanovan II and Orientalizing contexts in Etruria and at Bologna.

Cat. 804 and **805** are elliptical belt plaques also of late Villanovan type, with close parallels for example in the cemetery of Veii, Quattro Fontanili. A more unusual type of belt-plaque is **cat. 806**, also elliptical in shape, with an embossed decoration of bosses and concentric circles that is not known in Villanovan belt-plaques, whereas a good parallel can be found in the Latial cemetery of Riserva del Truglio (Marino, Rome), in the Alban Hills.

Cat. 807, an openwork disc formed by concentric rings joined by radial bars, is a relatively common type of ornament found in IA graves from Campania and Calabria.

A decorated armour disc of Adriatic type, that belongs to the *PBF* III, 3, Collarmele group, is **cat. 808** from Perugia, Umbria.

Cat. 809, a complete piece, and **cat. 810**, a finial from a similar object, are composite items made from a hollow sheet-bronze tube surmounted by an openwork globe. Similar objects, probably relative to a specific function, are known from important burials in Campania (Suessula, Capua), Etruria (Vetulonia, Tomba del Duce), and Bologna.

Two pieces representative of the Villanovan production of sheet-bronze vessels and other objects, usually with embossed decoration, are **cat. 811**, a crested helmet probably from southern Etruria, dating from Villanovan II, and **cat. 812**, a biconical vessel with its lid, of late Villanovan or Orientalizing date.

To the same industry belong **cat. 813–816**, bronze bands with inset plastic birds, probably originally riveted to the edges of wheeled incense burners. These are prestige objects, usually found in important burials of EIA, late, and Orientalizing date from Etruria, Lazio and Campania.

Cat. 817–819 are three 19th-century pastiches, all probably from Campania. They consist mainly of parts from composite parade fibulae, derived from the spectacle and four-spirals tradition and decorated with plastic figurines of humans and animals, that are specific to the metal industry of northern Campania (Suessula and Capua), dating from EIA, late and the Orientalizing period. The pastiches were further enriched with spiral pendants (*saltaleoni*), glass beads, sheet-bronze buds, and other ancient pieces. These objects have been described separately, according to their original function and association.

Cat. 820–822 are solid cast bronze figurines of humans and animals, which belong to the figurative tradition of central and, mainly, southern Italy during EIA, late and the Orientalizing period.

Note on Chronology

Due to the publication of several new series of calibrated BC 14C dates from secure contexts, both settlement stratigraphies and burials, by Italian, European and American laboratories, the definition of the absolute chronology of the Italian metal ages (Copper Age to Early Iron Age) has been significantly improved in the last few years. An important contribution also came from dendrochronology, although the application of this technique is strongly conditioned by the comparatively high, though not exclusive, concentration of BA lake settlements in northern Italy.

However, for different reasons, the generally higher chronology resulting from the adoption of dendrochronology and the calibration of 14C dates has not yet been explicitly accepted and adopted by all the specialists concerned, mainly as regards the crucial period between the Final Bronze and Early Iron ages.

Two main factors, both deeply rooted in the Italian research tradition, are responsible for this situation:

1 – The role of literary sources, the main basis for the absolute chronology of the Greek colonization in southern Italy and Sicily, and thus of the Greek Geometric pottery, which is found in Italian indigenous and colonial contexts. This combination of historical and archaeological factors is the main basis for the traditional absolute chronology of the Italian EIA and Orientalizing period.

Although in recent years this stronghold of Italian and European chronology was radically challenged especially by the dendro-dates of German and Swiss lake settlements, the authority of some ancient historians, mainly Thucydides, and the chronological framework which has been traditionally linked to his writings, are still perceived by many scholars as the only legitimate source of IA chronology, rather than as one of the factors which should be involved in this discussion.

2 – The established practice of founding the relative chronology of all archaeological complexes upon the typological classification of pottery and, mainly, metal artefacts, has been stretched to its extremes by Peroni and his collaborators. This method is meant to provide a detailed chronological framework which is explicitly considered as the necessary premise to the analysis and interpretation of the overall archaeological evidence from any given context. The obvious result of the widespread adoption of this procedure is that clearly identifiable types, especially bronze types included in the *Prähistorische Bronzefunde* Italian series, are strongly considered to be more reliable chronological indicators than the 14C dated stratigraphic layer, or, more generally, the archaeological context they belong to. Another implication of this approach is the chronologically parallel development of the cultural areas involved, including all the local subdivisions into periods and phases. Absolute dates are considered with scepticism, and often ignored or dismissed, especially if and when they do not conform to the relative sequence which has been already established on typological grounds.

No recent series of cal BC dates are at present available for Sicily; therefore, although the island's cultural sequences is definitely different from the Italian ones as regards both the archaeological aspects and their time span, the relative and absolute chronology of mainland Italy is currently used as the main point of reference (Albanese Procelli 2005).

This is not the proper place for a thorough discussion of the role of absolute chronology and its relationship with archaeologically based sequences of relative chronology; our purpose here is only to recall that in the recent Italian literature an absolute chronology based on 14C cal BC and dendro-dates is systematically adopted for CA contexts, whereas many publications on EBA, MBA, RBA, FBA and EIA complexes still rely on chrono-typological sequences and traditional absolute chronology. For a full discussion of the problem of LBA and IA absolute chronology, with papers devoted to the East Mediterranean, the Aegean region, Italy and Europe, see Bartoloni and Delpino 2005.

For a general assessment of Italian absolute dates see Skeates, Whitehouse 1994, and the updatings which appear regularly in the volumes of the *Accordia* series.

The following pages are a brief summary of the absolute chronology of the metal ages, based essentially on 14C cal BC and dendro-dates from Italian contexts. Neither the chrono-typological relationships between Italy and central Europe, nor the chronological implications of the occurrence of Mycenaean-Late Helladic artefacts and of Greek Geometric pottery in Italian Bronze Age and Iron Age contexts have been discussed in this text.

Moreover, it should be remembered that the absolute chronology which will be proposed is based on a limited number of reliable dates, and is only meant to provide a very general framework rather than a detailed account of the chronology of the Italian Copper Age, Bronze Age and Early Iron Age regional cultures. Moreover, the cal BC dates which are at present available are not uniformly calibrated with 1σ or 2σ. Therefore, in the following paragraphs, details on calibration depend on the present state of information relative to single regions and contexts.

The chronology of the Copper Age (CA) is based on a number of 14C cal BC dates, especially from northern Italy, and from new complexes in central Italy.

The earliest phase of the period in northern Italy (Remedello cemetery, phase I) can be dated between 3350 and 2900 cal BC; the second phase (Remedello II) between 2900 and 2500 cal BC, and the final phase (Bell beaker) between 2500 and 2200 cal BC (De Marinis 1998, table at fig. 1).

In central Italy the earliest complexes which can be archaeologically identified as eneolithic are dated to the first half of the 4th millennium BC: in the Marche the 14C cal BC dates

(Iσ) of the cemetery and settlement of Fontenoce-Area Guzzini range between 3760–3540 cal BC and 3360–3100 cal BC; those from the settlement of Conelle di Arcevia range between 3895–3650 cal BC and 3485–3100 cal BC; and the CA layers of the site of Maddalena di Muccia (Macerata), which include the advanced and late phases of the period, range between 2870–2580 cal BCand 2470–2310 cal BC (Cazzella and Silvestrini 2005, tab. I).

The absolute dates for the complexes of the central Tyrrhenian area are slightly later: the earliest date, from tomb 3 of the cemetery of Lunghezzina (Rome), is 3630–3380 cal BC (Anzidei *et al.* 2003, 383). The cemetery of Selvicciola (Ischia di Castro, Viterbo) ranges between 3500 and 2000 cal BC (Iσ) (Petitti *et al.* 2002; De Marinis 2001, fig. 5).

An overview of recent cal BC dates from eneolithic contexts from Sicily and southern Italy is presented by A. Cazzella (2000: 89, 92, 94). The dates for an early phase of the period, as represented in the Sicilian funerary complex of Piano Vento, are 3990–3370 (both Iσ). The central phase can be dated between the middle of the 4th and the beginning of the 3rd millennium BC both in Sicily and southern Italy : Toppo Daguzzo, Basilicata, 3653–3365 cal BC; Buccino, 3485–3040 cal BC (both Iσ). The approximate absolute dates for the final part of the period should range between *c.* 2600 and *c.* 2000 BC.

For the Early Bronze Age (EBA), the earliest absolute dates, marking the beginning of the period, are around 2200 BC in contexts from northern, central and southern Italy. Based on several 14C cal BC and dendro-dates, in northern Italy EBA I lasted until *c.* 1900 BC, while the second phase, EBA II, ended around 1700–1600 BC. (Gambari 1997; De Marinis 2005). Throughout the time span of the period, the main archaeological aspect which developed across the present territory of northern Italy was the so-called Polada culture.

The situation in southern Italy is definitely more complex: the earliest part of the period coincides with the final phase of the Laterza culture, a CA archaeological aspect extending from Apulia and Calabria to Lazio and Abruzzo. The immediately subsequent aspect is the so-called Proto-Apennine, with 14C cal BC dates from an important Apulian site, Coppa Nevigata (Foggia), around the 19th–17th century BC (Cazzella, Moscoloni 1998: 29–30). This high absolute chronology, which should place the beginnings of Proto-Apennine in the EBA, is not accepted by those scholars who would rather consider this archaeological aspect to be exclusive to the early and advanced phases of the Middle Bronze Age (MBA).

A stronghold of EBA chronology in Campania is represented by the 14C cal BC dates for the eruption of Mount Vesuvius that buried a number of villages characterized by the well-identified aspect of Palma Campania (the eponymous site discovered and excavated in the 70s of the last century: see Albore Livadie, D'Amore, 1980). The recent systematic excavation of the village of Nola – Croce del Papa (Naples) (Albore Livadie 2002; Albore Livadie, Vecchio 2005) is providing a complete documentation of the Palma Campania culture; the absolute chronology of the eruption is now established at 1782–1686 cal BC (Iσ) (Albore Livadie, Vecchio 2005, 44, fig. 48 and note 3; see Lubritto et al. 2003, in press). Whether or not the Palma Campania culture continued after the widespread destruction wrought by the eruption is still a matter of discussion.

From the EBA-MBA transition to the Final Bronze Age

another important component of the Italian relative chronology is constituted by the evidence of systematic relationships with Greece and the Aegean area; the best identifiable archaeological evidence is the occurrence possibly of Middle Helladic (MH), and mainly of Late Helladic (LH) and Mycenaean pottery in several contexts, especially in southern Italy and Sicily. Some imports of glass, faïence, ivory and bronze objects are also documented.

However, apart from the problems of the absolute dating of LH material in its areas of origin, the Italian situation is further complicated by the the fact that local productions of Aegean-style pottery became quite common in southern Italy in the Late Bronze Age, especially from LHIIIB.

The earliest part of the MBA, dating between 1700/1600 and 1500/1400 cal BC, corresponds to three main archaeological aspects: Palafitte-Terramare in northern Italy, Grotta Nuova in the central regions, essentially Tuscany, Umbria and Marche, Proto-Apennine in southern Italy, including Lazio south of the Tiber and Abruzzo. As already remarked, the beginning of Proto-Apennine probably dates from the EBA.

A substantial series of cal BC dates from Palafitte-Terramare contexts is assembled by De Marinis 1999, figs. 42–43. As regards southern Italy, the final date for the Proto-Apennine aspect at Coppa Nevigata, is *c.* 1500 cal BC.

During the final phase of the MBA the Palafitte-Terramare culture continued in northern Italy, while most of the territory of central and southern Italy was characterized by the so-called 'Apennine aspect', with its distinctive incised pottery. The range of absolute dates for the Apennine layers at Coppa Nevigata is *c.* 1500 to *c.* 1300 cal BC; in another series of dates, from the village of Portella di Salina (Aeolian Islands, Messina, Sicily), where Apennine pottery is associated with all the structures, the range is 1525–1320 cal BC (Iσ) (Martinelli 2005: 289–297).

The LBA is conventionally divided into Recent Bronze Age (RBA) and Final Bronze Age (FBA).

In archaeological terms, the RBA is generally associated with the appearance of a distinctive aspect, the so-called Sub-Apennine, which is specific to central and southern Italy; the main archaeological feature is a class of undecorated impasto (coarse hand-made) pottery with plastic protrusions on the handles of cups and bowls. Some features of Sub-Apennine style also appear in northern Italy in Terramare and Palafitte contexts. The dates for Piedmont range between *c.* 1350 and *c.* 1200 cal BC (Gambari 1997); in Lombardy, the RBA feature A from the site of Parre (Bergamo) has a 14C date of 1392–1329 cal BC (Poggiani Keller and Raposso 2004, 443). In central Italy, the RBA structure 61 of the settlement of Scarceta (Grosseto, Tuscany) is dated to *c.* 1312 cal BC (Poggiani Keller 2004, 469); 1407–1265 cal BC (Iσ) is the date presently available from the Sub-Apennine layers of the Capitol Hill at Rome (Baroni 2001, 294).

As regards southern Italy, the earliest RBA layers at Coppa Nevigata date from 1310–1140 cal BC (Iσ) (Muntoni 1997).

Overall, the absolute chronology of the period is considered to span *c.* 1350/1300 to *c.* 1200 cal BC.

FBA, the second part of the LBA, is characterized by a new style of decorated impasto pottery and by a distinctive bronze industry (so-called Protovillanovan), but also by the emergence of regional aspects in several areas of Italy. As already noted, the beginning of the period can be placed around *c.* 1200 BC, while the possible subdivisions into three or, more plausibly, two phases, can only be proposed by individual regional contexts.

The best available sequence of cal BC dates are all from the Groningen Laboratory. A number of cal BC dates have been obtained by the Groningen Laboratory on several LBA and EIA contexts (Bietti Sestieri and De Santis, forthcoming), from Latium Vetus (the part of the present Lazio region between the Tiber and Mount Circeo). FBA early is represented by cal BC dates from two 'Protovillanovan' contexts: a date of c. 1300–1100 BC (1σ) from the settlement of Quadrato (Rome), and two dates from the coastal site of Torre Astura (Latina): 1310–1000 cal BC and 1400–1080 cal BC (both 2σ) (Attema et al. 2003, 120). FBA late is known mainly from cremation burials found at Rome and in the adjacent area, which, unlike the earlier contexts, belong to a specifically local aspect (Latial period I). Tombs 1 and 2 from Quadrato: 1017–897 and 1041–901(both 1σ); tombs 1 and 2 from Foro di Cesare (central Rome): 1255–1013 and 995–833 (1σ) (Bietti Sestieri, De Santis 2003, 747–750).

An approximate chronological range for the period spans the 12th, 11th and possibly part of the 10th century BC.

On account of the complexity of the general historical framework, as well as of the co-existence of chronologically relevant factors originating from distant and inherently different areas (Italian archaeological sequences, dendro-chronological sequences from Switzerland and southern Germany, relative chronology of the Greek Geometric pottery, and historically based sequences from the east Mediterranean), the absolute chronology of the Italian EIA can be defined only in rather approximate terms. Moreover, given the wide range of regional cultures, which are unlikely to have started and developed simultaneously, it will only be possible to propose a general subdivision into two main periods, without considering the specific chronological details of the local sequences.

Some dates from the Groningen Laboratory are on bones from inhumation burials of the cemetery of Castiglione (Roma), which in terms of archaeological relative chronology apparently coincides with the greatest part of EIA early (Latial period II). Excluding those with an excessively wide range of oscillation, all the dates from tombs belonging to the whole archaeological range considered are rather close: tombs 71 and 86, phase IIA1: 919–833 and 999–876 cal BC (1σ); tomb 75, phase IIA: 1107–901 cal BC (1σ); tomb 85, phase IIB1: 1001–839 cal BC (1σ). A chronological range including most of the 10th and part of the 9th century BC seems likely for the early period of the EIA (Latial II, Villanovan I).

For the beginning of the second period (EIA late: Latial III, Villanovan II) a series of five 14C cal BC dates comes from the IA building of Fidenae (Rome), a closed context which was destroyed and sealed by a fire (Nijboer et al. 1999–2000: 168–170; Nijboer 2005: 530). Three dates, from wood, have a very wide range of oscillation: 1130–830 cal BC (2σ); the other two, both on cereal seeds, range between 1020 and 820 cal BC (2σ), and 970 and 835 cal BC (1σ). Thus EIA II should begin around 900 BC or slightly later.

The most difficult point is the transition EIA late–Orientalizing, which is traditionally dated to c. 730–720 BC on both archaeological and historical grounds: the archaeological dates for the Greek Geometric pottery found in central Mediterranean contexts: MG (from 830 BC), LGI (from 770 BC) and the beginning of LG II (which corresponds to EPC) around 730/720 BC; and the chronology based on Thucydides' historical account for the earliest foundations of Greek colonies in the west (Naxos 734, Syracuse 733, Cuma 730, Sybaris and Caulonia 709, Taras 706). No independent absolute dates from Italian contexts are available for this period, and many scholars would prefer to leave the traditional date unchanged.

An important new element which should be taken into account is the new, high absolute chronology for the earliest archaeological evidence relative to the foundation of Carthage: based on the presence of Greek LG pottery, the beginning of the Phoenician colony was usually dated to c. 760–740 BC, whereas the 14C cal BC dates obtained by the Groningen laboratory indicate a date within the 9th century (Nijboer 2005: 530–31, and pl. 2).

Moreover, as is well known, the absolute date for the HaB3–HaC transition (c. 700 BC), which has long been considered as a relatively close central European match to the EIA–Orientalizing transition in Italy, has been recently raised to c. 778 BC by a number of dendro-dates from tomb 8 at Wehringen (southern Germany)(Hennig 1995). This absolute date has been widely discussed, and its correlation to the Italian chronology has been usually dismissed, essentially because it seems too high for the beginning of the Orientalizing period in Italy (see for a brief summary of this discussion Peroni, Vanzetti 2005, 64–65).

Nevertheless, given the high cal BC dates for the Italian EIA, and the lack of independent absolute dates for the Greek Geometric pottery, the current retention of the traditional chronological term, 730–720 BC, for the end of the EIA and the beginning of the Orientalizing period should be considered merely as a temporary convention.

As regards Sardinia, the local absolute chronology is rather uncertain: recently, based on a series of cal BC dates (2σ), a chronological sequence from MBA to the Medieval period has been proposed by G. Webster (2001) for the settlement of Borore - Duos Nuraghes: MBA c. 1800–1300; LBA c. 1300–900; IA c. 900–500.

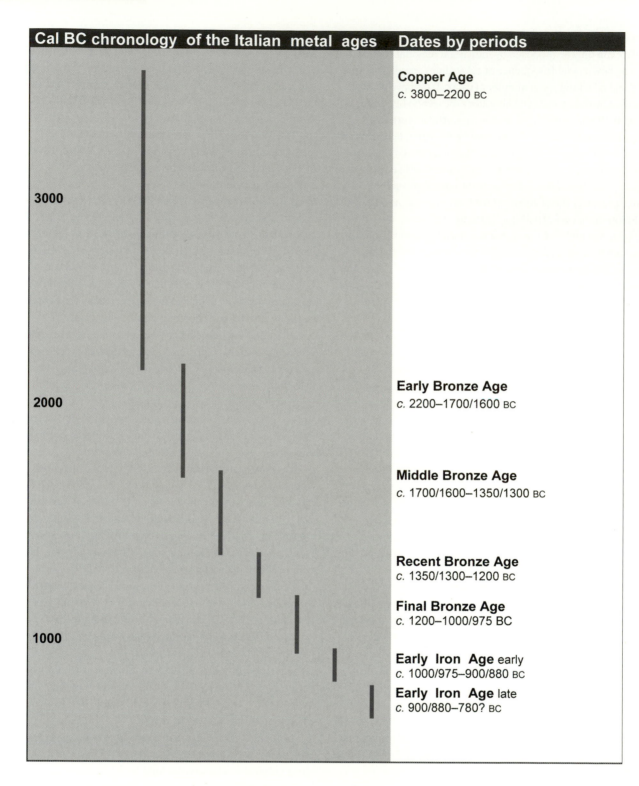

Cal BC chronology of the Italian metal ages	Dates by periods

Copper Age
c. 3800–2200 BC

Early Bronze Age
c. 2200–1700/1600 BC

Middle Bronze Age
c. 1700/1600–1350/1300 BC

Recent Bronze Age
c. 1350/1300–1200 BC

Final Bronze Age
c. 1200–1000/975 BC

Early Iron Age early
c. 1000/975–900/880 BC

Early Iron Age late
c. 900/880–780? BC

Note on the catalogue and illustrations

Under the Bibliography of individual objects, we have usually included only publications in which the object has been illustrated. Under the *comparanda* of the objects, we have given the author's or editor's name with the date of publication, all to be found in the Bibliography. The exceptions to this rule are some frequently mentioned sites, including Osteria dell' Osa, Pontecagnano, Cuma, Pithekoussai, Torre Galli, and Quattro Fontanili at Veii.

All line drawings are reproduced at 1:2 unless otherwise stated.

Copper Age

Axes

1.
PRB 1935.10-18.41. Transferred from GR (1916.6-1.23). Given by Lord Avebury. Acquired in Naples and probably from neighbourhood.
Campania.
Flat axe. **Axes type 1.**
Narrow triangular body with slightly convex faces and rounded sides, thin rounded butt, slightly rounded cutting edge. Surface irregular; dark green patina with incrustations.
L. 10.7cm Weight 133g
Analysis: Arsenical copper. See D. Hook report.
Close to De Marinis 1992, 389, fig. 1.2, unprovenanced, Bergamo Museum; fig. 1.3, from Campegine. Colini type I.
CA, early.

2.
PRB 1916.6-5.179. Given by Lord Avebury.
Naples, Campania.
Flat axe. **Axes type 2.**
Heavy narrow and elongated tool, with thin straight butt, elliptical profiles with central zone markedly thickened, and cutting edge nearly straight. Dull medium green patina with thick dark-green incrustations. Cutting edge damaged.
L. 20.3cm Weight 1027g
Analysis: Copper. See D. Hook report.
See Carancini 1993, 128, fig. 2.13, from Bibbona, type Bibbona. Also De Marinis 1992, 392, fig. 3.1-4, especially fig. 3.3, from Marendole, type Bocca Lorenza (with thicker butt and wider blade).
CA, early.

3.
PRB 1964.12-1.371(286). Sir Henry Wellcome Collection, no. 96448. Bought in Rome from Antichità delle Belle Arti by Captain Saint in April 1931. Given by the Wellcome Trustees.
Flat axe. **Axes type 4.**
Narrow elongated tool with central part of the faces dished, elliptical profiles with central zone thickened, thin straight butt, blade slightly widening towards almost straight cutting edge. Thick green patina with brown and green incrustations. Cutting edge damaged.
L. 18.5cm Weight 583g
Analysis: Copper. See D. Hook report.
Close to Carancini 1993, 128, fig. 2.20, from Poggio Aquilone, type Poggio Aquilone.
CA, late?

4.
PRB 1883.4-26.1. Given by Sir A.W. Franks.
Abruzzo.
Flat axe. **Axes type 4.**
Heavy tool with thin straight butt, elliptical profiles with central part thickened, central part of the faces dished, slightly flaring blade, and slightly rounded cutting edge. Coarse bright green patina.
L. 13.5cm Weight 526g
Analysis: Copper. See D. Hook report.
Close to Carancini 1993, 128, fig. 2.20, from Poggio Aquilone, type Poggio Aquilone; De Marinis 1992, 392ff, fig. 5.1, from Remedello, tomb 102, type Similaun (very similar in section, but less thick).
CA, late?
Bibliography: Bietti Sestieri and Giardino 2003, 412, 425, fig. 1.

5.
PRB WG1047. Canon W. Greenwell Collection, bought from the Rev. Greville J. Chester. Given by J. Pierpont Morgan in 1909.
Corneto (Tarquinia, Viterbo), Lazio.
Flat axe. Close to **Axes type 4.**
Trapezoidal tool with butt broken in antiquity, central zone thickened, slightly raised margins in the central part of the faces, blade widening towards the slightly rounded cutting edge. Rough green and turquoise patina with incrustations.
L. 10.4cm Weight 265g
Analysis: Arsenical copper. See D. Hook report.
See De Marinis 1992, 397ff., fig. 6.2, from Remedello, tomb 62 (with lower zone thickened and straight cutting edge; pure Cu). 'Asce a margini rialzati'; probably dating from an advanced phase of the cemetery of Remedello.
CA.

6.
PRB WG1048. Canon W. Greenwell Collection, bought from the Rev. Greville J. Chester. Given by J. Pierpont Morgan in 1909.
Ruvo (Bari), Apulia.
Flat axe. **Axes type 4.**
Heavy tool with dished butt, elliptical profiles with central zone thickened, central part of the faces lowered by a slightly marked step, slightly flaring blade, cutting edge nearly straight. Smooth black, white and green patina in various tones of green with incrustations and corroded zones.
L. 13.4cm Weight 504g
Analysis: Copper. See D. Hook report.
Close to Carancini 1993, 128, fig. 2.20, from Poggio Aquilone, type Poggio Aquilone.
CA, late?

7.
PRB 1889.2-1.2. Given by Sir A.W. Franks.
Capua (Caserta), Campania.
Flat axe. **Axes type 4.**
Heavy tool with thin straight butt, elliptical profiles with central part thickened, central part of the faces lowered by a slighly marked step, slightly flaring blade, slightly rounded cutting edge. Rough, bright green patina with incrustations. Cutting edge slightly damaged.
L. 14.9cm Weight 562g
Analysis: Copper. See D. Hook report.
Close to Carancini 1993, 128, fig. 2.20, from Poggio Aquilone, type Poggio Aquilone.
CA, late?

8.
PRB 1935.10-18.1. Transferred from GR (1856.12-26.974). Bequeathed by Sir William Temple.
Flat axe. **Axes type 5a.**
Thin trapezoidal tool with slightly dished butt, markedly flaring blade with thin rectangular section and rounded cutting edge. Remains of medium green patina.
L. 9.8cm Weight 97g
See Carancini 1993, 130, fig. 3.27, from Orvieto, 'flat axes with markedly flaring blade'.
Probably CA.
Bibliography: Walters 1899, no. 2911.

9.
PRB 1964.12-1.374(344). Sir Henry Wellcome Collection, no. 318. Bought in Rome from Arte Antica e Moderna by Captain Saint in November 1929. Given by the Wellcome Trustees.
Flat axe. **Axes type 5a.**
Small trapezoidal tool with thin, slightly dished butt, slightly flaring blade with thin rectangular section and rounded cutting edge. Dark green and black patina.
L. 5.5cm Weight 34g
See Carancini 1993, 128, fig. 2.14, from Città di Castello, type Città di Castello (longer and thicker in section).
Probably CA.

10.
PRB WG1064. Canon W. Greenwell Collection, bought from the Rev. Greville J. Chester. Given by J. Pierpont Morgan in 1909.
Pozzuoli (Naples), Campania.
Lugged axe. **Axes type 63.**
Heavy tool with long rectangular butt, two strong angular lugs, and thick trapezoidal blade, slightly dished on both faces and with marked bevel and rounded cutting edge. Surface corroded, with dark green and turquoise incrustations.
L. 15.4cm Weight 551g
Analysis: Copper. See D. Hook report. Note: this type has been often mistakenly associated with the much later trunnion axes of LBA date. The results of the analysis of the BM piece confirm its CA date.
See Carancini 1993, 130, fig. 3.33a, type Terni (this piece).
CA.
Bibliography: For lugged axes from Italy, see

Deshayes 1960, vol.I, 122; Harding 1975, 184–186; Petrie 1917, pl.18.107; Maryon 1938, 249, fig. 19; Maxwell-Hyslop 1953, 71, 79, fig. 3.6, pl. 8.2; Hammond 1967, 408, fig. 28.3; Carancini 1993, 130, fig. 3.33a; Giardino 1995, 200, footnotes 38 and 39, pl. 4.2 and 3.

11.
PRB 1964.12-1.215(299). Sir Henry Wellcome Collection no. 314. Bought in Rome from Arte Antica e Moderna by Captain Saint in November 1929. Given by Wellcome Trustees. Terni,Umbria.
Axe with thick lozenge lateral profile and protruding shoulders. **Axes type 64.**
Small thick-sectioned tool with straight butt, rectangular, slightly flanged haft, protruding shoulders, short blade with markedly concave sides and slightly rounded cutting edge. Shiny, bright green patina with corrosion and incrustations.
L. 10.5cm Weight 428g
Analysis: Arsenical copper. See D. Hook report.
See Peroni 1971, 179, fig. 40.3 (from Abruzzo), 4 (from Rome), and especially 5 (from Venafro, Campobasso); 181, fig. 41.15; 272, fig. 61.3, from Mirabella Eclano (Avellino), type Mirabella Eclano; Carancini 1993, 130, fig. 3.33, type Terni.
CA, late.

12.
PRB 1935.10-18.12. Transferred from GR. Bought from Sir William Hamilton.
Axe with thick lozenge lateral profile. **Axes type 65.**
Long straight butt with central area slightly dished, narrow trapezoidal blade with slight flanges converging at the joint with the butt and slightly curved cutting edge. Butt end and cutting edge hammered. Smooth dark green patina with light incrustations.
L.11.5cm Weight 281g
Analysis: Copper. See D. Hook report.
See Peroni 1971, 179, fig. 40.3 (from Abruzzo) and 4 (from Rome), not identical; Carancini 1993, 130, fig. 3.34a,b; Carancini 1999, 36, fig. 3.34a,b. Type Mirabella Eclano.
CA, late.
Bibliography: Walters 1899, no. 2922.

13.
PRB 1964.12-1.460(346). Sir Henry Wellcome Collection, no. 454. Bought in Florence from A. Ricardi by Captain Saint in December 1929.

Given by the Wellcome Trustees.
Miniature flat axe? **Axes type unclassified.**
Symmetrical form with straight edges and rounded ends. Trapezoidal section, probably made in one-piece mould. Green spotted patina with incrustations.
L. 3cm Weight 8g
No close parallels found.
Possibly CA.

Halberd

14.
PRB 1880.12-14.1. Given by Sir A. W. Franks. Calvatone (Cremona), Lombardy.
Halberd with large triangular blade with mid-rib. **Halberds type 1.**
Base of blade semicircular with three square rivet-holes and two large rivets with rounded heads extant; extension of the hilt-plates indicated by traces of wood. Blade with straight cutting edges, rounded tip and central rib with two lateral grooves. Smooth dark green patina with incrustations and corroded zones. Small parts missing.
L. 28.5cm Weight 366g
Analysis: Blade arsenical copper; rivet copper. See D. Hook report.
See *PBF* VI. 10, no. 84 (this piece), type Calvatone.
CA.
Bibliography: O'Riordain 1937, 284, fig. 67.2; *PBF* VI.10, no. 84, see for references.

Group of Associated Artefacts

1. **Group of two flat axes, Cat. 15 and 16, and the blade of a flat axe, Cat. 17, from Terni, Umbria; Axes type 3 and Unclassified.**

15.
PRB 1964.12-1.200(288). Sir Henry Wellcome Collection, no. 313. Bought in Rome from Arte Antica e Moderna by Captain Saint in November 1929. Given by the Wellcome Trustees.
Terni,Umbria.
Flat axe. **Axes type 3.**
Probably associated with **Cat. 16** and **17.**
Narrow trapezoidal faces, elliptical profiles with lower part slightly thickening and slightly rounded cutting edge. Dull light green patina with corroded zones. Butt and one of the faces

near the butt damaged in antiquity by hammering or chiselling.
L. 11cm Weight 191g
Analysis: Copper. See D. Hook report.
Close to Carancini 1993, 128, fig. 2.22b, from the province of Cremona, type Parlesca var. B (thicker in section); De Marinis 1992, 394ff., fig. 5.11, from Cumarola, type Cumarola (smaller, with butt straighter and thicker).
CA, late.
Bibliography: Bietti Sestieri 2004, 27 and fig. 2.1.

16.
PRB 1964.12-1.202(301). Sir Henry Wellcome Collection, no. 320. Bought in Rome from Arte Antica e Moderna by Captain Saint in November 1929. Given by the Wellcome Trustees.
Terni,Umbria.
Flat axe. **Axes type 3.**
Probably associated with **Cat. 15** and **17.**
Small tool with narrow trapezoidal faces, thin elliptical profiles slightly thickening toward the cutting edge; slightly rounded butt and cutting edge. Dull patina in various tones of green.
L. 4.2cm Weight 15g
Analysis: Copper. See D. Hook report.
Close to Carancini 1993, 128, fig. 2.12, from Tolfa, type Tolfa; De Marinis 1992, 394ff., fig. 5.11, from Cumarola; fig. 5.12, from Rivarolo Fuori. Type Cumarola.
CA, late.
Bibliography: Bietti Sestieri 2004, 28 and fig. 2.3.

17.
PRB 1964.12-1.201(300). Sir Henry Wellcome Collection, no. 317. Bought in Rome from Arte Antica e Moderna by Captain Saint in November 1929. Given by the Wellcome Trustees.
Terni,Umbria.
Blade from a flat axe. **Axes type unclassified.**
Probably associated with **Cat. 15** and **16.**
Thin, slightly flaring blade with rounded cutting edge. Patina smooth, dark-green on one side, coarse, black on the other.
L. 4cm Weight 39g
Analysis: Copper. See D. Hook report.
See Carancini 1993, 130, fig. 3.27 from Orvieto, 'flat axes with expanded cutting edge'.
CA. The composition of the metal (cf. analysis) confirms a CA date for this blade.
Bibliography: Bietti Sestieri 2004, 27 and fig. 2.2.

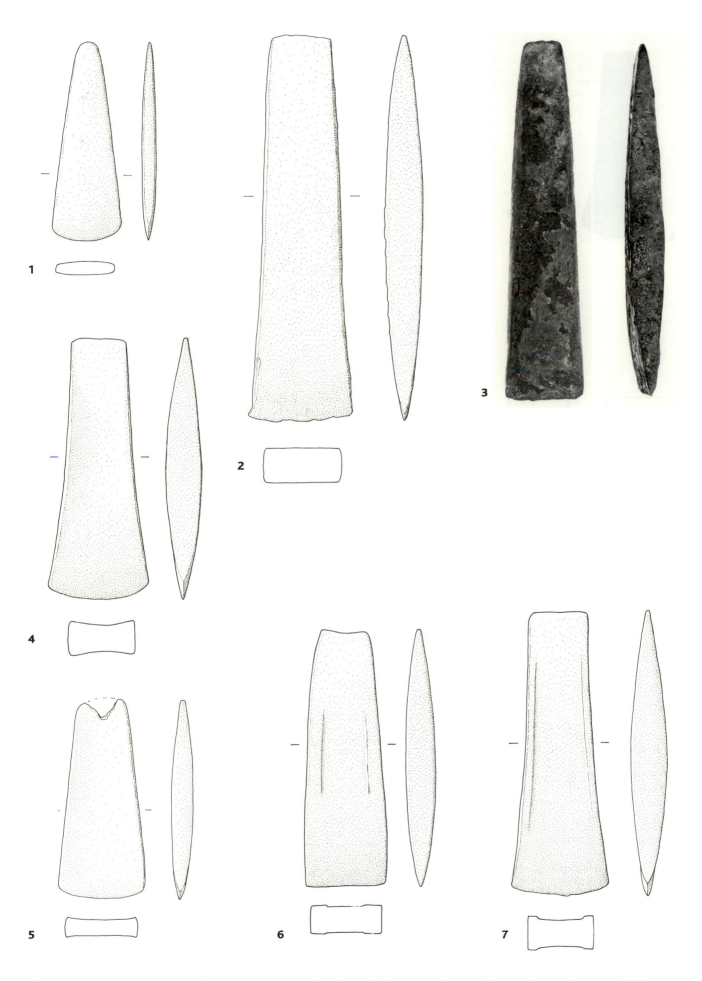

Plate 1   **Axes type 1**: - 1 Campania. **Axes type 2**: - 2 Naples, Campania. **Axes type 4**: - 3. - 4 Abruzzo. Close to **Axes type 4**: - 5 Corneto (Tarquinia, Viterbo), Lazio. **Axes type 4**: - 6 Ruvo (Bari), Apulia. - 7 Capua (Caserta), Campania.

Early Bronze Age

Axes

18.
PRB 1880.8-2.38. Given by Sir A.W. Franks.
Rome,Lazio.
Axe with slightly raised edges. **Axes type 6**.
Narrow trapezoidal tool with almost straight
profiles, straight butt and blade strongly flared
towards the rounded cutting edge. Thick
trapezoidal section, the smaller face flat, the
larger with slightly raised edges. Probably
made in one-piece mould. Cutting edge
damaged. Coarse dark green patina with
lighter zones.
L. 12.5cm Weight 241g
Analysis: Bronze. See D. Hook report.
See Albanese Procelli 1993, 31, 72ff., fig. 2.12,
isolated find from Taormina: 'axes with slightly
raised edges', type R2B. Very similar in shape,
but cast in a two-piece mould. See **cat. 50** from
Agrigento.
EBA?

19.
PRB WG1054. Canon W. Greenwell Collection,
bought from the Rev. Greville J. Chester. Given
by J. Pierpont Morgan in 1909.
Brescia, Lombardy.
Flanged axe. **Axes type 7**.
Axe with light flanges and straight butt, face
flaring, rounded bevel-line and cutting edge.
Smooth dark green patina.
L. 11.3cm Weight 222g
See Carancini and Peroni 1999, pl. 1.C, F. First
horizon of EBA hoards.
EBA, early.

20.
PRB 1935.10-18.43. Transferred from GR
(1916.6-1.25). Given by Lord Avebury.
Acquired in Naples and probably from
neighbourhood.
Campania.
Flanged axe. **Axes type 7**.
Small rounded butt, slightly flaring blade with
rounded cutting edge. Dull light green patina
and corroded irregular surface.
L. 16.9cm Weight 394g
See Carancini and Peroni 1999, pl. 1.C. First
horizon of EBA hoards.
EBA, early.

21.
PRB 1866.6-27.96.Henry Christy Collection.
Given by the Trustees under the will of Henry
Christy. Perhaps bought from G. Eastwood.
Flanged axe. **Axes type 8**.
Rounded butt with notch, slightly flaring blade
with rounded bevel-line and cutting edge.
Irregular, light green patina with incrustations.
L. 15.7cm Weight 384g
See Carancini and Peroni 1999, pl. 1.D, E. First
horizon of EBA hoards.
EBA, early.

22.
PRB 1935.10-18.42. Transferred from GR
(1916.6-1.24).Given by Lord Avebury.
Acquired in Naples and probably from
neighbourhood.
Campania.
Flanged axe. **Axes type 8**.
Small rounded butt with central notch, slightly
flared blade and rounded cutting edge. Dark
and light green patina, irregular surface,
probably from casting.
L. 9cm Weight 139g
See Carancini and Peroni 1999, pl. 1.E. First
horizon of EBA hoards.
EBA, early.

23.
PRB Old Acquistion 102. Registered OA on 19
July 1939.
Flanged axe. **Axes type 8**.
Small axe with rounded butt with central
notch, light flanges, slightly flaring blade and
rounded cutting edge. Cutting edge and one
side of blade damaged. Surface corroded, with
dark green patina.
L. 9cm Weight 129g
See Carancini and Peroni 1999, pl. 1.E. First
horizon of EBA hoards.
EBA, early.

24.
PRB 1935.10-18.6. Transferred from GR.
Flanged axe. **Axes type 8**.
Small axe with short, almost straight butt with
small notch, trapezoidal blade with almost
straight cutting edge. Smooth dark green
patina.
L. 9.4cm Weight 157g
See Carancini and Peroni 1999, pl. 1.E, F. First
horizon of EBA hoards.
EBA, early.
Bibliography: Walters 1899, no. 2916.

25.
PRB 1937.5-8.1. Bought from Sydney Burney.
Flanged axe. **Axes type 9**.
Very long, narrow axe with rounded butt with
central circular hole, blade slightly flared and
round cutting edge. Patchy patina with brown
and blue areas. Cutting edge worn.
L. 33.2cm Weight 1481g
Analysis: Bronze. See D. Hook report.
See Carancini 1993, 139, fig. 5.15, type Salerno,
identical in shape and size.
EBA.

26.
PRB 1935.10-18.2. Transferred from GR
(1856.12-26.973). Bequeathed by Sir William
Temple.

Flanged axe. **Axes type 10**.
Flanged axe with rounded butt with wide
notch, slightly flaring blade with rounded
cutting edge. Smooth dark green patina with
bright green zones.
L. 12.5cm Weight 228g
See Carancini and Peroni 1999, pl. 1.G. Second
horizon of EBA hoards.
EBA, early.
Bibliography: Walters 1899, no. 2912.

27.
PRB 1880.8-2.41.Given by Sir A.W. Franks.
Capua (Caserta), Campania.
Flanged axe. **Axes type 10**.
Flanged axe with rounded butt with notch,
slightly flaring blade with rounded bevel-line
and cutting edge. Patina smooth, dull green
with incrustations. Cutting edge damaged.
L. 12cm Weight 228g
Analysis: Bronze. See D. Hook report.
See Carancini and Peroni 1999, pl. 1.D, J. First
or second horizon of EBA hoards.
EBA, early.

28.
PRB 1935.10-18.4. Transferred from GR.
Flanged axe. **Axes type 10**.
Rounded butt with notch, slightly flared blade
with rounded bevel-line and cutting edge.
Smooth dark green patina with incrustations.
L. 15.8cm Weight 388g
See Carancini and Peroni 1999, pl. 1.K, Q.
Second–third horizon of EBA hoards.
EBA, early or later.
Bibliography: Walters 1899, no. 2914.

29.
PRB 1935.10-18.9. Transferred from GR.
Flanged axe. **Axes type 10**.
Rounded butt with notch, slightly flaring blade
with rounded bevel-line and cutting edge.
Medium green patina, lacking on sides.
L. 11.6cm Weight 213g
See Carancini and Peroni 1999, pl. 1.J, L, M.
Second horizon of EBA hoards.
EBA, early.
Bibliography: Walters 1899, no. 2919.

30.
PRB WG1055. Canon W. Greenwell Collection,
bought from the Rev. Greville J. Chester. Given
by J. Pierpont Morgan in 1909.
Corneto (Tarquinia, Viterbo), Lazio.
Flanged axe. **Axes type 10**.
Rounded butt with small central notch, flanges
widening towards the blade and hammered at
junction, short flared blade with rounded
cutting edge, probably reworked. Dull green
patina with light green zones.
L. 9.4cm Weight 123g
See Carancini and Peroni 1999, pl. 1.K, Q.
Second–third horizon of EBA hoards. Very

similar except for the hammered blade of this axe.
EBA, early or later.

31.
PRB 1935.10-18.8. Transferred from GR.
Flanged axe. **Axes type 10.**
Flanged axe with rounded butt and closed notch, slightly flaring blade with rounded bevel-line and cutting edge. Blackish patina with spotty incrustations of black and light green.
L. 16.3cm Weight 384g
See Carancini and Peroni 1999, pl. 1.L. Second horizon of EBA hoards.
EBA, early.
Bibliography: Walters 1899, no. 2918.

32.
PRB WG1057. Canon W. Greenwell Collection, bought from the Rev. Greville J. Chester. Given by J. Pierpont Morgan in 1909.
Anagni (Frosinone),Lazio.
Flanged axe. **Axes type 11.**
Distinct rounded butt with central notch, faceted sides and flared blade with rounded cutting edge. Smooth patina in various tones of green.
L.15.3cm Weight 366g
See Carancini and Peroni 1999, pl. 1.R, S. Third horizon of EBA hoards.
EBA, late.

33.
PRB 1964.12-1.216(289). Sir Henry Wellcome Collection, no. 103915. Bought via Mr. Comins at Steven's sale 3 October 1930, lot 82. Given by the Wellcome Trustees.
Bazzano (Bologna), Emilia Romagna.
Flanged axe. **Axes type 11.**
Small rounded butt with narrow notch, wide faceted flanges, slightly flaring blade with rounded cutting edge. Dark green patina with incrustations.
L. 17.4cm Weight 468g
See Carancini and Peroni 1999, pl. 1.R. Third horizon of EBA hoards; also Jurgeit 1999, no. 214, from Apulia.
EBA, late.

34.
PRB 1935.10-18.7. Transferred from GR. Charles Townley Collection. Bought from Peregrine Townley.
Flanged axe. **Axes type 11.**
Distinct rounded butt with small closed notch, slightly flaring blade with rounded cutting edge. Dull dark green patina with brown grey and dark green incrustations.
L. 15.5cm Weight 273g
See Carancini and Peroni 1999, pl. 1.R. Third horizon of EBA hoards.
EBA, late.
Bibliography: Walters 1899, no. 2917.

35.
GR 1969.12-31.86. Transferred from PRB.
Canon W. Greenwell Collection, no. 729, bought from W. Talbot Ready. Given by J. Pierpont Morgan in 1909.
'Athens', Greece.
Flanged axe. **Axes type 12.**
Concave sides, distinct rounded butt with notch-points closed, slightly faceted sides,

strongly rounded cutting edge. Smooth light green patina with areas of surface missing.
L. 14.7cm Weight 221g
See Carancini and Peroni 1999, pl. 1.S, T. Third–fourth horizon of EBA hoards.
EBA, late.

36.
PRB 1935.10-18.10. Transferred from GR.
Flanged axe. **Axes type 12.**
Distinct rounded butt, narrow notch, slightly concave sides with flaring blade and rounded cutting edge. Dark green dull patina with white incrustations.
L. 11.9cm Weight 241g
See **cat. 35**.
EBA, late.
Bibliography: Walters 1899, no. 2920.

37.
PRB 1935.10-18.3. Transferred from GR (1867.5-8.194). Blacas Collection.
Flanged axe. **Axes type 12.**
Concave sides, distinct rounded butt with notch-points once closed, one notch-point now missing, faceted sides, strongly rounded cutting edges. Elegant form, very accurately worked. Dark green patina with incrustations.
L. 17.1cm Weight 284g
See **cat. 35**.
EBA, late.
Bibliography: Walters 1899, no. 2913.

38.
PRB WG1056. Canon W. Greenwell Collection, bought from the Rev. Greville J. Chester. Given by J. Pierpont Morgan in 1909.
Albe, Magliano dei Marsi (L'Aquila), Abruzzo.
Flanged axe. **Axes type 12.**
Distinct rounded butt with narrow notch, slightly concave sides with flaring blade and rounded cutting edge. Smooth, dark green patina with blackish incrustations. Cutting edge and flanges damaged.
L. 13.5cm Weight 297g
See **cat. 35**.
EBA, late.
Bibliography: Bietti Sestieri and Giardino 2003, 413, fig. 4.

39.
PRB 1964.12-1.358(294). Sir Henry Wellcome Collection, no. 79647. Bought In Florence from A. Albizi in 1930. Given by the Wellcome Trustees.
Flanged axe. **Axes type 13.**
Elongated axe with small rounded butt with central notch, developed flanges with concave profile, slightly flaring blade with rounded cutting edge. Dark green patina with light earth incrustations, corrosion on the surface. Blade damaged.
L. 19.2cm Weight 483g
See Carancini and Peroni 1999, pl. 1.Q, Y. Third–fourth horizon of EBA hoards.
EBA, late.

40.
PRB 1880.8-2.40. Given by Sir A.W. Franks.
Bagni di Lucca, Tuscany.
Flanged axe. **Axes type 13.**
Elongated axe with small distinct butt with wide central notch, developed flanges with markedly concave profile, flaring blade with

rounded cutting edge. Smooth blackish patina.
L. 17.5cm Weight 419g
See **cat. 39**.
EBA, late.

Halberd and Daggers

41.
PRB WG1148. Canon W. Greenwell Collection, bought from Alessandro Castellani. Given by J. Pierpont Morgan in 1909.
Frosinone, Lazio.
Halberd with triangular blade with concave sides. **Halberds type 2.**
Semicircular base of blade with three large rivet-holes and two long rivets extant, separated from the functional part by a slightly raised line; thick-sectioned blade thinning towards the cutting edge. Smooth dark green and black patina, with dark green and whitish incrustations. Small parts missing.
L. 17cm Weight 150g
See *PBF* VI.10, no. 228 (this piece), type Cotronei, var. A.
According to Carancini 1993, 145, this type should belong to an advanced phase of the EBA.
EBA, late?
Bibliography: O'Riordain 1937, 284, fig. 67.5; *PBF* VI. 10, no. 228.

42.
PRB WG1135. Canon W. Greenwell Collection, given by the Earl of Northesk. Given by J. Pierpont Morgan in 1909.
Italy.
Dagger with socketed hilt for composite handle riveted to blade. **Daggers type 1.**
Lower part of hilt with oval section and one rivet-hole at centre, near edge; wide and shallow semicircular shoulder-cap with inner edge narrowing toward the blade and 10 rivets with separately cast rounded heads; long triangular blade with edges slightly concave below shoulder-cap, four converging ribs in central zone and slight gradation along the cutting edges. Complex incised decoration: curved band of dots and four hatched triangles, two with encircling row of dots, on base of blade; two hatched triangles hanging from a cross-hatched band at upper end of blade; row of dots and hatched triangles along blade edge; row of dots along the ribs; upper surface of ribs decorated with groups of parallel lines. Smooth dark green patina. Upper part of hilt missing and cutting edge slightly damaged.
L. 37.9cm Width 9.7cm max.Weight 406g
See *PBF* VI. 10, nos. 420, 421, from Ripatransone (especially 421), type Ripatransone var. B; also Carancini and Peroni 1999, pl. 1.10, from Ripatransone (Marche), third horizon of EBA hoards. See also *PBF* type Montemerano for the converging nervatures on the blade.
EBA, early or middle.

43.
PRB 1964.12-1.514. Sir Henry Wellcome Collection, no. R197/1937. Given by the Wellcome Trustees.
Dagger with cast hilt riveted to blade. **Daggers type 2.**
Elongated hilt with thick oval section, hammered rivet at centre of upper part and low distinct pommel with flat end; wide and

shallow semicircular shoulder-cap with inner edge slightly narrowing toward the blade and 13 rivets with separately cast rounded heads, all missing; triangular blade, narrower than shoulder-cap, with slight gradation in a wide band along the cutting edges. Complex incised decoration: curved cross-hatched bands alternating with rows of dots on end of pommel, shoulder-cap and upper part of blade base, also decorated with a row of hatched triangles; cross-hatched bands and a row of hatched triangles along central zone of blade. Shiny patina, dark green on hilt, and green-brown on blade. Parts of cutting edge missing.
L. 26.4cm Weight 261g
Close to *PBF* VI. 10, nos. 409, 411, from Ripatransone, type Cetona var. B; also Carancini and Peroni 1999, pl. 1.8, from Ripatransone (Marche), first–second horizon of EBA hoards. See also *PBF* type Montemerano var. B for the converging nervatures on the blade.
EBA, early–middle.

44.
PRB (P)1974.12-1.163. Pitt Rivers Collection. Italy.
Dagger with cast hilt riveted to blade. **Daggers type 4.**
Elongated hilt with wide oval section and low distinct pommel with flat end; semicircular shoulder-cap with inner edge markedly narrowing toward the blade and eight rivets with flat hammered heads; triangular blade with low section, slightly widening toward the central zone. Incised decoration: three parallel groups of a cross-hatched band and a row of hatched triangles on the base of the blade, two converging pairs of parallel lines along the edges of the blade. Smooth dark green patina. Small parts missing, cutting edges slightly damaged, possibly some ancient repairs.
L. 24.6cm Weight 235g
Analysis: Bronze. See D. Hook report.
Close to *PBF* VI. 10, no. 435, from the province of Siena, type Loreto Aprutino, var. B; also Carancini and Peroni 1999, pl. 2, hoard of Loreto Aprutino (Teramo, Abruzzo), third horizon of EBA hoards.
EBA, late.

45.
PRB Old Acquisition 98. Registered OA on 6 July 1939.
Part of dagger with cast hilt riveted to blade and tip of another weapon. **Daggers type 5.**
Elongated hilt with oval section and distinct widening pommel with flat top; semicircular shoulder-cap with inner edge narrowing toward the blade and seven rivets with separately cast rounded heads; only one rivet-head extant; triangular blade with thick central rib. Incised decoration: bands of oblique marks and dots on top of hilt and base of blade; two groups of parallel lines and hatched triangles along the cutting edges. Triangular tip of a different weapon, possibly a sword, with low diamond-shaped section and central swelling, has been attached to the dagger. Dark green and blackish patina. Cutting edges heavily damaged.
L. 12.4 + 9.1cm Weight 139g
Analysis: Hilt bronze; blade bronze; replacement blade tip arsenical copper. See D. Hook report.

Close to *PBF* VI. 10, no. 423, from Cella (Reggio Emilia), type Parco dei Monaci, var. A; also Carancini and Peroni 1999, pl. 1.7, from Matera (Basilicata), second–third horizon of EBA hoards.
EBA, late.

46.
PRB 1856.12-26.703.(W.T.703). Transferred from GR. Bequeathed by Sir William Temple. Torre Annunziata (Naples), Campania.
Dagger with cast hilt riveted to blade. **Daggers type 5.**
Hilt with thick oval section and low distinct pommel with flat end and rivet with separately cast conical head at centre; wide semicircular shoulder-cap with inner edge markedly narrowing toward the blade and eleven rivets with separately cast rounded heads; some rivet-heads missing; triangular blade with central rib widening toward the base of the blade and low section with central swelling. Complex incised decoration: narrow cross-hatched bands forming a cross pattern and rows of dots on the pommel end; cross-hatched band, rows of dots and row of hatched triangles on the shoulder-cap; parallel cross-hatched bands and lines on the base of the blade; four parallel lines and a row of hatched triangles along the blade edges; triangular pattern drawn with three converging pairs of parallel lines, a zigzag and a straight cross-hatched band alternating with a row of dots and one of hatched triangles, on the upper part of the central rib. Smooth dark green patina. Cutting edges slightly damaged.
L. 40.5cm Weight 600g
Analysis: Bronze. See D. Hook report.
Close to *PBF* VI. 10, no. 422, from Matera, type Parco dei Monaci, var. A. The triangular pattern at centre of blade, probably a relatively late feature, appears on *PBF* nos. 441, from Lodi?, and 442, from Lombardy.
EBA, late.

Groups of Associated Aretefacts

1. Group of three flat axes, cat. 47–49, and two flanged axes, cat. 50 and 51, from Agrigento, Sicily; Axes types 5b, 6 and 7.

47.
PRB WG1049. Canon W. Greenwell Collection, bought from the Rev. Greville J. Chester. Given by J. Pierpont Morgan in 1909.
Near Girgenti (= Agrigento), Sicily.
Flat axe. **Axes type 5b.**
Probably associated with **cat. 48, 49, 50** and **51**.
Elongated trapezoidal tool with narrow straight butt, slightly concave blade edges and flaring blade with rounded cutting edge. Small parts missing. Rough blackish patina.
L. 11.4cm Weight 104g
Analysis: Bronze. See D. Hook report.
Close to Albanese Procelli 1993, 30, 72ff., fig. 1.6, from Priolo. Type R1C1 (with thick-sectioned butt).
EBA or later.
Unlike those from mainland Italy, that date mainly from the CA, and are made of copper or arsenical copper, Sicilian flat axes are generally of BA date. A further element indicating a relatively late chronology for this piece is the

fact that it is made of bronze.
Bibliography: Bietti Sestieri 2004, 28 and fig. 3.1.

48.
PRB WG1050. Canon W. Greenwell Collection, bought from the Rev. Greville J. Chester. Given by J. Pierpont Morgan in 1909.
Near Girgenti (= Agrigento), Sicily.
Flat axe. **Axes type 5b.**
Probably associated with **cat. 47, 49, 50** and **51**.
Elongated trapezoidal tool with straight butt, markedly flaring blade with slightly concave edges and rounded cutting edge. Smooth green-turquoise patina with black zones.
L. 13.4cm Weight 200g
Analysis: Bronze. See D. Hook report.
Close to Albanese Procelli 1993, 31, 72ff., fig. 2.13, from Cesaro', type R1C (with markedly flaring blade).
See **cat. 47**.
EBA or later.
Bibliography: Bietti Sestieri 2004, 29 and fig. 3.2.

49.
PRB WG1051. Canon W. Greenwell Collection, bought from the Rev. Greville J. Chester. Given by J. Pierpont Morgan in 1909.
Near Girgenti (= Agrigento), Sicily.
Flat axe. **Axes type 5b.**
Probably associated with **cat. 47, 48, 50** and **51**.
Small trapezoidal tool, thick in section, with straight butt, strongly flared blade and rounded cutting edge marked by a slight bevel. Smooth black patina.
L. 6.9cm Weight 67g
Analysis: Bronze. See D. Hook report.
Close to Albanese Procelli 1993, 30f., 72, fig. 1.6, from Priolo; fig. 2.13, from Cesaro'. Flat axes, type R1C and var. R1C1.
See **cat. 47**.
EBA or later.
Bibliography: Bietti Sestieri 2004, 29 and fig. 3.3.

50.
PRB WG1052. Canon W. Greenwell Collection. Given by J. Pierpont Morgan in 1909.
Girgenti (= Agrigento), Sicily.
Axe with sightly raised edges. **Axes type 6.**
Probably associated with **cat. 47–49** and **51**.
Narrow trapezoidal tool with straight butt, slightly raised edges and blade strongly flared towards the rounded cutting edge. Rough blackish patina with brown incrustations.
L. 11.2cm. Weight 162g.
Analysis: Bronze. See D. Hook report.
See Albanese Procelli 1993, 31, 72, fig. 2.12, isolated find from Taormina. Axes with slightly raised edges, type R2B. See **cat. 18**. A similar piece is reported from Agrigento: De Gregorio 1917, 58, pl. 45.5.
EBA and later.
Bibliography: Bietti Sestieri 2004, 29 and fig. 3.4.

51.
PRB WG1053. Canon W. Greenwell Collection, bought from the Rev. Greville J. Chester. Given by J. Pierpont Morgan in 1909.
Near Girgenti (= Agrigento), Sicily.
Flanged axe. **Axes type 7.**
Probably associated with **cat. 47–50.**

Small trapezoidal tool with slightly dished butt, widely flaring blade with low flanges and rounded cutting edge. Rough blackish patina with bright green and reddish incrustations.
L. 6.6cm Weight 46g
Analysis: Bronze. See D. Hook report.
Close to Albanese Procelli 1993, 31, 72ff., fig. 2.11, from Reitana, Acireale. Slightly flanged axes, type R2A (with straight butt); also Carancini and Peroni 1999, pl. 1.F. First horizon of EBA hoards.
EBA.
Bibliography: Bietti Sestieri 2004, 30 and fig. 3.5.

2. Group of eight flanged axes, cat. 52–59, from Terni, Umbria; Axes type 12.

52.
PRB 1964.12-1.207(293). Sir Henry Wellcome Collection, no. 298. Bought in Rome from Arte Antica e Moderna by Captain Saint in November 1929. Given by the Wellcome Trustees.
Terni, Umbria.
Flanged axe. **Axes type 12.**
Associated with **cat. 53–59.**
Flanged axe with distinct rounded butt with notch, slightly concave sides with flaring blade and rounded bevel-line and cutting edge. Cutting edge hammered. Traces of dull light green patina.
L. 18.5cm Weight 484g
Analysis: Bronze. See D. Hook report.
See Carancini and Peroni 1999, pl. 1. S, T. Third–fourth horizon of EBA hoards.
EBA, late.
Bibliography: Bietti Sestieri 2004, 34 and fig. 5a.4.

53.
PRB 1964.12-1.208 (295). Sir Henry Wellcome Collection, no. 308. Bought in Rome from Arte Antica e Moderna by Captain Saint in November 1929. Given by the Wellcome Trustees.
Terni, Umbria.
Flanged axe. **Axes type 12.**
Associated with **cat. 52, 54–59.**
Distinct rounded butt with notch, slightly concave sides with flaring blade and rounded bevel-line and cutting edge. Dull light green patina with blue incrustations and earth. Cutting edge worn.
L. 18.2cm Weight 477g
Analysis: Leaded bronze. See D. Hook report.
See **cat. 52.**
EBA, late.
Bibliography: Bietti Sestieri 2004, 34 and fig. 5b.5.

54.
PRB 1964.12-1.211(298). Sir Henry Wellcome Collection, no. 309. Bought in Rome from Arte Antica e Moderna by Captain Saint in November 1929. Given by the Wellcome Trustees.
Terni, Umbria.
Flanged axe. **Axes type 12.**
Associated with **cat. 52, 53, 55–59.**
Distinct rounded butt with notch, slightly concave sides with flaring blade and rounded bevel-line and cutting edge. Cutting edge worn and points of butt and notch hammered. Dull

light green patina with blue incrustations and earth.
L. 18cm Weight 479g
Analysis: Bronze. See D. Hook report.
See **cat. 52.**
EBA, late.
Bibliography: Bietti Sestieri 2004, 34 and fig. 5b.8.

55.
PRB 1964.12-1.205(291). Sir Henry Wellcome Collection, no. 96446. Bought in Rome from Antichità delle Belle Arti by Captain Saint in April 1931. Given by the Wellcome Trustees.
Probably Terni, Umbria.
Flanged axe. **Axes type 12.**
Associated with **cat. 52–54, 56–59.**
Distinct rounded butt with notch, slightly concave sides with flaring blade and rounded bevel-line and cutting edge. Dull light green patina with blue incrustations and earth.
L. 18.4cm Weight 462g
Analysis: Bronze. See D. Hook report.
See **cat. 52.**
EBA, late.
Bibliography: Bietti Sestieri 2004, 34 and fig. 5a.2.

56.
PRB 1964.12-1.206(292). Sir Henry Wellcome Collection. Given by the Wellcome Trustees.
Probably Terni, Umbria.
Flanged axe. **Axes type 12.**
Associated with **52, 53, 54, 55, 57, 58** and **59.**
Distinct rounded butt with notch, slightly concave sides with flaring blade and rounded bevel-line and cutting edge. Dull light green patina with blue incrustations and earth.
Cutting edge worn.
L. 18.6cm Weight 419g
Analysis: Bronze. See D. Hook report.
See **cat. 52.**
EBA, late.
Bibliography: Bietti Sestieri 2004, 34 and fig. 5a.3.

57.
PRB 1964.12-1.204(290). Sir Henry Wellcome Collection, no. 96447. Bought in Rome from Antichità delle Belle Arti by Captain Saint in April 1931. Given by the Wellcome Trustees.
Probably Terni, Umbria.
Flanged axe. **Axes type 12.**
Associated with **cat. 52–56, 58** and **59.**
Distinct rounded butt with notch, slightly concave sides with flaring blade and rounded bevel-line and cutting edge. Dull light green patina with blue incrustations and earth.
Cutting edge worn.
L. 18.3cm Weight 442g
Analysis: Bronze. See D. Hook report.
See **cat. 52.**
EBA, late.
Bibliography: Bietti Sestieri 2004, 34 and fig. 5a.1.

58.
PRB 1964.12-1.209(296). Sir Henry Wellcome Collection, no. 67751. Bought from G. Pini November 1928. Given by the Wellcome Trustees.
Probably Terni, Umbria.
Flanged axe. **Axes type 12.**
Associated with **cat. 52–57** and **59.**

Distinct rounded butt with notch, slightly concave sides with flaring blade and rounded bevel-line and cutting edge. Cutting edge worn and flanges slightly damaged. Dull light green patina with blue incrustations and earth.
L. 18.6cm Weight 484g
Analysis: Bronze. See D. Hook report.
See **cat. 52.**
EBA, late.
Bibliography: Bietti Sestieri 2004, 34 and fig. 5b.6.

59.
PRB 1964.12-1.210(297). Sir Henry Wellcome Collection. Given by the Wellcome Trustees.
Probably Terni, Umbria.
Flanged axe. **Axes type 12.**
Associated with **cat. 52–58.**
Flanged axe with distinct rounded butt with notch, slightly concave sides with flaring blade and rounded bevel-line and cutting edge. Cutting edge worn. Dull light green patina with blue incrustations and earth.
L. 18.4cm Weight 455g
Analysis: Bronze. See D. Hook report.
See **cat. 52.**
EBA, late.
Bibliography: Bietti Sestieri 2004, 34 and fig. 5b.7.

3. Two daggers, cat. 60 and 61, probably from central Italy; Daggers types 2 and 3.

60.
PRB 1867.5-8.183. Blacas Collection.
Dagger with cast hilt riveted to blade. **Daggers type 2.**
Associated with **cat. 61**, same patina.
Elongated hilt with thick oval section and distinct widening pommel with flat end; wide semicircular shoulder-cap with inner edge slightly narrowing toward the blade and 21 rivets with separately cast rounded heads; one rivet-head missing; triangular blade with slight gradation in a wide band along the cutting edges. Incised decoration: rows of dots and bands of parallel lines on pommel and shoulder-cap; cross pattern of parallel lines with rows of dots in the resulting spaces on centre of pommel end; parallel lines, hatched bands and zigzag lines on base of blade; row of hatched triangles along central zone of blade. The blade was tinned to look like silver. Cutting edges damaged, with strike marks, tip of blade missing. Smooth green-brown patina, with marked azure incrustations.
L. 24cm Weight 233g
Analysis: Hilt bronze, blade tinned. See D. Hook report.
Close to *PBF* VI.10, no. 409, type Cetona, var. B; also Carancini and Peroni 1999, pl. 1.8, from Ripatransone (Marche). Second–third horizon of EBA hoards.
EBA, early–middle.
Bibliography: Bietti Sestieri 2004, 31 and fig. 4.1.

61.
PRB 1867.5-8.184. Blacas Collection.
Dagger with cast hilt riveted to blade. **Daggers type 3.**
Associated with **cat. 60.**
Hilt with oval section and low distinct pommel with flat end; shallow semicircular shoulder-

cap with inner edge markedly narrowing toward the blade and nine rivets with small separately cast rounded heads; triangular blade with low section, with three converging ribs in central zone and slight gradation in a narrow band along the cutting edges. Engraved decoration: bands of parallel lines and dots on end of pommel; parallel lines on hilt, shoulder-cap and base of blade; a row of hatched triangles on base of blade and along its central zone. Cutting edges damaged. Light green patina with marked azure incrustations.
L. 31.4cm Weight 328g

Analysis: Hilt bronze, blade bronze. See D. Hook report.
Close to *PBF* VI. 10, nos. 397, from Loreto Aprutino, 398–399, from Italy. Type Montemerano var. B; also Carancini and Peroni 1999, pl. 1.15, third horizon of EBA hoards. EBA, early or middle.
Bibliography: Bietti Sestieri 2004, 31 and fig. 4.2.

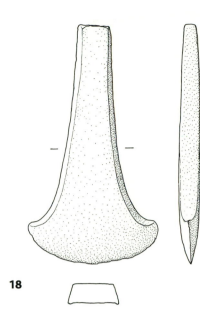

18

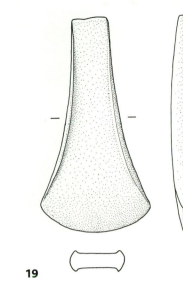

19

20

21

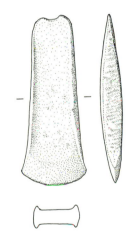

22

23

24

Plate 4   **Axes type 6**: - 18 Rome, Lazio. **Axes type 7**: - 19 Brescia, Lombardy. – 20 Campania. **Axes type 8**: - 21. - 22 probably near Naples, Campania. - 23. -24.

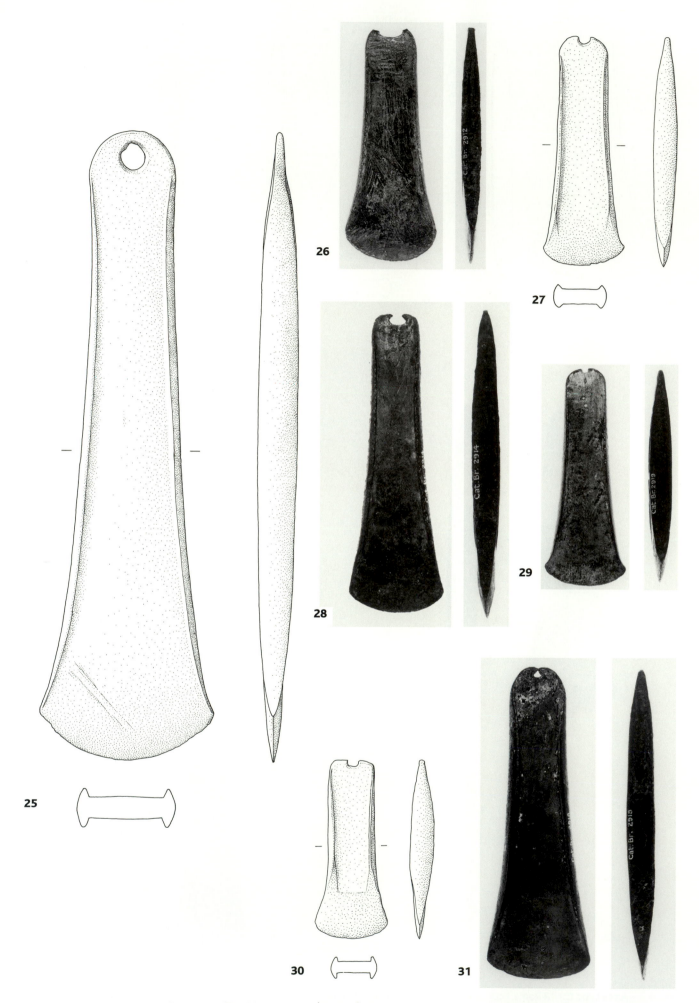

Plate 5 **Axes type 9**: - 25. **Axes type 10**: - 26. - 27 Capua (Caserta), Campania. - 28. - 29. - 30 Corneto (Tarquinia, Viterbo), Lazio. - 31.

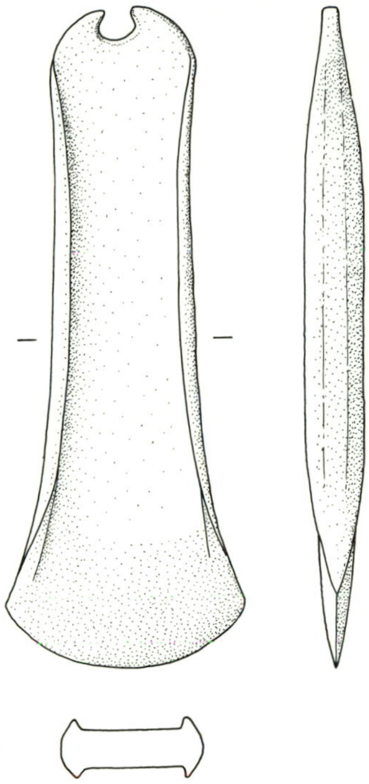

32

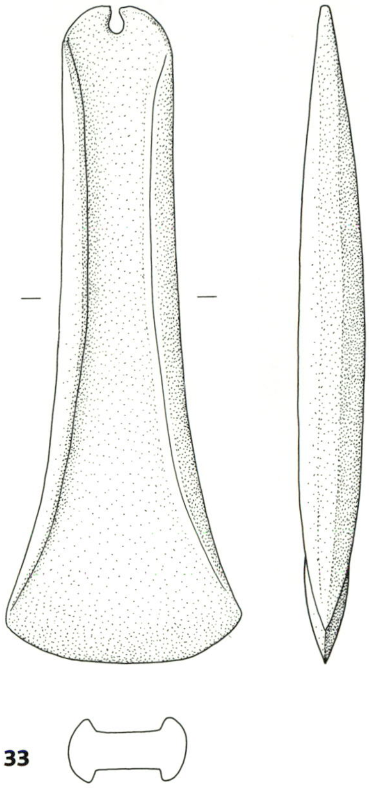

33

34

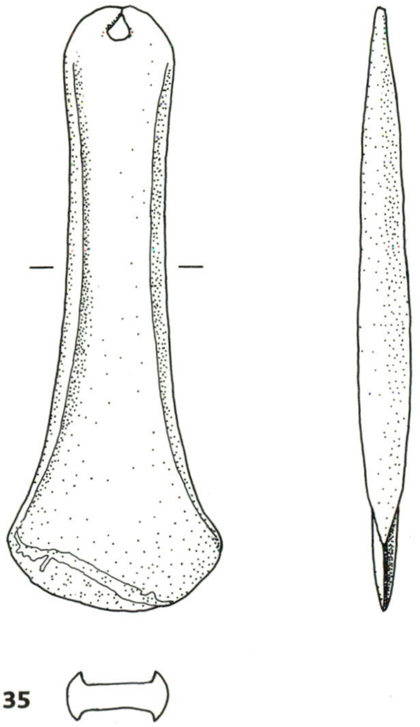

35

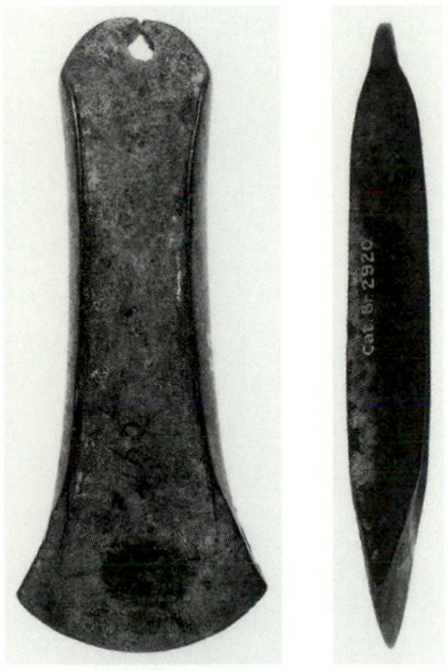

36

Plate 6 **Axes type 11**: - 32. Anagni (Frosinone), Lazio. - 33 Bazzano (Bologna), Emilia Romagna. - 34. **Axes type 12**: - 35 Athens, Greece. - 36.

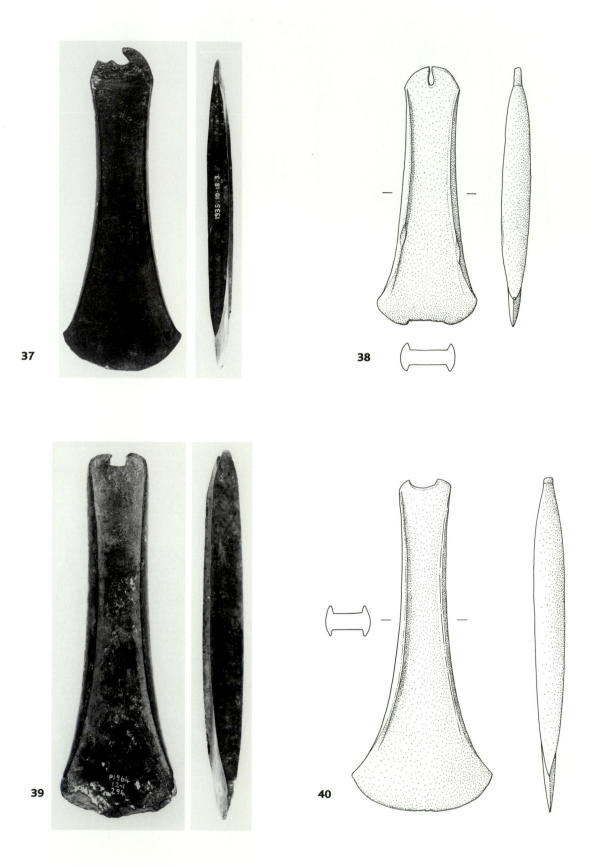

Plate 7   **Axes type 12**: - 37. - 38 Alba (L'Aquila), Abruzzo. **Axes type 13**: - 39. - 40 Bagni di Lucca (Tuscany).

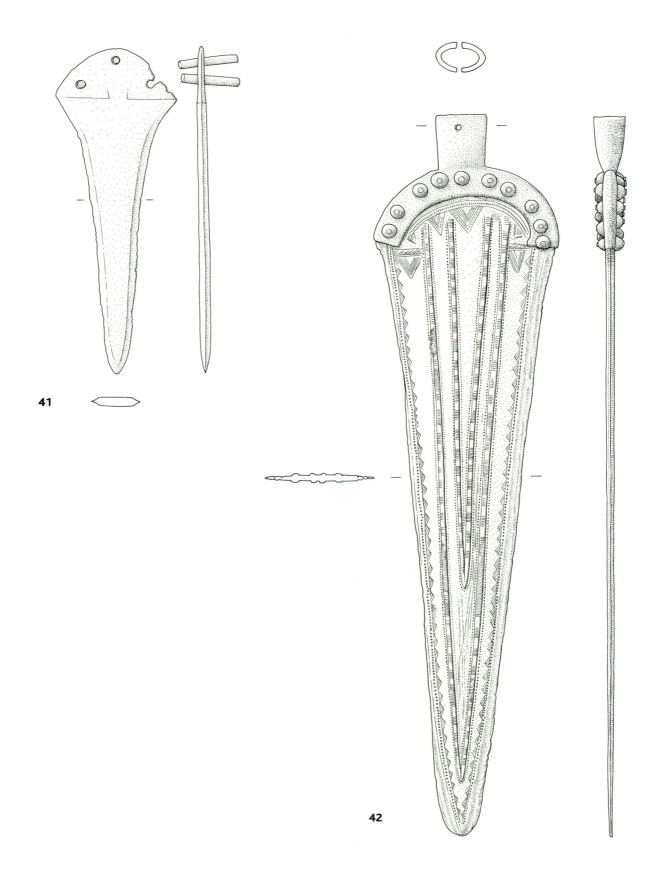

41

42

Plate 8 **Halberds type 2**: - 41 Frosinone, Lazio. **Daggers type 1**: - 42.

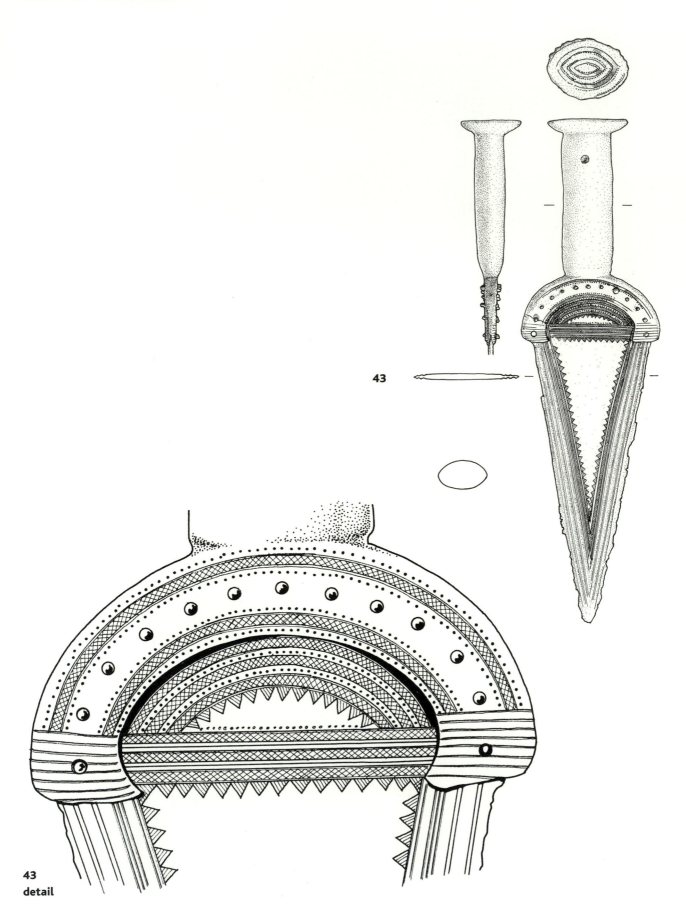

43

**43
detail**

Plate 9   Daggers type 2: - 43.

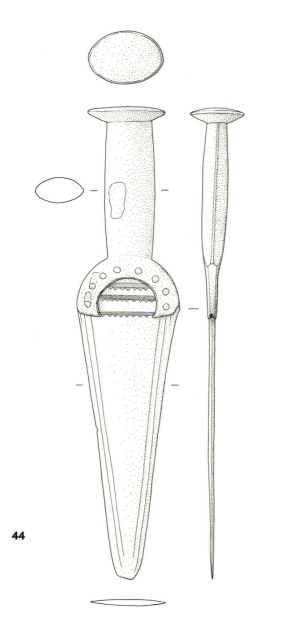

44

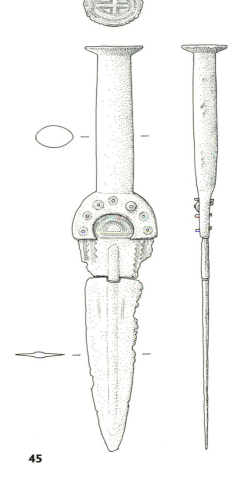

45

Plate 10   Daggers type 4: - 44. **Daggers type 5**: - 45

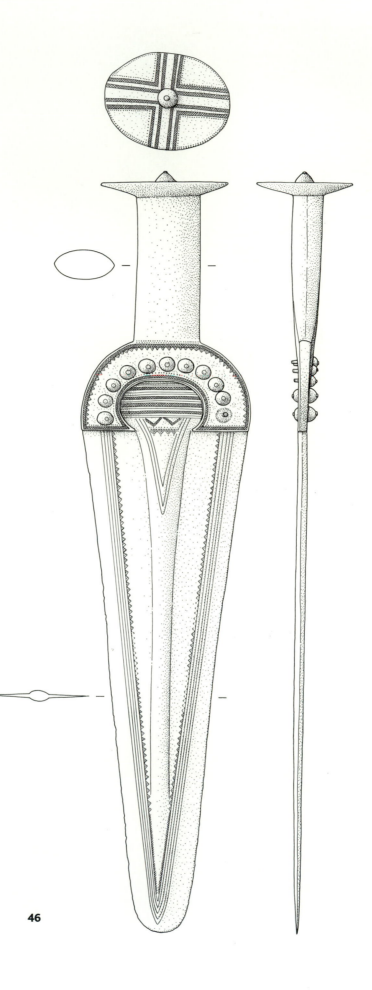

46

Plate 11   Daggers type 5: - 46 Torre Annunziata (Naples), Campania.

48 | Prehistoric Metal Artefacts from Italy (3500–720BC) in the British Museum

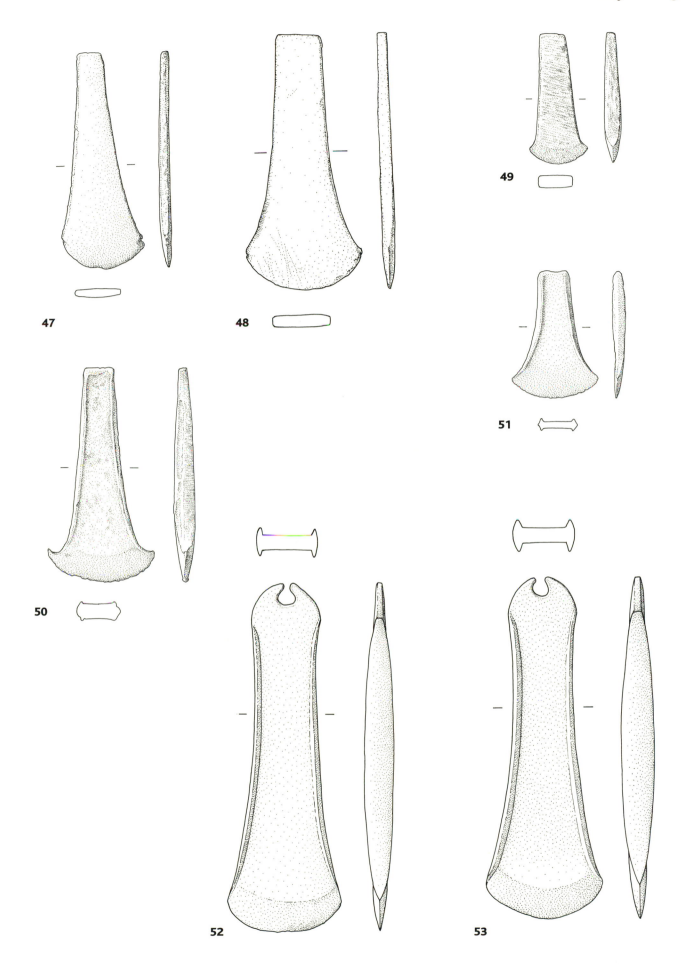

Plate 12   Group of five associated artefacts, Agrigento, Sicily. **Axes type 5b**: - 47. - 48. - 49. **Axes type 6**: - 50. **Axes type 7**: - 51. Group of eight associated artefacts, Terni, Umbria. **Axes type 12**: - 52. - 53.

Middle Bronze Age

Axes

62.
PRB 1935.10-18.11. Transferred from GR.
Flanged axe. **Axes type 14.**
Small rounded butt with central notch, faceted flanges widening towards the flaring blade, rounded cutting edge. Blackish rough patina with dark green incrustations. Circular hole below the notch.
L. 18.2cm Weight 580g
See Carancini and Peroni 1999, pl. 6.13, flanged axe from the Lodigiano hoard, EBA, late–MBA, early; pl. 12.4, flanged axe from Sezze (not identical, but see the side profile of the flanges).
MBA, early.
Bibliography: Walters 1899, no. 2921.

63.
PRB 1935.10-18.13. Transferred from GR (1867.5-8.193). Blacas Collection.
Flanged axe. **Axes type 14.**
Axe with developed flanges, rounded butt with wide notch, lower part of flanges and blade reworked by hammering, wide, rounded cutting edge. Light green patina with some brown and black incrustations.
L. 12.5cm Weight 310g
See Carancini and Peroni 1999, pl. 12.2, hoard of Cascina Ranza.
MBA, early.
Bibliography: Walters 1899, no. 2923.

64.
PRB 1883.4-26.6. Given by Sir A.W. Franks.
Flanged axe with distinct blade. **Axes type 15.**
Rounded butt with small notch, straight sides slightly flaring towards the blade, blade trapezoidal with concave edges and rounded cutting edge. Irregular surface, patina in various tones of green.
L. 12.1cm Weight 115g
See Carancini and Peroni 1999, pl. 12.1, hoard of Cascina Ranza (not identical).
MBA, early.

65.
PRB Old Acquisition 104. Registered OA on 21 July 1939.
Flanged axe with distinct blade. **Axes type 15.**
Narrow elongated tool with straight butt, sides slightly flaring towards the blade, long blade with concave edges and rounded cutting edge. Rough, dark green, patchy patina, surface with corroded areas.
L. 15.1cm Weight 147g
See Carancini and Peroni 1999, pl. 12.1, hoard of Cascina Ranza (not identical).
MBA, early.

66.
PRB 1964.12-1.214(306). Sir Henry Wellcome Collection, no. 311. Bought in Rome from Arte Antica e Moderna by Captain Saint in November 1929. Given by the Wellcome Trustees.
Terni,Umbria.
Flanged/winged axe. **Axes type 18.**
Almost straight butt, slightly concave sides flaring towards the distinct blade, blade rectangular with slightly concave edges and rounded cutting edge. Smooth dull green patina, partly corroded. Traces of wear.
L. 13.5cm Weight 184g
Analysis: Bronze. See D. Hook report.
See Carancini and Peroni 1999, pl. 9.18, Avigliana settlement (not identical).
MBA, middle.

67.
PRB Old Acquisition 103. Registered OA on 19 July 1939. Collection J.F. Lucas of Bentley Ashbourne, Co. Derby. Purchased from Mrs Ruth Faulkner, executor of J.F. Lucas.
Winged axe with contiguous wings. **Axes type 19.**
Straight butt with central cleft, wings faceted, widening towards the blade and hammered at junction with blade, short flaring blade with rounded cutting edge. Rough dark green patina. Sides of wings hammered.
L. 11.8cm Weight 227g
See Carancini and Peroni 1999, pl. 12.3, from Rome, type Sezze.
MBA, early.

68.
PRB 1935.10-18.14. Transferred from GR.
Winged axe with contiguous wings. **Axes type 19.**
Straight butt, wings widening towards the blade and hammered at junction with blade, short flared blade with rounded cutting edge. Dark green patina with dark brown incrustations.
L. 13cm Weight 359g
See Carancini and Peroni 1999, pl. 12.3, from Rome, type Sezze.
MBA, early.
Bibliography: Walters 1899, no. 2924.

69.
PRB 1964.12-1.357(287). Sir Henry Wellcome Collection, no. 96444. Bought in Rome from Antichità delle Belle Arti by Captain Saint in April 1931. Given by the Wellcome Trustees.
Winged axe with contiguous wings. **Axes type 20.**
Narrow elongated shape with parallel sides, straight butt, heavily hammered, low wings widening towards the blade and hammered at junction with blade, stop-bevel, short trapezoidal blade with slightly curved cutting edge. Blade broken and repaired, transverse grooves on one wing. Patina mixed with green and black areas. Probably Sardinian.
L. 20.6cm Weight 754g
See Carancini and Peroni 1999, pl. 12.5, type Orosei, MBA, early; Giardino 1995, 34, fig. 17 B.1, from Palermo, Sicily. Probably Sardinian.
MBA, early?

70.
PRB 1964.12-1.363(336). Sir Henry Wellcome Collection, no. 95405. Bought in Rome from Arte Antica e Moderna by Captain Saint in September 1930. Given by the Wellcome Trustees.
Winged axe with contiguous wings. **Axes type 20.**
Narrow elongated shape with parallel sides, straight butt, low wings widening towards the blade and hammered at junction with blade, stop-bevel, short trapezoidal blade with straight cutting edge. Dark green to black patina. Probably Sardinian.
L. 16.7cm Weight 458g
See **cat. 69.**
MBA, early?

71.
PRB 1883.4-26.4. Given by Sir A.W. Franks.
Nola (Naples), Campania.
Winged axe with contiguous wings.Close to **Axes type 20.**
Narrow shape with parallel sides, straight, hammered butt, low wings, very short trapezoidal blade with almost straight cutting edge. Smooth black patina with bright green spots.
L. 6.3cm Weight 62g
Close to Carancini and Peroni 1999, pl. 12.5, type Orosei, MBA, early.
MBA, early.

72.
PRB 1883.4-26.2. Given by Sir A.W. Franks.
Abruzzo.
Winged axe with contiguous wings. **Axes type 21.**
Narrow elongated tool with slightly flaring sides, straight, hammered butt, wings widening towards the blade and hammered at junction with blade, stop-bevel, very short flared blade with rounded cutting edge. Face of blade hammered. Smooth dark green patina.
L. 17.6cm Weight 703g
Close to Carancini and Peroni 1999, pl. 12.8, from Canterano, MBA, advanced; see also pl.12.4, from Sezze, MBA, early, for the narrow elongated shape of this piece.
The typological features of this axe seem to indicate its intermediate position between the early and middle phase of the MBA in the evolutionary sequence of axes with contiguous wings.

MBA, early or later.
Bibliography: *BM Guide* 1904, 116, fig. 116 left; *BM Guide* 1920a, 149, fig. 156 left; Bietti Sestieri and Giardino 2003, 416, fig. 6.

73.
PRB1935.10-18.15. Transferred from GR (1859.2-16.154). Bequeathed by Miss M.H.M. Auldjo.
Winged axe with contiguous wings. **Axes type 21.**
Rounded butt with very slight indentation, wings widening towards the blade and hammered at junction with blade, stop-bevel, very short flared blade with rounded cutting edge. Thin, dark green patina with light zones and some blackish incrustations.
L. 16.4cm Weight 545g
See **cat. 72** for the general shape and lateral profile.
Probably MBA, middle.
Bibliography: Walters 1899, no. 2925.

74.
PRB 1935.10-18.5. Transferred from GR.
Winged axe with contiguous wings. **Axes type 21.**
Rounded butt with slight indentation, wings widening towards the blade and slightly hammered at junction with blade, stop-bevel, very short flared blade with slightly rounded cutting edge. Traces of smooth blackish patina.
L. 13.6cm Weight 327g
See Carancini and Peroni 1999, pl. 12.8 (from Canterano, not identical). Type Canterano.
MBA, middle.
Bibliography: Walters 1899, no. 2915.

75.
PRB 1964.12-1.364(337). Sir Henry Wellcome Collection, no. 113254. Bought in Rome from A. Rocci by Captain Saint in April 1932. Given by the Wellcome Trustees.
Winged axe with contiguous wings. **Axes type 21.**
Narrow elongated tool; rounded butt with very slight indentation, wings widening towards the blade and hammered at junction with blade, very short flaring blade with slightly rounded cutting edge. Light, dark brown patina.
L. 16.7cm Weight 567g
Close to Carancini and Peroni 1999, pl. 12.8, from Canterano, MBA, advanced; see also pl. 12.4, from Sezze, MBA, early, for the narrow elongated shape of this piece. The typological features of this axe seem to indicate its intermediate position between the early and middle phase of the MBA in the evolutionary sequence of axes with contiguous wings.
MBA, early or later.

76.
PRB WG1061. Canon W. Greenwell Collection, bought from the Rev. Greville J. Chester. Given by J. Pierpont Morgan in 1909.
Poli (Rome), Lazio.
Winged axe with contiguous wings. **Axes type 21.**
Rounded butt with very slight indentation, wings widening towards the blade and hammered at junction with blade, stop-bevel, very short flared blade with rounded cutting edge. Dark green patina. Cutting edge damaged.
L. 13.1cm Weight 354g

See Carancini and Peroni 1999, pl. 12.10, 11, from Nemi. Type Nemi.
MBA, middle.

77.
PRB WG1058. Canon W. Greenwell Collection, bought from the Rev. Greville J. Chester. Given by J. Pierpont Morgan in 1909.
Palermo, Sicily.
Winged axe with contiguous wings. **Axes type 22.**
Elongated tool with continuous flaring profile. Short straight butt, wings faceted, short flaring blade with rounded cutting edge. Smooth patina almost black.
L. 17.7cm Weight 506g
See Carancini and Peroni 1999, pl. 12.7, from Avigliana; pl. 12.8, from Canterano.
MBA, middle.

78.
PRB 1889.11-1.159. T.W.V. Robinson Collection, mostly purchased from Dr V. Gross of Neufville, Lac de Berne. Bought from George House Esq., Trustee of the Robinson family.
Winged axe with contiguous wings. **Axes type 23.**
Small curved butt with wide notch, narrow haft with straight sides, light wings, wide trapezoidal blade with rounded cutting edge. Smooth brown patina.
L. 17.6cm Weight 416g
Close to *Terramare* 1997, 393, fig. 227. 19–22; Carancini and Peroni 1999, pl. 10.16, Fiavé settlement, phase VI; pl. 10. 10–12, hoard of Rocca di Badolo (not identical).
Probably MBA, middle.

Daggers

79.
PRB W. G.1149. Canon W. Greenwell Collection, bought from Alessandro Castellani. Given by J. Pierpont Morgan in 1909.
Magliano (L'Aquila), Abruzzo.
Dagger with triangular blade with slightly concave edges. **Daggers type 6.**
Thin elongated weapon; base of blade triangular with rounded angles with two rivet-holes and one large rivet with rounded heads extant; narrow blade, with raised central part. Smooth blackish patina, with light green incrustations.
L.18.4cm Weight 50g
See *PBF* VI.10, no. 736, from Castione dei Marchesi. Type Monte Castellaccio.
MBA.

80.
PRB WG264. Canon W. Greenwell Collection. Given by J. Pierpont Morgan in 1909.
Peschiera, Boccatura del Mincio (Verona), Veneto.
Dagger/short sword with tang. **Daggers type 7.**
Elongated trapezoidal tang with circular rivet hole, blade with slightly sloping shoulders, almost straight edges and low diamond-shaped section. No patina.
L. 26cm Weight 119g
Analysis: Bronze. See D. Hook report.
See *PBF* VI.10, nos. 1109 from Peschiera, 1119 from Cisano, 1153 from Peschiera and 1155 from S. Polo d'Enza.
MBA or RBA.

Sword

81.
PRB 1880.8-2.48. Given by Sir A.W. Franks.
Osor, Island of Cres, Croatia.
Short sword with trapezoidal butt. **Swords type 1.**
Shoulders with four rivets, blade with slightly curved sides, the central part raised and separated from the cutting edges by a slight step. Small parts missing. Green patina with brown patches and slight corrosion.
L. 25.2cm Weight 96g
Analysis: Blade bronze; rivets bronze. See D. Hook report.
See *PBF* IV.1, no. 11 from Pogrile di Monticelli (Parma, *terramara* settlement); Carancini and Peroni 1999, pl. 9.1, hoard of Cascina Ranza. Short swords with trapezoidal butt.
Probably MBA, early.

Groups of Associated Artefacts

1. Two flanged axes, cat. 82 and 83, from Lodi (Milan), Lombardy, part of a hoard; Axes types 16 and 17.

82.
PRB WG1062. Canon W. Greenwell Collection, bought from the Rev. Greville J. Chester. Given by J. Pierpont Morgan in 1909.
Lodi (Milan), Lombardy.
Flanged/winged axe. **Axes type 16.**
Associated with **cat. 83.**
Small rounded butt with notch surrounded by a slightly raised surface, straight sides ending in a wide flare, semicircular cutting edge. Small parts of the flanges/wings missing. Very accurate manufacture. Smooth light green patina with dark zones and incrustations.
L. 17cm Weight 300g
Analysis: Bronze. See D. Hook report.
See Carancini and Peroni 1999, pl. 13.1, hoard of Cascina Ranza (not identical).
This axe, and **cat. 83**, belong in all probability to the bronze hoard from the area of Lodi illustrated by Carancini and Peroni 1999, 24, pls. 2, 3.V, 4.11, 6; the hoard is dated by these authors to the fourth horizon of EBA hoards. The occurrence of the axes **cat. 82** and 83 is an indication that the hoard was buried in the MBA.
MBA, early.
Bibliography: Bietti Sestieri 2004, 35–36 and fig. 6.1.

83.
PRB WG1063. Canon W. Greenwell Collection, bought from the Rev. Greville J. Chester. Given by J. Pierpont Morgan in 1909.
Lodi (Milan), Lombardy.
Flanged axe. **Axes type 17.**
Associated with **cat. 82.**
Butt broken, with two small notches, straight sides ending in a wide flare, wide, almost circular blade. Smooth dark green patina with light incrustations.
L. 16.6cm Weight 395g
Analysis: Bronze. See D. Hook report.
See Carancini and Peroni 1999, pl. 7.7, type Auvernier, var.A; pl. 9.6, Cascina Ranza (not identical); *Terramare* 1997, 382, fig. 223. 5, 6.

See **cat. 82**.
MBA, early.
Bibliography: Bietti Sestieri 2004, 36 and fig. 6.2.

2. Two winged axes, cat. 84 and 85, from Nemi (Rome), Lazio, part of a hoard; Axes type 21.

84.
PRB WG 1059. Canon W. Greenwell Collection, bought from the Rev. Greville J. Chester. Given by J. Pierpont Morgan in 1909.
Nemi (Rome), Lazio.
Winged axe with contiguous wings. **Axes type 21**.
Associated with **cat. 85**. Greenwell recorded that the two axes were found with other examples.

Heavy tool with straight butt, slightly flaring faces, wings faceted and markedly hammered at junction with blade, short flaring blade with rounded cutting edge. Spotted patina with white and brown incrustations.
L. 16cm Weight 622g
Analysis: Bronze. See D. Hook report.
See Carancini and Peroni 1999, pl. 12.11 (this axe), from Nemi, MBA, early; cf. pl. 12.16 (from the settlement of Torre Castelluccia), MBA, late. The typological features of axe **cat. 84** seem to indicate its intermediate position between MBA middle and late in the evolutionary sequence of the axes with contiguous wings. See also Jurgeit 1999, no. 213, 'possibly Italian, MBA'.
MBA, middle–late.
Bibliography: Giardino 1985, 7, fig. 1.1 and fig. 2, right; Bietti Sestieri 2004, 37 and fig. 7.1.

85.
PRB WG1060. Canon W. Greenwell Collection, bought from the Rev. Greville J. Chester. Given by J. Pierpont Morgan in 1909.
Nemi (Rome), Lazio.
Winged axe with contiguous wings. **Axes type 21**.
Associated with **cat. 84**.
Heavy tool with straight butt, slightly flaring faces, wings faceted with lower part hammered, short flaring blade with rounded cutting edge. Dull green patina with whitish and rusty incrustations.
L. 16.3cm Weight 622g
Analysis: Bronze. See D. Hook report.
See Carancini and Peroni 1999, pl. 12.10 (this axe), 11 (from Nemi). Type Nemi.
MBA, middle.
Bibliography: Giardino 1985, 7, fig. 1, 2 and fig. 2 left; Bietti Sestieri 2004, 38 and fig. 7.2.

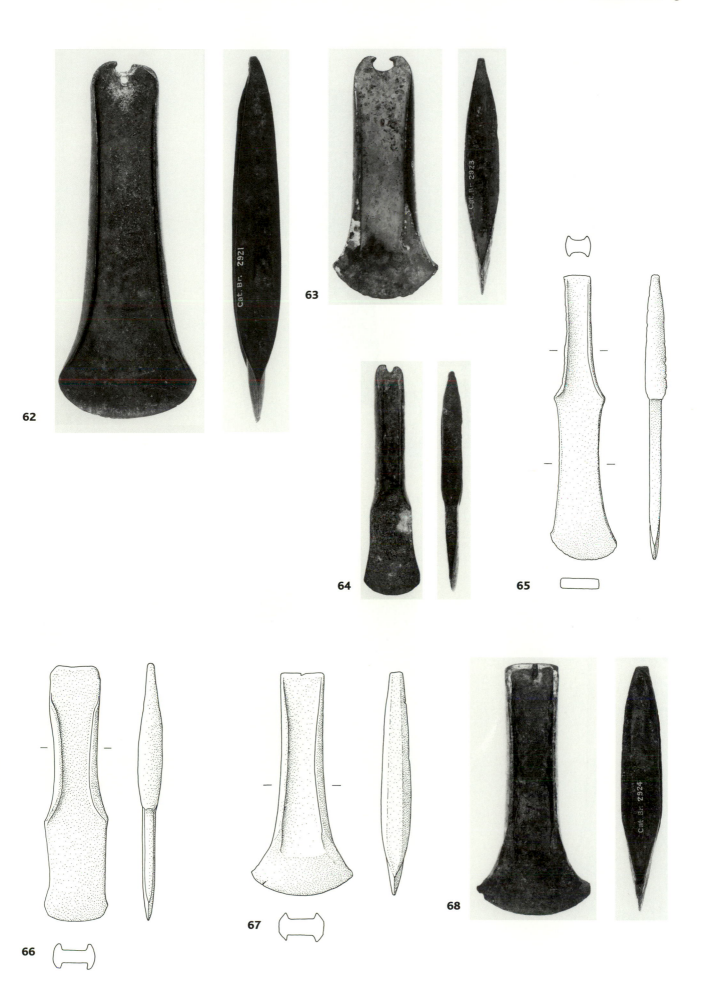

Plate 15 **Axes type 14**: - 62. - 63. **Axes type 15**: - 64. - 65. **Axes type 18**: - 66 Terni, Umbria. **Axes type 19**: - 67. - 68.

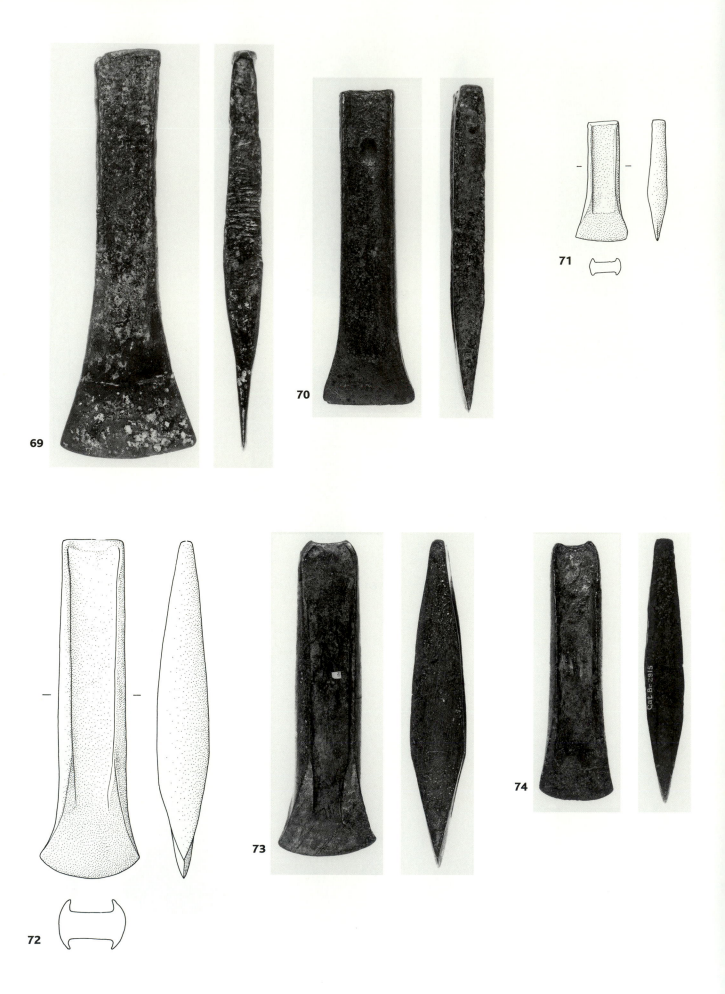

Plate 16 **Axes type 20**: - 69. - 70. Close to **Axes type 20**: - 71 Nola (Naples), Campania. **Axes type 21**: - 72 Abruzzo. - 73. - 74.

75

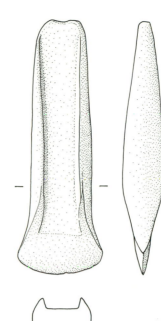

76

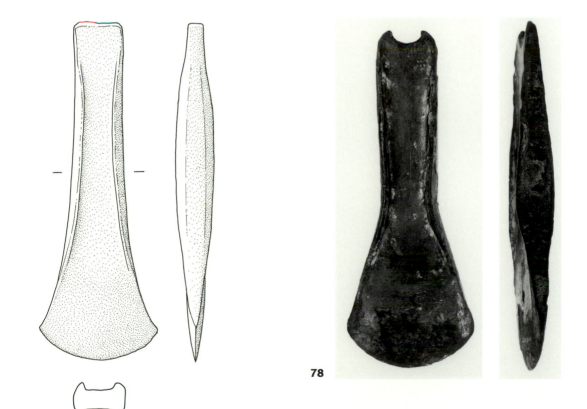

77

78

Plate 17   Axes type 21: - 75. - 76 Poli (Rome), Lazio. **Axes type 22**: - 77 Palermo, Sicily. **Axes type 23**: - 78.

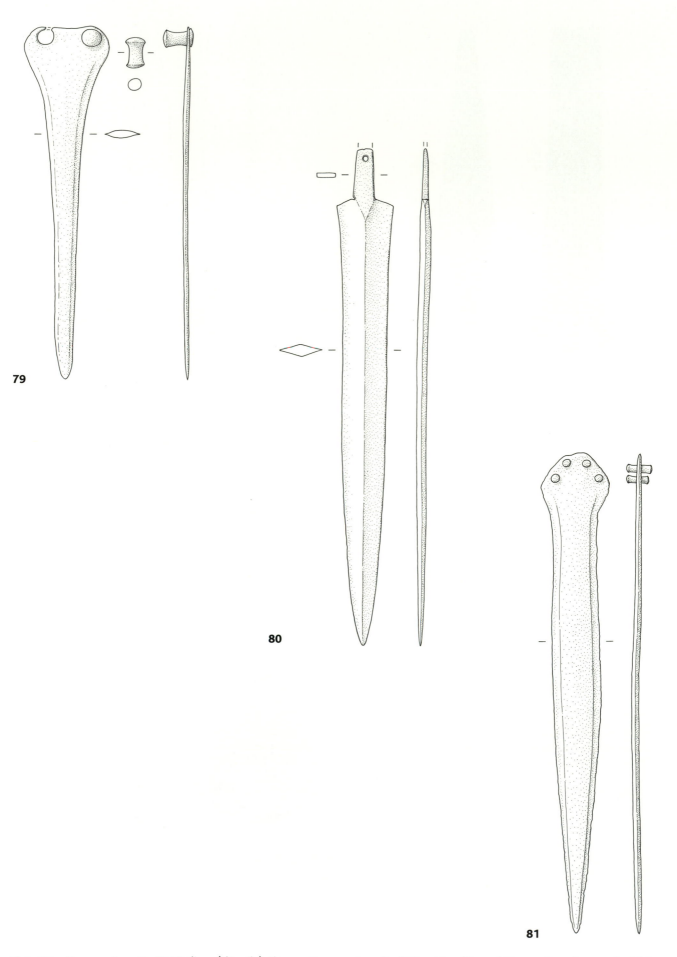

79

80

81

Plate 18   Daggers type 6: - 79 Magliano (L'Aquila), Abruzzo. **Daggers type 7**: - 80 Peschiera (Verona), Veneto. **Swords type 1**: - 81 Osor, Island of Cres, Croatia.

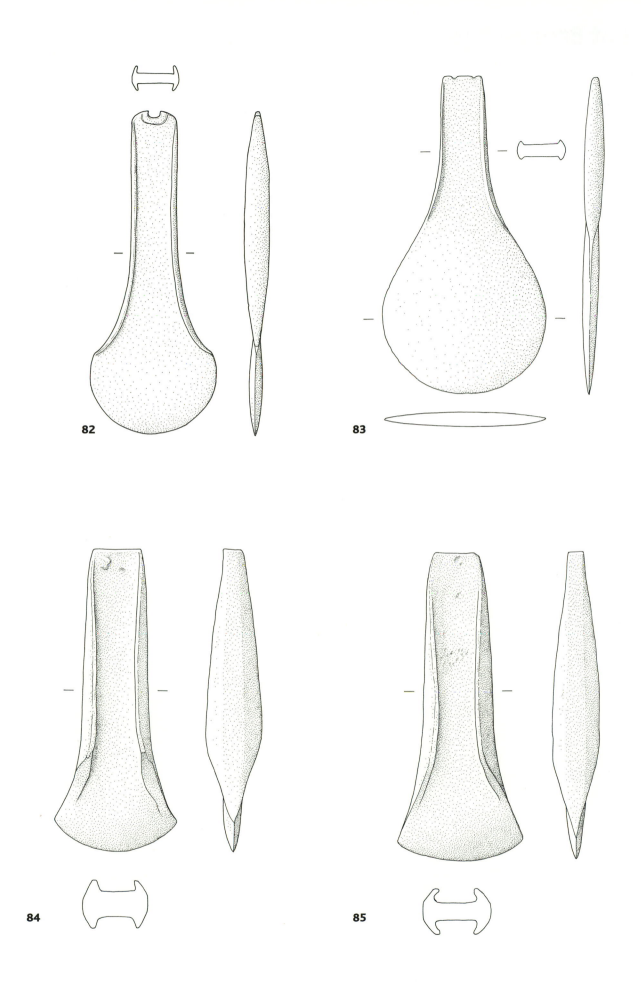

Plate 19 Group of two associated artefacts, Lodi (Milan), Lombardy. **Axes type 16**: - 82. **Axes type 17**: - 83. Group of two associated artefacts, Nemi (Rome), Lazio. **Axes type 21**: - 84. - 85.

Recent Bronze Age

Axes

86.
PRB 1964.12-1.394(339). Sir Henry Wellcome Collection, no. 96449. Bought in Rome from Antichità delle Belle Arti by Captain Saint in April 1931. Given by the Wellcome Trustees.
Winged axe with contiguous wings. **Axes type 24.**
Long trapezoidal butt with slightly dished end, wings with wide central zone, short, slightly flaring blade with straight cutting edge. Irregular surface, probably from casting. Thick-sectioned, dark green, patchy patina.
L. 14cm Weight 398g
See *Terramare* 1997, 400, fig. 236.99, from Noceto (Parma), Emilia Romagna.
RBA.

87.
PRB 1964.12-1.224 (307). Sir Henry Wellcome Collection, no. 172739. Bought at Steven's sale 9/10 September 1930, lot 425 (Mr Webb). Given by the Wellcome Trustees.
Italy.
Winged axe with medial wings. **Axes type 26.**
Long butt with straight sides and wide notch, short developed wings, separated from the blade by a slight step. Narrow elongated flaring blade with curved cutting edge. Shiny patina with dark green incrustations.
L. 12.8cm Weight 138g
See Carancini and Peroni 1999, 55, pls. 27.11; 29, with bibliography: close parallels include pieces from the RBA hoards of Castions di Strada 2, Friuli; Lipari, Aeolian islands; Surbo, Apulia; and from the settlement of Scoglio del Tonno, Apulia. See also Müller-Karpe 1959, pls. 83.9 and 103.36, 38, hoard of Merlara (Padova), Veneto and Peschiera lake settlement (Verona), Veneto.
RBA.

88.
PRB 1888.7-19.8. Bought at the sale of Lord Londesborough's Collection through Messrs. Rollin and Feuardent.
Winged axe with medial wings. **Axes type 27.**
Long butt with straight sides, slightly flaring towards the upper end, and with wide notch; short and wide wings separated from the blade by a slight step. Narrow elongated, slightly flaring blade with rectangular section and curved cutting edge. No patina.
L. 20cm Weight 584g
See *Terramare* 1997, 400, fig. 236.101, from Montirone di S. Agata (Bologna), RBA. The short and wide wings indicate a relatively low level of technological development in this series of winged axes.
RBA.

89.
PRB 1890.7-18.51. Given by the Earl of Derby, K.G.
Winged axe with medial wings. **Axes type 27.**
Heavy axe of elongated form and with long butt with straight end, short and wide wings, separated from the blade by a slight shoulder and step. Blade with rectangular section and almost parallel sides, lower section slightly flared with curved cutting edge. Smooth patina in various tones of green.
L. 17.2cm Weight 670g
See *Terramare* 1997, 400, fig. 236.101, from Montirone di S. Agata dei Goti (Bologna) RBA, similar to this axe in all main typological and technical features, except for the central notch on the butt. The short and wide wings indicate a low degree of technological development in this series of winged axes.
RBA, early?

90.
PRB 1873.6-2.14. Collection J.F. Lucas of Bentley Ashbourne, County Derby. Purchased from Mrs Ruth Faulkner, executor of J.F. Lucas. Said to have been found at 'Foxcote', England (see also **cat. 483**).
Winged axe with medial wings. **Axes type 28.**
Long butt with straight sides and a wide notch, elongated and moderately wide wings, separated from the blade by a slight step. Narrow elongated, slightly flaring blade with rectangular section and curved cutting edge. Smooth, almost black patina.
L. 23cm Weight 774g
For a close parallel see *Terramare* 1997, 384, fig. 224.12, type Pertosa. Proposed date: RBA. Some features of this axe, i.e., the height of the butt and the rectangular blade section, are technologically less advanced than those of the Pertosa type, which can probably be dated to the FBA.
Probably RBA.

91.
PRB 1964.12-6.75. Bequeathed by C.T. Trechmann.
Pozzuoli (Naples), Campania.
Winged axe with medial-butt wings. **Axes type 28.**
Butt with wide central notch and curved sides, narrow haft end with elongated oval wings, slightly marked stop-ridge, long flaring blade with thick rectangular section and curved cutting edge. Small hole on cutting edge. Patina light green, slightly corroded with dark zones.
L. 23.6cm Weight 756g
Close in overall shape and profile to *Terramare* 1997, 384, fig. 224.12, type Pertosa.
Some features of this axe, namely the height of the butt and the rectangular blade section, are technologically less advanced than those of the Pertosa type, which can probably be dated to the FBA.

Probably RBA.
Bibliography: Adinolfi 1988, 57; Albore Livadie, Bietti Sestieri and Marzocchella 2004, 486, fig. 3C.

92.
PRB WG1072. Canon W. Greenwell Collection, bought from the Rev. Greville J. Chester. Given by J. Pierpont Morgan in 1909.
Talamone, Maremma (Grosseto), Tuscany.
Winged axe with medial/butt wings. **Axes type 28.**
Butt with small central notch and curved sides, wide haft end with elongated oval wings, slightly marked stop-ridge, long and narrow blade, slightly flaring, with thick rectangular section and curved cutting edge. Decoration: row of oblique small notches along the edge of the wings. Smooth dull green patina.
L. 21.6cm Weight 755g
Close in overall shape and profile to *Terramare* 1997, 384, fig. 224.12, type Pertosa.
See **cat. 90** and **91**.
Probably RBA.

93.
PRB 1891.4-18.1. Given by Sir A.W. Franks. Bought at Palermo, Sicily.
Shaft-hole axe with flaring blade and nervature in the shaft-hole area. **Axes type 44.**
Continuous profile with markedly concave sides, hammered casting knob at centre of butt, wide oval shaft-hole, elongated blade, hexagonal in section, with markedly curved cutting edge. Central nervature on both sides of haft-end. Dark green patina with incrustations.
L. 18.6cm Weight 879g
See Albanese Procelli 1993, 50, 81ff., fig. 15. BM2, from the hoard of Badia Malvagna (Messina). Type R8A2, MBA–RBA; Giardino 1995, 17, fig. 7A.1 and 7B.1–2, hoards of Lipari (Messina), and Biancavilla (Catania), RBA.
RBA.

94.
PRB 1866.6-27.107. Henry Christy Collection. Given by the Trustees under the will of Henry Christy.
Shaft-hole axe with markedly concave sides and nervature in shaft-hole area. **Axes type 44.**
Continuous profile with markedly concave sides, hammered casting knob at the centre of the butt, wide elliptical shaft-hole, elongated blade, hexagonal in section, with markedly curved cutting edge. Central nervature on both sides of the haft-end. Light green patina with incrustations. Body twisted out of shape.
L. 14.5cm Weight 326g
See **cat. 93**.
RBA.

95.
PRB 1937.11-9.1. Bought from H.C. Audin.
Southbourne (Bournemouth), Dorset,
England. Found by vendor while beach-
combing in September 1937 at Southbourne,
Bournemouth, Hants, a short distance west of
Hengistbury Head. Due to recent alterations in
the boundaries of counties, Southbourne now
is in Dorset.
Shaft-hole axe with concave sides and
nervature in the shaft-hole area. Close to **Axes
type 44**.
Small, thick-sectioned tool with continuous
profile, hammered casting knob at centre of
butt, wide, irregular shaft-hole, thick-
sectioned, trapezoidal blade, flaring to pointed
corners, with markedly curved cutting edge.
On both faces, a central nervature on the upper
part of the haft-end. Smooth patina, dark green
with zones of a dull bronze colour.
L. 12.3cm Weight 596g
See Albanese Procelli 1993, 50, 81ff., fig. 15.
BM2,3,4, from the hoard of Badia Malvagna
(Messina). Type R8A (not identical).
RBA.
Bibliography: Hawkes 1938, 225–228, pl. 1.1;
Brailsford 1953, 28, fig. 8.2; Giardino 1995, 222,
footnotes 74 and 75, fig. 107.4; 327.

96.
PRB 1935.10-18.33. Transferred from GR
(1849.5-18.29). Bought from Campanari,
Blayd's sale 13.2.49. Probably part of Pizzati
Collection in Florence.
Shaft-hole axe with thick body decorated with
nervatures. **Axes type 45**.
Thick-sectioned tool with continuous profile,
hammered casting knob at centre of the butt,
wide oval shaft-hole, thick-sectioned,
elongated blade with slightly curved cutting
edge. On both faces, two central nervatures and
two outer curved nervatures running from butt
to blade corners. Surface irregular; dull green
patina with incrustations.
L. 15.7cm Weight 543g
See *PBF* IX. 12, no. 4249, from Cuma (Naples),
type Cuma, FBA?; Giardino 1995, 17, fig. 7A.2, 3,
hoard of Lipari, RBA.
Probably RBA.
Bibliography: Walters 1899, no. 2943.

97.
PRB 1935.10-18.36. Transferred from GR.
Bought from Sir William Hamilton.
Shaft-hole axe with thick body decorated with
nervatures. **Axes type 45**.
Thick-sectioned tool with continuous profile,
hammered casting knob at centre of butt, wide
oval shaft-hole, thick-sectioned, elongated
blade with slightly curved cutting edge. On
both faces, two central nervatures and two
outer curved nervatures running from butt to
blade corners. Smooth dark green patina with
dull green incrustations.
L. 14.5cm Weight 539g
See **cat. 96**.
RBA.
Bibliography: Walters 1899, no. 2946.

98.
GR 1951.6-6.18. Bequeathed by H. Swainson
Cowper.
Potenza, Basilicata.
Shaft-hole axe with thick body decorated with

nervatures. **Axes type 45**.
Thick-sectioned tool with continuous profile,
hammered casting knob at centre of butt, wide
oval shaft-hole, thick-sectioned, elongated
blade, hexagonal in section, with slightly
curved cutting edge. On both faces, the upper
part is decorated with five vertical nervatures.
The surface of the blade is heavily hammered.
Smooth, black patina.
L. 21.5cm Weight 1483g
See **cat. 96**.
Probably RBA.
Bibliography: Bietti Sestieri 1986, 'Weapons
and Tools', 6, no. 19, and fig. p. 19.

99.
PRB WG 1085. Canon W. Greenwell Collection,
bought from Alessandro Castellani. Given by J.
Pierpont Morgan in 1909.
Bologna, Emilia Romagna.
Socketed axe with thin continuous profile and
rounded socket. **Axes type 53**.
Elongated tool with slightly concave sides.
Elliptical mouth with raised collar and lateral
holes for cross-pin, end of socket slightly
discernible on face and sides, cutting edge
deformed and partly missing. Three
longitudinal nervatures on both faces. Smooth
blackish and dark green patina.
L. 12.2cm Weight 117g
See *PBF* IX.12, no. 3733, from Mugnano
(Perugia), type S. Polo var.; *Terramare* 1997,
385, fig. 224.13, type S. Polo, RBA.
RBA.

100.
PRB WG1086. Canon W. Greenwell Collection,
bought from Alessandro Castellani. Given by J.
Pierpont Morgan in 1909.
Near Ancona, Marche.
Socketed axe with thin continuous profile and
rounded socket. **Axes type 53**.
Elongated tool with slightly concave sides.
Circular mouth with raised collar and lateral
holes for cross-pin, cutting edge slightly curved.
Nervature forming a V on one face, below the
collar. Traces of dull patina in various tones of
green.
L. 12cm Weight 159g
See **cat. 99**.
RBA.

Tools

101.
PRB WG 413. Canon W. Greenwell Collection.
Given by J. Pierpont Morgan in 1909.
Peschiera, Boccatura del Mincio (Verona),
Veneto.
Needle with bent eye. **Needles type 1**.
Thin bronze wire with circular section,
diminishing toward the point. No patina.
L. 10.2cm Weight 1g
Probably RBA.

102.
GR 1887.11-1.23. Given by Sir A.W. Franks.
Borlace sale, Penzance, cat. no. 183.
Peschiera, Boccatura del Mincio (Verona),
Veneto.
Needle with bent eye. **Needles type 1**.
Thin bronze wire with circular section,
diminishing toward the point. No patina.
L. 8.6cm Weight 2g

Probably RBA.

103.
GR 1975.7-30.2. Found unregistered.
Rod chisel with square tang. **Chisels type 1**.
Thick rod with square section, diminishing at
tang, flattened and rectangular at lower end;
cutting edge slightly widened and curved. Red
brown and green patina with heavy corrosion.
L. 19.9cm Weight 165g
This type of rod-chisel without stop-ridge
probably belongs to the earlier group of chisels
of the same general shape, but usually with
circular or polygonal section in the central
portion: see for example **cat. 104** and Bietti
Sestieri 1973, 393, fig. 8.1, hoard of Poggio Berni
(Forlì), Emilia Romagna, FBA, early–middle.
Probably RBA or FBA, early.

104.
GR 1975.7-30.1. Found unregistered.
Rod chisel with square tang. **Chisels 1**.
Thick rod, section square at tang, circular in
central portion, flattened and rectangular at
lower end; cutting edge slightly widened and
curved. Smooth dark green patina.
L. 20.1cm Weight 132g
Close to Bietti Sestieri 1973, 388 f., figs. 1.6 and
2.13, hoards of Surbo (Lecce), Apulia and
Gualdo Tadino (Perugia), Umbria, RBA–FBA
transition.
For rod chisels from Italy, see Macnamara 1970,
247–248; Harding 1975,194.
RBA-FBA, early.
Bibliography: Bietti Sestieri 1986, 'Weapons
and Tools', 6, no. 18, and fig. p. 19.

105.
PRB WG1080. Canon W. Greenwell Collection,
bought from the Rev. Greville J. Chester. Given
by J. Pierpont Morgan in 1909.
Potenza, Basilicata.
Adze with medial-butt wings. **Winged adzes
type 1**.
Long butt with central notch and slightly
curved sides, narrow haft end with elongated
oval wings and straight, slightly marked stop-
ridge, narrow element rectangular in section at
junction of haft with blade. Blade long and
narrow, slightly flaring, with elliptical section,
sloping shoulders, curved cutting edge with
slight bevel. Patina originally smooth and dull
green, now scratched and corroded. Blade edge
and butt slightly damaged, butt ends cut and
hammered.
L. 18.4cm Weight 221g
Although no precise parallels could be found
for this type, the adze belongs to the same
functional and typological tradition of FBA axes
of **types 29 and 30**, for example c**at. 137 and
139**. The length of the butt of this piece might
indicate a relatively early date within the type.
A chisel with winged haft, probably of RBA
date, comes from Chiozzo di Pieve Velezzo
(Pavia), Lombardy: Montelius 1895–1910, col.
187f., pl. 35.6. A tool similar to this type in
general shape and style, although with a flat
elongated blade aligned with the haft, comes
from the FBA hoard of Casalecchio (Rimini),
Emilia Romagna: Bietti Sestieri 1973, 394f., fig.
9.8.
This type includes also two pieces probably of
FBA date, **cat. 183 and 184** (see below).
RBA.

Razors

106.
GR 1969. 12-31. 83. Transferred from PRB, 'Apparently unregistered.'
Narrow symmetrical razor. **Razors type 1.**
Flat elongated blade, slightly decreasing in width from butt to tip. Triangular tang, flat in section, with one rivet hole. Small parts missing. Dull green patina.
L. 9.9cm Weight 16g
See Giardino 1995, 225, fig. 109D.1, from Pantalica, type Pantalica; Turco 2000, 92, pl. 31, cemetery of Cassibile, type 22A.
RBA–FBA.

107.
PRB 1927.11-14.14. Bought from G.F. Lawrence. Lakenheath, Suffolk, England.
Narrow symmetrical razor. **Razors type 1.**
Narrow elongated shape. Distinct trapezoidal butt, broken in antiquity, with central rivet-hole; blade with slightly concave cutting edges, raised central part, end rounded with central notch. Smooth brown-yellowish patina. Small parts missing.
L. 10.7cm Weight 27g
See Giardino 1995, 17 ff., figs. 9.9, 109D.2, hoard of Niscemi, type Pantalica, RBA–FBA; Turco 2000, 92, pl. 31, cemetery of Cassibile, type 22A, RBA–FBA; Albanese Procelli 1993, 54, 99, fig. 16. N16, from the hoard of Niscemi, Sicily. Type R22, FBA.
RBA–FBA.
Bibliography: *PBF* VIII. 3, no. 231; Giardino 1995, 225–227, fig. 109D.4, and 327–328.

108.
GR 1975.7-30.17.Found unregistered.
Narrow symmetrical razor. **Razors type 1.**
Flat elongated blade; parts of cutting edges and tip missing. Tang missing. Dull green patina with some incrustation.
L. 7.6cm Weight 11g
Close to Giardino 1995, 225, fig. 109D.1, from Pantalica. Type Pantalica. See also *PBF* VIII. 2, no. 64, from Tropea, type Pertosa.
RBA–FBA.

109.
PRB W. G. 1151. Canon W. Greenwell Collection, bought from Alessandro Castellani. Given by J. Pierpont Morgan in 1909.
'Complio', probably Campli (Teramo), Abruzzo.
Narrow symmetrical razor. Close to **Razors type 1.**
Narrow elongated shape; cast flat butt, broken, with one rivet extant, separated from the blade by a marked rib; blade with slightly concave edges and V-shaped opening at the end, decorated with three slight nervatures; low diamond-shaped section with central swelling. Shiny dark-green patina. Blade broken in two pieces, small parts missing.
L. 9.1cm Weight 22g
Close to Giardino 1995, 17 ff., figs. 9.9, 109D.2, hoard of Niscemi, type Pantalica. See also *PBF* VIII. 2, no. 64, from Tropea, type Pertosa.
RBA–FBA.
Bibliography: Bietti Sestieri and Giardino 2003, 419.

110.
GR 1969.12-31.77. Transferred from PRB, 'Apparently unregistered'.
Narrow symmetrical razor. **Razors type 2.**
Elongated blade, flat except for slight central thickening and decreasing in width from butt to tip, which has a slight indentation. Tang rectangular in section. Dull green patina with some incrustation.
L. 12cm Weight 20g
See *PBF* VIII. 2, no. 60, from Grotta di Polla (Salerno), type Pertosa.
RBA–FBA.

111.
GR 1969.12-31.81. Transferred from PRB, 'Apparently unregistered.'
Narrow symmetrical razor. **Razors type 2.**
Elongated blade, flat except for slight central thickening, and slightly decreasing in width from butt to tip; tip broken. Tang rectangular in section. Vivid green corrosion and some incrustation.
L. 10.7cm Weight 22g
See **cat. 110.**
RBA–FBA.

112.
GR 1975.7-30.16.Found unregistered.
Narrow symmetrical razor. **Razors type 2.**
Flat elongated blade, of equal width throughout length. Tang rectangular in section. Small parts of cutting edges and tip missing. Dull green patina with areas of heavy incrustation.
L. 8.5cm Weight 12g
See *PBF* VIII. 2, no. 64, from Tropea, type Pertosa.
RBA–FBA.

Ornaments

113.
GR 1878.10-19.242. Given by General A.W.H. Meyrick.
Part of pin with globular head. **Pins type 1.**
Small head and thin shank, round in section; shank broken. Dull green patina.
L. 3cm Weight 7g
See *PBF* XIII. 2, nos. 1762 from Gorzano (Modena), 1785 from Rebbio (Como), types 'con capocchia ovoide liscia' and 'a globetto schiacciato'.
RBA.

114.
GR 1878.10-19.139. Given by General A.W.H. Meyrick.
Pin with globular head. **Pins type 2.**
Small distinct head, deeply incised decoration: oblique grooves on head; three encircling grooves on neck of shank. Smooth brown patina.
L. 11cm Weight 4g
See *PBF* XIII. 2, nos. 1717 from San Polo d'Enza (Reggio Emilia), 1725 from Cornocchio (Parma), type 'con piccola capocchia a papavero'.
RBA.

115.
GR 1850.1-17.57. Bought from M. Martin Rey.
Pin with thick disc head. **Pins type 3.**

Head with rounded edge, decorated on upper face with a row of small oblique grooves. Incised decoration on upper shank of pin: a zigzag line between two groups of encircling parallel lines. Smooth green patina.
L. 11.1cm Weight 10g
See *PBF* XIII. 2, nos. 1698–1700 from Tragno (Trento), type Tragno, var. A.
RBA, late.

116.
GR 1878.10-19.144. Given by General A.W.H. Meyrick.
Shank of a pin with two ridges at neck. **Pins type 4.**
Head missing, probably conical; two sharp ridges on neck of shank. Dull green patina.
L. 9.2cm Weight 5g
See *PBF* XIII. 2, no. 1336 from Montale (Modena), type 'con capocchia biconica e collo ingrossato'.
RBA.

Daggers

117.
GR 1916.6-1.20. Given by Lord Avebury.
Dagger with open triangular tang. **Daggers type 8.**
Small instrument with continuous profile, foliate blade with rounded edges and low section, slightly thickening toward centre. Short tang with elongated rivet-hole. Blade edge damaged. Smooth green patina.
L. 12.2cm Weight 30g
See *PBF* VI. 10, no. 1227, from Peschiera (Verona). Type Torre Castelluccia var. C.
RBA.

118.
PRB W. G. 1152.Canon W. Greenwell Collection, bought from Alessandro Castellani. Given by J. Pierpont Morgan in 1909.
Bologna, Emilia Romagna.
Dagger with triangular tang. **Daggers type 8.**
Small instrument; narrow pointed tang, thinner than the blade, with lowered area and elongated rivet-hole at centre; triangular blade forming an obtuse angle at junction with tang; low section with slightly raised central part. Smooth light green patina with dark green incrustations. Small parts missing.
L. 11.3cm Weight 23g
See *PBF* VI. 10, no. 941, from Peschiera (Verona), type Campegine, var. B.
MBA or RBA.

119.
PRB W. G. 1150. Canon W. Greenwell Collection, bought from Alessandro Castellani. Given by J. Pierpont Morgan in 1909.
Teramo, Abruzzo.
Dagger with elongated tang. **Daggers type 9.**
Short and narrow triangular tang with rounded end and circular rivet-hole at base; wide blade with angular, slightly sloping shoulders, almost parallel edges, slightly rounded toward the tip, and raised central part. Smooth blackish patina with dark green incrustations.
L. 14.2cm Weight 37g
See *PBF* VI. 10, nos.1359 from Gualdo Tadino (Perugia), 1369 from Campegine (Reggio Emilia), type Glisente var. A, and 1384 from

Isolone del Mincio (Mantova), type Glisente var.E. RBA or beginning of FBA.
RBA, late, or FBA, early.
Bibliography: Bietti Sestieri and Giardino 2003, 419.

120.
PRB W. G. 265. Canon W. Greenwell Collection. Given by J. Pierpont Morgan in 1909.
Peschiera, Boccatura del Mincio (Verona), Veneto.
Dagger with flanged hilt terminating in a ring.
Daggers type 10.
Elongated hilt, narrowing toward the end and with four irregular holes, surmounted by a ring with diamond-shaped section; one cylindrical rivet with rounded heads extant. Blade slightly narrower than lower end of hilt, with raised central part and low diamond-shaped section. No patina, some blackish zones. Cutting edges slightly damaged.
L. 23.6cm Weight 58g
Analysis: Bronze. See D. Hook report.
Close to *PBF* VI. 10, no. 1650 from Calerno (Reggio Emilia), very similar in general shape, but no ring at end of hilt. Close to type Toscanella, var. C.
Probably RBA.

121.
PRB (P)1974.12-1.264.Pitt Rivers Collection. Bought from Egger Collection. (See Egger sale catalogue, Sotheby's 25 June 1891, lot. 64).
Steiermark, Austria.
Dagger with flanged hilt (Peschiera dagger).
Daggers type 11.
Long and narrow hilt with upper end widely open and widening toward the blade; one circular rivet-hole at base; elongated triangular blade sharply narrowing below junction with hilt, with raised central part and low diamond-shaped section. Dull blackish patina, with traces of organic material on the blade (sheath?).
L. 21.3cm Weight 61g
Analysis: Bronze. See D. Hook report.
Close to *PBF* VI. 10, no. 1600 from Castelbonafisso (Mantua), type Bertarina, var. II.
RBA.

122.
PRB W. G. 266. Canon W. Greenwell Collection. Given by J. Pierpont Morgan in 1909.
Peschiera, Boccatura del Mincio (Verona),Veneto.
Dagger with flanged hilt (Peschiera dagger).
Daggers type 11.
Short hilt with V-shaped upper end and strongly widening toward the blade; three circular rivet-holes and one cylindrical rivet with rounded heads extant; elongated blade sharply narrowing below junction with hilt, with low diamond-shaped section. No patina, black incrustations. The dagger was dredged up by W.F. Foster in 1879.
L. 17.9cm Weight 49g
Analysis: Blade bronze; rivet bronze. See D. Hook report.
See *PBF* VI. 10, no. 1657 (this piece), type Verona.
RBA.
Bibliography: Harding 1973, 142–3, fig. 2.1; *PBF* VI. 10, no. 1657.

123.
PRB 1853.4-12.11. Bought from R. Mantell. Near Lewes, Sussex, England.
Dagger with flanged hilt (Peschiera dagger).
Daggers type 11.
Long hilt with parallel sides, broken at end and widening toward the blade; one rivet-hole at base; elongated triangular blade sharply narrowing below junction with hilt, with distinct raised central part and thick swelling on section. Shiny blackish and discontinuous patina. Parts missing.
L. 18cm Weight 65g
Analysis: Bronze. See D. Hook report.
Close to *PBF* VI. 10, no. 1570, from Castelnuovo di Sotto (Reggio Emilia), type Bertarina.
RBA.
Bibliography: Harding 1973, 143, fig. 2.3 and pl. 67.C.

124.
GR 1935.8-23.3.Transferred from the Department of British and Medieval Antiquities. Canon W. Greenwell Collection, no. 762, bought from F.E. Whelan. Given by J. Pierpont Morgan in 1909.
Naxos,Greece.
Dagger with flanged hilt (Peschiera dagger).
Daggers type 12.
Long narrow hilt with parallel sides, the upper end open and with parts missing, the flanges at the lower end continuing along the margin of the rounded shoulders. One rivet survives at the middle of the shoulder area, with traces of two or more on the hilt. Ivory or bone hilt-plates with parts missing survive on both sides of the hilt; the patina shows the hilt-plates covered part of the shoulder area. The blade is flame-shaped with the section thickening in steps towards the middle. Parts of the blade margins are missing. Smooth brown patina with areas of corrosion and some incrustations.
L. 24.7cm Weight 97g
Analysis: Blade bronze, rivet bronze. See D. Hook report.
Close to *PBF* VI. 10, no. 1484, from Grotta Pertosa (Salerno), type Pertosa var. A. This is a type of Peschiera dagger which is specifically linked to the Aegean area.
RBA.
Bibliography: Greenwell 1902, 6–7, fig. 7; *BM Guide* 1920a, 162, fig. 172; Cline 1994, 226, no. 829, see for references.

Swords

125.
GR 1975.5-18.1. Found unregistered.
Short sword with flanged hilt. **Swords type 2.**
Slender hilt with upper ends widely open and curved profile, wide rounded shoulder; four rivet holes; blade with upper part narrower than the shoulder and markedly curved edges, widening towards the lower part, section with raised central part and a wide groove on either side. Cutting edge damaged. No patina; cleaned in modern times. Surface pitted.
L. 33.5cm Weight 202g
See *PBF* IV. 1, no. 124, from S. Marco di Belvedere (Aquileia), type Montegiorgio. Some parallels for this sword can be found in FBA–EIA pieces: *PBF* IV. 1, no. 187, from Populonia, and *PBF* XX. 1, no. 187A, both Contigliano type. However, the main

typological features, wide shoulder, curved blade edges and the two marked grooves on the blade, make a BA date more plausible.
Probably RBA.
Bibliography: Walters 1899, no. 2707; *BM Guide* 1920, 99, fig. 99 c.; Bietti Sestieri 1986, 'Weapons and Tools', 4, no. 4, and fig. p. 15.

126.
GR 1880.2-28.1. Given by C. West.
Scutari, Albania.
Sword with flanged hilt. **Swords type 3.**
Butt of hilt missing, hilt edges almost straight, triangular shoulders, four rivet holes, sides of blade almost straight, lenticular section with central part raised, separated from the cutting edges by a step. Cutting edges damaged, end of tip missing. Dark green patina.
L. 57.2cm Weight 445g
Close to *PBF* IV. 1, nos. 133, from Cherasco (Cuneo), 134, from Casier (Treviso), type Treviso. The sword belongs to the wide European Naue II group (see discussion in *PBF* IV. 12, 100–105), which has been divided into regional groups distributed over continental Europe, Italy and the Aegean. The possibility of it being an Italian import is based on the similarity to the north Italian Treviso type and on the intense Adriatic connections which linked Italy to the coastal regions of the Balkan peninsula throughout the Bronze Age.
RBA.
Bibliography: Walters 1899, no. 2754; *BM Guide* 1920, 96, fig. 96a; Catling 1956, 117, pl. 9d; Catling 1961, 118, no. 32; Hammond 1967, 324, fig. 19.D; Catling 1968, 99–104; *PBF* IV. 12, no. 265.

127.
PRB W. G. 1262. Canon W. Greenwell Collection, bought from Alessandro Castellani. Given by J. Pierpont Morgan in 1909.
Frosinone, Lazio.
Sword with flanged hilt and pommel tang.
Swords type 4.
Rectangular tang, hilt with curved sides, triangular sloping shoulders; four rivet holes, long blade with almost straight edges and diamond shaped section with sharp step separating cutting edge from central part. Smooth black patina with incrustations in dark green; traces of organic material in hilt area. Small parts missing.
L. 69.5cm Weight 714g
Analysis: Bronze. See D. Hook report.
See *PBF* IV. 1, nos. 153–163, type Allerona.
RBA–FBA.
Bibliography: *PBF* XX. 1, 31, pl. 9B.2.

Arrowheads

128.
GR 1975.6-5.85. Found unregistered.
Socketed arrowhead with conical socket and triangular blade. **Arrowheads type 1.**
Socket elongated with wide circular base, blade ending in angled points. Parts of blade missing. Green patina.
L. 4.9cm Weight 6g
See Montelius 1895–1910, pl. 15.6 from Campegine (Reggio Emilia); *Terramare* 1997, 403, fig. 237.125 (sporadic, Reggio Emilia).
RBA.

129.
PRB W. G. 1159. Canon W. Greenwell
Collection, bought from the Rev. Greville J.
Chester. Given by J. Pierpont Morgan in 1909.
Lake Trasimeno (Perugia), Umbria.
Socketed arrowhead with triangular blade.
Arrowheads type 1.
Socket with one pin-hole; blade angled at base.
Small parts missing. Smooth dark green patina.
L. 4.2cm Weight 8g
See **cat. 128**.
Probably RBA.

130.
GR 1975.6-5.81. Found unregistered.
Socketed arrowhead with triangular blade.
Arrowheads type 1, variant.
Solid blade with lozenge section and slightly
pointed ends, socket elongated, with wide
circular base. Small parts of blade and socket
missing. Smooth dark green patina.
L. 6.4cm Weight 12g
See **cat. 128**.
Probably RBA.

131.
GR 1975.6-5.80. Found unregistered.
Socketed arrowhead with triangular blade.
Arrowheads type 1, variant.
Wide blade, socket markedly elongated below
junction with blade; wide circular base. Ends of
blade damaged. Smooth green patina with
areas of metal showing.
L. 5.8cm Weight 9g
See **cat. 128**, and Montelius 1895–1910, pl. 19.5,
javelin head from the *terramara* of Montale
(Modena), Emilia Romagna.
Probably RBA.

132.
GR 1975.6-5.84. Found unregistered.
Socketed arrowhead with triangular blade.
Arrowheads type 2.
Blade ending in angled wing, socket markedly
elongated below junction with blade; circular
base. Dark green patina.
L. 4.5cm Weight 7g

See Montelius 1895–1910, cols. 188f., and pl. 35,
9 and 11, from a *terramara* in the territory of
Modena, and from Reggio Emilia; also
Terramare 1997, 403, fig. 237, 125, RBA. A
similar shape is also found in FBA contexts, see
Bietti Sestieri 1973, 394f. and fig. 9.9, hoard of
Casalecchio (Rimini), Emilia Romagna.
RBA to FBA.

133.
GR 1975.6-5.86. Found unregistered.
arrowhead with conical socket and triangular
blade, ending in angled points. **Arrowheads
type 2.**
Socket elongated below junction with blade;
wide circular base. Dark green-brown patina.
L. 6cm Weight 16g
See **cat. 132** and Montelius 1895–1910, cols.
601–602, pl. 126.13, from Chiusi, sporadic; note
that a relatively similar type also appears in EIA
contexts: Müller-Karpe 1959, pl. 73Q.2 from
Bologna, Savena cemetery, tomb 92.
RBA.

86

87

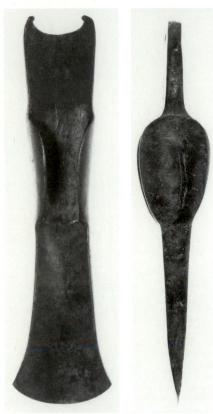

88

89

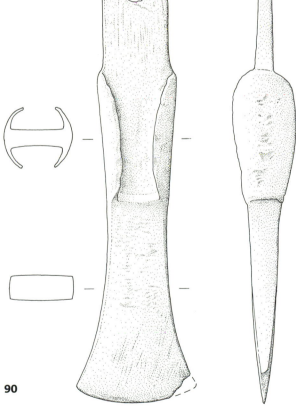

90

Plate 20   Axes type 24: - 86. **Axes type 26**: - 87. **Axes type 27**: - 88. - 89. **Axes type 28**: - 90 'Foxcote', England.

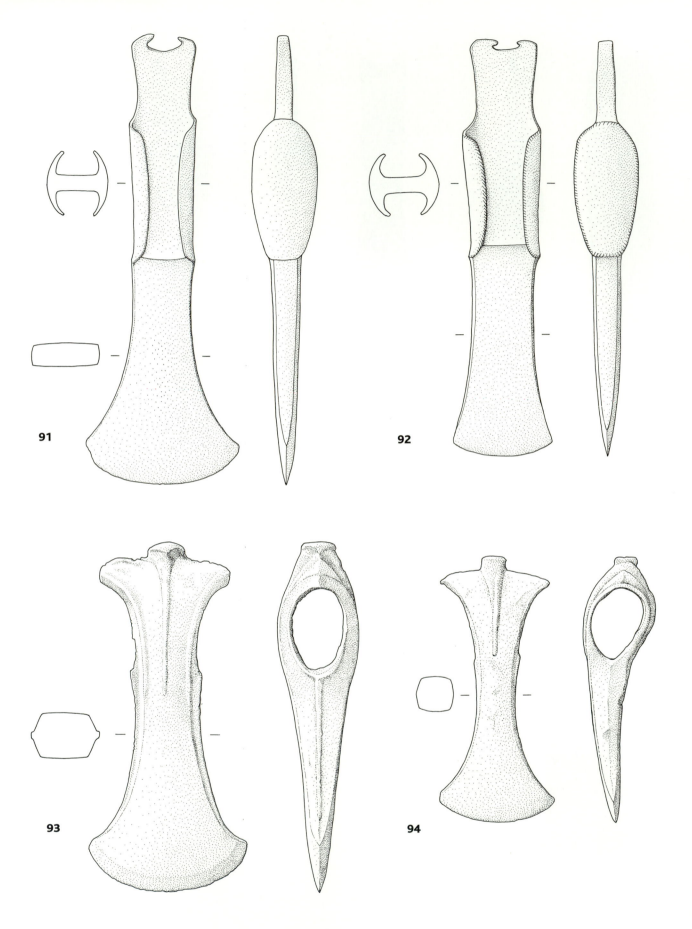

Plate 21   Axes type 28: - 91 Pozzuoli (Naples), Campania. - 92 Talamone (Grosseto), Tuscany. **Axes type 44**: - 93 probably Sicily. - 94.

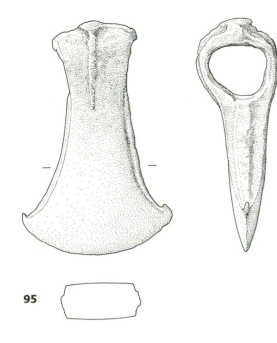

95

96

97

98

Plate 22   Close to **Axes type 44**: - 95 Southbourne (Bournemouth), Dorset, England. **Axes type 45**: - 96. - 97. - 98 Potenza, Basilicata.

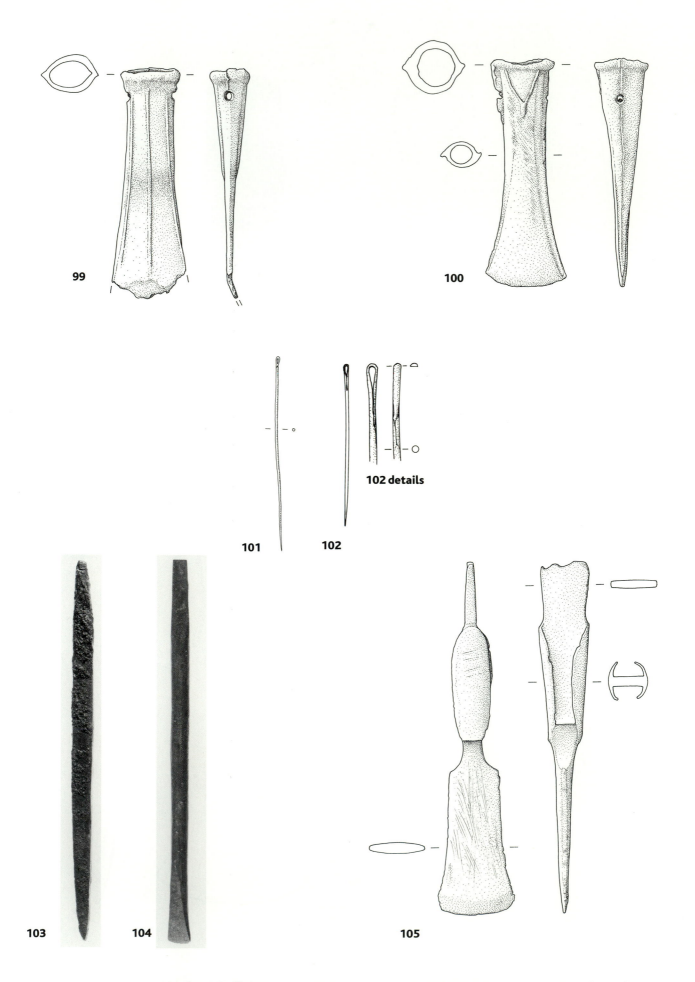

Plate 23   **Axes type 53**: - 99 Bologna, Emilia Romagna. - 100 near Ancona, Marche. **Needles type 1**: - 101 Peschiera (Verona), Veneto. - 102 Peschiera (Verona), Veneto. **Rod-chisels type 1**: - 103. - 104. **Winged adzes type 1**: - 105 Potenza (Basilicata).

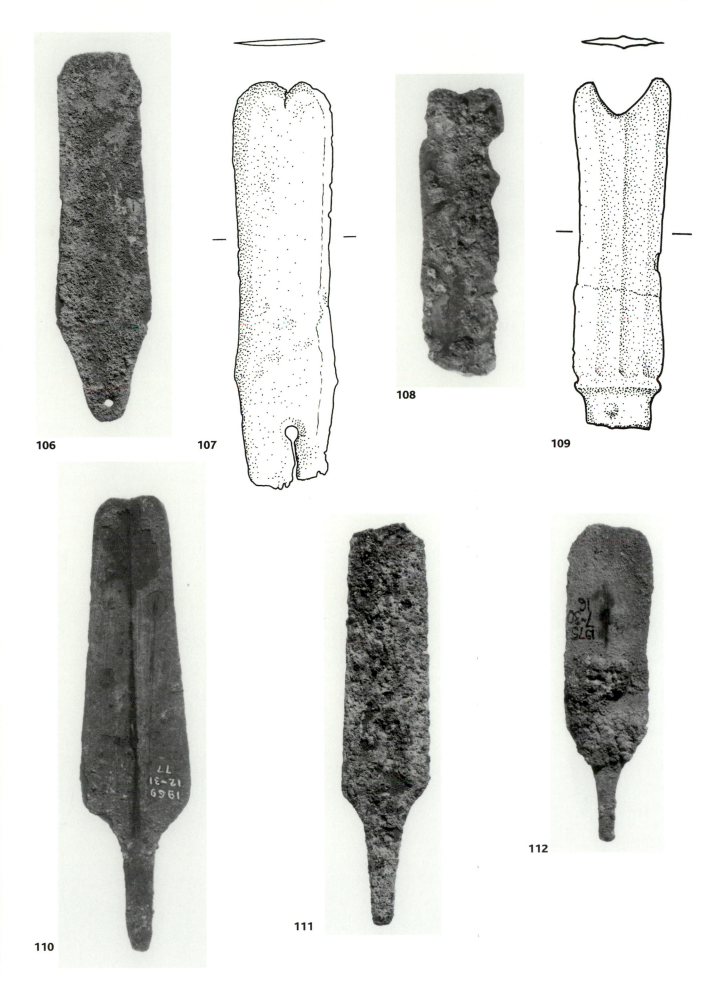

Plate 24 **Razors type 1**: - 106. - 107 Lakenheath, Suffolk, England - 108. Close to **Razors type 1**: - 109 Campli (Teramo), Abruzzo. **Razors type 2**: - 110. - 111. - 112. All at scale 1:1.

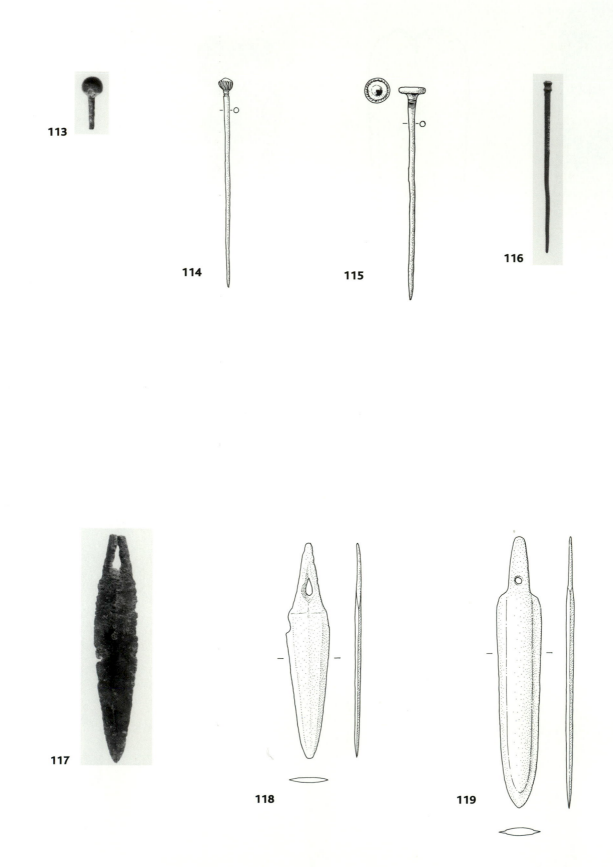

113

114

115

116

117

118

119

Plate 25   Pins type 1: - 113. **Pins type 2**: - 114. **Pins type 3**: - 115. **Pins type 4**: - 116. **Daggers type 8**: - 117. - 118 Bologna, Emilia Romagna. **Daggers type 9**: - 119 Teramo, Abruzzo.

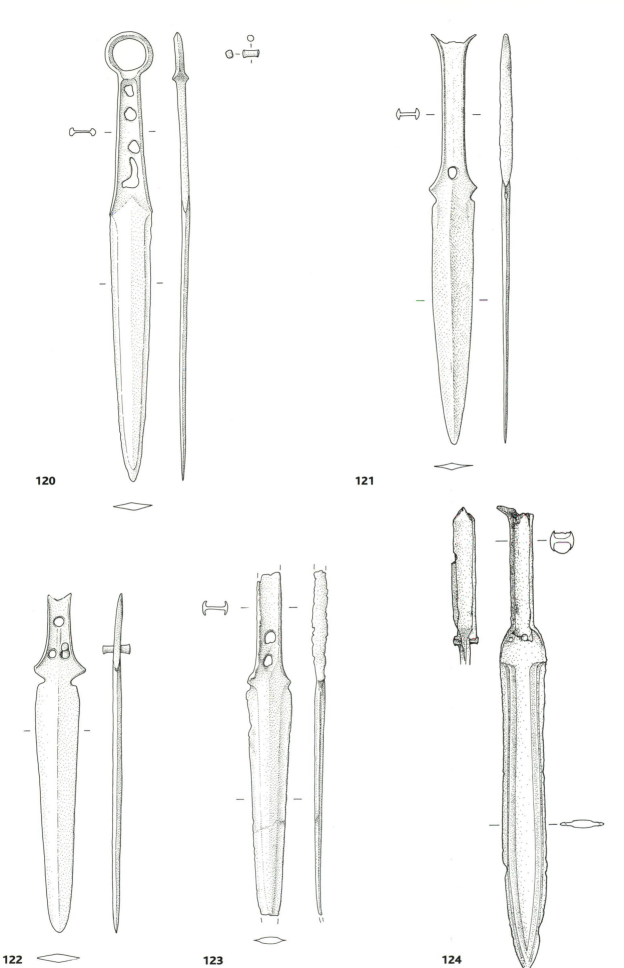

120

121

122

123

124

Plate 26 **Daggers type 10**: - 120 Peschiera (Verona), Veneto. **Daggers type 11**: - 121 Steiermark, Austria. -122 Peschiera (Verona), Veneto. - 123 near Lewes, Sussex, England. **Daggers type 12**: - 124 Naxos, Greece.

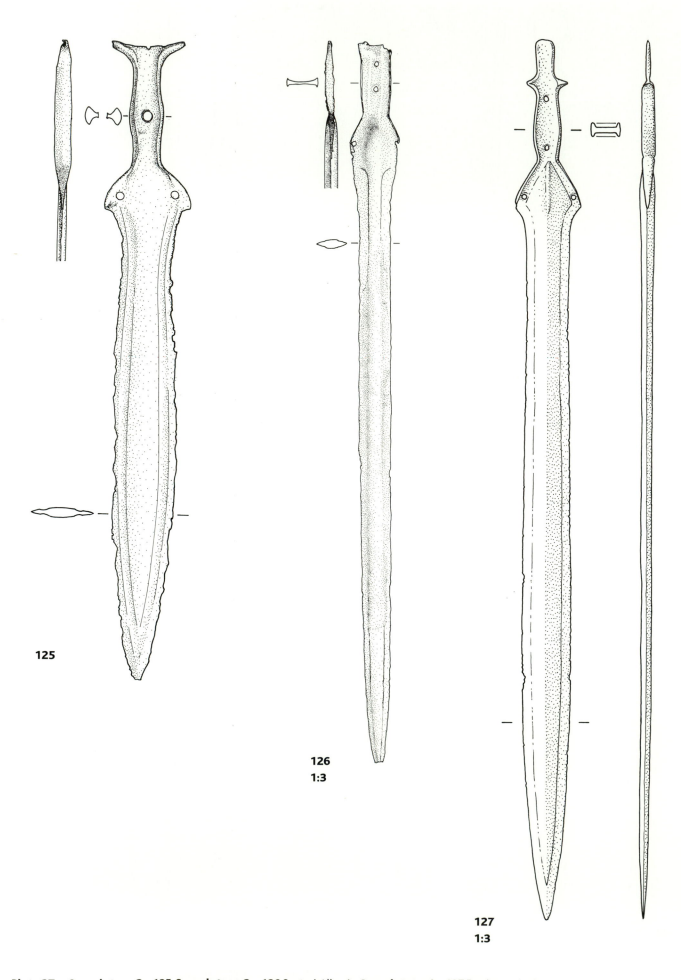

125

126
1:3

127
1:3

Plate 27   Swords type 2: - 125. **Swords type 3**: - 126 Scutari, Albania. **Swords type 4**: - 127 Frosinone, Lazio.

128

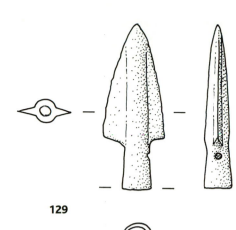

129

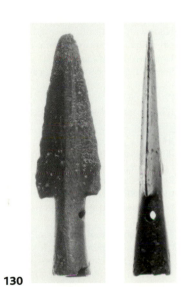

130

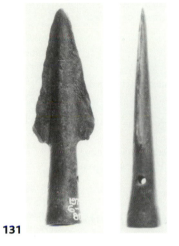

131

132

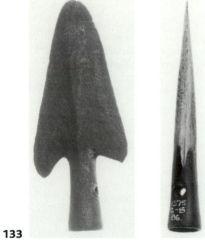

133

Plate 28   **Arrows type 1**: - 128. - 129 Lake Trasimeno (Perugia), Umbria. **Arrows type 1 variant**: - 130. - 131. **Arrows type 2**: - 132. - 133. All at scale 1:1.

Final Bronze Age

Axes

134.
PRB 1916.6-5.180. Given by Lord Avebury.
Perugia, Umbria.
Winged axe with medial-butt wings. **Axes type 29.**
Large, heavy tool. Butt with large central notch and curved sides, narrow haft with elongated oval wings, very slight shoulder at joint to blade, and slightly marked stop-ridge. Long flaring blade with thick oval section and curved cutting edge. Light green patina, surface corroded with turquoise incrustations. Small parts missing.
L. 22.7cm Weight 629g
See Bietti Sestieri 1973, figs. 13.2-4; 14; 15. Type Ortucchio, especially fig.14.1, from Grotta Pertosa (Salerno), Campania; very close in shape and size.
FBA, early.

135.
PRB WG1065. Canon W. Greenwell Collection, bought from the Rev. Greville J. Chester. Given by J. Pierpont Morgan in 1909.
'Massica' (probably Marsica, L'Aquila), Abruzzo.
Winged axe with medial-butt wings. **Axes type 29.**
Butt with small central notch and curved sides, narrow haft end with elongated oval wings, slight shoulder at junction with blade, and slightly marked stop-ridge. Long, slightly flaring blade with elliptical section and curved cutting edge. Incised decoration: two double rows of dots on the upper part of the blade. Dull green patina with very light incrustations.
L. 16.5cm Weight 200g
See Bietti Sestieri 1973, figs. 13.2-4; 14; 15. Type Ortucchio, especially fig. 15.4, from Blera, (Viterbo), Lazio; close in shape and size; similar pattern of pointillé decoration on the blade.
FBA, early.
Bibliography: Bietti Sestieri and Giardino 2003, 419, fig. 8.

136.
PRB WG1066. Canon W. Greenwell Collection, bought from the Rev. Greville J. Chester. Given by J. Pierpont Morgan in 1909.
Canino (Viterbo), Lazio.
Winged axe with medial-butt wings. **Axes type 29.**
Long distinct butt with curved sides and dished end, narrow haft with elongated wings, slight shoulder at junction to blade, and slight stop-ridge. Short trapezoidal blade with oval section and almost straight cutting edge, probably reworked. Traces of hammering on the surface; wings hammered and with parts missing. Smooth blackish patina with incrustations.
L. 12.4cm Weight 156g

See Bietti Sestieri 1973, figs. 13.2-4; 14; 15. Type Ortucchio, especially fig. 13.4, from Urbino, Marche, similar in general shape and size. The height of the butt is an early feature in the evolutionary sequence of this type.
FBA, early.

137.
PRB WG1071. Canon W. Greenwell Collection, bought from the Rev. Greville J. Chester. Given by J. Pierpont Morgan in 1909.
Naples, Campania.
Winged axe with medial-butt wings. **Axes type 29.**
Butt with large central notch and curved sides, narrow haft with elongated oval wings, slight shoulder at junction to blade, and slightly marked stop-ridge, long flaring blade with elliptical section and almost straight cutting edge. Smooth dull green patina. Hammered wings.
L. 18.7cm Weight 222g
See **cat. 134.**
FBA, early.

138.
PRB 1935.10-18.19. Transferred from GR (1856.12-26.972). Bequeathed by Sir William Temple.
Italy.
Winged axe with medial-butt wings. **Axes type 29.**
Butt with large central notch and curved sides, narrow haft with elongated oval wings, with slight shoulder at junction with blade, long flaring blade with oval section and slightly curved cutting edge. Smooth dark green patina with light zones.
L. 16.5cm Weight 194g
See Bietti Sestieri 1973, figs. 13.2-4; 14; 15. Type Ortucchio, especially fig. 14.1, from Grotta Pertosa (Salerno), Campania; very close in shape.
FBA, early.
Bibliography: Walters 1899, no. 2929.

139.
PRB 1935.10-18.20. Transferred from GR (1853.2-18.4). Bought from H.O. Cureton, who acquired it at Count Milano's sale at Sotheby's, 10 February 1853.
Italy.
Winged axe with medial-butt wings. **Axes type 29.**
Large heavy tool. Butt with central notch and curved sides, narrow haft with slightly concave sides, elongated oval wings, slight shoulder at junction to blade and slightly marked stop-ridge; long, slightly flaring blade with thick oval section and slightly curved cutting edge. Blackish patina with incrustations and light green zones. Small parts missing.
L. 24cm Weight 851g

See **cat. 134.**
FBA, early.
Bibliography: Walters 1899, no. 2930.

140.
PRB 1935.10-18.21. Transferred from GR.
Bought from Sloane Collection, 459.
Italy.
Winged axe with medial-butt wings. **Axes type 29.**
Butt with large central notch and curved sides, narrow haft with elongated oval wings and slight shoulder at junction to blade, long flaring blade with elliptical section and curved cutting edge. Smooth dark green patina.
L. 18.5cm Weight 270g
See Bietti Sestieri 1973, figs. 13.2-4; 14; 15. Type Ortucchio.
FBA, early.
Bibliography: Walters 1899, no. 2931.

141.
PRB 1964.12-1.384(382). Sir Henry Wellcome Collection, no. 113259. Bought in Rome from A. Rocci by Captain Saint in April 1932. Given by the Wellcome Trustees.
Winged axe with medial-butt wings. **Axes type 29.**
Thin elongated tool or weapon. Butt with central notch and concave sides, narrow haft with elongated elliptical wings, slight shoulder at junction with blade and slightly marked stop-ridge; thin flaring blade with elliptical section, and slightly curved cutting edge. Shiny almost black patina; surface corroded. Wings, cutting edge and end of butt hammered.
L. 17cm Weight 197g
See Bietti Sestieri 1973, figs. 13.2-4; 14; 15, type Ortucchio, especially fig. 13.3, from Aquileia, Friuli-Venezia Giulia, very close in shape and overall proportions.
FBA, early.

142.
PRB 1964.12-1.383(308). Sir Henry Wellcome Collection, no. 96454. Bought in Rome from Antichità delle Belle Arti by Captain Saint in April 1931. Given by the Wellcome Trustees.
Winged axe with medial-butt wings. **Axes type 29, variant.**
Large heavy tool. Butt with wide central notch and slightly curved sides, narrow haft with elongated oval wings, slightly marked stop-ridge, and protruding shoulder, blade oval in section, with markedly concave sides and curved cutting edge. Smooth patina in various tones of green. Blade scratched in antiquity.
L. 22.7cm Weight 765g
Close to Bietti Sestieri 1973, figs. 13.2-4; 14; 15. Type Ortucchio, especially fig. 14.2, from Gubbio, Umbria, very close in shape. The markedly concave edges of the blade could be an evolutionary late feature in this series, as

they characterize the slightly later Poggio Berni type, ibid. fig. 16.
FBA, early–middle?

143.
PRB 1868.12-28.280. Purchased from M. Gustav Klemm of Dresden. Acquired by his father Dr Klemm. The axe was no. 834 of the Klemm Collection and probably was bought from Baron Von Stackelburg, who collected in Greece.
Greece.
Winged axe with medial-butt wings and concave profiles to blade. **Axes type 30**.
Butt with wide central notch and curved sides, narrow haft with elongated oval wings, slightly marked stop-ridge, and sharply protruding shoulder, blade with markedly concave edges and almost straight cutting edge. Smooth light green patina with dark incrustations. Small parts missing.
L. 15cm Weight 186g
See Bietti Sestieri 1973, 393 ff., pl. 41.1, hoard of Poggio Berni (Forlì), Emilia Romagna, 2 (this axe), fig. 16. Type Poggio Berni; Carancini and Peroni 1999, pls. 28.13; 30.13.
FBA, middle.
Bibliography: Klemm 1854, 103, fig. 180; Deshayes 1960, vol.I, 251, no. 1997; Bietti Sestieri 1973, 393, pl. 41.2; Harding 1975, 187–188.

144.
PRB 1880.8-2.46.Given by Sir A.W. Franks.
Winged axe with medial-butt wings? **Axes type 31**.
Butt probably cut and hammered in antiquity, haft longer than blade, with elongated oval wings, heavily damaged, and slight stop-ridge, narrow slightly flaring blade with rounded cutting edge. Smooth dark green patina with corrosions and incrustations.
L. 16cm Weight 369g
See Bietti Sestieri 1973, 395, fig. 9.3, hoard of Casalecchio (Rimini), Emilia Romagna; Peroni *et al.* 1980, pl. 13 B. Type Teor.
FBA, middle.

145.
PRB WG1073. Canon W. Greenwell Collection, bought from the Rev. Greville J. Chester. Given by J. Pierpont Morgan in 1909.
River Ticino, near Milan, Lombardy.
Winged axe with medial-butt wings. **Axes type 32**.
Thick-sectioned tool. Narrow trapezoidal butt with central notch, elongated haft with wide wings, hammered on the faces, marked stop-ridge, and slightly marked shoulder; short trapezoidal blade with slightly curved cutting edge. Almost no patina. Small parts missing.
L.15.9cm Weight 576g
See Müller-Karpe 1959, pls. 171A.3, 175C.3, hoards of Asperg and of Hohenhewen, Baden Württemberg, phase HaB1, roughly corresponding to the Italian FBA, late.
This is a transalpine type also found in northern Italy.
FBA, late.

146.
PRB WG1042. Canon W. Greenwell Collection, bought from D. Egger of Paris. Given by J. Pierpont Morgan in 1909.

Prettau, the Tyrol, Austria.
Winged axe, with wide body and medial-butt wings. **Axes type 33**.
Heavy thick-sectioned tool. Butt, narrower than haft, with wide central notch, haft with elongated oval faceted wings, diminishing towards blade, and marked shoulder. Wide trapezoidal blade with slightly concave sides and curved cutting edge. Dark green, shiny patina with corroded zones and earth incrustations.
L. 18.4cm Weight 643g
This is an Alpine type found in the Tyrol and Trentino-Alto Adige. See Marzatico 2001, 401, fig. 29,3.
FBA.

147.
PRB 1964.12-1.395(232). Sir Henry Wellcome Collection. Given by the Wellcome Trustees.
Winged axe with medial-butt wings. **Axes type Unclassified**.
Broken butt, narrower than the haft, wide wings hammered on faces, stop-ridge, slightly marked shoulder and very short trapezoidal blade, reworked, with rounded cutting edge. Dark green shiny patina.
L. 9.4cm Weight 324g
See Bietti Sestieri 1973, 394, fig. 8.9 (broken and reworked axe), hoard of Poggio Berni (Forlì), Emilia Romagna, FBA, middle. Based on the overall shape of this axe, including the wings, that prior to hammering should have been relatively short and wide, a comparison to RBA types is possible (see **Axes type 27**).
FBA?

148.
PRB 1866.6-27.98. Henry Christy Collection. Given by the Trustees under the will of Henry Christy. Perhaps bought from G. Eastwood.
Winged axe with medial-butt wings. **Axes type 34**.
Butt with central notch, narrower than haft, haft with elongated oval wings, marked shoulder and stop-ridge; wide trapezoidal blade with slightly curved cutting edge. No patina.
L. 13.5cm Weight 190g
See Carancini and Peroni, 1999, pl. 31.48 (not identical). FBA, late; Müller-Karpe 1959, pl. 50.5-8. Hoard of Piediluco (Terni), Umbria. FBA–EIA transition.
FBA, late.

149.
PRB 1878.11-1.208. Given by General A.W.H. Meyrick.
Winged axe with butt wings and trapezoidal blade. **Axes type 34**.
Straight butt, oval wings, marked stop-ridge and shoulders, wide trapezoidal blade with slightly curved cutting edge. Irregular blackish patina with zones in various tones of green. Parts missing.
L. 14.8cm Weight 496g
See for the general shape, especially the wide blade, the hoard of Gabbro, Tuscany, dating from the final phase of the FBA. See Delpino 1997, 202, fig. 133, 1, 2. A few similar pieces also appear in the hoard of Piediluco (Terni), Umbria, FBA–EIA transition: Müller-Karpe 1959, pls. 50.5, 8; 51.11, 13.
FBA, late.

150.
PRB. No registration number. Transferred from GR. Charles Townley Collection. Bought from Peregrine Townley
Winged axe with butt wings and trapezoidal blade. **Axes type 34**.
Short concave butt, narrow haft-end with oval wings, slightly marked stop-ridge, protruding shoulders, wide trapezoidal blade with slightly rounded cutting edge. Smooth blackish patina.
L.12.7cm Weight 156g
See **cat. 149**.
FBA, late.

151.
PRB 1964.12-1.387 (377). Sir Henry Wellcome Collection, no. 113261. Bought in Rome from A. Rocci by Captain Saint in April 1932. Given by the Wellcome Trustees.
Winged axe with butt wings and trapezoidal blade. **Axes type 34**.
Short markedly concave butt, oval wings, marked stop-ridge and shoulders, wide trapezoidal blade with almost straight cutting edge. Dull, light green patina with brown incrustations.
L. 20.6cm Weight 674g
See for the general shape, especially the wide blade, the hoard of Gabbro, Tuscany, dating from the final phase of the FBA: Delpino 1997, 202, fig. 133, 1, 2. Some very close parallels in the hoard of Piediluco (Terni), Umbria; Müller-Karpe 1959, pl. 50.2,5.
FBA, late.

152.
PRB 1866.6-27.97. Henry Christy Collection. Given by the Trustees under the will of Henry Christy. Perhaps bought from G. Eastwood.
Winged axe with butt wings and blade with concave profiles. **Axes type 34, variant**.
Short hammered butt, elongated oval wings, low stop-ridge, protruding shoulders, wide blade with concave sides and almost straight cutting edge. Irregular green patina with corrosion.
L. 11.5cm Weight 143g
See for the general shape, especially the wide blade, the hoards of Gabbro, and of Limone (hoards 1 and 2) Tuscany, dating from the late or final phase of the FBA: Delpino 1997, 202, fig. 133, 2, 3; Cateni 1997, 210, fig. 140, 26. For the markedly concave sides of the blade, see **Axes type 30**.
FBA, late.

153.
PRB 1964.12-1.223(309). Sir Henry Wellcome Collection, no. 72566. Bought at Sotheby's sale 14 March 1929, lot 103. (Mr Webb). Given by the Wellcome Trustees.
Italy.
Winged axe with elongated body and protruding shoulders. **Axes type 35**.
Large heavy tool, with short rounded butt with side indentations and central notch, wide, closed oval wings, marked stop-ridge and protruding shoulders, narrow blade with concave sides and almost straight cutting edge, hammered. Shiny dark green patina.
L. 24.6cm Weight 1075g
See Müller-Karpe 1959, pl. 51.24, hoard of Piediluco (Terni), Umbria, FBA–EIA transition.
This is a well identifiable axe type which characterizes the hoards of Campese (Isola del

Giglio) Tuscany; Santa Marinella (Rome) Lazio, Piediluco (Terni), Umbria, dating from the final phase of the FBA and the FBA–EIA transition. See Carancini and Peroni 1999, 63, pl. 31.43 and tab. 32. Type Campese.
FBA, late.

154.
PRB 1866.6-27.99. Henry Christy Collection. Given by the Trustees under the will of Henry Christy. Perhaps bought from G. Eastwood.
Winged axe with short butt and butt wings. **Axes type 36**.
Butt with wide central notch, narrower than haft, narrow elongated wings and slightly marked shoulder and stop-ridge; trapezoidal blade, thin in section, with slightly curved cutting edge. Smooth dark green patina.
L. 15.3cm Weight 239g
See Müller-Karpe 1959, pl. 47.26, 27, hoard of Goluzzo (Siena), Tuscany. FBA, late; pl. 50.1-5, hoard of Piediluco (Terni), Umbria. FBA–EIA transition.
FBA, late.

155.
PRB 1964.12-1.385(312). Sir Henry Wellcome Collection, no. 67752. Bought from G. Pini in November 1928. Given by the Wellcome Trustees.
Winged axe with short butt and trapezoidal blade. **Axes type 36**.
Short concave butt, oval wings, marked stop-ridge and shoulders, trapezoidal blade with slightly rounded cutting edge. Tranverse groove on the blade. Dull blackish patina with incrustations in various tones of green and brown. Small parts missing.
L. 19cm Weight 601g
See Müller-Karpe 1959, pl. 47.30, hoard of Goluzzo (Siena), Tuscany. FBA, late; pl. 51.6, 18, hoard of Piediluco (Terni), Umbria.
FBA–EIA transition.

156.
PRB 1964.12-1.213(314). Sir Henry Wellcome Collection, no. 312. Bought in Rome from Arte Antica e Moderna by Captain Saint in November 1929. Given by the Wellcome Trustees.
Terni,Umbria.
Winged axe with short butt and trapezoidal blade. **Axes type 36**.
Short butt with small central notch, oval wings, marked stop-ridge and angular shoulders, short trapezoidal blade, probably reworked, with rounded cutting edge. Irregular green patina, thick incrustations between the wings. Small parts missing.
L. 9.5cm Weight 141g
See Müller-Karpe 1959, pl. 50.7, 16, hoard of Piediluco (Terni), Umbria.
FBA–EIA transition.

157.
PRB WG1095. Canon W. Greenwell Collection, bought from the Rev. Greville J. Chester. Given by J. Pierpont Morgan in 1909.
Castrovillari (Cosenza), Calabria.
Shaft-hole axe with thick body decorated with nervatures. Close to **Axes type 45**.
Small, thick-sectioned tool with continuous profile, hammered casting knob at centre of butt, wide, circular shaft-hole, thick

trapezoidal blade with markedly curved cutting edge. On both faces, three thick nervatures on the haft-end. Smooth discontinuous blackish patina.
L. 16.5cm Weight 864g
See *PBF* IX. 12, no. 4251, from Reggio Calabria, not identical. Type Cuma.
Probably FBA.
Bibliography: Giardino 1994, 782, pls. 167,3; 168,2.

158.
PRB WG1092. Canon W. Greenwell Collection, bought from the Rev. Greville J. Chester. Given by J. Pierpont Morgan in 1909.
Paternò (Catania), Sicily.
Shaft-hole axe with thick body decorated with nervatures. Close to **Axes type 45**.
Thick-sectioned tool with continuous profile, hammered casting knob at centre of butt, wide oval shaft-hole, thick, trapezoidal blade, hexagonal in section, with slightly curved cutting edge. On both faces, a central nervature on the upper part of the haft-end. Surface hammered. Smooth blackish patina.
L. 21cm Weight 915g
See *PBF* IX. 12, no. 4250, unprovenanced, not identical. Type Cuma, FBA; Albanese Procelli 1993, 38, 82–84, fig. 6.45, from Paternò, Sicily. Type R8A3, FBA. The present piece might be from the same context as the axe published by Albanese Procelli 1993; it is similar in shape, without central nervature.
FBA.

159.
PRB WG1093. Canon W. Greenwell Collection, bought from the Rev.Greville J. Chester. Given by J. Pierpont Morgan in 1909.
'Massica' (probably Marsica, L'Aquila), Abruzzo.
Shaft-hole axe with thick body and slightly flaring butt and blade. **Axes type 46**.
Probably associated with **160**.
Continuous profile, angular hammered butt, wide oval shaft-hole, thick blade hexagonal in section, curved cutting edge. Dull light green patina with incrustations.
L. 18.2cm Weight 1066g
See *PBF* IX. 12, nos. 4238–4244, from Abruzzo and Umbria. Type Menaforno.
FBA.
Bibliography: *PBF* IX. 12, no. 4239.

160.
PRB WG1094. Canon W. Greenwell Collection, bought from the Rev. Greville J. Chester. Given by J. Pierpont Morgan in 1909.
'Tesi', Magliano dei Marsi (L'Aquila), Abruzzo.
Shaft-hole axe with thick body and slightly flaring butt and blade. **Axes type 46**.
Probably associated with **cat. 159**.
Continuous profile, angular hammered butt with cast residues, wide oval shaft-hole, thick blade hexagonal in section, curved cutting edge. Discontinuous light green patina with dark incrustations.
L. 16.7cm Weight 872g
See **cat. 159**.
FBA.
Bibliography: *PBF* IX. 12, no. 4240.

161.
PRB 1935.10-18.40. Transferred from GR. Bought from Sir William Hamilton.
Shaft-hole axe with angular butt and rounded blade section. **Axes type 47**.
Elongated tool with wide elliptical shaft-hole, haft-end separated from the blade with a slight step, blade slightly widening toward the rounded cutting edge. Smooth dark green patina.
L. 17.3cm Weight 786g
See *PBF* IX. 12, no. 4259, from Taranto. Type Zinzulusa var. B, very accurately made.
FBA, early.
Bibliography: Walters 1899, no. 2950.

162.
PRB 1880.8-2.47.Given by Sir A.W. Franks.
Cuma (Naples), Campania.
Shaft-hole axe with angular hammered butt and trapezoidal blade. **Axes type 47**.
Heavy tool. Haft-end separated from the blade by a step, elliptical shaft-hole, blade with slightly rounded cutting edge, damaged. Dull green patina with whitish and brown incrustations.
L. 17.2cm Weight 1080g
See *PBF* IX. 12, no. 4258, hoard of Mottola (Taranto), type Zinzulusa var. B.
FBA.

163.
PRB WG1091. Canon W. Greenwell Collection, bought from the Rev. Greville J. Chester. Given by J. Pierpont Morgan in 1909.
Bovino, Capitanata (Foggia), Apulia.
Shaft-hole axe with angular butt and trapezoidal blade. **Axes type 47**.
Heavy, elongated body with elliptical shaft-hole, haft-end separated from the blade by a slight step, blade with slightly rounded cutting edge. Smooth black patina with dark green zones. Small part of the blade missing.
L. 20cm Weight 1314g
See *PBF* IX. 12, no. 4272, hoard of Scorrano (Lecce), Apulia, type 'axes with pentagonal profile to haft-end'; also Jurgeit 1999, no. 215, from Apulia, FBA?
FBA, late.

164.
PRB 1889.2-1.1. Given by Sir A.W. Franks.
Pozzuoli (Naples), Campania.
Shaft-hole axe with angular hammered butt and trapezoidal blade. **Axes type 47**.
Haft-end separated from the blade by a slight step, elliptical shaft-hole, wide blade with slightly rounded cutting edge. Groove between butt and blade. Cast marks, a cross and a two-pronged fork respectively, on either face of the haft-end. Dark green patina with incrustations.
L. 16.5cm Weight 953g
See *PBF* IX. 12, no. 4271, hoard of Reinzano (Lecce), Apulia, type 'axes with pentagonal profile to haft-end'.
FBA, late.
Bibliography: Petrie 1917, pl. 9.4; *BM Guide* 1920a, 150, fig. 158.

165.
PRB 1935.10-18.37. Transferred from GR (1856.12-26.971). Bequeathed by Sir William Temple.
Magna Graecia , Southern Italy.

Shaft-hole axe with angular butt and trapezoidal blade. **Axes type 47.**
Heavy, elongated body with elliptical shaft-hole, haft-end separated from the blade by a step, blade with slightly rounded cutting edge. Surface very irregular with corrosion. Dull patina in various tones of green.
L. 17.7cm Weight 918g
See cat. 163.
FBA, late.
Bibliography: Walters 1899, no. 2947.

166.
GR 1982.6-17.22. Received from PRB. Sir Henry Wellcome Collection, no. 25951. Bought at Sotheby's sale 6–7 December 1920, lot 120. Given by the Wellcome Trustees.
Lake Trasimeno (Perugia), Umbria.
Shaft-hole axe with angular butt and trapezoidal blade. **Axes type 47.**
Elliptical shaft-hole, haft-end separated from the blade by a slight step, blade with slightly rounded cutting edge. Green patina with some areas of corrosion.
L. 15.5cm Weight 870g
See PBF IX. 12, no. 4312, hoard of Reinzano (Lecce), Apulia, not identical. Type S. Francesco var. B.
FBA, late.

167.
PRB 1866.6-27.108. Henry Christy Collection. Given by the Trustees under the will of Henry Christy.
Shaft-hole axe with angular butt and trapezoidal blade. **Axes type 47.**
Elliptical shaft-hole, haft-end separated from the blade by a very slight step, blade with slightly rounded cutting edge and faceted section. Dark green discontinuous patina.
L. 15.5cm Weight 675g
See cat. 163.
FBA, late.

168.
GR 1982.6-17.21. Received from PRB. Sir Henry Wellcome Collection, no. 79646. Bought in Florence from A. Albizi in April 1930. Given by the Wellcome Trustees.
'Populonia' (Livorno), Tuscany.
Shaft-hole axe with wide oval shaft-hole and trapezoidal blade. **Axes type 48.**
Heavy tool with angular hammered butt, wide shaft-hole, almost circular, trapezoidal blade with angular section and rounded cutting edge. Green patina with some corrosion and incrustations. L.16.2cm Weight 1013g
See PBF IX. 12, nos. 4292, hoard of Reinzano (Lecce), Apulia; 4295, unprovenanced. Type Chiusi var. A.
FBA, late.

169.
GR 1982.6-17.23. Received from PRB. Sir Henry Wellcome Collection, no. 79492. Bought in Athens from G. Polychronopoulos in March 1930. Given by the Wellcome Trustees.
'Corinth', Greece.
Shaft-hole axe with angular hammered butt and trapezoidal blade. **Axes type 48**
Oval shaft-hole, blade with curved cutting edge. Fracture in the socket area, and small part of the cutting edge missing. Green patina with some incrustation.

L. 15.2cm Weight 802g
See PBF IX. 12, no. 4294, from Lavello (Potenza), Basilicata. Type Chiusi var. A.
FBA, late.

170.
GR 1982.6-17.25. Received from PRB. Sir Henry Wellcome Collection, no. 96443. Bought in Rome from Antichità delle Belle Arti in April 1931. Given by the Wellcome Trustees.
Shaft-hole axe with angular hammered butt and trapezoidal blade. **Axes type 48.**
Oval shaft-hole, blade with slightly curved cutting edge. Dull green patina with some areas of corrosion.
L. 13.2cm Weight 650g
See PBF IX. 12, no. 4294, from Lavello (Potenza), Basilicata. Type Chiusi var. A.
FBA, late.

171.
PRB 1935.10-18.39. Transferred from GR (1756.1-1.458). Bought from Sloane Collection, 458.
Shaft-hole axe with angular hammered butt and continuous profile. **Axes type 48.**
Elliptical shaft-hole, blade with slightly curved cutting edge. Smooth dull green patina.
L. 13.4cm Weight 715g
See PBF IX. 12, no. 4357, hoard of Manduria (Taranto), Apulia, (with asymmetrical blade). Type Soleto var. B.
FBA, late, or EIA.
Bibliography: Walters 1899, no. 2949.

172.
PRB WG1090. Canon W. Greenwell Collection, bought from the Rev. Greville J. Chester. Given by J. Pierpont Morgan in 1909.
Mineo (Catania), Sicily.
Shaft-hole axe with angular butt and trapezoidal blade. **Axes type 49.**
Heavy, elongated body with elliptical shaft-hole, haft-end separated from the blade by a slight step, blade trapezoidal, with slightly rounded cutting edge. Smooth blackish patina.
L. 21cm Weight 1374g
See PBF IX. 12, no. 4280, unprovenanced. Type Cerchiara, FBA, late; Albanese Procelli 1993, 38, 83, 86, fig. 7.43, from Paternò, Sicily. Type R8F, EIA.
FBA, late, or EIA.

173.
PRB 1935.10-18.38. Transferred from GR.
Shaft-hole axe with hammered butt and straight sides. **Axes type 49.**
Small tool, probably reworked, angular, hammered butt, elliptical shaft-hole, straight cutting edge. Dull blackish patina with incrustations.
L. 9.7cm Weight 497g
Probably FBA, late, or EIA.
Bibliography: Walters 1899, no. 2948.

174.
PRB 1935.10-18.45. Transferred from GR (1916.6-1.27). Given by Lord Avebury. Acquired in Naples and probably from neighbourhood.
Campania.
Shaft-hole axe with hammered butt and slightly flaring blade. **Axes type 49.**
Wide body with continuous profile, large oval

shaft hole and curved cutting edge. Smooth brown patina with reddish and green spots.
L. 17cm Weight 1380g
See PBF IX. 12, no. 4284, hoard of Reinzano (Lecce), Apulia. Type Cerchiara, var; also Jurgeit 1999, no. 216, from Apulia, FBA?
FBA, late.

175.
PRB 1935.10-18.40A. Transferred from GR. Bought from Sir William Hamilton.
Shaft-hole axe with angular hammered butt and continuous profile. **Axes type 49.**
Heavy elongated tool with continuous profile, oval shaft-hole, blade with slightly rounded cutting edge. Smooth dark green patina; transverse break on one face.
L. 18.5cm Weight 1108g
See PBF IX. 12, no. 4280, unprovenanced. Type Cerchiara, FBA, late; Albanese Procelli 1993, 38, 83, 86, fig. 7.43, from Paternò. Type R8F, EIA.
FBA, late.
Bibliography: Walters 1899, no. 2950.

176.
PRB 1880.8-2.39. Given by Sir A.W. Franks. Enna, Sicily.
Lugged axe ['trunnion axe']. **Axes type 66.**
Narrow trapezoidal body with two lugs set near the butt. Butt and cutting edge slightly rounded. Dull, dark green patina. Lugs cut and hammered in antiquity.
L. 15.2cm Weight 210g
See Albanese Procelli 1993, 52, 78–9, fig. 16.N5, hoard of Niscemi (Caltanissetta), Sicily. Type R6B; Giardino 1995, 205, fig. 93. 1–3, 5–10, Sicily; 4, hoard of Monte Rovello (Tolfa, Rome); 11–14, Sardinia; 15–18, France; fig. 94A, Iberian peninsula; fig. 95, distribution map. See especially fig. 93. 5, hoard of Niscemi (Caltanissetta), Sicily, 'Asce piatte a spuntoni laterali'.
FBA, middle.
Bibliography: Giardino 1995, 205, fig. 93.7.

177.
PRB 1889.2-1.3. Given by Sir A.W. Franks. 'Massica' (probably Marsica, L'Aquila), Abruzzo.
Tanged axe. **Axes type 67.**
Long rectangular tang, rectangular blade with rounded section, slightly sloping shoulders and concave sides. Probably two symmetrical, circular holes set at the shoulders. Rounded cutting edge. Smooth black patina with dark green zones. One shoulder recently broken off, traces of hammering on the tang.
L. 12.7cm Weight 219g
See Carancini and Peroni 1999, 67, pl. 33. 76, tab. 34, hoards of Manduria I (Taranto), Scorrano (Lecce) and 'Foggiano', all in Apulia. Type 'Ascia piatta con lama espansa tipo Scorrano'.
FBA, middle–late.
Bibliography: Bietti Sestieri and Giardino 2003, 421.

178.
PRB 1880.8-2.43. Given by Sir A.W. Franks. 'Castro Giovanni' = Enna, Sicily.
Axe with one lateral loop. **Axes type 68.**
Heavy tool. Rectangular body with slightly concave sides. Large loop at middle of one side.

Slightly rounded cutting edge. Smooth blackish patina with calcareous incrustations.
L. 19cm Weight 819g
See Giardino 1995, 200, fig. 91A.1, this piece; 2, Quintana de Bureba (Burgos), and 3. Debesa de Romanos (Palencia), Spain; fig. 92A, distribution map, 'Asce piatte con un occhiello laterale'.
FBA, late, and beginning of EIA.
The PRB Registration book notes the provenance as Viterbo but Castro Giovanni, modern Enna, is written in ink above the patina on the bronze. However, although a provenance from Sicily would not be unlikely, this would be the only axe of this type at present known from the island.
Bibliography: Giardino 1995, 198–200, footnote 25, fig. 91A.1 and pl. 4.1.

179.
PRB 1964.12-1.440 (187). Sir Henry Wellcome Collection, no. 96456. Bought in Rome from Antichità delle Belle Arti by Captain Saint in April 1931. Given by the Wellcome Trustees.
Sardinian double axe. **Axes type 69.**
Perhaps associated with **cat. 180.**
Heavy tool with two converging blades. Nearly parallel cutting edges, upper side straight and slightly dished, lower side curved, large, circular shaft-hole with raised ring on lower face. Smooth blackish patina. Irregular hammer-marks along the edges and socket.
L. 19.5cm Weight 805g
See Taramelli 1922, 288, fig. 1, hoard of Chilivani, near Ozieri, Sardinia; Lo Schiavo, Macnamara and Vagnetti 1985, 20–22, fig. 8.3, 'Doppie asce a tagli paralleli o convergenti'; Lo Schiavo 1988, 78, pl. I. 3–8; Giardino 1995, 46–48, fig. 21A.3, 'Doppie asce a tagli paralleli o convergenti'.
This double axe and the similar piece **cat. 180** have continuous numbers in the Inventory of the Wellcome collection, and may have been originally found together.
FBA or EIA.

180.
PRB 1964.12-1.441. Sir Henry Wellcome Collection, no. 96457. Given by the Wellcome Trustees.
Sardinia?
Sardinian double axe. **Axes type 69.**
Perhaps associated with **cat. 179.**
Two converging blades, with nearly parallel cutting edges; upper side straight, lower side curved, large, circular shaft-hole with raised ring on lower face. Dull dark green patina with light zones. Ancient break on the shaft-hole.
L. 26cm Weight 1241g
See **cat. 179.**
FBA or EIA.

181.
PRB WG1089. Canon W. Greenwell Collection, bought from F.E. Whelan. Given by J. Pierpont Morgan in 1909.
Cagliari, Sardinia.
Sardinian double axe. **Axes type 70.**
Orthogonal cutting edges (axe-adze), blades rectangular in section, large circular shaft-hole with raised ring on lower face. Surface irregular, probably from the casting. Smooth dark green patina with light zones.
L. 17cm Weight 397g

See Taramelli 1922, 289, fig. 2, hoard of Chilivani, near Ozieri, Sardinia; Lo Schiavo, Macnamara and Vagnetti 1985, 20–22, fig. 8.4, 'doppie asce a tagli ortogonali'; Lo Schiavo 1988, 80, pl. 6.7, from Chilivani, Loc. Baldosa; Giardino 1995, 46–48, figs. 21A.4, 26.8. See also fig. 17B.2, from Taormina (Messina), Sicily. 'Doppie asce a tagli ortogonali'.
FBA–EIA
Bibliography: Petrie 1917, pl. 14.48.

Tools

182.
GR 1856.12-26.975. Bequeathed by Sir William Temple.
Rod chisel with stop-ridge and square tang. **Chisels type 2.**
Thick rod with square section, slightly diminishing at tang, flattened and rectangular at lower end; marked stop-ridge, cutting edge slightly widened, with small parts missing. Green patina.
L. 17.8cm Weight 204g
See Bietti Sestieri 1973, 392, fig. 6.4, 5, hoard of Mottola (Taranto), Apulia. FBA, advanced; Müller-Karpe 1959, pl. 49.17, hoard of Piediluco (Terni), Umbria, FBA late–EIA early.
FBA, middle–late.

183.
PRB 1935.10-18.22. Tranferred from GR. Bought from Sir William Hamilton.
Adze with medial-butt wings. **Winged adzes type 1.**
Long butt with central notch and curved sides, narrow haft end with elongated oval wings and straight, slightly marked stop-ridge, narrow element hexagonal in section at junction of haft with blade. Blade narrow and slightly flaring, with sloping shoulders and slightly curved cutting edge and angular section, due to a longitudinal crest at centre of both faces, which continues from the central element. Dark green patina. Wings hammered.
L. 15cm Weight 172g
See **cat. 105** and **184.**
FBA, early–middle.
Bibliography: Walters 1899, no. 2932.

184.
PRB 1964.12-1.356(381). Sir Henry Wellcome Collection, no. 829. Bought in Florence from A. Albizi by Captain Saint in November 1929. Given by the Wellcome Trustees.
Tuscany?
Adze with medial-butt wings. **Winged adzes type 1.**
Butt with central notch and slightly curved sides, narrow haft end with elongated oval wings and convex, slightly marked stop-ridge, narrow cylindrical element at junction of haft with blade. Blade narrow and slightly flaring, with elliptical section, sloping shoulders, and curved cutting edge. Incised decoration on the outer faces of the wings: row of short oblique traits along the edge, framing three vertical rows of double zigzag lines. Shiny discontinuous dark green patina. Blade edge and butt slightly damaged.
L. 15.5cm Weight 177g
See **cat. 105** and **183.**
FBA, early–middle.

185.
GR 1976.12-31.232. Found unregistered.
Straight socketed tool. **Sicilian socketed tools type 1.**
Hollow tool, probably a plough-head, with distinct, slightly bulging edge to upper end, wide rounded point and elliptical section; large irregular oval hole below the edge at centre of each face. Irregular casting. Dull green patina with some corrosion.
L. 12.8cm Weight 538g
Close to Albanese Procelli 1993, 54, 55, 89–90, figs. 16. N18, 17. NA3, hoards of Niscemi (Gela) and Noto Antica (Syracuse), both in Sicily. Type R11B.
FBA, middle.

186.
PRB 1888.9-1.5.Given by Sir A.W.Franks.
Syracuse, Sicily.
L-shaped socketed tool. **Sicilian socketed tools type 2.**
Hollow flat socketed tool with thickened rim, blunt tip and narrow oval section. Two wide triangular openings below the rim. Smooth dark green patina.
L. 12.3cm Weight 169g
See Albanese Procelli 1993, 54, 55, 90, figs. 16. N19, N20, and 17. NA4, hoards of Niscemi (Gela) and Noto Antica (Syracuse), both in Sicily. Type R12.
FBA, middle.

187.
GR 1842.7-28.705. Bought from Mr. Burgon.
Said to be from Florence, Tuscany.
Hammer-head with narrow shaft-hole. **Hammers type 1.**
Elongated tool with rectangular section and blunt ends; central area slightly raised on all sides, probably meant to reinforce the narrow longitudinal shaft-hole. Green patina with corrosion and incrustations.
L. 13.5cm Weight 1048g
See Bietti Sestieri 1973, 392, fig. 6.2, hammer-head of similar shape, with no raised central area; hoard of Mottola (Taranto), Apulia. For hammer-heads from Italy, see Macnamara 1970, 248–249; Harding 1975, 194–195.
FBA, middle?

188.
PRB 1894.7-27.7.
Given by Sir A. W. Franks.
Tanged sickle with continuous profile. **Sickles type 1.**
Short straight tang with central hole and small triangular protrusion on the back side, blade wide and markedly curved, with blunt rounded tip; two parallel nervatures on tang and blade, joining at the tip of the blade. Cast in a one-piece mould. Discontinuous blackish patina with zones of corrosion.
L. 14cm Weight 128.5g
Close to Bietti Sestieri 1973, 394f. and fig. 9.14, hoard of Casalecchio (Rimini), Emilia Romagna, FBA middle–late; Giardino 1995, 10, fig. 3.14, type Piediluco, FBA late–EIA; *Dizionari Terminologici* 1980, 105, pl. 102.5, hoard of Limone (Livorno), Tuscany, FBA, late.
FBA, middle–late.

Knives

189.
GR 1856.5-14.1. Bought from H.O. Cureton, Sotheby's sale 2 April, lot 8.
Knife with serpentine blade and tang. **Knives type 1.**
Back of blade firmly thickened and with a strong nervature below running parallel to the back; back decorated with an incised herring bone pattern and dotted transverse lines. Tang round in section near blade and flattened at end. Ancient break across centre of blade. Smooth green patina.
L. 16.8cm Weight 35g
Close to *PBF* VII. 2, nos. 262, from S. Antonino Casier, (Treviso), Veneto, type Bismantova, var. A, and 233, type Iseo.
FBA.
Bibliography: Walters 1899, no. 2757.

190.
GR 1850.1-17.85. Bought from M. Martin Rey.
Knife with slightly curved blade and tang. **Knives type 1.**
Narrow elongated blade with firm thickening towards the back and a groove below running parallel to the back. Tang round in section. Broken across centre of blade; tip missing. Smooth dark green patina.
L. 18.1cm Weight 44g
Close to *PBF* VII. 2, nos. 261, from Castagnaro (Verona), Veneto, type Bismantova var. A, and 233, type Iseo.
FBA.
Bibliography: Walters 1899, no. 2756.

191.
PRB 1867.10-11.9. Bought from Dr Florian Romer of Budapest. Objects belonged chiefly to his friend M. Bakitich.
Knife with serpentine blade and flat tang. **Knives type 1.**
Cast in one-piece mould, with thickened rounded side, two wide grooves along the blade, tang thinned towards butt, made of two parallel parts. Shiny dark green patina.
L. 12.9cm Weight 27g
Close to *PBF* VII. 2, no. 233, unprovenanced. Type Iseo, FBA?
Probably FBA.

192.
GR 1847.8-6.140. Bought from the Executors of J. Millingen.
Knife with serpentine blade and tang. **Knives type 2.**
Thin blade of narrow elongated shape with slightly upturned tip and back with a narrow T-shaped profile. Narrow tang with very slight flanges. Dull green patina.
L. 20.8cm Weight 38g
Close to *PBF* VII. 2, nos. 272 and 273, from L'Aquila, Abruzzo. Type Bismantova, var. B. FBA, middle.
Bibliography: Walters 1899, no. 2758.

193.
PRB 1880.5-1.29. Bought from the Rev. G.J. Chester.
Regalbuto (Enna), Sicily.
Knife with serpentine blade and flanged tang. **Knives type 3.**
Serpentine blade with markedly curved profile

and T-section, slender rectangular tang with four rivet holes. Incised decoration: groups of longitudinal multiple chevrons separated by transversal lines and empty zones on back of blade; zigzag lines and rows of dots on blade. Smooth black patina with zones in light green. End of tang missing.
L. 22.2cm Weight 80g
No parallels found in Albanese Procelli 1993.
Close to *PBF* VII. 2, no. 42, from Castel Beseno, type Fontanella, FBA. Not identical.
FBA.

194.
GR 1975.7-30.19. Found unregistered.
Knife with curved blade and tang ending in a ring. **Knives type 4.**
Cast in one piece. Narrow elongated shape with serpentine blade and slightly thickened back. Tang with rectangular section ending in a flat ring. Dull dark green patina.
L. 13.5cm Weight 7g
Although the shape of this piece is rather close to a well-known type from the earliest Latial phases (*PBF* VII. 2, nos. 250, 251, 253, from different localities in the Alban hills, near Rome, type Fontana di Papa; *Osteria dell'Osa* 1992, 398–399, pl. 41, type 58, phase IIA1, EIA, early), apparently some better parallels can be found in several Sicilian contexts dating from a middle–late phase of the FBA: see Turco 2000, cemetery of Cassibile, 92 and pl. 30, type 20, tombs CS 82.1 and SP 46.2. See for distribution of this type and bibliography, notes 153–158.
Probably FBA, middle–late.
Bibliography: Walters 1899, no. 2762.

Razors

195.
PRB 1880.8-2.30. Given by Sir A.W. Franks. Probably obtained from A. Castellani.
Symmetrical razor. **Razors type 3.**
Cast ring handle, wide blade with slightly rounded shoulders, straight upper edge interrupted by an opening into a wide circular hole. Rough blackish patina with light incrustations. Blade edges damaged.
L. 10.3cm Weight 37g
See *PBF* VIII. 2, no. 216, from Pianello. Type Pianello.
FBA, late.

196.
PRB 1880.8-2.31. Given by Sir A. W. Franks. Probably obtained from A. Castellani.
Symmetrical razor. **Razors type 4.**
Ring handle of twisted wire, attached to the blade with a semicircular plate held by two rivets, rectangular blade with slightly rounded lower and lateral edges, straight upper edge interrupted by an opening into a wide circular hole. Smooth dark green patina with blackish incrustations. Blade edges damaged.
L. 9.4cm Weight 17g
See *PBF* VIII. 2, no. 99, from Tolfa. Type Terni. FBA, late - EIA.

197.
PRB 1880.8-2.34. Given by Sir A. W. Franks. Probably obtained from A. Castellani.
Symmetrical razor. **Razors type 4.**
Ring handle of twisted wire, attached to the blade with a small circular plate held by three

rivets; only the central part of the blade remains. Decoration on both sides at centre of blade, incised with three parallel lines: double axe enclosing an elongated element. Smooth green-brown patina.
L. (preserved) 8.5cm Width (preserved) 4.9cm Weight 13g
Close to *PBF* VIII. 2, nos. 94, from Terni, Umbria, 95–96. Type Terni, FBA–EIA; see also no. 80, from Timmari (Matera), Basilicata, type Croson di Bovolone, FBA.
FBA, late–EIA.

Ornaments

198.
GR 1878.10-19.140. Given by General A.W.H. Meyrick.
Pin with pointed globular head. **Pins type 5.**
Small head and thin shank, slightly diminishing below head and decorated with a group of slight encircling grooves. Dull green patina.
L. 10.8cm Weight 3g
See *PBF* XIII. 2, no. 1749, from 'provincia di Trento', Trentino-Alto Adige, type Sarteano. FBA.

199.
GR 1878.10-19.143. Given by General A.W.H. Meyrick.
Pin with pointed head. **Pins type 6.**
Small head and swollen neck of shank; shank round in section and distorted in shape. Dull green to brown patina.
L. 9.8cm Weight 3g
See *PBF* XIII. 2, no. 1391 from Fontanella Grazioli (Mantova), Lombardy, type Fontanella.
FBA.

200.
GR 1867.5-8.142. Blacas Collection.
Nail-headed pin. **Pins type 7.**
Small head and thin shank, round in section. Little patina with some corrosion.
L. 15.3cm Weight 6g
See *PBF* XIII. 2, no. 1674, from Fontanella Grazioli (Mantova), Lombardy, type 'a capocchia di chiodo'.
FBA.

201.
GR 1935.8-23.68. Transferred from the Department of British and Medieval Antiquities. Canon W. Greenwell Collection, no. 1167, bought from the Rev. Greville J. Chester. Given by J. Pierpont Morgan in 1909.
'Massica' (probably Marsica, L'Aquila), Abruzzo.
Sheet disc with embossed decoration. **Sheet disc type 1.**
Flat sheet with hole at centre, probably once circular. Decoration: punched row of dots along the edge and two crossing rows of dots dividing the disc into four sections, each with an encircled dot at centre. Small parts missing. Smooth green patina.
See Bernabò Brea and Cavalier, 1960, Lipari, Piazza Monfalcone, tomb 31. FBA. Orsi 1905, 118, fig. 22; Bernabò Brea, Militello and La Piana 1969, 262, figs. 15c, 20e, necropolis of Molino della Badia- Madonna del Piano (Catania), Sicily, tomb 24. FBA, late or EIA, early.
Probably FBA.

Fibulae

202.
GR 1994.8-3.4. Transferred from PRB.
P. Corwen-Britton, 1910.
Heightened violin-bow fibula with two knobs.
Fibulae type 1.
Catch-plate missing, probably symmetrical, thin bow with front portion stilted, rounded elbow and upper portion curved and slightly thickened, large one-coiled spring and straight pin, partly missing. Incised encircling decoration on central portion of bow: transverse chevrons between two groups of parallel lines. Dull green patina.
L. 7.5cm Weight 9g
See Bietti Sestieri 1973, fig. 20.2 from Milazzo (Messina), Sicily.
PBF XIV. 5, nos. 62 and 63 from northern Italy. Type: 'Fibule ad arco di violino rialzato'.
PBF XIV, forthcoming, II. (11), 'Fibula ad arco con due noduli e gomito al di sopra della staffa', no. 31, from Milazzo, Sicily; II. (12) Tipo Caltagirone/Monte Dessueri. (12)A, nos. 32, 34 from Caltagirone (Catania), Sicily, cemetery of Montagna Alta; 33 from the cemetery of Monte Dessueri (Caltanissetta), Sicily, tomb 59 Palombara; (12)B. Transitional type from violin- to stilted-bow.
FBA, early.

203.
GR 1976.2-5.19. Found unregistered.
Elbow fibula with two coils and symmetrical catch-plate ('fibula a gomito'). **Fibulae type 2.**
Small catch-plate, thin bow straight above the catch-plate and slightly bent between the coils. Incised decoration: groups of encircling lines and chevrons between the coils. Seven small cast bronze rings threaded on to the pin. Dull green to brown patina.
L. 11.5cm Weight 42g
See Bernabò Brea, Militello and La Piana 1969, 263, fig. 20g, Molino della Badia-Madonna del Piano (Catania), Sicily, tomb 27; Lo Schiavo and Peroni 1979, 560f., fig. 2.6, Vibo Valentia, Calabria, sporadic; *PBF* XIV, forthcoming, XXXVI. I (299), 'Fibule serpeggianti con occhiello, spillone dritto e staffa simmetrica'. (299)A, no. 5300, sporadic from the cemetery of Molino della Badia (Grammichele, Catania), Sicily; (299) B, nos. 5301, from the cemetery of Cassibile (Syracuse), Sicily, tomb 17; 5302, from the cemetery of Madonna del Piano (Mineo, Catania), Sicily, tomb 27.
FBA, late.
Bibliography: Walters 1899, no. 2065; Montelius 1895–1910, Series A, pl. XVI. no. 219; Sundwall 1943, 142, D II alpha a 1, fig. 207.

204.
GR 1867.5-8.169. Blacas Collection.
Heightened violin-bow fibula with multiple coils. Close to **Fibulae type 2.**
Triangular profile, large semicircular catch-plate; bow above catch-plate vertical with rectangular section; the upper part forms a series of eight loops descending to the spring. Embossed pointillé decoration in two parallel rows on catch-plate. Small parts missing. Dull brown patina with green areas.
L. 17.1cm Weight 97g
Close to **cat. 203** in general shape and probably in date.

See for a relatively similar type of EIA date Montelius 1895–1910, pl. 355.3, from Rome; Müller-Karpe 1959, pl. 42G.4, Terni, Umbria, cemetery of the Acciaierie, tomb 154: large fibulae of thin bronze wire with low elongated arch forming a series of loops, and spiral disc catch-plate; chains of rings attached to each loop.
FBA, late.
Bibliography: Walters 1899, no. 2066; Montelius 1895–1910, Series A, pl. XVI, no. 220; Sundwall 1943, 156, D III alpha a 1, fig. 237.

205.
GR 1878.10-19.163. Given by General A.W.H. Meyrick.
Arch fibula with two knobs and symmetrical catch-plate. **Fibulae type 3.**
Small catch-plate, thin symmetrical bow with two double knobs, large one-coiled spring with square section. Incised decoration: groups of encircling lines and chevrons. Catch-plate partly missing. Smooth dark green patina.
L. 8.6cm Weight 29g
Analysis: Bronze. See D. Hook report.
See Bietti Sestieri 1973, 404, fig. 20.9, from Pantalica (Sicily); Carancini and Peroni 1999, 63, no. 35, pl. 31.35, 'fibula ad arco con noduli' (not identical); *PBF* XIV, forthcoming, III. 2 (20), 'Fibule ad arco semplice con due noduli, tipo Gargano'; (20) B, no. 70, from Campania.
FBA, late.
Bibliography: Bietti Sestieri 1986, 'Fibulae', 6, no. 1, and fig. p. 20.

206.
GR 1856.12-26.745. Bequeathed by Sir William Temple.
Arch fibula with two flat knobs and symmetrical catch-plate. **Fibulae type 4.**
Very large fibula with semicircular catch-plate, thin symmetrical bow with two large flat cylindrical knobs, large one-coiled spring with square section. Embossed pointillé decoration in three parallel rows on the catch-plate; groups of encircling incised lines and chevrons on the bow. Small parts of catch-plate missing. Dull green patina with brown patches.
L. 31.7cm Weight 112g
Analysis: Bronze. See D. Hook report.
Close to Lo Schiavo and Peroni 1979, 556, fig. 4.1, sporadic, from Sibari, Calabria, and *PBF* XIV, forthcoming, V (30), 'Fibule ad arco semplice di grandi dimensioni'. (30) A, no. 134, sporadic from the cemetery of Castellace (Oppido Mamertina, Reggio Calabria); (30) B, no. 135 from Sibari (Cassano Jonio, Cosenza), Calabria.
FBA, late.
Bibliography: Walters 1899, no. 2003; Bietti Sestieri 1986, 'Fibulae', 6, no. 2, and fig. p. 20.

207.
GR 1757.8-15.40A. Given by Thomas Hollis.
Thickened stilted arch fibula with symmetrical catch-plate. **Fibulae type 5.**
Large catch-plate, bow slightly asymmetrical, widened and bent in the central part, stilted above the catch-plate, small one-coiled spring. Incised decoration: double zigzag and groups of encircling lines and chevrons on the sides; lozenge grid in the central space. Small parts of catch-plate and pin missing. Dull green patina.
L. 10.2cm Weight 60g

See *PBF* XIV, forthcoming, VI (38), 'Fibule ad arco con doppia piegatura, tipo Fucino'. (38) A, no. 45, from the cemetery of Pantalica (Syracuse), Sicily.
See also, for a similar type of EIA date, *Torre Galli* 1999, 41, fig. 10, type OB5D, phase IA. FBA, late, and beginning of EIA.
Bibliography: Walters 1899, no. 1999; Bietti Sestieri 1986, 'Fibulae', 8, no. 15, and fig. p. 21.

208.
GR 1976.2-8.8. Found unregistered.
Thickened arch fibula with symmetrical catch-plate. Probably **Fibulae type 5.**
Broken and completely distorted. Small catch-plate, now detached, bow probably once stilted or semicircular, with central zone thickened, one-coiled spring. Incised decoration: encircling lines alternating with groups of chevrons on the whole surface of the bow. Tip of pin missing. Dull green patina.
L. 9.5cm total. Weight 14g
See **cat. 207**.
FBA–EIA transition?
Bibliography: Bietti Sestieri 1986, 'Fibulae', 8, no. 19, and fig. p. 21, incorrectly numbered 20.

209.
GR 1982.6-17.61. Received from PRB. Sir Henry Wellcome Collection. Given by the Wellcome Trustees.
Arch fibula with diverging ends and symmetrical catch-plate. **Fibulae type 6.**
Catch-plate partly missing, thin raised bow with diverging ends, one-coil spring with square section. Bow with cast and incised decoration: groups of cast encircling lines at ends, incised hatched bands lengthwise. Pin missing. Green to brown patina with some corrosion.
L. 13.5cm Weight 42g
Close to Bernabò Brea, Militello and La Piana 1969, fig. 17a: Molino della Badia-Madonna del Piano (Catania), Sicily, sporadic; see also a group of sporadic pieces from Calabria, Lo Schiavo and Peroni 1979, fig. 3.1-5; *PBF* XIV, forthcoming, VIII (46), 'Fibule ad arco fortemente ingrossato, tipo Realmese'. (46), no. 488 (not identical), from the cemetery of Torre Galli (Vibo Valentia), Calabria; IX, 'Fibule ad arco ingrossato con costolature longitudinali e sezione poligonale o quadrangolare'.
Both shape and decoration are specific to eastern Sicily and western Calabria.
FBA, late?

210.
GR 1772.3-9.36. Bought from Sir William Hamilton.
Slightly thickened arch fibula with coil above spring and terminal disc of spiral sheet. **Fibulae type 16.**
Small disc, thin, slightly asymmetrical bow, forming an inward loop near the spring; large one-coiled spring. A ring of thin bronze wire is suspended from the pin. Dull green patina.
L. 5.7cm Weight 9g
Close to *PBF* XIV, forthcoming, XII. I (68), 'Fibule ad arco con occhielli e staffa a disco-spirale'. (68), no. 687 (arch forming a series of loops). See also Peroni et al. 1980, pl. 23C for the distribution of this type, which is found mainly in southern Etruria and Abruzzo during

FBA, late, and FBA–EIA transition.
FBA, late, or EIA.
Bibliography: Walters 1899, no. 2010; Bietti Sestieri 1986, 'Fibulae', 10, no. 35, and fig. p. 22.

211.
PRB Morel 2139. Bought from Léon Morel, April–May 1901.
Probably found in France.
Serpentine fibula with straight pin and terminal disc of spiral wire. **Fibulae type 38.**
Small disc, thin bow with triangular contour, forming a small coil above the catch-plate and a pronounced curve in the upper part, large one-coiled spring and straight pin. Incised decoration of encircling lines on whole surface. Plain green patina.
A large bead of clear blue-green glass, probably later in date than the fibula, threaded on pin.
L. 6.8cm Weight 18g (with bead).
See in general *PBF* XIV, forthcoming, XXXVIII, (310), 'Fibule serpeggianti con occhiello, spillone dritto, staffa a spirale o a disco-spirale e arco di verga, tipo Caggiano'.
Pontecagnano 1988, 51, pl. 18; 103, fig. I. B, types 32B1, 32B2.
Peroni *et al.* 1980, pl. 28C (pieces from Campania, Cuma, Amendolara, Chiaromonte S. Pasquale, Caggiano, prov. Cosenza, Potenza).
Close parallel: *PBF* XIV, forthcoming, XXXVIII, (310e), no. 5409, sporadic from Cuma (Naples). This is a central and south Italian type, especially found in FBA–EIA tombs in Umbria, Lazio and Campania.
FBA–EIA transition.

212.
GR 1976.2-5.8. Found unregistered.
Serpentine fibula with straight pin and terminal disc of spiral wire. **Fibulae type 38.**
Small disc; thin bow with triangular contour, forming a small coil above the catch-plate and a pronounced curve in the upper part; large one-coiled spring and straight pin. Incised decoration of encircling lines on the whole surface. Smooth brown patina.
L. 6.2cm Weight 7g
See *PBF* XIV, forthcoming, XXXVIII, (310) E, no. 5409, sporadic from Cuma (Naples), Campania.
See **cat. 211.**
FBA–EIA transition.
Bibliography: Walters 1899, no. 2018; Bietti Sestieri 1986, 'Fibulae', 7, no. 5, and fig. p. 20.

213.
GR 1772.3-9.42. Bought from Sir William Hamilton.
Serpentine fibula with straight pin and terminal disc. **Fibulae type 38.**
Disc missing, probably a wire spiral; bow with triangular contour, forming a small coil above the catch-plate and a slight curve in the upper part; large one-coiled spring and straight pin. Coils with squarish section. Cast decoration of groups of encircling nervatures on the whole surface. Light green patina.
L. 11.6cm Weight 57g
Analysis: Craddock 1986, 144.
See **cat. 211,** and *PBF* XIV, forthcoming, XXXVIII, (310) D, no. 5407 from Capua (Caserta), Campania.
FBA–EIA transition.

Bibliography: Walters 1899, no. 2020; Bietti Sestieri 1986, 'Fibulae', 7, no. 3, and fig. p. 20.

214.
GR 1856.12-26.904. Bequeathed by Sir William Temple.
Serpentine fibula with straight pin and terminal disc of spiral wire. **Fibulae type 38.**
Small disc; bow with triangular contour, forming a small coil above the catch-plate and a pronounced curve in the upper part; large one-coiled spring and straight pin. Incised decoration of encircling lines on straight section of bow above the catch-plate. Slightly deformed. Light green patina.
L. 12.3cm Weight 40g
Analysis: Bronze. See D. Hook report.
See **cat. 211** and *PBF* XIV, forthcoming, XXXVIII, (310) E, no. 5409 from Cuma (Naples), Campania.
FBA–EIA transition.
Bibliography: Walters 1899, no. 2019; Bietti Sestieri 1986, 'Fibulae', 7, no. 6, and fig. p. 20.

215.
PRB 1944.7-2.7. Henry Christy Collection. Given by the Trustees under the will of Henry Christy. Bought by them from T.A. Glenn.
May have been excavated in Dorset, England, by Captain Sabine.
Serpentine fibula with straight pin and terminal disc. **Fibulae type 38.**
Disc missing, probably a sheet bronze spiral, thin bow with triangular contour and oblique front portion, forming a small coil above the catch-plate and a pronounced curve in the upper part, large one-coiled spring and straight pin. Traces of incised decoration of encircling parallel lines. Light green patina.
L. 7.7cm Weight 9g
See **cat. 211** and *PBF* XIV, forthcoming, XXXVIII, (310e), no. 5409 from Cuma (Naples), Campania.
FBA–EIA transition.
Bibliography: Hull and Hawkes 1987, 35, no. 6694, pl. 14. See 26, no. 7260, for comment on the provenance of this fibula.

216.
GR 1814.7-4.262. Charles Townley Collection. Bought from Peregrine Townley.
Serpentine fibula with large spring and terminal disc of spiral wire. **Fibulae type 39.**
Small disc; bow with triangular contour, forming a small coil above the catch-plate and a pronounced curve in the upper part; large one-coiled spring and straight pin. Cast decoration of single and double encircling nervatures on the whole surface. Catch-plate deformed. Little patina.
L. 14cm Weight 50g
Analysis: Craddock 1986, 144.
See *PBF* XIV, forthcoming, XXXVII.1, no. 5412 from the cemetery of Torre Galli (Vibo Valentia), Calabria: very close in shape, but with disc of coiled sheet; Peroni *et al.* 1980, pl. 22A (especially the fibula from Allumiere, Rome).
FBA–EIA transition.
Bibliography: Walters 1899, no. 2021; Bietti Sestieri 1986, 'Fibulae', 7, no. 4, and fig. p. 20.

217.
GR 1824.4-34.43. Bequeathed by R. Payne Knight.
Two-piece serpentine fibula with plastic decoration and terminal disc of spiral wire. **Fibulae type 42.**
Catch-plate and disc missing, bow with trapezoidal contour with two coils and attached to separate pin, straight, ending in a solid semi-globe. Decoration: groups of encircling raised nervatures on the whole surface of the bow. Dark green patina with some corrosion.
L. 12cm Weight 105g
Analysis: Bronze. See D. Hook report.
See for parallels Sundwall D IV alpha.b; Peroni *et al.* 1980, pl. 10C, no. 28; Bietti Sestieri 1986, 7, nos. 11 and 12. This distinctive type of two-piece fibula is found mainly in central Italian hoards dating from FBA, late, and FBA–EIA transition, although some pieces appear over the whole Italian territory: hoards of Campese and Limone, and a sporadic piece from Saturnia, Tuscany; hoard of Piediluco-Contigliano (Terni), Umbria; cemeteries of Alfedena, Abruzzo, and Fontanella, Lombardy; a sporadic piece from Molise. Some of the latest finds are from tomb 4 of the cemetery of Celano (L'Aquila), Abruzzo: D'Ercole, Cairoli 1998, 159, fig. 5.
No precise parallels in *PBF* XIV, forthcoming; XXXVIII.1 (321), no. 5480 from tomb 104, cemetery of Torre Galli (Vibo Valentai), Calabria, is partly similar, with curved pin.
FBA–EIA transition.
Bibliography: Walters 1899, no. 2064; Bietti Sestieri 1986, 'Fibulae', 7, no. 12 and fig. p. 20.

218.
GR 1910. 10-15. 2. Bought from W.C. Bacon and Co., London.
Two-piece serpentine fibula with plastic decoration and terminal disc of spiral wire. **Fibulae type 42.**
Small disc, bow with trapezoidal contour with two coils; opposing end of bow round in section, which once fitted into a separate pin, straight, now missing. Decoration: encircling double raised nervatures on the whole surface of bow; a row of encircling incised chevrons on both sides of the coils, impressed circlets on the back of the catch-plate coils. Dull green patina.
L. 10.7cm Weight 66g
See **cat. 217.**
FBA–EIA transition.
Bibliography: Bietti Sestieri 1986, 'Fibulae', 7, no. 11, and fig. p. 20.

Swords and Sheath

219.
PRB WG1143. Canon W. Greenwell Collection, bought from the Rev. Greville J. Chester. Given by J. Pierpont Morgan in 1909.
Bisignano (Cosenza), Calabria.
Short sword with flanged hilt and pommel tang. Close to **Swords type 4.**
Rectangular tang, hilt with slightly curved edges, rounded sloping shoulders; eight rivet holes, three rivets extant, short blade with almost straight edges, lenticular section and decorated with a band of nervatures. Rough dark green patina. Small part of blade missing.
L. 40cm Weight 359g

148

149

150

151

152

Plate 32   Axes type 34: - 148. - 149. - 150. -151. **Axes type 34 variant**: -152.

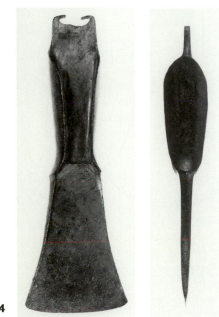

154

153

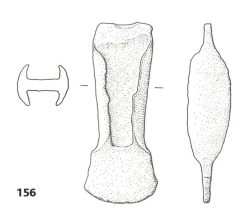

155

156

Plate 33   Axes type 35: - 153. **Axes type 36**: - 154. - 155. - 156 Terni , Umbria.

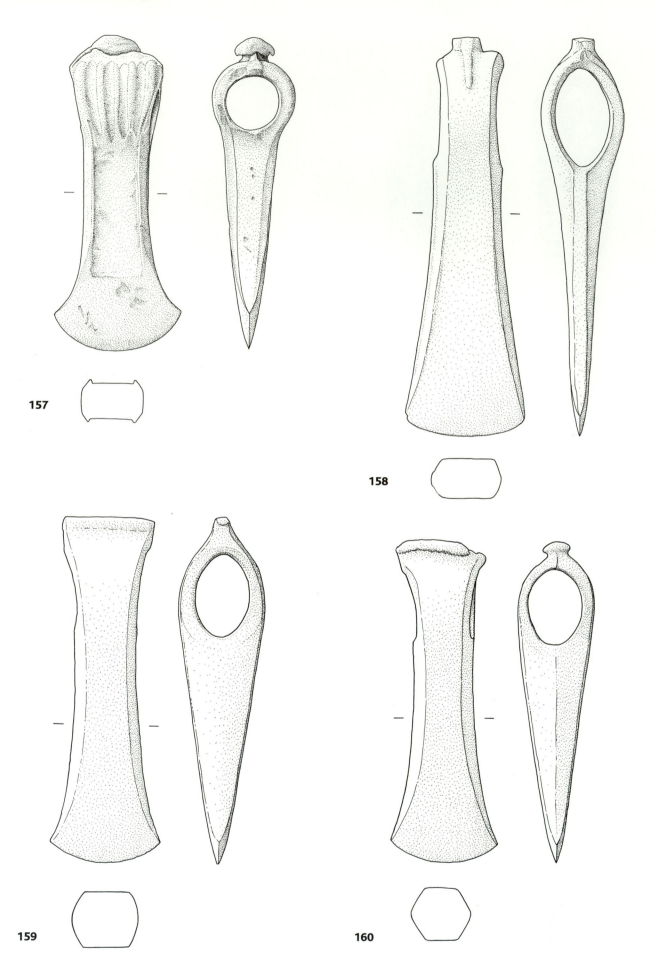

Plate 34   Close to **Axes type 45**: - 157 Castrovillari (Cosenza), Calabria. - 158 Paternò (Catania), Sicily. **Axes type 46**: - 159 Marsica (L'Aquila), Abruzzo. - 160 Tesi, Magliano dei Marsi (L'Aquila), Abruzzo.

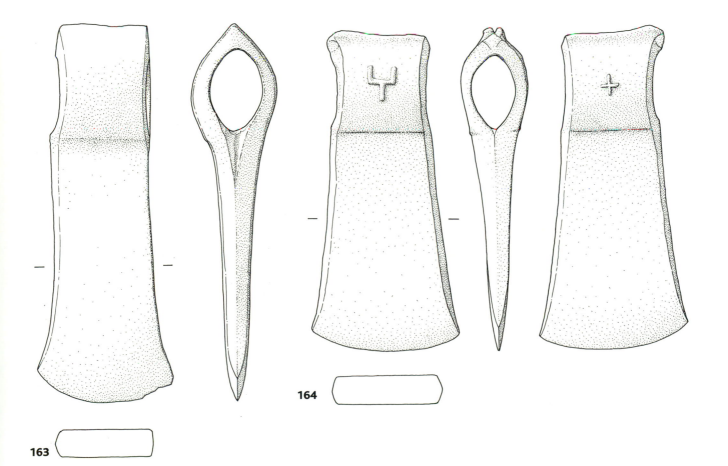

Plate 35 **Axes type 47**: - 161. - 162 Cuma (Naples), Campania. - 163 Bovino (Foggia), Apulia. - 164 Pozzuoli (Naples), Campania.

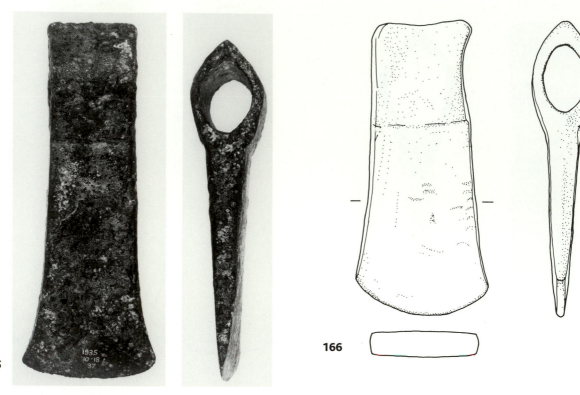

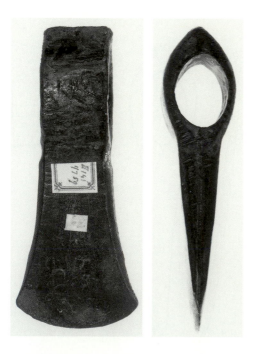

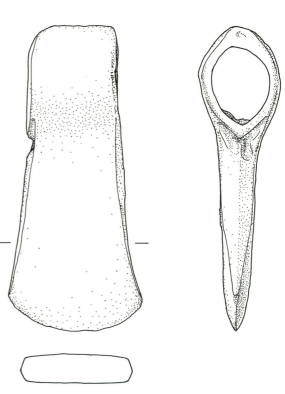

Plate 36   Axes type 47: - 165 'Magna Graecia'. - 166 Lake Trasimeno (Perugia), Umbria. - 167. **Axes type 48**: - 168 Populonia (Livorno), Tuscany.

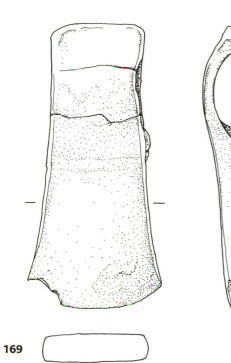

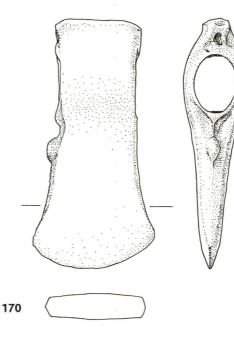

169

170

171

173

172

Plate 37 **Axes type 48**: - 169 Corinth, Greece. - 170. - 171. **Axes type 49**: - 172 Mineo (Catania), Sicily. - 173.

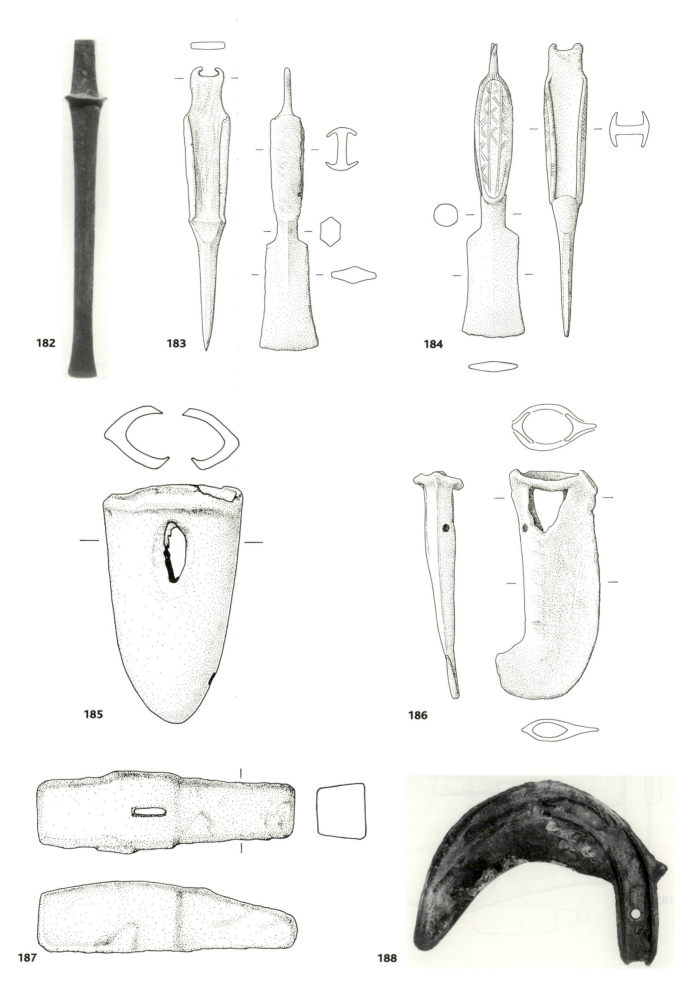

182

183

184

185

186

187

188

Plate 40   **Chisels type 2**: - 182. **Winged adzes type 1**: - 183. - 184 Tuscany?. **Sicilian socketed tools type 1**: - 185. **Sicilian socketed tools type 2**: - 186 Syracuse, Sicily. **Hammers type 1**: - 187 probably Florence, Tuscany. **Sickles type 1**: - 188.

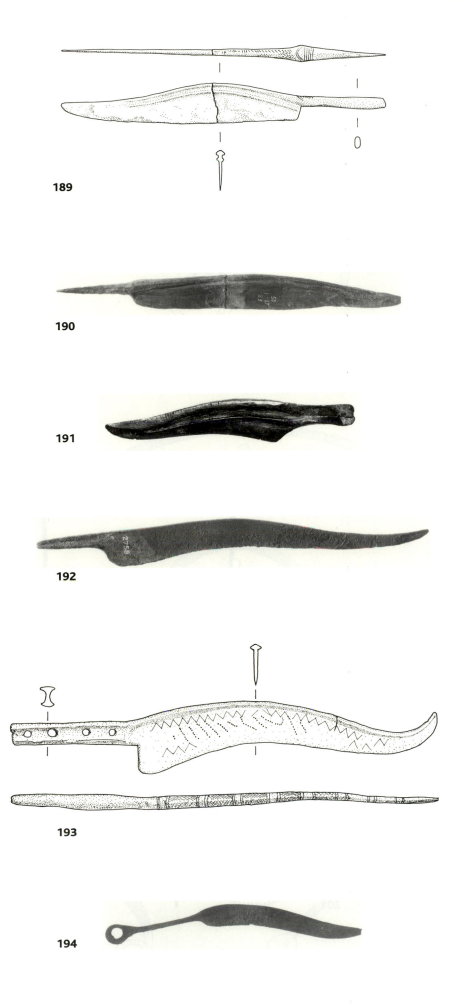

Plate 41   **Knives type 1**: - 189. - 190. -191. **Knives type 2**: - 192. **Knives type 3**: - 193 Regalbuto (Enna), Sicily. **Knives type 4**: - 194.

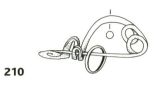

210

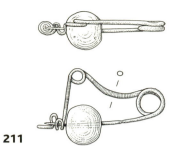

211

212

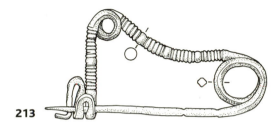

213

214

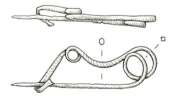

215

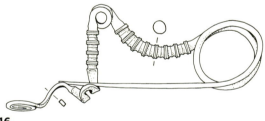

216

217

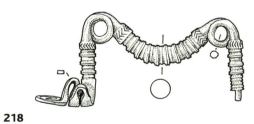

218

Plate 44 **Fibulae type 16**: - 210. **Fibulae type 38**: - 211 probably France. - 212. - 213. - 214. - 215 possibly Dorset, England. **Fibulae type 39**: - 216. **Fibulae type 42**: - 217. - 218.

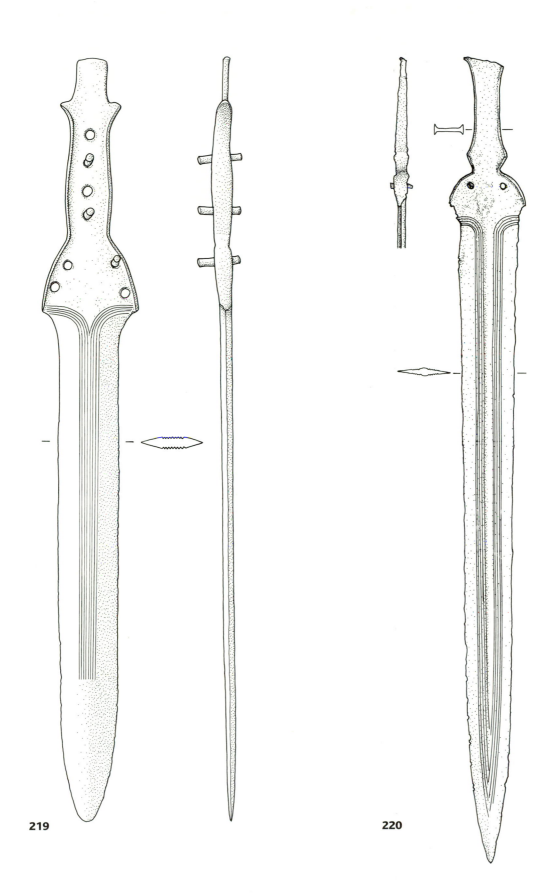

219

220

Plate 45   Close to **Swords type 4**: - 219 Bisignano (Cosenza), Calabria. **Swords type 5**: - 220 Naples, Campania.

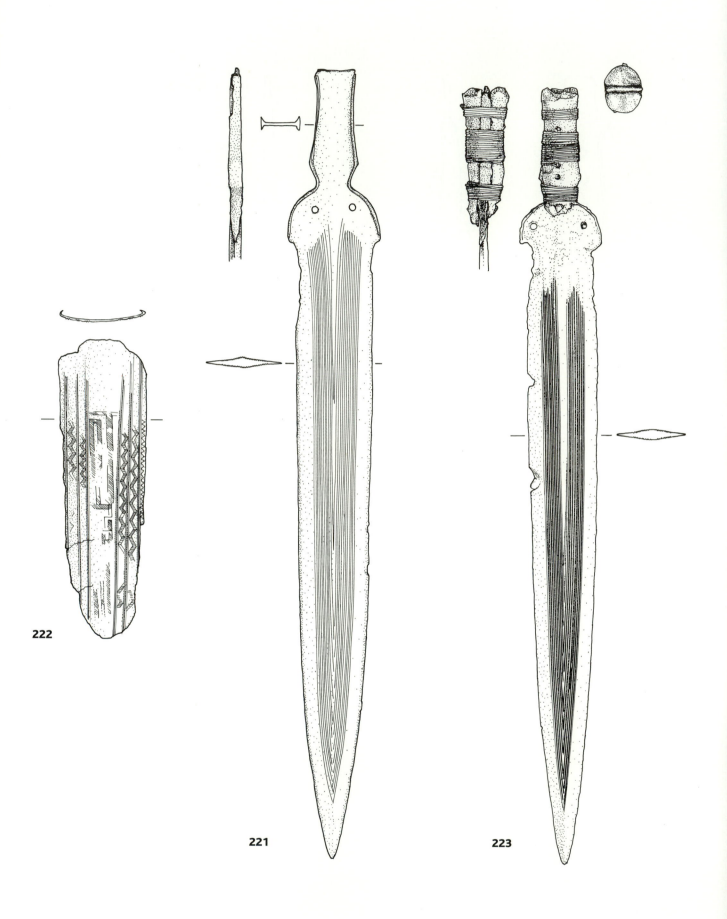

222

221

223

Plate 46   Swords type 5: - 221. Probably **Sheaths type 1**; - 222. **Swords type 5**: - 223.

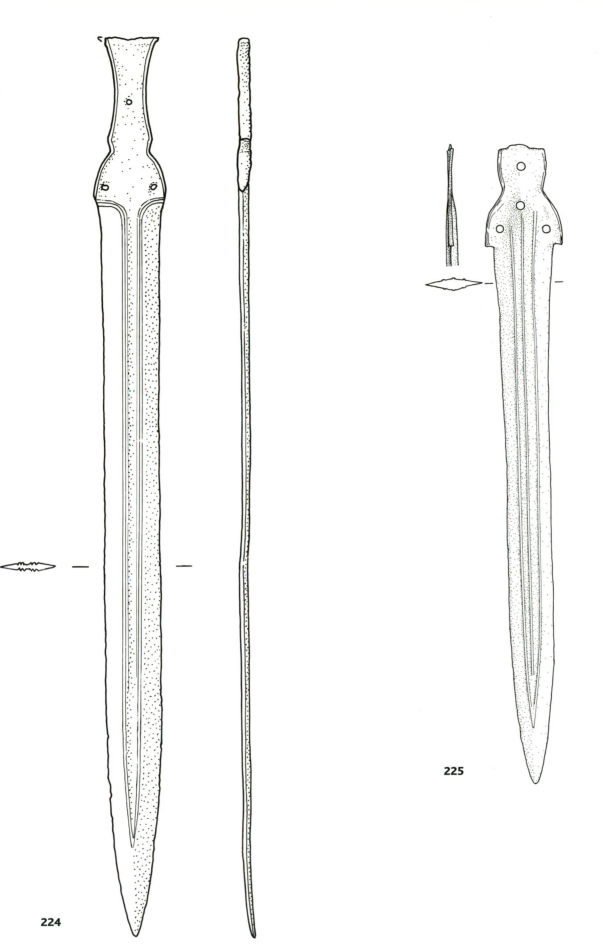

Plate 47   Swords type 5: - 224 near Perugia, Umbria. - 225.

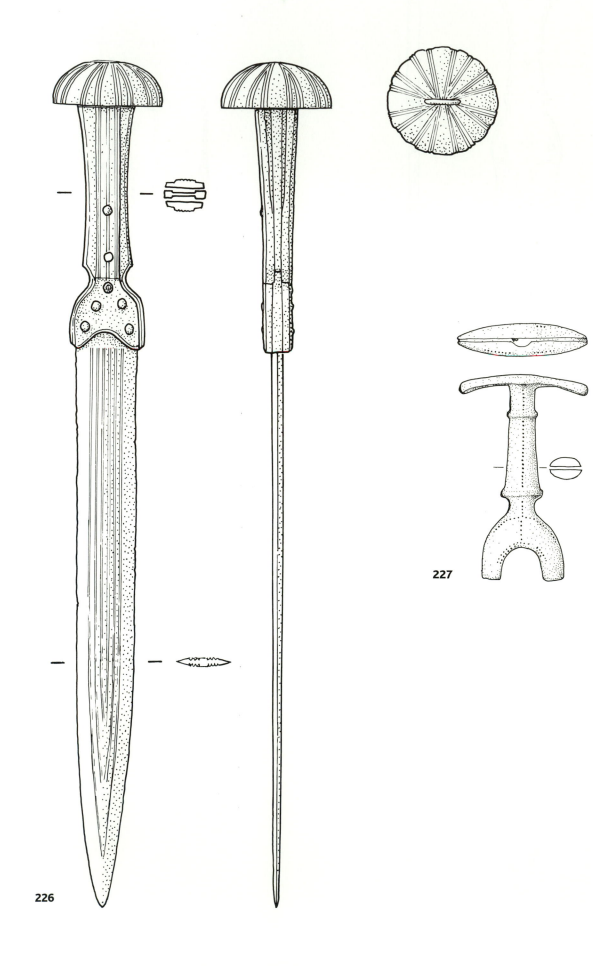

226

227

Plate 48 Close to **Swords type 5**: - 226. **Swords type 6**: - 227 Armento (Potenza), Basilicata.

229

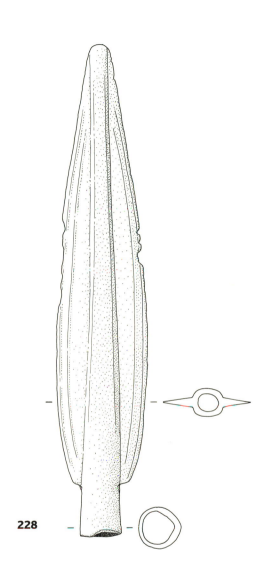

228

230

Plate 49   Spearheads type 1: - 228 River Tiber, Rome, Lazio. **Spearheads type 2**: - 229. - 230.

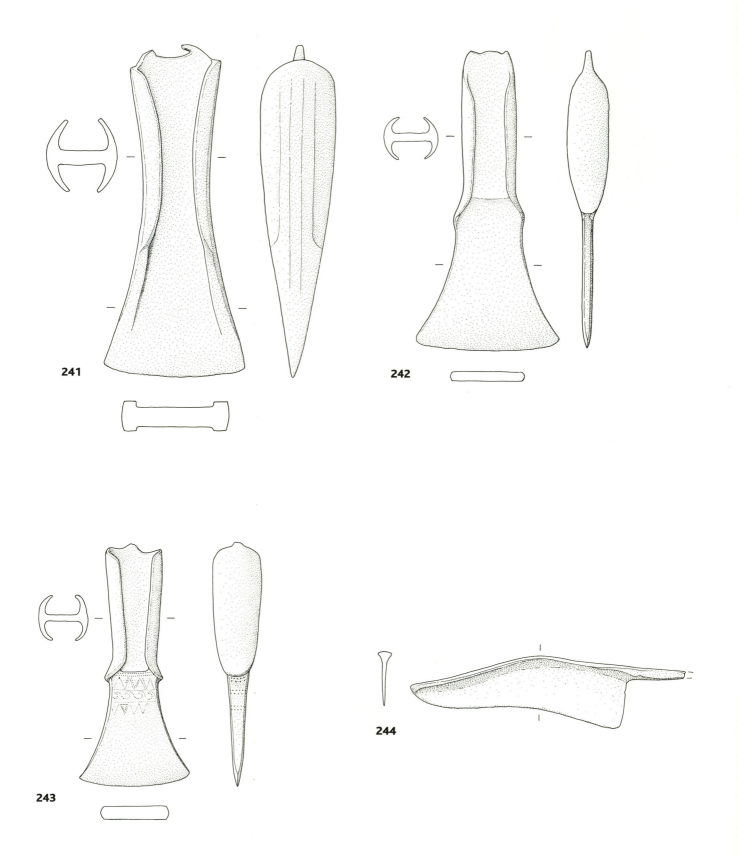

241

242

243

244

Plate 52   Group of associated artifacts, Lake Como, Lombardy. **Axes type 25**: - 241. Close to **Axes type 30**: - 242. - 243. **Knives type 1**: - 244.

Early Iron Age, Early

Axes

245.
PRB WG1070. Canon W. Greenwell Collection.
Given by J. Pierpont Morgan in 1909.
Rome, Lazio.
Winged axe with butt wings and blade with concave profiles. **Axes type 43.**
Short rounded butt, oval wings with side facets and flattened at junction with blade, low stop-ridge, protruding shoulders, blade with concave sides slightly raised in section, slightly curved cutting edge. Smooth green patina with black zones.
L. 16cm Weight 367g
See *PBF* IX. 12, nos. 3596, from Monte Reale (Mazzone, Bolzano), 3597, from Mezzolombardo (Trento), both in Trentino-Alto Adige. Type Mazzone.
EIA.

246.
PRB WG1097. Canon W. Greenwell Collection, bought from the Rev. Greville J. Chester. Given by J. Pierpont Morgan in 1909.
Mineo (Catania), Sicily.
Shaft-hole axe with hammered butt and wide irregular shaft-hole. **Axes type 50.**
Wide tool with parallel sides, slightly widening towards cutting edge, hammered butt, slightly curved cutting edge. Surface irregular. Dark green patina with light green zones.
L. 14.2cm Weight 1000g
No close parallels in *PBF* IX. 12, see no. 4373, hoard of Soleto (Lecce) Apulia. Type Crichi var. C, EIA.
Probably EIA.

247.
PRB 1935.10-18.32. Transferred from GR (1859.2-16.155). Bequeathed by Miss M.H.M. Auldjo.
Shaft-hole axe with angular hammered butt and continuous profile. **Axes type 51.** Elliptical shaft-hole, blade with slightly rounded cutting edge. Dull green patina with blackish zones.
L. 15cm Weight 612g
See *PBF* IX. 12, no. 4360, hoard of Manduria (Taranto), Apulia. Type Manduria.
EIA, early?
Bibliography: Walters 1899, no. 2942.

248.
PRB WG1096. Canon W. Greenwell Collection, bought from the Rev. Greville J. Chester. Given by J. Pierpont Morgan in 1909.
Capua (Caserta), Campania.
Shaft-hole axe with angular hammered butt and continuous profile. **Axes type 51.**
Haft-end separated from blade by a very slight step, oval shaft-hole, blade with marked bevel and slightly rounded cutting edge. Smooth

discontinuous patina in various tones of green.
L. 15.3cm Weight 705g
See *PBF* IX. 12, nos. 4360, hoard of Manduria (Taranto), Apulia, 4364, unprovenanced. Type Manduria.
EIA, early?

249.
PRB 1964.12-6.76. Bequeathed by C.T. Trechmann.
Calabria.
Shaft-hole axe with angular hammered butt and continuous profile. **Axes type 51.**
Oval shaft-hole, blade with slightly rounded cutting edge. Damaged surface covered with striations, probably ancient. Patina discontinuous in various tones of green. Small parts missing.
L.14.9cm Weight 788g
See *PBF* IX. 12, no. 4407, from Pertosa (Salerno), Campania. Type Ardea var. B.
EIA, early?

250.
PRB 1964.12-1.426 (371). Sir Henry Wellcome Collection, no. 113255. Bought in Rome from A. Rocci by Captain Saint in April 1932. Given by the Wellcome Trustees.
Socketed axe with continuous profile and rounded socket. **Axes type 54.**
Mouth almost circular in section, with raised double collar and lateral loop, broken in antiquity, short trapezoidal blade with slightly curved cutting edge. Decorated on both faces with multiple nervatures in the form of Vs. Smooth blackish patina with incrustations of earth. Cutting edge and body slightly damaged by hammering.
L. 13.1cm Weight 420g
See *PBF* IX. 12, nos. 3798–3820, hoards of Manduria (Taranto) and Soleto (Lecce), both in Apulia, and unknown locality. Type Manduria, var. H. This is a very distinctive Apulian type, not known elsewhere.
EIA.

251.
PRB 1964.12-1.212 (322). Sir Henry Wellcome Collection, no. 310. Bought in Rome from Arte Antica e Moderna by Captain Saint in November 1929. Given by the Wellcome Trustees.
Terni, Umbria.
Socketed axe with continuous profile and rounded socket. **Axes type 56.**
Small tool with concave sides, wide circular mouth with low collar and closed lateral loop, short blade with slightly rounded cutting edge. Dull dark green patina with brown earth incrustations.
L. 8.1cm Weight 187g
See *PBF* IX. 12, nos. 3759–3774, hoard of Manduria (Taranto), Apulia; see especially no.

3772. Type Manduria, var. C.
EIA, early?

252.
PRB WG1081. Canon W. Greenwell Collection.
Given by J. Pierpont Morgan in 1909.
Perugia, Umbria.
Socketed axe with separated blade and conical socket. **Axes type 60.**
Mouth with raised collar and square inner section, rounded socket base visible on upper blade, thin, slightly flaring blade with rounded shoulders and lateral protrusions and rounded cutting edge. Dull dark green patina with whitish incrustations.
L. 14.9cm Weight 368g
See *PBF* IX. 12, nos. 3899, from Cuma (Naples), Campania; 3900–3901, unprovenanced. Type Cuma.
EIA, early.

253.
PRB WG1082. Canon W. Greenwell Collection.
Given by J. Pierpont Morgan in 1909.
Near Rome, Lazio.
Socketed axe with separated blade and conical socket. **Axes type 60.**
Mouth with raised collar and square inner section, rounded socket base visible on upper blade, thin, trapezoidal blade with squared shoulders and lateral protrusions and slightly rounded cutting edge. Irregular patina in various tones of green.
L. 13.5cm Weight 280g
See **cat. 252.**
EIA, early?

254.
PRB 2000.1-1.36. Found unregistered.
Socketed axe with separated blade and conical socket. **Axes 60.**
Mouth with raised collar and oval inner section, rounded socket base visible on upper blade, thin, slightly flaring blade with rounded shoulders and lateral protrusions, almost straight cutting edge. Dull, dark green patina. Socket damaged and both socket and blade have parts missing.
L. 15cm Weight 312g
See **cat. 252.**
EIA, early?

Tools

255.
GR 1873.8-20.237. Bought from Alessandro Castellani.
Spindle with three discs set upon the shaft. **Spindles type 1.**
Rod with circular section, thickened in lower portion and slightly diminishing at upper end, discs of different size: a small one set upon the

lower end, a large and a small one upon the upper end. Incised decoration on discs and rod: on the upper faces of the discs, concentric rows of parallel oblique traits, hatched triangles and zigzag lines; on the rod, horizontal rows of chevrons, with two plain zigzag lines framing a central undecorated zone. Dull green patina.
L. 23cm Weight 101g
See *Pontecagnano* 1988, 73, pl. 23, type 46A1b. Phase IB to period II. See **cat. 256**.
Not identical: *Quattro Fontanili* 1967, 217, fig. 76.24, tomb Z 11-12.24, *Quattro Fontanili* 1986, 96, fig. 24, type XVIII, 1. Phase IIA-C.
EIA, early–late.
Bibliography: *BM Guide* 1920, 144, fig. 173 left.

256.
GR 1976.1-3.1. Found unregistered.
Spindle with two discs set upon the shaft.
Spindles type 2.
Thin rod, slightly diminishing at ends, discs of different size, with smaller one set upon lower end; rod with circular section, plain at ends, twisted between the discs. Incised decoration on the upper face of larger disc: two concentric rows of circles and hatched triangles. Traces of wear at middle and towards the lower end of the shaft. Dull green to brown patina.
L. 26.5cm Weight 56g
See *Pontecagnano* 1988, 73, pl. 23, type 46A1NC. Phase IB to period II; *Ibid.*: 95, footnote 288 for usage of spindles and for further references.
Not identical: *Quattro Fontanili* 1986, 96, fig. 24, type XVIII, 1. Phase IIA-C.
EIA early to late.
Bibliography: *BM Guide* 1920, 144, fig. 173 right.

Knives

257.
GR 1856.12-26.1088. Bequeathed by Sir William Temple.
Knife with serpentine blade and tang. **Knives type 5.**
Narrow elongated blade with slightly thickened back and a light T-shaped profile. Narrow tang with rectangular section. Small parts of cutting edge missing. Green patina with some corrosion.
L. 27.1cm Weight 101g
Close to *PBF* VII. 2, no. 320, from Cenna (San Marco dei Gavoti, Benevento), Campania. Type Piediluco var. B.
Probably EIA, early.
Bibliography: Walters 1899, no. 2755.

258.
GR 1975.7-30.20. Found unregistered.
Knife with wide serpentine blade and flat tang. **Knives type 6.**
Back of blade and tang with continuous markedly convex profile; blade with slightly thickened back. Tang almost entirely missing, with two small rivet-holes at junction with blade. The original position of the tang-plates is still visible on the butt of the blade. Small parts of cutting edge missing. Dull green patina with areas of corrosion.
L. 21cm Weight 70g
Close to *PBF* VII. 2, nos. 391, from Spezzano Calabro (Cosenza), and 392, from S. Onofrio (Roccella Ionica, Reggio Calabria), both in Calabria. Type Spezzano Calabro.
EIA, early.

Razors

259.
GR 1982.6-17.56. Received from PRB. Sir Henry Wellcome Collection, no. 5985. 40400 (also marked R. 12918. 1936). Ex Lovatt Collection 'Athens'. Bought at Sotheby's sale 17 April 1929, lot 174. Given by the Wellcome Trustees.
Athens, Greece.
Symmetrical razor. **Razors type 5.**
Ring handle of twisted wire, attached to the blade with small circular plates on either face and one rivet; narrow trapezoidal blade with rounded lower edge; parts of lateral and upper edges missing. Small circular hole at centre of upper part of blade. No decoration. Smooth green to brown patina.
L. 11.3cm Weight 30g
See *PBF* VIII. 2, no. 102, from Capua (Caserta), Campania. Type Capua.
EIA, early.

260.
PRB 1880.8-2.33. Given by Sir A.W. Franks. Probably obtained from A. Castellani.
Symmetrical razor. **Razors type 5.**
Ring handle of twisted wire, attached to the blade with a semicircular plate held by three rivets, rectangular blade slightly wider at the handle end, with straight upper edge interrupted by an opening into a wide circular hole; smaller hole at centre. Dark green patina with black incrustations.
L. 12cm Weight 35g
Close to *PBF* VIII. 2, nos. 105, and 107, from Vulci (Viterbo), Lazio. Type Capua.
EIA, early.

261.
GR 1865.7-20.51. Bought from C. Merlin.
Athens, Greece.
Symmetrical razor. **Razors type 6.**
Ring handle of twisted wire, attached to the blade with triangular plates on either face; wide trapezoidal blade with slightly rounded lower and lateral edges, almost straight upper edge. Three circular holes, one large and two small, at centre of the upper part of the blade. Incised decoration, principally visible on one face: bands of hatched triangles and multiple zigzag lines arranged in a semicircular area at the attachment of the handle, with a hatched meander band above. Cutting edges damaged. Bright areas of surface and green patina with some corrosion.
L. 14.5cm Weight 72g
See *PBF* VIII. 2, nos. 108, from Sala Consilina (Salerno), Campania; 109, 110; 111 from Bologna, Emilia Romagna. Type Savena.
EIA, early.
Bibliography: Walters 1899, no. 2420, fig. 74; Petrie 1917, pl. 60.6l; *BM Guide* 1920, 141, fig. 167.

262.
PRB 1880.8-2.32. Given by Sir A.W. Franks. Probably obtained from A. Castellani.
Symmetrical razor. **Razors type 6.**
Ring handle of twisted wire, attached to the blade with a semicircular plate held by three rivets, wide trapezoidal blade with slightly rounded lower and lateral edges, almost straight upper edge. Circular hole at centre of the upper part of the blade. Rough dark green patina with blackish incrustations. Handle distorted, blade edges damaged.
L. 13.4cm Weight 66g
See *PBF* VIII. 2, nos. 108, from Sala Consilina (Salerno), Campania, 112, from Tarquinia (Viterbo), Lazio. Type Savena.
EIA, early.

263.
GR 1839.11-9.45. Bought from C. Campanari.
Symmetrical razor. **Razors type 6.**
Ring handle of twisted wire, attached to the blade with triangular plates on either face and two rivets; wide trapezoidal blade with slightly rounded lower edge; parts of lateral and upper edges missing. Large circular hole at centre of upper part of blade, surrounded by two lightly incised lines on both faces of blade. Green patina with some corrosion and much incrustation.
L. 12.3cm Weight 78g
See *PBF* VIII. 2, no. 112, from Tarquinia (Viterbo), Lazio. Type Savena.
EIA, early.
Bibliography: Walters 1899, no. 2421.

264.
GR 1867.5-8.382. Blacas Collection.
Symmetrical razor, miniature. **Razors type 7.**
Flat bronze sheet, cut in one piece. Semicircular handle with central hole; part of blade missing. Surface of blade scratched. Dull green patina.
L. 4.5cm Weight 5g
Close to *PBF* VIII. 2, nos. 243, from Villa Cavalletti (Grottaferrata, Rome), 245, from Castel Gandolfo (Rome), both in Lazio, 'Rasoi bitaglienti in miniatura'.
FBA–EIA.

265.
PRB 1880.8-2.29. Given by Sir A.W. Franks. Probably obtained from A. Castellani.
Symmetrical razor. **Razors type 8.**
Ring handle of bronze wire with rectangular section, partly missing, attached to the blade with a small circular plate, irregular rectangular blade with slightly rounded angles, three small circular holes below the upper edge. Dull green patina. Blade damaged.
L. 7.8cm Weight 11g
See *PBF* VIII. 2, nos. 163, 164, from Castiglione di Paludi (Cosenza), Calabria. Type Spezzano Calabro.
EIA.

266.
PRB 1880.8-2.35. Given by Sir A.W. Franks. Probably obtained from A. Castellani. Lunate razor. **Razors 10.**
Cast ring handle with two elongated protrusions on outer side of ring; blade with slightly thickened back, straight edge in correspondence with the handle and curved cutting edge ending in an angle; profile of blade back slightly concave towards the point and straight towards the handle, where it ends in a right angle. Two small holes (one open) near the back of the blade. Smooth dark green patina. Small parts missing.
L. 11.4cm Width 3.8cm max. Weight 26g
Close to *PBF* VIII. 2, no. 408, from Cerveteri (Rome), Lazio. Type Tarquinia.
EIA, early.

267.
GR 1935.8-23.54. Transferred from the Department of British and Medieval Antiquities (1880. 8-2.36). Given by Sir A.W. Franks. Probably obtained from A. Castellani.
Lunate razor. **Razors type 11.**
Cast ring handle. Shallow blade, flat in section; back with concave profile, interrupted by an angled spur and probably once straightened and ending in a right angle towards handle. Circular hole at centre of blade. Small parts missing; some scratches on surface. No decoration. Dull green patina.
L. 12cm Weight 24g
See *PBF* VIII. 2, no. 573, from Tarquinia (Viterbo), Lazio. Type Vulci var.A.
EIA, early.

268.
GR 1838.6-8.80. Bought from C. Campanari.
Lunate razor. **Razors type 11.**
Cast handle broken. Shallow blade, flat in section; back with concave profile, interrupted by an angled spur, straightened and ending in a right angle towards handle. Blade distorted; parts of cutting edge missing. No decoration. Dark green patina.
L. 12.3cm Weight 35g
See *PBF* VIII. 2, no. 384, from Bologna, Emilia Romagna, type 'Tarquinia con sperone laminare'; no. 574, from Bologna, type Vulci var.A.
EIA, early.

269.
GR 1982.6-17.58. Received from PRB. Sir Henry Wellcome Collection, no. 89163 (also marked R1801/1937). Bought in Rome from Antichità delle Belle Arti in October 1930. Given by the Wellcome Trustees.
Rome, Lazio.
Lunate razor, miniature. **Razors type 11.**
Bronze sheet, cut in one piece. Ring handle. Shallow blade with slightly thickened back; back with concave profile, ending towards the handle in a truncated angle with a V-shaped opening; tip of blade missing. Cutting edge damaged; surface of blade scratched. Light green patina.
L. 6.6cm Weight 2g
Close to *PBF* VIII. 2, nos. 613, 617, from Bisenzio (Viterbo), Lazio. 'Rasoi lunati in miniatura'; *Osteria dell'Osa* 1992, 402, pl. 42, type 62a, phase IIA.
There is a good correspondence between the specific characteristics of this piece and the indications of its provenance.
EIA, early.

270.
GR 1935.8-23.59. Transferred from the Department of British and Medieval Antiquities. Canon W. Greenwell Collection, no. 1142, bought from the Rev. Greville J. Chester. Given by J. Pierpont Morgan in 1909. Etruria (Tuscany or northern Lazio).
Lunate razor. **Razors type 12.**
Handle missing but once attached by rivets; two rivet holes at butt of blade with one rivet surviving. Wide blade, flat in section; back with concave profile, interrupted by an angled spur and straightened towards butt of blade. Cutting edge damaged. No decoration. Dull green patina with incrustations.

L. 7.7cm Weight 18g
See *PBF* VIII. 2, nos. 314, from central Italy, 315, from Tarquinia (Viterbo), Lazio. Type Sirolo-Numana var. B.
EIA.

271.
GR 1975.7-10.1A and 1B. Found unregistered.
Two fragments from a lunate razor. **Razors type 13.**
Cast ring handle with two straight protrusions at outer side of ring. Back of blade slightly thickened, with concave profile interrupted by a markedly raised knob, straightened and ending with a right angle towards the handle. Finely incised decoration on both faces: row of hatched triangles and band of hatched meander elements between double lines along the back of the blade; traces of decoration on the blade. Green patina with some shiny areas.
L. 9.5cm surviving. Weight 20g
See *PBF* VIII. 2, no. 484, from Bologna, Emilia Romagna. Type Fermo, var. A.
EIA.

Ornaments

272.
GR 1772.3-7.316. Bought from Sir William Hamilton.
Pin-head in the form of a spoked wheel. **Pins type 8.**
Wheel with eight beams meeting at right angles and conical socket. Dull brownish patina.
Diam. 3.5cm Weight 13g
Close to *PBF* XIII. 2, nos. 2744 from Vulci (Viterbo), Lazio, with polygonal profile, and 2746 from Este (Padova), Veneto. Type Vulci.
EIA, early or later.

273.
GR 1994.8-3.9. Transferred from PRB.
Hair-ring of double wire with undulating ends. **Hair rings type 1.**
Very fine wire, rounded in section, doubled and twisted into a coil and a half with further undulating ends. Dull green patina.
Diam. 4.5cm Weight 8g
Hair-rings of this type are known from several Iron Age cemeteries over the whole Italian territory.
See for parallels *Osteria dell'Osa* 1992, 388, pl. 40, type 47a. Period II.
EIA, early.

274.
GR 1856.12-26.716. Bequeathed by Sir William Temple.
Ruvo (Bari), Apulia.
Spectacle pendant. **Pendants type 1.**
Two coils of wire, diminishing in thickness at the centre, linked by a suspension loop. Dull green patina.
L. 13.6cm Weight 163g
Coiled pendants of this simple form are known from BA and EIA contexts.
See *Dizionari Terminologici* 1980, 102, pl. 81.2, from Allumiere (Rome), Lazio. FBA; Marzocchella 2004, fig. 1, Carinaro (Caserta), Campania, tomb 12, FBA, late; Johannowsky 1983, 108-111, pls. 4b, left, and XVI.18, Capua (Caserta), Campania, tomb 253. Phase IIA; *Pontecagnano* 1988, 67, type 40E1, fig. 153.10,

tomb 2057. Phase IB.
Probably EIA, early or later.

275.
GR 1878.10-19.249. Given by General A.W.H. Meyrick.
Pendant or bead (*saltaleone*), cylindrical. **Unclassified.**
Tightly coiled wire of plano-convex section forming a tube of equal diameter throughout length. Dull green patina.
L. 8cm Weight 16g
Similar simple ornaments are known from several Italian contexts through the IA and later. For the cylindrical type see *Pontecagnano* 1988, 65, pl. 21, type 37E1a,b. Phase IB to period II; *Osteria dell'Osa* 1992, 422–423, pl. 45, type 88 l. Periods II-III.
For the conical type, see **cat. 817,5c,6b,8d and 8g.**
EIA, early or later.

276.
GR 1856.12-26.734. Bequeathed by Sir William Temple.
Rod torque with flattened coiled ends. **Torques type 1.**
Thin rod with square section; ends hammered to a thick ribbon, with tightly coiled butts. Closely incised spiral grooves on whole surface of rod. Six cast solid rings with thick triangular section (3.4cm max. diameter: weight 12–21g each), attached. Patina in different shades of green with whitish incrustations. Brown incrustations on rings.
Diam. 12.5cm max. Weight: torque 56g Total 172g
Close to Peroni 1987, 104f., fig. 88.8, 12, from Castellace (Oppido Mamertina, Reggio Calabria), Calabria. FBA, late?
See also *Torre Galli* 1999, 31ff., fig. 6.1, sporadic, cemetery at contrada La Rota. Phase IIA.
For the rings, see Buffa 1994, pl. 158.8-11, Torre Mordillo (Cosenza), Calabria, tomb CLX; Müller-Karpe 1962, pl. 6.10, 14, 15, Rome, Esquilino cemetery. Phase IIB; *Osteria dell'Osa* 1992, 385, pl. 39, type 46e. Phase IIA-IIB.
EIA, early or later.

277.
GR 1975.7-12.35. Transferred from PRB, July 1975. Sir Henry Wellcome Collection. Given by the Wellcome Trustees.
Cuma (Naples), Campania.
Rod torque with flattened ends. **Torques type 1.**
Thin rod with circular section, ends flattened with terminal coils missing. Tightly incised oblique grooves on the whole surface. Dull light green patina with incrustations.
Diam. 11cm max. Weight 26g
See **cat. 276.**
Probably EIA, early or later.

Fibulae

278.
GR 1867.5-8.172. Blacas Collection.
Thickened and slightly stilted arch fibula with symmetrical catch-plate. **Fibulae type 7.**
Semicircular arch, slightly asymmetrical, thickened and slightly bent in the central part; one-coiled spring, pin and catch-plate partly

missing. Dark green patina with some corrosion.

L. 4.6cm Weight 6g

Some features of this fibula, such as the raised, slightly asymmetrical arch and the large spring with circular section probably indicate a date slightly earlier than the other pieces in this group (**Fibulae type** 7). See Bietti Sestieri 1986, 8, for discussion and references.

EIA, early or FBA–EIA transition.

Bibliography: Bietti Sestieri 1986, 'Fibulae', 8, no. 16, and fig. p. 21; Bartoloni 1986, 235, fig. 3b.

279.

PRB 1964.12-6.117. Bequeathed by C.T. Trechmann.

Belgrade, Serbia. **Fibulae type** 7.

Thickened arch fibula with symmetrical catch-plate.

Large catch-plate, partly missing, raised bow with central part markedly thickened, large one-coiled spring and straight pin. Deeply incised decoration on whole surface of bow: longitudinal chevrons and a band with reticulate pattern at each end, band with reticulate pattern at centre, bands of chevrons on the remaining surface, all separated by groups of incised parallel lines. Small parts missing. Rough dark green discontinuous patina with corroded zones.

L. 9.8cm Weight 93g

See *Osteria dell'Osa* 1992, 356, pl. 33, type ip15 (decoration), 358, pl. 36, type 38d, phase IIA.

PBF XIV, forthcoming, X (62), no. 595, from Vicari (Palermo), Sicily, 'Fibule ad arco ingrossato e rialzato, tipo Cuma Osta'.

Possibly an import from Lazio.

EIA, early.

280.

GR 1922.4-13.39. Given by E. Sanders.

Thickened arch fibula with symmetrical catch-plate. **Fibulae type** 7.

Large catch-plate, bow thickening in central part, large one-coiled spring.Incised decoration: deeply incised encircling lines, incised chevrons and a hatched band at each end of the bow; incised parallel and zigzag lines along the edge of the catch-plate. Small parts missing. Shiny brown patina.

L. 9.2cm Weight 60g

Analysis: Bronze. See D. Hook report.

See *Osteria dell'Osa* 1992, 356, pl. 33, type ip15 (decoration), 358, pl. 36, type 38d, phase IIA.

Torre Galli 1999, 131, fig. 35, type Ob15, phase IA. *PBF* XIV, forthcoming, see **cat. 279.**

EIA, early.

Bibliography: Bietti Sestieri 1986, 'Fibulae', 8, no. 18, and fig. p. 21.

281.

PRB 2000.1-1.2. P. Curwen Britton 1910, 3.

Thickened arch fibula with symmetrical catch-plate. **Fibulae type** 7.

Small catch-plate, mostly missing, bow with central part slightly thickened, small two-coiled spring and straight pin, slightly bent at centre. Incised decoration: groups of encircling parallel lines and chevrons on the whole surface of the bow. Dull patina in various tones of green.

L. 6cm Weight 17g

See *Osteria dell'Osa* 1992, 360–61, pl. 36, type 38k, phase IIA to period III.

Quattro Fontanili 1986, 78, fig. 19, type I.5, phases IC-IIA.

PBF XIV, forthcoming, X (59 var.b), no. 556, from Cuma (Naples), Campania, tomb 4 Osta, 'Fibule ad arco ingrossato leggermente ribassato, decorato con motivi a spina di pesce'.

EIA, early–late.

282.

PRB 1964.12-1.510(210). Sir Henry Wellcome Collection. Given by the Wellcome Trustees. Previous Registration stated 'possibly from Zurich' but the source of this information is not known.

Thickened arch fibula with symmetrical catch-plate. **Fibulae type** 7.

Small catch-plate, partly missing, bow with central part slightly thickened, two-coiled spring with rectangular section at joint with bow, and straight pin. Incised decoration: groups of encircling parallel lines and chevrons on whole surface of bow. Smooth patina, dark green.

L. 6.3cm Weight 23g

See **cat. 281.**

EIA, early–late.

283.

GR 1976.2-8.5. Found unregistered.

Thickened arch fibula with symmetrical catch-plate. **Fibulae type** 7.

Semicircular arch, thickened at centre, one coil spring with square section, symmetrical foot. Undecorated. Smooth green patina.

L. 4.5cm Weight 10g

See *Osteria dell'Osa* 1992, 360–61, pl. 36, type 38k, phase IIA to period III.

PBF XIV, forthcoming, XIII (86), 'Fibule piccole ad arco leggermente ingrossato ed inornato'. (86), no. 1269, from the cemetery of Sala Consilina (Salerno), Campania, tomb S. Antonio 68.

EIA, early–late.

Bibliography: Bietti Sestieri 1986, 'Fibulae', 8, no. 17, and fig. p. 21.

284.

GR 1772.3-9.71. Bought from Sir William Hamilton.

Thickened arch fibula with wide symmetrical catch-plate. **Fibulae type** 8.

Low and wide catch-plate, raised bow slightly narrowing at ends, small two-coiled spring. Incised decoration on the whole surface of the bow: groups of transverse parallel lines and dots. Small parts missing. Smooth green patina.

L. 8.7cm Weight 43g

See *Cuma* 1913, col. 87, pl. 20.1, from the pre-Hellenic cemetery.

Müller-Karpe 1959, pls. 17B.11; 18B.1,2, 14; 19A.21, Cuma, Osta graves 4, 7 and 36. *PBF* XIV, forthcoming, X (64b), no. 625, from Suessula (Sessa Aurunca, Caserta), Campania, 'Fibule ad arco ingrossato a tutto sesto, con fitta decorazione incisa'.

The main typological features of these fibulae indicate a provenance from Campania, probably from a fossa-grave context.

EIA, early–late.

Bibliography: Walters 1899, no. 2002; Bietti Sestieri 1986, 'Fibulae', 9, no. 24, and fig. p. 21.

285.

GR 1814.7-4.250. Charles Townley Collection. Bought from Peregrine Townley.

Thickened arch fibula with large symmetrical catch-plate. **Fibulae type** 8.

Low and wide catch-plate, partly missing; raised bow slightly narrowing at ends, large two-coiled spring. Incised decoration: the whole surface of the bow is covered with double oblique lines separating hatched areas. Dark green patina with some corrosion.

L. 17.8cm Weight 293g

See **cat. 284** for references. Also Müller-Karpe 1959, pl. 19A.21 (general shape), Cuma (Naples), Campania, Osta grave 36.

PBF XIV, forthcoming, X (64) A, no. 624, Archaeological Museum of Palermo (Sicily), 'Fibule ad arco ingrossato a tutto sesto, con fitta decorazione incisa'.

EIA, early–late.

Bibliography: Walters 1899, no. 1998; Bietti Sestieri 1986, 'Fibulae', 9, no. 23, fig. p. 21.

286.

GR 1772.3-9.72. Bought from Sir William Hamilton.

Thickened arch fibula with large symmetrical catch-plate. **Fibulae type** 9.

Large catch-plate, partly missing, bow slightly lowered and thickened in central part, large two-coiled spring; pin missing. Incised decoration: groups of encircling lines and chevrons on the whole surface of the bow. Smooth green patina.

L. 11cm Weight 56g

See for the type in general Müller-Karpe 1959, pls. 16–19, fibulae with lowered bow and large symmetrical catch-plate from Cuma (Naples), Campania, Osta graves.

Close parallel: Johannowsky 1983, 102 and pl. XI.14; Capua (Caserta), Campania, tomb 930, EIA, late.

PBF XIV, forthcoming, X (64) C, no. 675, from Suessula (Sessa Aurunca, Caserta), Campania, 'Altre fibule ad arco ingrossato e ribassato, dalla Campania'.

Also *Osteria dell'Osa* 1992, 360, pl. 36, type 38i var.I, period II.

Quattro Fontanili 1986, 78, fig. 19, type I 6, phases IC-IIA.

This is a specific Campanian type of EIA date; the resemblances to fibulae of slightly earlier date from Lazio and Etruria depend on the fact that the type belongs to the class of thickened arch fibulae, dating mainly from EIA, early.

EIA, early–late.

287.

GR 1976.2-5.6. Found unregistered.

Thickened and lowered arch fibula with large symmetrical catch-plates. **Fibulae type** 9.

Low and wide catch-plate, partly missing; low bow with central part thickened, large two-coiled spring. Deeply incised decoration: encircling parallel lines on the whole surface of the bow. Dark green patina.

L. 14.2cm Weight 170g

See **cat. 286** for general parallels and references.

Close parallels: *Cuma* 1913, cols. 72 and 135, pl. 19.3: Stevens collection, no. 45.

PBF XIV, forthcoming, X (59) B, no. 556, from Suessula (Sessa Aurunca, Caserta), Campania, 'Fibule ad arco ingrossato leggermente ribassato'.

EIA, early–late.
Bibliography: Walters 1899, no. 2000; Bietti Sestieri 1986, 'Fibulae', 9, no. 21, and fig. p. 21.

288.
GR 1772.3-9.44. Bought from Sir William Hamilton.
Thickened and lowered arch fibula with large symmetrical catch-plate. **Fibulae type 9**.
Low and wide catch-plate; low bow with central part thickened, large two-coiled spring. Deeply incised decoration: encircling parallel lines on each side of the bow, and double oblique lines and hatched bands in the central section. Small parts and pin missing. Dull green patina.
L. 16.5cm Weight 168g
See **cat. 286** for general parallels and references.
PBF XIV, forthcoming, X (61)B, no. 570, from Capua (Caserta), Campania, 'Fibule ad arco ingrossato leggermente ribassato, decorato con sottili costolature, tipo Anfiteatro Campano'.
EIA, early–late.
Bibliography: Walters 1899, no. 1997; Bietti Sestieri 1986, 'Fibulae', 9, no. 22, and fig. p. 21.

289.
GR 1975.7-12.36. Transferred from PRB, July 1975. Sir Henry Wellcome Collection, 165919. Bought at Sotheby's 17 February 1931, lot 551. Given by the Wellcome Trustees.
Thickened and slightly lowered arch fibula with symmetrical catch-plate. **Fibulae type 10**.
Small catch-plate, partly missing, bow slightly thickened in central zone, spring and pin missing. Incised decoration: groups of encircling lines and chevrons on the whole surface of bow. Heavy corrosion and incrustation.
L. 7.4cm Weight 24g
See in general *Osteria dell'Osa* 1992, 362, pl. 36, type 38n, periods I I-III.
Quattro Fontanili 1986, 78, fig. 19, type I 6, phases IC-IIA.
PBF XIV, forthcoming, X (59) B, no. 555, from Capua (Caserta), Campania, 'Fibule ad arco ingrossato leggermente ribassato, decorato con motivi a spina di pesce'.
EIA, early–late.

290.
GR 1824.4-34.10. Bequeathed by R. Payne Knight.
Thickened and lowered arch fibula with symmetrical catch-plate. **Fibulae type 10**.
Small catch-plate partly missing; low bow with central part thickened, small two-coiled spring. Incised decoration: groups of encircling parallel lines and chevrons on the whole surface of bow. Smooth green patina.
L. 6cm Weight 26g
See **cat. 289** for parallels and references.
Also *PBF* XIV, forthcoming, XIII (78) B, no. 797, from Sala Consilina (Salerno), Campania, tomb A101, 'Piccole fibule ad arco ingrossato con decorazione a spina di pesce'.
EIA, early–late.
Bibliography: Walters 1899, no. 1992; Bietti Sestieri 1986, 'Fibulae', 9, no. 26, and fig. p. 22.

291.
GR 1920.11-18.6. Given by the Committee of the Guildhall Museum.
Thickened and lowered arch fibula with symmetrical catch-plate. **Fibulae type 10**.
Catch-plate partly missing; low bow with central part thickened, small two-coiled spring and small symmetrical catch-plate. Incised decoration: encircling parallel lines on the whole surface of the bow, with a superimposed pattern of double oblique lines. Pin broken. Dull green patina.
L. 5.7cm Weight 14g
See **cat. 289** for parallels and references. Also *PBF* XIV, forthcoming, XIII (86) B, no. 1338, unprovenanced, Museum of Palermo (Sicily), 'Altre piccole fibule ad arco ingrossato'.
EIA, early–late.
Bibliography: Bietti Sestieri 1986, 'Fibulae', 10, no. 33, and fig. p. 22.

292.
GR 1976.2-8.6. Found unregistered.
Thickened and lowered arch fibula with symmetrical catch-plate. **Fibulae type 10**.
Bow thickened in central part and round in section. Small catch-plate and two-coiled spring, broken; pin missing. Dull green patina.
L. 6.3cm Weight 24g
See **cat. 289** for parallels and references.
EIA, early–late.
Bibliography: Bietti Sestieri 1986, 'Fibulae', 9, no. 29, and fig. p. 22.

293.
GR 1867.5-8.171. Blacas Collection.
Thickened and lowered arch fibula with symmetrical catch-plate. **Fibulae type 11**.
Small catch-plate, slightly lowered bow with central part thickened, small two-coiled spring and slightly curved pin. Incised decoration: groups of encircling parallel lines and chevrons on the whole surface of the bow. Smooth green patina.
L. 5.6cm Weight 14g
See in general *Osteria dell'Osa* 1992, 362, pl. 36, types 38n, 38o, 38p, phase IIB to period III.
PBF XIV, forthcoming, XIII (78) B, no. 797, from Sala Consilina (Salerno), Campania, tomb A101, 'Piccole fibule ad arco ingrossato con decorazione a spina di pesce'.
Quattro Fontanili 1986, 78, fig. 19, type I 7, phases IC-IIA (close parallel).
EIA, early–late transition.
Bibliography: Walters 1899, no. 1993; Bietti Sestieri 1986, 'Fibulae', 9, no. 27, and fig. p. 22.

294.
GR 2001.3-30.1. Found with incorrect Registration number, and re-registered in 2001.
Thickened and lowered arch fibula with symmetrical catch-plate. **Fibulae type 11**.
Small catch-plate; slightly lowered and thickened bow. Incised decoration whole surface of bow: transverse parallel lines and two bands filled with chevrons. Two-coiled spring. Dull green patina.
L. 5.7cm Weight 16g
See **cat. 293**.
EIA, early–late transition.
Bibliography: Bietti Sestieri 1986, 'Fibulae', 10, no. 31 with incorrect Registration number, and fig. p. 22.

295.
GR 1920.11-18.5. Given by the Committee of the Guildhall Museum.
Said to be from the Rhineland.
Thickened and lowered arch fibula with wide symmetrical catch-plate. Close to **Fibulae type 11**.
Low and wide catch-plate, thick and slightly lowered bow, two-coiled spring. Incised decoration on the whole surface of bow: groups of encircling parallel lines except for six thin zones. Pin and catch-plate broken. Smooth green patina.
L. 8cm Weight 68g
See **cat. 293**; also *PBF* XIV, forthcoming, XIII (85) A, no. 1253, from Sala Consilina (Salerno), Campania, tomb S. Antonio 68, 'Fibule ad arco ingrossato e ribassato con decorazione a fasce di linee incise, tipo S. Nicola'.
EIA, early–late transition?
Bibliography: Bietti Sestieri 1986, 'Fibulae', 10, no. 32, and fig. p. 22.

296.
GR 1920.11-18.4. Given by the Committee of the Guildhall Museum.
Thickened and lowered arch fibula with symmetrical catch-plate. **Fibulae type 11**.
Large catch-plate, partly missing. Bow thickened and slightly lowered. Incised decoration on bow: groups of transverse parallel lines between plain areas. Two-coiled spring; pin broken. Dull green patina with areas of corrosion.
L. 5.7cm Weight 28g
Close to *Osteria dell'Osa* 1992, 362, pl.36, type 380, phase IIB.
PBF XIV, forthcoming, XIII (85) B, no. 1248, from Sala Consilina (Salerno), Campania, tomb S. Nicola 10, 'Fibule ad arco ingrossato e ribassato, con decorazione a fasci di linee incisi, tipo S. Nicola'.
EIA, early–late transition.
Bibliography: Bietti Sestieri 1986, 'Fibulae', 9, no. 30 with incorrect Registration number, and fig. p. 22.

297.
PRB BM.23. Bowsfield Collection, 1865.
? England.
Thickened and lowered arch fibula with symmetrical catch-plate. **Fibulae type 11**.
Catch-plate and pin broken, slightly lowered bow with central part thickened, three-coiled spring, probably restored in antiquity, and straight pin. Surface corroded in various tones of green.
L. 9cm Weight 54g
See **cat. 293**.
Also *Osteria dell'Osa* 1992, 362, pl. 36, type 38n, phase IIB to period III.
EIA, early–late transition.
Bibliography: Hull and Hawkes 1987, 16, no. 7318, pl. 3.

298.
GR 1814.7-4.249. Charles Townley Collection. Bought from Peregrine Townley.
Thickened arch/leech fibula with large symmetrical catch-plate. **Fibulae type 12a**.
Low and wide catch-plate, thick raised bow, two-coiled spring. Incised decoration on bow: groups of transverse parallel lines, dots, chevrons in central part. Lower face

pattern along the edge. Small parts missing. Smooth green patina with some corrosion.
L. 13.5cm Weight 76g
See *Pontecagnano* 1988, 55, pl.19, 103ff., fig. I.18, type 32B18a, phase IA.
PBF XIV, forthcoming, XVII. 2 (106a), no. 1440 (with transverse bar above disc), Sala Consilina (Salerno), Campania, tomb A302 (Kilian 1970, pl. 87.II.3a), 'Fibule ad arco rivestito da dischi di lamina e staffa a disco intagliato o a disco'.
EIA, early.

318.
GR 1856.12-26.898. Bequeathed by Sir William Temple.
Ruvo, (Bari), Apulia.
Leech-shaped fibula, bow formed of graduated discs, with terminal disc missing. **Fibulae type 37.**
Catch-plate broken and mended with two rivets in antiquity; catch-plate now detached from bow and has a Roman medallion attached. Thin sheet discs of bronze threaded on bow, probably square in section. Two-coiled spring. Patina: dark green (bow), green (catch-plate).
L. 12.7cm Weight 98g (bow). 38g (catch-plate and medallion).
See *PBF* XIV, forthcoming, XVII. 2 (107), nos. 1460, 1461, Sala Consilina (Salerno), Campania, tomb A256 (Kilian 1970, pl. 75.II.4a), 'Fibule ad arco rivestito da dischi di lamina, con contorno passante alla sanguisuga e staffa a disco'.
Pontecagnano 1988, 55, pl. 19, 103ff, fig. L-M.34, type 32B19; disc solid. Phase IB.
This is a well-known Villanovan type.
EIA, early.
Bibliography: Walters 1899, no. 1973.

319.
GR 1976.2-5.9. Found unregistered.
Serpentine fibula with two coils and terminal disc of spiral sheet. **Fibulae type 39.**
Large disc; bow with straight front portion, forming a small coil above the catch-plate and a pronounced curve in the upper part; very large one-coiled spring and straight pin. Incised decoration of encircling lines on the whole surface of bow. Small parts missing. Smooth green to brown patina.
L. 15cm Weight 56g
See *PBF* XIV, forthcoming, XXXVII. 1, (313), no. 5416, from Capua (Caserta), Campania, not identical.
Pontecagnano 1988, 51–52, pl. 18, 103, fig. I.B and 3, types 32B2, 32B3, phase IA.
Torre Galli 1999, fig. 10, type Od2, phase IA.
EIA, early.
Bibliography: Walters 1899, no. 2022, fig. 35; *BM Guide* 1920, 132, fig. 148; Bietti Sestieri 1986, 'Fibulae', 7, no. 9, and fig. p. 20.

320.
GR 1772.3-9.40. Bought from Sir William Hamilton.
Serpentine fibula with terminal disc of spiral sheet. **Fibulae type 39.**
Small disc, bow with triangular contour with small coil above catch-plate and a curve in the upper part, which is round in section. Large one-coiled spring, pin missing. Smooth light green patina.
L. 10cm Weight 21g
See **cat. 319.**

EIA, early.
Bibliography: Walters 1899, no. 2023; Bietti Sestieri 1986, 'Fibulae', 7, no. 7, and fig. p. 20.

321.
GR 1865.11-18.153. Given by George Witt.
Serpentine fibula with two coils and terminal disc. **Fibulae type 39.**
Large disc, missing; bow with straight front portion, forming a small coil above the catch-plate and a pronounced curve in the upper part; very large one-coiled spring and straight pin. Incised decoration of encircling lines on the whole surface of bow. Dull green to brown patina.
L. 7.5cm Weight 14g
See **cat. 319.**
EIA, early.
Bibliography: Bietti Sestieri 1986, 'Fibulae', 7, no. 8, and fig. p. 20.

322.
GR 1915.12-28.1. Anonymous donation.
Serpentine fibula with two coils and terminal disc. **Fibulae type 39.**
Disc missing; bow with straight front portion, forming a small coil above the catch-plate and a slight curve in the upper part; very large one-coiled spring with square section, and straight pin. Incised decoration of encircling chevrons on the whole surface of bow. Dull green patina.
L. 6.8cm Weight 16g
See **cat. 319.**
EIA, early.
Bibliography: Bietti Sestieri 1986, 'Fibulae', 7, no. 10, and fig. p. 20.

323.
GR 1890.5-12.13. Bought from the Rev. Greville J. Chester.
Found near Rome.
Serpentine fibula with three loops and terminal disc of spiral sheet. **Fibulae type 40.**
Small disc of sheet bronze, low bow of thin wire forming three small loops with four, three and two coils respectively; pin slightly curved. Five beads threaded on the pin, three of blue-green glass-paste, two of amber. Dull green patina with some corrosion.
L. 5.9cm Weight 5g
See for a close parallel *PBF* XIV, forthcoming, XLII (363.2), no. 6646, cemetery of S. Marzano (Salerno), Campania, tomb 245, 'Fibule serpeggianti con tre occhielli e staffa a disco-spirale'.
Gastaldi 1979, 30, fig. 7, type B1 (cemeteries of the Sarno Valley, Campania). EIA, early.
Pontecagnano 1988, 53, pl.18, 103, fig. I.C, type 32B8 (not identical), phase IA.
EIA, early.
Bibliography: Walters 1899, no. 2028; Strong 1966, 60, no. 32, pl.13; Bietti Sestieri 1986, 'Fibulae', 11, no. 45, and fig.p.23

324.
GR 1824.4-34.41. Bequeathed by R. Payne Knight.
Serpentine fibula with curved pin, large spring and terminal disc of spiral sheet. **Fibulae type 41a.**
Large disc of sheet bronze, front portion of bow straight, with a small coil, upper part curved; very large one-coiled spring, curved pin with bronze wire wound around the upper part. Bow

surface decorated with sharp encircling nervatures. Almost no patina.
L. 14.9cm Weight 83g
Analysis: Bronze. See D. Hook report.
Close parallels: Müller-Karpe 1959, pl.48. 6, hoard of Piediluco (Terni), Umbria.
Roma 1976, 335, no. 109, pl. 90.10, Satricum (Borgo Le Ferriere, Latina), Lazio, tomb 17. EIA, early.
Bibliography: Walters 1899, no. 2026; Bietti Sestieri 1986, 'Fibulae', 7, no. 13, and fig. p. 21.

325.
GR 1872.6-4.722bis. Bought from Alessandro Castellani.
Serpentine fibula with curved pin and terminal disc of spiral sheet. **Fibulae type 41b.**
Large disc of sheet bronze, front portion of bow straight, with a small coil, upper part curved; large three-coiled spring, curved pin partly missing, with bronze wire wound around the upper part. Front portion of bow decorated with a band of deeply incised parallel lines. Green to brown patina.
L. 10.5cm Weight 30g
Analysis: Craddock 1986, 144.
See *PBF* XIV, forthcoming, XXXVII. 2 (314), no. 5449, Cuma (Naples), Campania, tomb Osta 8, 'Fibule serpeggianti con occhiello, spillone ricurvo, grande molla rialzata e staffa a disco intagliato'.
Pontecagnano 1988, 52, pl. 18, 103, fig. I.12, type 32B4, 32B4a, phase IA.
Osteria dell'Osa 1992, 373, pl. 38, type 40b, phase IIA-B.
See Bietti Sestieri 1986, 'Fibulae', 8, no. 14 for further parallels.
This is the most popular type of serpentine fibula found in male burials in Villanovan Etruria, Lazio and the Villanovan cemeteries of Campania.
EIA, early.
Bibliography: Walters 1899, no. 2025; Bietti Sestieri 1986, Fibulae, 8, no. 14, and fig. p. 21.

326.
GR 1772.3-9.38. Bought from Sir William Hamilton.
Two-piece serpentine fibula with solid terminal disc. **Fibulae type 43.**
Very large disc with traces of incised diamonds, linked together and hatched; bow with trapezoidal contour, now distorted, with two coils, all rectangular in section except for round end, which once fitted into a separate pin. Smooth green patina on bow, areas of disc covered with incrustations.
L. 27.3cm Weight 178g
Analysis: Craddock 1986,144.
See *PBF* XIV, forthcoming, XXXVIII. 4 (333b), no. 5540, from the cemetery of S. Marzano, Campania, tomb 4 (very close, except for the attachment of the disc), 'Fibule serpeggianti con staffa a disco e spillone con testa a vaso, tipo S. Marzano'.
Pontecagnano 1988, 50, pl. 18, type 32A2. EIA, early.
This is a south Italian type, especially found in fossa-grave cemeteries.
EIA, early–late transition.
Bibliography: Walters 1899, no. 2027; Montelius 1895–1910, Series A, pl. XIV, no. 202; Sundwall 1943,153, see DII beta c 7.

327.
GR 1876.11-7.1. Given by Sir A. W. Franks.
Nola (Naples), Campania.
Two-piece serpentine fibula with parallel bars
to bow and solid terminal disc (*fibula a ponte*).
Fibulae type 44.
Large solid disc with small protrusion to hold
the pin, low elongated bow with trapezoidal
profile; two short transverse bars with flat ends
join the parallel bars forming the upper part of
the bow; pin ending with two solid discs. Finely
incised decoration on the disc: parallel and
tremolo lines along the edge, hatched squares
on centre. Small parts missing, pin deformed.
Little patina.
L. 20.4cm Weight 158g
Close to Gastaldi 1979, 29, fig. 7, type A2a
(cemeteries of the Sarno valley, Campania).
Pontecagnano 1988, 51, pl. 18, 103ff., fig. L-M.
45, type 32A5, phase IB to period II.
PBF XIV, forthcoming, XXXIX (336), no. 5555,
from Cairano (Avellino), Campania, 'Fibule
serpeggianti a due pezzi con arco doppio
massiccio e staffa a disco, tipo S. Marzano'.
As **Fibulae type 43**, this is a south Italian type;
it is found both in fossa-grave and Villanovan
cemeteries.
EIA, early and later.
Bibliography: Walters 1899, no. 2053;
Montelius 1895–1910, Series A, pl. XV, no. 216;
Sundwall 1943, 161, D IV alpha d 2, fig. 248.

328.
GR 1856.12-26.1074. Bequeathed by Sir William
Temple.
Part of two-piece serpentine fibula. **Fibulae
type 45.**
Symmetrical trapezoidal bow with two loops.
Lateral ends of thick wire with circular section,
central zone flat and widened at centre.
Engraved decoration: encircling lines on sides.
One end of bow flattened to form catch-plate,
now missing; opposing end round in section
and once fitted into separate pin, now missing.
Dull green patina.
L. 10.5cm Weight 30g
See for the general shape Lo Schiavo 1984, 228,
fig. 4.1, Salapia (Foggia), Apulia, tomb 231.
PBF XIV, forthcoming, XXXVIII. 3, (332), no.
5524B, from Cuma (Naples), Campania, tomb
Osta 9, 'Fibula serpeggiante a due pezzi con
arco a contorno trapezoidale, parte centrale
dell'arco appiattata e staffa a disco.'
Close parallels: Montelius 1895–1910, cols.
636–637, pl. 131.8, two-piece fibula with
flattened upper bow from Lame (L'Aquila),
Abruzzo; pl. 131.15, fragment from a similar
piece from Colle Cardeto (Ancona), Marche.
EIA, early and later.

329.
PRB 1964.12-1.513. Sir Henry Wellcome
Collection. From Schleichen Collection,
A.D. Lacaills. Given by the Wellcome Trustees.
Serpentine fibula with two coils and elongated
catchplate. **Fibulae type 46.**
Narrow catch-plate, partly missing, circular
section to bow; both portions of bow and pin
curved. Incised decoration: encircling chevrons
on whole surface of bow. Dull brown-black
patina.
L. 10.8cm Weight 16g
See *PBF* XIV, forthcoming, XLI (341), no. 5737,
from Cuma (Naples), Campania, Stevens
collection, 'Fibule serpeggianti meridionali di

verga a sezione circolare con decorazione a
spina di pesce'.
This is a south Italian type also found in central
Italy (Lazio, Etruria).
EIA, early.

330.
GR 1976.2-5.13. Found unregistered.
Serpentine fibula with two coils and elongated
catch-plate. **Fibulae type 46.**
Narrow catch-plate with tip missing; both
portions of bow and pin curved. Bow, coils and
pin round in section. Smooth green patina.
L. 15cm Weight 60g
Analysis: Craddock 1986, 144.
See **cat. 329.**
EIA, early.
Bibliography: Walters 1899, no. 2041.

331.
GR 1976.2-5.12. Found unregistered.
Serpentine fibula with two coils and elongated
catch-plate. **Fibulae type 46.**
Narrow catch-plate, partly missing; circular
section to bow. Front portion of the bow
oblique, portion between coils and pin curved.
Incised decoration: encircling chevrons on the
whole surface of the bow. Various shades of
green patina.
L. 17.5cm Weight 32g
Analysis: Craddock 1986,144.
See **cat. 329.**
Close parallel : *Osteria dell' Osa* 1992, 376, pl.
39, 529ff., type 42a, phase IIA-B.
EIA, early.
Bibliography: Walters 1899, no. 2036, fig. 36.

332.
GR 1976.2-5.16. Found unregistered.
Serpentine fibula with two coils and elongated
catch-plate. **Fibulae type 47.**
Narrow catch-plate; both portions of bow and
pin curved; coils with rectangular section.
Incised decoration: encircling chevrons on the
whole surface of the bow. Small parts missing.
Smooth dark green patina.
L. 18.5cm Weight 96g
See *PBF* XIV, forthcoming, XLI (349a), nos.
6482, 6502, both from Suessula (Sessa
Aurunca, Caserta), Campania, 'Fibule
serpeggianti meridionali arco a sezione
circolare, occhiello e molla a sezione
quadrangolare, con decorazione a spina di
pesce'.
Osteria dell' Osa 1992, 377, pl. 39, 529ff., type
42f, phase IIIA.
Quattro Fontanili 1986, 82, fig. 25, type III 12,
phase IIB.
Pontecagnano 1988, 60, pl. 20 and fig. M-L. 37
and 52, types 32E1a1 and 32E1a3, phase IB. EIA,
(early)–late.
Bibliography: Walters 1899, no. 2044;
Macnamara 1990, 9, fig. 6c.

333.
GR 1772.3-9.43. Bought from Sir William
Hamilton.
Serpentine fibula with two coils and elongated
catch-plate. **Fibulae type 47.**
Catch-plate partly missing; both portions of the
bow and pin curved; coils with rectangular
section. Incised decoration: encircling
chevrons on the whole surface of the bow. Pin
partly missing. Green patina with some

corrosion.
L. 19cm Weight 79g
Analysis: Craddock 1986, 144.
See **cat. 332.**
EIA, (early)–late.
Bibliography: Walters 1899, no. 2040.

334.
GR 1976.2-5.15. Found unregistered.
Serpentine fibula with two coils and elongated
catch-plate. **Fibulae type 47.**
Narrow catch-plate, partly missing; both
portions of the bow and pin curved; coils with
rectangular section. Incised decoration:
encircling chevrons on the whole surface of the
bow. Smooth dark green patina.
L. 21.5cm Weight 112g
See **cat. 332.**
EIA, (early)–late.
Bibliography: Walters 1899, no. 2043.

335.
GR 1975.7-12.41. Transferred from PRB , July
1975. Sir Henry Wellcome Collection,
F 18098. Given by the Wellcome Trustees.
Serpentine fibula with two coils and elongated
catch-plate. **Fibulae type 47.**
Catch-plate partly missing; both portions of the
bow almost straight, pin curved; coils with
rectangular section. Incised decoration:
encircling chevrons on the whole surface of the
bow. Small parts missing. Dark green patina
with much corrosion.
L. 9.6cm Weight 12g
See **cat. 332.**
EIA, (early)–late.

336.
GR 1938.3-31.8. Transferred from the Dept. of
British and Medieval Antiquities. Canon W.
Greenwell Collection, no. 1965. Given by J.
Pierpont Morgan in 1909.
Italy.
Serpentine fibula with two coils and elongated
catch-plate. **Fibulae type 47.**
Narrow catch-plate with tip missing. Both
portions of bow and pin curved; coils
rectangular in section. Various shades of green
patina and some corrosion.
L. 20cm Weight 85g
The lack of decoration characterizes a
Calabrian type; see *PBF* XIV, forthcoming, XLI
(343), no. 5863, from Torre Mordillo
(Cosenza), Calabria.
See also for the general shape **cat.332.**
EIA, (early)–late.

337.
GR 1976.2-5.11. Found unregistered.
Serpentine fibula with two coils and elongated
catch-plate. **Fibulae type 48.**
Catch-plate partly missing; front portion of the
bow oblique and slightly curved, portion
between coils and pin almost straight,
decorated on side and upper faces with a
longitudinal zigzag line; coils and upper
portion of bow square in section. Smooth green
patina.
L. 7.3cm Weight 11g
See *PBF* XIV, forthcoming, XLI. 2 (346 var.), no.
6191, S. Marzano (Salerno), Campania, tomb
46, 'Fibule serpeggianti meridionali di verga a
sezione quadrangolare'.
Osteria dell' Osa 1992, 376, pl. 39, 529ff., types

Smooth dark green to brown patina with areas of corrosion and incrustation.
L. 54.2cm Weight 416g
See *PBF* IV. 1, nos. 214–237. Type Cuma, Bietti Sestieri 1986, 'Weapons and Tools', 5, nos. 7, p. 16, and 8, p. 17.
EIA, early.
Bibliography: Walters 1899, no. 2737, fig. 78; *PBF* IV. 1, no. 235.

361.
PRB 1916.6-5.186. Given by Lord Avebury.
Naples, Campania.
Sword with flanged hilt and crescent-shaped pommel (T-hilt sword). **Swords type 8a.**
Curved pommel, hilt widening in central part, curved shoulders; seven rivet holes and four rivets extant; long blade with almost straight edges and low diamond-shaped section, decorated with two groups of incised lines.
Dark patina, incrustations in various tones of green.
L. 54.6cm Weight 398g
See *PBF* IV. 1, nos. 234–235. Type Cuma.
EIA, early.

362.
GR 1856.12-26.619. Bequeathed by Sir William Temple.
Ruvo (Bari), Apulia.
Short sword with flanged hilt and crescent-shaped pommel (T-hilt sword). **Swords type 8a.**
Wide curved pommel, slender hilt slightly widening in central part, curved sloping shoulders; four rivet holes; blade with almost straight edges and low diamond-shaped section with central swelling, decorated with two groups of thin nervatures ending with incised lines in the upper part. Blade damaged.
No patina; cleaned in modern times.
L. 40.5cm Weight 186g
See *PBF* IV. 1, no. 218, from L'Aquila, Abruzzo. Type Cuma.
EIA, early.
Bibliography: Walters 1899, no. 2735; Bietti Sestieri 1986, 'Weapons and Tools', 4, no. 7, and fig. p. 16.

363.
PRB 1916.6-5.187. Given by Lord Avebury.
Naples, Campania.
Sword with flanged hilt and crescent shaped pommel (T-hilt sword). **Swords type 8a.**
Curved pommel broken and twisted out of shape, hilt widening in central part, wide curved shoulders; at least one rivet hole in pommel, one at center of hilt, two pairs on base of the blade and three rivets extant; blade with almost straight edges and low lenticular section, decorated with two groups of nervatures and two groups of incised and zigzag lines towards shouder. Tip of blade missing. Opaque black patina.
L. 46cm Weight 381g
See *PBF* IV. 1, nos. 231–235. Type Cuma.
EIA, early.

364.
GR 1975.5-18.5. Found unregistered.
Part of a sword with flanged hilt (probably T-hilt sword). Probably **Swords type 8a.**
Hilt and point missing; wide curved shoulders with two rivet-holes, blade with straight edges

and low diamond-shaped section, decorated with two groups of thin nervatures ending with incised lines towards the upper edges. Dull dark brown patina.
L. 36.8cm Weight 352g
See *PBF* IV. 1, nos. 233, from Campli (Teramo), Abruzzo, 232 and 235. Type Cuma.
EIA, early.
Bibliography: Walters 1899, no. 2738; Bietti Sestieri 1986, 'Weapons and Tools', 5, no. 11, and fig. p. 16.

365.
GR 1856.12-26.618A. Bequeathed by Sir William Temple.
Armento (Potenza), Basilicata.
Part of sword blade. Probably **Swords type 8a.** Associated with sheath **cat. 366.**
Pommel, hilt and lower part of the blade missing; wide curved shoulders with one large rivet hole on each side, probably the original ones, and four central small ones, probably used to restore the sword after breaking. Blade with straight edges narrowing towards the tip and low diamond-shaped section, decorated with two groups of thin nervatures and incised zigzag lines. Dull green to brown patina.
L. 15.3cm Weight 140g
See *PBF* IV. 1, no. 231, from Celano (L'Aquila), Abruzzo. Type Cuma.
EIA, early.
Bibliography: Walters 1899, no. 2742; *BM Guide* 1920, 99, fig. 99b.; Bietti Sestieri 1986, 'Weapons and Tools' , 4, no. 9, and fig. p. 16.

366.
GR 1856.12-26.618B. Bequeathed by Sir William Temple.
Armento (Potenza), Basilicata.
Sword sheath with globular terminal. **Sheaths type 3.**
Associated with sword **cat. 365.**
Bronze sheet in one piece, broken unevenly at the top, and folded to form the rear face. Point ending in a large cast globe surmounted by a disc. Front face decorated on either side with three pairs of converging incised grooves and chevrons near the point. Dull green patina with some corrosion.
L. 28cm Weight 153g
See *PBF* IV. 1, no. 248a. Type Guardia Vomano.
EIA.
Bibliography: Walters 1899, no. 2742; *BM Guide* 1920, 99, fig. 99f; Bietti Sestieri 1986, 'Weapons and Tools', 5, no. 10, and fig. p. 16.

367.
GR 1849.5-18.30A. Bought from Campanari, Blayd's sale 13 February 1849. The greater part of the objects formed part of the Pizzati Collection in Florence.
Short sword with flanged hilt and crescent-pommel (T-hilt sword). **Swords type 8b.** Associated with sheath **cat. 368.**
Wide curved pommel, slender hilt slightly widening in central part, wide curved shoulders; five rivet holes and two rivets extant; short blade narrowing below the shoulders, with almost straight edges and low section with central swelling, decorated with two groups of thin nervatures and incised zigzag lines. Bronze wire originally holding the hilt-plates still attached to the hilt. Small parts missing. Smooth, shiny, brown patina.

L. 37cm Weight 241g
Analysis: Sword bronze; rivets bronze; wire spirals bronze. See D. Hook report.
See *PBF* IV. 1, nos. 205, from Pontecagnano (Salerno), Campania, and 212, from Abruzzo? Type Pontecagnano.
EIA, early.
Bibliography: Walters 1899, no. 2751; Bietti Sestieri 1986, 'Weapons and Tools', 5, no. 12, and fig. p. 17; Macnamara 1990, 10, fig. 7 b.

368.
GR 1849.5-18.30B. Bought from Campanari, Thomas Blayd's sale 13 February 1849. The greater part of these objects formed part of the Pizzati Collection in Florence.
Sword sheath with globular terminal. **Sheaths type 2.**
Associated with sword **cat. 367.**
Bronze sheet in one piece, folded to form the rear face. Point ending in a cast double globe surmounted by a cylindrical extension, decorated with five raised horizontal nervatures. Front face decorated on either side with three converging grooves, enclosing incised double zigzag lines and a hatched meander pattern in the centre; one incised line parallel to both edges of the sheet on the rear face. Smooth green patina.
L. 29.3cm Weight 163g
Analysis: Sword sheath bronze; terminal bronze. See D. Hook report.
See *PBF* IV. 1, no. 205a. Type Pontecagnano.
EIA, early.
Bibliography: Walters 1899, no. 2710; Bietti Sestieri 1986, 'Weapons and Tools', 5, no. 13, and fig. p.17.; Macnamara 1990, 10, fig. 7 b.

369.
GR 1975.5-18.6. Found unregistered.
Part of a short sword with flanged hilt (probably T-hilt sword). **Swords type 8b.**
Hilt and point of blade missing; wide sloping shoulder with three rivet-holes, blade with straight edges decorated with two groups of thin nervatures or grooves, with low diamond-shaped section at centre.Smooth dark green patina.
L. 23.3cm Weight 137g
See *PBF* IV. 1, no. 211. Type Pontecagnano.
EIA, early.
Bibliography: Bietti Sestieri 'Weapons and Tools' 1986, 4, no. 8, and fig. p. 16.

370.
PRB (P)Old Acquisition 205. Apparently from the collection of Sir William Hamilton.
Sword with separately cast hilt ending in opposed spirals (antennae sword). **Swords type 12.**
Hilt cast in one piece, central spur set between coils, grip of hilt oval in section with three low raised bands, semicircular shoulder cap with three extant rivets, blade with almost straight edges, lenticular in section with four sharp nervatures. No patina.
L. 57.7cm Weight 538 g
Analysis: Blade bronze; hilt bronze; rivets bronze. See D. Hook report.
See *PBF* IV. I, nos. 306 from Gombito (Cremona), Lombardy, and 307 from Preara (Vicenza), Veneto. Type Tarquinia.
EIA.
Bibliography: *BM Guide* 1904, 105, fig. 110; *BM*

Guide 1920a, 134, fig. 143; Jenkins and Sloan, 1996, 181, no. 57.

371.
GR 1873.8-20.229A. Bought from Alessandro Castellani.
Sword with cast hilt ending in opposed spirals (antennae sword). **Swords type 12.**
Associated with sheath fragment **372.**
Pommel with central spur, coils of spirals missing; solid hilt with central part swelling and raised decoration recalling encircling wire; narrow, almost square shoulder cap with two rivets; slender blade, narrower than the shoulders, with straight edges sharply narrowing towards the tip, and diamond-shaped section with central swelling.
Decoration: two pairs of nervatures enclosing an incised hatched band. No patina. Probably broken in antiquity in three pieces.
L. 55cm Weight 480g
See *PBF* IV. 1, nos. 321–329. Type Fermo.
EIA, early.
Bibliography: Walters 1899, no. 2744; *BM Guide* 1920, 99, fig. 99 d.; Hencken 1956, 167, fig. 20A; *PBF* IV.1, no. 328, type Fermo.

372.
GR 1873.8-20.229B. Bought from Alessandro Castellani.
Part of a sword sheath. **Sheaths Unclassified.**
Associated with sword **cat. 371.**
Bronze sheet in one piece, folded to form the rear face; broken unevenly at the top. Point ending in a cast globe surmounted by a disc. No decoration. Areas of shiny surface, green patina with some corrosion.
L. 21cm Weight 146g
EIA, early.
Bibliography: Walters 1899, no. 2744.

373.
GR 1865.7-22.9. Bought from Alessandro Castellani.
Sword sheath with globular terminal. **Sheaths type 2.**
Bronze sheet in one piece, broken towards the point, and folded to form the rear face. Point ending in a cast globe surmounted by a disc. Front face decorated on either side with three pairs of converging incised grooves, enclosing incised zigzag lines and a hatched meander pattern in the centre. Dull green patina.
L. 29.5cm Weight 192g
See *PBF* IV.1, nos. 352, 355, 356. Type Pontecagnano.
EIA, early.
Bibliography: Walters 1899, no. 2745; Bietti Sestieri 1986, 'Weapons and Tools', 5, no. 15, and fig. p. 18.

Spearheads and Spear-butts

374.
PRB 1964.12-1.327(324). Sir Henry Wellcome Collection. Given by the Wellcome Trustees.
Spearhead with conical socket and foliate blade. **Spearheads type 2.**
Blade with rounded profile towards lower end, upper part of socket slightly faceted, outer lateral angles at base of socket and two lateral pin-holes. Blackish patina.

L. 16.7cm Weight 139g
Close to *Pontecagnano* 1988, 77–78, pl. 24, types 58A1, 59A1. Phase IB.
EIA, early or later.

375.
PRB 1964.12-1.328(325). Sir Henry Wellcome Collection. Given by the Wellcome Trustees.
Spearhead with conical socket and foliate blade. **Spearheads type 2.**
Blade with rounded profile towards lower end, upper part of socket slightly faceted, outer lateral angles at base of socket and two lateral pin-holes. Blackish discontinuous patina with dark green incrustations.
L. 16.3cm Weight 127g
See **cat. 374.**
EIA, early or later.

376.
PRB W. G.1110. Canon W. Greenwell Collection, bought from the Rev. Greville J. Chester. Given by J. Pierpont Morgan 1909.
Capua (Caserta), Campania.
Spearhead with conical socket and flame-shaped blade. **Spearheads type 2.**
Blade with rounded profile towards lower end, upper part of socket slightly faceted, pin-holes set near the junction of blade and socket, outer lateral angles at base of socket. Light brown patina, with dark green and blackish incrustations.
L. 18.3cm Weight 136g
See **cat. 374.**
EIA, early or later.

377.
GR 1859.2-16.152. Bequeathed by Miss M.H.M. Auldjo.
Spearhead with conical socket and foliate blade. **Spearheads type 2.**
Blade with slightly rounded profile towards lower end, plain socket with two lateral pin-holes. Small parts missing. Light green patina with brown areas.
L. 23.6cm Weight 231g
See **cat. 374.**
EIA, early or later.

378.
GR 1916.6-1.16. Given by Lord Avebury.
Spearhead with conical socket and foliate blade. **Spearheads type 2.**
Blade with slightly rounded profile towards lower end, wide plain flattened socket with two lateral pin-holes. Part of one of the blades missing. Green to brown patina with some incrustation.
L. 19.3cm Weight 145g
See **cat. 374.**
EIA, early or later.

379.
GR 1975.6-27.3. Found unregistered.
Spearhead with conical socket and foliate blade. **Spearheads type 2.**
Blade with rounded profile towards lower end, plain flattened socket with two low lateral pin-holes. Blade edges heavily damaged. Dull green patina.
L. 18.6cm Weight 155g
See **cat. 374.**
EIA, early or later.

380.
GR 1975.6-27.26. Found unregistered.
Spearhead with conical socket and foliate blade. **Spearheads type 2.**
Long blade with rounded profile towards lower end, long and slender plain socket with two lateral pin-holes. Small parts missing. Smooth brown patina with green areas.
L. 27.4cm Weigh 225g
See **cat. 374.**
EIA, early or later.

381.
GR 1975.6-27.31. Found unregistered.
Spearhead with conical socket and foliate blade. **Spearheads type 2.**
Narrow blade with rounded profile towards lower end, plain elongated socket with slight lateral angles near butt and two lateral pin-holes. Blade edges heavily damaged. Rough green to brown patina.
L. 24.2cm Weight 280g
See **cat. 374.**
EIA, early or later.

382.
GR 1975.6-27.39. Found unregistered.
Spearhead with conical socket and foliate blade. **Spearheads type 2.**
Narrow blade with slightly rounded profile towards lower end, plain long and wide socket with cruciform incisions at lateral pin-holes. Nick out of the edge of the socket, small hole at junction with blade. No patina.
L. 21cm Weight 132g
See **cat. 374.**
EIA, early or later.

383.
GR 1975.6-27.41. Found unregistered.
Spearhead with conical socket and foliate blade. **Spearheads type 2.**
Long and narrow blade with rounded profile towards lower end, socket very slightly faceted with cruciform incisions at lateral pin-holes. Small parts missing. Smooth light green patina.
L. 33.1cm Weight 368g
See **cat. 374.**
EIA, early or later.
Bibliography: Walters 1899, no. 2712.

384.
GR 1975.6-27.5. Found unregistered.
Javelin-head with conical socket and foliate blade. **Spearheads type 3.**
Wide and relatively short blade with rounded profile towards lower end, wide plain socket with lateral angles at base and two lateral pin-holes. Blade edges damaged. Smooth brown patina.
L. 14.8cm Weight 94g
Close to *Pontecagnano* 1988, 77–78, pl. 24, types 58A1, 59A2. Phase IB to period II.
EIA, early or later.

385.
GR 1975.6-27.28. Found unregistered.
Javelin-head with conical socket and foliate blade. **Spearheads type 3.**
Wide and relatively short blade with rounded profile towards lower end, wide plain socket with two lateral pin-holes near base. Small circular hole (possibly a casting fault) on socket, part of blade missing. Green to brown

patina with incrustations.
L. 13cm Weight 85g
See **cat. 384**.
EIA, early or later.

386.
GR 1859.2-16.153. Bequeathed by Miss M.H.M.
Auldjo.
Javelin-head with conical socket and foliate
blade. **Spearheads type 3, variant**.
Wide and relatively short blade with rounded
profile towards lower end, short and wide plain
socket with two low lateral pin-holes. Point
missing. Dull green patina.
L. 9.2cm Weight 65g
See **cat. 384**.
EIA, early or later.
Bibliography: Walters 1899, no. 2711.

387.
GR 1856.12-26.620. Bequeathed by Sir William
Temple.
Bari, Apulia.
Spearhead with conical socket and foliate
blade. **Spearheads type 4**.
Narrow blade with rounded profile, faceted
socket with lateral facets ending in slightly
raised angles at junction of blade with socket
and central facet continuing below the
junction; outer lateral angles at base of socket.
Groove encircling the socket in correspondence
with the pin-holes. Complex incised
decoration: on lower part of socket, three
circles and rows of dots encircling margins and
other features. The decoration creates the
approximation of a human face. Cutting edge
slightly damaged. Light green to blue patina.
L. 33.4cm Weight 330g
See **cat. 458** for a close parallel and discussion
of this type. For a general parallel:
Pontecagnano 1988, 78, pl. 24, type 59A1b.
Phase IB to period II.
EIA, early.
Bibliography: Walters 1899, no. 2785.

388.
GR 1853.2-18.3. Bought from H.O. Cureton, who
had acquired it at Count Milano's sale,
Sotheby's 10 February 1853, lot 9.
Spearhead with conical socket and foliate
blade. **Spearheads type 4**.
Narrow blade with rounded profile, faceted
socket in blade area with central facet
extending below the junction with the lower
socket, outer lateral angles at base of socket.
Engraved decoration: hatched triangles on the
blade; deeply incised herringbone pattern on
socket at base of blade, on both sides; on the
lower part of the socket, punched circles and
rows of dots encircling both pin-holes and
along margins. Cutting edge slightly damaged.
Smooth green to brown patina with spots of
corrosion.
L. 29.7cm Weight 378g
See **cat. 387** and **458**.
EIA, early or later.
Bibliography: Walters 1899, no. 2715.

389.
GR 1916.6-1.21. Given by Lord Avebury.
Miniature spearhead with narrow, straight-
sided blade. **Spearheads type 4, variant**.
Cast in one piece; elongated blade with straight
edges and diamond-shaped section, shaft with

circular section. Engraved decoration on the
blade: two incised lines and rows of small
punched triangles along the central edge, two
circles at base. Tip broken and end of shaft
missing. Smooth green patina.
L. 6.8cm Weight 10g
Close to *Osteria dell'Osa* 1992, 408, pl. 42,
miniature spear with cast shaft, type 72c.
This is probably a miniature version of a
prestige weapon similar to the decorated pieces
here classified as **type 4**, especially **cat. 388**,
458 and **754**; it could have been part of the
funerary set of a male cremation burial with
miniature grave-goods, as found in the EIA,
early, in Lazio and Campania.
A provenance of this piece from Campania is
possible, since part of the Avebury collection
was assembled in Naples.
EIA, early.

390.
GR 1975.6-27.25. Found unregistered.
Spearhead with conical socket and foliate
blade. **Spearheads type 4, variant**.
Blade slightly expanded in the lower part, not
sharply separated from the socket; socket
faceted in the blade area, lower socket with
outer lateral angles at the base and two lateral
pin-holes. Engraved decoration: double lines
along the facets and the base of the lower
socket; raised band of deeply incised lines
encircling the base of the blade. Smooth green
to brown patina.
L. 23.3cm Weight 245g
See *Pontecagnano* 1988, 132–133, fig. 56.10,
tomb 180. Phase IA-B.
EIA, early.

391.
GR 1975.6-27.42. Found unregistered.
Spearhead with conical socket and foliate
blade. **Spearheads type 4, variant**.
Narrow blade with rounded lower part, slightly
faceted socket in blade area, with lateral facets
ending in slightly raised angles below the
junction of blade with socket, outer lateral
angles at base of socket and two lateral pin-
holes surrounded by cruciform incisions.
Engraved decoration: small circles on lower
part of blade and on socket, rows of dots at the
base of the blade and along the raised angles.
Edges of the blade slightly damaged. Mottled
green and brown patina with some corrosion.
L. 35.1cm Weight 436g
Close to *Pontecagnano* 1988, 78, pl. 24, type
59A1b. Phase IB to period II.
EIA, early and later.
Bibliography: Walters 1899, no. 2793.

392.
PRB 2000.1-1.33. Found unregistered.
Spearhead with conical socket and foliate
blade. **Spearheads type 5**.
Narrow blade with rounded lower end and two
small circular holes at the base, upper socket
faceted to junction of blade and socket, outer
lateral angles at base of socket and two lateral
pin-holes surrounded by cruciform incisions.
Decoration: four circles on each face of the
socket; irregular longitudinal *a tremolo* on
blade and socket. Smooth dark green patina
with light zones.
L. 29.5cm Weight 341g

Close to *Pontecagnano* 1988, 78, pl. 24, type
59A1b. Phase IB to period II; *Torre Galli* 1999,
fig. 10, type P6B (with holes on lower blade).
Phase IA.
The faceted upper socket is a specifically south
Italian feature, while in Villanovan spearheads
the whole socket is usually faceted.
EIA, early.

393.
PRB 1964.12-1.217(328). Sir Henry Wellcome
Collection, no. 21077. Bought at Steven's sale 8
October 1918, lot 140. Given by the Wellcome
Trustees.
Capua (Caserta), Campania.
Spearhead with conical socket and foliate
blade. **Spearheads type 5**.
Narrow blade with rounded lower end, upper
socket faceted to junction of blade and socket,
outer lateral angles at base of socket and two
pin-holes. Smooth green-black patina. Small
parts missing from blade.
L. 33cm Weight 434g
See **cat. 392**.
EIA, early.

394.
PRB W. G.1114. Canon W. Greenwell Collection,
bought from the Rev. Greville J. Chester. Given
by J. Pierpont Morgan in 1909.
Popoli (Pescara), Abruzzo.
Javelin head with conical socket and foliate
blade. **Spearheads type 5**.
Narrow blade with rounded lower end, upper
socket faceted to junction of blade and socket,
outer lateral angles at base of socket and two
pin-holes. Smooth patina in dark copper
colour, with marked green and whitish
incrustations. Edge of blade and tip damaged.
L. 15.7cm Weight 125g
See **cat. 392**.
EIA, early.

395.
GR 1865.7-20.54. Bought from C. Merlin.
Olympia, Greece.
Spearhead with conical socket and foliate
blade. **Spearheads type 5**.
Narrow blade with rounded profile, socket
lightly faceted in blade area and wide towards
butt with two lateral pin-holes surrounded by
cruciform incisions. Green patina with some
corrosion.
L. 20.6cm Weight 174g
See **cat. 392**.
EIA, early.
Bibliography: Walters 1899, no. 2772.

396.
GR 1975.6-27.24. Found unregistered.
Javelin-head with conical socket and foliate
blade. **Spearheads type 5**.
Blade expanded with slightly rounded lower
part and wide socket, lightly faceted in blade
area; two lateral pin-holes. Dull green patina.
L. 14.2cm. Weight 122 g.
See **cat. 392**.
EIA, early.

397.
PRB 1916.6-5.178. Given by Lord Avebury.
Naples, Campania.
Spearhead with conical socket and foliate
blade. **Spearheads type 6**.

Blade with rounded profile towards lower end, faceted socket, two lateral pin-holes. Blade decorated with rows of incised hatched triangles. Smooth blackish patina with dark green incrustations.
L. 20.5cm Weight 172g
See for spearheads and javelins with faceted socket *Pontecagnano* 1988, 174, fig. 150, tomb 2052.6. Phase IB; 202–203, fig. 164, tomb 2157.9. Period II.
EIA, early or later.

398.
PRB WG1127. Canon W. Greenwell Collection, given by the Earl of Northesk. Given by J. Pierpont Morgan in 1909.
Bovino, Capitanata (Foggia), Apulia.
Spearhead with conical socket and foliate blade. **Spearheads type 6, variant**. Associated with spear-butt **cat. 399**.
Narrow blade with rounded profile, faceted socket. Decoration: parallel grooves on the facets, incised lines at the base of the socket, vertical and horizontal band with herringbone pattern on each side of the socket, the horizontal band surmounted by a zigzag line, the vertical band pierced by two lateral pin-holes. Smooth black patina with green and dark blue incrustations. Edge of blade damaged.
L. 20.9cm Weight 264g
Analysis : Bronze. See D. Hook report.
Close to *Torre Galli* 1999, 41, figs. 10, 12, and 134, fig. 36, types P7 (for the general shape) and P5B (for the incised decoration). Phases IA and IA-B. See also *Pontecagnano* 1988, 78, pl. 24, type 59A1b. Phase IB to period II.
EIA, early or later.

399.
PRB W. G.1128. Canon W. Greenwell Collection, given by the Earl of Northesk. Given by J. Pierpont Morgan in 1909.
Bovino, Capitanata (Foggia), Apulia.
Spear-butt, conical faceted. **Spear-butts type 5**. Associated with spearhead **cat. 398**.
Elongated socket with slightly marked encircling groove below the rim, faceted body and rounded tip. Decoration: encircling band of incised lines. Smooth black patina with green and dark blue incrustations. Tip damaged.
L. 23cm Weight 88g
Analysis: Leaded bronze. See D. Hook report.
See for general parallels **cat. 766**.
EIA, early or later.
The accurately made and decorated spearhead and spear-butt probably belonged to the burial of a high ranking man.

400.
PRB 2000.1-1.34. Found unregistered.
Spearhead with conical socket and foliate blade. **Spearheads type 8**.
Long, narrow blade with rounded lower part and outer lateral angles at base of socket. Smooth blackish patina with black incrustations and corroded zones. Blade edges damaged.
L. 29.1cm Weight 327g
Close to *Pontecagnano* 1988, 78, pl. 24, type 59A1a. Phase IB to period II.
EIA, early or later.

401.
PRB 2000.1-1.35. Found unregistered.
Spearhead with conical socket and foliate blade. **Spearheads type 8**.
Long, narrow blade with rounded lower part and two lateral holes at the base. Outer lateral angles at base of socket and two pin-holes. Dark green and brown discontinuous patina with incrustations. Cutting edge damaged.
L. 27.3cm Weight 321g
See **cat. 400**.
EIA, early or later.

402.
PRB W. G.1099. Canon W. Greenwell Collection, bought from the Rev. Greville J. Chester. Given by J. Pierpont Morgan in 1909.
Capua (Caserta), Campania.
Spearhead with conical socket and foliate blade. **Spearheads type 8**.
Long, narrow blade with rounded lower part and wide socket with two lateral pin-holes. Smooth blackish discontinuous patina with corroded zones.
L. 27.7cm Weight 360g
See **cat. 400**.
EIA, early or later.

403.
GR 1916.6-1.17. Given by Lord Avebury.
Naples, Campania.
Spearhead with conical socket and foliate blade. **Spearheads type 8**.
Patina suggests a possible association with javelin-head **cat. 426**.
Long, narrow blade with slightly rounded lower part and outer lateral angles at base of socket and two lateral pin-holes. Blade edges damaged; twisted out of shape, perhaps intentionally. Little patina; large areas with colour of metal showing.
L. 19cm Weight 213g
See **cat. 400**.
EIA, early or later.

404.
PRB W. G.1119. Canon W. Greenwell Collection, bought from the Rev. Greville J. Chester. Given by J. Pierpont Morgan in 1909.
'Massica' (probably Marsica, L'Aquila), Abruzzo.
Javelin-head with conical socket and foliate blade. **Spearheads type 9**.
Blade almost straight at base, elliptical in section, with socket not distinct on blade zone, two incised lines along the edges of the blade, pin-holes set near the junction of blade and socket. Smooth patina in dark copper colour. Socket missing.
L. 8.5cm Weight 33g
No precise parallels.
Probably EIA, early or later.

405.
PRB W. G.1113. Canon W. Greenwell Collection, bought from the Rev. Greville J. Chester. Given by J. Pierpont Morgan in 1909.
Cuma (Naples), Campania.
Spearhead with conical socket and foliate blade. **Spearheads type 9**.
Blade almost straight at base, elliptical in section, with socket not distinct on blade zone, marked nervatures along the edges of the blade, pin-holes set near the junction of blade and socket. Smooth black patina, with light green spots.
L. 15.6cm Weight 112g
See **cat. 404**.
Probably EIA, early or later.

406.
PRB 1880.8-2.42. Given by Sir A.W. Franks. Bought at Pozzuoli, probably from Cuma (Naples), Campania.
Javelin-head with conical socket and foliate blade. **Spearheads type 10**.
Narrow blade with rounded profile, wide socket with two lateral pin-holes. Light green patina
L. 14.8cm Weight 108g
Close to *Pontecagnano* 1988, 77, pl. 24, type 58A1. Periods I–II.
EIA, early or later.

407.
PRB W. G.1116. Canon W. Greenwell Collection, bought from the Rev. Greville J. Chester. Given by J. Pierpont Morgan in 1909.
Calabria.
Javelin-head with conical socket and foliate blade. **Spearheads type 10**.
Possibly associated with spear-butt **cat. 778**, with similar patina, also from Calabria.
Narrow blade with rounded profile, long conical socket with two lateral pin-holes. Dull patina in various tones of green, with brown incrustations.
L. 12.6cm Weight 82g
See **cat. 406**.
EIA, early or later.

408.
PRB W. G.1118. Canon W. Greenwell Collection, bought from the Rev. Greville J. Chester. Given by J. Pierpont Morgan in 1909.
'Massica' (probably Marsica, L'Aquila), Abruzzo.
Javelin-head with conical socket and foliate blade. **Spearheads type 10**.
Narrow blade with rounded profile, very wide conical socket with outer edges at base and two lateral pin-holes. Smooth olive-green patina with green-brown incrustations.
L. 10.3cm Weight 112g
See **cat. 406**.
EIA, early or later.

409.
GR 1814.7-4.1577. Charles Townley Collection. Bought from Peregrine Townley.
Javelin-head with conical socket and foliate blade. **Spearheads type 10**.
Narrow blade with rounded profile, very wide conical socket with two lateral pin-holes. Both socket and blade damaged, with small parts missing. Dull green patina with some corrosion.
L. 10.3cm Weight 57g
See **cat. 406**.
EIA, early or later.

410.
GR 1867.5-8.186. Blacas Collection.
Javelin-head with conical socket and foliate blade. **Spearheads type 10**.
Wide blade with rounded profile, wide conical socket with two lateral pin-holes. Small parts

missing. Dark green patina with some corrosion.
L. 11.9cm Weight 80g
See **cat. 406**.
EIA, early or later.
Bibliography: Walters 1899, no. 2789.

411.
GR 1975.6-27.17. Found unregistered.
Spearhead with conical socket and foliate blade. **Spearheads type 10**.
Blade with rounded profile, conical socket with two lateral pin-holes. Blade edges damaged. Patchy patina with green and brown areas and some corrosion.
L. 28cm Weight 405g
See **cat. 406**.
EIA, early or later.

412.
GR 1975.6-27.7. Found unregistered.
Spearhead with conical socket and with foliate blade. **Spearheads type 10, variant**.
Blade very narrow with rounded profile, elongated conical socket and two lateral pin-holes. Butt damaged and small parts missing. No patina.
L. 25.2cm Weight 220g
See **cat. 406**.
EIA, early or later.

413.
GR 1975.6-27.11. Found unregistered.
Javelin-head with conical socket and foliate blade. **Spearheads type 10, variant**.
Blade very narrow with slightly rounded profile, wide conical socket with two lateral pin-holes. Smooth green patina.
L. 10.5cm Weight 44g
See **cat. 406**.
EIA, early or later.

414.
PRB 1964.12-1.329(329). Sir Henry Wellcome Collection. Given by the Wellcome Trustees.
Spearhead with conical socket and foliate blade. **Spearheads type 11**.
Narrow blade with rounded lower part, slender elongated socket flattened in the blade zone, with casting fault and two lateral pin-holes. Smooth spotted patina in various tones of green, with earthy incrustations. Small parts of the blade missing.
L. 35cm Weight 299g
See *Torre Galli* 1999, 41, fig. 10, and 134, fig. 36, type P2. Phase 1A.
EIA, early or later.

415.
PRB W. G.1100. Canon W. Greenwell Collection, bought from the Rev. Greville J. Chester. Given by J. Pierpont Morgan in 1909.
Pozzuoli (Naples), Campania.
Spearhead with conical socket and foliate blade. **Spearheads type 11**.
Narrow blade with rounded profile, socket elongated below junction with blade and with wide base and two lateral pin-holes. Rough patina in various tones of green. Blade partly missing.
L. 26.7cm Weight 264g
See **cat. 414**.
EIA, early or later.

416.
PRB W. G.1102. Canon W. Greenwell Collection, bought from the Rev. Greville J. Chester. Given by J. Pierpont Morgan in 1909.
Near Metaponto (Matera), Basilicata.
Spearhead with conical socket and foliate blade. **Spearheads type 11**.
Narrow blade with rounded lower part, socket elongated below junction with blade, with wide base and two lateral pin-holes. Smooth olive green patina.
L. 23.5cm Weight 263g
See **cat. 414**.
EIA, early or later.

417.
PRB W. G.1103. Canon W. Greenwell Collection, bought from the Rev. Greville J. Chester. Given by J. Pierpont Morgan in 1909.
Near Naples, Campania.
Spearhead with conical socket and foliate blade. **Spearheads type 11**.
Narrow blade with rounded lower part, socket elongated below junction with blade and with wide base and two lateral pin-holes. Smooth dull green patina. Edges of blade damaged.
L. 24cm Weight 190g
See **cat. 414**.
EIA, early or later.

418.
PRB W. G.1104. Canon W. Greenwell Collection, bought from the Rev. Greville J. Chester. Given by J. Pierpont Morgan in 1909.
Capua (Caserta), Campania.
Spearhead with conical socket and foliate blade. **Spearheads type 11**.
Narrow blade with rounded profile, socket elongated below junction with blade; wide base with outer lateral edges and two lateral pin-holes. Small parts missing. Smooth patina in various tones of green.
L. 23.7cm Weight 339g
See **cat. 414**.
EIA, early or later.

419
PRB W. G.1115. Canon W. Greenwell Collection, bought from the Rev. Greville J. Chester. Given by J. Pierpont Morgan in 1909.
'Massica' (probably Marsica, L'Aquila), Abruzzo.
Javelin-head with conical socket and foliate blade. **Spearheads type 11**.
Possibly associated with spear-butt **779**.
Narrow blade with rounded profile, socket widening towards the base, which is missing. Smooth dull green patina, with iron incrustations. Heavily damaged (socket and edges of blade).
L. 13.5cm Weight 76g
See **cat. 414**.
EIA, early or later.

420.
GR 1975.6-27.4. Found unregistered.
Spearhead with conical socket and foliate blade. **Spearheads type 11**.
Narrow blade with rounded profile, wide elongated socket flattened with two lateral pin-holes. Small parts of the blade missing. Shiny green patina.
L. 16.3cm Weight 110g
See **cat. 414**.

EIA, early or later.

421.
GR 1975.6-27.2. Found unregistered.
Javelin-head with conical socket and foliate blade. **Spearheads type 11**.
Very narrow blade with slightly rounded profile, wide elongated socket with two lateral pin-holes. Casting fault at base of socket and small parts of the blade missing. Dark green patina.
L. 14.7cm Weight 80g
See **cat. 414**.
EIA, early or later.

422.
PRB 1883.4-26.3. Given by Sir A. W. Franks.
Abruzzo.
Spearhead with conical socket and flame-shaped blade. **Spearheads type 13**.
Large weapon with long, expanded blade and long socket with two lateral pin-holes. Discontinuous patina in various tones of green with dark green incrustations.
L. 28.5cm Weight 342g
See Müller-Karpe 1959, pls. 40A.1, 41B.4, Terni, Umbria, cemetery of the Acciaierie, tombs 97 and 94. Phase Terni II, for the flame-shaped blade. Also *Pontecagnano* 1988, 78, pl. 24, types 59B1 and 59B2. Phase IB to period II.
EIA, early or later.

423.
PRB W. G.1098. Canon W. Greenwell Collection, bought from the Rev. Greville J. Chester. Given by J. Pierpont Morgan in 1909.
Girgenti (= Agrigento), Sicily.
Spearhead with conical socket and flame-shaped blade. **Spearheads type 13**.
Very large weapon with long expanded blade and long socket with two lateral pin-holes; surface of bronze corroded and cutting edges damaged. Smooth dark green patina with lighter incrustations.
L. 36cm Weight 473g
See **cat. 422**.
EIA, early or later.

424.
PRB W. G.1101. Canon W. Greenwell Collection, bought from the Rev. Greville J. Chester. Given by J. Pierpont Morgan in 1909.
Near Naples, Campania.
Spearhead with conical socket and flame-shaped blade. **Spearheads type 13**.
Long, very narrow blade and long socket with outer lateral angles at the base and two lateral pin-holes. Two deeply incised lines joining at the base of the blade, on both sides. Smooth dull green discontinuous patina with blackish zones.
L. 24.8cm Weight 214g
See **cat. 422**.
EIA, early or later.

425.
GR 1849.5-18.46. Bought from Campanari, Blayd's sale 13 February 1849. The greater part of these objects formed part of the Pizzati Collection in Florence.
Spearhead with conical socket and flame-shaped blade. **Spearheads type 13**.
Long blade, slightly rounded and expanded at base, long plain socket, with two lateral pin-

holes and the pin still in place. Dull green patina with some corrosion.
L. 33.7cm Weight 293g
See **cat. 422.**
EIA, early or later.
Bibliography: Walters 1899, no. 2713.

426.
GR 1916.6-1.19. Given by Lord Avebury.
Naples, Campania.
Javelin-head with conical socket and flame-shaped blade. **Spearheads type 13.**
Patina suggests a possible association with spearhead **cat. 403.**
Slightly expanded blade with rounded lower part, wide socket with outer lateral angles at base and two lateral pin-holes. Slight curved grooves on the lower part of blade, on both sides. Little patina; areas with colour of metal showing.
L. 14.3cm Weight 90g
See **cat. 422.**
EIA, early or later.

427.
GR 1975.6-27.12. Found unregistered.
Javelin-head with conical socket and flame-shaped blade. **Spearheads type 13.**
Expanded blade with rounded lower part, slender socket with two lateral pin-holes, decorated at base with an incised band of oblique parallel lines. Socket and blade slightly damaged. Smooth green patina.
L. 14.7cm Weight 118g
See **cat. 422.**
EIA, early or later.

428.
GR 1975.6-27.19. Found unregistered.
Spearhead with conical socket and flame-shaped blade. **Spearheads type 13.**
Long blade, rounded and expanded at base, and long, flattened socket, with outer lateral angles at base and two lateral pin-holes surrounded by cruciform incisions. Smooth dark brown patina.
L. 25cm Weight 347g
See **cat. 422.**
EIA, early or later.

429.
GR 1975.6-27.20. Found unregistered.
Spearhead with conical socket and flame-shaped blade. **Spearheads type 13.**
Long blade, rounded and expanded at base, and long, flattened socket with two lateral pin-holes. Blade and socket edges much damaged. Green patina with areas of corrosion.
L. 22cm Weight 210g
See **cat. 422.**
EIA, early or later.

430.
GR 1975.6-27.21. Found unregistered.
Spearhead with conical socket and flame-shaped blade. **Spearheads type 13.**
Long blade, rounded and expanded at base, and long, flattened socket, with outer lateral angles at base and two lateral pin-holes. Small parts missing from the blade edges. Smooth green to brown patina.
L. 36cm Weight 398g
See **cat. 422.**
EIA, early or later.

431.
GR 1975.6-27.23. Found unregistered.
Javelin-head with conical socket and foliate blade. **Spearheads type 13.**
Blade expanded with curved lower part, slight lateral facets continuing past base of blade and forming two raised elements on either side of the socket, which has two low lateral pin-holes. Blade edges damaged. Smooth green patina.
L. 10.6cm Weight 65g
See **cat. 422.**
EIA, early or later.

432.
GR 1975.6-27.29. Found unregistered.
Spearhead with conical socket and flame-shaped blade. **Spearheads type 13.**
Long blade, rounded and expanded at base, and long, flattened socket, lower socket with outer lateral angles at base and two lateral pin-holes. Lightly incised herringbone decoration on one side of the blade only. Dull green patina.
L. 28.9cm Weight 259g
See **cat. 422.**
EIA, early or later.

433.
GR 1975.6-27.18. Found unregistered.
Spearhead with conical socket and flame-shaped blade. **Spearheads type 14.**
Short, expanded blade and long plain socket with two lateral pin-holes. Small parts missing from the blade edges and tip. Smooth brown patina.
L. 22cm Weight 189g
See Müller-Karpe 1959, pls. 40A.1, 41B.4, Terni, Umbria, cemetery of the Acciaierie, tombs 97 and 94. Phase Terni II; *Pontecagnano* 1988, 78, pl. 24, types 59B1 and 59B2. Phase IB to period II.
EIA, early or later.

434.
GR 1975.6-27.36. Found unregistered.
Spearhead with conical socket and flame-shaped blade. **Spearheads type 14.**
Expanded blade and flattened socket in blade area, lower socket with a wide base and outer lateral angles; no lateral pin-holes. Series of small nicks on one of the blade edges and on the socket. Dark green to brown patina.
L. 20.8cm Weight 170g
See **cat. 433.**
EIA, early or later.

435.
PRB W. G.1124. Canon W. Greenwell Collection, bought from the Rev. Greville J. Chester. Given by J. Pierpont Morgan in 1909.
Capua (Caserta), Campania.
Spearhead with conical socket and flame-shaped blade. **Spearheads type 16.**
Expanded blade and faceted socket with two lateral pin-holes. Engraved decoration: five horizontal lines and a row of hatched triangles at the base of the socket; a line and a row of hatched triangles along the lower part of the blade. Smooth dull green and grey patina. Cutting edge and base of the socket damaged.
L. 22.1cm Weight 167g
Close parallels for this piece are to be found in the distinctive metal production of the Piediluco-Contigliano group, dating from the FBA–EIA transition. See Müller-Karpe 1959, pl.

49.23, hoard of Piediluco (Terni), Umbria; Ponzi Bonomi 1972, 106ff., figs. 5.9 and 4.1 (so-called Contigliano hoard, probably also from Piediluco).
FBA–EIA transition.

436.
PRB 1925.10-17.3. Bought from Fenton Ltd, 33 Cranbourne St, London WC.
Spearhead with conical socket and flame-shaped blade. **Spearheads type 16.**
Long, expanded blade and socket faceted in the blade zone; lower socket with two lateral pin-holes. Engraved line along the edge of the blade. Discontinuous dull green patina. Hammer marks and edge of blade damaged.
L. 32cm Weight 286g
See **cat. 435** for the general shape; see also Müller-Karpe 1959, pls. 39B.1, 40B.3, 40C.4, Terni, Umbria, cemetery of the Acciaierie, tombs 160, 167 and 184, Terni II; *Pontecagnano* 1988, 78, pl. 24, type 59B2. Phase IB to period II.
EIA, early or later.

437.
PRB 1964.12-6.78. Bequeathed by C.T. Trechmann.
Viterbo, Lazio.
Spearhead with conical socket and flame-shaped blade. **Spearheads type 16.**
Expanded blade with squared ends, wide faceted socket with two lateral pin-holes. Decorated with incised lines along the sides of the facets and the lower part of the blade and around the base of the socket. Smooth pale green patina with azure and iron incrustations.
L. 28.2cm Weight 352g
See **cat. 435** and **436.**
EIA, early or later.

438.
PRB W. G.1125. Canon W. Greenwell Collection, bought from the Rev. Greville J. Chester. Given by J. Pierpont Morgan in 1909.
Mineo (Catania), Sicily.
Spearhead with conical socket and flame-shaped blade. **Spearheads type 16.**
Associated with spear-butt **cat. 439.**
Narrow curved blade, slender socket faceted in blade zone; lower socket with two lateral pin-holes. Spotted green patina with blue incrustations. Blade edge damaged.
L. 25cm Weight 189g
See **cat. 435** and **436.**
EIA, early or later.

439.
PRB W. G.1126. Canon W. Greenwell Collection, bought from the Rev. Greville J. Chester. Given by J. Pierpont Morgan in 1909.
Mineo (Catania), Sicily.
Spear-butt, conical faceted. **Spear-butts type 5.**
Associated with spearhead **cat. 438.**
Straight upper end, partly missing, with three slightly marked encircling grooves below the rim and two pin-holes; faceted body ending in a rounded tip. Spotted green patina with blue incrustations.
L. 19.8cm Weight 112g
Close to *Pontecagnano* 1988, 78–79, pl. 24, type 60A2. Phase IB to period II.
EIA, early or later.

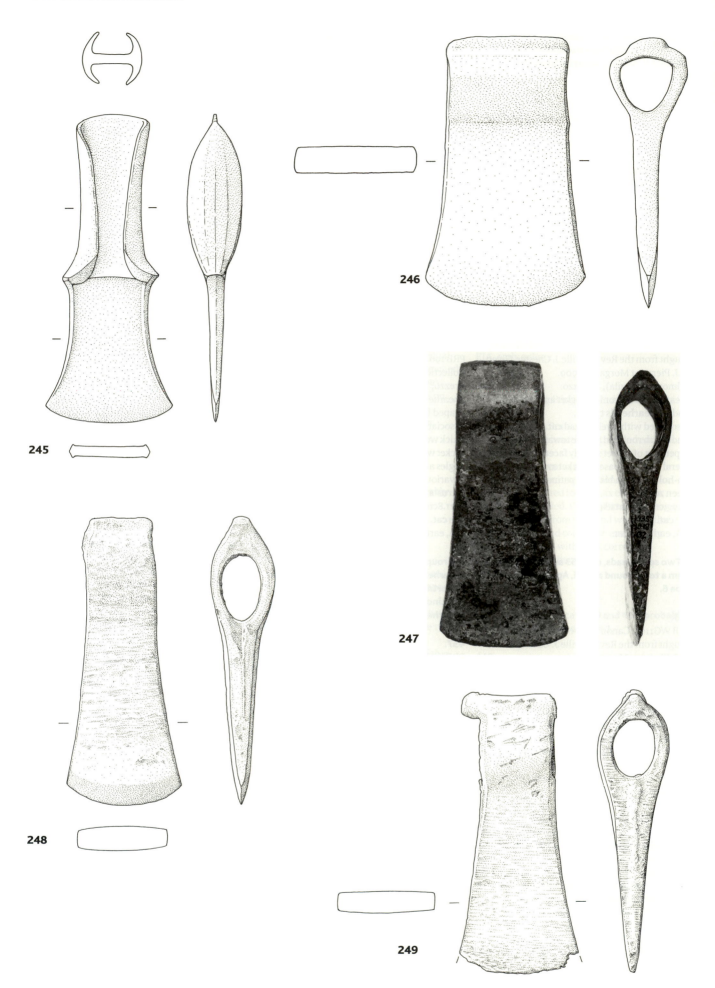

Plate 53   Axes type 43: - 245 Rome, Lazio. **Axes type 50**: - 246 Mineo (Catania), Sicily. **Axes type 51**: - 247. - 248 Capua (Caserta), Campania. 249 Calabria.

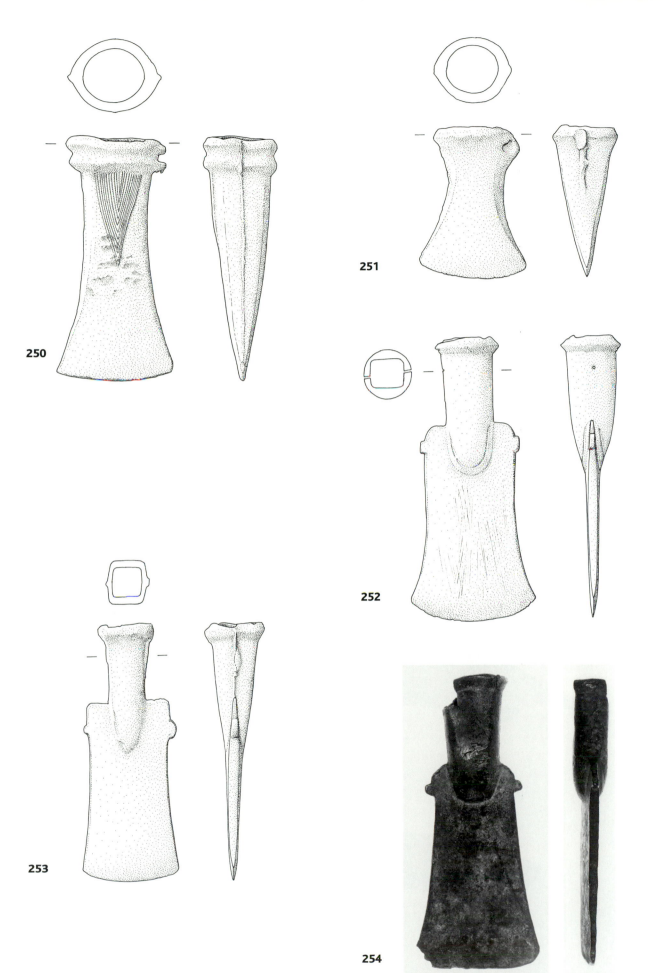

Plate 54   **Axes type 54**: - 250. **Axes type 56**: - 251 Terni, Umbria. **Axes type 60**: - 252 Perugia, Umbria. - 253 near Rome, Lazio. - 254.

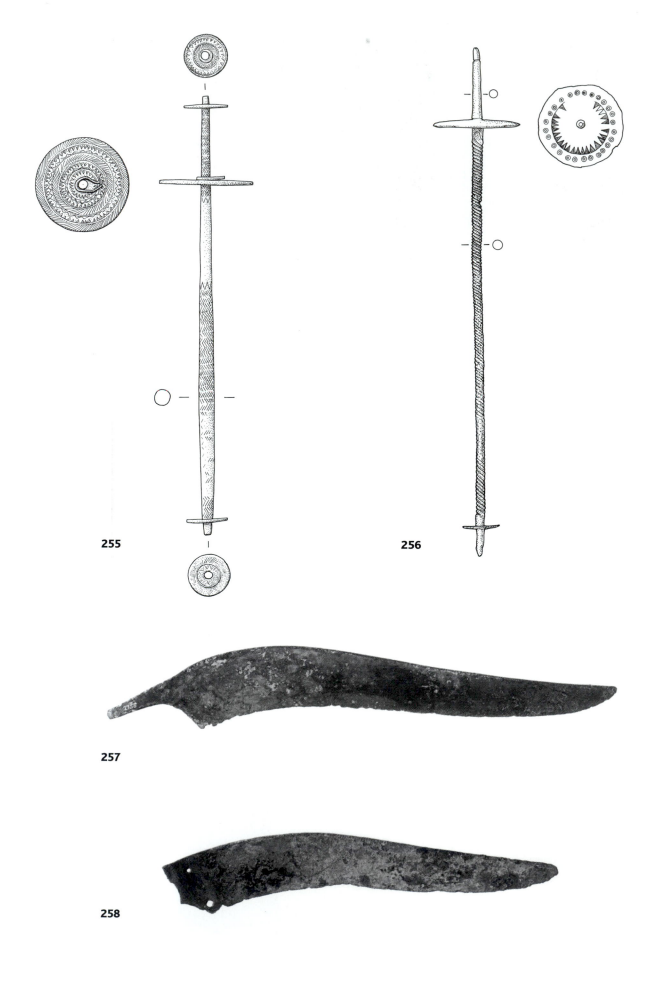

255

256

257

258

Plate 55   Spindles type 1: - 255. **Spindles type 2**: - 256. **Knives type 5**: - 257. **Knives type 6**: - 258.

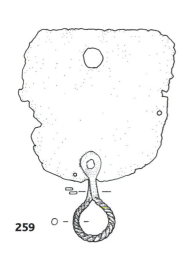

259

260

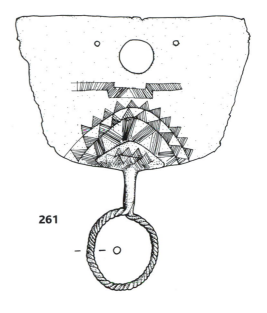

261

262

263

264

265

Plate 56   Razors type 5: - 259 Athens, Greece. - 260. **Razors type 6**: - 261 Athens, Greece. - 262. - 263. **Razors type 7**: - 264. **Razors type 8**: - 265.

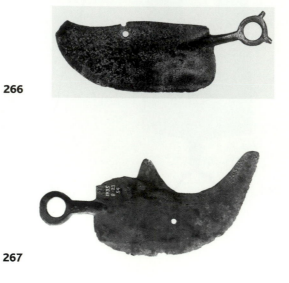

266

267

268

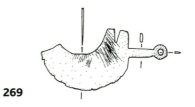

269

270

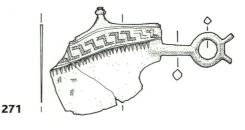

271

Plate 57   Razors type 10: - 266. **Razors type 11**: - 267. - 268. - 269 Rome, Lazio. **Razors type 12**: - 270 'Etruria'. **Razors type 13**: - 271.

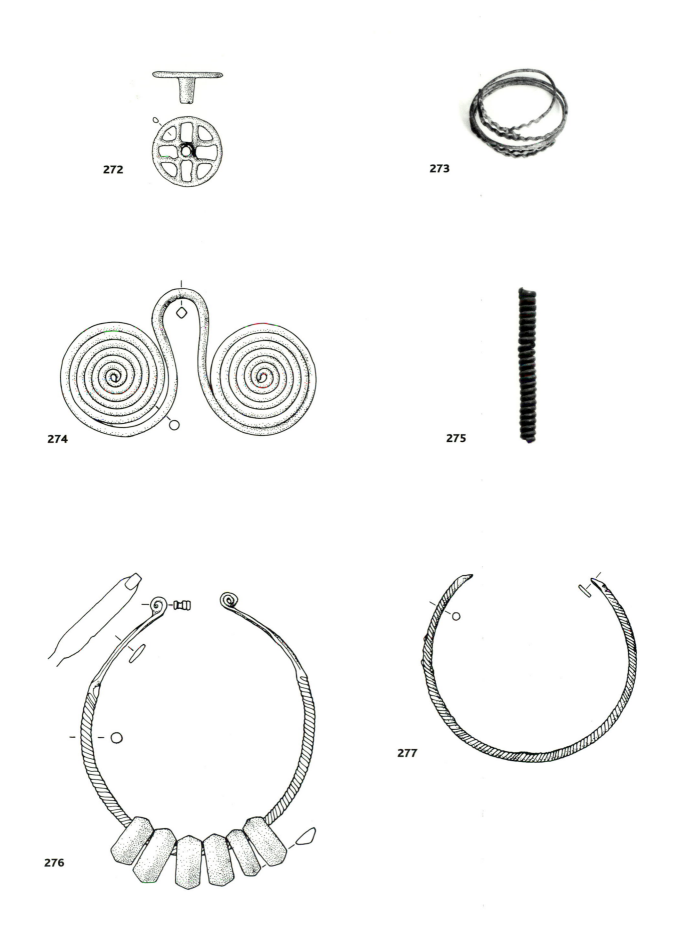

Plate 58   Pins type 8: - 272. **Hair-rings type 1**: - 273. **Pendants type 1**: - 274 Ruvo (Bari), Apulia. **Unclassified ornament**: - 275. **Torques type 1**: - 276. - 277 Cuma (Naples), Campania.

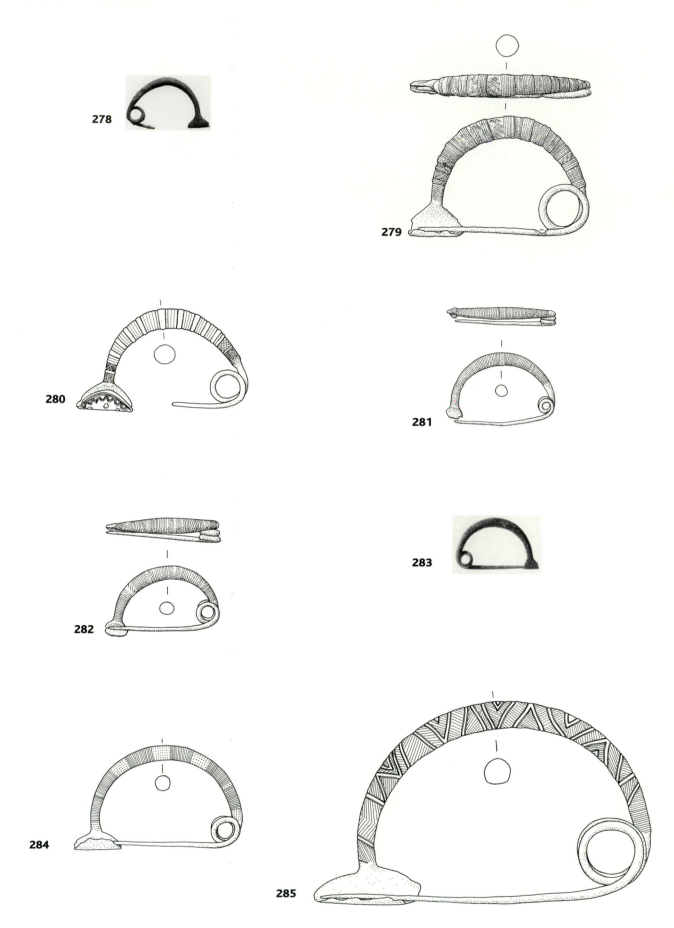

278

279

280

281

282

283

284

285

Plate 59   **Fibulae type 7**: - 278. - 279 Belgrade, Serbia. - 280. - 281. - 282 possibly Zürich, Switzerland. -283. **Fibulae type 8**: - 284–285.

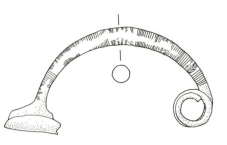

286

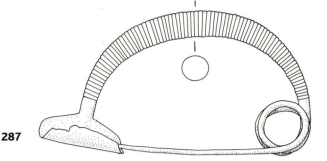

287

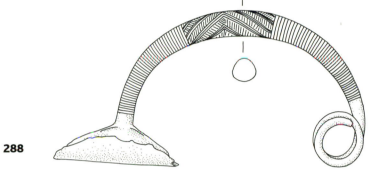

288

289

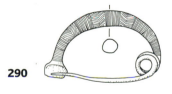

290

291

292

Plate 60 **Fibulae type 9**: - 286. - 287. - 288. **Fibulae type 10**: - 289. - 290. - 291. - 292.

293

294

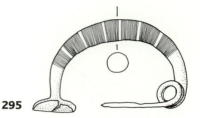

295

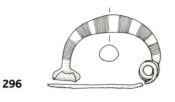

296

297

298

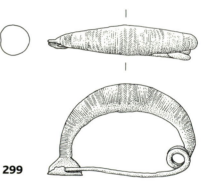

299

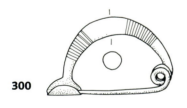

300

301

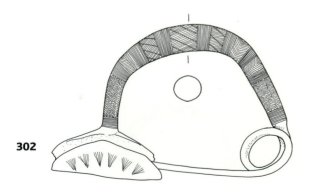

302

303

Plate 61 **Fibulae type 11**: - 293. - 294. Close to **Fibulae type 11**: - 295 possibly Rhineland, Germany. **Fibulae type 11**: - 296. - 297 probably England. **Fibulae type 12a**: - 298 - 299 Steiermark, Austria. - 300. - 301. **Fibulae type 13**: - 302. **Fibulae type 14**: - 303.

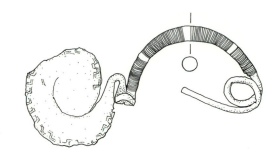

304

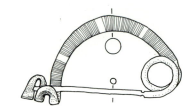

305

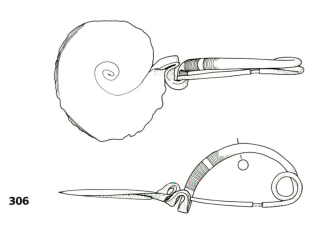

306

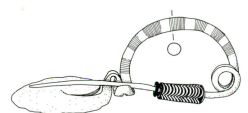

307

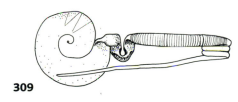

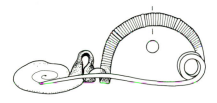

308

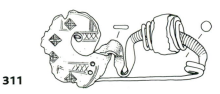

309

311

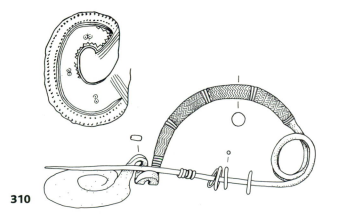

310

312

Plate 62   Fibulae type 17: - 304. - 305. - 306. - 307. - 308 near Rome, Lazio. - 309. - 310. - 311 near Rome. - 312.

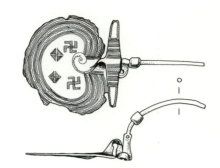

313

314

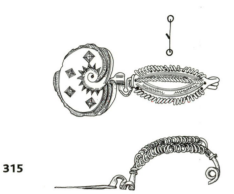

315

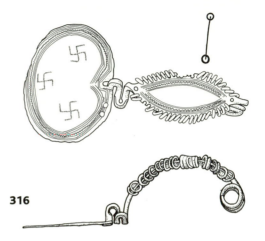

316

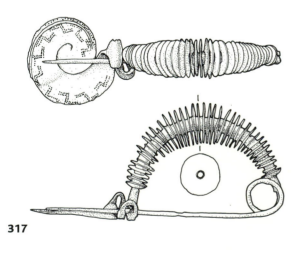

317

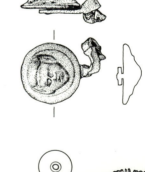

318

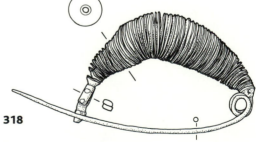

318

Plate 63   Fibulae type 18: - 313 near Rome, Lazio. **Fibulae type 32**: - 314. **Fibulae type 33**: - 315 near Rome. - 316 near Rome. **Fibulae type 36**: - 317. **Fibulae type 37**: - 318 Ruvo (Bari), Apulia.

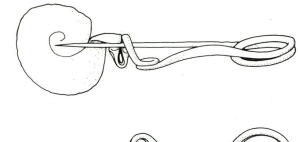

319

320

321

322

323

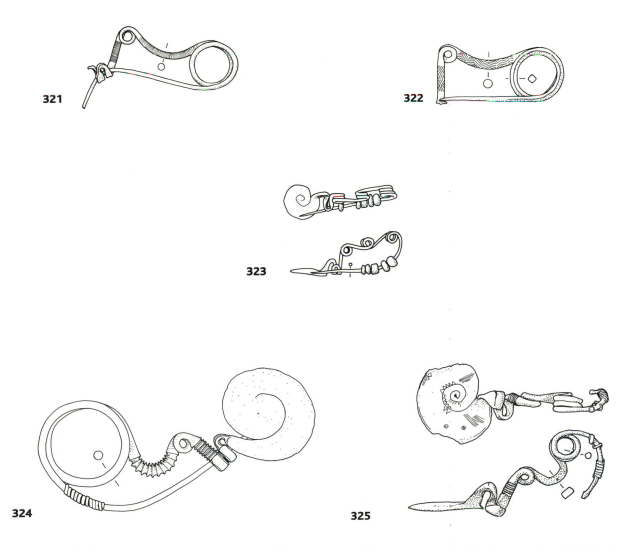

324

325

Plate 64 Fibulae type 39: - 319. - 320. - 321. - 322. **Fibulae type 40**: - 323 near Rome, Lazio. **Fibulae type 41a**: - 324. **Fibulae type 41b**: - 325.

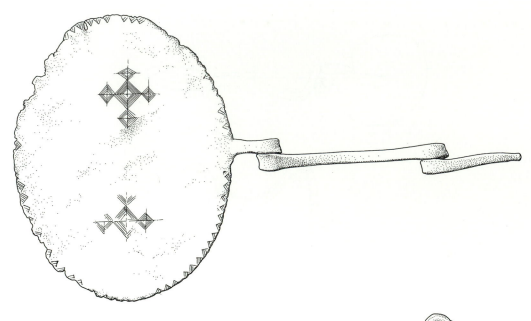

326

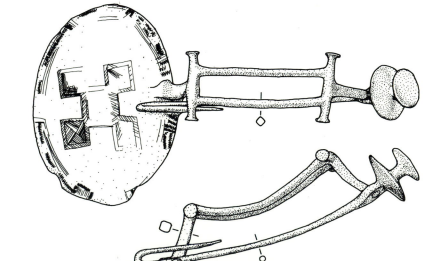

327

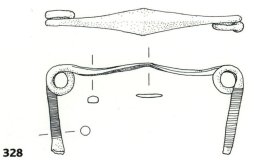

328

Plate 65   Fibulae type 43: - 326. **Fibulae type 44**: - 327 Nola (Naples), Campania. **Fibulae type 45**: - 328.

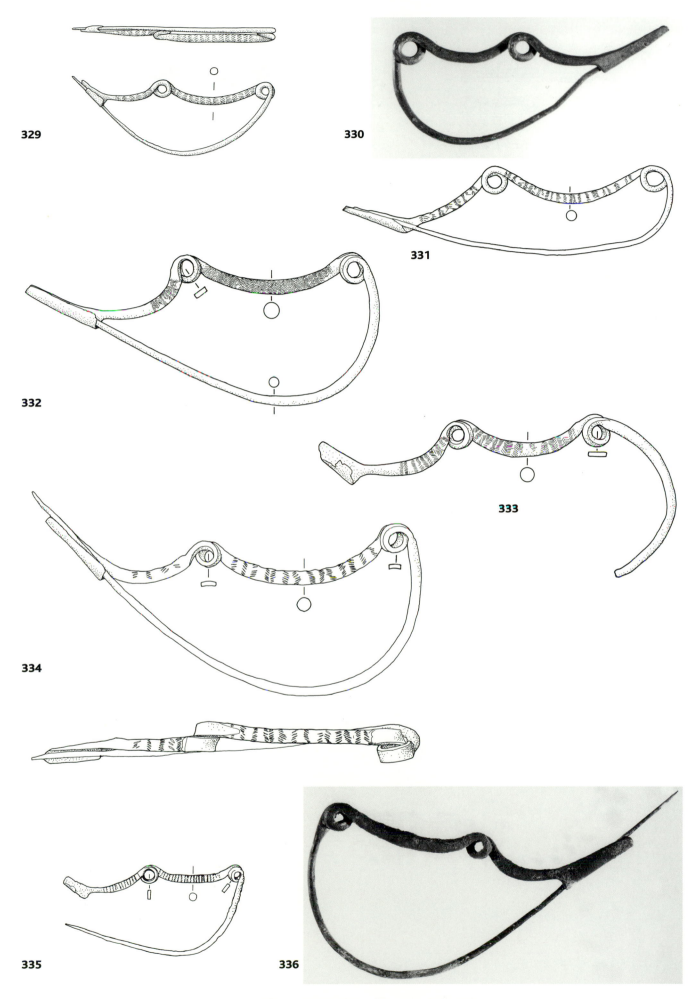

329

330

331

332

333

334

335

336

Plate 66   Fibulae type 46: – 329. – 330. – 331. **Fibulae type 47**: – 332. – 333. – 334. – 335. – 336.

337

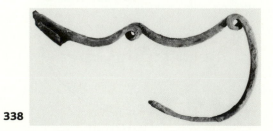

338

339

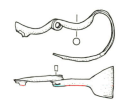

340

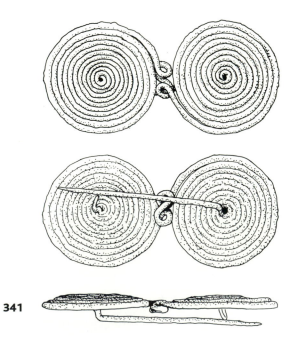

341

Plate 67   Fibulae type 48: - 337. - 338. - 339. **Fibulae type 49**: - 340. **Fibulae type 52**: - 341 Paestum (Salerno), Campania.

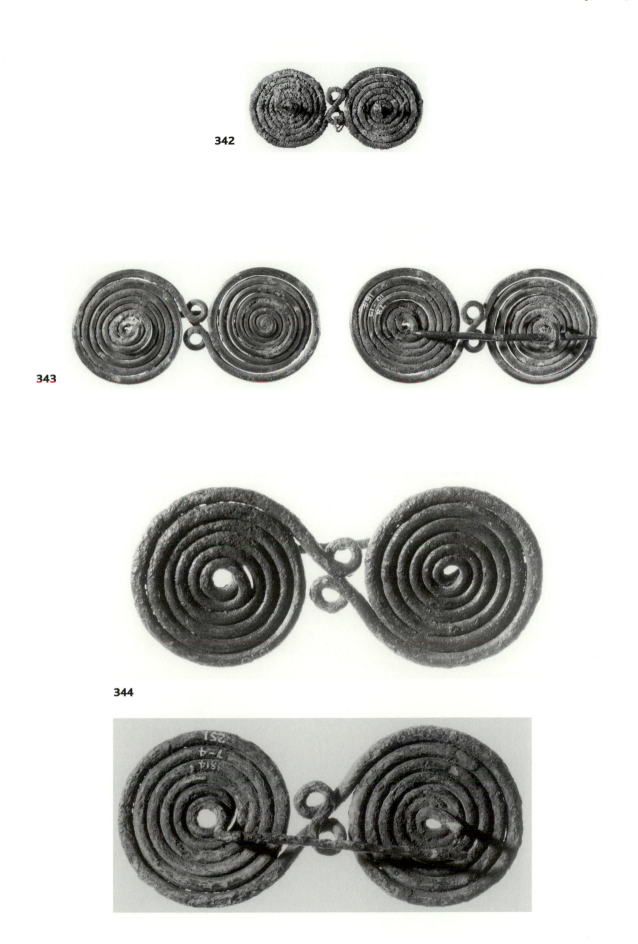

342

343

344

Plate 68   Fibulae type 52: - 342. - 343. - 344. All at scale 1:1.

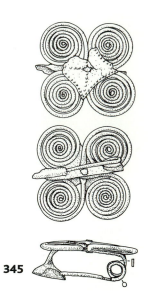

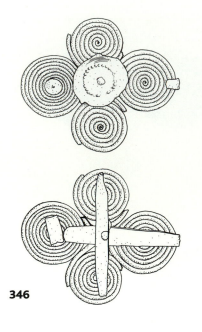

345

346

347

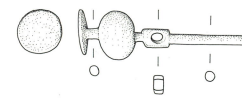

348

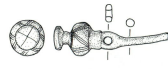

349

350

Plate 69   Fibulae type 57: - 345. - 346 S. Maria Maggiore, Capua (Caserta), Campania. **Fibulae type 56 or 57**: - 347. **Fibulae unclassified**: - 348 Marsica (L'Aquila), Abruzzo. - 349. - 350.

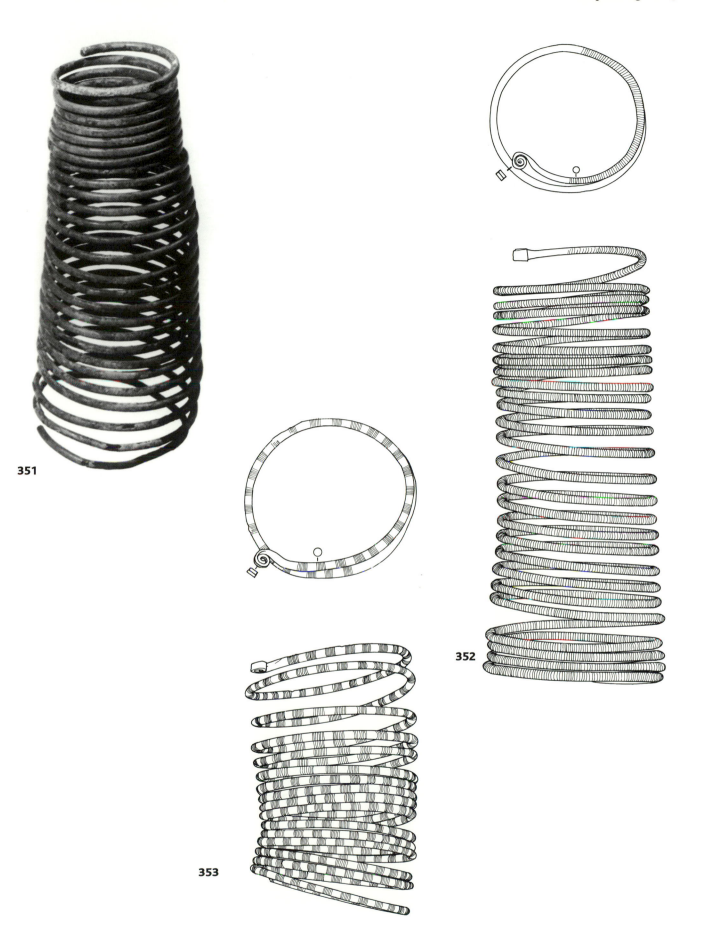

351

352

353

Plate 70 Bracelets type 2a: - 351. - 352. - 353.

354

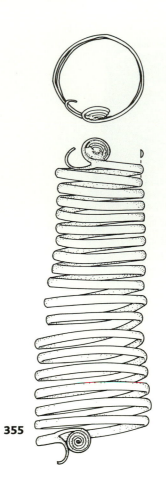

355

356

357

Plate 71   Close to **Bracelets type 2a**: - 354. **Bracelets type 2b**: -355 Cuma (Naples), Campania. **Bracelets type 3a**: - 356 Armento (Potenza), Basilicata. **Bracelets type 3b**: - 357.

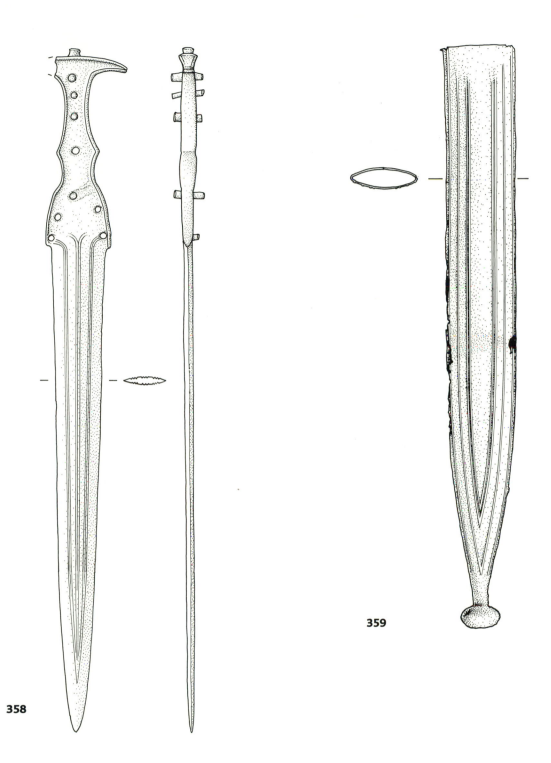

358

359

Plate 72   **Swords type 7**: - 358 probably Naples, Campania. **Sheaths type 1**: - 359 probably Naples, Campania.

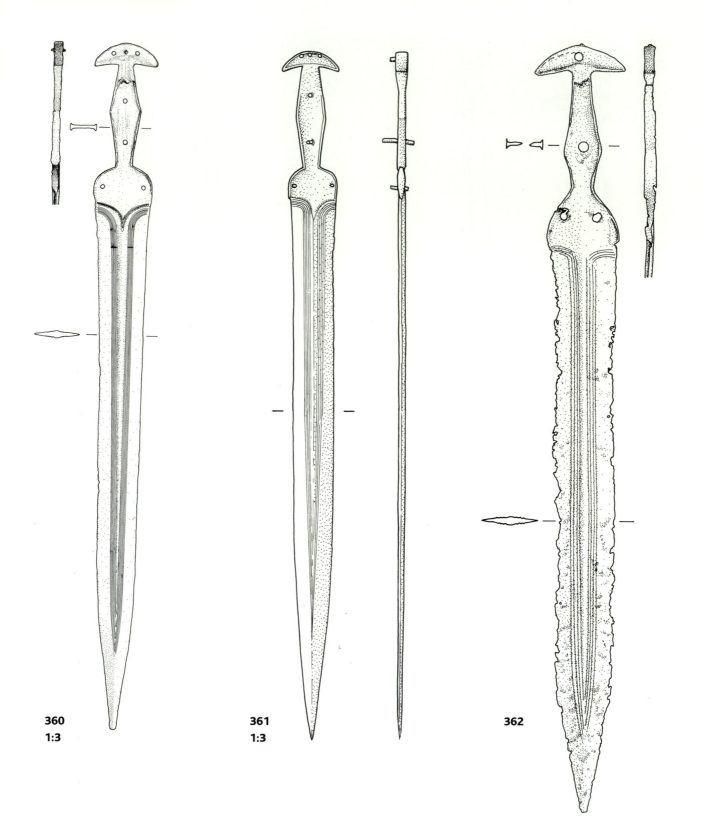

360
1:3

361
1:3

362

Plate 73   Swords type 8a: - 360. - 361 Naples, Campania. - 362 Ruvo (Bari), Apulia.

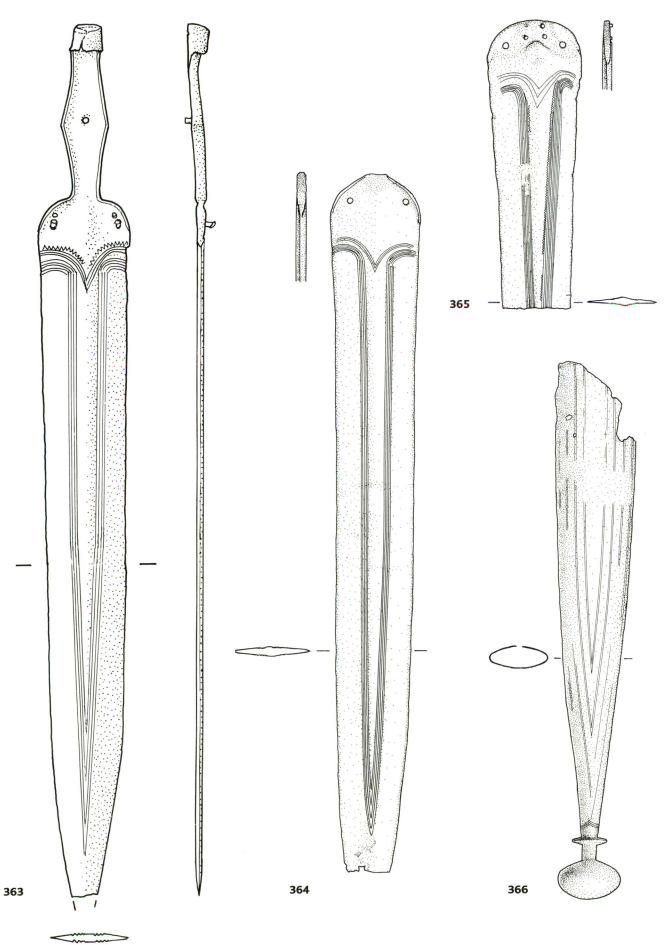

363

365

364

366

Plate 74   Swords type 8a: -363 Naples, Campania.. Probably **Swords type 8a**: -364. -365 Armento (Potenza), Basilicata. **Sheaths type 3**: - 366 Armento, (Potenza), Basilicata.

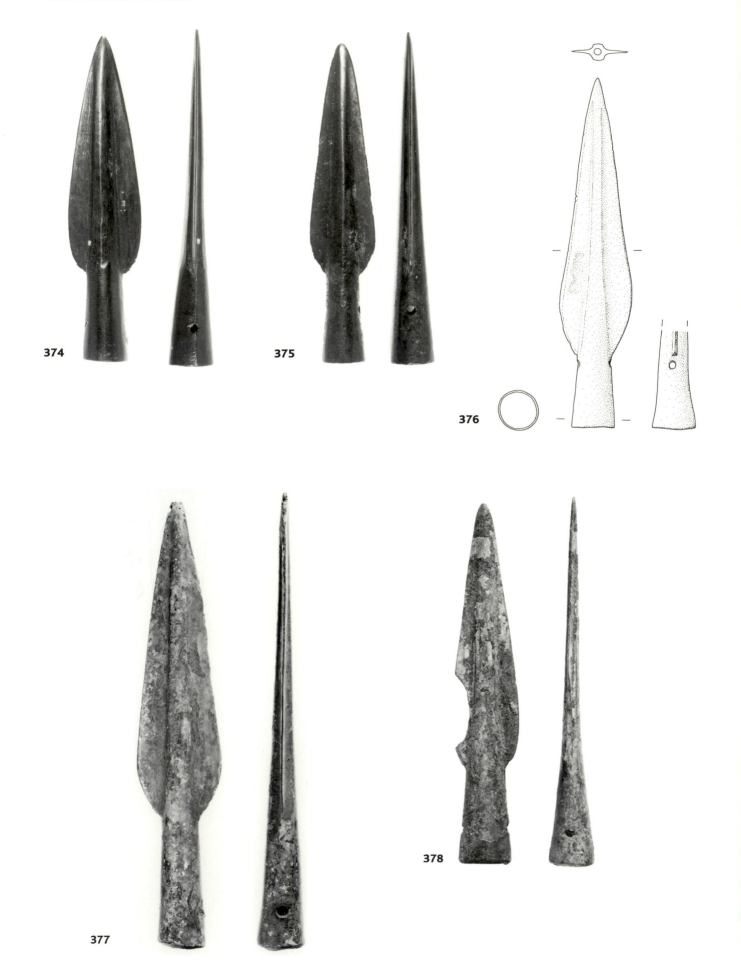

Plate 77 **Spearheads type 2:** - 374. -375. -376 Capua (Caserta), Campania. - 377. -378.

379

380

381

Plate 78   Spearheads type 2: - 379. - 380. - 381.

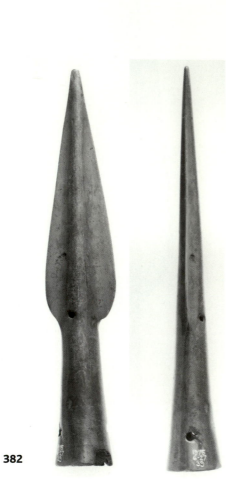

382

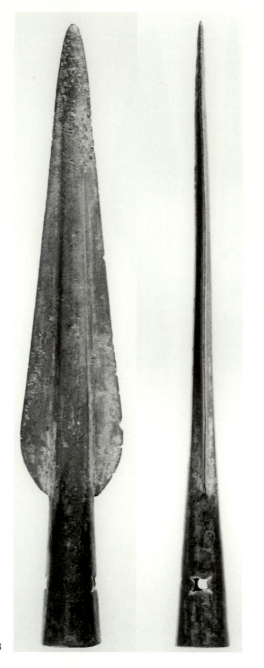

383

Plate 79   Spearheads type 2: - 382. - 383.

384

385

386

Plate 80   Spearheads type 3: - 384. -385. **Spearheads type 3 variant**: -386. All at scale 1:1.

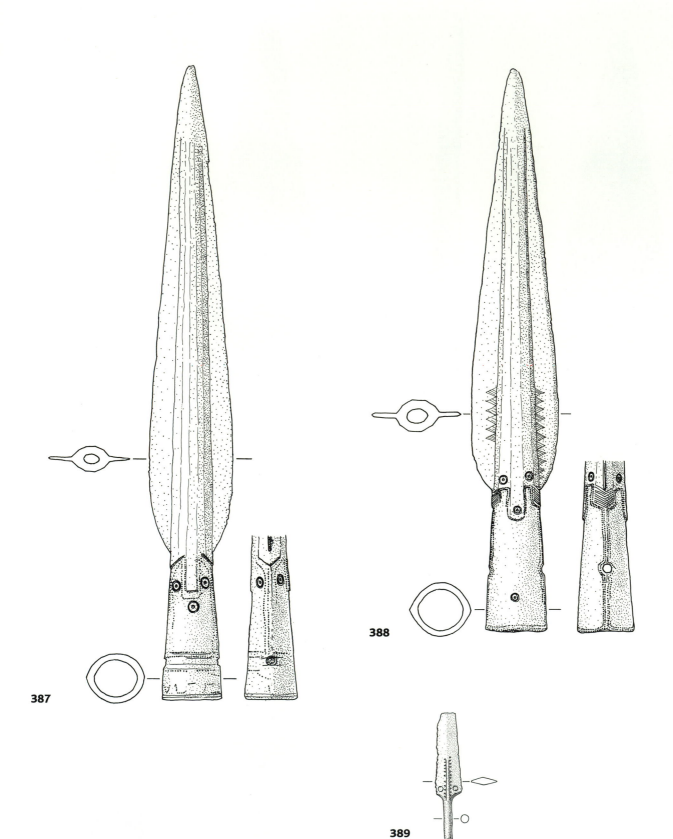

Plate 81   Spearheads type 4: - 387 Bari, Apulia. - 388. **Spearheads type 4 variant**: - 389.

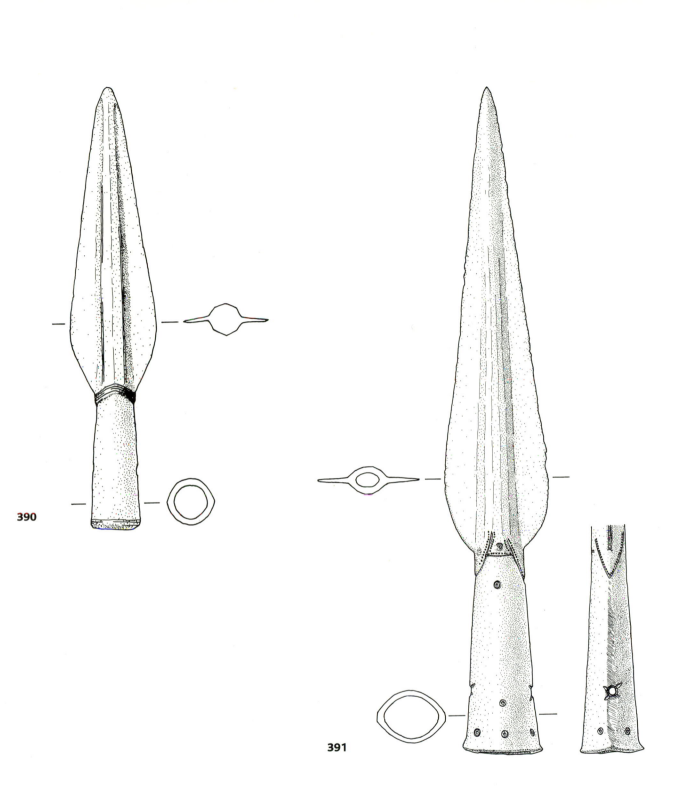

390

391

Plate 82   Spearheads type 4 variant: - 390. - 391.

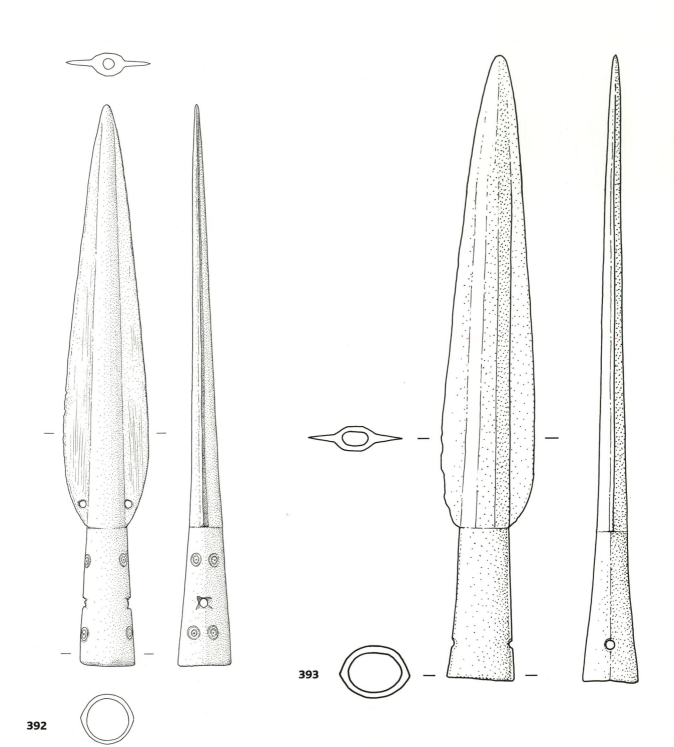

Plate 83   Spearheads type 5: - 392. - 393 Capua (Caserta), Campania.

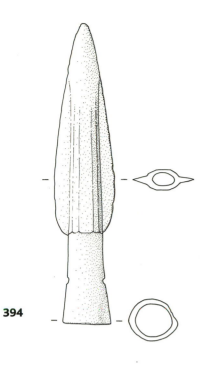

394

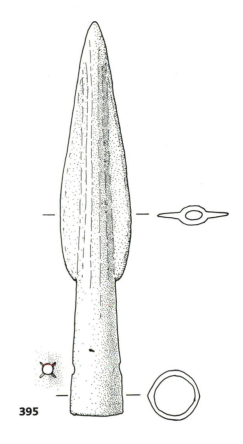

395

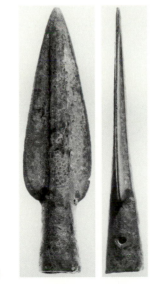

396

Plate 84   **Spearheads type 5**: - 394 Popoli (Pescara), Abruzzo. - 395 Olympia, Greece. - 396.

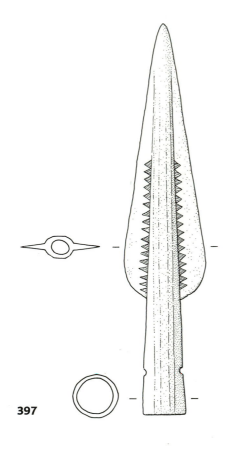

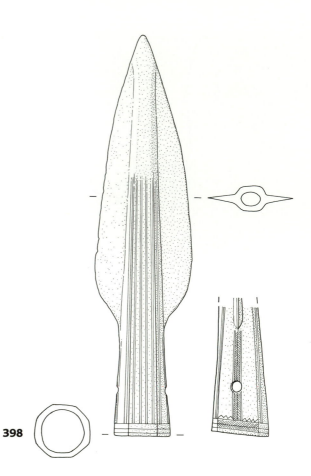

397

398

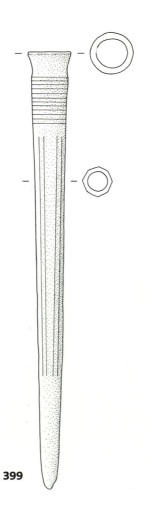

399

Plate 85   Spearheads type 6: - 397 Naples, Campania. **Spearheads type 6 variant**: - 398 Bovino (Foggia), Apulia. **Spear-butts type 5**: - 399 Bovino (Foggia), Apulia.

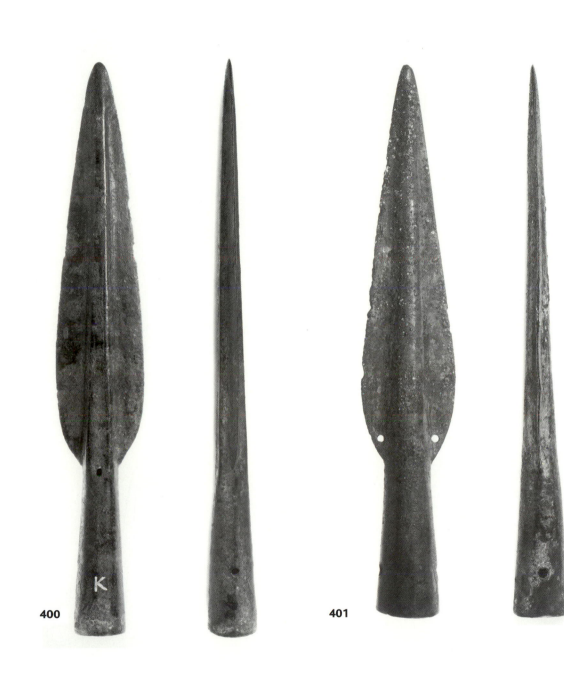

Plate 86   Spearheads type 8: - 400. - 401.

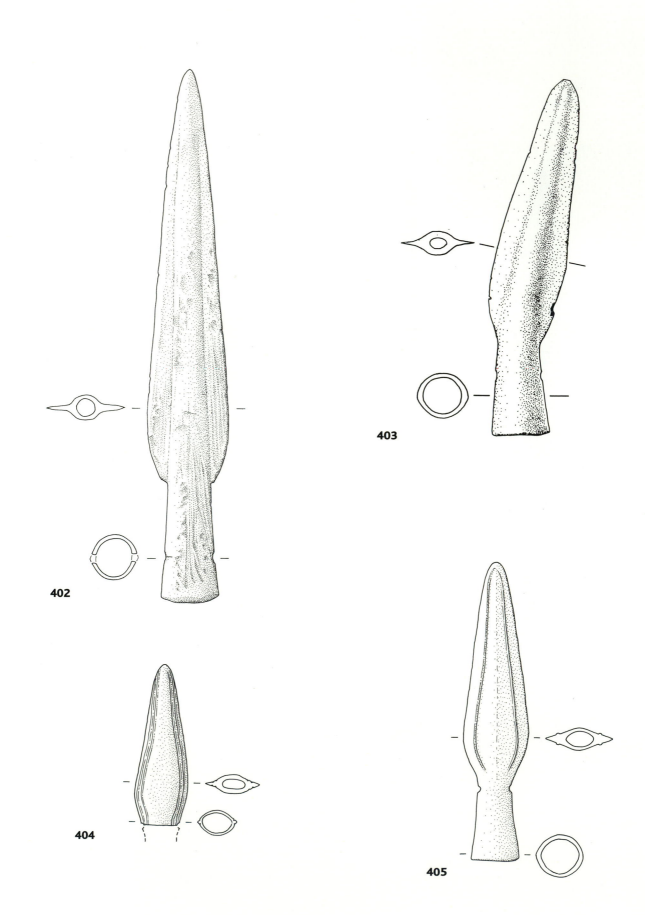

Plate 87   Spearheads type 8: - 402 Capua (Caserta), Campania. - 403 Naples, Campania. **Spearheads type 9**: - 404 Marsica (L'Aquila), Abruzzo. - 405 Cuma (Naples), Campania.

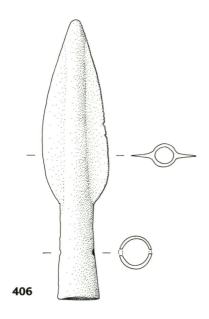

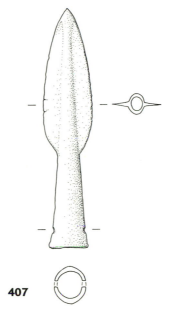

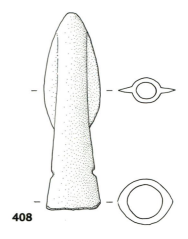

406

407

408

409

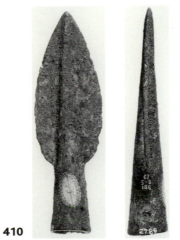

410

Plate 88   Spearheads type 10: - 406 probably Cuma (Naples), Campania. - 407 Calabria. - 408 Marsica (L'Aquila), Abruzzo. - 409. - 410.

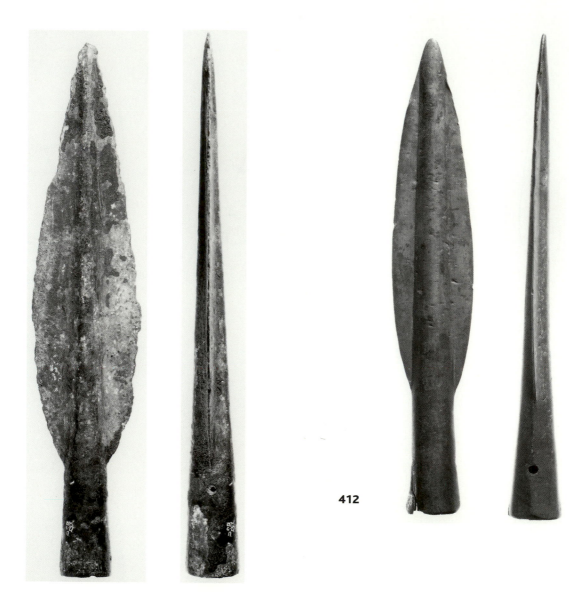

411

412

413

Plate 89   Spearheads type 10: - 411. Spearheads type 10 variant: - 412. - 413.

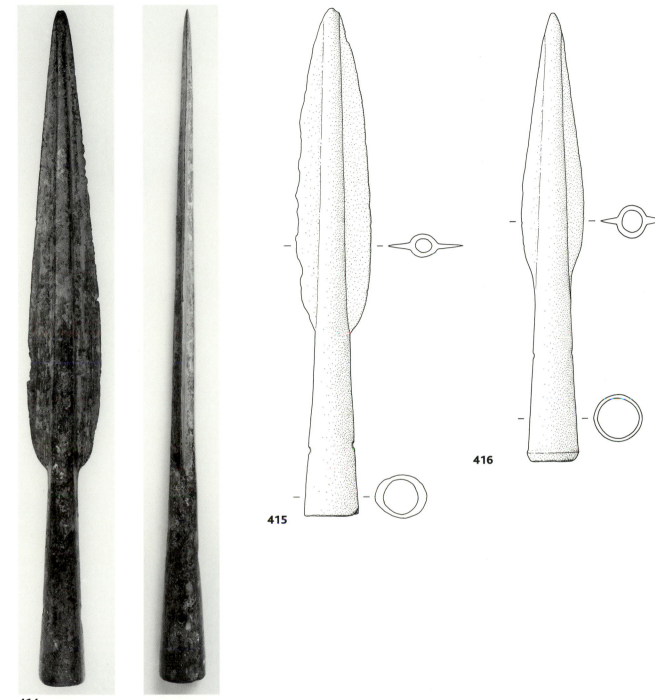

414

415

416

Plate 90   Spearheads type 11: - 414. – 415 Pozzuoli (Naples), Campania. - 416 near Metaponto (Matera), Basilicata.

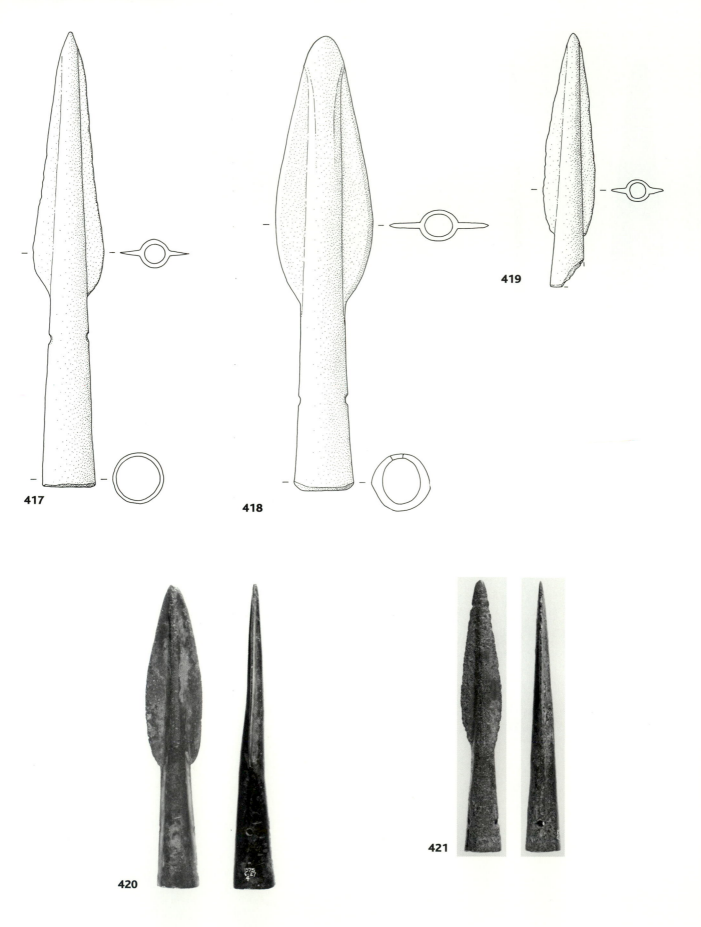

Plate 91   **Spearheads type 11**: - 417 near Naples, Campania. - 418 Capua (Caserta), Campania. - 419 Marsica (L'Aquila), Abruzzo. - 420. - 421.

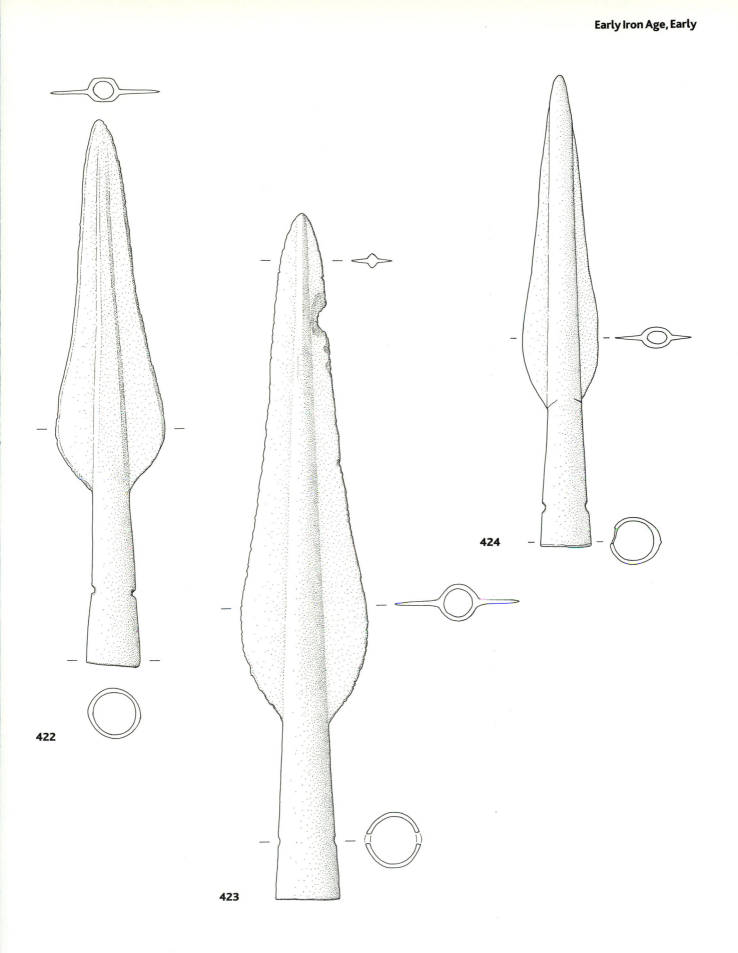

Plate 92   Spearheads type 13: - 422 Abruzzo. - 423 Agrigento, Sicily. - 424 near Naples, Campania.

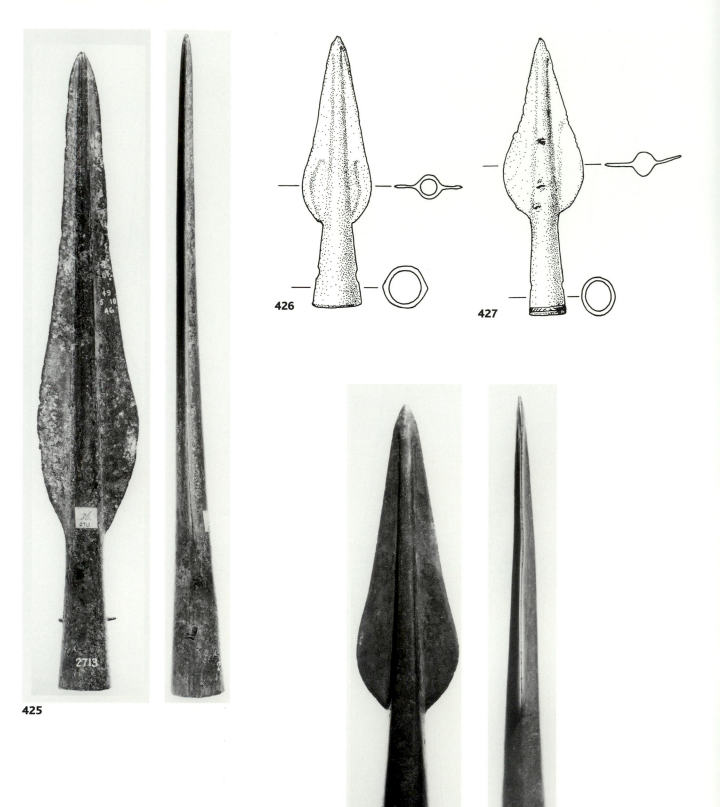

Plate 93   Spearheads type 13: - 425. - 426 Naples, Campania. - 427. - 428.

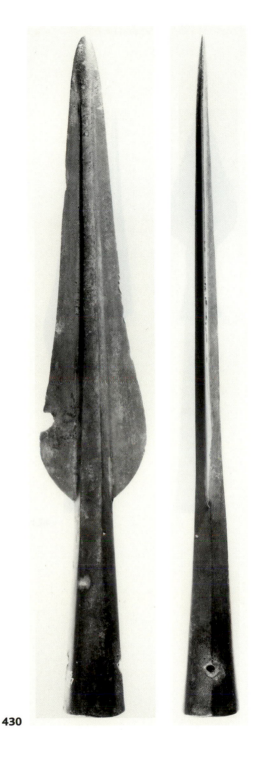

429

430

Plate 94   Spearheads type 13: - 429. - 430.

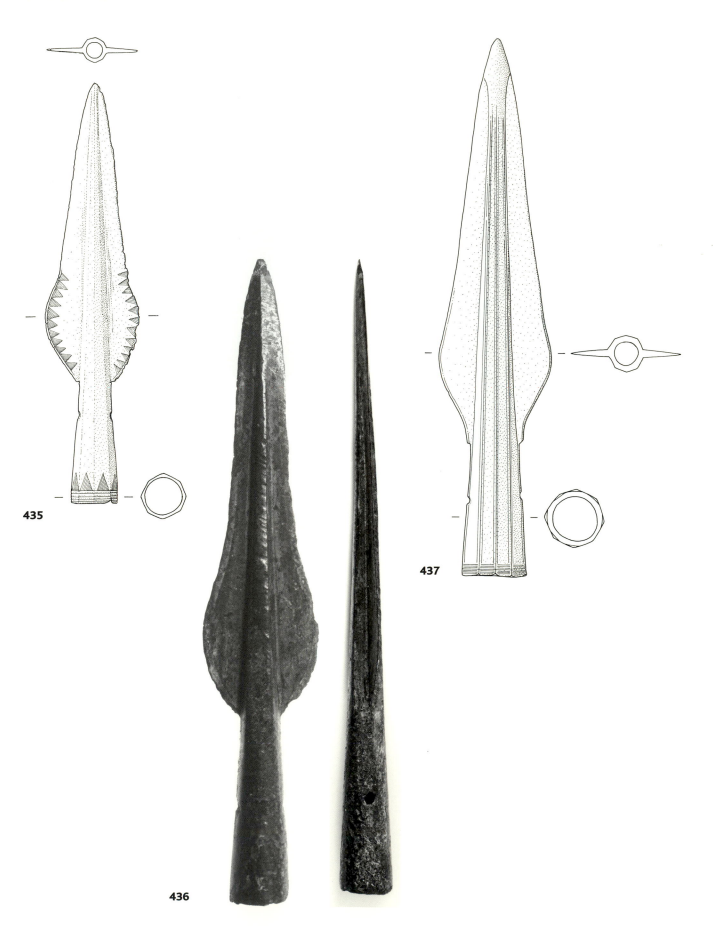

435

436

437

Plate 97   Spearheads type 16: - 435 Capua (Caserta), Campania. - 436. - 437 Viterbo, Lazio.

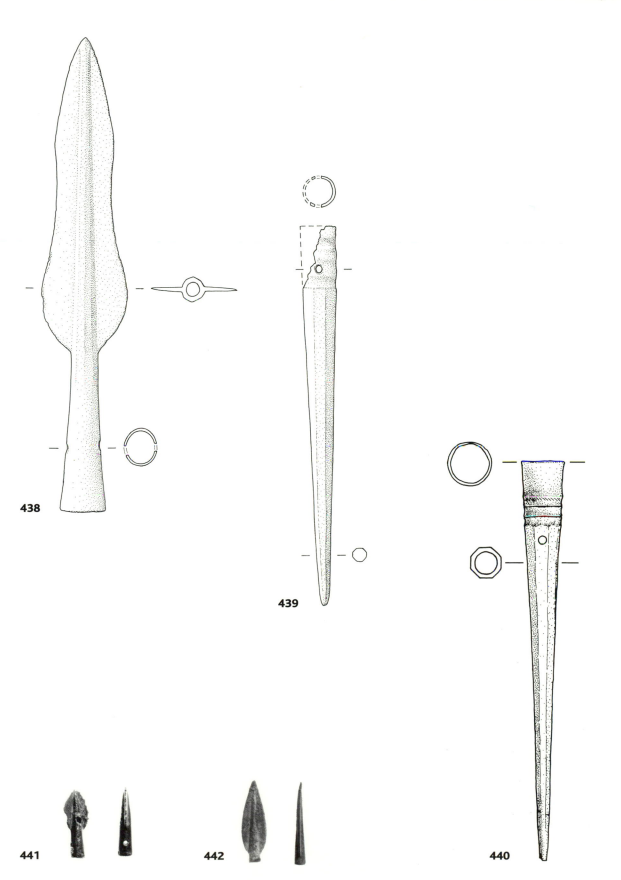

438

439

441　　**442**

440

Plate 98 **Spearheads type 16**: - 438 Mineo (Catania), Sicily. **Spear-butts 5**: - 439 Mineo (Catania), Sicily. **Spear-butts 4** - 440.
Arrowheads 3: - 441. - 442.

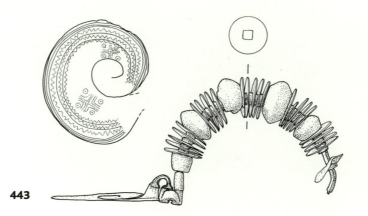

443

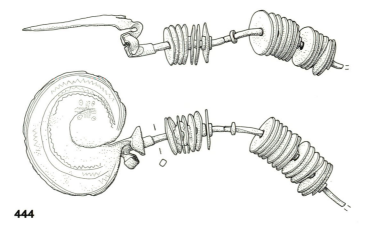

444

445

446

Plate 99   Group of two associated artefacts. **Fibulae type 35**: - 443. - 444. Group of two associated artefacts . **Fibulae type 37**: - 445. - 446.

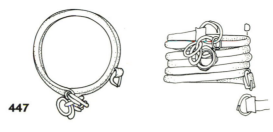

447

448

449

450

Plate 100   Group of two associated artefacts, Bologna, Emilia Romagna. **Bracelets type 1**: - 447. - 448. Group of two associated artefacts . **Bracelets type 1**: - 449. - 450.

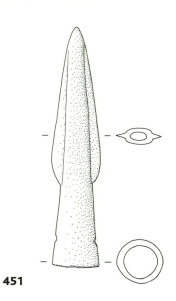

451

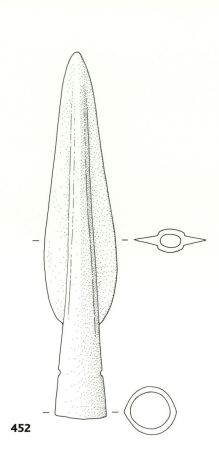

452

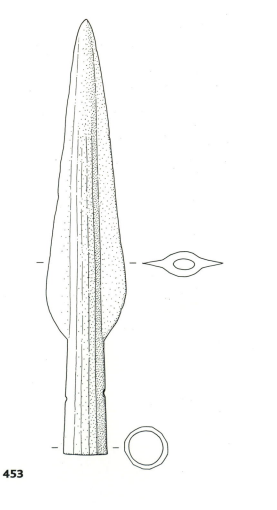

453

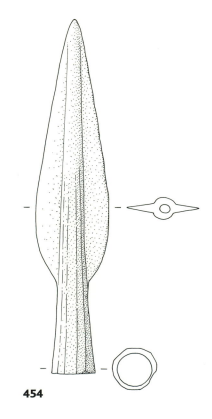

454

Plate 101   Group of two associated artefacts, Sulmona (L'Aquila), Abruzzo. **Spearheads type 2**: - 451. - 452. Group of two associated artefacts, Bari, Apulia. **Spearheads type 6**: - 453. - 454.

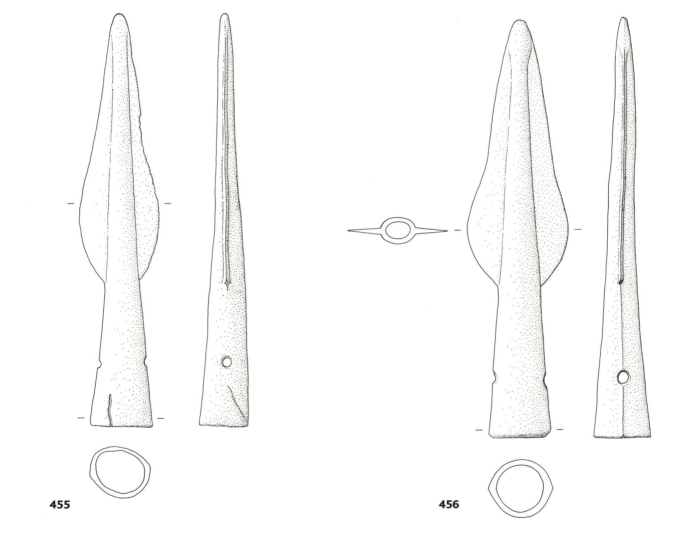

455

456

Plate 102   Group of two associated artefacts, Arezzo, Tuscany. **Spearheads type 13:** - 455. **Spearheads type 14:** - 456.

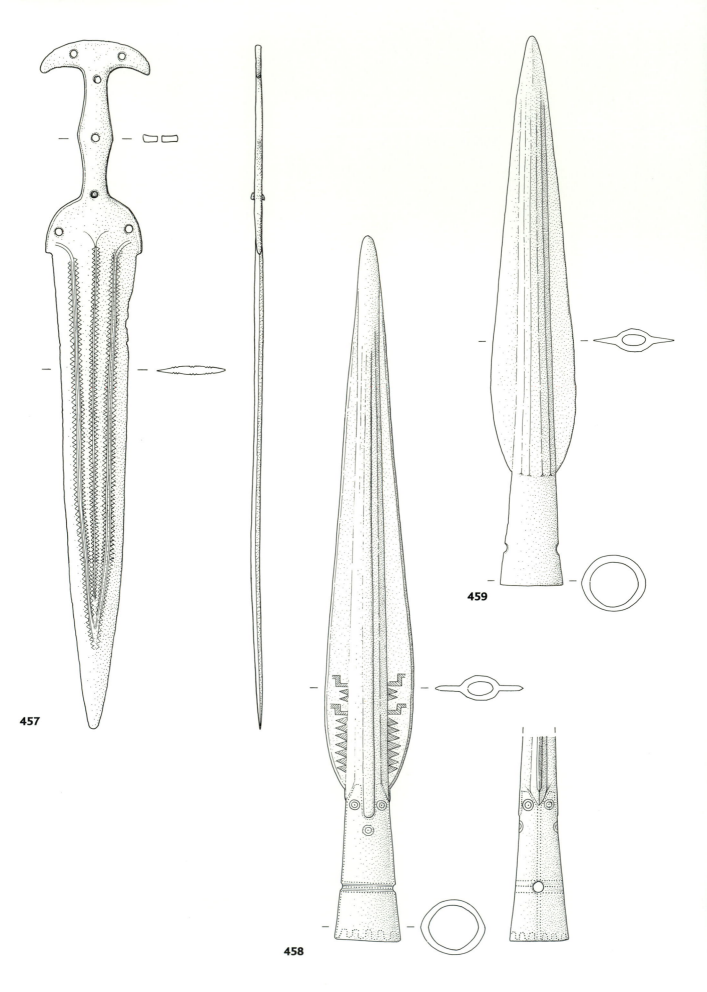

457

459

458

Plate 103   Group of three associated artefacts, Cassino (Frosinone), Lazio. **Swords type 8a**: - 457. **Spearheads type 4**: - 458. **Spearheads type 5**: - 459.

Early Iron Age, Late

Axes

460.
PRB 1868.12-28.279. Purchased from M. Gustav Klemm of Dresden. Collected by his father Dr Klemm.
Fiesole (Florence), Tuscany.
Winged axe with butt wings and trapezoidal blade. **Axes type 37.**
Straight butt, widening beyond the end of the wings, oval wings, marked stop-ridge and shoulders, trapezoidal blade with slightly curved cutting edge. Blackish patina with light green zones.
L. 18.5cm Weight 685g
See *PBF* IX. 12, nos. 2056-2060, type Grottazzolina var. A.
EIA.
Bibliography: *BM Guide* 1904, 116, fig. 116 right; *BM Guide* 1920a, 149, fig. 156 right; *PBF* IX. 12, no. 2058.

461.
PRB 1875.12-29.2. Given by Sir A. W. Franks.
Tarascon, Provence, France.
Winged axe with butt wings and trapezoidal blade. **Axes type 37.**
Straight butt, oval wings, marked stop-ridge and shoulders,trapezoidal blade with almost straight cutting edge. Shiny, dark green patina with bright green incrustations and corroded zones. Faces flattened, probably by hammering, part of a wing missing.
L. 16.5cm Weight 438g
See *PBF* IX. 12, no. 2057, from the Tronto or Vibrata valleys (Marche or Abruzzo), type Grottazzolina var. A; no. 3362, from Veii, Grotta Gramiccia, Tomb 517. Type Narce.
EIA.

462.
PRB 1935.10-18.26. Transferred from GR. Bequeathed by Richard Payne Knight in 1824.
Winged axe with butt wings and trapezoidal blade. **Axes type 37.**
Straight butt, oval wings, marked stop-ridge and shoulders, wide trapezoidal blade with slightly curved cutting edge. Dark green smooth patina. Parts missing.
L. 17.5cm Weight 543g
See *PBF* IX. 12, no. 2058, type Grottazzolina var.A.
EIA.
Bibliography: Walters 1899, no. 2936.

463.
PRB 1964.12-1.388(374). Sir Henry Wellcome Collection, no. 113258. Bought in Rome from A. Rocci by Captain Saint in April 1932. Given by the Wellcome Trustees.
Winged axe with butt wings and trapezoidal blade. **Axes type 37.**

Straight butt, widening beyond the end of the wings, oval wings, marked stop-ridge and shoulders, trapezoidal blade with slightly curved cutting edge. Incised parallel lines and two lines crossing on the blade, and series of lines at an angle on the wings. Dark green patina with incrustations of earth. Small parts missing.
L. 12.1cm Weight 98g
See *PBF* IX. 12, no. 2054, from Veii, type Bambolo, var.; Giardino 1995, fig. 62B.1,2, decorated axes of similar type from Lustignano and Volterra, Tuscany.
EIA.

464.
PRB 1964.12-1.391(375). Sir Henry Wellcome Collection, no. 113264. Bought in Rome from A. Rocci by Captain Saint in April 1932. Given by the Wellcome Trustees.
Winged axe with butt wings and trapezoidal blade. **Axes type 37.**
Straight butt, widening beyond the wing ends, wide oval wings, marked stop-ridge and protruding shoulders, wide trapezoidal blade with slightly curved cutting edge. Incised lines along the edges of the blade. Shiny brown patina with green incrustations. Small parts missing.
L. 14cm Weight 246g
See *PBF* IX. 12, nos. 2060, from Tarquinia (Viterbo), Lazio; 2061, from Roccalbegna (Grosseto), Tuscany. Type Grottazzolina.
EIA.

465.
PRB WG1046. Canon W. Greenwell Collection, bought from the Rev. Greville J. Chester. Given by J. Pierpont Morgan in 1909.
Tuscany.
Winged axe with butt wings and trapezoidal blade. **Axes type 38.**
Concave butt, wide oval wings, marked stop-ridge and shoulders, trapezoidal blade with slightly curved cutting edge. Smooth blackish patina; surface with corroded zones. Parts of wings missing.
L. 16cm Weight 545g
See *PBF* IX. 12, no. 2137 from Cignano (Arezzo), Tuscany, type Cignano.
EIA, late.

466.
PRB 1964.12-1.220(315). Sir Henry Wellcome Collection, no. 79449. Bought in Florence from A. Albizi by Captain Saint in April 1930. Given by the Wellcome Trustees.
Populonia (Livorno), Tuscany.
Winged axe with butt wings and trapezoidal palette blade. Close to **Axes type 38.**
Straight butt, oval wings, marked stop-ridge and shoulders, long and thin trapezoidal blade with slightly curved cutting edge. Incised

circles on blade and wings; incised and *tremolo* zigzags on wings. Olive green patina with incrustations. Small parts of blade missing.
L. 20cm Weight 262g
Analysis: Bronze. See D. Hook report.
See *PBF* IX. 12, no. 3389, from Bologna, Emilia Romagna (not identical). Type Benacci var B.
EIA, late.

467.
GR 1865.7-20.105. Bought from C. Merlin.
Olympia, Greece.
Winged axe with butt wings and trapezoidal blade. **Axes type 38.**
Straight butt, oval wings, slightly marked shoulders, wide trapezoidal blade with slightly curved cutting edge. Dull olive green patina with dark green incrustations. Butt damaged in antiquity.
L. 12.4cm Weight 215g
See *PBF* IX. 12, no. 2137, from Cignano (Arezzo), Tuscany. Type Cignano, EIA, late. The BM piece is very close to this type, except that it has no stop-ridge.
EIA.
Bibliography: Walters 1899, no. 2926, fig. 82; Bietti Sestieri 1986, 'Weapons and Tools', 6, no. 20, and fig. p. 19.

468.
PRB 1866.6-27.100. Henry Christy Collection. Given by the Trustees under the will of Henry Christy. Perhaps bought from G. Eastwood.
Winged axe with butt wings and trapezoidal blade. **Axes type 38.**
Straight butt, widening beyond the end of the wings, oval wings, marked stop-ridge and shoulders, trapezoidal blade with straight cutting edge. Traces of grooved decoration on blade and wings. Irregular patina, green and black incrustations.
L. 14cm Weight 246g
See **cat. 467**; for the decoration see also *PBF* IX. 12, nos. 3362, from Veii; 3385, 3386, from Bologna, Benacci cemetery.
EIA.

469.
PRB WG1075. Canon W. Greenwell Collection, bought from the Rev. Greville J. Chester. Given by J. Pierpont Morgan in 1909.
'Maremma di Toscana', Province of Siena, Tuscany (note that now the Maremma, i.e. the coastal strip of central and northern Tuscany, is part of the province of Livorno).
Winged axe with butt wings and trapezoidal blade. **Axes type 39.**
Straight butt with two slight side indentations, wide oval wings, marked stop-ridge and protruding shoulders, wide trapezoidal blade with almost straight cutting edge.Incised lines along the edge of the blade. Smooth dark green patina. Blade broken in antiquity, both parts

preserved. Probably from a hoard.
L. 15.7cm Weight 313g
See *PBF* IX. 12, nos. 3055–3355, mainly from the
San Francesco hoard, Bologna, Emilia
Romagna. Type San Francesco.
EIA, late.

470.
PRB WG1076. Canon W. Greenwell Collection,
bought from the Rev. Greville J. Chester. Given
by J. Pierpont Morgan in 1909.
Salso (Parma), Emilia Romagna.
Winged axe with butt wings and trapezoidal
blade. **Axes type 39**.
Thick-sectioned tool. Straight butt, wide oval
wings, marked stop-ridge and protruding
shoulders, wide and short trapezoidal blade,
probably reworked, with curved cutting edge.
On both faces, incised zigzag pattern on the
stop-ridge. Smooth olive green patina. Wings
broken intentionally in antiquity.
L. 13.8cm Weight 494g
See **cat. 469**.
EIA, late.

471.
PRB WG1077. Canon W. Greenwell Collection.
Given by J. Pierpont Morgan in 1909.
Bologna, Emilia Romagna.
Winged axe with butt wings and trapezoidal
palette blade. **Axes type 39**.
Slightly concave butt, wide oval wings with
small central hole between the wings, marked
stop-ridge and protruding shoulders, thin,
wide trapezoidal blade, broken at end. Blackish
patina with thick green and turquoise
incrustations.
L. 12.2cm Weight 196g
See **cat. 469**.
EIA, late.

472.
PRB 1964.12-6.86. Bequeathed by C.T.
Trechmann.
Poszory, Hungary.
Winged axe with butt wings and trapezoidal
blade. **Axes type 39**.
Straight butt, wide oval wings, marked stop-
ridge and protruding shoulders, wide
trapezoidal blade with almost straight cutting
edge. On both faces, three nicks on the stop-
ridge, a series of fine vertical nervatures and a
cast mark (letter?) between the wings. Dull
patina, dark green in various tones.
L. 15.7cm Weight 646g
See **cat. 469**.
EIA, late.

473.
PRB 1866.6-27.102. Henry Christy Collection.
Given by the Trustees under the will of Henry
Christy. Perhaps bought from G. Eastwood.
Winged axe with butt wings and trapezoidal
blade. **Axes type 39**.
Straight butt, oval wings, marked stop-ridge
and shoulders, trapezoidal blade with almost
straight cutting edge. Incised decoration on the
whole surface: concentric circles on the faces of
the blade; alternating rows of concentric
circles, dots and parallel lines on the wings;
parallel lines and dots on the sides of the blade.
Irregular green and black patina.
L. 17cm Weight 663g
See **cat. 469**. Decoration: *PBF* IX. 12, no. 3395,

type Benacci, var.
EIA, late.

474.
PRB 1878.11-1.207. Given by General A.W.H.
Meyrick.
Winged axe with butt wings and trapezoidal
blade. **Axes type 39**.
Straight butt with small central hole, wide oval
wings, marked stop-ridge and protruding
shoulders, wide trapezoidal blade with almost
straight cutting edge. Blackish patina with
white incrustations and very dark corroded
surface.
L. 17cm Weight 511g
See **cat. 469**.
EIA, late.

475.
PRB 1935.10-18.24. Transferred from GR.
Bequeathed by R. Payne Knight in 1824.
Winged axe with butt wings and trapezoidal
blade. **Axes type 39**.
Straight hammered butt, wide oval wings,
marked stop-ridge and protruding shoulders,
wide and short trapezoidal blade, probably
reworked, with slightly curved cutting edge.
Smooth dark green patina with incrustations.
L. 13.3cm Weight 514g
See *PBF* IX. 12, especially nos. 3297–3299,
mainly from the hoard of San Francesco,
Bologna, Emilia Romagna. Type San Francesco.
EIA, late.
Bibliography: Walters 1899, no. 2934.

476.
PRB 1935.10-18.27. Transferred from GR.
Charles Townley Collection. Bought from
Peregrine Townley.
Winged axe with butt wings and trapezoidal
blade. **Axes type 39**.
Straight butt, wide oval wings, marked stop-
ridge and protruding shoulders, wide
trapezoidal blade with almost straight cutting
edge. Smooth dark green patina. Wings, blade
edges and cutting edge all damaged.
L. 16.7cm Weight 637g
See **cat. 469**.
EIA, late.
Bibliography: Walters 1899, no. 2937.

477.
PRB 1964.12-1.389(373). Sir Henry Wellcome
Collection, no. 113263. Bought in Rome from
A. Rocci by Captain Saint in April 1932. Given by
the Wellcome Trustees.
Winged axe with butt wings and trapezoidal
blade. **Axes type 39**.
Straight butt, wide oval wings, marked stop-
ridge and protruding shoulders, wide and short
trapezoidal blade, reworked, with slightly
curved cutting edge. Dull, dark green patina
with incrustations in various tones of green and
brown. Small parts missing from the wings,
casting fault (one wing asymmetrical).
L. 10.4cm Weight 229g
See **cat. 469**.
EIA, late.

478.
PRB 1964.12-1.392 (376). Sir Henry Wellcome
Collection. Given by the Wellcome Trustees.
Winged axe with butt wings and trapezoidal
blade. **Axes type 39**.

Straight butt, wide oval wings, marked stop-
ridge and protruding shoulders, wide
trapezoidal blade with almost straight cutting
edge. Between the wings on one side, an incised
mark (star). Smooth blackish patina with
bright green incrustations. Small parts missing.
L. 16.2cm Weight 638g
See **cat. 469**.
EIA, late.

479.
PRB WG1078. Canon W. Greenwell Collection,
bought from the Rev. Greville J. Chester. Given
by J. Pierpont Morgan in 1909.
Sarzana (La Spezia), Liguria.
Winged axe, thick with elongated body and
trapezoidal butt. **Axes type 40**.
High butt, wide oval wings, marked stop-ridge
and shoulders, elongated trapezoidal blade
with slightly rounded cutting edge. Smooth
patina in various tones of green, surface with
corroded zones. Butt hammered. Part of
cutting edge missing.
L. 19.6cm Weight 795g
See *PBF* IX. 12, nos. 2146–2523, mainly from the
hoards of San Francesco, Bologna, Emilia
Romagna, and Ardea (Rome), Lazio. Type
Ardea.
EIA, late.

480.
PRB WG1079. Canon W. Greenwell Collection,
bought from the Rev. Greville J. Chester. Given
by J. Pierpont Morgan in 1909.
'Alba della Massa', probably Massa d'Albe
(L'Aquila), Abruzzo.
Winged axe, thick, with elongated body and
trapezoidal butt. **Axes type 40**.
Medium butt, wide oval wings, marked stop-
ridge and shoulders, wide and elongated
trapezoidal blade with slightly rounded cutting
edge. Small hollow at centre of the upper part
of the blade. Smooth blackish patina.
L. 19.2cm Weight 661g
See **cat. 479**.
EIA, late.

481.
PRB 1935.10-18.44. Transferred from GR
(1916.6-1.26). Given by Lord Avebury.
Acquired in Naples and probably from
neighbourhood.
Campania.
Winged axe, thick-sectioned, with elongated
body and trapezoidal butt. **Axes type 40**.
Medium butt, wide oval wings, marked stop-
ridge and shoulders, elongated trapezoidal
blade with rounded cutting edge. Dull green
patina with corroded surface. Small parts
missing.
L. 21.3cm Weight 759g
See **cat. 479**.
EIA, late.

482.
PRB WG2263. Canon W. Greenwell Collection,
bought from Bryce Knight of Regent Street.
Given by J. Pierpont Morgan in 1909.
Tarascon, Provence, France.
Winged axe, thick-sectioned, with elongated
body and trapezoidal butt. **Axes type 40**.
Medium butt, wide oval wings, marked stop-
ridge and shoulders, elongated blade with
rounded cutting edge. Incised lines along the

edges of the blade. Shiny, dark green patina with bright green incrustations and corroded zones.
L. 19.5cm Weight 708g
See **cat. 479**.
EIA, late.

483.
PRB 1873.6-2.15. Collection J.F. Lucas of Bentley Ashbourne, Derbyshire. Purchased from Mrs. Ruth Faulkner, executor of J.F. Lucas.
Said to have been found at Foxcote, England (see also **cat. 91**).
Winged axe, thick with elongated body and trapezoidal butt. **Axes type 40**.
Medium butt, wide oval wings, marked stop-ridge and shoulders, elongated blade with slightly rounded cutting edge. Irregular patina, dark green with green and white incrustations, corroded zones. Cutting edge damaged.
L. 21.5cm Weight 813g
See **cat. 479**.
EIA, late.

484.
PRB 1866.6-27.103. Henry Christy Collection. Given by the Trustees under the will of Henry Christy. Perhaps bought from G. Eastwood.
Winged axe, thick-sectioned, with elongated body and trapezoidal butt. **Axes type 40**.
Short butt, wide oval wings with hammered faces, marked stop-ridge and slightly marked shoulders, short blade with rounded cutting edge. Probably reworked. Smooth, yellowish patina with thick green incrustations. Bronze fragments adhering between wings.
L. 15cm Weight 559g
See **cat. 479**.
EIA, late.

485.
PRB 1935.10-18.23. Transferred from GR. Bought from Sir William Hamilton.
Winged axe, thick with elongated body and trapezoidal butt. **Axes type 40**.
Medium butt, wide oval wings, marked stop-ridge and shoulders, elongated blade with rounded cutting edge. Smooth light green patina. Butt and wings damaged.
L. 18.7cm Weight 675g
See **cat. 479**.
EIA, late.
Bibliography: Walters 1899, no. 2933.

486.
PRB 1935.10-18.25. Transferred from GR.
Winged axe, thick with elongated body and trapezoidal butt. **Axes type 40**.
Medium butt, wide oval wings, marked stop-ridge and shoulders, elongated blade with rounded cutting edge. Incised lines along edges of both faces and sides of blade. Smooth dark green patina. Wings damaged.
L. 18.5cm Weight 694g
See **cat. 479**.
EIA, late.
Bibliography: Walters 1899, no. 2935.

487.
PRB 1964.12-1.386(311). Sir Henry Wellcome Collection, no. 79450. Bought in Florence from A. Albizi by Captain Saint in April 1930. Given by the Wellcome Trustees.
Winged axe with elongated body and

protruding shoulders. **Axes type 40**.
Butt probably short and rounded, broken in antiquity, wide oval wings, marked stop-ridge and protruding shoulders, narrow blade with concave sides and curved cutting edge. Smooth and discontinuous dark green patina with light green, brown and whitish incrustations.
L. 18.3cm Weight 704g
See *PBF* IX. 12, nos. 2146–2523, mainly from the hoards of San Francesco, Bologna, and Ardea (Rome); especially nos. 2146–2157, blade with slightly concave sides.
EIA, late.

488.
PRB 1964.12-1.382 (378). Sir Henry Wellcome Collection, no. 113260. Bought in Rome from A. Rocci by Captain Saint in April 1932. Given by the Wellcome Trustees.
Winged axe, thick with elongated body and trapezoidal butt. **Axes type 40**.
Medium butt with central notch, wide oval wings, marked stop-ridge and shoulders, elongated blade with rounded cutting edge. Shiny brown patina with green areas, bronze visible.
L. 17.3cm Weight 678g
See *PBF* IX. 12, nos. 2146–2523, mainly from the hoards of San Francesco, Bologna, Emilia Romagna, and Ardea (Rome), Lazio, especially no. 2528, type Ardea, var. A.
EIA, late.

489.
PRB 1866.6-27.101. Henry Christy Collection. Given by the Trustees under the will of Henry Christy. Perhaps bought from G. Eastwood.
Winged axe with butt wings and sloping shoulders. **Axes type 41**.
Straight butt, oval wings, marked stop-ridge, slightly marked shoulders, trapezoidal blade with slightly rounded cutting edge. Smooth dark green patina.
L. 16.8cm Weight 560g
See *PBF* IX. 12, nos. 2540–2841, from Marsiliana d'Albegna (Grosseto), Tuscany, and the hoard of San Francesco, Bologna, Emilia Romagna. Type Marsiliana d'Albegna.
EIA, late.

490.
PRB 1964.12-1.393 (313). Sir Henry Wellcome Collection, no. 96453. Bought in Rome from Antichità delle Belle Arti by Captain Saint in April 1931. Given by the Wellcome Trustees.
Winged axe with butt wings and sloping shoulders. **Axes type 41**.
Straight butt, wide, oval wings, marked stop-ridge, slightly marked shoulders, rectangular blade with slightly rounded cutting edge. Dull discontinuous patina, with green and azure incrustations and surface corrosion. Part of wings missing.
L. 18cm Weight 682g
See **cat. 489**.
EIA, late.

491.
PRB WG1074. Canon W. Greenwell Collection, bought from G.F. Lawrence. Given by J. Pierpont Morgan in 1909.
Lake Trasimeno (Perugia), Umbria.
Winged axe with butt wings and trapezoidal blade. **Axes type 42**.

Short butt with two small indentations, oval wings, marked stop-ridge and slightly marked shoulders, wide and short trapezoidal blade, probably reworked, with slightly rounded profile and cutting edge. Incised decoration on the blade: concentric circles, parallel lines and triangles. Smooth grey patina with dark green and turquoise incrustations. Small parts missing.
L. 12.4 Weight 234g
Analysis: Bronze. See D. Hook report.
See *PBF* IX. 12, no. 3375, from Roselle (Grosseto), Tuscany. Type Roselle, similar shape and decoration.
EIA, late to early Orientalizing.

492.
PRB 1935.10-18.18. Transferred from GR.
Winged axe with butt wings and trapezoidal blade. **Axes type 42**.
Straight butt, widening beyond end of wings, very wide oval wings, marked stop-ridge and protruding shoulders, wide, thin trapezoidal blade with almost straight cutting edge. Covered with thick black and dark green incrustations.
L. 14.8cm Weight 276g
See *PBF* IX. 12, nos. 3371–3376, from Roselle and Vetulonia (Grosseto), and Chiusi (Siena), both in Tuscany. Type Roselle.
EIA, late to early Orientalizing.
Bibliography: Walters 1899, no. 2928.

493.
PRB 1935.10-18.34. Transferred from GR (1865.7-22.10). Bought from Alessandro Castellani.
Decorated shaft-hole axe with circular shaft-hole. **Axes type 52**.
Elongated trapezoidal shape with continuous profile, asymmetrical angular butt, straight cutting edge. Surface, with the exception of the lower part of the blade, covered with decoration - a series of continuous incised zigzag lines on the haft-end, and concentric circles on the faces and sides of the haft and blade. Rough patina in various tones of olive green.
L. 18.5cm Weight 940g
See *PBF* IX.12, no. 4460, San Francesco hoard, Bologna, Emilia Romagna. Type Doss Trento.
EIA, late.
Note: this piece could be a ceremonial axe made in bronze in the Orientalizing period and reminiscent of EIA types; see for a similar piece the group of ceremonial objects from Tarquinia, Bonghi Jovino and Chiaramonte Trere 1997, 172, pl.126.5.
Bibliography: Walters 1899, no. 2944.

494.
PRB 1964.12-1.407(363). Sir Henry Wellcome Collection, no. 113257. Bought in Rome from A. Rocci by Captain Saint in April 1932. Given by the Wellcome Trustees.
Socketed axe with continuous profile and oval socket. **Axes type 55**.
Small tool, socket with raised band at mouth, slightly marked upwards-pointing shoulders, short flaring blade with curved cutting edge. Black shiny patina with green areas.
L. 8.6cm Weight 154g
No close parallels, but see *PBF* IX. 12, no. 4197, from Bologna, Emilia Romagna. Type San

Francesco (without shoulders).
EIA, late.

495.
PRB 1964.12-1.404 (362). Sir Henry Wellcome Collection, no. 113256. Bought in Rome from A. Rocci by Captain Saint in April 1932. Given by the Wellcome Trustees.
Socketed axe with continuous profile and oval socket. **Axes type 56**.
Small tool with concave sides, oval socket with slightly thickened mouth edge, short blade with curved cutting edge. Spotted green patina with earth incrustations.
L. 7.5cm Weight 115g
See *PBF* IX. 12, no. 4213, unprovenanced. Type Ripatransone.
EIA, late.

496.
PRB WG1084. Canon W. Greenwell Collection, bought from the Rev. Greville J. Chester. Given by J. Pierpont Morgan in 1909.
'Fondi Lavoro', probably Fondi (Latina), Lazio.
Socketed axe with continuous profile, square socket and lateral lugs. **Axes type 57**.
Mouth with raised collar, base of the socket visible at top of blade, sloping lugs, elongated trapezoidal blade with slightly rounded cutting edge. Smooth blackish patina. Surface covered with ancient striations, one lateral hole on socket (a casting defect).
L. 14.3cm Weight 268g
See *PBF* IX. 12, nos. 3947–3956, mainly from the hoards of Ardea (Rome), Lazio, and San Francesco, Bologna, Emilia Romagna; see especially no. 3949, unprovenanced. Type Cortona var. A.
EIA, late.

497.
PRB 1935.10-18.29. Transferred from GR.
Socketed axe with continuous profile, square socket and lateral lugs. **Axes type 57**.
Mouth with raised collar, base of the socket visible at top of blade, sloping lugs, elongated trapezoidal blade with slightly rounded cutting edge. Smooth patina in various tones of green.
L. 14.4cm Weight 298g
See *PBF* IX. 12, nos. 3947–3956, mainly from the hoards of Ardea (Rome) and San Francesco, Bologna, Emilia Romagna; see especially no. 3956, from Foiano della Chiana (Arezzo), Tuscany. Type Cortona, var. A.
EIA, late.
Bibliography: Walters 1899, no. 2939.

498.
PRB Morel 1239. Bought from Léon Morel, April–May 1901.
Bari, Apulia.
Socketed axe with continuous profile and squared socket. **Axes type 58**.
Miniature axe. Mouth with raised collar with lateral loop, square in section, slightly widening towards the blade, slightly curved cutting edge. Lateral hole on the socket.
Smooth dull green, brown and whitish patina.
L. 4.3cm Weight 14g
See *PBF* IX. 12, nos. 3912–3913, from Città della Pieve (Perugia), Umbria, and from the Marche. Type Città della Pieve.
EIA.

499.
PRB 1866.6-27.86. Henry Christy Collection. Given by the Trustees under the will of Henry Christy.
Verona, Veneto.
Socketed axe with continuous profile and squared socket. **Axes type 58**.
Small axe. Mouth with raised double collar with lateral loop, square in section, elongated trapezoidal blade with almost straight cutting edge. Dull dark green patina with clay incrustations. Socket hole filled with light red clay. Casting residues on mouth and sides.
L. 7.7cm Weight 84g
See *PBF* IX. 12, no. 3913, from the Marche (with single collar). Type Città della Pieve.
EIA.

500.
PRB 1883.8-2.7. Given by Sir A.W. Franks.
Naples, Campania.
Socketed axe with continuous profile and squared socket. **Axes type 58**.
Small axe with sides slightly widening towards the blade. Mouth with raised collar, rectangular in section, very short blade, reworked, with upturned corners and rounded cutting edge. Smooth, discontinuous brown and dark green patina.
L. 6.2cm Weight 80g
No close parallels, but see *PBF* IX. 12, nos. 3916 to 3927, hoard of Ardea (Rome), Lazio. Type Ardea var. A (with lateral loops).
EIA, late.

501.
PRB 1964.12-1.408 (310). Sir Henry Wellcome Collection. Given by the Wellcome Trustees.
Socketed axe with continuous profile and squared socket. **Axes type 58**.
Mouth with raised collar, base of the socket visible at the top of the blade, semicircular lateral loops, elongated trapezoidal blade with slightly rounded cutting edge. Thick green patina with incrustations of iron, probably from contact with iron objects.
L. 17.6cm Weight 786g
See *PBF* IX. 12, no. 3926, hoard of San Francesco, Bologna, Emilia Romagna. Type Ardea, var. A.
EIA, late.

502.
PRB 1880.8-2.44. Given by Sir A.W. Franks.
Grosseto, Maremma di Toscana, Tuscany.
Socketed axe with continuous profile and squared socket. **Axes type 59**.
Half the length of the socket missing, perhaps due to an unsuccessful casting, socket rectangular in section, slightly marked sloping shoulders, narrow trapezoidal blade with almost straight cutting edge. Decorated with reticulated pattern on both faces of the socket, the vertical nervatures continuing on the blade. Discontinuous brown patina with earth incrustations.
L. 12.4cm Weight 534g
See *PBF* IX. 12, no. 4179, hoard of San Francesco, Bologna, Emilia Romagna (with wider blade). Type San Francesco.
EIA, late.

503.
PRB 1935.10-18.28. Transferred from GR.
Socketed axe with separated blade and conical socket. Close to **Axes type 60**, but probably slightly later.
Mouth with raised double collar and square inner section, rounded socket base visible on upper blade, thin, trapezoidal blade with irregular lateral protrusions and straight cutting edge. Smooth dark green patina with light zones.
L. 8.4cm Weight 102g
See *PBF* IX. 12, nos. 3973–3974, hoard of Ardea (Rome), Lazio, not identical. Type Ardea, var. B.
EIA, late.
Bibliography: Walters 1899, no. 2938.

504.
PRB 1935.10-18.30. Transferred from GR.
Socketed axe with separated blade and conical socket. Close to **Axes type 60**.
Mouth with raised collar and square inner section, rounded socket base visible on upper blade, thin, slightly flaring blade with squared shoulders and slightly rounded cutting edge. Smooth almost black patina.
L. 12.6cm Weight 251g
See *PBF* IX. 12, no. 3985, hoard of San Francesco, Bologna. Type Ardea, var. (with angular shoulder). EIA, advanced ? See also *PBF* IX. 12, nos. 3899–3901. Type Cuma, EIA.
EIA.
Bibliography: Walters 1899, no. 2940.

505.
PRB 1883.8-2.8. Given by Sir A.W. Franks.
Talamone (Grosseto), Tuscany.
Socketed axe with separated blade and socket square in section. **Axes type 61**.
Mouth with raised double collar, rounded socket base just visible on upper blade, angular protruding and sloping shoulders, trapezoidal blade with slightly curved cutting edge. Decorated with reticulated nervatures on both faces of the socket. Rough green patina with brown areas.
L. 15cm Weight 356g
See *PBF* IX. 12, nos. 4057–93, mainly from the hoard of San Francesco, Bologna, Emilia Romagna. Type San Francesco, var.E.
EIA, late.

506.
PRB WG1083. Canon W. Greenwell Collection, bought from G.F. Lawrence. Given by J. Pierpont Morgan in 1909.
Orvieto, Umbria.
Socketed axe with separated blade and socket square in section. **Axes type 61**.
Mouth with raised double collar, lateral pin-holes in socket, rounded socket base visible on upper blade, angular protruding and sloping shoulders, trapezoidal blade with slightly curved cutting edge. Decorated with incised concentric circles on the socket and the upper part of the blade. Smooth bright green patina with black and reddish incrustations, surface partly corroded.
L. 15.2cm Weight 370g
See *PBF* IX. 12, no. 4045, from Vetulonia (Grosseto), Tuscany, not identical. Type San Francesco, var. E.
EIA, late.

507.
PRB 1964.12-1.398 (316). Sir Henry Wellcome Collection, no. 67750. Bought from G. Pini in November 1928. Given by the Wellcome Trustees.
Socketed axe with separated blade and socket square in section. **Axes type 61.**
Mouth with raised double collar, rounded socket base just visible on upper blade, angular protruding and sloping shoulders, trapezoidal blade with slightly curved cutting edge. Decorated with reticulated nervatures on both faces of the socket. Thick spotted patina with incrustations in various tones of green and black.
L. 14.1cm Weight 326g
See *PBF* IX. 12, nos. 4057–93, mainly from the hoard of San Francesco, Bologna, Emilia Romagna. Type San Francesco, var. E.
EIA, late.

508.
PRB 1964.12-1.400 (319). Sir Henry Wellcome Collection, no. 96452. Bought in Rome from Antichità delle Belle Arti by Captain Saint in April 1931. Given by the Wellcome Trustees.
Socketed axe with separated blade and socket square in section. **Axes type 61.**
Mouth with raised double collar, rounded socket base visible on upper blade, sloping, protruding shoulders, trapezoidal blade with slightly curved cutting edge. Decorated with herringbone nervatures on both faces of the socket. Patina dull green with some corrosion; dark green incrustations. Small parts missing.
L. 14.2cm Weight 310g
See *PBF* IX. 12, nos. 4061–4070, mainly from the hoard of San Francesco, Bologna, Emilia Romagna. Type San Francesco, var. E.
EIA, late.

509.
PRB 1964. 12-1. 402 (317). Sir Henry Wellcome Collection, no. 79451. Bought in Florence from A. Albizi by Captain Saint in April 1930. Given by the Wellcome Trustees.
Socketed axe with separated blade and socket square in section. **Axes type 62.**
Mouth with raised double collar and two lateral lugs, angular protruding shoulders, trapezoidal blade with slightly curved cutting edge. Decorated with indistinct herringbone nervatures on both faces of the socket and three small indentations on the upper part of the blade. Dull dark green patina with incrustations of earth.
L. 13.7cm Weight 311g
See *PBF* IX. 12, no. 4013, hoard of San Francesco, Bologna, Emilia Romagna. Type San Francesco, var. C.
EIA, late.

510.
PRB 1964.12-1.403(318). Sir Henry Wellcome Collection, no. 67577. Bought from G. Pini in November 1928. Given by the Wellcome Trustees.
Socketed axe with separated blade and socket square in section. **Axes type 62.**
Mouth with raised double collar, protruding shoulders, trapezoidal blade, separated from the socket by a straight step, and with almost straight cutting edge. Dark green-black patina with brown and dark green incrustations and

surface in part corroded.
L. 14.1cm Weight 320g
See *PBF* IX. 12, nos. 4027–4040, mainly from the hoard of San Francesco, Bologna, Emilia Romagna. Type San Francesco, var. E; see especially no. 4031.
EIA, late.

511.
PRB Old Acquisition 135. Registered OA on 21 August 1946.
Socketed axe with separated blade and socket square in section. **Axes type 62.**
Mouth with raised double collar, sloping protruding shoulders, trapezoidal blade, separated from the socket by a straight step, and with almost straight cutting edge. Decorated on both faces of the socket with two circles below the collar and opposed triangular nervatures below. Irregular, blackish patina. Small part of the blade missing.
L. 12.7cm Weight 267g
See *PBF* IX. 12, no. 4028, hoard of San Francesco, Bologna, Emilia Romagna. Type San Francesco, var. E.
EIA, late.

512.
PRB 1964.12-1.401(320). Sir Henry Wellcome Collection, no. 79452. Bought in Florence from A. Albizi by Captain Saint in April 1930. Given by the Wellcome Trustees.
Socketed axe with separated blade and socket square in section. **Axes type 62.**
Mouth with raised collar, protruding shoulders, trapezoidal blade, separated from the socket by a straight step, and with almost straight cutting edge; pin-hole on two sides of the socket and indistinct cast decoration on both faces of the socket. Dull green spotted patina with traces of iron.
L. 13.2cm Weight 301g
See *PBF* IX. 12, nos. 4098–4100, hoard of San Francesco, Bologna, Emilia Romagna. Type San Francesco, var. F; see especially no. 4098.
EIA, late.

513.
PRB 1964.12-1.399(321). Sir Henry Wellcome Collection, no. 96451. Bought in Rome from Antichità delle Belle Arti by Captain Saint in April 1931. Given by the Wellcome Trustees.
Socketed axe with separated blade and socket square in section. **Axes type 62.**
Mouth with raised double collar, protruding shoulders, trapezoidal blade separated from the socket by a straight step, with almost straight cutting edge. Decorated with incised concentric circles on both faces of the socket and upper part of the blade and with circles and groups of parallel lines on both sides of the socket and blade. Light green patina with corrosion in parts. Parts of blade and socket missing.
L. 15.5cm Weight 272g
Analysis: Bronze. See D. Hook report.
See *PBF* IX. 12, nos. 4027–4040, mainly from the hoard of San Francesco, Bologna, Emilia Romagna. Type San Francesco, var. E.
EIA, late.

Tools

514.
PRB 1876.7-6.10. Given by Sir A.W. Franks.
Socketed chisel. **Chisels type 3.**
Conical socket with square internal section and two angular cordons at mouth; blade with square section and slightly flaring cutting edge. Rough dull green patina with whitish incrustations.
L. 13.3cm Weight 112g
Close to Pontecagnano 1992, 28, fig. H, type 51B; 109ff. Pontecagnano-S. Antonio, tomb 3284. 14, fig. 123.14. Phase IIB. See 31–32, notes 38–40 for references.
See also Albore Livadie 1985, 67 and pl. 12, no. 9.13, Cuma (Naples), Campania, sporadic; Montelius 1895–1910, pl. 68.8, hoard of San Francesco, Bologna, Emilia Romagna.
EIA, late.

515.
PRB 1883.4-26.5. Given by Sir A.W. Franks. Near Naples, Campania.
Socketed chisel. **Chisels type 4.**
Conical socket with circular internal section and rounded cordon at mouth, thick blade with square section and slightly flaring cutting edge. Smooth dull green patina with rusty, black and light green incrustations.
L. 12.6cm Weight 92g
See Montelius 1895–1910, pl. 68.9, hoard of San Francesco, Bologna, Emilia Romagna.
Socketed chisels are known from the FBA, for example in the hoard of Limone (Livorno, Tuscany), but with square section to socket: see Giardino 1995, 10 and fig. 3.10.
EIA, late.

Knives

516.
GR 1982.6-17.63. Received from PRB. Sir Henry Wellcome Collection, no. 67764. Bought in Florence from Guido Pini in November 1928. Given by the Wellcome Trustees.
Knife with up-curving blade and flat tang.
Knives type 7.
Blade with concave, slightly thickened back. Narrow flat tang, partly missing, with low rectangular section and three holes for rivets. Cutting edge heavily damaged. Dark green patina with some corrosion.
L. 21.8cm Weight 52g
Close to *PBF* VII. 2, no. 65 from Leprignano (Capena, Rome), Lazio. Type Leprignano.
EIA, late and Orientalizing.

517.
PRB WG1146. Canon W. Greenwell Collection, bought from F.E. Whelan. Given by J. Pierpont Morgan in 1909.
Castiglione del Lago (Perugia), Umbria.
Knife with serpentine blade and socketed handle. **Knives type 8.**
Thin blade with thickened oval section along back, pointed spur at end near the handle, made separately, hammered socket of bronze sheet. Rough, bright green patina, with incrustations.
L. 24.4cm Weight 81g
Close to *PBF* VII. 2, no. 183, from Este (Padova), Veneto. Type Morlungo.
EIA, late and Orientalizing.

518.
GR 1975.5-18.8. Found unregistered.
Knife with separately cast handle of rectangular form. **Knives type 9**.
Solid handle, made of a thick bar with rectangular section, ending with a short segment of bronze bar bent at right angles, with a tiny eyelet cast above the first angle. Curved blade, upper edge slightly thickened, with T-profile. The upper edge and the butt of the blade near the attachment to the handle are decorated with a plain zigzag line. Little patina.
L. 41.3cm Weight 337g
See *PBF* VII. 2, no. 151 from Caracupa (Latina), Lazio. Type Caracupa.
This is a specific Latial and Campanian type. EIA, late and Orientalizing.
Bibliography: Walters 1899, no. 2760; Petrie 1917, pl. 26.165; Bietti Sestieri 1986, 'Weapons and Tools', 6, no. 17, and fig. p. 18.

519.
GR 1814.7-4.701. Charles Townley Collection. Bought from Peregrine Townley.
'Praeneste' (= Palestrina, Rome), Lazio.
Knife with separately cast handle of rectangular form. **Knives type 9**.
Solid handle, made of a thick bar with rectangular section bent at right angles to form the upper end and the blade attachment. The upper end termination is a ring; a tiny eyelet is cast above the opposite angle. Curved blade, its upper edge is slightly thickened, with T-profile. The upper edge and the butt of the blade near attachment to the handle are decorated with a row of incised hatched triangles. The tip is missing. No patina. Cleaned in modern times.
L. 43cm Weight 291g
See **cat. 518**. See too *PBF* VII. 2, nos. 146–155, type Caracupa, especially no. 149, in Naples National Museum.
EIA, late and Orientalizing.
Bibliography: Walters 1899, no. 2759; Bietti Sestieri 1986, 'Weapons and Tools', 5, no. 16, and fig. p. 18; Bailey 1986, 134, figs. 2 and 4.

Razors

520.
PRB 1880.8-2.28. Given by Sir A. W. Franks. Probably obtained from A. Castellani. Symmetrical razor. **Razors type 9**.
Cast ring handle, almost square blade with slightly rounded shoulders, straight upper edge. Dark green patina with whitish incrustations. Part of upper edge missing.
L. 10.5cm Weight 27g
See *PBF* VIII. 2, no. 257, from S. Marzano sul Sarno (Salerno), Campania. Type Suessula var. A.
EIA, late.

521.
GR 1935.8-23.56. Transferred from the Department of British and Medieval Antiquities. Canon W. Greenwell Collection, no. 1139, bought from the Rev. Greville J. Chester. Given by J. Pierpont Morgan in 1909. Chiusi, Tuscany.
Lunate razor. **Razors type 14**.
Cast ring handle with two birds' heads at sides of ring, with long curved beaks and eyes marked by a small hole. Wide blade, slightly thickened towards the back; back with markedly concave profile, ending towards the handle in a truncated angle. Incised decoration, now scarcely visible: band of multiple zigzag lines and row of hatched triangles along the back of the blade. Heavily damaged, with parts missing. Green patina with much corrosion and incrustation.
L. 12.3cm Weight 40g
Close to *PBF* VIII. 2, nos. 722, from Narce (Viterbo), 747, from Veii (Rome), both in Lazio. Type Grotta Gramiccia, var. A.
EIA, late.

522.
GR 1875.3-13.8. Bought from Rollin and Feuardent.
Lunate razor. **Razors type 14**.
Cast ring handle with two simplified birds' heads indicated at sides of ring. Wide blade, almost circular and slightly thickened towards the back; back with markedly concave profile, ending towards the handle in a truncated angle. No decoration. Dull green patina.
L. 9.8cm Weight 30g
See *PBF* VIII. 2, no. 1006, from Sarteano (Siena), Tuscany, type San Francesco; nos. 751, from Volterra, Tuscany, 753, from Vulci (Viterbo), Lazio, type Grotta Gramiccia var. A. EIA, late.
Bibliography: Walters 1899, no. 2422, fig. 75; *BM Guide* 1920, 140, fig. 166.

523.
GR 1935.8-23.55. Transferred from the Dept. of British and Medieval Antiquities (1880.8-2.37). Given by Sir A. W. Franks. Probably obtained from A. Castellani.
Lunate razor. **Razors type 14**.
Cast ring handle with two simplified birds' heads at side of ring. Wide blade, flat in section; back with concave profile, once ending towards handle in a protruding angle, now broken. No decoration. Smooth green patina with some corrosion.
L. 10cm Weight 42g
See *PBF* VIII. 2, no. 753, from Vulci (Viterbo), Lazio. Type Grotta Gramiccia var. B, EIA. EIA, late.

524.
GR 1935.8-23.57. Transferred from the Department of British and Medieval Antiquities. Canon W. Greenwell Collection, no. 1140, bought from W. Talbot Ready. Given by J. Pierpont Morgan in 1909. Chiusi, Tuscany.
Lunate razor. **Razors type 15**.
Cast ring handle with two birds' heads at sides of ring. Wide blade, slightly thickened towards the back; back with concave profile, interrupted by a protruding knob and ending in a right angle towards the handle. Incised decoration: oblique parallel lines on the handle, band of hatched triangles and row of dots along the back of the blade, dotted circle at the handle end of the blade. Cutting edge slightly damaged. Green patina with smooth surface areas.
L. 11.4cm Weight 26g
See *PBF* VIII. 2, no. 710, from Tarquinia (Viterbo), Lazio. Type Valle La Fata. EIA, late.

525.
GR 1840.2-12.18. Bought at the Bishop of Lichfield's Sale, Bishop S. Butler.
Lunate razor. **Razors type 16**.
Cast ring handle with two simplified birds' heads at sides of ring. Blade almost circular, slightly thickened towards the back; back forming a narrow U-shaped opening, ending near the handle with a truncated angle, surmounted by a small knob. Incised decoration on both faces: three lines parallel to the back of the blade. Cutting edge damaged. Dark green patina with some corrosion.
L. 11.1cm Weight 40g
Close to *PBF* VIII. 2, nos. 870, from Vulci (Viterbo), Lazio, 905, from Bologna, Emilia Romagna. Type Benacci, var. A and B. EIA, late.
Bibliography: Walters 1899, no. 2423.

526.
GR 1982.6-17.57. Transferred from PRB. Sir Henry Wellcome Collection, no. 168124. Given by the Wellcome Trustees.
Lunate razor. **Razors type 16**.
Cast ring handle with two simplified birds' heads at sides of ring. Blade almost circular, slightly thickened towards the back; back forming a narrow U-shaped opening, ending near the handle with a truncated angle surmounted by a small knob. Incised decoration on both faces: five lines and a hatched band parallel to the back of the blade. Cutting edge and back of blade damaged. No patina. Cleaned in modern times.
L. 12cm Weight 22g
See *PBF* VIII. 2, nos. 842, from Vulci (Viterbo), Lazio, 866, from Bologna, Emilia Romagna, 868, from Tarquinia (Viterbo), Lazio. Type Benacci, var. A-B. EIA, late.

527.
GR 1982.6-17.59. Transferred from PRB. Sir Henry Wellcome Collection, no. 301 (also marked R. 12917.1936). Bought in Rome from Arte Antica e Moderna. Given by the Wellcome Trustees.
Lunate razor with deeply curved back. **Razors type 16**. Cast handle broken in antiquity. Blade almost circular, slightly thickened towards the back and with a T-profile; back forming a narrow U-shaped opening, ending near the handle with a truncated angle surmounted by a small knob. Two circular holes set high in the blade. Fine incised decoration on both faces: three lines enclosing a band of hatched triangles parallel to the back of the blade. Terminal of handle and parts of the blade missing. No patina. Cleaned in modern times.
L. 7.2cm Weight 18g
See *PBF* VIII. 2, no. 862, from Vulci (Viterbo), Lazio. Type Benacci var. A-B. EIA, late.

528.
GR 1935.8-23.58. Transferred from the Department of British and Medieval Antiquities. Canon W. Greenwell Collection, no. 1141, bought from the Rev. Greville J. Chester. Given by J. Pierpont Morgan in 1909. Etruria (Tuscany or northern Lazio).
Lunate razor. **Razors type 16**.
Cast handle missing. Blade much damaged but

thickened towards the back and with a T-profile; back with markedly concave profile, ending near the handle with a truncated angle surmounted by a small knob. No decoration. Dull green patina with much incrustation.
L. 8.7cm Weight 17g
See *PBF* VIII. 2, nos. 773, from Verucchio (Forlì), Emilia Romagna, 796, from Vetralla (Viterbo), Lazio, type Grotta Gramiccia var. B; no. 891, from Narce (Viterbo), Lazio, type Benacci.
EIA, late.

Ornaments

529.
GR 1927.11-15.36. Given by Dr. W.L. Hildburgh. Florence, Tuscany.
Pin-head in the form of a spoked wheel. **Pins type 9**.
Wheel with seven thick spokes separated by irregular holes, and conical socket. Small parts missing. Dull green patina.
Diam. 3.4cm Weight 21g
See *PBF* XIII. 2, nos. 2705 Vetulonia (Grosseto), Tuscany, 2724 (Orvieto), Umbria. Type Vetulonia.
EIA, late and Orientalizing.

530.
GR 1975.7-12.45. Transferred from PRB, July 1975. Sir Henry Wellcome Collection, F 3252. Given by the Wellcome Trustees.
'Gela, 1887', Sicily.
Pendant in the form of a shaft-hole axe. **Pendants type 2**.
Cast replica of an axe with flat, trapezoidal blade and circular shaft-hole acting as suspension loop. Little patina.
L. 4.7cm Weight 15g
No precise parallels found. A number of pendants in the form of shaft-hole axes are known from Sicily. Some pieces are known from the hoard of Modica (Ragusa); Giardino 1995, 21, fig. 10B.2, 3, FBA late; several others come from the cemetery of Cassibile (Syracuse); Turco 2000, 93, pl. 32, type 25A, FBA late–EIA early. See for references.
The circular shaft-hole of this pendant might indicate that it should be dated in late phase of the EIA: see for example the shaft-hole axes from the hoard of Ardea (Rome), *Inventaria Archaeologica* 1967, nos. 189, 190, 193–196. Probably EIA, late.

531.
GR 1824.4-99.20. Bequeathed by R. Payne Knight.
Solid pointed globe pendant. **Pendants type 3**.
Cast solid with slight steps or nervatures around neck, round in section, at top of globe and below suspension loop. Dark brown patina.
L. 3cm Weight 7g
This is a common type in central and southern Italy. See for example Cuma 1913, col. 72, pl. 21.2, Stevens Collection; *Osteria dell'Osa* 1992, 426, pl. 45, type 88bb. Period III; *Quattro Fontanili* 1975, 95, fig. 19.16, tomb F 9.16 Phase IIB; *Quattro Fontanili* 1986, 96, fig. 24, type XX 3 (composite pendant including three smaller pendants of this type). Phases IIA-IIC.
EIA, late.

532.
GR 1878.10-19.244. Given by General A.W.H. Meyrick.
Hollow tube with three solid biconical pendants, one missing. **Pendants type 4**.
Tube cast hollow with three loops, two now broken, at base; exterior decorated with seven pairs and one single encircling incised lines. Cast biconical pendants. Dull green patina.
L. 8cm Weight 22g
Similar pendants or ornaments, all with slight variations, are known from several IA Italian cemeteries. See *Quattro Fontanili* 1986, 96 and fig. 24, type XX.3. Phases II A-C. For example, *Quattro Fontanili* 1965, 129, fig. 55.s, Tomb HH11–12.s. Phase IIB; *Cerveteri-Sorbo* 1972, 205–206, fig. 183.3, Tomb 443; Dohan 1942, 12, pl. 4.31, Narce (Viterbo), Lazio, tomb 18B. 31.
EIA, late.

533.
GR 1772.3-7.210. Bought from Sir William Hamilton.
Globular pendant surmounted by two opposed heads of birds. **Pendants type 5**.
Cast solid with opposed heads of birds indicated, their necks turning at right angles and merging with a suspension hole at the center. Below a narrow waist and globe. One head slightly damaged. Smooth green to brown patina.
L. 6.5cm Weight 128g
Close to Colucci Pescatori 1971.I, 479.9, fig. 3.1, Bisaccia (Avellino), Campania, EIA; see also Peroni 1967, 125 and fig. 27.3, probably from Apulia, Bellak Collection, EIA.
EIA, late or later.

534.
GR 1856.12-26.696. Bequeathed by Sir William Temple.
Torre Annunziata (Naples), Campania.
Globular pendant surmounted by a tranverse bar with angular extensions. **Pendants type 5**.
Cast solid with a broken suspension loop at the top and a small hole below loop; below a shaft and globe. Green patina with some corrosion.
L. 5.4cm Weight 81g
See **cat. 533**.
EIA, late or later.

535.
GR 1958.8-22.8. Found unregistered.
Globular pendant surmounted by two opposed bird's head. **Pendants type 5, variant**.
Cast solid with suspension loop and shaft below, from which branches on either side the necks and heads of schematic birds. Below a shaft and small globe. Dull green patina with some corrosion.
L. 5.6cm Weight 33g
No precise parallels found; see **cat. 533** and **534** for broadly similar pieces (with parallels).
EIA, late or later.

536.
GR 1974.12-3.11. Found unregistered.
Globular pendant terminating in two aquatic birds. **Pendants type 6**.
Cast solid with schematic heads of two birds out-facing and with their bodies united above; a flattened globe above and a flange, flattened in section, pierced by a hole for suspension. Dark green patina.

L. 4cm Weight 10g
Similar pendants hang from an unpublished openwork pendant from Suessula (Caserta), Campania (Naples Archaeological Museum). For the openwork pendant, see von Duhn 1887, 250, fig. 19.13 and those from **cat. 817** and **818**. See also Suessula (von Duhn 1887, 251, fig. 20.17) and Capua (Caserta), Campania, Tomb 502 (Johannowsky 1983, 115f. and pl. XIX.3) for fibulae with similar pendants, though terminating in single, not two opposed, aquatic birds.
EIA, late.

537.
GR 1975.10-5.18. Found unregistered.
Hollow globular pendant. **Pendants type 7**.
Globe cast hollow with a hole at centre of base; neck with cast nervatures and ending in a suspension loop. Smooth green to brown patina with shiny areas.
L. 6.2cm Weight 48g
Close to *Pithekoussai* 1993, 726, pl. 259.12, sporadic from the cemetery. See also Colucci Pescatori 1971.II, 535, fig. 44.18, sporadic from the cemetery of Cairano (Avellino), Campania. See for partly similar types *PBF* XI. 2, nos. 330 and 331, from Serbia; 336, from Philia, Thessaly.
Plain, hollow globular pendants, with or without holes in the globe, are rare in Italy and Greece.
EIA, late.

538.
GR 1772.3-7.72. Bought from Sir William Hamilton.
Hollow globular pendant with ring for suspension. **Pendants type 7**.
Globe cast hollow with four opposed holes set at line of maximum diameter and with a suspension loop at the top, through which is threaded a penannular ring with encircling incised striations. Globe: smooth green patina. Ring: green patina with corrosion.
L. 6.5cm with ring. Weight 45g
See **cat. 537**.
EIA, late.

539.
GR 1975.10-5.20. Found unregistered.
Hollow globular pendant. **Pendants type 7**.
Globe cast hollow; one side damaged and parts missing. Neck round in section and ending in a suspension loop. Patchy patina with dark green areas and some corrosion.
L. 5.4cm Weight 32g
See **cat. 537**.
EIA, advanced-late.

540.
GR 1856.12-26.1053. Bequeathed by Sir William Temple.
Pendant in the form of a horse. **Pendants type 8**.
Cast solid with four separated legs, one now broken, schematic head, tail curved downwards and suspension loop above centre of back. Decoration on both sides of incised lines indicating mane and at throat; series of punched dots surrounded by circles on body. Shiny green patina.
L. 5.5cm Weight 29g
Analysis: Craddock 1986, 144.

562.
PRB 2000.1-1.23. Found unregistered.
Solid leech fibula with lowered bow. **Fibulae type 21.**
Catch-plate, spring and pin missing, thick lowered and expanded bow. Deeply incised decoration on upper side of bow: transverse parallel grooves on the whole upper surface. Dull dark green to black patina with bright green and white incrustations.
L. 4cm Weight 27g
Close to *PBF* XIV. 5, no. 646 (provenance unknown).
EIA, late.

563.
PRB 1964.12-6.94. Bequeathed by C.T. Trechmann.
Semlin, Hungary.
Solid lowered leech fibula with symmetrical catch-plate. **Fibulae type 21.**
Low and wide catch-plate, partly missing, thick slightly expanded bow, small two-coiled spring and straight pin. Deeply incised decoration on bow: groups of transverse parallel lines separated by plain bands; lower side undecorated. Rough dark green patina with incrustations in azure (malachite) and various tones of green.
L. 4.7cm Weight 49g
See *PBF* XIV. 5, no. 680, (provenance unknown). Undecorated.
EIA, late.

564.
GR 1878.10-19.159. Given by General A.W.H. Meyrick.
Solid lowered and flattened arch fibula with symmetrical catch-plate. **Fibulae type 22.**
Bow stilted and lowered with sides slightly expanded. Two-coiled spring. Light green patina.
L. 3cm Weight 8g
See *PBF* XIV. 5, no. 569, from Este (Padova, Veneto).
PBF XIV, forthcoming, XIX. 1, (113a,b) 'Fibule ad arco ribassato e schacciato', nos. 1541 from Suessula (Caserta), Campania, 1546 from Montecorvino Rovella (Salerno), Campania.
EIA, late.

565.
PRB 2000.1-1.4. P. Curwen Britton, 1910. 5.
Hollow leech fibula with symmetrical catch-plate. **Fibulae type 23.**
Low large catch-plate, raised expanded bow, probably hollow with a clay filling, small two-coiled spring and straight pin. Deeply incised decoration on upper side of bow: transverse bands of chevrons separated by plain zones. Small parts missing. Dull patina in various tones of green, with the colour of metal showing in some areas.
L. 8cm Weight 117g
See *PBF* XIV, forthcoming, XIX. 3 (126.2), no. 1650 (with wide catch-plate), from Suessula (Caserta), Campania, 'Grandi fibule a sanguisuga cava con staffa larga e simmetrica'.
PBF XIV. 5, 'Fibule a sanguisuga a staffa corta', no. 660, provenance unknown. EIA, late.
Quattro Fontanili 1986, 79, fig. 25, type I 19, phase IIB.
EIA, late.

566.
PRB (P) 1974.12-1.322. Pitt Rivers Collection. Bought from Egger Collection. (See Egger sale catalogue, Sotheby's 25 June 1891, lot 122, pl. xix.122).
'Tirol', Austria.
Hollow leech fibula with symmetrical catch-plate. **Fibulae type 23.**
Wide catch-plate, probably restored in antiquity by attaching it to a small cleft in the end of the bow, thick raised and expanded bow with clay core and a hole at centre of lower side, small three-coiled spring, straight pin. Deeply incised decoration on upper side of bow: transverse bands of parallel lines, chevrons and concentric circles, separated by plain bands. Shiny dark green patina with blackish incrustations.
Thin ring with diamond section suspended from the pin.
L. 9cm Weight 176g
See for the general type *PBF* XIV. 5, nos. 655–667, 'Fibule a sanguisuga a staffa corta', 8th century and later.
Quattro Fontanili 1986, 79, fig. 25, type I 22, phase IIB (very similar in shape and decoration); 80, fig. 29, type I 28, phase IIB-IIC; 80, fig. 31, type I 33, phase IIC.
PBF XIV, forthcoming, XIX. 3, (126.1), nos. 1647, 1648, from Suessula (Caserta), Campania, 'Grandi fibule a sanguisuga cava con breve staffa simmetrica'.
EIA, late.

567.
GR 1920.11-18.3. Given by the Committee of the Guildhall Museum.
?Reculver, Kent, England.
Hollow leech fibula with symmetrical catch-plate. **Fibulae type 23.**
Low and wide catch-plate, partly missing, thick raised bow with clay core and two holes on upper side. Small spring, probably two-coiled, pin missing. Deeply incised decoration on upper side of bow: transverse chevron bands alternating with two rows of impressed concentric circles. Smooth light green patina, with the colour of the metal showing on most of the surface.
L. 8.8cm Weight 159g
See **cat. 566.**
EIA, late.

568.
GR 1916.6-1.8. Given by Lord Avebury.
Perugia, Umbria.
Hollow leech fibula probably with symmetrical catch-plate. **Fibulae type 23.**
Catch-plate missing, thick raised bow with clay core and a hole at centre of lower side, small, probably three-coiled spring, and pin missing. Deeply incised decoration on upper side of bow: alternate transverse bands of reticulate pattern, chevrons, opposed hatched triangles, concentric circles. Dull green patina.
L. 8cm Weight 200g
For general parallels see **cat. 566.** Also *PBF* XIV. 5, no. 666, from Este (Padova), Veneto, period II.
Probably a north Italian type.
EIA, late.

569.
GR 1976.2-6.1. Found unregistered.
Hollow leech fibula. **Fibulae type 23.**
Catch-plate missing; an ancient restoration of this part is probably indicated by a small cleft in the end of the bow. Thick raised bow with slight protrusion on the lower side, large spring, probably three-coiled, separated from the bow by a step and also restored in antiquity; pin missing. Deeply incised encircling decoration on the whole surface of bow: alternate bands of chevrons and hatched triangles. Smooth dark green patina.
L. 9cm Weight 212g
See **cat. 566.**
EIA, late.
Bibliography: Walters 1899, no. 1972.

570.
GR 1991.12-18.21. Given by Mrs C. Marchionne and Dr E.H. Walker. From the collection of H. Dewey.
Hollow leech fibula with elongated catch-plate. **Fibulae type 23.**
Small catch-plate, partly missing, thick raised bow, probably with clay filling, small two-coiled spring and straight pin. Deeply incised decoration on upper side of bow: transverse bands of hatched and plain triangles and meanders. Small parts missing. Dull brown patina on the upper face of the bow, thick green incrustations on lower face.
L. 6cm Weight 74g
See for general parallels **566.** Also *PBF* XIV. 5, no. 656, from Santa Cristina (Bergamo), Lombardy. EIA, late.
Probably a north Italian type.
EIA, late.

571.
GR 1916.6-1.7. Given by Lord Avebury.
Hollow leech fibula with symmetrical catch-plate. **Fibulae type 23.**
Catch-plate partly missing, raised bow with hole on upper side for inserting a clay filling. Spring and pin missing. Deeply incised decoration on upper side of bow: groups of parallel transverse lines at ends; hatched triangles and herringbone pattern on central zone. A small longitudinal cleft at the attachment of the spring and pin indicates that these had been broken and restored in antiquity. Smooth green patina.
L. 5.4cm Weight 50g
See **cat. 566.**
EIA, late.

572.
GR 1909.6-22.1. Bought from A. Decaristo.
Hollow leech fibula with lateral expansions and elongated catch-plate. **Fibulae type 24.**
Catch-plate partly missing, raised bow with slight lateral expansions, small three-coiled spring and straight pin. Small protrusion, probably connected with casting, at centre of inner side of bow. Deeply incised decoration on bow: a group of transverse parallel lines at each side; longitudinal bands with parallel lines, concentric circles and chevrons on upper side; concentric circles and parallel lines forming a rectangle in central zone. Small parts missing. Shiny green patina with brown areas.
L. 8cm Weight 40g
See *PBF* XIV, forthcoming, XXI.2 (139), no.

1928, from Suessula (Caserta), Campania, 'Grandi fibule a sanguisuga cava con staffa allungata'.
PBF XIV. 5, 'fibule a navicella', nos. 722, 723, from Este (Padova, Veneto).
EIA, late.

573.
GR 1876.9-2.1. Given by Sir A. W. Franks.
Hollow leech fibula with elongated catch-plate.
Fibulae type 24.
Catch-plate broken, raised and expanded bow with wide opening in lower side, spring and pin missing. The centre of the upper side of the bow has a large hole, mended in antiquity with a small plate attached from the inner side with three rivets. Incised decoration on bow: transverse bands of parallel lines at each end; longitudinal bands with parallel lines and multiple zigzag lines on each side, wide band with transverse and longitudinal chevrons and longitudinal parallel lines in central zone. Dark green patina with thick incrustations.
L. 13.8cm Weight 300g
See **cat. 572.**
PBF XIV, forthcoming, XXI. 2 (139), no. 1930, from Oliveto Citra (Salerno), Campania, tomb 2.
EIA, late.
Bibliography: Walters 1899, no. 1958.

574.
PRB 1911.4-1.1. Given by Alfred Jones of Bath.
'Box', Wiltshire, England.
Boat fibula with elongated catch-plate.
Fibulae type 25.
Wide catch-plate, wide raised and expanded bow, with large irregular opening on lower side, small spring, mostly missing, pin missing. Deeply incised decoration on bow: a group of transverse parallel bands of single chevrons at each end, opposed oblique bands of chevrons with a large concentric circle at centre, and a band of concentric circles, on each side of central zone; wide central band divided into zones with bands of concentric circles and chevrons and three large concentric circles. Small parts missing. Dark green patina.
L. 10.4cm Weight 80g
See *PBF* XIV. 5, 'Fibule a navicella', nos. 720, 723, from Este (Padova), Veneto.
Possibly a north Italian piece.
EIA, late.
Bibliography: Hull and Hawkes 1987, 22–24, no. 7286, pl. 7. See for comments on provenance and references.

575.
GR 1905.1-15.1 Given by Mrs. W. Kench-Welch.
Orvieto, Umbria.
Hollow leech fibula with elongated catch-plate.
Fibulae type 25.
Slightly elongated catch-plate, raised and expanded bow, small two-coiled spring and straight pin. Deeply incised decoration on bow: transverse bands of parallel lines, single chevrons, opposed hatched triangles and concentric circles at each side; longitudinal bands with reticulate pattern in central zone. Small parts missing. Smooth light green patina with some areas of blue-green corrosion.
L. 7.3cm Weight 42g
Analysis: Bronze. See D. Hook report.
Close parallel: *PBF* XIV, forthcoming, XXVII. 1

(209), no. 3812, from Pontecagnano (Salerno), Campania, 'Grandi fibule a navicella e a sanguisuga decorate, con staffa lunga'.
See also *PBF* XIV. 5, 'Fibule a navicella', nos. 715–728; also no. 667, from Manerbio (Brescia), Lombardy (hollow leech type, but with very similar decoration).
EIA, late.

576.
GR 1814.7-4.797. Charles Townley Collection.
Bought from Peregrine Townley.
Boat fibula. **Fibulae type 25.**
Catch-plate missing, wide raised and expanded bow, with large irregular opening on lower side, small two-coiled spring, pin missing. Deeply incised decoration on bow: a group of transverse parallel lines at each end, longitudinal bands of opposed oblique lines and concentric circles on each side of central zone, wide central band divided into longitudinal and transverse bands of oblique lines, concentric circles and chevrons. Smooth dark brown-green patina with light green incrustation on one side.
L. 9.5cm Weight 67g
See *PBF* XIV. 5, no. 719, from an unknown provenance.
EIA, late and Orientalizing.
Bibliography: Walters 1899, no. 1963.

577.
GR 1814.7-4.800. Charles Townley Collection.
Bought from Peregrine Townley.
Boat fibula. **Fibulae type 25.**
Catch-plate, spring and pin missing, raised and slightly expanded bow, with large irregular opening on lower side. Deeply incised decoration on bow: a group of transverse parallel grooves and a band of concentric circles at each end, longitudinal bands with reticular pattern and concentric circles on each side of central zone, wide central band divided into longitudinal and transverse bands of reticulate and parallel lines and concentric circles. Smooth dark green patina.
L. 7.5cm Weight 53g
See *PBF* XIV, forthcoming, XXVII. 1 (210a) A, no. 3832, provenance unknown (quite similar, with small lateral protrusions), 'Grandi fibule a navicella scanalata, con staffa lunga'. Probably a south Italian piece.
EIA, late and Orientalizing.
Bibliography: Walters 1899, no. 1964.

578.
PRB 1916.10-14.1. Given by Charles Hercules Read.
Found near 'Taunton', Somerset, England.
Boat fibula with long catch-plate. **Fibulae type 25.**
Narrow catch-plate with pointed end, wide raised and expanded bow, with large irregular opening on lower side, small three-coiled spring, pin missing. Deeply incised decoration on bow: a group of transverse parallel lines at each end, opposed oblique hatched bands, a band of oblique lines and a row of concentric circles on each side of central zone; wide central band divided into zones of parallel oblique and straight lines and chevrons; a large square at centre of bow is decorated with multiple square lines crossed by two diagonal lines. Smooth patina dark green and blackish.

Part of bow missing, and end of catch-plate deformed.
L. 15.6cm Weight 82g
See *PBF* XIV. 5, nos. 720, 722, both from Este (Padova), Veneto; for the decoration see also no. 719.
EIA, late and Orientalizing.
Bibliography: Hull and Hawkes 1987, 22–24, no. 7261, pl. 8.

579.
GR 1920.11-18.2. Given by the Committee of the Guildhall Museum.
Hollow leech fibula with elongated catch-plate.
Fibulae type 25.
Catch-plate almost entirely missing, raised and slightly expanded bow with wide opening on lower side. No spring coils, pin end flattened and attached to bow with a rivet (probably restored in antiquity); the rest of the pin has a circular section. Deeply incised decoration on bow: transverse parallel grooves at each side, a few longitudinal and transverse lines visible in central zone. Small parts missing. Smooth dark green patina. The fibula is heavily worn from use.
L. 8cm Weight 39g
See **cat. 577.** Probably a south Italian piece.
EIA, late and Orientalizing.

580.
PRB 1944.7-2.5. Henry Christy Collection. Given by the Trustees under the will of Henry Christy.
Bought by them from T. A. Glenn.
May have been excavated in Dorset, England, by Captain Sabine.
Boat fibula with long catch-plate. **Fibulae type 25.**
Catch-plate missing, raised bow with lateral knobs and wide irregular opening on lower side, small three-coiled spring with rectangular section, and straight pin. Deeply incised decoration on bow: transverse parallel grooves at sides, longitudinal parallel grooves on sides of central zone; traces of incised decoration on central longitudinal and transverse bands. Small parts missing. Covered with incrustations in various tones of green.
L. 9.2cm Weight 58g
See **cat. 577.**
See *PBF* XIV, forthcoming, XXVII.1 (210a) A, no. 3832 from Marsiconuovo (Potenza), Basilicata (quite similar, with small lateral protrusions). Possibly a south Italian type.
EIA, late and Orientalizing.
Bibliography: Hull and Hawkes 1987, 26, no. 7287, pl. 7. See no. 7260 for comment on the provenance of this fibula.

581.
GR 1824.4-34.37. Bequeathed by R. Payne Knight.
Boat fibula with marked lateral protrusions and long catch-plate. **Fibulae type 26.**
Narrow catch-plate with rounded tip, raised bow with angular expansions and wide opening on lower side, small two-coiled spring, straight pin. Small hole at centre of upper side of bow. Incised decoration: longitudinal parallel lines covering the whole bow surface.
Green to brown patina.
L. 11.5cm Weight 53g
Close to *PBF* XIV. 5, 'Fibule a navicella a losanga tipo Este', nos. 1086–1089 (from Este, Chiavari,

three-coiled spring and curved pin with foliate arch bow. Incised decoration: two bands of plain and multiple zigzag lines alternate with plain zones along edge of disc and bow; row of hatched triangles with band of parallel lines at base, and two multiple squares with lines crossing at right angles on disc; two opposed rows of hatched triangles at centre of bow. Bow slightly distorted and small parts missing. Smooth dark green patina.

L. 24.2cm Weight 135g

Close parallel for both shape and decoration: Montelius 1895–1910, col. 634, pl. 130.10, large sporadic fibula (33cm long), one of a pair from a tomb found at Basciano (Teramo), Abruzzo. See Müller-Karpe 1959, pls. 44C.4, 45D.5, Terni (Umbria), cemetery of the Acciaierie, foliate fibulae with solid disc from tombs 9 and 75, phase II.

Piceni 1999, 193–4, nos. 66, from Lama dei Peligni (Chieti), Abruzzo; 68, sporadic from Loreto Aprutino (Pescara), Abruzzo: large foliate fibulae with solid disc, period Piceno II. The fibula was probably an import from the central Adriatic area of Italy.

EIA, late.

604.

GR 1920.11-18.18. Given by the Committee of the Guildhall Museum.

Serpentine fibula with lateral knobs and lozenges, and long catch-plate. **Fibulae type 50.**

Catch-plate partly missing, thin bow square in section, with lozenge expansions and central elbow marked by lateral knobs with flat ends; small one-coiled spring and curved pin, partly missing, with upper part wound with thin bronze wire. Dull dark green patina with incrustations.

L. 6.8cm Weight 9g

See *Osteria dell'Osa* 1992, 378, pl. 39, types 42i-j, phase IIIA.

Quattro Fontanili 1986, 82, fig. 29, type III 16, phase IIB-C.

EIA, late.

605.

GR 1872.6-4.912. Bought from Alessandro Castellani.

Serpentine fibula with transverse knobs, double spring and upper pin and long catch-plate. **Fibulae type 51a.**

Catch-plate missing, both portions of bow curved, small spring coils and markedly curved pin. Bow, knobs, coils and upper pin covered and bound with thin silver wire. Small parts missing. Light green patina with incrustations.

L. 6.6cm Weight 11g

See *PBF* XIV, forthcoming, XLV. 2 (380b), no. 6811 (not identical), S. Marzano sul Sarno (Salerno), Campania, tomb 174, 'Fibule a drago con coppia di bastoncelli alternati a espansioni romboidali, e parte posteriore bifida'.

Quattro Fontanili 1986, 82, fig. 29, type III 15 (not identical), phases IIB-IIC.

Pontecagnano 1988, 61–62, pl. 20 and fig. N.73, type 32F1b, period II.

EIA, late.

Bibliography: Walters 1899, no. 2046.

606.

GR 1910.10-15.3. Bought from W.C. Bacon and Co., London.

Serpentine fibula with knobs and lozenges on bow and double upper pin. **Fibulae type 51b.** Narrow catch-plate partly missing, saw-tooth edge on upper side near junction with bow. Bow with two lozenge expansions and central elbow marked by lateral knobs with flat ends. Opposed double spring, each spring with one coil, and double upper pin; pin curved. Dull dark green patina.

L. 12.3cm Weight 32g

See *PBF* XIV, forthcoming, XLV. 2 (381a), no. 6825 from tomb 539 of Capua (Caserta), Campania, 'Fibule a drago con una coppia di bastoncelli con dischetti alternati a cuscinetti romboidali, e parte posteriore bifida con fermapieghe'.

Pontecagnano 1988, 61, pl. 20 and fig. N. 63, type 32E3b1a, period II.

Osteria dell'Osa 1992, 378, pl. 39, types 42i-j, phases IIIA-B.

EIA, late and later.

607.

GR 1856.12-26.1038. Bequeathed by Sir William Temple.

Serpentine fibula with knobs and lozenges on bow and double upper pin. **Fibulae type 51b.** Long catch-plate partly missing; saw-tooth edge on upper side near junction with bow and pierced by a large hole, probably for ancient mending. Bow with two lozenge expansions and central elbow marked by lateral knobs with flattened ends. Opposed double spring, each spring with one coil, pin missing. Smooth green patina.

L. 6cm Weight 6g

See cat. 606.

EIA, late and later.

608.

GR 1976.3-1.5. Found unregistered.

Serpentine fibula with knobs and lozenges on bow and double upper pin. **Fibulae type 51b.** Long catch-plate bent and partly missing, saw-tooth edge on upper side near junction with bow. Bow with two ridged lozenge expansions and central elbow marked by lateral knobs with flattened ends. Opposed double spring, each spring with one coil, and double upper pin; much of pin missing. Dull green patina.

L. 7.5cm Weight 8g

See cat. 606.

EIA, late and later.

609.

GR 1824.4-34.42. Bequeathed by R. Payne Knight.

Spectacle fibula with backing-plate. **Fibulae type 53a.**

Coils and figure-of-eight of wire with circular section and rather uneven thickness. Flat, circular discs, decorated with punched dots at the rim, at centre of coils; discs pierced by rivets, which attach the backing-plate. Backing-plate of violin-bow shape with narrow back, rectangular in section, one-coil spring, round in section, and small catch-plate. Dull green patina.

L. 11.8cm Weight 94g

See *PBF* XIV, forthcoming, LIV. 1 (434), no 7674, from Lavello (Potenza), Basilicata, 'Fibule a occhiali con raccordo a 8, con sostegno a fascetta, con molla'.

EIA, late.

Bibliography: Walters 1899, no. 1938.

610.

GR 1814.7-4.252. Charles Townley Collection. Bought from Peregrine Townley.

Spectacle fibula with backing-plate. **Fibulae type 53b.**

Coils of wire with circular section and decreasing in thickness from edge to centre; figure-of-eight rectangular in section. Hemispherical caps at centre of both coils, pierced by rivets, which also attach the backing-plate. Backing-plate of violin-bow shape, no spring and pin and catch-plate missing. Dark green patina.

L. 8.6cm Weight 37g

See *PBF* XIV, forthcoming, LIV. 1 (435), no. 7682 'Valle dell'Ofanto' (from inner Campania to the Apulian coast), 'Fibule a occhiali con raccordo a 8, con sostegno a fascetta, senza molla'.

EIA, late.

Bibliography: Walters 1899, no. 1936.

611.

GR 1772.3-9.37. Bought from Sir William Hamilton.

Spectacle fibula with backing-plate. **Fibulae type 53b.**

Coils of wire with circular section and decreasing in thickness from edge to centre; figure-of-eight rectangular in section. Hemispherical caps at centre of both coils pierced by iron rivets, which also attach the backing-plate. Backing-plate of violin-bow shape, the back slightly widening at centre, no spring, pin of circular section partly missing and small catch-plate. Smooth light green patina with some corrosion.

L. 9.2cm Weight 54g

See cat. 610.

EIA, late.

Bibliography: Walters 1899, no. 1937.

612.

GR 1872.6-4.1089. Bought from Alessandro Castellani.

Spectacle fibula with backing-plate. **Fibulae type 54.**

Coils of wire with circular section and even thickness; no central figure-of-eight. Bands once encircled both spirals, one now missing half its length; bands attached by rivets, which pass through centre of both coils and also attach the backing-plate, which is set at right angles to the bands. Backing-plate of violin-bow shape with no spring, pin circular in section and slightly widened catch-plate. Green patina with some corrosion.

L. 8.4cm Weight 43g

See *PBF* XIV, forthcoming, LIV. 2 (439, 440), nos. 7729 from tomb 2, cemetery of Castiglione di Paludi (Cosenza), Calabria; 7731 from tomb 231, cemetery of Salapia (Foggia), Apulia, 'Fibule a occhiali con raccordo obliquo e sostegno a fascetta, senza molla'.

EIA, late.

Bibliography: Walters 1899, no. 1935, fig. 29. *BM Guide* 1920, 133, fig.151.

613.
GR 1856.12-26.718 and 719. Bequeathed by Sir William Temple.
Ruvo, (Bari), Apulia.
Two spirals from a large spectacle fibula with backing-plate missing. **Fibulae type 55**.
Broken near figure-of-eight. Coils of wire with circular section, decreasing in thickness from edge to centre; figure-of-eight with rectangular section. High conical cap, pierced by a rivet, at centre of one coil. Green patina with corrosion and heavy incrustations.
L. 11.8 and 12cm Weight together: 474g
See *PBF* XIV, forthcoming, LIV. 1 (435a), nos. 7682, from the Ofanto valley (Foggia, northern Apulia); 7684B and 7684D, tombs from Ordona (Foggia), Apulia, 'Fibule a occhiali con raccordo a 8 e sostegno a fascetta, senza molla'.
EIA, late.
Bibliography: Walters 1899, no. 1929 (refers to GR 1856.12-26.719 only).

614.
GR 1814.7-4.253. Charles Townley Collection. Bought from Peregrine Townley.
Two spirals from a large spectacle fibula once with backing-plate. **Fibulae type 55**.
Coils of wire with circular section and decreasing in thickness from edge to centre; figure-of-eight rectangular in section. Hemispherical cap at the centre of one coil; traces of iron rivets at centre of both coils. Backing-plate missing. Green patina with heavy corrosion.
L. 20.4cm Weight 336g
See **cat. 613**.
EIA, late.
Bibliography: Walters 1899, no. 1933.

615.
GR 1824.4-98.19. Bequeathed by R. Payne Knight.
Spectacle fibula probably once with backing-plate. Probably **Fibulae type 55**.
Coils of wire with circular section and decreasing in thickness from edge to centre; figure-of-eight rectangular in section. Wire broken at centre of both coils at back; backing plate missing. Dark green patina with some corrosion.
L. 18.3cm Weight 305g
See **cat. 613**.
EIA, late.

616.
GR 1824.4-98.18. Bequeathed by R. Payne Knight.
Spiral, perhaps from a large spectacle fibula. See **Fibulae type 55**.
Large wire spiral, circular in section and decreasing in thickness from edge to centre, with a small coil rectangular in section at the outer end. Smooth dark green patina.
Diam 12.5cm Weight 260g
EIA, late.
Bibliography: Walters 1899, no. 1930.

617.
GR 1884.10-11.45. Bought from Rev. Greville J. Chester.
Naples, Campania.
Spiral, held within an outer band, from a large spectacle fibula. See **Fibulae type 55**.
Large wire spiral circular in section and

decreasing in thickness from edge to centre, with small coil with rectangular section at outer end. Inner coil broken; outer coil is held by a penannular outer band, U-shaped in section, with coiled ends, perforations along outer face and an incised line parallel to the margin at the back. Light green patina.
Diam. 13.5cm Weight 306g
See Colucci Pescatori 1971.I, 476, fig. 2.1, from Bisaccia (Avellino), Campania, sporadic; same type.
EIA, late.
Bibliography: Walters 1899, no. 1931.

618.
GR 1772.3-9.115. Bought from Sir William Hamilton.
Spiral from a large spectacle fibula. See **Fibulae type 55**.
Large wire spiral circular in section and decreasing in thickness from edge to centre. Outer coil has a series of round perforations for two-thirds of its length and is broken at the end. Small conical cap at the centre, pierced by an iron rivet. Green patina with some corrosion.
Diam. 12cm Weight 282 g
See **cat. 613** and **617**.
EIA, late.
Bibliography: Walters 1899, no. 1932.

619.
GR 1856.12-26.762. Bequeathed by Sir William Temple.
Torre Annunziata (Naples), Campania.
Backing-plate of a large spectacle fibula. See **Fibulae type 55**.
Narrow violin-bow shape; upper side flat, widening at centre, with two rivet holes with remains of iron rivets to fasten the coils and two rivet holes at centre, probably to attach the figure-of-eight element. Incised line parallel to outer margin of back of upper side. No spring, pin with circular section and small catch-plate. Smooth green to brown patina.
L. 25cm Weight 74g
See **cat. 613**. Also *PBF* XV, forthcoming, no. 7690, from Mattinata (Foggia), Apulia.
EIA, late.
Bibliography: Walters 1899, no. 1943.

620.
GR 1856.12-26.763. Bequeathed by Sir William Temple.
Torre Annunziata (Naples), Campania.
Backing-plate of a spectacle fibula. See **Fibulae type 55**.
Narrow violin-bow shape; upper side flat, lozenge-shaped, with two rivet holes with remains of iron rivets. No spring, pin with circular section and small catch-plate. Smooth green to brown patina with small areas of corrosion.
L. 15.9cm Weight 28g
See **cat. 613** and **619**.
EIA, late.
Bibliography: Walters 1899, no. 1942.

621.
GR 1856.12-26.764. Bequeathed by Sir William Temple.
Torre Annunziata (Naples), Campania.
Backing-plate from large spectacle fibula. See **Fibulae type 55**.
Narrow violin-bow shape; upper side flat,

slightly widening at centre, with two rivet holes, one with remains of iron rivet visible on underside. No spring, pin with circular section and small catch of wire. Smooth green to brown patina with areas of corrosion.
L. 19.7cm Weight 31g
See **cat. 613** and **619**.
EIA, late.
Bibliography: Walters 1899, no. 1944, fig. 30.

622.
GR 1772.3-18.23. Given by Sir William Hamilton.
Backing-plate from large spectacle fibula. See **Fibulae type 55**.
Violin-bow shape; upper side flat in section, slightly widening at centre and with a right angled turn at catch end. Two conical caps to attach coils, one with inner end of coil surviving. At centre two rivet holes, one rivet with button-head surviving, which probably attached figure-of-eight element. Traces of incised line parallel to outer margin of back of upper side. No spring, pin with circular section, catch of wire. Mainly brown patina with corrosion on underside.
L. 20.6cm Weight 90g
See **cat. 613** and **619**.
EIA, late.
Bibliography: Walters 1899, no. 1945.

623.
GR 1856.12-26.717. Bequeathed by Sir William Temple.
Ruvo (Bari), Apulia.
Spiral from a spectacle fibula with backing-plate. **Fibulae types 54** or **55**.
One coil of wire, broken at the outer end, with circular section and even thickness; two bands set at right angles once encircled the coil. Rivet at centre of coil, joining it with the encircling bands and backing-plate, partly extant, broken at both ends; pin and catch-plate missing. Green patina with much corrosion.
Diam. 7.3cm Weight 71g
See **cat. 612** and **619**.
EIA, late.

624.
PRB 1916.6-5.184. Given by Lord Avebury.
Four-spiral fibula with central disc. **Fibulae type 56**.
Coils of bronze wire with circular section and thickness decreasing from edge to centre; a small disc is attached to the upper central joint of the spirals with a rivet. Pin and hook missing, once probably springing diagonally from the centre of two opposing spirals. Decoration of small bosses on disc: a row around the edge and two straight rows crossing at right angles at centre. Black patina with dark green incrustations.
L. 9.3cm Weight 63g
See *PBF* XIV, forthcoming, LV. 1 (445), 7926, Incoronata (Matera), Basilicata, tomb 34, 'Grandi fibule a quattro spirali tipo Incoronata'.
EIA, phase IIA.
Kilian 1970, 165 ff., only one four-spiral fibula in two pieces with central disc (type M5c) is recorded by Kilian at Sala Consilina (Salerno), Campania, from the cremation burial of a woman, dating from the beginning of period II. EIA, late.

625.
GR 1824.4-98.20. Bequeathed by R. Payne Knight.
Four-spiral fibula with pin and hook once springing from centre of opposing spirals. **Fibulae type 56.**
Two pairs of two coils of wire with circular section and thickness decreasing from edge to centre; both pairs flattened at the central junction and pierced by a rivet uniting them. Wire broken at centre of two coils at back; pin and hook missing. Smooth dark green patina.
L. 9.8cm and 9.5cm Weight 114g
See **cat. 624.**
Also *PBF* XIV, forthcoming, no. 7935, Incoronata (Matera), Basilicata, tomb 24. Ibid. (447), no. 7992, from Suessula (Caserta), Campania, 'Grandi fibule con arco a fascetta tipo Amendolara'. EIA, phase IIA.
EIA, late.

626.
GR 1938.3-31.2. Transferred from the Department of British and Medieval Antiquities. Canon W. Greenwell Collection, no. 1164, bought from the Rev. Greville J. Chester. Given by J. Pierpont Morgan in 1909. Terra di Lavoro, (Caserta), Campania.
Four-spiral fibula with pin and hook springing from centre of opposing spirals. **Fibulae type 56.**
Two pairs of two coils of wire with circular section and thickness decreasing from edge to centre; a small fragment from a plate is attached to the front of the flattened central junction and is pierced by a rivet, which unites the two pairs of spirals. The inner end of two of the spirals is bent to form the catch-plate (a simple hook) and the pin on the back of the fibula. Light green patina.
L. 5.6cm Weight 26g
See **cat. 624.**
EIA, late.
Bibliography: Bietti Sestieri 1986, Fibulae, 12, no. 50, and fig. p. 23.

627.
GR 1772.3-18.16. Given by Sir William Hamilton.
Backing-plate from four-coil fibula with horned bird attached on upper side. **Fibulae type 58.**
Backing-plate of narrow violin-bow shape; upper side flat, slightly widening at centre, small two-coiled spring and symmetrical catch-plate. Circular hole at centre of upper side and inset cast solid figurine of horned bird (L.6.1cm) with straight rounded beak, curved horns and plump body with below a vertical element for attachment. Backing-plate and figurine are genuine, but probably have been attached recently. Smooth green-brown patina with a little corrosion.
L. 15.7cm Weight 97g
Fibulae of this type are known mainly from Suessula (Caserta), Campania and from other sites of Campania.
See *PBF* XIV, forthcoming, (450b1 and b2), nos. 8061, 8065, both from Suessula, 'Fibule da parata con quattro spirali'. (450) B1, nos. 8061–8064.
Suessula 1878, pl. 6.4 and 5.
Comstock and Vermeule 1971, no. 333, from Suessula.
Cuma 1913, cols. 72 and 140, pl. 22.5.
See Hencken 1968, 519–531 for a discussion of

horned birds and other animals. Similar backing-plates of fibulae with differing central figurines are worthy of note: from Capua (Caserta), Campania, Tomb 363 (Johannowsky 1983, 133ff., pl. XXXV,59–61) and Suessula (Sundwall 1943, 257, fig. 435) fibulae with a human figure standing on a 'sun-boat' at the centre and a fibula with a bull set on the upper side (Sundwall 1943, 257, fig. 436).
EIA, late.
Bibliography: Walters 1899, no. 348; Kemble 1855, 361, pl. 27.4; *PBF* XIV, forthcoming, no. 8068.

628.
GR 1974.12-3.9. Found unregistered.
Horned bird from a fibula. See **Fibulae type 58.**
Cast solid figurine with rounded beak, curved horns and plump body with below a vertical element, narrowed at the base, and originally used to insert the figurine into the hole in the supporting object, probably a fibula. Base partly missing and with traces of iron. Smooth green-brown patina.
L. 5.8cm Weight 68g
Close to **627.**
EIA, late.
Bibliography: Walters 1899, no. 351; Hencken 1968, 529, fig. 485a.

629.
GR 1878.10-19.166. Given by General A.W.H. Meyrick.
Spiral, perhaps once part of a fibula. **Fibulae unclassified.**
Coil of wire, round in section, diminishing in thickness towards the centre. Probably once a cap at the centre; where traces of an iron rivet survive. Outer end terminates in a small coil, with rectangular section, and a flat extension, broken at the end. Dull green patina.
Diam. 11.1cm without extension. Weight 248 g
See **Fibulae types 54** and **55.**
EIA, late?

630.
GR 1772.3-9.116. Bought from Sir William Hamilton .
Spiral, probably once part of a fibula. **Fibulae unclassified.**
Coil of wire, round in section, diminishing in thickness towards the centre; conical cap at the centre, pierced by an iron rivet. Outer end terminates in a small coil, with rectangular section, and a short, flat extension. Dull green patina with a 'shadow' line across centre of back, which might indicate the position of a backing-plate of a fibula.
Diam. 11cm Weight 236g
See **Fibulae types 54** and **55.**
EIA, late?

631.
PRB 1964.12-6.79. Bequeathed by C.T. Trechmann. Hilton Price Collection.
Maremma, near Veii (Rome), Lazio.
Large wire spiral, probably from a spectacle or a four-spiral fibula.
Fibulae unclassified.
Large wire spiral, round in section, with small coil with rectangular section at outer end; hemispherical bronze cap with iron rivet at centre of outer coil. Possibly part of a spectacle fibula. Smooth light green patina with earth

incrustations.
Diam. 9.5cm Weight 118 g
See **Fibulae types 54** and **55.**
EIA, late?

632.
GR 1772.3-9.132. Bought from Sir William Hamilton (H.132).
Spiral, probably from a fibula. **Fibulae unclassified.**
Five coils of oval section; broken at both ends. Green patina with some corrosion.
Diam. 9.8cm Weight 105g
See **Fibulae types 54** and **55.**
EIA, late?

633.
GR 1976.2-5.1. Found unregistered.
Spiral, probably from a fibula. **Fibulae unclassified.**
Coil of wire, broken at the outer end, circular in section and diminishing in thickness from edge to centre. Dark green patina.
Diam. 3.4cm Weight 9g
See **Fibulae types 54** and **55.**
EIA, late?

634.
GR 1878.10-19.167. Given by General A.W.H. Meyrick.
Spiral, possibly from a fibula. **Fibulae unclassified.**
Coil of wire, broken at the outer end, of circular section and even thickness. Dull green patina.
Diam. 2.6cm Weight 6g
See **Fibulae types 54** and **55.**
EIA, late?

Bracelets

635.
GR 1856.12-26.722. Bequeathed by Sir William Temple.
Armento (Potenza), Basilicata.
Spiral ribbon bracelet. **Bracelets type 2c.**
Thin ribbon of rectangular section, hammered to form 19 coils with decreasing diameter; one end broken, the other end tapers to a point. Smooth light green patina.
Diam. min. 6cm max. 7cm Weight 242g
Close to *Cuma* 1913, col. 88, pl. 25.6.
See Colucci Pescatori 1971. II, 534 ff., fig. 44.14, Cairano (Avellino), Campania, Zigarelli collection.
Probably EIA, late.

636.
GR 1772.3-7.178. Bought from Sir William Hamilton.
Spiral rod bracelet with coiled ends. **Bracelets type 2d.**
Rod with triangular section, hammered to form seven coils of decreasing diameter and ending in two small coils of thin wire with round section. Green patina with areas of corrosion.
Height 5.4cm Diam. max. 4.8cm Weight 89g
Close to *Quattro Fontanili* 1967, 131, fig. 25.6 tomb EE 7-8 B.6. Phase IIB.
See also *Quattro Fontanili* 1965, 201, fig. 103.r, tomb II 9-10.r.; (not identical, with similar section). Phase IIB.
EIA, late.

637.
GR 1772.3-7.123. Bought from Sir William Hamilton.
Coiled ribbon and wire bracelet with coiled ends. **Bracelets type 3a, variant**.
One and a half coils extant; two thirds of the main coil is hammered ribbon with central ridge, which then reduces to thin hammered wire with round section ending in a small coil. Ribbon broken and mended in antiquity with two rivets. Delicately incised decoration: double zigzag chevrons on whole surface of ribbon. A large part of the bracelet is missing. Smooth green patina.
Diam. 8cm Weight 33g
See for a ribbon bracelet with central ridge and terminal coils *Torre Galli* 1999, fig. 6.8, cemetery from Contrada La Rota, sporadic. Phase IIA.
Probably EIA, late.

638.
GR 1772.3-7.133. Bought from Sir William Hamilton.
Coiled double-wire bracelet with ends wrapped together. **Bracelets type 4**.
Thick wire with round section, doubled to form two parallel strands and hammered to form one and a half double coils; at one end, the wires thinned and one wrapped closely around the other. A small, plain penannular coil, is attached to the bracelet, its max. diam is 4.3cm. Green patina with much corrosion and some earth adhering.
Diam. 10.4cm Weight 128g
See Colucci Pescatori 1971.I, 476, fig. 2.7, from Bisaccia (Avellino), Campania, sporadic; Colucci Pescatori 1971.II, figs. 27, 31, 40, from Cairano (Avellino), Campania, tombs 12, 8, 22; *Pithekoussai* 1993, 340, pl. 109.9, tomb 283.9 LGI-II; *Cuma* 1913, col. 73, fig. 17, Stevens Collection, not identical. See Bailey 1986, 136 and Jurgeit 1999, no. 1013 for further references and comments.
EIA, late.

639.
GR 1772.3-7.174. Bought from Sir William Hamilton.
Coiled double-wire bracelet with ends wrapped together. **Bracelets type 4**.
Thick wire with round section, doubled to form two parallel strands and hammered to form one and a half double coils; at one end, the wires thinned and one wrapped closely around the other. Smooth brown to green patina.
Diam. 8.7cm Weight 52g
See **cat. 638**.
EIA, late.

640.
GR 1814.7-4.233. Charles Townley Collection. Bought from Peregrine Townley.
Coiled double-wire bracelet with ends wrapped together. **Bracelets type 4**.
Thick double-wire with round section, hammered to form two coils; at one end, the wires thinned and one wrapped closely around the other. Dull green patina with some corrosion.
Diam. 9.4cm Weight 112g
See **cat. 638**.
EIA, late.

641.
GR 1814.7-4.238. Charles Townley Collection. Bought from Peregrine Townley.
Coiled double-wire spiral bracelet with ends wrapped together. **Bracelets type 4**.
Double-wire with round section, hammered to form one and a half coils; at one end the wire thinned and one wrapped closely around the other. Dull green patina with some corrosion.
Diam. 7cm Weight 28g
See **cat. 638**.
EIA, late.

642.
GR 1772.3-7.135. Bought from Sir William Hamilton.
Coiled double-wire bracelet or hair ring with ends wrapped together. **Bracelets type 4**.
Wire with round section, doubled to form two parallel strands and hammered to form nearly two double coils; at one end, the wires thinned and one wrapped closely around the other. A small break in outer coil. Dull green patina.
Diam. 3.5cm Weight 14g
See **cat. 638**.
EIA, late.

643.
GR 1814.7-4.234. Charles Townley Collection. Bought from Peregrine Townley.
Coiled double-wire bracelet once with ends wrapped together. **Bracelets type 4**.
Double-wire with round section, hammered to form coils; both wires broken. Dull green patina with some corrosion.
Diam. 9cm Weight 44g
See **cat. 638**.
EIA, late.

644.
GR 1856.12-26.724. Bequeathed by Sir William Temple.
Armento (Potenza), Basilicata.
Coiled double-wire bracelet once with ends wrapped together. **Bracelets type 4**.
Double-wire with round section; one end missing. Damaged and parts missing. Dull green patina.
Diam. 9cm Weight 69g
See **cat. 638**.
EIA, late.

645.
GR 1975.9-5.10. Found unregistered.
Coiled rod bracelet with overlapping ends. **Bracelets type 5**.
Rod of roughly round section (diam. 0.4cm) with ends narrowing and overlapping. Thick incrustations covering the whole surface.
Diam. 4.3cm Weight 10g
See *Cuma* 1903, col. 269, fig. 51, Greek inhumation burial 103bis.
Also *Quattro Fontanili* 1965, 114 and fig. 45 j, tomb GG 13-14 j. Phase IIB.
Probably EIA, late.

646.
GR 1814.7-4.237. Charles Townley Collection. Bought from Peregrine Townley.
Coiled rod bracelet with overlapping ends. **Bracelets type 5**.
Thick rod of roughly square section with ends narrowing and overlapping. Dull green-brown patina.
Diam. 9cm Weight 62g
Close to Hencken 1968, 175, fig. 160b, from Tarquinia (Viterbo), Lazio, Impiccato, Grave II. Phase IIB. See also *Pithekoussai* 1993, 491, pl. 145.4,5, tomb 488.4 and 5. LGI or II. Also Cuma 1903, col. 269, fig. 51, though smaller; Greek inhumation burial 103bis.
See also similar pieces (not identical) from Etruria: *Quattro Fontanili* 1963, 239, fig. 106.f, tomb KKLL 18-19.f. Phase II C; 252, fig. 117.e, tomb LL 18.e. Phase II B. Also Jurgeit 1999, nos. 1020 and 1021.
EIA, late.

647.
GR 1814.7-4.230. Charles Townley Collection. Bought from Peregrine Townley.
Coiled rod bracelet with overlapping ends. **Bracelets type 5**.
Thick rod of roughly plano-convex section (diam. 1cm) with ends narrowing and overlapping. Ends flat. Dull green patina.
Diam. 8.5cm Weight 138g
See **cat. 646**.
EIA, late.

648.
GR 1838.6-8.73. Bought from C. Campanari.
Coiled rod bracelet with overlapping ends. **Bracelets type 5**.
Rod of roughly plano-convex section (diam. 0.7cm) with ends narrowing and overlapping. Rough green patina with areas of corrosion.
Diam. 7.5cm Weight 77g
See **cat. 646**.
EIA, late.

649.
GR 1975.9-5.15bis. Found unregistered.
Coiled thin rod bracelet with overlapping ends. **Bracelets type 5, variant**.
Rod of round section (diam. 0.5cm). Smooth green-brown patina.
Diam. 9cm Weight 28g
See Hencken 1968, 73, fig. 60a, Tarquinia (Viterbo), Lazio, Selciatello Sopra, tomb 125. Phase I B; Kilian 1977 b, 28, nos. 10 and 11, fig. 5.3 and 4, Tarquinia, Monterozzi (M1), Tomb of the Warrior.
EIA, late.

650.
GR 1772.3-7.149. Bought from Sir William Hamilton.
Coiled thick rod bracelet with overlapping ends. **Bracelets type 6**.
Thick rod with rounded section, slightly diminishing at ends, and hammered to form one and a quarter coils. Deeply incised decoration on outer surface of ends: groups of transverse parallel grooves separated by slightly bulging areas. Light green patina with some corrosion.
Diam. 9.7cm Weight 567g
See von Duhn 1887, 252, fig. 22 from Suessula (Caserta), Campania, very similar but rod of even thickness.
See, too, *Pithekoussai* 1993, 470, pl. 138.10, tomb 469.10 and 11, though smaller. LGI.
EIA, late.

651.
GR 1772.3-7.151. Bought from Sir William Hamilton.
Coiled thick rod bracelet with overlapping ends. **Bracelets type 6.**
Thick rod with round section slightly diminishing at ends and hammered to form one and a quarter coils. Deeply incised decoration on outer surface of ends: groups of transverse parallel grooves separated by slightly bulging areas. Dark green patina.
Diam. 5.2cm Weight 70g
See *Pithekoussai* 1993, 470, pl. 138.10. tomb 469. 10 and 11. LGI.
EIA, late.

652.
GR 1824.4-6.2. Bequeathed by R. Payne Knight.
Coiled rod bracelet with overlapping ends. **Bracelets type 6.**
Rod with oval section, hammered to form one and a fifth circular coils, ends flat with deeply incised cross pattern. Incised decoration on outer surface of ends: groups of transverse parallel lines. Dark green patina.
Diam. 8cm Weight 112g
See *Pithekoussai* 1993, 356, pl. 114.10, tomb 298.10 and 11, though smaller. LGII; *Pontecagnano* 2001, 40, pl. 23, 23,24, tomb 4894. 23, 34. Similar to Pontecagnano, type 36A (*Pontecagnano* 1988, 64, pl. 21, period II).
EIA, late.

653.
GR 1814.7-4.231. Charles Townley Collection. Bought from Peregrine Townley.
Coiled faceted rod bracelet. **Bracelets type 7.**
Thin rod with approximately octagonal section, hammered to form one and a half coils, ends slightly rounded. Deeply incised decoration on outer side of ends: groups of transverse parallel lines separated by slightly bulging areas: see **Bracelets type 6.** A ring of bronze sheet with five holes, circular or figure-of-eight in form, suspended from the bracelet. Dull green patina.
Diam. 8.6cm Weight (including the ring) 117g
For faceted section, see *Pithekoussai* 1993, 491, pl. 145.4, tomb 488.4. LGI or II.
For decoration, see *Pithekoussai* 1993, 356, pl. 114.10, tomb 298. 10 and 11. LGII.
EIA, late.

654.
GR 1878.10-19.180. Given by General A.W.H. Meyrick.
Coiled faceted rod bracelet. **Bracelets type 7.**
Rod with square section with rounded angles, hammered to form almost two circular coils, ends slightly diminished with straight butts. Small solid cast ring and circular bulla of folded sheet bronze attached to the bracelet. Smooth dark green patina.
Diam. 9.2cm Weight (including the bulla and ring) 134g
See **cat. 653.**
EIA, late.

655.
GR 1772.3-7.122. Bought from Sir William Hamilton.
Coiled thick rod bracelet. **Bracelets type 8.**
Small, heavy, rod with round section (diam. 0.8cm). Two and a third coils, flat ends. Plain. Green patina with some earth adhering.

Diam. 5.2cm Weight 140g
See *Pontecagano* 1988, 222, fig. 209.5, tomb 4870.5, type 36A. Period II.
EIA, late.

656.
GR 1772.3-7.121. Bought from Sir William Hamilton.
Coiled thick rod bracelet. **Bracelets type 8.**
Thick rod with round section (diam. 1.5cm). Almost two coils with somewhat straightened ends. Plain. Brown-green patina.
Diam. 9.4cm Weight 462g
See *Pithekoussai* 1993, 491 and pl. 145.4, tomb 488.4, though this example is faceted. LGI or II.
EIA, late.

657.
GR 1772.3-7.167. Bought from Sir William Hamilton.
Coiled rod bracelet with moulded ends. **Bracelets type 9a.**
Rod with round section, hammered to form one and a quarter coils; ends narrowing with plano-convex section and somewhat rounded ends, decorated on outer face with three transverse grooves. Dark green patina with some corrosion.
Diam. 5.4cm Weight 33g
Close to *Quattro Fontanili* 1965, 202, fig. 103.ee, tomb II 9-10.ee. Phase IIB.
Hencken 1968, 139, fig. 127.e, from Tarquinia (Viterbo), Lazio, Sopra Selciatello, tomb 140.e. Phase IIA.
EIA, late.

658.
GR 1772.3-7.157. Bought from Sir William Hamilton.
Coiled rod bracelet with moulded ends. **Bracelets type 9a.**
Small, rod with roughly plano-convex section (diam. 0.45cm). One and a quarter coils, ends narrowing with slightly moulded rounded butts. Tip of one end misssing. Light green patina.
Diam. 4cm Weight 14g
See **cat. 657.**
EIA, late.

659.
GR 1772.3-7.156. Bought from Sir William Hamilton.
Coiled rod bracelet with moulded ends. **Bracelets type 9a.**
Small, rod with round section (diam. 0.55cm). One and a quarter coils and distinct knobbed ends. Smooth green patina.
Diam. 4.4cm Weight 26g
See **cat. 657.**
EIA, late.

660.
GR 1772.3-7.165. Bought from Sir William Hamilton.
Coiled rod bracelet with moulded ends. **Bracelets type 9a.**
Small, thin rod with round section (diam. 0.4cm). Two coils with distinct knobbed ends. Smooth dark green patina.
Diam. 4.6cm Weight 34g
See **cat. 657.**
EIA, late.

661.
GR 1772.3-7.126. Bought from Sir William Hamilton.
Coiled rod bracelet with moulded ends. **Bracelets type 9b.**
Rod with round section, slightly thickened at centre and bent to form one coil with overlapping, knobbed ends. Probably once incised decoration on whole outer surface: encircling parallel lines. Dull green patina with some corrosion.
Diam. 9cm Weight 68g
Close (not identical) to Johannowsky 1983, 117, pl. XX.9, Capua (Caserta), Campania, tomb 213.13. See also *Pontecagnano* 1992, 109, fig. 125.12, tomb 3280.12, though smaller. Phase IIA; *Quattro Fontanili* 1972, 378, fig. 122.6, tomb QR beta.6. Phase IIA.
EIA, late.

662.
GR 1772.3-7.141. Bought from Sir William Hamilton.
Annular wire bracelet. **Bracelets type 10a.**
Wire with round section (diam. 0.2cm). Plain. Smooth dark green patina.
Diam. 7.5–8cm Weight 10g
Close to *Quattro Fontanili* 1970, 296, fig. 69.16; tomb Z I alpha. 16. Phase IIB. See also Jurgeit 1999, no. 1045.
EIA, late.

663.
GR 1772.3-7.145. Bought from Sir William Hamilton.
Annular thin wire bracelet. **Bracelets type 10a.**
Wire with round section (max. diam. 0.2cm). Plain. Smooth dark green patina.
Diam. 8cm Weight 6g
See **cat. 662.**
EIA, late.

664.
GR 1772.3-7.162. Bought from Sir William Hamilton.
Annular wire bracelet. **Bracelets type 10a.**
Wire with four-sided faceted section (max. diam. 0.3cm). Plain. Dark green patina.
Diam. 8.8cm Weight 13g
See **cat. 662.**
EIA, late.

665.
GR 1975.9-5.14. Found unregistered.
Annular wire bracelet. **Bracelets type 10a.**
Wire of rectangular section (diam. 0.3cm). Smooth green-brown patina.
Diam. 9.3cm Weight 12g
See **cat. 662.**
EIA, late.

666.
GR 1975.9-5.15. Found unregistered.
Annular wire bracelet. **Bracelets type 10a.**
Wire of round section (diam. 0.2cm). Smooth green-brown patina.
Diam. 8.1cm Weight 8g
See **cat. 662.**
EIA, late.

667.
GR 1975.9-5.16. Found unregistered.
Annular rod bracelet or suspension ring. **Bracelets type 10b.**

Rod of roughly square section(diam. 0.5cm).
Smooth dull green patina.
Diam. 6.9cm Weight 14g
Close to *Pontecagnano* 1988, 63, pl. 21, type 35A;
tomb 211.40, fig. 64.40. Period II.
Also *Osteria dell'Osa* 1992, 394, pl. 40, type 49e.
Period III.
EIA, late.

668.
GR 1772.3-7.168. Bought from Sir William
Hamilton.
Penannular rod bracelet. **Bracelets type 11**.
Rod with rounded section (diam. 0.9cm). Bent
to form one coil, with the section narrowing
towards the ends and the straight ends
touching. Plain, smooth light green patina.
Diam. 10cm Weight 158g
See *Cuma* 1903, col. 269, nos. 14–17, figs. 49–50
from Greek inhumation burial 103bis. Similar
in form but of smaller size.
EIA, late.

669.
GR 1772.3-7.153. Bought from Sir William
Hamilton.
Penannular rod bracelet. **Bracelets type 11**.
Rod with slightly faceted section, bent to form
one coil with the straight ends touching. Deeply
incised decoration on outer face: transverse
groups of chevrons and parallel lines separated
by slightly bulging areas with circle at centre.
Green patina.
Diam. 10.3cm Weight 160g
See Colucci Pescatori 1971. II, 536 and fig. 44. 22
from Cairano (Avellino), Campania, Zigarelli
Collection.
EIA, late.

670–723.
GR 1814.7-4.1579 (672). Charles Townley
Collection. Bought from Peregrine Townley.
GR 1975.9-4.14-66. Found unregistered.
Penannular rod bracelet in form of a capital D
with in-curved back. **Bracelets type 12a**.
Rod of rounded section on inner and outer
faces and flattened sides (diam. 0.45cm): flat
open ends. Light green patina with brown areas
and some corrosion.
Total 54 pieces. The bracelets can be divided in
three groups according to maximum width:
Width under 6cm:
Cat. 670, 671, 673–676. Weight: 5–19g
Width 6–8cm:
Cat. 677, 678–705. Weight: 13–43g
Width 8cm or over:
Cat. 672, 706–723. Weight: 32–56g
This type of bracelet, without decoration, is
known chiefly from tombs of the Oliveto-
Cairano culture, often with several examples in
a grave. From Oliveto Citra (Salerno),
Campania, D'Agostino 1964, 42, 'bracciali ad
arco inflesso' from tombs 1, 3, 7, 10 (see fig. 23,
14–17) and 25. From Cairano (Avellino),
Campania, Colucci Pescatori 1971.II. 488, Type
C2, tomb 11, fig. 14; tomb 7, fig. 31; tomb 13, fig.
31 and tomb 2, fig. 40. From Cairano, Bailo
Modesti 1980, 40, type 35 BI (see for
references); from tombs V and VI, pl. 18; tomb
IX, pl. 76.3. From Bisaccia (Avellino),
Campania, Colucci Pescatori 1971. I, fig. 2.4.
D'Agostino 1964, 95–96 notes the type probably
reached Campania from the east and is related
to forms north of the Adriatic.

See for a similar type and distribution,
Bracelets type 12b.
EIA, late or later.

724.
GR 1975.9-4.12. Found unregistered.
Penannular rod bracelet in the form of a capital
D with in-curved back. **Bracelets type 12a,
variant**.
Plain thick rod with triangular section,
irregular open ends. Light green patina.
Width 6.5cm Weight 76g
EIA, late or later.

725.
GR 1964.12-21.4. Found unregistered.
Penannular thick rod bracelet in the form of a
capital D with in-curved back. **Bracelets type
12b**.
Thick and wide rod with triangular section,
slightly convex open ends. Deeply incised
decoration: oblique parallel lines on whole
outer surface. Dark green patina.
Like **bracelets type 12a**, very similar in general
shape, this type is rather standardized, except
for some variation in weight. Total 13 pieces.
maximum width: 6.7 – 7.8cm
weight: 76 – 254g
This heavy type of bracelet decorated by
incision on the outer side is known from the
Cairano area (Avellino), Campania. See Colucci
Pescatori 1971. II. 488 'bracciali ad arco inflesso'
Type C I, from Cairano, sporadic, fig. 36 and
from the Zigarelli collection, fig. 44.19. See, too,
an example without incised decoration from
Calitri (Avellino), Campania, fig. 43.9. Also
Bailo Modesti 1980, 40, type 35A, pl.18,
sporadic 2, from necropoli Vignale, Cairano.
EIA, late or later.

726.
GR 1935.8-23.66. Transferred from the
Department of British and Medieval Antiquities
(1904.3-12.5). Given by Max Rosenheim.
Tarquinia (Viterbo), Lazio.
Penannular thick rod bracelet in the form of a
capital D with in-curved back. **Bracelets type
12b**.
Thick and wide rod, section triangular at
centre, plano-convex at sides, flat open ends.
Deeply incised decoration: oblique parallel
lines, originally on whole outer surface. One
end broken. Smooth green patina with some
corrosion.
Max. width 7.8cm Weight 173g
See **cat. 725**.
Although the possibility of this piece being an
import to Etruria should not be excluded, the
provenance from Tarquinia must be considered
with caution, since this type is specific to the
Campanian Oliveto-Cairano culture.
EIA, late or later.

727.
GR 1975.9-4.1. Found unregistered.
Penannular thick rod bracelet in the form of a
capital D with in-curved back. **Bracelets type
12b**.
Thick rod with rounded section, flat open ends.
Deeply incised decoration: oblique parallel
lines, originally on whole outer surface. Dark
green patina with some corrosion.
Max. width 7.9cm Weight 159g
See **cat. 725**.

EIA, late or later.

728.
GR 1975.9-4.2. Found unregistered.
Penannular thick rod bracelet in the form of a
capital D with in-curved back. **Bracelets type
12b**.
Thick rod with rounded section, flat open ends.
Deeply incised decoration: oblique parallel
lines, originally on whole outer surface. Dark
green patina with some corrosion.
Max. width 7.5cm Weight 178g
See **cat. 725**.
EIA, late or later.

729.
GR 1975.9-4.3. Found unregistered.
Penannular thick rod bracelet in the form of a
capital D with in-curved back. **Bracelets type
12b**.
Thick rod with plano-convex section. Deeply
incised decoration: oblique parallel lines
originally on whole outer surface. Dark green
patina.
Max width 7.1cm Weight 254g
See **cat. 725**.
EIA, late or later.

730.
GR 1975.9-4.4. Found unregistered.
Penannular thick rod bracelet in the form of a
capital D with in-curved back. **Bracelets type
12b**.
Thick rod with plano-convex section. Deeply
incised decoration: oblique parallel lines
originally on whole outer surface. Dark green
patina.
Max. width 6.8cm Weight 153g
See **cat. 725**.
EIA, late or later.

731.
GR 1975.9-4.5. Found unregistered.
Penannular thick rod bracelet in the form of a
capital D with in-curved back. **Bracelets type
12b**.
Thick rod with plano-convex section. Deeply
incised decoration: oblique parallel lines
originally on whole outer surface. Dark green
patina.
Max. width 7cm Weight 178g
See **cat. 725**.
EIA, late or later.

732.
GR 1975.9-4.6. Found unregistered.
Penannular thick rod bracelet in the form of a
capital D with in-curved back. **Bracelets type
12b**.
Rod with plano-convex section, flat ends.
Deeply incised decoration: oblique parallel
lines originally on whole outer surface. Dark
green patina with areas of corrosion.
Max. width 6.7cm Weight 76g
See **cat. 725**.
EIA, late or later.

733.
GR 1975.9-4.7. Found unregistered.
Penannular thick rod bracelet in the form of a
capital D with in-curved back. **Bracelets type
12b**.
Rod of plano-convex section. Deeply incised
decoration: oblique parallel lines originally on

discontinuous patina with bright green incrustations.
L. 18.3cm Weight 183g
See **cat. 754**.
EIA, late.
Bibliography: *BM Guide* 1920a, 149, fig. 157.

756.
PRB 1916.6-5.177. Given by Lord Avebury.
Naples, Campania.
Spearhead with conical socket and foliate blade. **Spearheads type 4**.
Narrow blade with rounded profile, faceted socket with central facet extending below the junction with the blade, outer lateral angles at base of socket and two lateral pin-holes surrounded by cruciform incisions. Decoration: very deeply incised herringbone pattern at the base of the blade, on both sides. Smooth blackish patina with dark green incrustations.
L. 20.7cm Weight 180g
See **cat. 754**.
EIA, late.

757.
PRB 1891.5-14.65. Purchased from Rollin and Feuardent; Roots Sale, Christies 20 April 1891.
Spearhead with conical socket and foliate blade. **Spearheads type 4**.
Note: all the pieces in this type have very fine workmanship and decoration.
Narrow blade with rounded profile, faceted socket with central facet extending below the junction with the blade, outer lateral angles at base of socket and two lateral pin-holes. Decorated with four nervatures on the socket and lateral herringbone incision below junction of blade with socket. Smooth patina in various tones of green.
L. 21.5cm Weight 217g
See **cat. 754**.
EIA, late.

758.
PRB 1883.4-26.7. Given by Sir A. W. Franks.
Spearhead with conical socket and foliate blade. **Spearheads type 4, variant**.
Blade slightly expanded in the lower part, not sharply separated from the faceted socket; outer lateral angles at the base of the socket and two lateral pin-holes surrounded by cruciform incisions. Decoration: incised circles in two different sizes on the socket, deeply incised herringbone pattern at the base of the blade, on both sides, and row of parallel marks on both sides of the socket. Smooth patina in various tones of green with brown incrustations.
L. 19.9cm Weight 169g
See for a general similarity **cat. 757**.
Probably EIA, late.

759.
GR 1856.12-26.1087. Bequeathed by Sir William Temple.
Spearhead with conical socket and foliate blade. **Spearheads type 6**.
Narrow elongated blade with rounded lower profile, faceted socket; lateral pin-hole on one side only. One side of blade heavily damaged. Green to grey patina with some corrosion.
L. 36cm Weight 437g
The narrow elongated profile, for which see **Spearheads type 7**, probably indicates that this is a late version of the type already found in

EIA, early.
EIA, late.

760.
GR 1865.7-22.11. Bought from Alessandro Castellani.
Spearhead with conical socket and narrow foliate blade. **Spearheads type 6, variant**.
Very narrow elongated blade with slightly angular profile at lower end, slender faceted socket. Two lateral pin-holes in socket. Dull green to brown patina.
L. 32.2cm Weight 393g
See **cat. 759**.
Bibliography: Walters 1899, no. 2790.

761.
GR 1975.6-27.15. Found unregistered.
Spearhead with conical socket and foliate blade. **Spearheads type 7**.
Long, narrow blade with slightly rounded lower part and plain socket with two lateral pin-holes. Smooth dull green patina.
L. 20.2cm Weight 202g
See for the general shape *Pontecagnano* 1988, 78, pl. 24, type 59A1a. Phase IB.
For a close parallel, *Pontecagnano* 1992, 54ff., fig. 102.17, tomb 3191. Phase IIA.
EIA, late.

762.
GR 1975.6-27.33. Found unregistered.
Spearhead with conical socket and foliate blade. **Spearheads type 7**.
Long, narrow blade with slightly rounded lower part and plain socket with two lateral pin-holes. Small parts missing. Rough green patina.
L. 20.9cm Weight 194g
See **cat. 761**.
EIA, late.

763.
GR 1982.6-17.27. Received from PRB. Sir Henry Wellcome Collection, no. 172737. Bought at Sotheby's sale 16 September 1930, lot 425. Given by the Wellcome Trustees.
Arezzo, Tuscany.
Javelin-head with conical socket and foliate blade. **Spearheads type 7**.
Long, narrow blade with slightly rounded lower part and faceted socket with two lateral pin-holes. Slight damage at butt. Smooth green patina.
L. 15cm Weight 130g
See **cat. 761**.
EIA, late.

764.
GR 1865.7-20.53. Bought from C. Merlin.
Olympia, Greece.
Spearhead with conical socket and foliate blade. **Spearheads type 7**.
A small fragment of charcoal, probably from the wooden shaft, is associated with this spearhead. Long, narrow blade with slightly rounded lower part and slender faceted socket throughout length. Two lateral pin-holes in socket. Dark green patina with some corrosion.
L. 28.6cm Weight 322g
See **cat. 761**.
EIA, late.
For Italian spearheads from Olympia, see Herrmann 1984, 282–283, figs. 15–17.

765.
GR 1873.8-20.231. Bought from Alessandro Castellani.
Spearhead with conical socket and foliate blade. **Spearheads type 7**.
Long, narrow blade with slightly rounded lower part and two wide longitudinal grooves; slender faceted socket with no lateral pin-holes. Several oblique marks on one side of the central ridge of the socket. Bent, probably intentionally; blade edges slightly damaged. Uneven dark and light green patina.
L. 44.5cm when straight. Weight 301g
Identical in general shape, decoration and size to the spearhead from the Tomb of the Warrior, Monterozzi (M1) of Tarquinia (Viterbo), Lazio: Kilian 1977b, 24ff, 63–64, fig. 7.5 and Hencken 1968, 204, fig. 180g, phase IIC.
See for the general EIA type *Pontecagnano* 1988, 78, pl. 24, type 59A1a. Phase IB.
This is an oversize weapon, probably found with its butt, **cat. 766**, formally belonging to the EIA tradition of bronze weaponry; similar pieces are found in Etruria in some important male burials dating from the final phase of the EIA and the Orientalizing period. See Kilian 1977b, 63–64, footnotes 134–143. Compare the two spearheads from Bomarzo (Viterbo), Lazio, **cat. 799** and **800**.
EIA, late or Orientalizing.
Bibliography: Walters 1899, no. 2796.

766.
GR 1873.8-20.238. Bought from Alessandro Castellani.
Spear-butt, conical faceted. **Spear-butts type 5**.
Probably found with spearhead **cat. 765**.
Very long and slender piece, with distinct, slightly flaring rim, lightly faceted body and pointed tip. No pin-holes. Upper part decorated with an encircling band of incised lines. Upper end broken. Dark green patina with much corrosion.
L. 44.6cm Weight 307g
See *Pontecagnano* 1988, 78–79, pl. 24, type 60A2. Phase IB to period II. For size and general shape see the Monterozzi (M1), Tomb of the Warrior of Tarquinia (Viterbo), Lazio: Kilian 1977b, 24ff, 63–64, fig. 7.6; and Hencken 1968, 204, fig. 180e, phase IIC.
EIA, late or Orientalizing.

767.
GR 1975.6-27.9. Found unregistered.
Spearhead with conical socket and narrow foliate blade. **Spearheads type 12**.
Narrow blade with rounded profile, joining to socket at right angles, socket flattened in blade area and with lateral facets continuing past base of blade and forming two raised pointed elements on either side of the socket; no pin-holes in the socket. Traces of incised decoration of lines and dots on the socket: two lines along the central facet in blade area, groups of encircling parallel lines separating bands of zigzag and meander patterns on lower socket. Blade heavily damaged. Some shiny surface areas; elsewhere green patina with heavy corrosion.
L. 32.1cm Weight 351g
See *Quattro Fontanili* 1975, 143, fig. 51.7, tomb AB11-12. 7. Phase IIB.
EIA, late.

768.
GR 1975.6-27.27. Found unregistered.
Spearhead with conical socket, foliate blade
and squared-off butt. **Spearheads type 12.**
Narrow blade with rounded profile, joining to
socket at right angles, plain conical socket with
central zone flattened in blade area, outer
lateral angles and two lateral pin-holes
surrounded by cruciform incisions in lower
socket. Smooth green patina.
L. 29.5cm Weight 386g
See **cat. 767.**
EIA, late.

769.
GR 1975.6-27.32. Found unregistered.
Spearhead with conical socket and foliate
blade. **Spearheads type 12.**
Narrow blade with rounded profile, joining to
socket at right angles, plain conical socket with
two lateral pin-holes. Little patina with colour
of metal showing in some areas.
L. 16cm Weight 92g
See **cat. 767.**
EIA, late.

770.
PRB 1964.12-6.84. Bequeathed by C.T.
Trechmann.
Capua (Caserta), Campania.
Large spearhead with conical socket and foliate
blade. **Spearheads type 12.**
Narrow blade with rounded profile, joining to
socket at right angles, socket with high lateral
nervatures continuing past base of blade and
forming two raised pointed elements on either
side of the socket and two lateral pin-holes. Two
incised lines along edges of lower blade?
Discontinuous black and dark green patina.
Parts of the blade missing.
L. 48.5cm Weight 624g
See **cat. 767.**
EIA, late.

771.
GR 1824.4-7.2. Bequeathed by R. Payne Knight.
Spearhead with conical socket and flame-
shaped blade. **Spearheads type 15.**
Expanded blade and slender flattened socket
with outer lateral angles at the base and two
lateral pin-holes surrounded by cruciform
incisions. Decoration: band of thin incised lines
along the edges of the blade. Smooth dark
green patina.
L. 34.7cm Weight 348g
The slender elongated shape, as seen also in
Spearheads type 7, probably indicates a
relatively late date in the EIA; this seems to be
confirmed by the two oversize spearheads of
similar shape from Bomarzo, **cat. 799** and **800,**
probably of Orientalizing date.
Close to *Pontecagnano* 1988, 77, pl. 24, type
58A2, tomb 2157. Period II.
EIA, late.
Bibliography: Walters 1899, no. 2791.

772.
GR 1867.5-8.185. Blacas Collection.
Spearhead with conical socket and flame-
shaped blade. **Spearheads type 15.**
Similar patina and proportions suggests
association with spear-butt **cat. 773.**
Blade with rounded profile towards lower end,
faceted socket with two lateral pin-holes.

Decoration: row of incised circles along the
lower edge of the blade, four circles around
each pin-hole; flat nervatures with incised
herringbone pattern along the edges of the
socket facets; double band with incised
herringbone pattern at the base of the socket.
Small parts missing. Light green patina with
corrosion and incrustations; earth adhering.
L. 36.2cm Weight 622g
See **cat. 771.**
EIA, late.
Bibliography: Walters 1899, no. 2786.

773.
GR 1867.5-8.190. Blacas Collection.
Spear-butt, conical faceted. **Spear-butts type 4.**
Similar patina suggests association with
spearhead **cat. 772.**
Upper end of socket plain, with three encircling
grooves alternating with encircling nervatures
enclosing bands of deeply incised lines; faceted
body with pointed tip. No pin-holes. Broken in
two pieces; two strike marks. Light green patina
with corrosion and incrustations; earth
adhering.
L. 37.7cm Weight 419g
Close to *Pontecagnano* 1988, 78–79, pl. 24, type
60A2. Period II.
EIA, late.

774.
GR 1867.5-8.188. Blacas Collection.
Spearhead with conical socket and flame-
shaped blade. **Spearheads type 15.**
Long, slender blade with slightly angular
expansions in the lower part and an incised line
parallel to lower edge of blade. Faceted socket
ending in a raised cordon decorated with
oblique grooves; two lateral pin-holes. Smooth
green to brown patina with a little corrosion.
L. 29.3cm Weight 267g
See **cat. 771.**
EIA, late.
Bibliography: Walters 1899, no. 2788.

775.
GR 1867.5-8.189. Blacas Collection.
Spearhead with conical socket and flame-
shaped blade. **Spearheads type 15.**
Long, slender blade with slightly angular lower
expansions; faceted socket with two lateral pin-
holes. Dull green patina with a little corrosion.
L. 26.7cm Weight 354g
See **cat. 771.**
EIA, late.
Bibliography: Walters 1899, no. 2787.

776.
GR 1975.6-27.38. Found unregistered.
Spearhead with conical socket and flame-
shaped blade. **Spearheads type 15.**
Long, slender blade with slight rounded lower
expansions, long and wide faceted socket with
two lateral pin-holes. Small parts missing.
Green patina with spots of corrosion.
L. 23.2cm Weight 170g
See **cat. 771.**
EIA, late.

777.
PRB W. G.1109. Canon W. Greenwell Collection,
bought from the Rev. Greville J. Chester. Given
by J. Pierpont Morgan in 1909.
Capua (Caserta), Campania.

Spearhead with conical socket and flame-
shaped blade. **Spearheads type 15.**
Probably a javelin; long, narrow blade and
faceted socket with two lateral pin-holes, two
smaller holes beneath and a wide base.
Discontinuous smooth patina in two shades of
green.
L. 21cm Weight 141g
See **cat. 771.**
EIA, late.

778.
PRB W. G.1130. Canon W. Greenwell Collection,
bought from the Rev. Greville J. Chester. Given
by J. Pierpont Morgan in 1909.
Calabria.
Spear-butt, conical. **Spear-butts type 1.**
Possibly associated with javelin-head **cat. 407,**
with similar patina.
Short piece, plain, with flaring upper end, two
large pin-holes and rounded point. Light green
patina with areas of corrosion.
L. 10.5cm Weight 55g
Close to *Pontecagnano* 1988, 78–79, pl. 24, type
60A1. Period II.
EIA, late.

779.
PRB W. G.1131. Canon W. Greenwell Collection,
bought from the Rev. Greville J. Chester. Given
by J. Pierpont Morgan in 1909.
'Massica' (probably Marsica, L'Aquila),
Abruzzo.
Spear-butt, conical. **Spear-butts type 1.**
Possibly associated with javelin-head **cat. 419.**
Plain piece, with straight rim, partly missing,
one or two pin-holes and pointed tip; traces of
wood in the socket. Rough light green patina
with black areas and corroded zones.
L. 14.9cm Weight 56g
See **cat. 778.**
EIA, late.

780.
PRB W. G.1132. Canon W. Greenwell Collection,
bought from the Rev. Greville J. Chester. Given
by J. Pierpont Morgan in 1909.
Bolsena (Viterbo), Lazio.
Spear-butt, conical. **Spear-butts type 1.**
Short plain piece, with rounded tip. Upper end
possibly cut off with a saw. Dark green patina
with black, bright green and yellowish
incrustations.
L. 7.3cm Weight 55g
See **cat. 778.**
EIA, late.

781.
PRB WG1129. Canon W. Greenwell Collection,
bought from the Rev. Greville J. Chester. Given
by J. Pierpont Morgan in 1909.
Calabria.
Spear-butt with flattened end. **Spear-butts
type 2.**
Short piece, plain, with flaring lower end
forming a slightly convex circular surface; a
single hole below the rim and one lower down.
Light green patina with azure incrustations,
and areas of corrosion.
L. 12.5cm Weight 7g
Close to *Pontecagnano* 1988, 78–79, pl. 24, type
60C. Period II.
EIA, late.

slightly widening at centre, two-coil spring, rectangular in section, symmetrical catch-plate. Three circular holes in upper side with horned bird inset in central hole. Small parts missing. Dark green patina.

3 – Cast figurine of horned bird (L. 6cm); bird probably a duck with broad, flattened beak, curved horns and plump body with below a vertical element for attachment. Chains, all with attachment ring, one link and outer three rings, suspended from small flanges below beak and horns. Dark green patina.

4 – Ten cast figurines of aquatic birds, probably ducks (L. 3.6–3.6cm): the birds have up-turned beaks, all pierced with a hole, schematic body, ending in a vertical element for attaching each bird to its support; seven birds still have chains suspended from a hole in the beak, all with an attachment ring, one link and outer coil of two circuits. Small parts missing. Dark green patina.

5 – Eight globular glass-paste beads (Diam. 1.1cm), attached to modern disc (1) by wire, probably modern, with wire ring attached at upper end.

Parallels for **cat. 819**:

2 and 3 – See **cat. 627** and **628**, **Fibulae type 58** (four-coil fibulae with horned bird) and **cat. 817.2**. Both 2 and 3 probably from fibulae of this type.

4 – See **cat. 817.3** and **817.4**, for similar figurines of aquatic birds; see for references.
EIA, later.
Bibliography: Kemble 1855, 360, pl. 27.2; Walters 1899, no. 347; Aigier Foresti 1986, 37–38, fig. 2; *PBF* XIV, forthcoming, no. 8070.

820.
GR 1974.12-3.17. Found unregistered.
Two seated figurines connected by their adjacent arms.
Cast figurines, poorly modelled and of uncertain sex. Head of one figure missing; the right hand of this figure rests on the right knee and the left arm, modelled in a curious flattened form, passes behind the back of the second figure and clasps the torso. The head of the second figure has protruding facial features and ears indicated; the left arm is broken above the elbow and the right arm, modelled in flattened form, passes across the back and rests on the right shoulder of the adjacent figure. Upper legs of both figures raised and broken at the knees. A hole pierces the centre of the junction of the arms. Green patina with areas of corrosion.
L. 4.4cm Width 4.5cm Weight 52g
Analysis: Craddock 1986, 144. Heavily leaded bronze.
See linked pair of standing figurines from Torre Mordillo, Tombs 21.1 and 78.1 (Pasqui 1888, 256, pl. 15.22; 472, pl. 19.1). Two identical figurines are mentioned from Tomb 17.18, 19, from La Motta near Francavilla Marittima (De

la Genière 1992, 113 pl. 13,2); from Torano (De la Genière 1968, 83, pl. 65; Peroni 1987, 128, fig. 104). See Frasca 1992 for further references. Apart from the magnificent series of cast bronze figurines from Sardinia (Lilliu 1966) Italy has no sustained tradition of casting small figurines, either singly or in groups, until the later EIA. Then, there appear a number of examples of bronze pendants or amulets in the form of linked human couples, found mainly in Calabria and Sicily, which might have been inspired by east Mediterranean originals. Towards the end of the EIA, both groups and individual bronze figurines of humans and of animals are known (see **cat. 817, 818, 821** and **822**): many of the earlier of these examples come from Campania and it seems likely the origin of their style was influenced by that of the contemporary Greek world (Macnamara 2002, 169).
EIA, late.
Bibliography: Walters 1899, no. 339; Hanfmann 1937, 164, pl. 123.15, left. Kilian 1966, pl. 8.2.

821.
GR 1772.3-5.22. Bought from Sir William Hamilton
Figurine of wolf carrying a small animal in its mouth.
The cast figurine, probably representing a wolf, has an animal of prey, perhaps a lamb, held between its jaws. The jaws are long and widely opened to hold the small, plump animal, the head only sketched and with all its legs broken off. The larger animal has eyes indicated by punched dots surrounded by circles, lightly incised lines on the forehead and pricked ears; the body is sturdy with male genitals shown, the tail is curved downwards and the legs, one partly missing, end in feet with canine pads. A vertical hole between the shoulders may indicate the figurine was mounted upon an upright pin. Dull green patina with some surface pitting.
L. 7.8cm Weight 105g
Analysis: Craddock 1986, 144.
This figurine has been believed to belong to a group of bronzes said to have been found at Lucera in 1800 by Cavaliere Bonghi (Gerhard 1830,15) and illustrated by Gerhard (Gerhard 1840, vol.1, pl. 18. 5-13). The group included figurines of men and animals with peg feet, a pierced disc of sheet bronze and three pairs of wheels, embellished with animal's heads and struts rising above. Many of these bronzes were bought in Naples and subsequently acquired by W.M. Wylie in Rome in 1865–66; Wylie donated them to the Ashmolean Museum, Oxford, where they remain (Garrucci 1867, 275–282; Brown 1980, 29, pl. 9). These bronzes were the subject of an exhibition and seminar held at Lucera (Pietropaolo 2002). However, the

bronzes in the Ashmolean do not include a wolf with a small animal in its mouth, which was included among Gerhard's drawings of the bronzes from Lucera, and the whereabouts of the figurine of a wolf has remained in doubt. Some authors have accepted the example in the British Museum to be that illustrated by Gerhard (Wylie in Garrucci 1867, 278, note a; Petersen 1897, 5, fig. 2; Walters 1899, 58, no. 394), while others, though noting its similarity of style, have expressed doubts of this identification (Hill 1956, 35, footnote 4). The British Museum figurine reached the Museum before 1778, when D'Hancarville described many pieces in the Hamilton collection, including this figurine of a wolf (Manuscript, vol. 1, 308), and thus before the Lucera bronzes were said to have been found; nor does the wolf in Gerhard's drawing correspond in detail with the British Museum example, which has an open jaw, male genitals and canine padded feet, not suitable for fixing into holes of a bronze sheet like those of the Ashmolean figurines. Thus the British Museum figurine cannot be accepted as once belonging to the Lucera group and it is now seen that a similar figurine of a wolf with an animal in its mouth, now in the Ortiz Collection, is the missing Lucera example (Ortiz 1993, no. 187; Vickers 2002, 74–75).

Though not from a composite group once attached to a bronze sheet, like the Lucera group or the figurines of the pastiches, discussed in this catalogue (see **cat. 817** and **818** above), nevertheless this figurine is in a similar style and in all probability from Campania. If indeed it is a single piece, then it may have been a votive dedication, perhaps as has been suggested for the Lucera group, a votive to do with the welfare of flocks and their protection from wolves.
EIA, late.
Bibliography: Walters 1899, no. 394.

822.
GR 1912.11-25.51. Bought from Léon Morel (Morel 34).
Standing male figurine.
Cast. The large head is poorly modelled with protruding facial features, the nose and mouth lightly indicated, neck thick, long torso, well-formed legs bent at the knee and small feet. Wiry arms; the right hand clutches the prominent penis, while the left arm is raised with the hand resting on the side of the head. Green patina with brown areas.
From the style, proportions and attitude, Richardson included this figurine in her Archaic II phase, when Greek Geometric models influenced Italic figurines.
L. 6.2cm Weight 32g
EIA, late or later.
Bibliography: Richardson 1962, 172, fig. 24.

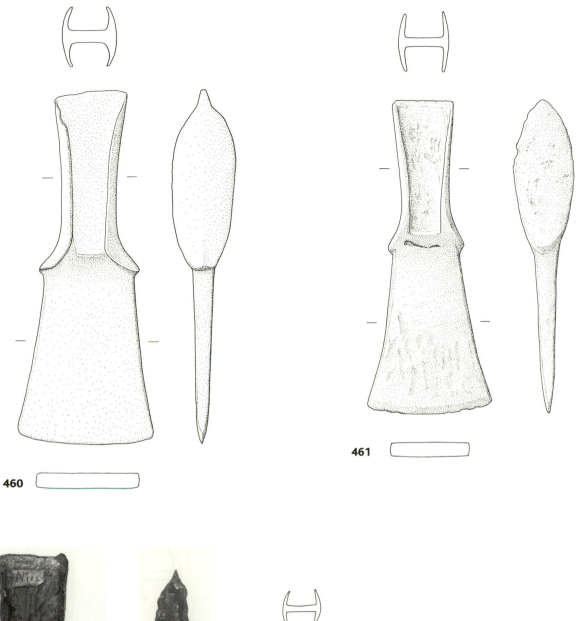

460

461

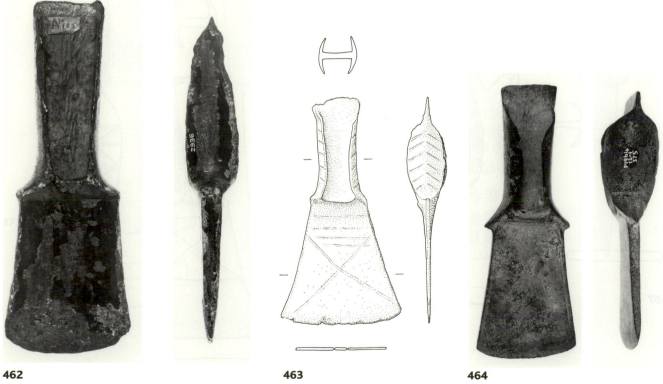

462   463   464

Plate 104   Axes type 37: - 460 Fiesole (Florence), Tuscany. - 461 Tarascon, Provence, France. - 462. - 463. - 464.

474

475

477

476

478

Plate 107   **Axes type 39**: - 474. - 475. - 476. - 477. - 478.

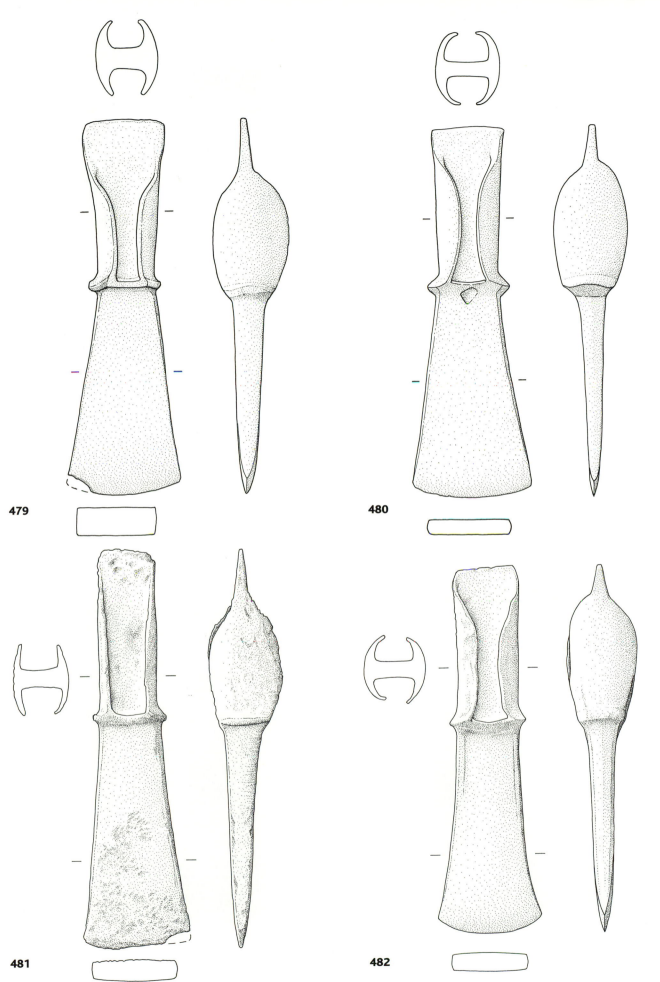

479

480

481

482

Plate 108   Axes type 40: - 479 Sarzana (La Spezia), Liguria. - 480 probably Massa d'Albe (Aquila), Abruzzo. - 481 probably near Naples, Campania. - 482 Tarascon, Provence, France.

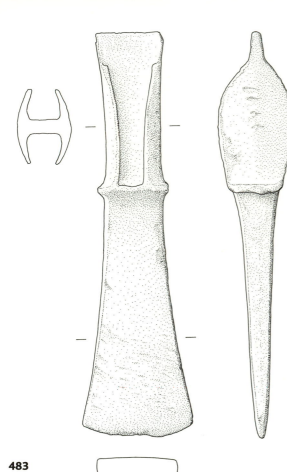

483

484

485

486

Plate 109   Axes type 40: - 483 'Foxcote', England. - 484. - 485. - 486.

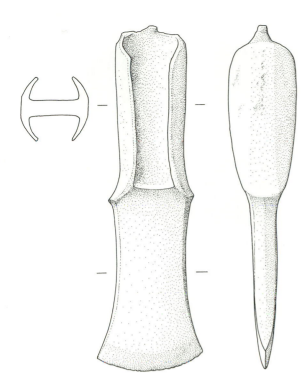

487

488

489

490

Plate 110   Axes type 40: - 487. - 488. **Axes type 41**: - 489. - 490.

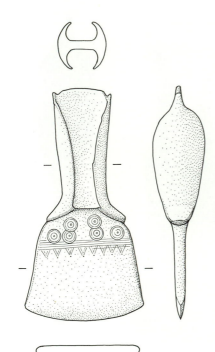

491

492

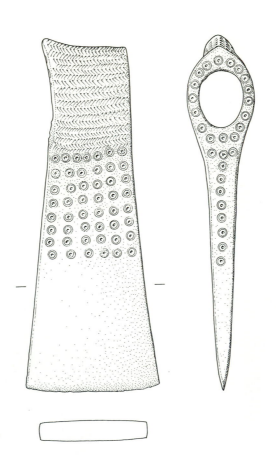

493

Plate 111 **Axes type 42**: - 491 Lake Trasimeno (Perugia), Umbria. - 492. **Axes type 52:** - 493.

494

495

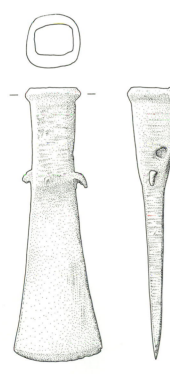

496

497

Plate 112   **Axes type 55:** - 494. **Axes type 56**: - 495. **Axes type 57**: - 496 Fondi (Latina), Lazio. - 497

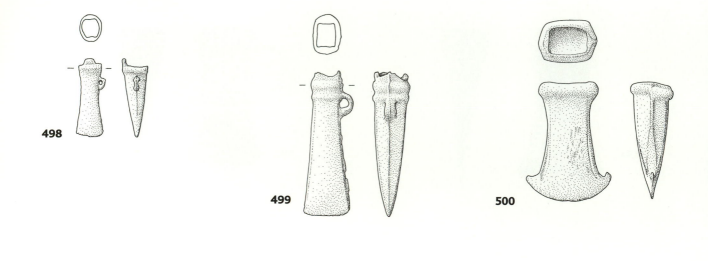

498

499

500

501

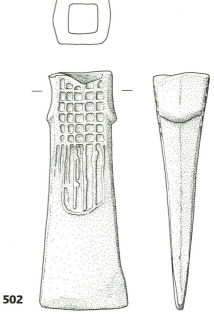

502

503

504

Plate 113   Axes type 58: - 498 Bari, Apulia. - 499 Verona, Veneto. - 500 Naples, Campania. - 501. **Axes type 59**: - 502 Grosseto, Tuscany. Close to **Axes type 60**: - 503. - 504.

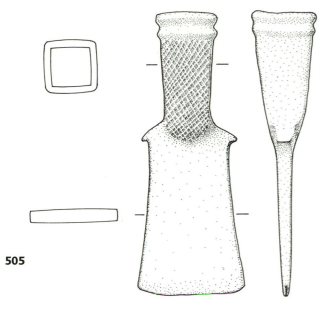

505

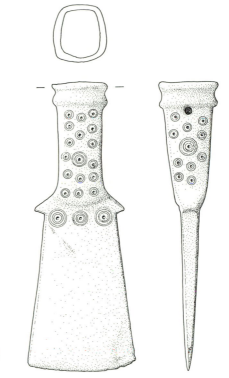

506

507

508

Plate 114 **Axes type 61**: - 505 Talamone (Grosseto), Tuscany. - 506 Orvieto, Umbria. - 507. - 508.

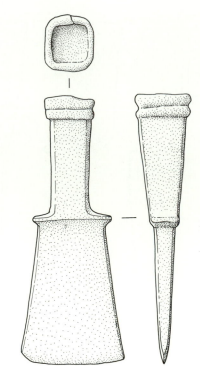

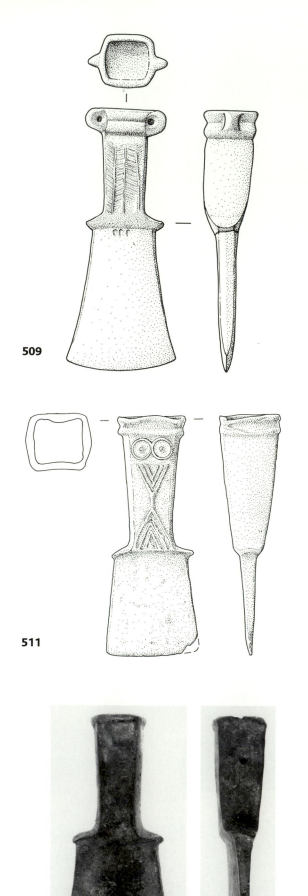

509

510

511

513

512

Plate 115   **Axes type 62**: - 509. - 510. - 511. - 512. - 513.

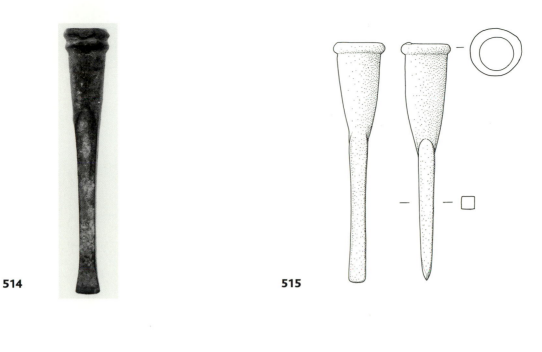

514 515

516

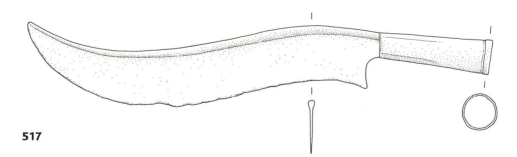

517

Plate 116   Chisels type 3: 514. **Chisels type 4**: 515 near Naples, Campania. **Knives type 7**: 516. **Knives type 8**: 517 Castiglione del Lago (Perugia), Umbria.

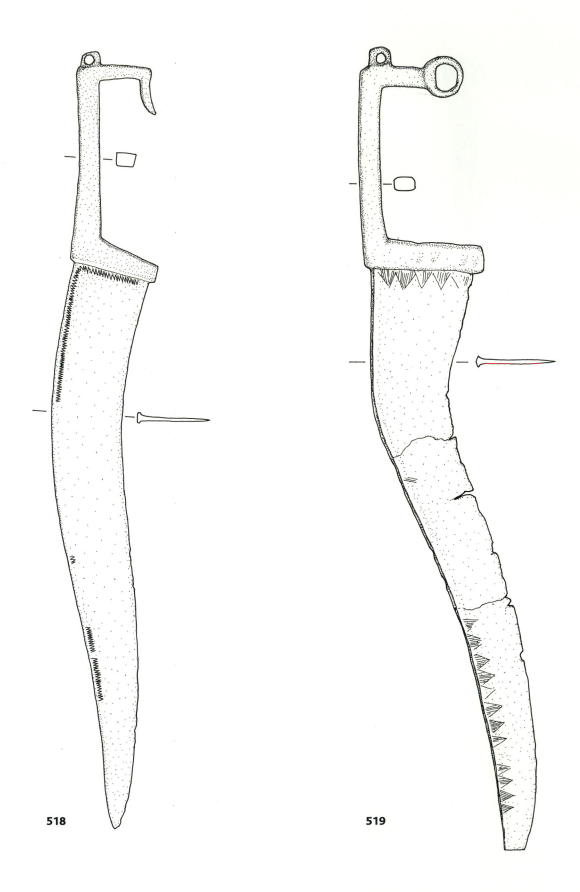

518

519

Plate 117   Knives type 9: - 518. - 519 Palestrina (Rome), Lazio.

520

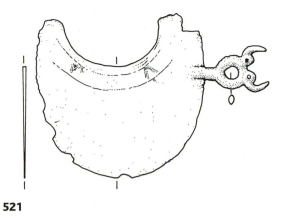

521

522

523

Plate 118   **Razors type 9**: - 520. **Razors type 14**: - 521 Chiusi, Tuscany. - 522. - 523.

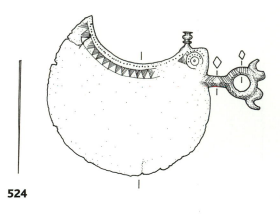

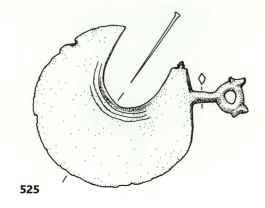

524

525

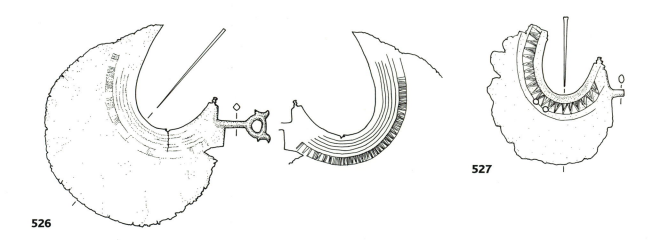

526

527

528

Plate 119   Razors type 15: - 524 Chiusi, Tuscany. **Razors type 16**: - 525. - 526. - 527. - 528 'Etruria'.

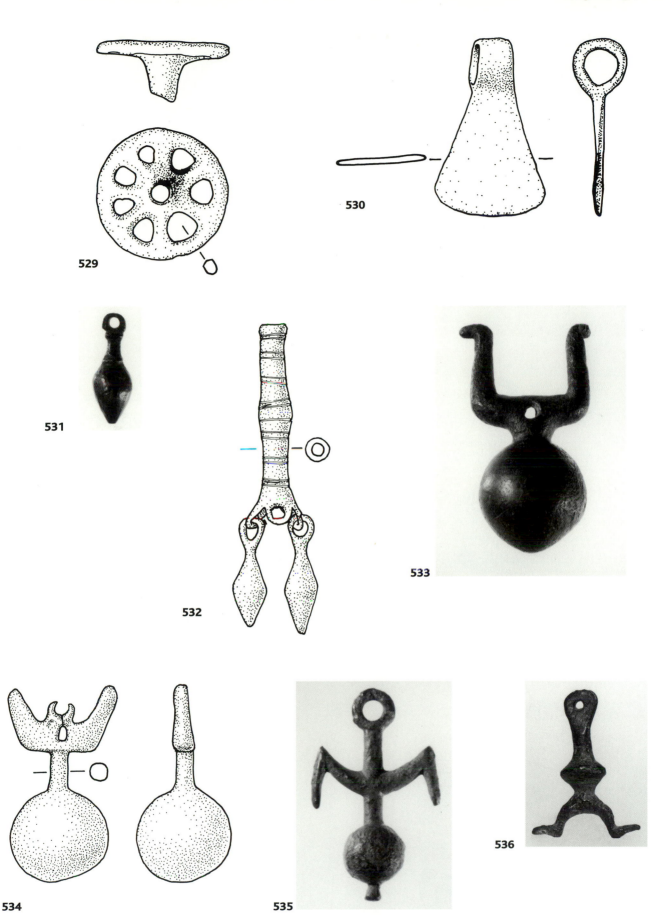

Plate 120   **Pins type 9**: - 529 Florence, Tuscany. **Pendants type 2**: - 530 Gela, Sicily. **Pendants type 3**: - 531. **Pendants type 4**: - 532.
Pendants type 5: - 533. - 534 Torre Annunziata (Naples), Campania. **Pendants type 5 variant**: - 535. **Pendants type 6**: - 536. All at scale 1:1.

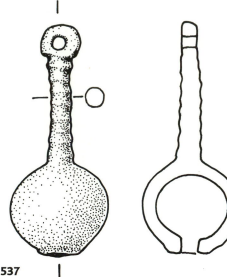

537

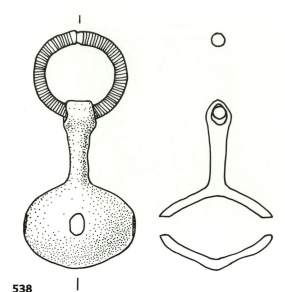

538

539

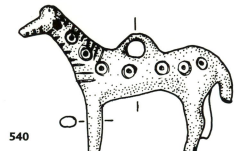

540

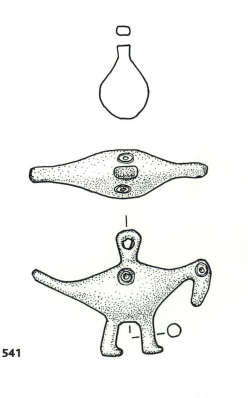

541

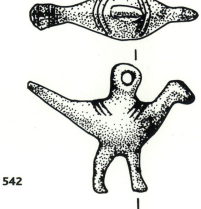

542

Plate 121   **Pendants type 7**: - 537. -538. - 539. **Pendants type 8**: - 540. **Pendants type 9**: - 541. - 542. All at scale 1:1.

543

544

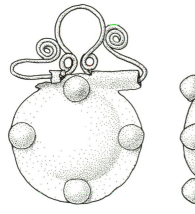

545

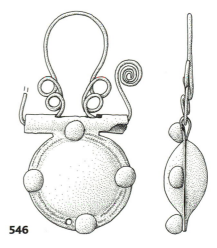

546

Plate 122   Pendants type 10: - 543. **Pendants type 11**: - 544. - 545 Ruvo (Bari), Apulia. - 546.

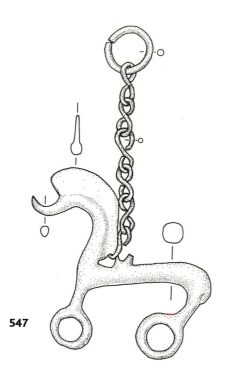

547

548

549

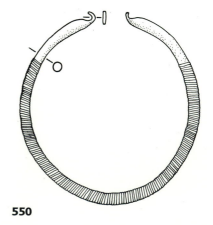

550

Plate 123 Pendants type 12: - 547. - 548. **Belt clasp ring**: - 549. **Torques type 2**: - 550.

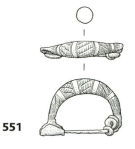

551

552

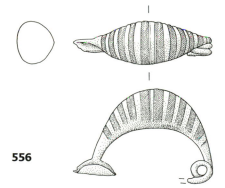

553

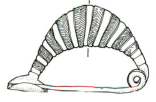

554

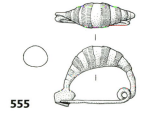

555

556

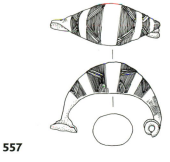

557

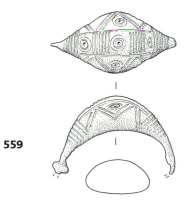

558

559

Plate 124 Fibulae type 12b: - 551. **Fibulae type 15**: - 552. **Fibulae type 19**: - 553. - 554. - 555 Kosice, Slovakia. - 556 Orvieto, Umbria. - 557. - 558 Steiermark, Austria. - 559.

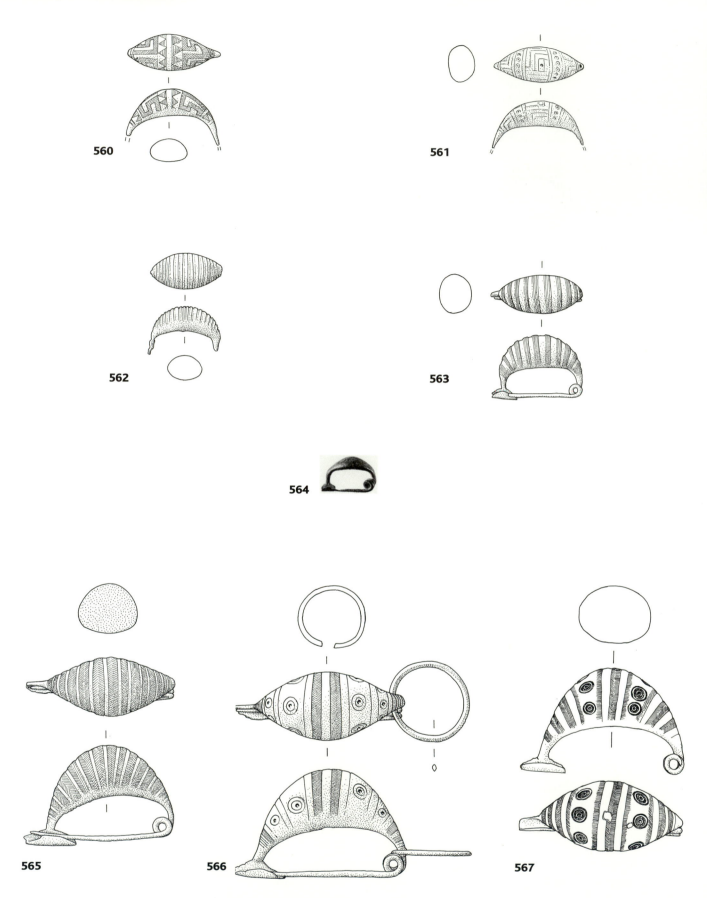

Plate 125   Fibulae type 20: - 560. - 561 York, England. **Fibulae type 21**: - 562. - 563 Semlin, Hungary. **Fibulae type 22**: - 564. **Fibulae type 23**: - 565. - 566 Tirol, Austria. - 567 ' Reculver', Kent, England.

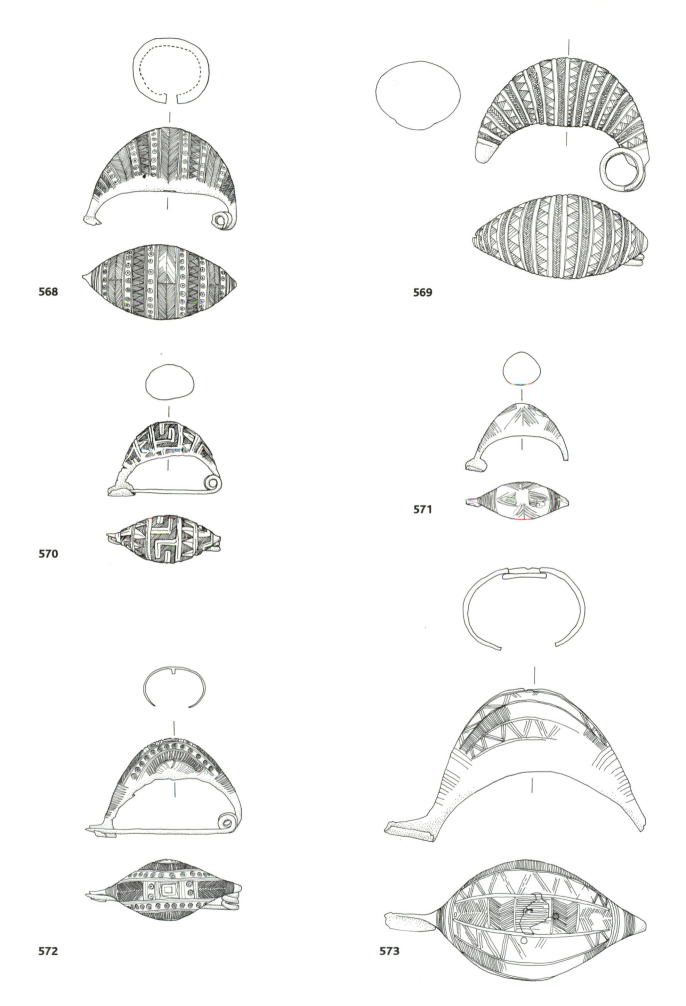

568

569

570

571

572

573

Plate 126 **Fibulae type 23**: - 568 Perugia, Umbria. - 569. - 570. - 571. **Fibulae type 24**: - 572. - 573.

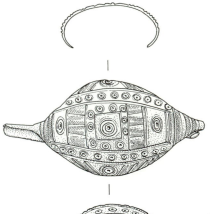

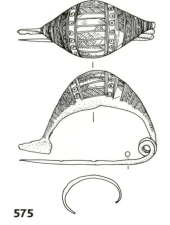

575

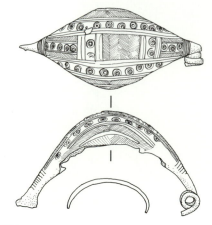

576

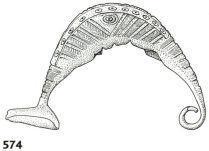

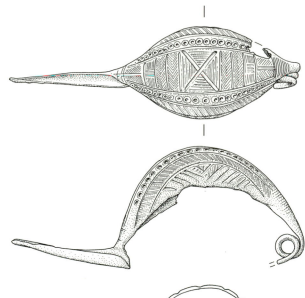

574

577

578

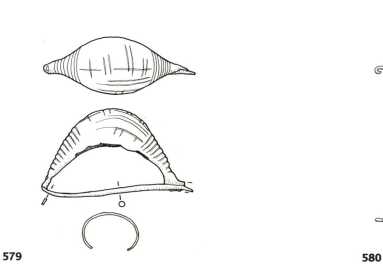

579

580

Plate 127   Fibulae type 25: - 574 Box, Wiltshire, England. - 575 Orvieto, Umbria. - 576. - 577. - 578 Taunton, Somerset, England. - 579. - 580 possibly Dorset, England.

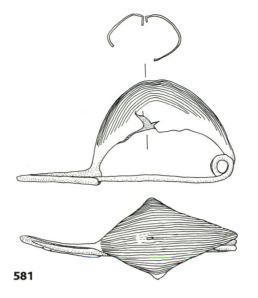

581

582
1:1

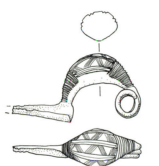

583

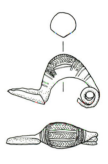

584

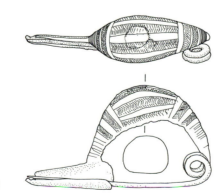

585

Plate 128   **Fibulae type 26**: - 581. **Fibulae type 27**: - 582. - 583. - 584. - 585 Athens, Greece.

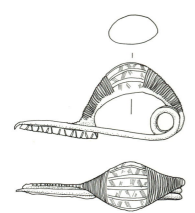

586

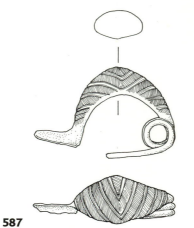

587

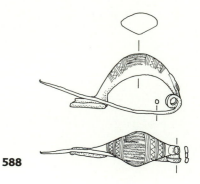

588

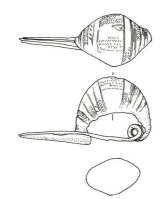

589

590

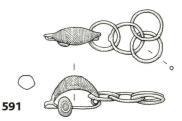

591

592

593

594

595

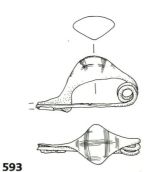

596

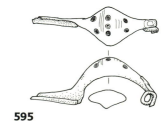

597

Plate 129   Fibulae type 28: - 586. - 587. - 588. **Fibulae type 28 variant**: - 589. - 590. - 591. **Fibulae type 29**: - 592. - 593. - 594. - 595. - 596. - 597.

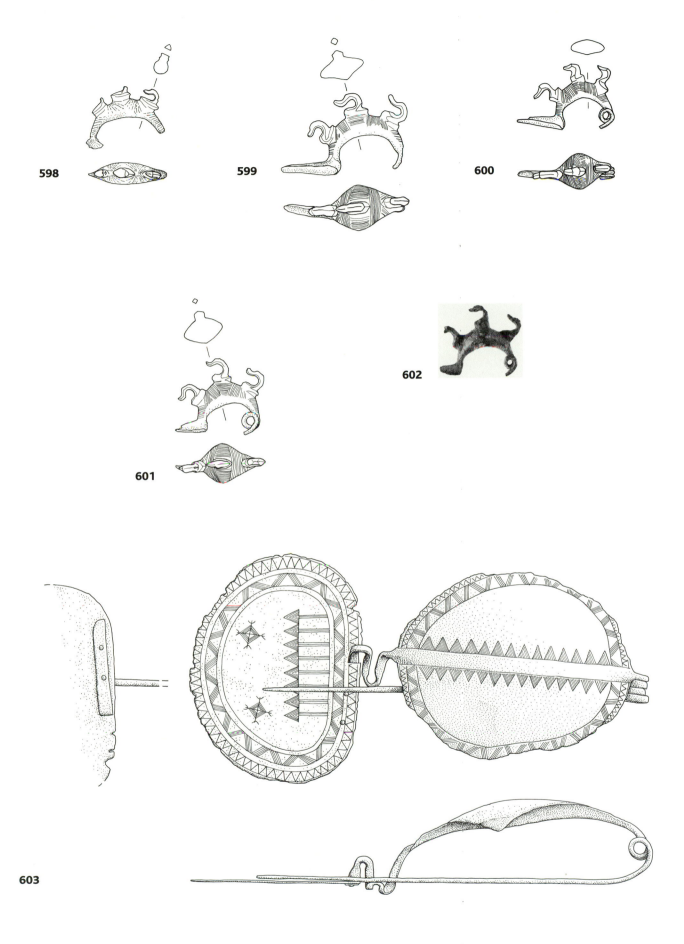

598

599

600

602

601

603

Plate 130   **Fibulae type 30a**: - 598. **Fibulae type 30b**: - 599. - 600. - 601. - 602. **Fibulae type 34**: - 603 Gorizia, Friuli Venezia Giulia.

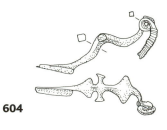

604

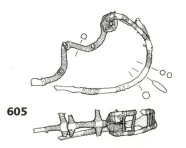

605

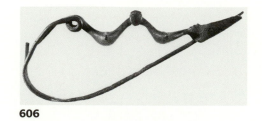

606

607

608

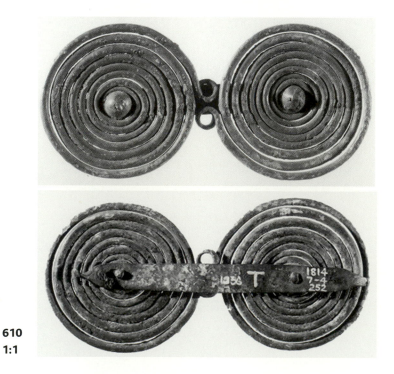

609

610

1:1

Plate 131 Fibulae type 50: - 604. **Fibulae type 51a**: - 605. **Fibulae type 51b**: - 606. - 607. - 608. **Fibulae type 53a**: - 609. **Fibulae type 53b**: - 610.

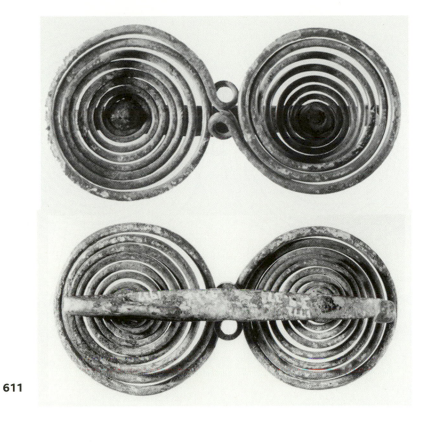

611

612

Plate 132   **Fibulae type 53b**: - 611. **Fibulae type 54**: - 612. Both at scale 1:1.

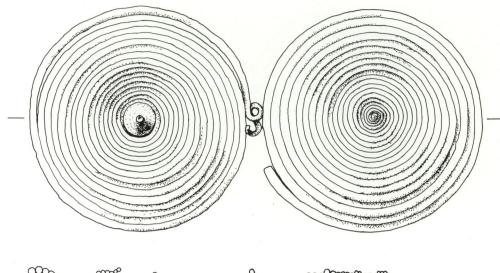

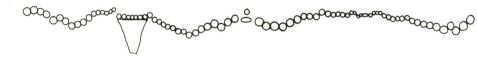

613

614

615

Plate 133 **Fibulae type 55**: - 613 Ruvo (Bari), Apulia. - 614. Probably **Fibulae type 55**: - 615.

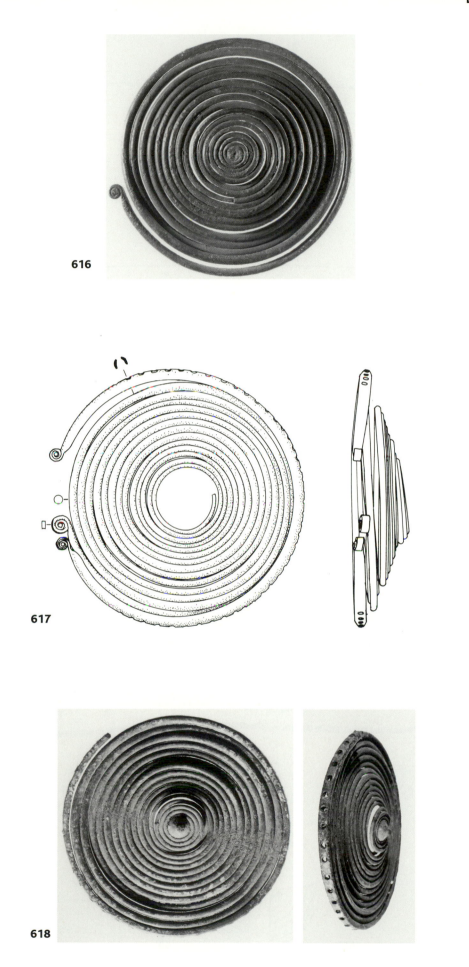

616

617

618

Plate 134 *See* **Fibulae type 55**: - 616. - 617 Naples, Campania. - 618.

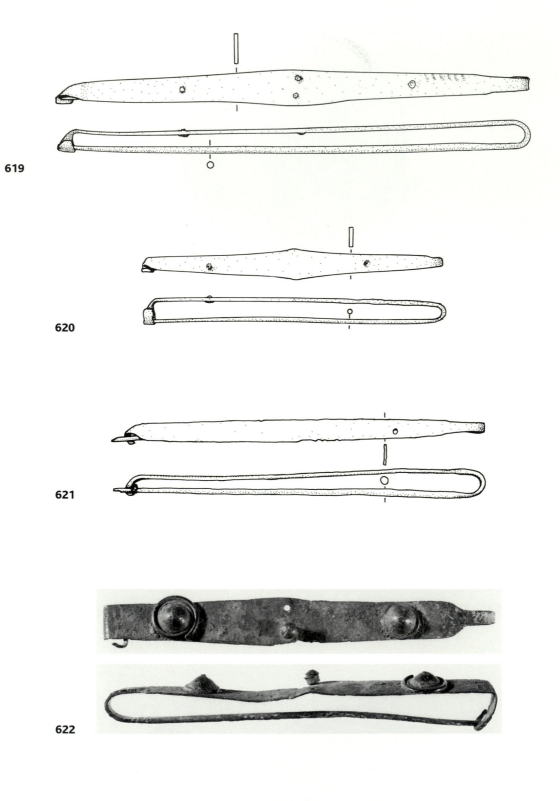

619

620

621

622

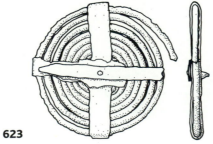

623

Plate 135   See Fibulae type 55: - 619 Torre Annunziata (Naples), Campania. - 620 Torre Annunziata. - 621 Torre Annunziata. - 622. **Fibulae type 54** or **55**: - 623 Ruvo (Bari), Apulia.

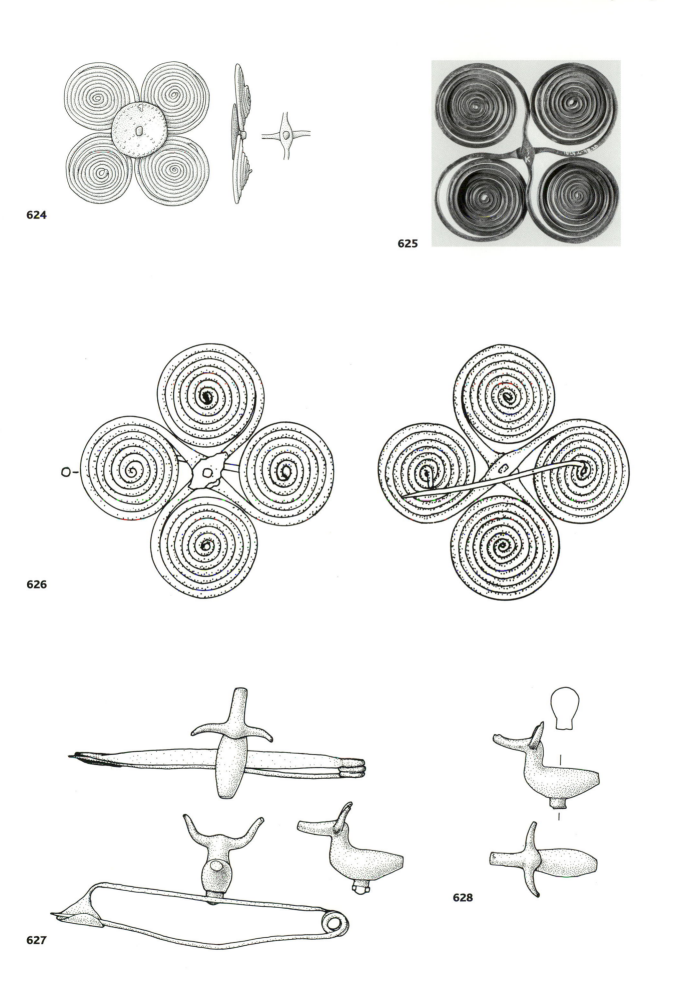

624

625

626

627

628

Plate 136   **Fibulae type 56**: - 624. - 625. - 626 Terra di Lavoro (Caserta), Campania. **Fibulae type 58**: - 627. *See* **Fibulae type 58**: - 628.

Prehistoric Metal Artefacts from Italy (3500–720BC) in the British Museum | 241

629

630

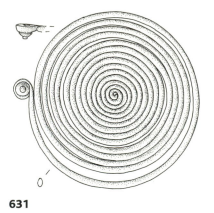

631

632

633

634

Plate 137   Fibulae unclassified: - 629. - 630. - 631 Maremma, Veii, Lazio. - 632. - 633. - 634.

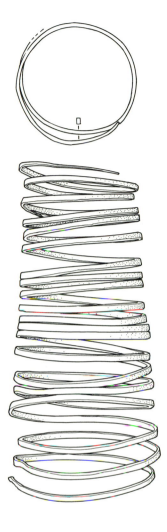

635

636

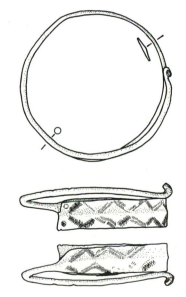

637

Plate 138   **Bracelets type 2c**: - 635 Armento (Potenza), Basilicata. **Bracelets type 2d**: - 636. **Bracelets type 3a variant**: - 637.

638

639

640

Plate 139   Bracelets type 4: - 638. - 639. - 640. All at scale 1:1.

641

642

643

644

Plate 140 **Bracelets type 4**: - 641. - 642. - 643. - 644 Armento (Potenza), Basilicata.

645

646

647

648

649

Plate 141   **Bracelets type 5**: - 645. - 646. - 647. - 648. **Bracelets type 5 variant**: - 649. All at scale 1:1.

651

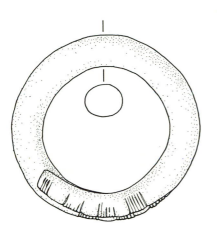

650

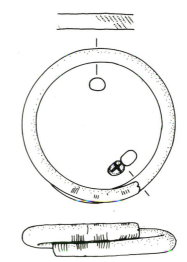

652

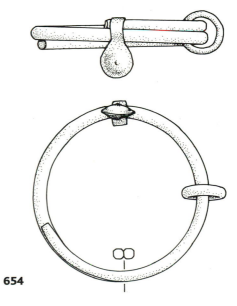

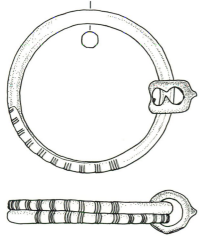

653

654

Plate 142   **Bracelets type 6**: - 650. - 651. - 652. **Bracelets type 7**: - 653. - 654.

655

656

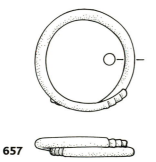

657

658

659

660

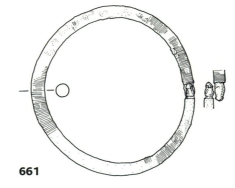

661

Plate 143   **Bracelets type 8**: - 655. - 656. **Bracelets type 9a**: - 657. - 658. - 659. - 660. **Bracelets type 9b**: - 661.

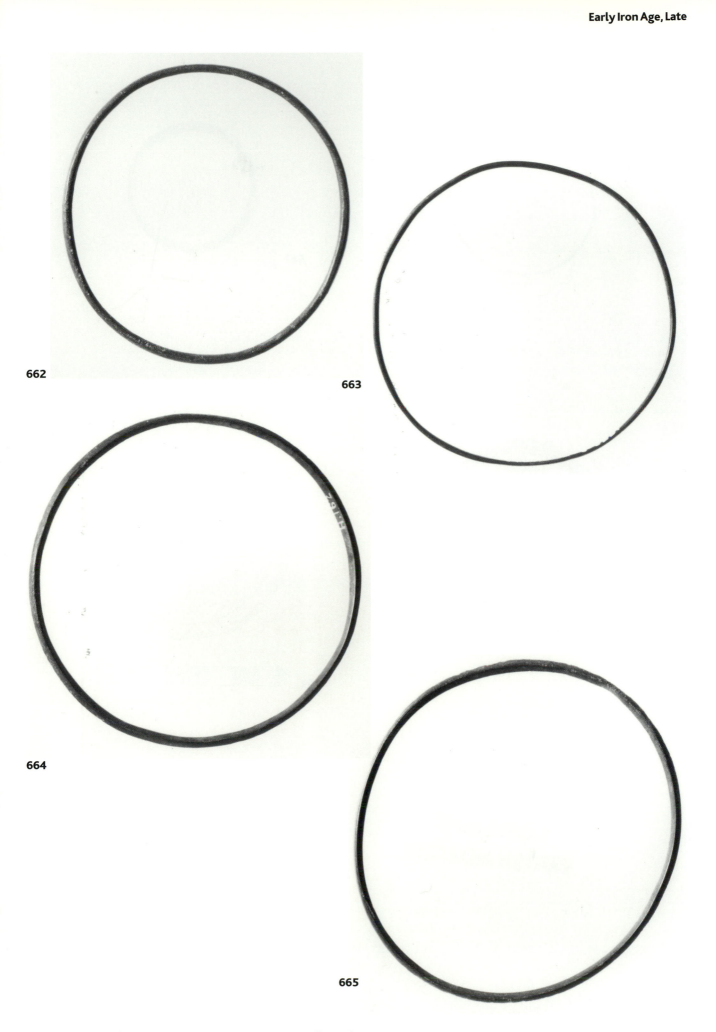

662

663

664

665

Plate 144 **Bracelets type 10a**: - 662. - 663. - 664. - 665. All at scale 1:1.

666

667

668

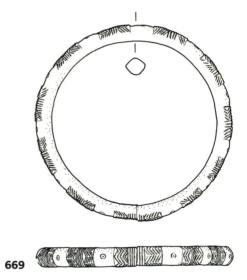

669

Plate 145   Bracelets type 10a: - 666. **Bracelets type 10b**: - 667. **Bracelets type 11**: - 668. - 669.

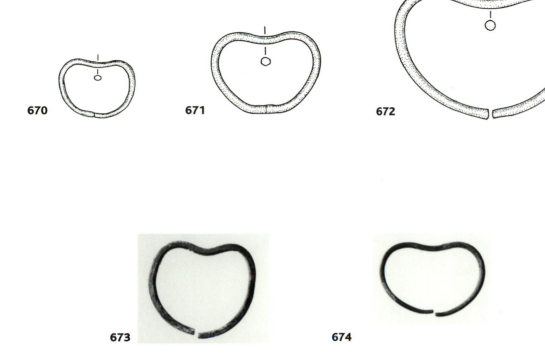

Plate 146 **Bracelets type 12a**: - 670. - 671. - 672. - 673. - 674. - 675. - 676.

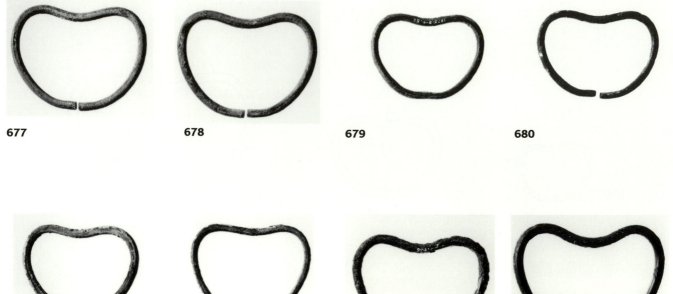

677   678   679   680

681   682   683   684

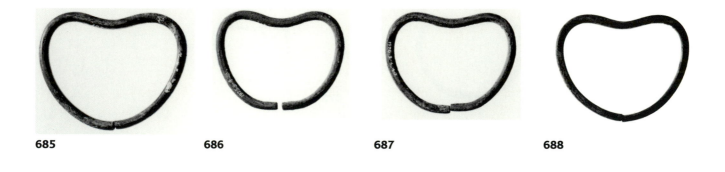

685   686   687   688

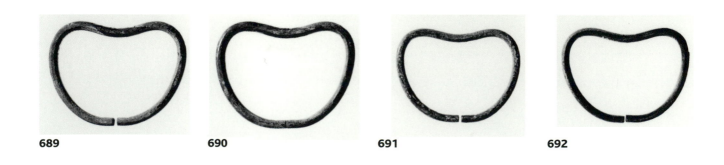

689   690   691   692

Plate 147   Bracelets type 12a: - 677. - 678. - 679. - 680. - 681. - 682. - 683. - 684. - 685. - 686. - 687. - 688. - 689. - 690. - 691. - 692.

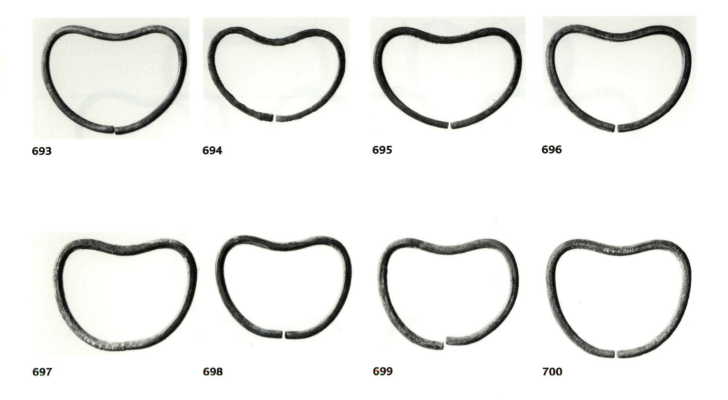

693 694 695 696

697 698 699 700

701 702 703

704 705

Plate 148 **Bracelets type 12a**: - 693. - 694. - 695. - 696. - 697. - 698. - 699. - 700. - 701. - 702. - 703. - 704. - 705.

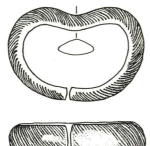

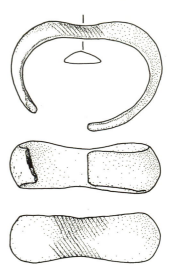

725

726

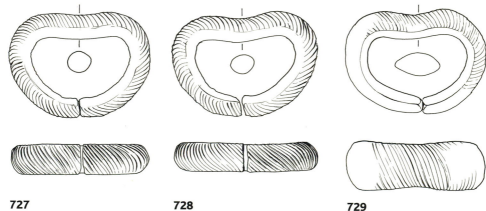

727

728

729

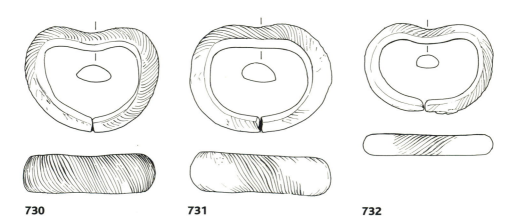

730

731

732

Plate 151 **Bracelets type 12b**: - 725. - 726 Tarquinia (Viterbo), Lazio. - 727. - 728. - 729. - 730. - 731. - 732.

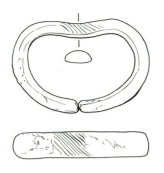

733

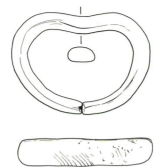

734

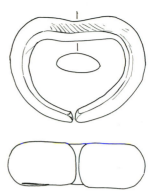

735

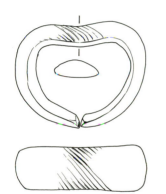

736

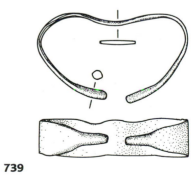

737

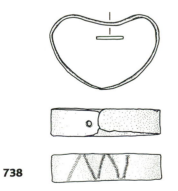

738

739

Plate 152   Bracelets type 12b: - 733. - 734. - 735. - 736. - 737. **Bracelets type 12c**: - 738. **Bracelets type 12d**: - 739.

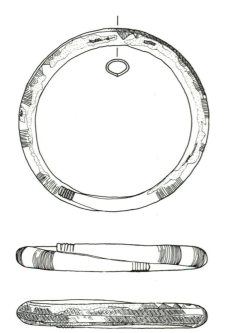

740

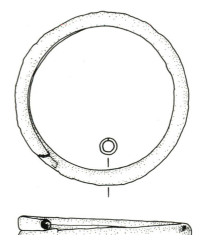

741

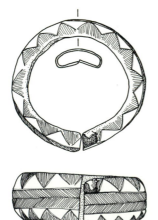

742

Plate 153   Bracelets type 13a: - 740. **Bracelets type 13b**: - 741. **Bracelets type 13d**: - 742 Locri (Reggio Calabria), Calabria.

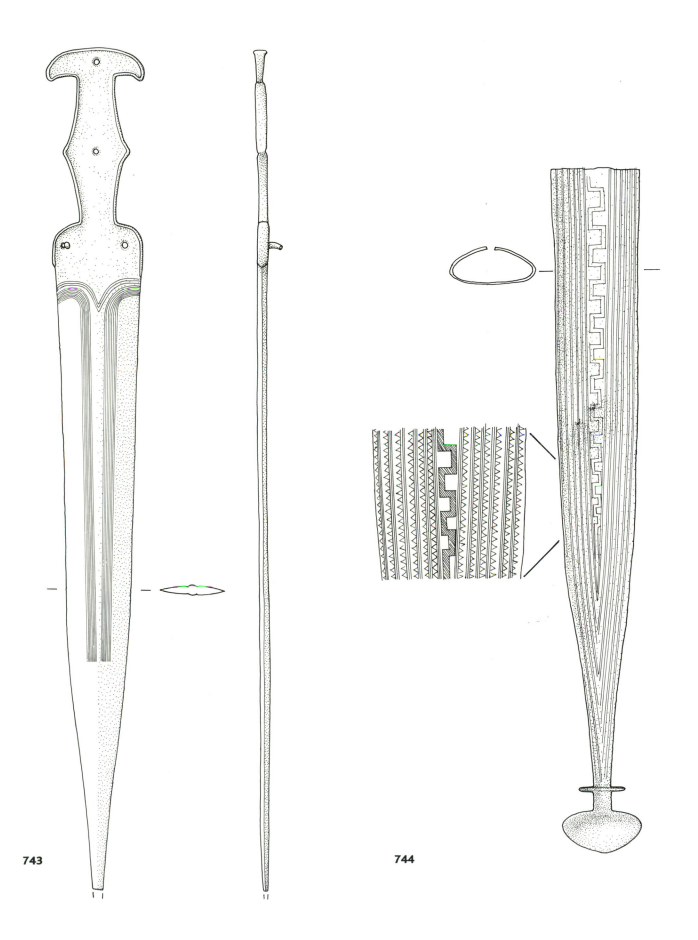

743

744

Plate 154 **Swords type 9a**: - 743 Locri (Reggio Calabria), Calabria. **Sheaths type 3**: - 744 Locri (Reggio Calabria), Calabria.

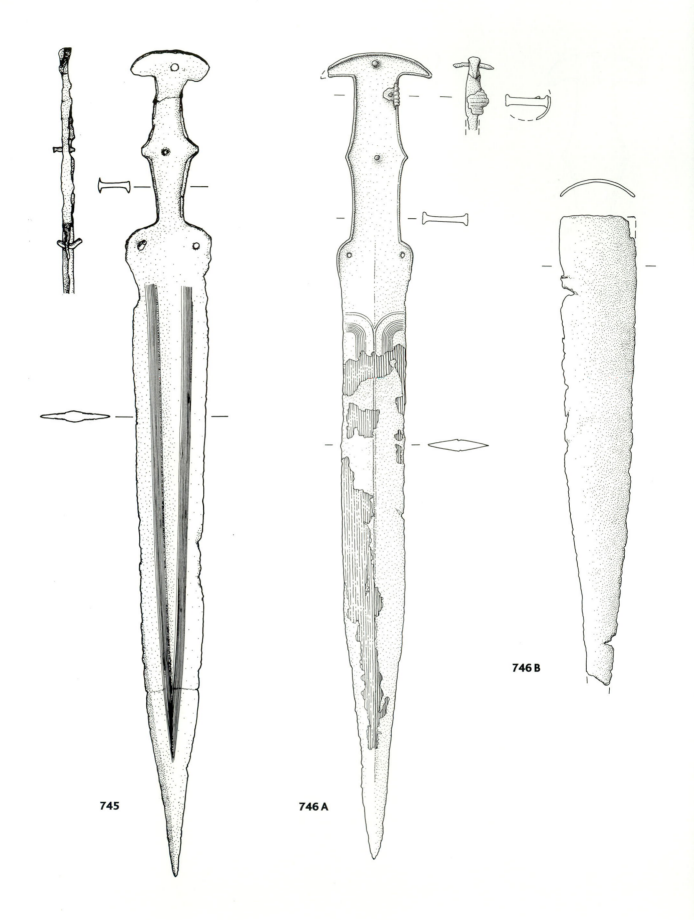

745

746 A

746 B

Plate 155   Swords type 9b: - 745. - 746 Sticna, Slovenia.

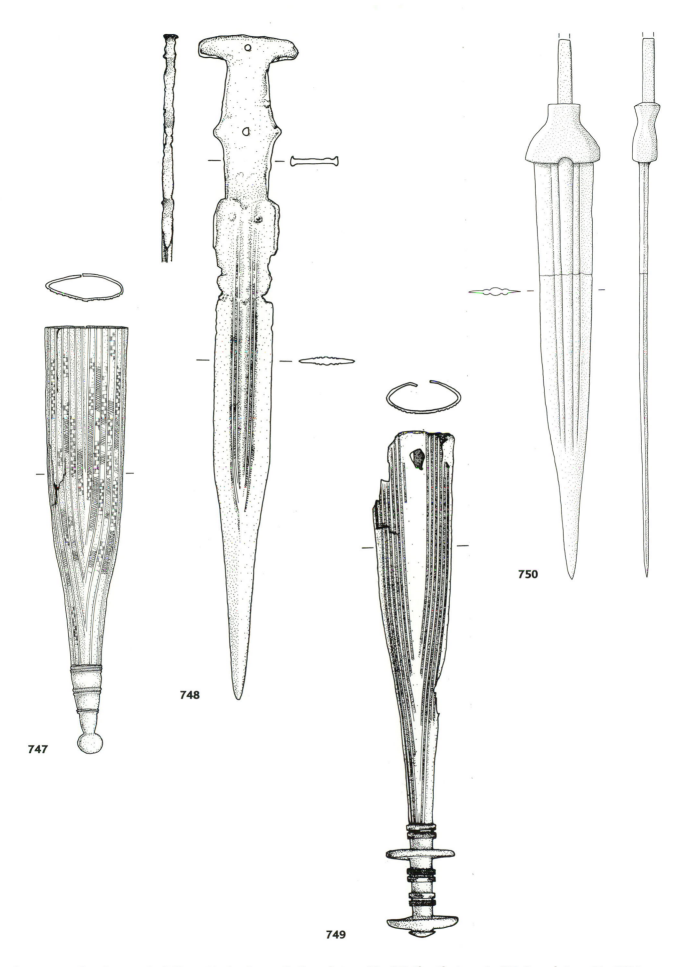

Plate 156 **Sheaths type 3**: - 747 near Naples, Campania. **Swords type 10**: - 748. **Sheaths type 4**: - 749. **Swords type 11**: - 750 Acerra (Naples), Campania.

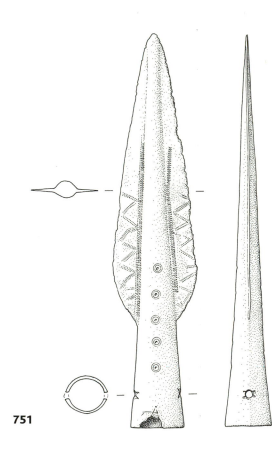

751

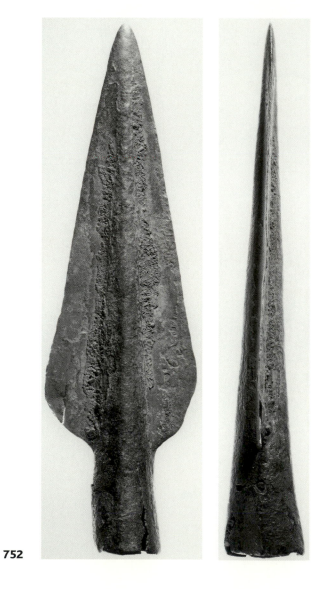

752

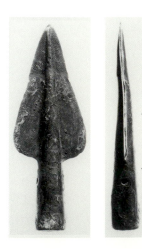

753

Plate 157 **Spearheads type 2**: - 751. **Spearheads type 3**: - 752. **Spearheads type 3 variant**: - 753.

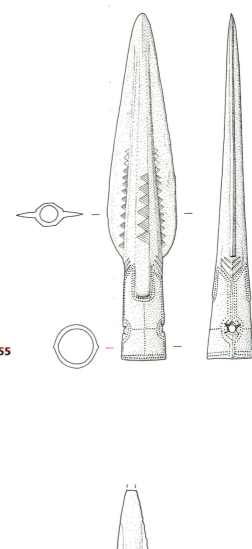

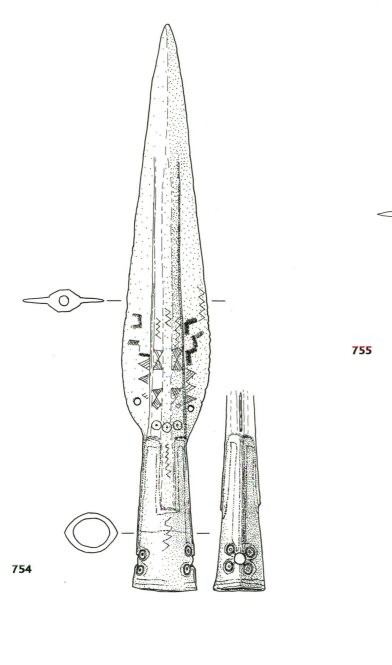

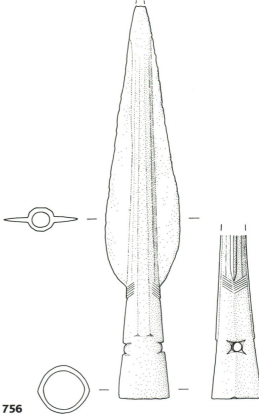

Plate 158   Spearheads type 4: - 754. - 755 Bari, Apulia. - 756 Naples, Campania.

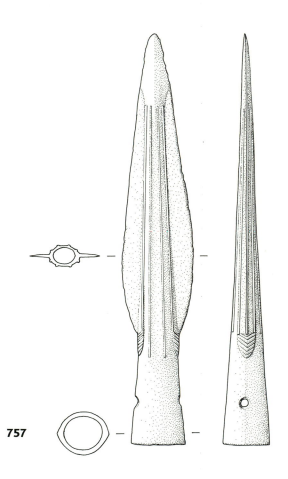

757

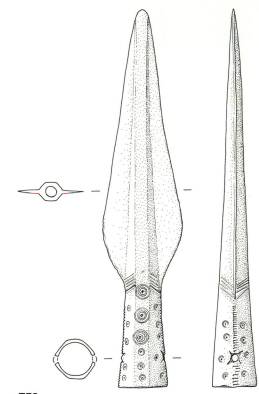

758

Plate 159   Spearheads type 4: - 757. Spearheads type 4 variant: - 758.

759

760

Plate 160   Spearheads type 6: - 759. **Spearheads type 6 variant**: -760.

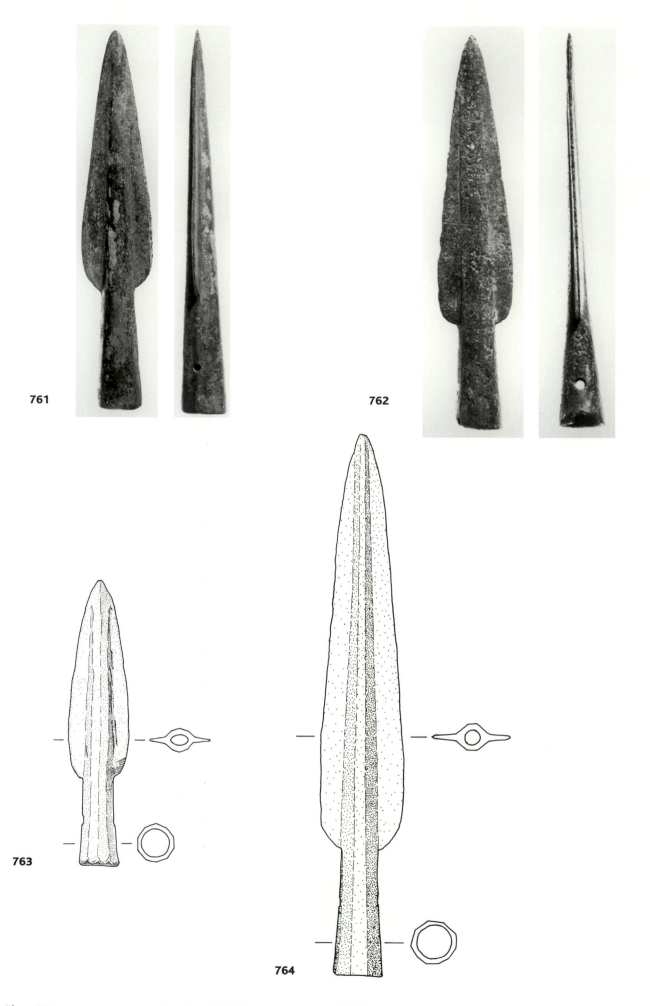

Plate 161   Spearheads type 7: - 761. - 762, 763 Arezzo, Tuscany. - 764 Olympia, Greece.

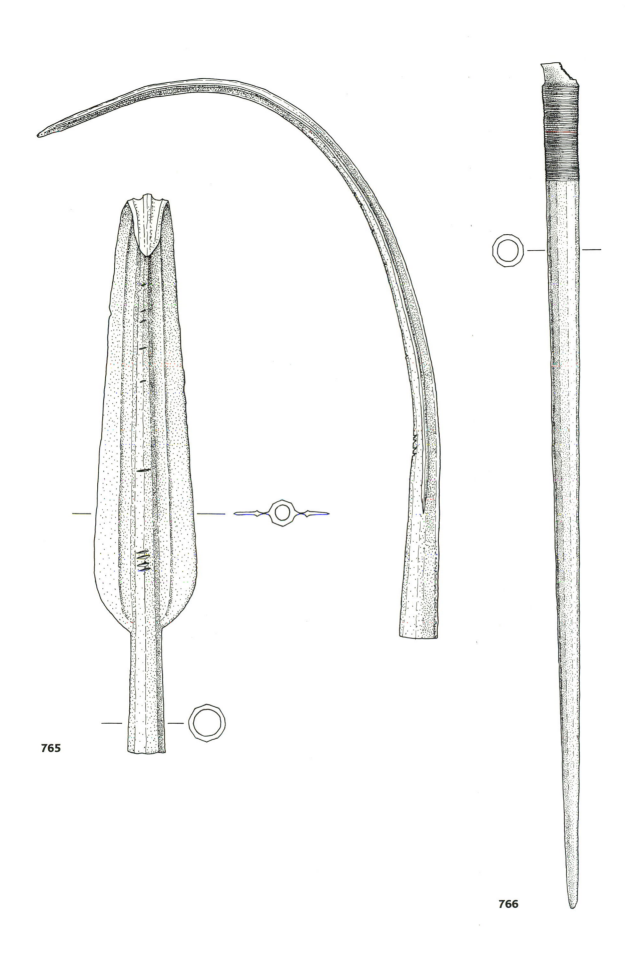

765

766

Plate 162 **Spearheads type 7**: - 765. **Spear-butts type 5**: - 766.

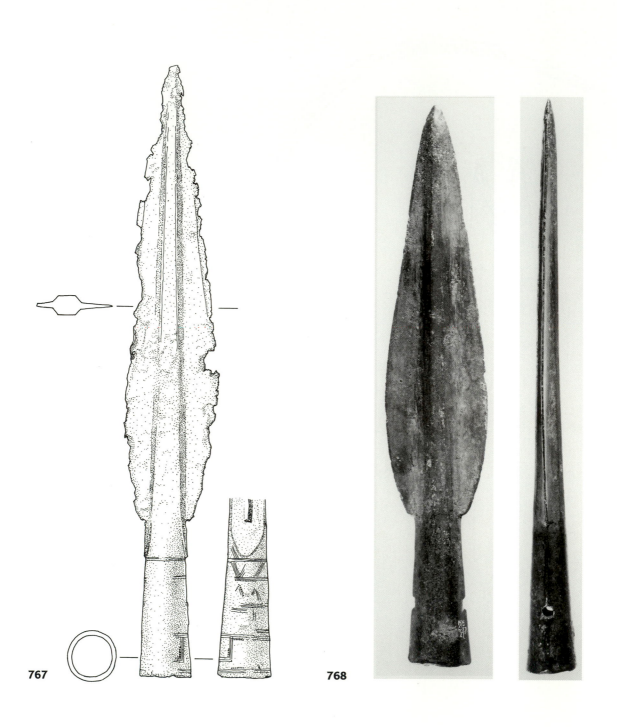

Plate 163   Spearheads type 12: - 767. - 768.

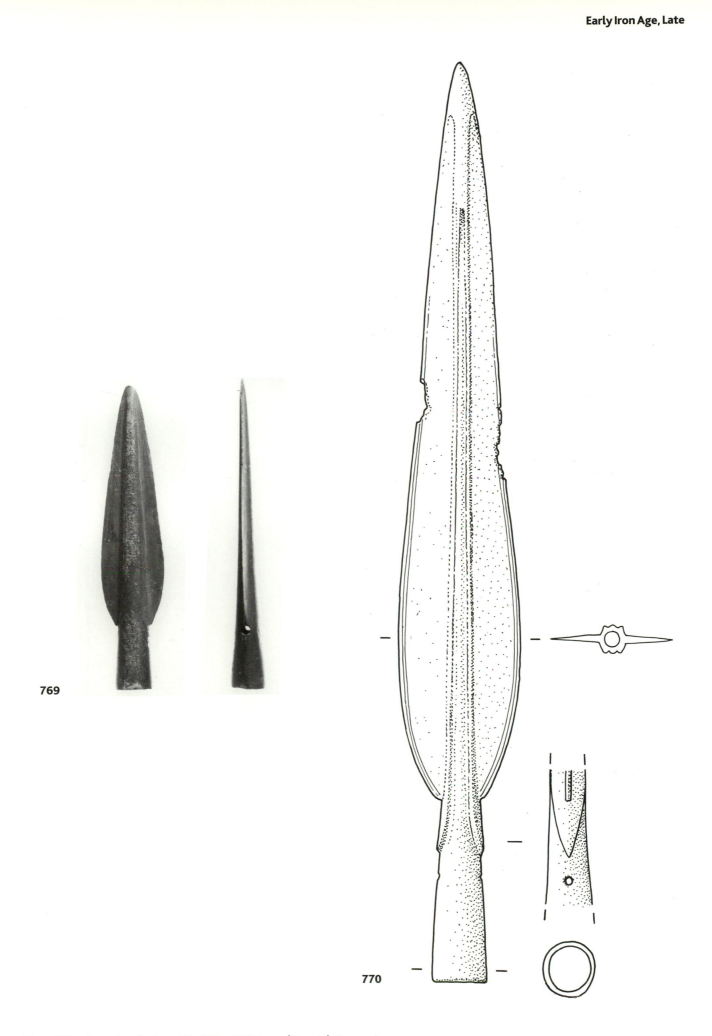

769

770

Plate 164   Spearheads type 12: - 769. - 770 Capua (Caserta), Campania.

Prehistoric Metal Artefacts from Italy (3500–720BC) in the British Museum | 269

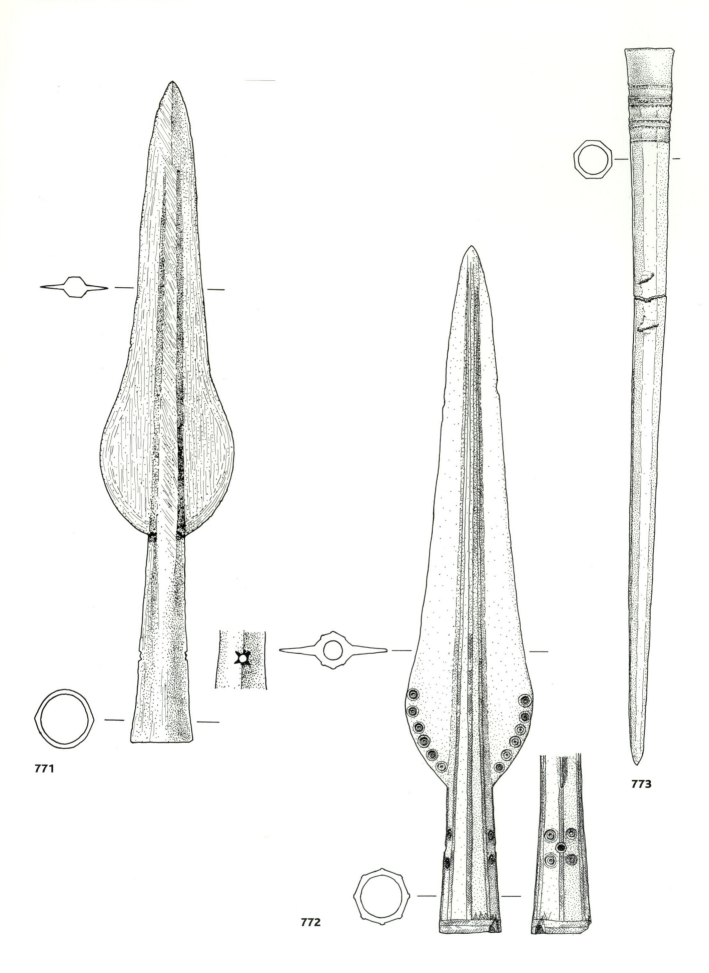

Plate 165 **Spearheads type 15**: - 771. - 772. **Spear-butts type 4**: - 773.

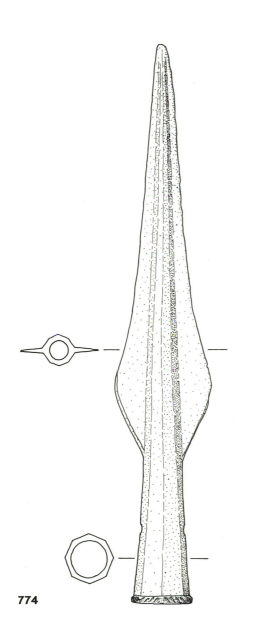

774

775

Plate 166   Spearheads type 15: - 774. - 775.

776

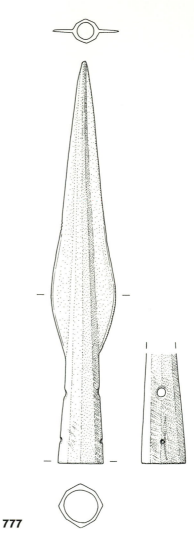

777

Plate 167   Spearheads type 15: - 776. - 777 Capua (Caserta), Campania.

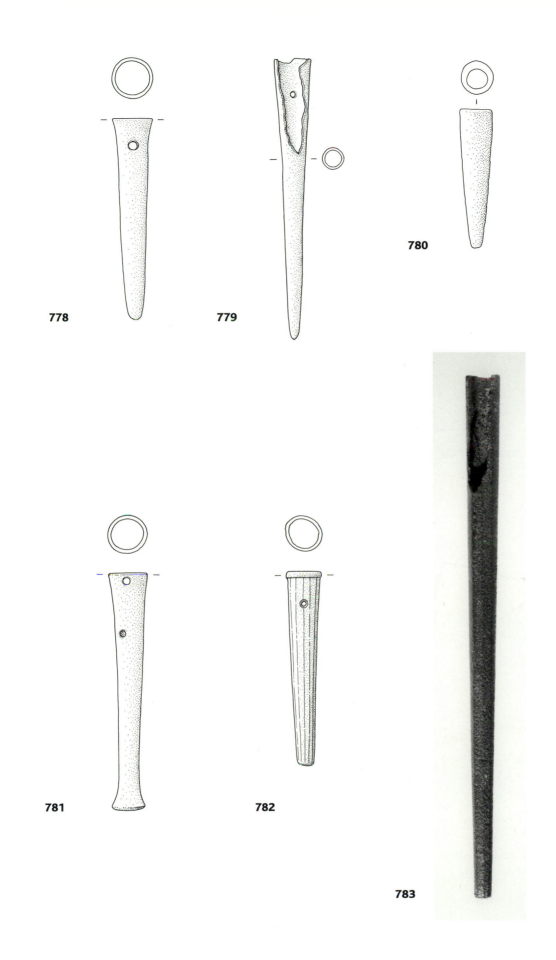

778

779

780

781

782

783

Plate 168   **Spear-butts type 1**: - 778 Calabria. - 779 Marsica (L'Aquila), Abruzzo. - 780 Bolsena (Viterbo), Lazio. **Spear-butts type 2**: - 781 Calabria. **Spear-butts type 3**: - 782 Orvieto, Umbria. - 783.

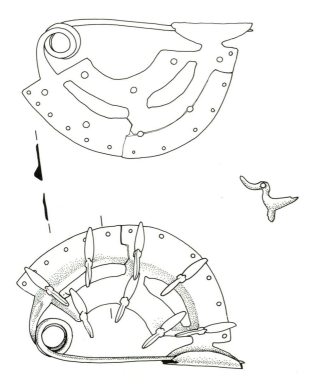

784

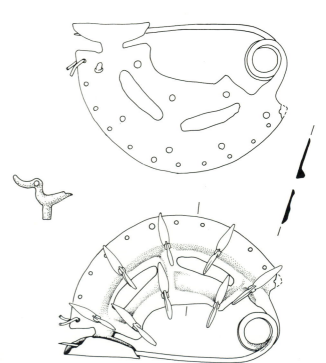

785

Plate 169 Group of two associated artefacts. **Fibulae type 31**: - 784. - 785.

786

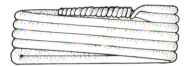

787

788

789

Plate 170   Group of two associated artifacts, Palestrina (Rome), Lazio. **Bracelets type 4**: - 786. - 787. Group of two associated artifacts. **Bracelets type 4**: - 788. - 789.

790

791

792

794

793

Plate 171 Group of five associated artefacts. **Bracelets type 5**: - 790. - 791. - 792. - 793. - 794. All at Scale 1:1.

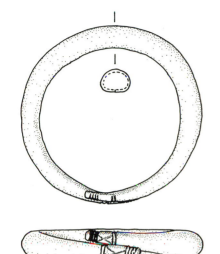

795

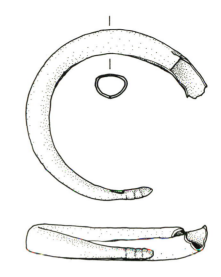

796

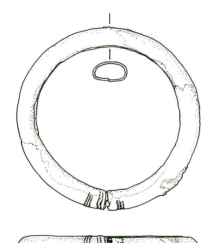

797

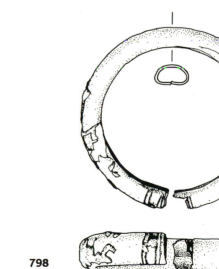

798

Plate 172   Group of two associated artifacts. **Bracelets type 13a**: - 795. -796. Group of two associated artifacts. **Bracelets type 13c**: - 797. - 798.

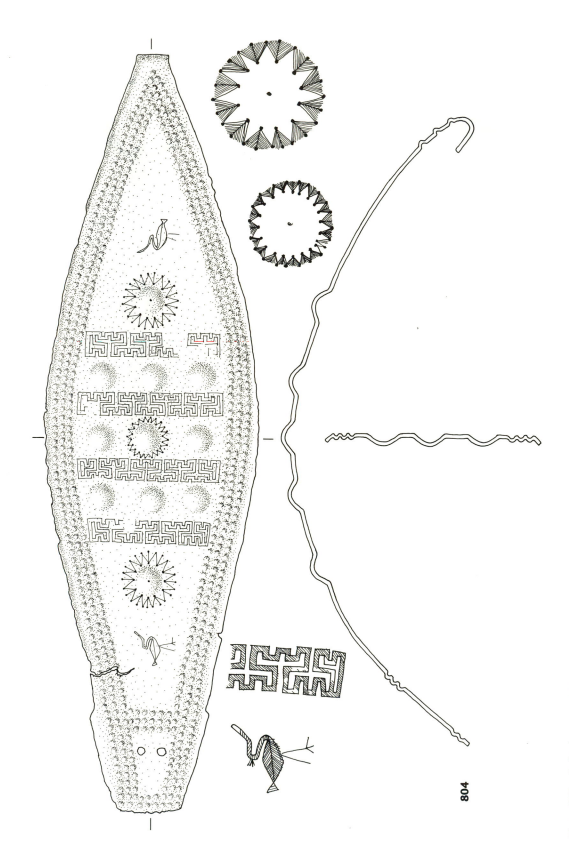

804

Plate 175   Belt plaques: - 804.

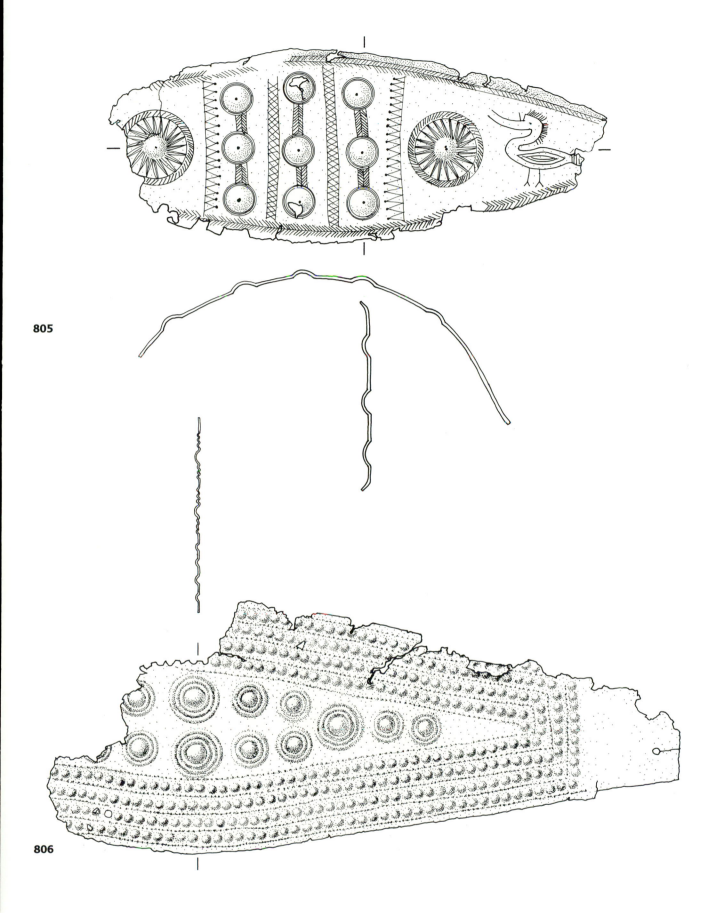

805

806

Plate 176   Belt plaques: - 805. - 806.

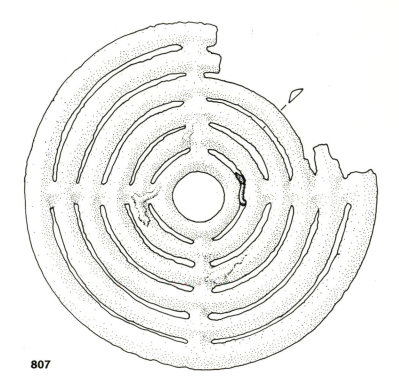

807

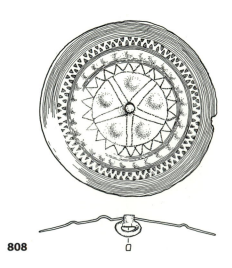

808

Plate 177   Openwork disc: - 807 Caserta, Campania. **Armour disc**: - 808 Perugia, Umbria.

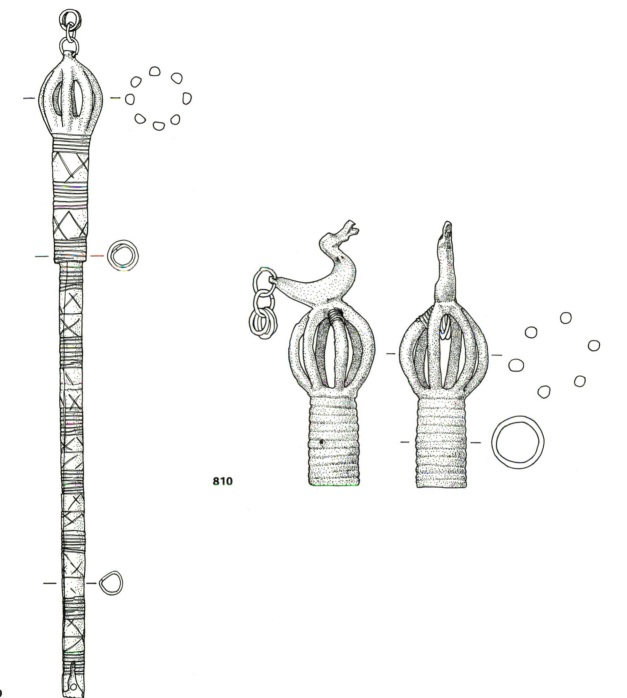

809

810

Plate 178   Tube with finial: - 809 Campania. **Finial**: - 810.

811

Plates 179 Villanovan helmet: - 811 probably Vulci (Viterbo), Lazio.

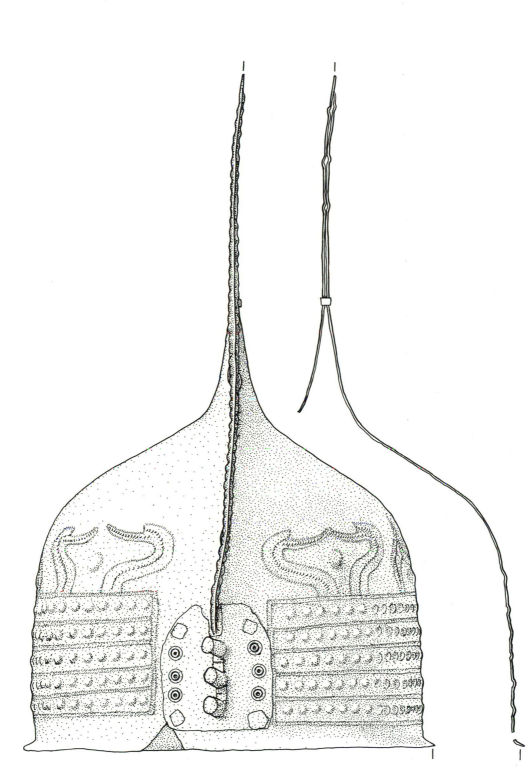

811

Plate 180   Villanovan helmet: - 811 probably Vulci (Viterbo), Lazio.

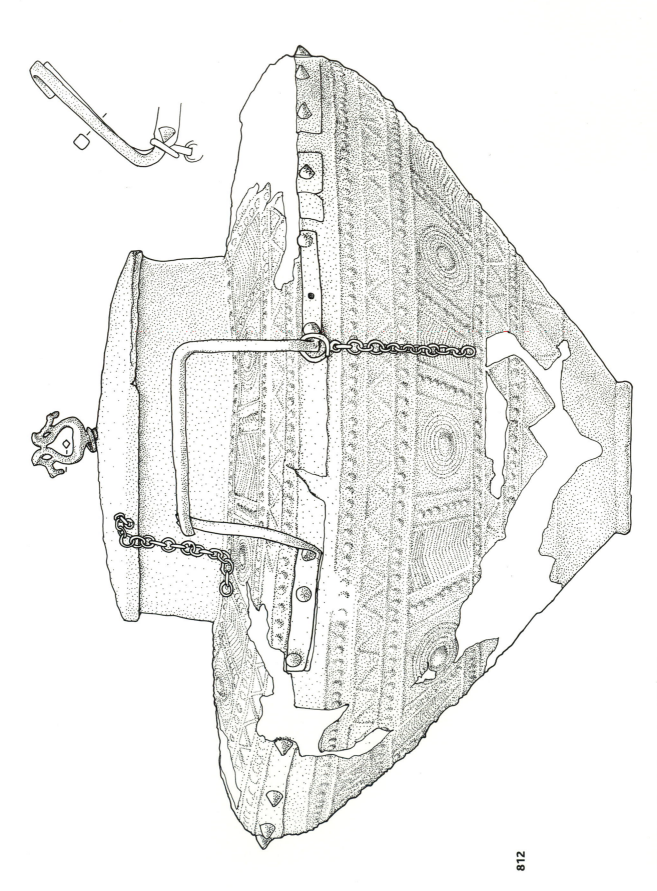

812

Plate 181   Biconical vessel and lid: - 812.

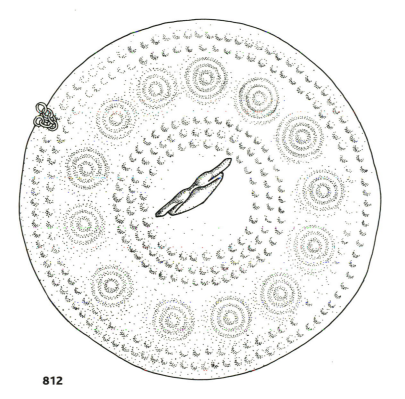

812

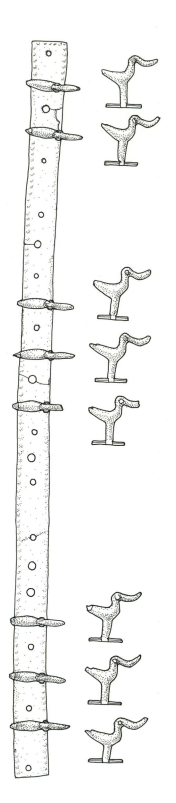

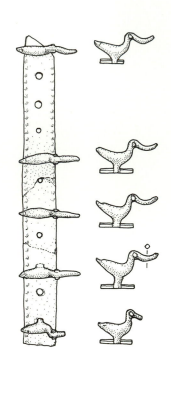

814

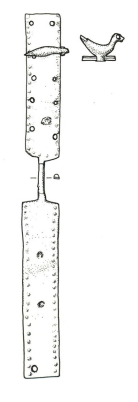

813

815

Plate 183   Band with inset birds: - 813. - 814. - 815.

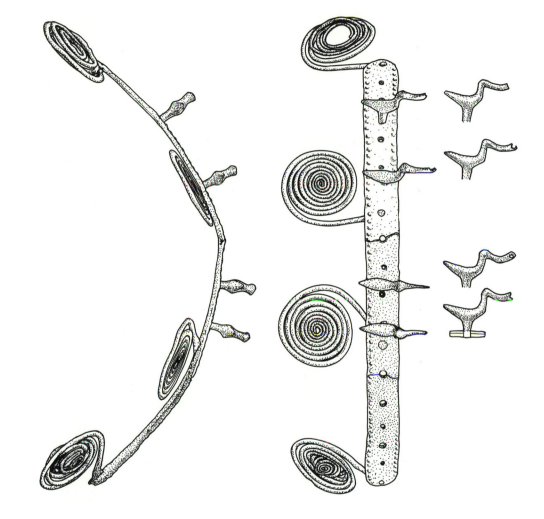

816

Plate 184   Band with inset birds and attached coils: - 816.

817

Plate 185   Pastiche: - 817 Campania.

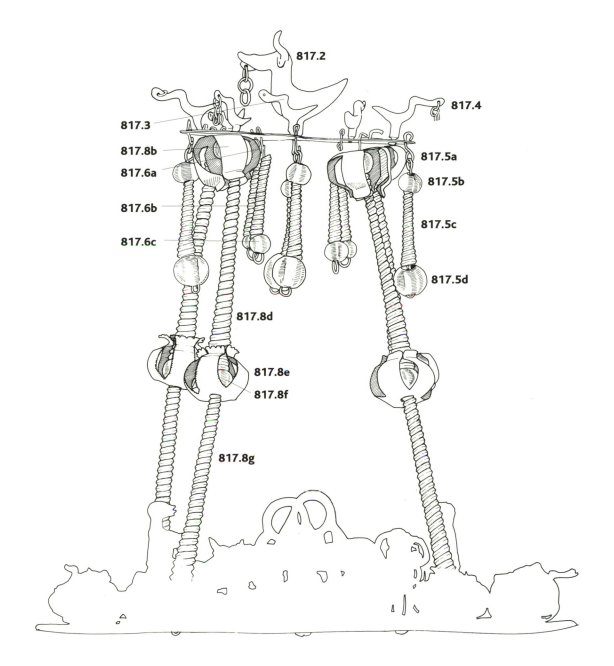

817.2

817.3
817.8b
817.6a
817.6b
817.6c

817.4
817.5a
817.5b
817.5c
817.5d

817.8d
817.8e
817.8f

817.8g

817

Plate 186   **Pastiche**: -817 (detail). Arrangement of upper decorative elements.

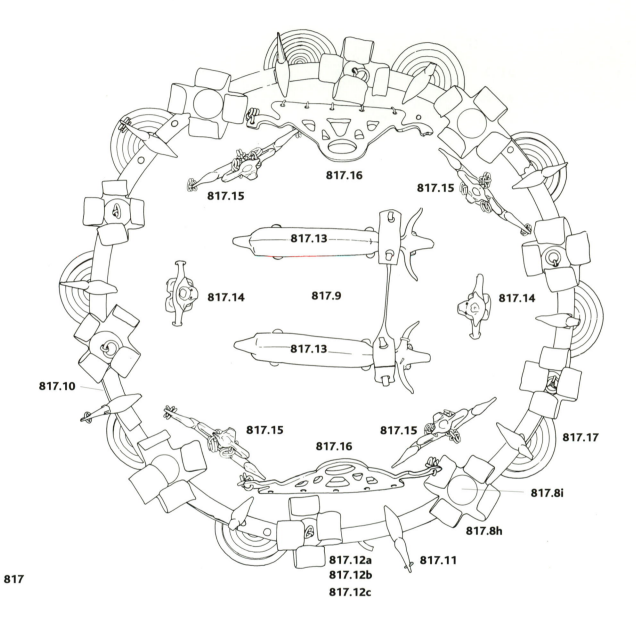

817.16

817.15

817.15

817.13

817.14

817.9

817.14

817.13

817.10

817.15

817.15

817.16

817.17

817.8i

817.8h

817.11

817.12a
817.12b
817.12c

817

Plate 187   **Pastiche**: -817 (detail). Arrangement of decorative elements on upper side of lower disc, 817.9.

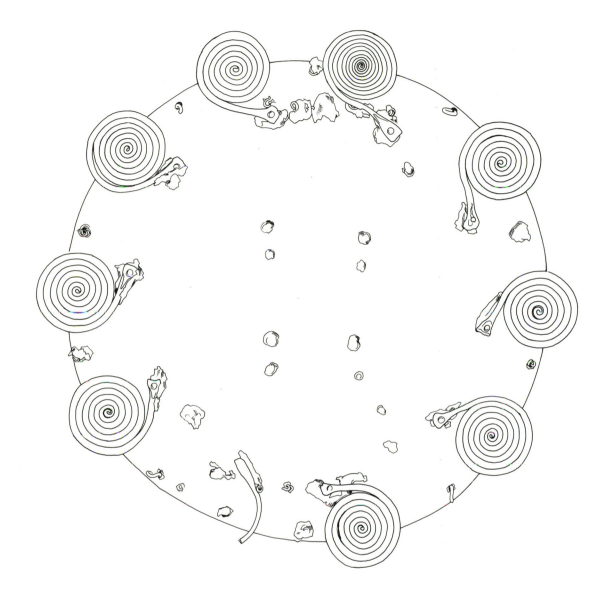

817

Plate 188 **Pastiche**: -817 (detail). Arrangement of decorative elements on lower side of lower disc, 817.9.

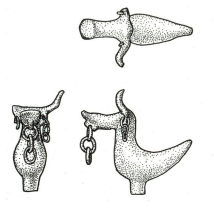

817.2

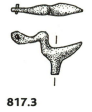

817.3

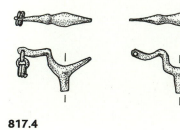

817.4

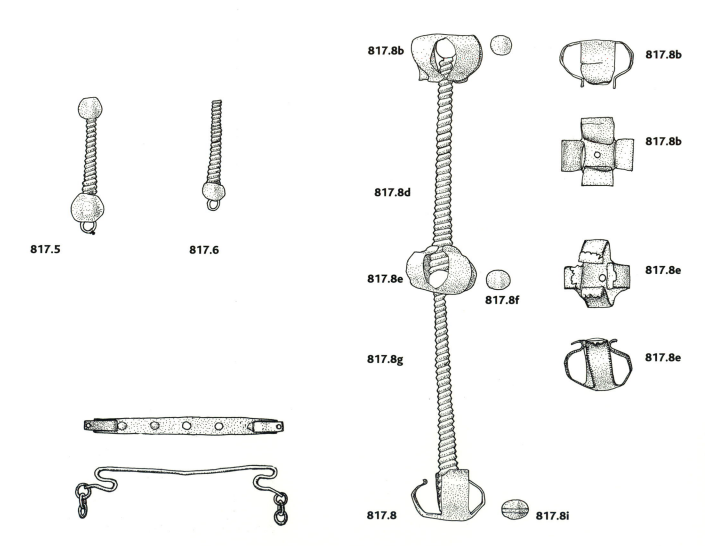

817.5

817.6

817.7

817.8b

817.8d

817.8e

817.8f

817.8g

817.8

817.8i

817.8b

817.8b

817.8e

817.8e

Plate 189   **Pastiche**: -817 (detail). Objects from the upper decorative elements.

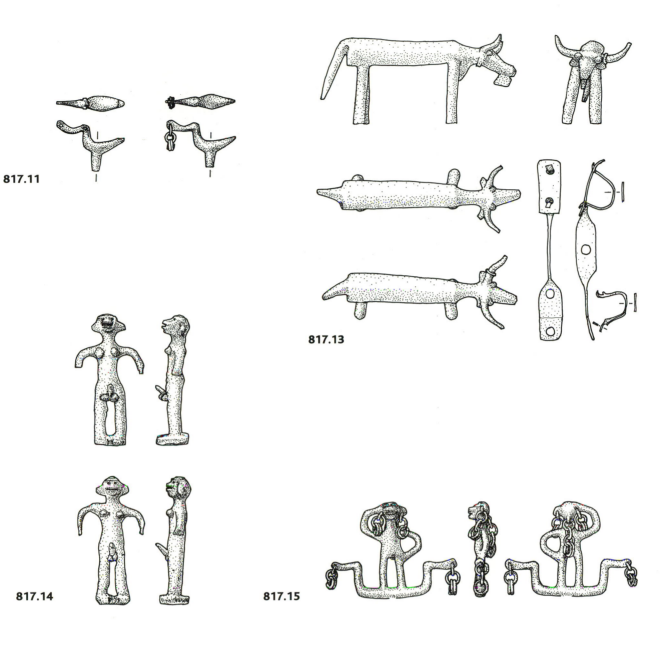

817.11

817.13

817.14

817.15

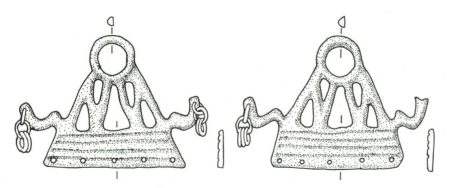

817.17

817.16

Plate 190   **Pastiche:** -817 (detail). Objects from the lower decorative elements.

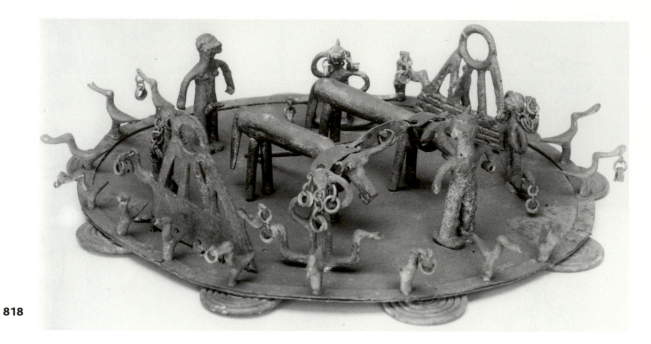

818

Plate 191   Pastiche: - 818 Campania.

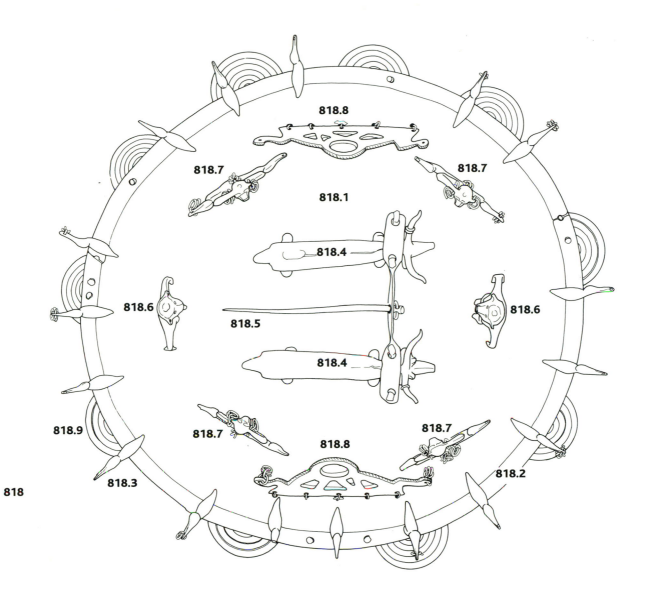

818

818.8
818.7   818.7
818.1
818.4
818.6   818.5   818.6
818.4
818.9   818.7   818.7
818.8
818.3   818.2

Plate 192   Pastiche: -818 (detail). Arrangement of decorative elements on upper side of disc, 818.1.

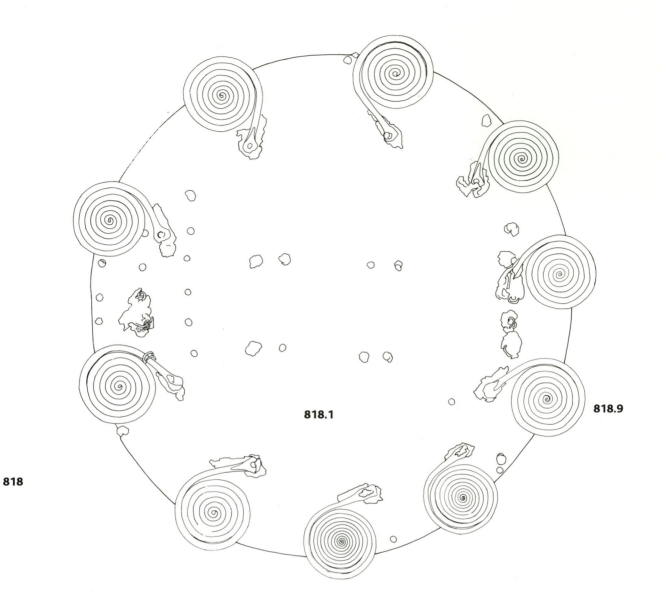

818

818.1

818.9

Plate 193   **Pastiche:** -818 (detail). Arrangement of decorative elements on lower side of disc, 818.1.

818.3

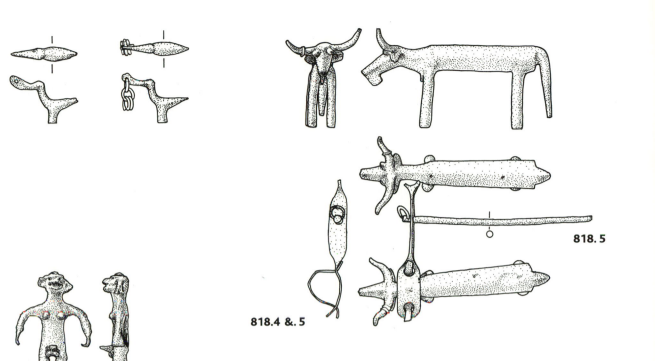

818. 5

818.4 &. 5

818.6

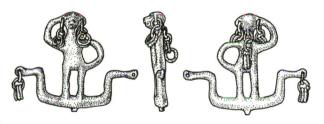

818.7

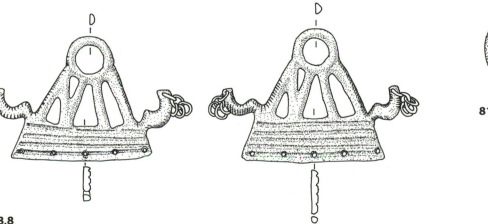

818.8

818.9

Plate 194 **Pastiche**: -818 (detail). Decorative elements.

819
1:1

819
1:1

Plate 195 **Pastiche:** - 819.

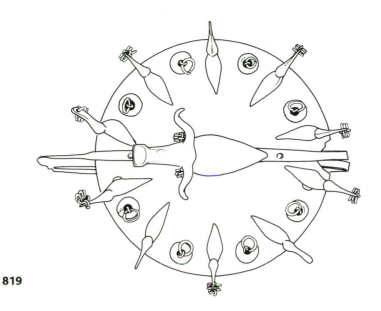

819

819.2

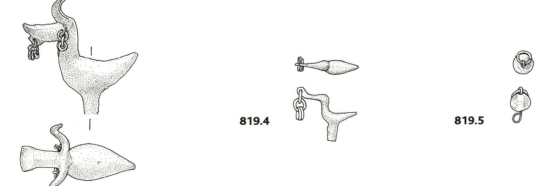

819.3

819.4

819.5

Plate 196   **Pastiche**: -819 (detail). Arrangement of decorative elements on upper side of disc, 819.1 and individual elements.

820

821

822

Plate 197 **Figurines**: - 820. - 821. - 822. All at scale 1:1.

Unclassified Objects

Axes

823.
PRB 1883.8-2.6. Given by Sir A.W. Franks.
Naples, Campania.
Axe blade, probably from a winged axe. **Axes unclassified**.
Small trapezoidal slightly flaring blade, probably reworked, with upper end slightly dished, cutting edge nearly straight. Smooth blackish patina.
L. 5.8cm Weight 62g
Analysis: Bronze. See D. Hook report.

824.
PRB Old Acquistion 101. Registered OA on 19 July 1939.
Axe blade. **Axes unclassified**.
Narrow flaring blade with faceted sides and round cutting edge. Smooth dark green patina.
L 10.3cm Weight 197g

Tools

825.
PRB 1964.12-1.377(305). Sir Henry Wellcome Collection. Given by the Wellcome Trustees.
Axe blade? **Tools unclassified**.
Very wide, trapezoidal, with strongly curved cutting edge; surface curved at joint to the shaft. Thick dull patina, bright green, discontinuous.
L. 9.8cm W. 12.7cm Weight 539g
Analysis: Copper. See D. Hook report.
Probably CA, but no precise parallels found.

826.
PRB 1964.12-1.459(345). Sir Henry Wellcome Collection, no. 453. Bought in Florence from A. Riccardi by Captain Saint in December 1929. Given by the Wellcome Trustees.
Tip of chisel blade. **Chisels unclassified**.
Tip of blade of a chisel, broken in antiquity: rectangular section, cutting edge slightly curved. Discontinuous patina, brown and light green.
L. 2.4cm Weight 17g
See **cat. 103, 104**, and **182**.
FBA or EIA.

827.
PRB 1964.12-1.203(302). Sir Henry Wellcome Collection, no. 321. Bought in Rome from Arte Antica e Moderna by Captain Saint in November 1929. Given by the Wellcome Trustees.
Terni, Umbria.
Tip of chisel blade. **Chisels unclassified**.
Tip of a chisel, possibly broken and reshaped in antiquity. Rod with square section, cutting edge blunt and curved. Shiny patina, dark green to black.

L. 3.6cm Weight 20g
Analysis: Bronze. See D. Hook report.
See **cat. 826**.
FBA or EIA.
Bibliography: Bietti Sestieri 2004, 28 and fig. 2.4.

Bracelets

828.
GR 1886.3-9.6. Given by Sir Henry Layard.
Sesto Calende (Varese), Lombardy, near a tomb.
Coiled wire bracelet. **Bracelets unclassified**.
Wire of round section, hammered to form one and a half circular coils extant, ends slightly diminished. Broken in two fragments, one end missing. Green patina with some corrosion.
Diam. 5.5cm Weight 14g
Probably EIA, late.

829.
GR 1867.5-8.216 and 217. Blacas Collection.
Coiled thick wire bracelet. **Bracelets unclassified**.
Fragments of a bracelet: thick wire coils of rectangular section and even diameter (diam. 0.4cm.). Broken at centre and at both ends. Dull green patina with some corrosion and heavy incrustations.
Diam. 8cm Weight 129g
See **cat. 828**.

Swords

830.
GR 1909.6-21.1. Bought from D. Komter of Amsterdam.
Sword with cast hilt ending in opposed spirals (antennae sword). **Swords type 12?**
Thick-sectioned weapon; pommel with high conical central spur, coils of spirals made of thick bronze ribbon; solid hilt with central part swelling decorated with two raised encircling bands; rounded shoulder cap with two rivets; blade narrower than the shoulders, with curved edges, rounded tip, and diamond-shaped section with central swelling. Decoration: two pairs of grooves along the central part of the blade. Dull green patina with some corrosion. Blade edges heavily damaged.
L. 51.4cm Weight 1047g
Analysis: Gunmetal. See D. Hook report. The copper-tin-zinc alloy of this sword, as well as the casting in one piece, strongly indicate that it is a modern fake.
Similar to *PBF* IV. 1, no. 330, from Lake Sirio (Ivrea), Piedmont. Zürich type, EIA. Not a very close parallel.
EIA or fake.

831.
PRB W. G.1149A. Canon W. Greenwell Collection. Given by J. Pierpont Morgan in 1909.
Point of a sword blade. **Swords unclassified**.
Section with central part raised, separated from the cutting edges by a slight step. Point hammered, cutting edges damaged. Modern break. Blackish patina.
L. 12.9cm Width 2.7cm Weight 91g
Blade section: see eg *PBF* IV. 1, nos. 113, 116, from Aquileia (Udine), Friuli Venezia Giulia, and Manaccora (Foggia), Apulia. Type Sacile, MBA–LBA transition.

Spearheads

832.
GR 1842.7-28.682. Bought from Mr Burgon.
Rome, Lazio.
Javelin-head with conical socket and foliate blade. **Spearheads unclassified**.
Upper part of the blade missing; narrow blade with rounded profile; socket faceted in blade zone and widening towards the base with two lateral pin-holes. Incised line along the edges of the blade. Dull green patina with heavy corrosion.
L. 10.7cm Weight 86g
Bibliography: Walters 1899, no. 2782.

833.
GR 1867.5-8.143. Blacas Collection.
Spearhead, miniature? **Unclassified**.
Foliate blade, shaft broken near blade. Dark green patina.
L. 3.3cm Weight 2g

834.
GR 1916.6-1.22. Given by Lord Avebury.
Perugia, Umbria.
Point of spearhead. **Spearheads unclassified**.
Solid point, once the tip of a spear blade, probably re-used as an arrowhead. Smooth green patina.
L. 4.1cm Weight 13g

835.
GR 1772.3-3.1000. Bought from Sir William Hamilton.
Little St. Bernard, Temple of Jupiter Poeninus (Aosta), Val d'Aosta.
Conical socket of a spearhead. **Spearheads unclassified**.
Socket cut from base of the blade. Two lateral pin-holes, one surrounded by cruciform incisions and the other by six irregular radial incisions. Dull green patina.
L. 10.2cm Weight 118g

Arrowheads

836.
PRB W. G. 1158. Canon W. Greenwell
Collection, bought from the Rev. Greville J.
Chester. Given by J. Pierpont Morgan in 1909.
Corneto (= Tarquinia, Viterbo), Lazio.
Tanged arrowhead. **Arrowheads unclassified**.
Narrow tang with flattened section; triangular
and elongated blade with angled points at base
and raised central part. Dull green patina with
brown incrustations (earth ?).
L. 6.3cm Weight 6g
No precise parallels. See **cat. 837**.
Possibly EIA.

837.
PRB W. G. 1157. Canon W. Greenwell Collection,
bought from the Rev. Greville J. Chester. Given
by J. Pierpont Morgan in 1909.
Cuma (Naples), Campania.
Tanged arrowhead. **Arrowheads unclassified**.
Tang with circular section, which becomes a
nervature on the blade; blade triangular with
parts missing. Smooth dark green patina.
L. 5.3cm Weight 8g
No precise or well-dated parallels found; see for
example Montelius 1895–1910, 602 pl. 126.10,
from Bisenti (Teramo), Abruzzo, pl. 126.18,
from Norcia (Perugia) Umbria, Collezione
Bellucci.
Possibly EIA.

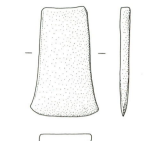

823

824

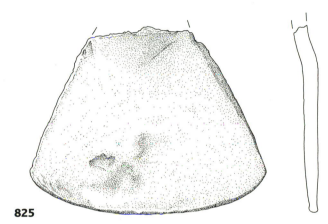

825

826

827

828

829

Plate 198   Unclassified objects. **Axes**: - 823 Naples, Campania. - 824. **Tools**: - 825. **Chisels**: - 826. - 827 Terni, Umbria . **Bracelets**: - 828 Sesto Calende (Varese), Lombardy. - 829.

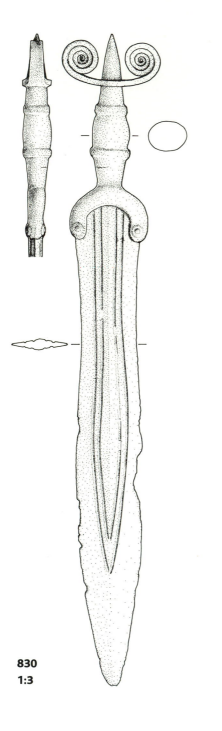

830
1:3

831

Plate 199 Unclassified objects. **Swords:** Close to **Swords type 12:** - 830. **Unclassified:** -831.

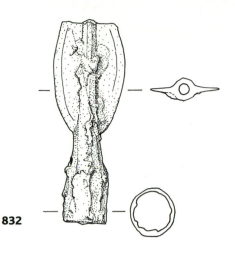

832

833
2:1

834

835

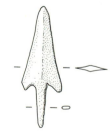

836

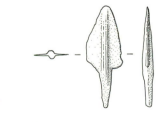

837

Plate 200   Unclassified objects. **Spearheads**: - 832 Rome, Lazio. - 833. - 834 Perugia, Umbria. - 835 Little St. Bernard, Temple of Jupiter Poeninus (Aosta), Val d'Aosta. **Arrowheads**: - 836 Corneto (Tarquinia, Viterbo), Lazio. - 837 Cuma (Naples), Campania.

The Composition and Technology of Selected Bronze Age and Early Iron Age Copper Alloy Artefacts from Italy

Duncan Hook

Introduction

This contribution to the catalogue concerns the composition and technological examination of over 100 prehistoric copper alloy artefacts, dating from the Copper Age through to the Early Iron Age (approximately from the late 4th to the beginning of the 1st millennium BC). A wide range of artefact types have been examined, including axes and blades from the earlier periods, to swords, spearheads and fibulae from the Final Bronze Age and Early Iron Age. Geographically, the artefacts represent many areas in Italy, with some having recorded provenances of either a region or a particular site.

The analyses add significantly to the analyses of pre-Etruscan Italian material published previously (for a discussion of many of the most significant publications, see the **Classification** section of this volume, pages 5–26), although not all of the published analyses are fully quantitative. The scientific work reported here has allowed an accurate technical description of the material to be made, including the identification of the alloys and often the fabrication methods used in their manufacture. The analyses allow compositional changes to be investigated with reference to typological chronology, the investigation of the compositions of material forming geographical groups, and enable comparisons to be made with material from across Europe.

The scientific work has also facilitated investigations into the authenticity of a number of the pieces and has identified several that have been repaired in recent times.

Methods of analysis

The majority of the artefacts examined were analysed using inductively coupled plasma atomic emission spectrometry (ICP-AES). The technique is capable of giving accurate and precise quantitative results for a range of major, minor and trace elements, but requires that a sample is removed from the object being analysed. This was achieved by drilling using a 1 mm diameter steel drill bit fitted to a small electric drill, discarding any potentially unrepresentative surface metal. Approximately 10–15 milligrams of the drillings were then accurately weighed, dissolved in *aqua regia* and diluted to volume using deionised water. More details about the technique and procedures used can be found in Hook (1998). Fourteen of the objects in the catalogue had been analysed some years previously using atomic absorption spectrophotometry (AAS, see Hughes *et al.* 1976 for details of the analytical technique used). These were mostly serpentine or other fibulae or figurines/items of small metalwork (Craddock 1986a). AAS has generally similar analytical capabilities to ICP-AES, but is less sensitive for some important elements such as tin and arsenic, and cannot easily measure elements such as sulphur and phosphorus. However, the analyses from the two techniques should be directly comparable. The analytical results in **Table 1** below (containing the results for both ICP-AES and the older AAS analyses) have a precision of approximately ±2% for copper, ±5–10% for tin and lead when present in amounts greater than 1%, and ±10–30% for the remaining minor and trace elements, deteriorating to ±50% at their respective detection limits.

Some of the artefacts were considered unsuitable for sampling for full quantitative analysis, usually because the metal was too thin to be sampled safely or because they were heavily corroded. In these cases, the artefacts were analysed using energy dispersive X-ray fluorescence spectrometry (XRF), using the system described by Cowell (1998). The analyses were carried out on uncleaned surfaces, without the removal of the patina or corrosion products, or of any potentially unrepresentative surface metal. These analyses were therefore only qualitative and hence the results (also summarized in **Table 1**) were restricted to indications of which elements were present and descriptive terms of the alloys used.

Most of the artefacts were also examined under a binocular optical microscope, especially to look for evidence of the method of manufacture used if this was in doubt. This was assisted by the use of radiography in some cases (Lang and Middleton 2005). Optical microscopy was also used to identify any remaining organic components, such as sword hilt plates. The scanning electron microscope (SEM) was also used to examine the silver-coloured coating on an EBA dagger (**cat. 60**).

Results and discussion

The results of the analyses (see **Table 1**) are listed in order of catalogue number and have been grouped on typological grounds as Copper Age (CA), Early Bronze Age (EBA), Middle Bronze Age (MBA), Recent Bronze Age (RBA), Final Bronze Age (FBA) and Early Iron Age (EIA), the latter category further divided into early and late (see the **Note on Chronology** section of this volume, pages 27–30). A statistical summary of the quantitative data grouped by approximate date is presented in **Table 2**, and illustrated as 'box and whisker plots' in **Figures 1–11**. In these Figures, the 'box' represents the inter-quartile range (i.e. the middle 50% of values) and the horizontal line in each box represents the median value, which will be less affected by extreme outlying values than the arithmetic mean. The 'whiskers' extend from the quartiles to the value not further than 1.5 times the inter-quartile range. Any values beyond this range are plotted as individual points. It should be noted that the numbers of analyses presented here are relatively small and therefore any conclusions drawn from the statistical analysis should be regarded with caution.

The arsenic levels are generally low from the EBA through to the RBA, but show a step up in values from the FBA onwards, to a median value of over 0.5 % in the later EIA (**Figure 1** and **Table 2**). The 15 analyses of Copper Age material (mostly axes and one halberd), were found to be copper or arsenical copper.

Most of these artefacts had low or undetectable arsenic, although four artefacts (**axes cat. 1, 5, 11** and the blade of **halberd cat. 14**) were found to have higher arsenic concentrations, in the range of 1.6–2.8%. (This bimodal nature of arsenic distribution for the CA material means that the use of the arithmetic mean (or simple average) is potentially misleading and therefore has been omitted in **Table 2**, and is also illustrated by the large box and spread in **Fig. 1**). The presence of even a few percent of arsenic would have increased the hardness of such alloys, especially if they had been work hardened, and given them a more silvery appearance. The different components of the CA halberd from Calvatone (**cat. 14**) were found to have very different arsenic contents: the blade was found to contain 2.74% whilst the rivet analysed was found to be of almost pure copper with no detectable arsenic. The blade would have certainly benefited from the increased hardness as a result of the higher arsenic content, and a deliberate choice of alloy appears to have been made. This difference between arsenic contents of blades and rivets in early metalwork from elsewhere in Europe has been discussed previously (e.g. McKerrell and Tylecote, 1972, and Hook *et al.* 1987). A similar tendency for blades to have higher arsenic contents than axes has been noticed previously (e.g. Pearce 1998).

None of the CA material (perhaps almost by definition) contained more than a slight trace of tin. The 22 analyses of EBA material have a median tin content approaching 7%, but show a large spread, with several containing 2–3% and ranging up to the 14.9% of the hilt of dagger **cat. 45**. Most of the subsequent periods have similar overall median values (*c.* 7 or 8%), but have smaller overall ranges than in the EBA (see **Fig. 2**), possibly suggesting a greater degree of control over alloy production or perhaps an increase in recycling. The period of highest tin content appears to be the RBA, with a median value of *c.* 10%. However, all these artefacts are daggers and swords which would benefit from the increased hardness resulting from higher tin contents, thus their tin contents may well reflect the use of an alloy designed with object functionality in mind rather than being part of a chronological trend.

The lead content of much of the worked metalwork is low as might have been expected, as the presence of large amounts of lead is detrimental to the mechanical properties of copper alloys. However, the presence of some lead improves the fluidity of molten copper making it easier to cast (Gregory 1932), which might explain the slight increase in lead contents from the FBA/EIA onwards (**Fig. 3**). Only one item of heavily leaded bronze appears in the artefacts analysed here (the 24.3% of lead in the two seated figurines, **cat. 820**), otherwise the highest lead content is less than 5%. This is perhaps surprising given the occurrence of higher lead alloys elsewhere, e.g. in the Greek world (e.g. Craddock 1976 and 1977) in material from nearby Slovenia (e.g. Trampuz-Orel 1996)and from the edges of western Europe in the Atlantic Bronze Age (Craddock 1979).

None of the artefacts analysed were found to be brasses, all the artefacts having zinc contents of less than 1%. Zinc should therefore be regarded as a trace impurity, presumably entering into the copper metal from the original copper ore. The highest zinc contents of EBA artefacts are from Terni, Umbria **cat. 52** and **58**, the highest overall being a later EIA winged axe from Populonia, Tuscany (**cat. 466, Fig. 4**).

The remaining trace elements tend to be low in the CA and EBA material, but appear at higher levels in the artefacts analysed from the subsequent phases of the Bronze and Iron Ages. The iron levels of the CA material are virtually undetectable in many cases, and are generally low in the EBA. From the MBA onwards they tend to be slightly higher, and by the Iron Age several artefacts approach the 1–2% level (**Table 2** and **Fig. 5**). For nickel and cobalt, most values are low or not detectable in the CA/EBA, rising slightly until the earlier EIA, before possibly dropping back (**Figs. 6** and **7**). However, the visual pattern in **Figs. 6** and **7** is dominated by the large 'box' in the FBA which indicates a large spread of values, caused by the very high nickel and cobalt contents of three winged axes from near Lake Como (**cat. 241–243**), with similarly high antimony and silver values (**Figs. 8** and **10**). It should be noted that these high values will have a greater effect on the mean values shown in **Table 2** than the median values (shown as the horizontal line in the boxes in the Figures). Antimony is again very low in the CA, slightly higher during the EBA, MBA and RBA, increases in the FBA and then stays at a relatively high level in the EIA (**Fig. 8**). For bismuth no obvious pattern could be observed (**Fig. 9**). Silver is generally low in the CA, EBA and MBA, being possibly slightly higher in the RBA and subsequent periods (**Fig. 10**). Sulphur again is very low or not detected in the CA, is slightly higher in the EBA, and higher still in the MBA and following periods (**Fig. 11**).

The levels of trace elements in the artefacts are related to the trace element concentrations of the ores being utilised at a given period, but they are also related to other factors such as whether and how the copper ore was roasted before smelting (leading to the loss of volatile elements), the smelting technology itself (especially smelting temperature and duration, the reducing conditions and the addition of fluxes), the degree of subsequent refining of the smelted metal and the possible mixing of copper from different sources through recycling and the use of scrap. Although the amount of data presented here is small, an attempt may be made to interpret some of the broader changes in trace element composition outlined above. For example, the rising sulphur concentrations from the CA through the EBA to the MBA and later may reflect a change in the nature of the copper ores being processed, from oxide/carbonate to sulphide-based ores. The iron content of copper has previously been used as an indicator of the sophistication of the smelting process employed (Craddock and Meeks 1987; Craddock and Burnett 1998), and appears to be applicable here. Early copper smelting was probably carried out at relatively low temperatures using high grade ore, leaving little debris behind as evidence for the process. Later processes are thought to have been carried out at higher temperatures, for longer times, under more reducing conditions and with the production of an iron-rich slag (e.g. by the addition of a flux) to help remove the gangue material originating from the use of lower grade ores. Under these conditions more iron becomes incorporated into the copper, and whilst some may be removed during subsequent refining, the artefacts made from copper produced in this way tend to have elevated iron contents. As mentioned above, the iron levels of the CA material are virtually undetectable, indicating the use of a simple smelting process, but rise to a mean of 0.35% in the early part of the EIA, suggesting the use of a more sophisticated process.

The main ore sources exploited in the Italian peninsula south of the Alps are likely to have been those in the Colline Metallifere (e.g. Davies 1935), although it is uncertain when they were first exploited (mining was certainly taking place by the mid-4th millennium in the north-west in Liguria (Maggi and Pearce 2005) and other sources such as those on Sardinia must also not be ignored (Tylecote *et al*. 1983). However, it is likely to remain either difficult or impossible to use the trace element content of a particular copper alloy object to relate it to the ore from which it was originally produced. Never the less, some groupings of artefacts based on trace element content appear to be significant, although not necessarily indicative of a particular source. The most striking of these groups is formed by the three FBA winged axes from near Lake Como, mentioned above, which all have high levels of silver, antimony, nickel, cobalt, bismuth and arsenic, along with detectable zinc. They are unlike any other metalwork analysed here, but are compositionally similar to several examples of published Alpine metalwork (e.g. Junghans, Sangmeister and Schröder (1968 and 1974), Giumlia-Mair (1998) and Northover (2004)). Other groups include four of the EBA axes from near Girgenti, Agrigento, Sicily (**cat. 47, 48, 50** and **51**) which all have detectable cobalt and similar levels of the other trace elements. Also a further group of eight EBA bronze axes, either from or probably from Terni, Umbria, contain similar trace element levels, including detectable bismuth and zinc. None of the analyses are sufficiently close to suggest that the axes were produced from the same melt, but the combined analyses give an indication of the likely variations that might be expected in a stock of metal or the production of a localised industry.

Comments referring to specific artefacts or small groups

Cat. 3

Copper Age flat axe **cat. 3** was found to be copper, with most other elements at or below the limit of detection of the analytical technique. However, the flat axe does contain low but detectable levels of selenium (*c*. 0.056%), tellurium (*c*. 0.006%) and vanadium (*c*. 0.0012%). Selenium and tellurium often occur in trace amounts in copper ores, often associated with sulphur, and it has been suggested that their abundance and ratio may be characteristic of different ore deposits (Loftus-Hills and Solomon 1967). Unfortunately, these elements are rarely sought or are present at detectable levels in ancient copper alloys, but the presence of selenium and tellurium in Bronze Age ingots from Crete and Sardinia has been reported by Rehren and Northover (1991), who suggested that selenium and tellurium are likely to be concentrated in sulphide inclusions in the metal (although in this case the low sulphur content suggests that there will be few sulphide inclusions present). It appears that these elements, and especially their ratio, may be of use in the characterization and grouping of ancient metalwork once a reliable, large database has been established.

It has also been suggested that this flat axe resembles the axe found with 'Ötzi', the mummified iceman in the Italian Alps (Egg 1992), although the British Museum axe is almost twice as long. The iceman's axe has only been analysed using XRF, with no indication of whether the analysis is of surface metal and therefore possibly susceptible to errors due to the surface metal not being representative of the axe as a whole. The reported result of copper 99.7%, arsenic 0.22% and silver 0.08% indicates that the iceman's axe is higher in both arsenic and silver, but it is difficult to draw further conclusions.

Cat. 44

Radiography of EBA dagger **cat. 44** (**Fig. 12**) showed a run of metal extending from the repair visible in the hilt up towards the pommel. Two cracks approximately 0.5cm long extend from the dagger edges in towards the centre of the blade. The blade exhibits less porosity than the larger dagger, **cat. 46**.

Cat. 45

The detached blade fragment of the dagger was found to be arsenical copper, unlike the upper part of the blade which is a tin bronze. The lower part of the blade is clearly of a very different alloy and therefore should not be re-attached. The hilt was found to be hollow during sampling. A small sample of core material removed from the hilt was analysed using X-ray diffraction (XRD) and identified as calcite containing a little quartz. Radiography (**Fig. 13**) showed the unsuspected presence of two large rivets in the hilt, although their purpose is not immediately apparent. The radiograph also shows the decoration at the top of the blade and also the hole drilled into the rib of the dagger as part of the modern repair.

Cat. 46

Radiography of EBA dagger **cat. 46** (**Fig. 14**) revealed the presence in the hilt of a bar tapering from *c*. 3.5 to 2mm across the upper part of the hilt, also showing the dimensions of the pin set into the top of the hilt (*c*. 23 x 2mm). Some porosity in the blade was also present, presumably a result from insufficient degassing during the casting process and possibly accentuated by corrosion during burial.

Cat. 60

EBA dagger **cat. 60** consists of a relatively high tin bronze blade and a low tin bronze hilt, joined together using bronze rivets. The higher tin content of the blade presumably represents a deliberate choice of alloy, as the higher tin would result in a greater hardness level after working.

The dagger blade has large areas of its surface that are smooth and silver-grey coloured. The coloration also extends to the parallel grooved decoration around the perimeter near to the cutting edge (**Fig. 15**), although some areas of high relief have worn away. Analysis of the silver-grey coloured areas in the SEM indicated that the coating was a copper alloy which was very high in tin (*c*. 45%), with only traces of other elements present. The durability of the coating, its corrosion resistance, colour and composition strongly suggest that it consists of mixed tin/copper intermetallic compounds (ϵ and η) that form at elevated temperatures during tinning. Therefore it is thought likely that the silver-grey coloration was the result of deliberate surface tinning of the original worked and decorated blade, rather than either tin sweat (no eutectoid structures were seen) or corrosion phenomena. The dagger would originally have been visually striking with a decorated silver-coloured polished blade contrasting with the bronze of the hilt.

Deliberate tinning is rare in the European EBA – the published examples include an axe from Barton Stacey, Hampshire, England (Kinnes *et al*. 1979) and a group of Scottish flat axes (Tylecote 1985). Some work on tin-rich surfaces of daggers was carried out by McKerrell (see Close-Brooks and Coles 1980), and a fuller discussion on the surface characterization of tinned bronzes has been published by Meeks (1993).

Cat. 124

The dagger from Naxos, Greece, **cat. 124**, was too thin to be sampled for quantitative analysis. XRF showed that both the blade and central rivet were tin bronze. The hilt plates were also examined to try to identify the organic material. Unfortunately, no transverse section was visible for microscopic examination. The longitudinal surface matched reference collection specimens of ivory but there was insufficient structural detail visible to make an unequivocal attribution specifically to elephant ivory, although it remains a strong possibility.

Cat. 223

XRF confirmed that the blade and hilt rivet of this tanged sword are bronze and that the three coils of wire on the hilt are of gold containing silver and a little copper. No transverse section of the organic hilt plates was visible for microscopic examination. The longitudinal surface matched reference collection specimens of ivory but there was insufficient structural detail visible to make an unequivocal attribution specifically to elephant ivory, although it remains a strong possibility.

Cat. 226

XRF confirmed that the blade and collar rivets of this tanged sword are bronze. The rivets in the hilt are unusual: the rivet nearest the pommel appears to be bronze on one side and lead on the other, the lower rivet appears to be lead on both sides. It is possible that the lead represents a repair filling rather than proper rivets. Microscopic examination of a transverse surface of the organic component of the hilt revealed the intersecting arc structure which is characteristic of elephant ivory as displayed in a reference collection specimen, and described by

MacGregor (1985).

Cat. 227

The sword hilt consists of two bronze plates joined by a lead-tin alloy. The distribution of the lead-tin alloy was revealed using radiography, although it may not necessarily be original. XRF of the bronze plates shows the presence of a little lead, traces of silver, antimony and arsenic, and an unusually large trace of bismuth.

Cat. 280, 310, 316,

These three fibulae were all found to be bronzes containing a little lead using XRF. Only **cat. 310** was considered suitable for quantitative analysis, which confirmed its alloy identification as bronze and also revealed the surprising presence of more than 2% of iron, presumably indicating relatively poor refining of the copper prior to alloying and casting.

A radiograph of **cat. 280** indicates that the fibula is solid. The catchplate is decorated with punched dots and incised lines. It is likely that the fibula was cast as a fairly simple shape and then worked and decorated.

Cat. 367 and 368

The blade, rivets and spirals of wire on the hilt of the sword (**cat. 367**) are all bronze. The scabbard (**cat. 368**) is hammered and incised bronze, and is similar in composition to the thicker terminal which appears to have been hard soldered or cast on. Radiography of the scabbard revealed the final 3 or 4mm of the scabbard cavity to be solid.

Cat. 398 and 399

The spearhead and spear-butt from Bovino, Apulia are bronzes, although the spearhead has noticeably lower lead (a high lead content would be detrimental to a cutting tool). Their arsenic, antimony and nickel contents are sufficiently different to suggest that they are not closely related analytically.

Cat. 457–459

The sword and spearheads from 'San Germano', Cassino, Lazio are bronzes, the two spearheads having reasonably similar levels of trace elements. No evidence was seen to suggest that the decoration on these objects had been cast in and it seems more likely that the decoration had been added by engraving after casting.

Cat. 466, 491 and 513

The three decorated axes are all bronzes with variable tin contents, but all contain around 2% of lead. **cat. 466 and 491** contain relatively high traces of iron (c. 0.8%) and **cat. 466** also contains a relatively high trace of zinc. The concentric circle decoration appears sharp, with the circles overlapping in some places, suggesting engraving. No evidence was found to suggest that the decoration was partly applied at the moulding stage.

Cat. 554 and 575

Radiography indicated that the leech fibula **cat. 554 and 575** are hollow. **Cat. 554** contains four small bars, three of which appear to be mobile. Some fine casting porosity was also revealed.

Cat. 750

The tang and collar of short sword **cat. 750** appear to have slightly different tin contents, but otherwise are analytically identical in terms of their trace elements. There is a visible join which runs across the upper part of the blade. XRF analysis of either side of the join showed that the upper and lower parts of the blade are analytically similar. Analysis of the join area showed elevated lead and tin, with some zinc, indicative of the use of modern solder. Radiography (**Fig. 16**) revealed that the joint had additionally been strengthened by the insertion of a solid peg between the two parts of the blade.

Cat. 799 and 800

The two large spearheads from Bomarzo, Lazio are bronzes with around 6% tin and have similar trace element contents. The closeness of the two analyses of spearhead **cat. 800** shows that the object does not suffer from gross heterogeneity and also illustrates the precision (a measure of reproducibility) of the analytical procedures used.

Cat. 813–816

The laminated strips consist of a very thin bronze ribbon soldered using a tin-lead soft solder to a thicker copper backing plate. The copper backing plates have little depth of corrosion and are likely to be modern. The bronze coils have then been riveted to the strips and the birds soldered in position, again using soft solder.

Cat. 817 and 818

a) Larger pastiche (**cat. 817**)
Several areas of the largest pastiche were analysed using XRF. These included the large lower disc, its attached circumferential strip, one of the spirals, the sheet metal 'bud' ornaments, and the 'bud' ornaments of thicker metal on the hanging pendants. All were found to be tin bronze with traces of lead, iron, silver, arsenic and antimony. This composition is not particularly distinctive, and is consistent with the compositions of ancient alloys from many periods and cultures. It was not possible to analyse the central oxen due to the geometry of the piece.

b) Smaller pastiche (**cat. 818**)
The disc of the smaller pastiche was analysed using XRF and found to be copper, containing traces of lead, iron, nickel, silver, arsenic and antimony. A small amount of mercury was also detected on the surface, possibly present as a result of an artificial patination process or from a cleaning solution. The bronze circumferential strip was found to be bronze containing traces of lead, iron, silver, arsenic and antimony, with a small amount of mercury again present on the surface. The strip was attached to the disc by rivets, four of which were found to be copper alloys containing both tin and high levels of zinc suggesting that they may be relatively modern. One of the oxen was analysed and found to be bronze with traces of lead, iron, silver, arsenic and antimony, again with mercury present.

Several of the separate fragments were also analysed, including the two triangular openwork plaques, four standing androgynous figures, two male figures, two birds and two loose strips of metal. These fragments were all found to be tin bronzes, containing traces of lead, iron, silver, arsenic and antimony, again with a small amount of mercury present on their surfaces. A number of these pieces had the remains of a tin/lead soft solder (in some cases disguised with green paint) visible where they once had been attached. The compositions of these fragments (and by inference, similar components of the two pastiches) are again consistent with those of alloys of many periods and cultures.

Cat. 830

XRF of the surface of the sword was found to give very variable results. Copper, tin and zinc were found to be present in varying amounts along the length of the blade, at the hilt and at the rivets. Lead, arsenic and iron were also present, but in extremely variable amounts. Analysis of the antennae itself at two areas (one area of relatively bare metal and one area of heavily patinated metal) showed that the bare metal was of fairly pure copper containing only trace amounts of tin and lead and no detectable zinc or iron, whereas analysis of the patinated area showed the presence of substantial amounts of lead, arsenic and iron and a trace of zinc. The patina has an unnatural appearance and was found to be easily removed on gentle rubbing with methylated spirits. The patina did not fluoresce under ultraviolet light, suggesting that an organic binder had not been applied. In an attempt to unequivocally identify the alloy of the sword, a sample was removed from the hilt by drilling, discarding the surface drillings and analysing the remainder using XRF. The analysis indicated that the sword is a copper-tin-zinc alloy with a little lead, in modern terms an alloy known as a 'gunmetal'. No other artefact analysed here has been found to be a gunmetal (the alloy only became widespread during the Roman period), and therefore the sword should be regarded with suspicion. Radiography of the sword showed no evidence of joins or discontinuities at the rivets and it appears to be cast, possibly as a single piece (apart from the copper antennae).

Conclusions

The results of the compositional analysis of over 100 prehistoric copper alloy artefacts from Italy has allowed the alloys used to be characterized and enabled accurate technical descriptions of the alloys to be made in the catalogue entries. A wide range of artefact types have been studied, ranging from the CA through to the EIA in date (with many geographical regions of Italy being represented) and when studied in conjunction with previous studies of Italic, Sardinian and Etruscan metalwork (Craddock 1986a and b) gives an overview of the metallurgy of the Italian peninsula from the CA to the Roman Republican period.

The earliest artefacts were found to be virtually pure copper or copper containing arsenic as the only other element present in significant amounts. Tin bronze becomes ubiquitous with the onset of the EBA. None of the artefacts analysed were found to contain more than trace levels of zinc. Lead contents were found to be generally low, the higher lead contents tending to be found in the IA.

The analyses have also revealed a number of trends in the trace element contents, some of which are suggestive of changes in smelting technology over time. The levels of many of the trace elements were found to be virtually undetectable in the CA material but were higher in the later periods, as exemplified by iron and antimony. Sulphur also exhibits this trend and may well reflect a change in the nature of the copper ores being processed, from oxide/carbonate to sulphide-based deposits.

Some geographical groupings of artefacts were found to have similar levels of trace elements. These include a group of four EBA axes from near Girgenti, Agrigento, Sicily, eight EBA axes from near or probably near Terni, Umbria, and three FBA winged axes from near Lake Como, Lombardy.

A CA flat axe was found to consist of copper containing low but detectable levels of selenium, tellurium and vanadium. This unusual composition may have significance in the origin or processing of the original copper.

Examination of a number of the artefacts using radiography and optical and scanning electron microscopy facilitated the identification of the methods of manufacture employed and materials used. In some cases the presence of unsuspected features, such as a rare early example of tinning have been revealed and the presence of ivory on a sword hilt was also confirmed.

Acknowledgements

The scientific aspects of this project have benefited greatly from the archaeological and typological knowledge of Anna Maria Bietti Sestieri and Ellen Macnamara. I would like to thank Josephine Turquet and Fiona Campbell for their editing and production skills, and their patience. I am also very grateful for the help received from colleagues in the British Museum, especially Judith Swaddling and Stuart Needham, and from present and former colleagues in my own department, Paul Craddock, Andrew Middleton, Nigel Meeks, Sheridan Bowman, Caroline Cartwright, Janet Ambers, Tony Simpson, Janet Lang and Louise Joyner.

Notes

[1] Short summaries of the results have been published in Hook (2003) and Hook (2005), although these publications do not include the full analyses. Changes in the geographical and chronological attribution of some artefacts have also occurred whilst the catalogue was being prepared.

Table 1: Analyses of Italian Bronze Age/Iron Age metalwork

Cat.	Description (part analyzed)	Provenance	Cu	Sn	As	Pb	Zn	Fe	Ni	Co	Sb	Bi	Ag	S	Total	Alloy
Copper Age:																
1	Flat axe	Campania	98.6	0.04	1.68	0.14	<0.01	0.708	0.008	0.003	0.01	<0.02	0.005	0.27	101.4	Arsenical copper
2	Flat axe	Naples, Campania	99.5	<0.01	<0.01	<0.01	<0.01	<0.003	<0.003	<0.003	<0.01	<0.01	0.017	<0.01	99.5	Copper
3	Flat axe		97.4	0.01	<0.01	<0.01	0.01	0.017	<0.005	<0.002	<0.01	<0.02	0.023	<0.01	97.4	Copper
4	Flat axe	Abruzzo	100.9	<0.01	<0.01	<0.01	<0.01	0.005	<0.003	<0.003	<0.01	<0.01	0.022	<0.01	100.9	Copper
5	Flat axe	Corneto, Lazio	94.5	0.01	1.81	0.03	<0.01	<0.005	0.010	<0.002	0.02	0.12	0.088	<0.01	96.5	Arsenical copper
6	Flat axe	Ruvo, Apulia	100.0	<0.01	0.03	<0.01	<0.01	0.009	<0.003	<0.003	0.04	<0.01	0.033	<0.01	100.0	Copper
7	Flat axe	Capua, Campania	100.0	<0.01	<0.02	<0.01	<0.02	<0.003	<0.003	<0.003	<0.01	<0.01	0.030	<0.02	100.0	Copper
10	Lugged axe	Pozzuoli, Campania	93.5	<0.01	0.18	<0.01	<0.01	<0.005	0.022	<0.001	0.03	0.03	0.056	<0.01	93.8	Copper
11	Axe, protruding shoulders	Terni, Umbria	95.3	<0.01	1.99	0.01	<0.01	<0.005	0.009	<0.002	<0.01	0.13	0.097	<0.01	97.5	Arsenical copper
12	Axe		97.0	<0.01	0.03	<0.01	<0.01	<0.005	0.010	<0.002	<0.01	<0.02	0.096	<0.01	97.1	Copper
14	Halberd (blade)	Calvatone, Lombardy	97.3	<0.01	2.74	<0.01	<0.02	<0.003	0.023	<0.003	<0.01	0.023	0.024	<0.02	100.1	Arsenical copper
	(rivet)		100.0	<0.01	<0.01	<0.01	<0.01	<0.003	0.027	<0.003	<0.01	<0.01	0.008	<0.01	100.0	Copper
15	Flat axe	Terni, Umbria	100.0	<0.01	<0.01	0.01	<0.01	<0.003	0.007	<0.003	<0.01	0.058	0.047	<0.01	100.1	Copper
16	Flat axe	Terni, Umbria	100.0	<0.01	<0.02	<0.01	<0.02	<0.003	0.015	<0.003	<0.01	<0.01	0.090	<0.02	100.0	Copper
17	Blade from a flat axe	Terni, Umbria	100.0	<0.01	0.02	<0.01	<0.02	<0.003	0.006	<0.003	0.07	<0.01	0.035	<0.01	100.1	Copper
Early Bronze Age:																
18	Axe with raised edges	Rome, Lazio	90.3	5.56	0.09	0.06	<0.01	<0.005	0.019	0.016	0.13	<0.02	0.019	0.05	96.2	Bronze
25	Flanged axe		88.6	6.52	0.16	1.42	0.14	0.018	0.015	<0.002	0.05	0.02	0.034	0.09	97.1	Bronze
27	Flanged axe	Capua, Campania	92.7	6.47	0.10	0.25	0.137	0.261	0.012	<0.003	0.04	0.020	0.007	0.07	100.0	Bronze
44	Dagger		Cu, Sn, tr. As, tr. Pb													
45	Dagger (hilt)		83.8	14.9	<0.02	0.25	<0.03	0.007	<0.005	<0.005	<0.02	<0.02	<0.003	0.03	98.9	Bronze
	(blade)		80.1	10.1	<0.01	0.25	<0.01	<0.003	0.004	<0.003	<0.01	<0.01	0.003	0.03	90.4	Arsenical copper
	(replacement blade tip)		Cu, As, tr. Pb, tr. Fe, tr. Ag													
46	Dagger	Torre Annunziata, Campania	Cu, Sn, tr. As, tr. Pb													
47	Flat axe	Near Girgenti (Agrigento), Sicily	85.3	11.8	0.12	0.43	<0.02	0.009	0.024	0.009	0.04	0.014	0.016	0.11	97.8	Bronze
48	Flat axe	Near Girgenti (Agrigento), Sicily	90.5	10.2	0.06	0.04	<0.01	0.023	0.015	0.014	0.03	<0.01	0.007	0.07	100.9	Bronze
49	Flat axe	Near Girgenti (Agrigento), Sicily	90.1	6.31	0.39	0.32	<0.01	0.018	0.025	0.003	0.61	<0.01	0.316	0.05	98.0	Bronze
50	Axe with slightly raised edges	Near Girgenti (Agrigento), Sicily	95.4	2.91	0.08	0.03	<0.02	0.026	0.019	0.012	0.08	<0.01	0.025	0.06	98.5	Bronze
51	Flanged axe	Near Girgenti (Agrigento), Sicily	98.5	2.05	0.09	0.05	<0.02	0.010	0.022	0.014	0.11	<0.02	0.022	0.04	100.8	Bronze
52	Flanged axe	Terni, Umbria	92.3	5.17	0.24	1.20	0.727	0.049	0.011	<0.003	0.09	0.024	0.013	0.15	100.0	Bronze
53	Flanged axe	Terni, Umbria	88.1	7.01	0.14	4.09	0.061	0.004	0.019	<0.003	0.04	0.131	0.105	0.11	99.8	Leaded bronze
54	Flanged axe	Terni, Umbria	90.2	7.82	0.09	0.47	0.042	0.004	0.023	<0.003	0.11	0.037	0.074	0.08	99.0	Bronze
55	Flanged axe	Probably Terni, Umbria	89.5	7.50	0.47	0.69	0.220	0.031	0.030	<0.003	0.17	0.024	0.021	0.11	98.8	Bronze
56	Flanged axe	Probably Terni, Umbria	91.4	5.64	0.11	1.60	0.116	0.067	0.017	0.003	0.02	0.018	0.031	0.18	99.2	Bronze
57	Flanged axe	Probably Terni, Umbria	88.4	7.57	0.18	0.90	0.072	0.007	0.031	<0.003	0.09	0.042	0.041	0.09	97.4	Bronze
58	Flanged axe	Probably Terni, Umbria	93.0	4.48	0.15	2.17	0.486	0.200	0.013	<0.003	0.17	0.019	0.026	0.23	100.9	Bronze
59	Flanged axe	Probably Terni, Umbria	88.5	8.44	0.10	1.65	0.180	0.021	0.015	<0.003	0.07	0.052	0.027	0.15	99.2	Bronze
60	Dagger (hilt)		96.7	2.57	<0.02	<0.01	<0.02	0.006	<0.005	<0.005	<0.02	<0.02	<0.003	<0.02	99.3	Bronze
	(blade tinned)		89.0	11.2	<0.03	<0.01	<0.03	0.015	0.007	<0.006	<0.02	<0.03	<0.003	<0.03	100.3	Bronze
61	Dagger (hilt)		93.5	5.92	0.09	0.70	<0.03	<0.007	0.013	<0.007	<0.03	<0.03	0.011	<0.03	100.2	Bronze
	(tinned blade)		88.6	9.35	0.16	1.03	<0.02	<0.004	0.016	<0.004	0.09	0.029	0.026	<0.02	99.3	Bronze

Table 1 cont. Analyses of Italian Bronze Age/Iron Age metalwork

Cat.	Description (part analyzed)	Provenance	Cu	Sn	As	Pb	Zn	Fe	Ni	Co	Sb	Bi	Ag	S	Total	Alloy
Middle Bronze Age:																
66	Flanged/winged axe	Terni, Umbria	91.4	5.70	0.12	0.47	0.034	0.052	0.109	0.028	0.12	0.043	0.084	0.19	98.3	Bronze
80	Dagger/short sword with tang	Peschiera, Veneto	88.1	8.77	0.06	1.37	<0.02	0.005	0.061	<0.003	0.05	0.017	0.058	0.07	98.6	Bronze
81	Short sword (blade)	Osor, Island of Cres, Croatia	90.9	7.52	0.79	0.08	<0.01	0.214	0.543	0.029	0.35	<0.02	0.011	0.16	100.6	Bronze
	(4 rivets)	Cu, Sn, As, tr. Pb, tr. Sb, tr. Ni, tr. Fe, str. Ag														Bronze
82	Flanged/winged axe	Lodi, Lombardy	91.8	7.23	0.19	0.82	0.045	0.005	0.170	<0.003	0.15	0.018	0.116	0.10	100.6	Bronze
83	Flanged axe	Lodi, Lombardy	92.7	7.07	0.03	0.04	<0.01	0.109	0.021	<0.003	0.12	0.018	0.022	0.41	100.6	Bronze
84	Winged axe	Nemi, Lazio	92.4	6.58	0.06	0.04	<0.01	0.105	0.019	0.013	<0.01	0.012	0.008	0.31	99.6	Bronze
85	Winged axe	Nemi, Lazio	89.5	8.93	0.08	<0.01	<0.01	0.252	0.016	0.048	<0.01	<0.01	0.002	0.26	99.1	Bronze
Recent Bronze Age:																
120	Dagger	Peschiera, Veneto	92.6	7.70	0.03	<0.01	<0.01	0.058	0.031	0.005	<0.01	<0.02	0.006	0.48	101.0	Bronze
121	Dagger	Steiermark, Austria	87.1	10.8	0.04	0.33	0.029	0.033	0.029	0.021	0.07	0.040	0.054	0.37	98.9	Bronze
122	Dagger (blade)	Peschiera, Veneto	88.7	10.4	0.04	0.30	0.086	0.522	0.006	0.020	0.04	0.034	0.077	0.40	100.7	Bronze
	(rivet)		92.5	5.69	0.04	2.03	<0.02	0.025	0.079	0.012	0.12	0.029	0.102	0.08	100.7	Bronze
123	Dagger	Lewes, Sussex, England	86.7	11.2	0.08	0.49	0.093	0.201	0.035	0.029	0.16	0.044	0.090	0.18	99.2	Bronze
124	Dagger (blade)	Naxos, Greece	Cu, Sn, tr. As, tr. Pb, tr. Fe													Bronze
	(rivet)		Cu, Sn, tr. As, tr. Fe													Bronze
127	Sword	Frosinone, Lazio	88.9	9.57	0.26	0.58	<0.01	0.009	0.128	0.024	0.12	0.019	0.042	0.09	99.8	Bronze
Final Bronze Age:																
205	Arch fibula		Cu, Sn, tr. As, Pb, tr. Sb, tr. Ni, tr. Fe, str. Ag													Bronze
206	Arch fibula		Cu, Sn, tr. As, Pb, tr. Sb, tr. Ni, tr. Fe, str. Ag													Bronze
213	Serpentine fibula		92.5	7.50	0.18	0.22	<0.01	0.16	0.050	0.040	0.14	0.005	0.080		100.9	*Bronze
214	Serpentine fibula		90.5	6.90	0.03	0.71	0.020	0.36	0.050	0.020	0.03	0.005	<0.1		98.6	*Bronze
216	Serpentine fibula		89.5	9.50	0.01	0.01	<0.01	0.03	0.050	0.010	0.15	0.004	0.060		99.3	*Bronze
217	Two-piece serpentine fibula		91.4	7.23	0.17	0.73	0.009	0.308	0.264	0.086	0.33	<0.01	0.102	0.10	100.8	Bronze
219	Short sword (blade)	Bisignano, Calabria	89.8	7.04	0.28	2.40	0.078	0.091	0.040	0.026	0.15	0.021	0.175	0.27	100.4	Bronze
	(rivet)		88.5	10.0	0.45	1.59	<0.01	0.017	0.031	0.033	0.02	0.014	0.067	0.14	100.9	Bronze
223	Short sword (blade)		Cu, Sn, tr. Pb, tr. Zn, tr. Sb, tr. Ni, tr. Fe, tr. Ag													Bronze
	(hilt rivet)		Cu, Sn, tr. Pb, tr. Zn, tr. Sb, tr. Ni, tr. Fe, tr. Ag													Bronze
	(wire)		Au, Ag, Cu													Gold alloy
226	Short sword (blade)		Cu, Sn, tr. As, tr. Pb, tr. Sb, tr. Fe													Bronze
	(collar rivets)		Cu, Sn, tr. As, tr. Pb, tr. Sb, tr. Fe													Bronze
	(hilt rivet)		Pb													Lead
227	Sword hilt	Armento (Potenza), Basilicata	Cu, Sn, tr. As, Pb, tr. Sb, tr. Ag, tr. Bi.													Bronze
241	Winged axe	Near Lake Como, Lombardy	88.6	5.66	0.67	1.22	0.015	0.096	0.618	0.143	0.93	0.034	0.211	0.04	98.2	Bronze
242	Winged axe	Near Lake Como, Lombardy	85.0	7.98	0.48	1.20	0.014	0.127	0.553	0.149	0.66	0.028	0.181	0.18	96.6	Bronze
243	Winged axe	Near Lake Como, Lombardy	86.8	5.14	0.32	4.35	0.086	0.476	0.449	0.164	0.38	0.031	0.151	0.28	98.7	Leaded bronze
244	Knife	Near Lake Como, Lombardy	83.8	11.5	0.29	0.91	0.023	0.087	0.083	0.030	0.54	0.034	0.188	0.16	97.6	Bronze

Table 1 cont. Analyses of Italian Bronze Age/Iron Age metalwork

Cat.	Description (part analyzed)	Provenance	Cu	Sn	As	Pb	Zn	Fe	Ni	Co	Sb	Bi	Ag	S	Total	Alloy
Early Iron Age (early):																
280	Thickened arch fibula		Cu, Sn, tr.As, tr.Pb, tr.Sb, tr.Fe													Bronze
305	Thickened arch fibula		95.0	4.90	0.15	0.68	<0.01	0.045	0.110	0.025	0.15	0.006	0.070		101.1	*Bronze
310	Thickened arch fibula (body)		91.2	5.81	0.18	0.42	0.028	2.07	0.187	0.066	0.18	<0.03	0.063	0.17	100.3	Bronze
	(rings)		Cu, Sn, tr.As, tr.Sb, tr.Ni, tr.Fe													Bronze
316	Foliate arch fibula (body)	Near Rome, Lazio	Cu, Sn, tr.As, tr.Pb, tr.Sb, tr.Ni, tr.Fe, tr.Ag													Bronze
	(disc)		Cu, Sn, tr.As, tr.Pb, tr.Sb, tr.Ni, tr.Fe, tr.Ag													Bronze
	(rivets)		Cu, Sn, tr.As, tr.Pb, tr.Sb, tr.Ni, tr.Fe, tr.Ag													Bronze
	(ring)		Cu, Sn, tr.As, tr.Pb, tr.Sb, tr.Ni, tr.Fe, tr.Ag													Bronze
324	Serpentine fibula		92.0	7.20	0.15	0.70	0.007	0.12	0.160	0.050	0.25	0.004	0.150		100.8	*Bronze
325	Serpentine fibula		87.5	9.00	0.25	1.30	<0.01	0.05	0.180	0.035	0.33	0.002	0.190		98.8	*Bronze
326	Two piece serpentine fibula		89.5	8.70	0.30	0.48	0.040	0.06	0.110	0.005	0.35	0.015	0.210		99.8	*Bronze
330	Serpentine fibula		90.5	7.60	0.12	0.80	0.060	0.17	0.110	0.020	0.35	0.015	0.100		99.8	*Bronze
331	Serpentine fibula		94.5	4.20	0.18	1.00	<0.01	0.15	0.070	0.035	0.14	0.008	0.060		100.3	*Bronze
333	Serpentine fibula		92.0	6.80	0.27	0.40	0.300	0.27	0.035	0.008	0.15	0.013	0.075		100.3	*Bronze
339	Serpentine fibula		91.5	7.10	0.15	0.80	0.190	0.12	0.110	0.030	0.35	0.015	0.090		100.5	*Bronze
367	T-hilt sword (hilt)		93.7	5.93	0.12	0.75	<0.01	0.087	0.122	0.045	0.19	<0.01	0.055		100.9	Bronze
	(rivets)		Cu, Sn, tr.As, tr.Pb													Bronze
	(wire spirals)		Cu, Sn, tr.As, tr.Pb													Bronze
368	Sword sheath (sheath)		Cu, Sn, tr.As, tr.Pb, tr.Sb, tr.Ni, tr.Fe, tr.Ag													Bronze
	(terminal)		Cu, Sn, tr.As, tr.Pb, tr.Sb, tr.Ni, tr.Fe, tr.Ag													Bronze
370	Antennae sword (blade)		83.1	9.01	0.05	3.10	<0.01	0.082	0.010	0.031	0.04	0.011	0.026	0.28	95.7	Bronze
	(hilt)		86.1	10.3	0.14	0.74	<0.02	0.025	0.101	0.044	0.24	<0.02	0.055	0.18	97.9	Bronze
	(rivets)		Cu, Sn, tr.As, Pb, tr.Sb, tr.Ni, tr.Fe, tr.Ag													Bronze
398	Spearhead	Bovino, Apulia	93.9	3.39	0.10	1.34	0.045	1.49	0.068	0.064	0.05	<0.01	0.029	0.30	100.8	Bronze
399	Spear-butt	Bovino, Apulia	84.5	9.29	0.46	4.85	0.048	0.132	0.231	0.040	0.90	0.017	0.160	0.30	100.9	Leaded bronze
457	T-hilt sword (hilt)	'San Germano', Cassino, Lazio	90.2	6.72	0.15	1.79	0.043	0.862	0.095	0.057	0.07	<0.01	0.041	0.21	100.2	Bronze
	(rivet)		Cu, Sn, tr.As, tr.Pb, tr.Sb, tr.Ni, tr.Fe, tr.Ag													Bronze
458	Spearhead	'San Germano', Cassino, Lazio	86.1	10.8	0.39	1.43	0.342	0.147	0.056	0.012	0.35	0.022	0.097	0.20	99.9	Bronze
459	Spearhead	'San Germano', Cassino, Lazio	91.4	7.22	0.31	0.99	0.177	0.106	0.116	0.019	0.32	0.015	0.089	0.15	100.9	Bronze
Early Iron Age (late):																
466	Winged axe	Populonia, Tuscany	91.2	3.64	0.78	2.03	0.797	0.769	0.041	0.009	0.47	0.025	0.094	0.32	100.2	Bronze
491	Winged axe	Lake Trasimeno, Umbria	84.6	10.3	0.19	2.34	0.018	0.839	0.107	0.161	0.02	<0.02	0.023	0.21	98.8	Bronze
513	Socketed axe		86.0	5.63	1.17	1.93	0.131	0.066	0.079	0.022	0.54	0.028	0.089	0.32	96.0	Bronze
540	Pendant in the form of a horse		87.5	7.80	0.30	4.10	<0.01	0.13	0.060	<0.005	0.40	<0.01	0.065		100.4	*Leaded bronze
554	Leech fibula		Cu, Sn, tr.As, tr.Pb, tr.Sb, tr.Ni, tr.Fe, tr.Ag													Bronze
575	Hollow leech fibula	Orvieto, Umbria	Cu, Sn, tr.Pb, tr.Sb, tr.Ni, tr.Fe, tr.Ag													Bronze
750	Short sword (tang)	Acerra, Campania	90.0	7.54	0.17	0.53	0.086	0.007	0.054	0.005	0.15	0.034	0.133	0.27	99.0	Bronze
	(collar)		89.7	8.87	0.17	0.54	0.099	0.006	0.055	0.005	0.17	0.017	0.127	0.28	100.1	Bronze
799	Large spearhead	Bomarzo (Viterbo), Lazio	87.0	6.13	0.93	0.83	0.021	0.114	0.030	0.005	0.27	0.024	0.059	0.05	95.5	Bronze
800	Large spearhead (top of blade)	Bomarzo (Viterbo), Lazio	88.2	5.70	1.03	0.66	<0.01	0.030	0.022	0.004	0.29	0.024	0.063	0.05	96.0	Bronze
	(tip of blade)		88.4	5.90	1.07	0.61	<0.04	0.052	0.020	<0.007	0.29	0.052	0.064	0.06	96.4	Bronze
810	Finial with aquatic bird		90.0	7.50	0.55	2.00	0.110	0.04	0.095	0.005	0.50	0.010	0.090		100.9	*Bronze

Table 1 cont. Analyses of Italian Bronze Age/Iron Age metalwork

Early Iron Age (late) cont.:

Cat.	Description (part analyzed)	Provenance	Cu	Sn	As	Pb	Zn	Fe	Ni	Co	Sb	Bi	Ag	S	Total	Alloy
813	Band with inset birds		Bronze strip soldered to copper support													Bronze
814	Band with inset birds		Bronze strip soldered to copper support													Bronze
815	Band with inset bird		Bronze strip soldered to copper support													Bronze
816	Band with inset birds & coils		Bronze strip soldered to copper support													Bronze
817	C19th pastiche (lower disc)	Campania	Cu, tr. Sn, tr.As, Pb, tr. Zn, tr. Sb, tr. Ni, tr. Fe, tr. Ag													Low tin bronze
	(strip on lower disc)		Cu, Sn, tr.As, Pb, tr. Sb, tr. Ni, tr. Fe, tr. Ag													Bronze
	(mid bud)		Cu, tr. Sn, tr.As, tr. Pb, tr. Zn, tr. Sb, tr. Fe, tr. Ag													Bronze
	(lower bud)		Cu, Sn, tr.As, Pb, tr. Sb, tr. Fe, tr. Ag													Bronze
818	C19th pastiche (disc)	Campania	Cu, tr.As, tr. Pb, tr. Sb, tr. Ni, tr. Fe, tr. Ag, tr. Hg													Copper
	(strip)		Cu, Sn, tr.As, tr. Pb, tr. Sb, tr. Fe, tr. Ag, tr. Hg													Bronze
	(rivet)		Cu, Sn, tr.As, Pb, Zn, tr. Sb, tr. Fe, tr. Ag, tr. Hg													Gunmetal
	(oxen)		Cu, Sn, tr.As, tr. Pb, tr. Sb, tr. Fe, tr. Ag, tr. Hg													Bronze
	(pendant?)		Cu, Sn, tr.As, tr. Pb, tr. Sb, tr. Fe, tr. Ag, tr. Hg													Bronze
	(androgynous figure)		Cu, Sn, tr.As, Pb, tr. Sb, tr. Fe, tr. Ag, tr. Hg													Bronze
	(male figure)		Cu, Sn, tr.As, Pb, tr. Sb, tr. Fe, tr. Ag, tr. Hg													Bronze
	(bird)		Cu, Sn, tr.As, tr. Pb, tr. Zn, tr. Sb, tr. Fe, tr. Ag, tr. Hg													Bronze
820	Two seated figurines		66.5	8.90	0.45	24.3	0.080	0.05	0.020	0.003	0.27	0.005	0.070		100.7	*Heavily leaded bronze

Unclassified:

Cat.	Description (part analyzed)	Provenance	Cu	Sn	As	Pb	Zn	Fe	Ni	Co	Sb	Bi	Ag	S	Total	Alloy
823	Axe blade	Naples, Campania	92.4	3.10	1.52	1.22	0.013	0.388	0.078	0.009	0.03	0.011	0.035	0.15	98.8	Bronze
825	Axe blade?		100.0	<0.01	<0.01	<0.01	<0.01	<0.003	<0.003	<0.003	<0.01	<0.01	0.004	<0.01	100.0	Copper
827	Tip of chisel blade	Terni, Umbria	89.4	5.99	0.66	1.32	0.182	0.806	0.061	0.011	0.56	0.027	0.114	0.15	99.2	Bronze
830	Antennae sword		Cu, Sn, tr.As, Pb, Zn, tr. Sb, tr. Ni, tr. Fe, tr. Ag													Gunmetal

Notes

The quantitative analyses were carried out using inductively coupled plasma atomic emission spectrometry, ICP-AES, except for the older analyses marked '*' which were by atomic absorption spectophotometry, AAS. Bismuth was by AAS in all cases. X-ray fluorescence, XRF, was used for the qualitative analyses.

ICP-AES and AAS have a precision of approximately ±2% for copper and ±5-10% for tin and lead when present in amounts greater than 1%. The remaining minor and trace elements have a precision of ±10-30%, deteriorating to ±50% at their respective detection limits. The following elements were also looked for but not found above their detection limits: Mn (0.001), P (0.02), Cd (0.002), Au (0.004).

< denotes an element not present above the quoted detection limit.

Semi-quantitative ICP-AES analyses showed that the flat axe cat. no. 3 contains approximately 0.056% Selenium, 0.006% Tellurium and 0.0012% Vanadium.

Table 2: Summary statistics of analyses of Italian Bronze Age/Iron Age metalwork

	Sn	As	Pb	Zn	Fe	Ni	Co	Sb	Bi	Ag	S
CA (n=15)											
Mean	nd	nd	nd	nd	nd	0.010	nd	nd	nd	0.045	nd
Standard Deviation	nd	nd	nd	nd	nd	0.008	nd	nd	nd	0.033	nd
RSD %	nd	nd	nd	nd	nd	84.8	nd	nd	nd	73.2	nd
Minimum	0.01	0.01	0.005	0.007	0.002	0.002	0.002	0.005	0.005	0.005	0.007
Maximum	0.04	2.74	0.14	0.010	0.708	0.027	0.003	0.07	0.13	0.097	0.27
EBA (n=22)											
Mean	7.25	0.13	0.80	0.103	0.036	0.016	0.005	0.09	0.022	0.037	0.08
Standard Deviation	3.14	0.11	0.97	0.179	0.066	0.008	0.005	0.127	0.028	0.067	0.060
RSD %	43.3	87.2	120.8	174.5	184.6	50.3	105.2	143.3	128.8	178.3	76.0
Minimum	2.05	0.01	0.005	0.007	0.002	0.002	0.002	0.005	0.005	0.001	0.007
Maximum	14.9	0.47	4.09	0.727	0.261	0.031	0.016	0.61	0.131	0.316	0.23
MBA (n=7)											
Mean	7.40	0.19	0.40	0.016	0.106	0.134	0.018	0.11	0.017	0.043	0.21
Standard Deviation	1.15	0.27	0.52	0.016	0.097	0.189	0.018	0.119	0.013	0.044	0.121
RSD %	15.5	141.2	129.2	99.2	91.3	141.0	100.8	105.4	76.0	102.5	56.8
Minimum	5.70	0.03	0.005	0.007	0.005	0.015	0.002	0.005	0.005	0.002	0.066
Maximum	8.9	0.79	1.37	0.045	0.252	0.543	0.048	0.35	0.043	0.116	0.41
RBA (n=6)											
Mean	9.22	0.08	0.62	0.038	0.141	0.051	0.019	0.08	0.029	0.062	0.27
Standard Deviation	2.12	0.09	0.72	0.041	0.199	0.045	0.009	0.057	0.014	0.035	0.172
RSD %	23.0	105.5	115.0	106.8	140.8	87.2	47.6	68.4	50.6	57.3	64.5
Minimum	5.69	0.03	0.005	0.007	0.009	0.006	0.005	0.005	0.005	0.006	0.079
Maximum	11.2	0.26	2.03	0.093	0.522	0.128	0.029	0.16	0.044	0.102	0.48
FBA (n=10, except for sulphur, where n=7)											
Mean	7.85	0.29	1.33	0.027	0.175	0.219	0.070	0.33	0.018	0.132	0.17
Standard Deviation	1.97	0.21	1.26	0.030	0.153	0.235	0.060	0.298	0.013	0.056	0.084
RSD %	25.1	71.8	94.4	111.5	87.6	107.5	85.6	89.6	71.6	42.4	50.8
Minimum	5.14	0.01	0.01	0.007	0.017	0.031	0.010	0.020	0.004	0.060	0.041
Maximum	11.5	0.67	4.35	0.086	0.476	0.618	0.164	0.93	0.034	0.211	0.28
EIA - early (n=17, except for sulphur, where n=8)											
Mean	7.29	0.20	1.27	0.078	0.352	0.110	0.034	0.26	0.010	0.092	0.23
Standard Deviation	2.06	0.11	1.13	0.107	0.581	0.056	0.019	0.199	0.006	0.055	0.062
RSD %	28.3	53.3	88.9	138.0	165.0	50.9	54.1	76.4	59.1	59.7	27.6
Minimum	3.39	0.05	0.40	0.007	0.025	0.010	0.005	0.035	0.002	0.026	0.152
Maximum	10.8	0.46	4.85	0.342	2.075	0.231	0.066	0.90	0.022	0.210	0.30
EIA - late (n=11, except for sulphur, where n=8)											
Mean	7.08	0.62	3.63	0.124	0.191	0.053	0.020	0.31	0.021	0.080	0.20
Standard Deviation	1.89	0.39	6.94	0.228	0.306	0.030	0.047	0.161	0.015	0.032	0.122
RSD %	26.7	63.1	191.5	184.1	159.9	57.2	231.5	52.7	69.5	39.8	62.2
Minimum	3.64	0.17	0.53	0.007	0.006	0.020	0.002	0.018	0.005	0.023	0.051
Maximum	10.3	1.17	24.3	0.797	0.839	0.107	0.161	0.54	0.052	0.133	0.32

Notes

n = number of artefacts analysed. 15 items were analysed previously using atomic absorption, which cannot measure sulphur.

RSD % = relative standard deviation expressed as a percentage of the mean.

nd = value not determined, usually because of insufficient measurable data.

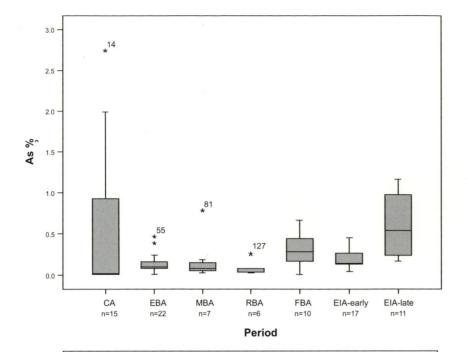

Figure 1 Box and whisker plot of arsenic content by period. (The 'box' represents the inter-quartile range (i.e. the middle 50% of values) and the thick horizontal line in each box represents the median value. The 'whiskers' extend from the quartiles to the observation not further than 1.5 times the inter-quartile range. Any values beyond this range are plotted as individual points).

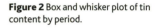

Figure 2 Box and whisker plot of tin content by period.

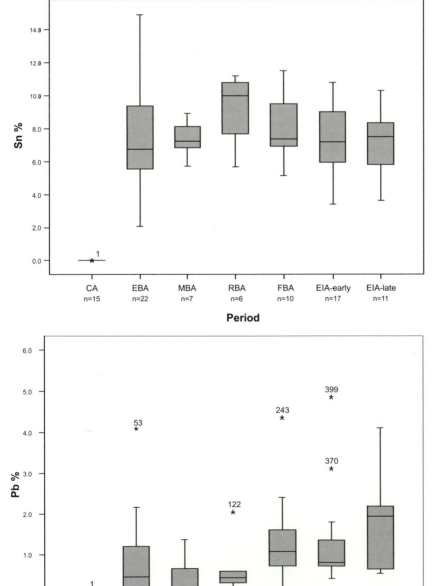

Figure 3 Box and whisker plot of lead content by period. (Note that one extreme value of 24.3% from the EIA – later period (**cat. 820**) has not been plotted).

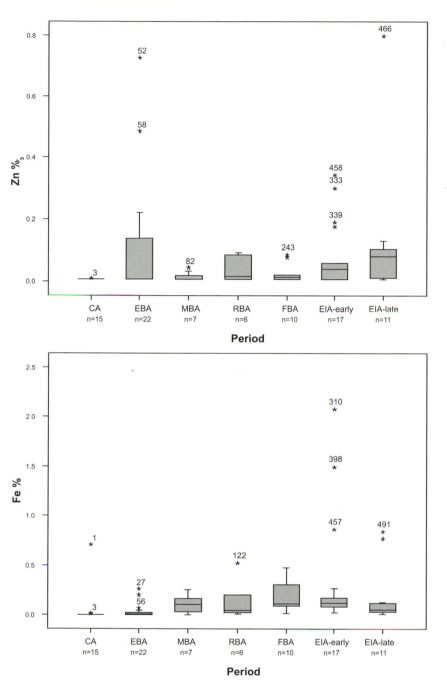

Figure 4 Box and whisker plot of zinc content by period.

Figure 5 Box and whisker plot of iron content by period.

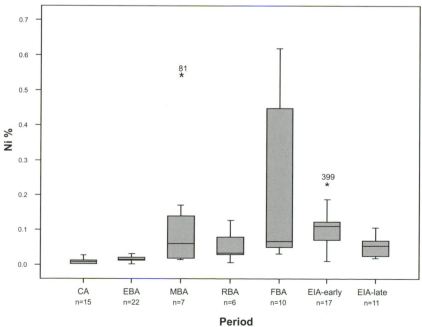

Figure 6 Box and whisker plot of nickel content by period.

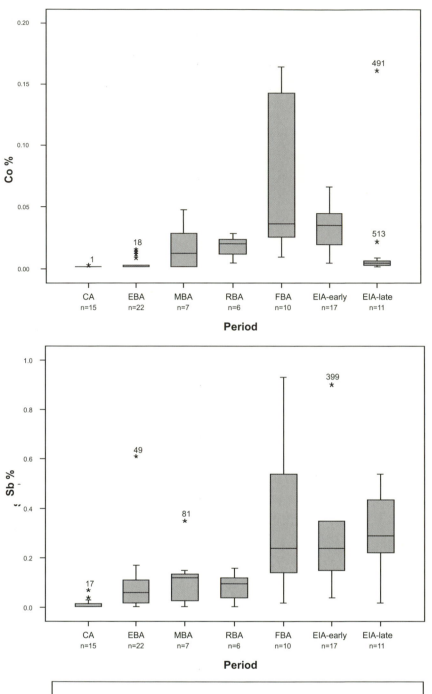

Figure 7 Box and whisker plot of cobalt content by period.

Figure 8 Box and whisker plot of antimony content by period.

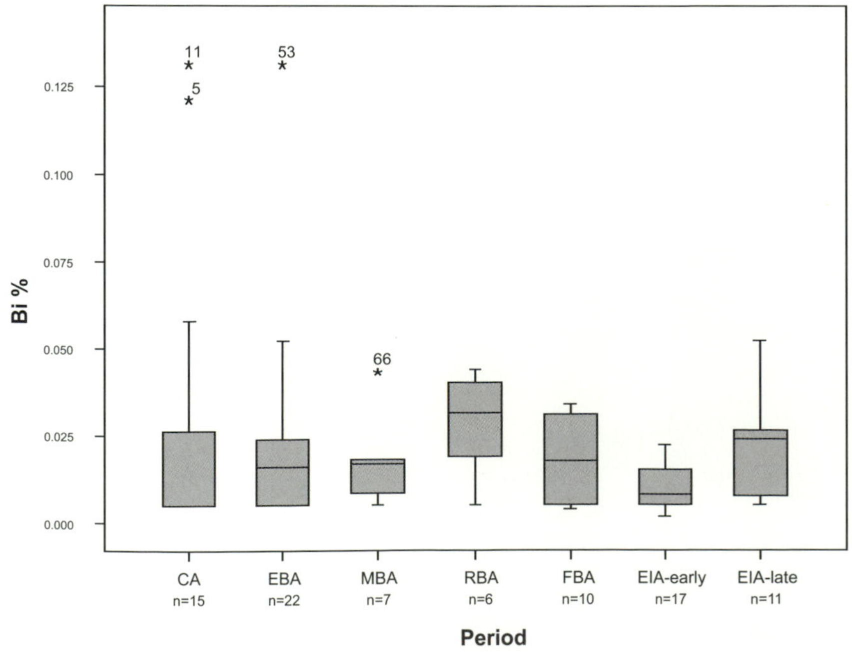

Figure 9 Box and whisker plot of bismuth content by period.

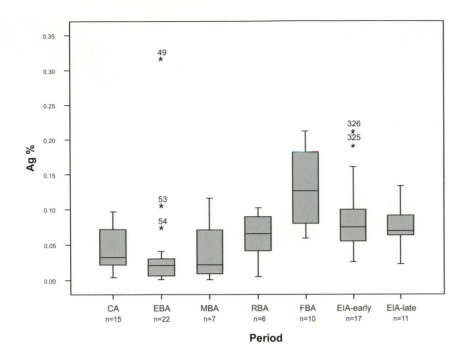

Figure 10 Box and whisker plot of silver content by period.

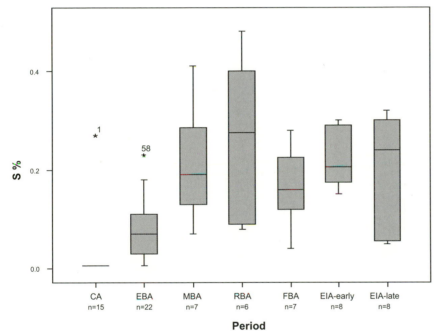

Figure 11 Box and whisker plot of sulphur content by period.

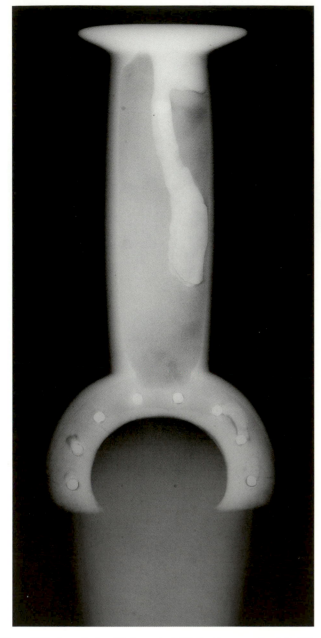

Figure 12 Radiograph of an EBA dagger (**cat**. **44**), showing a run of metal in hilt. (Horizontal field of view = *c*. 70mm).

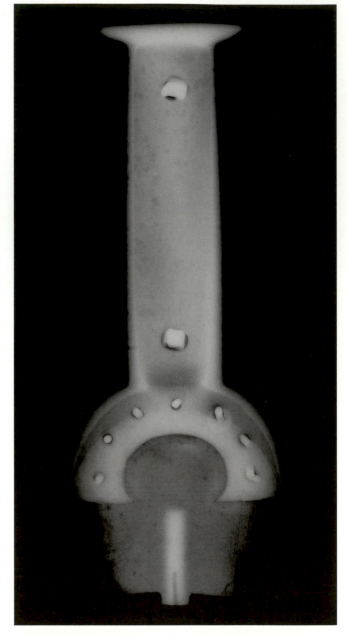

Figure 13 Radiograph of an EBA dagger (**cat**. **45**), showing the two large rivets in the hilt. The radiograph also shows the decoration at the top of the blade and also the hole drilled into the rib of the dagger as part of a modern repair. (Horizontal field of view = *c*. 72 mm).

Figure 15 Photomicrograph taken in the scanning electron microscope of the surface of an EBA dagger (**cat**. **60**) showing light coloured areas due to tinning. (Horizontal field of view = 5 mm).

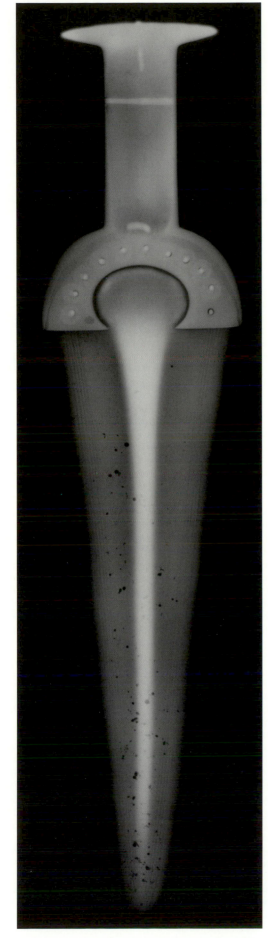

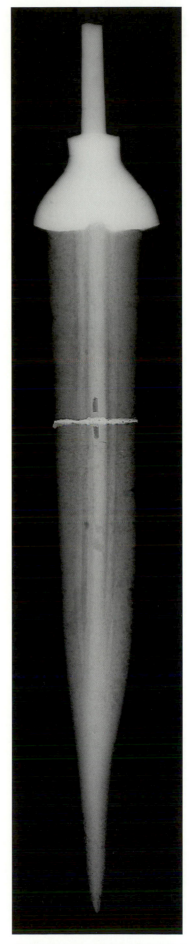

Figure 14: Radiograph of an EBA dagger (**cat. 46**), showing a bar and rivet in hilt. (Horizontal field of view = c. 90 mm)

Figure 16 Radiograph of an EIA (late) short sword (**cat. 750**), showing the join which runs across the upper part of the blade. The white areas along the join are indicative of the use of a lead-rich soft solder. The joint has been additionally strengthened by the insertion of a small peg between the two parts of the blade. (Horizontal field of view = c. 60 mm).

Bibliography

Under the Bibliography of individual objects, we have usually included only publications in which the object has been illustrated. Under the Comparanda of the objects, we have given the author's or editor's name with the date of publication, all to be found in the following bibliography. The exceptions to this rule are some frequently mentioned sites, including Osteria dell' Osa, Pontecagnano, Cuma, Pithekoussai, Torre Galli, and Quattro Fontanili at Veii.

This bibliography was completed in 2007 and includes authors cited in Duncan Hook's contribution.

Adam, A.M., 1984. *Bronzes Etrusques et Italiques*. Bibliothèque Nationale, Paris.

Adinolfi, R., 1988. *Cuma*. Marano.

Aigner Foresti, L., 1986. 'Su un arredo della Campania'. In Swaddling 1986: 37–41.

Albanese Procelli, R.M., 1993. *Ripostigli di bronzi della Sicilia nel Museo Archeologico di Siracusa*. Accademia Nazionale di Scienze, Lettere ed Arti, Palermo.

Albanese Procelli, R.M., 2003. 'La metallurgie du bronze en Sicile (Italie)'. In F. Lo Schiavo and A. Giumlia Mair (eds), *Le problème de l'étain à l'origine de la métallurgie*. Proceedings of the XIV UISPP Conference, Colloquium 11.2, Liège 2001: 139–45.

Albanese Procelli, R.M., 2005. 'Fasi e facies della prima età del Ferro in Sicilia: dati e problemi interpretativi'. In Bartoloni and Delpino 2005: 517–25.

Albore Livadie, C., 2002. 'A first Pompeii: the Early Bronze Age village of Nola-Croce del Papa (Palma Campania phase)'. *Antiquity* 76: 941–2.

Albore Livadie, C. and D'Amore, L., 1980. 'Palma Campania (Napoli). Resti di abitato dell'età del bronzo antico'. *Notizie Scavi*: 59–101.

Albore Livadie, C., Bietti Sestieri, A.M. and Marzocchella, A., 2004. 'Testimonianze del bronzo recente in Campania'. In D. Cocchi Genick (ed.), *L'età del bronzo recente in Italia*, Viareggio-Lucca: 481–90.

Ancona, A, 1886. *Le armi, le fibule e qualche altro cimelio della sua collezione archeologica*. Milan.

Anderson, J.K., 1961. *Ancient Greek Horsemanship*. University of California Press, Berkeley and Los Angeles.

Antonacci Sanpaolo, E. (ed.), 1992. *Archeometallurgia, ricerche e prospettive*. Atti del colloquio Internazionale di Archeometallurgia Bologna-Dozza Imolese 1989. Bologna.

Anzidei, A.P., Carboni, G., Catalano, P., Celant, A., Lemorini, C. and Musco, S., 2003. 'La necropoli eneolitica di Lunghezzina (Roma)'. In *Atti della XXXV Riunione Scientifica dell'Istituto Italiano di Preistoria e Protostoria*, Lipari 2000. Florence: 379–91.

Attema, P., De Haas, T. and Nijboer, A., 2003. 'The Astura project, interim report of the 2001 and 2002 campaigns of the Groningen Institute of Archaeology along the coast between Nettuno and Torre Astura (Lazio, Italy.)'. *Babesch* 78: 107–40.

Bailo Modesti, G., 1980. *Cairano nell'età arcaica. L'abitato e la necropoli*. Istituto Universitario Orientale, Naples.

Bailey, D.M., 1986. 'Charles Townley's *cista mystica*'. In Swaddling 1986: 131–41.

Barfield, L.H., 1969. 'Two Italian halberds and the question of the earliest European halberds'. *Origini* 3: 67–80.

Barker, G., 1971. 'The first metallurgy in Italy in the light of the metal analyses from the Pigorini Museum'. *Bullettino di Paletnologia Italiana, n.s.* XXII–80: 183–212.

Baroni, I., 2001. 'I livelli di occupazione dell'età del bronzo nel Giardino Romano: il Bronzo Recente'. *Bullettino dei Musei Comunali di Roma* 102: 291–8.

Bartoloni, G., 1986. 'Le urne a capanna: ancora sulle prime scoperte nei Colli Albani'. In Swaddling 1986: 235–48.

Bartoloni, G. and Delpino, F. (eds), 2005. *Oriente e Occidente: metodi e discipline a confronto. Riflessioni sulla cronologia dell'età del ferro italiana*. Pisa-Rome.

Bellintani, P. and Moser, L., 2003. *Archeologie Sperimentali. Metodologie ed esperienze fra verifica, riproduzione, comunicazione e simulazione*. Provincia Autonoma di Trento, Servizio Beni Archeologici. Trento.

Berlin 1988. Die Welt der Etrusker. Archäologische Denkmäler aus Museen der sozialistischen Länder. Staatliche Museen zu Berlin, Hauptstadt der DDR, Altes Museum. Berlin.

Bernabò Brea, L. and Cavalier, M., 1960. *Meligunis Lipara 1*. Flaccovoa. Palermo.

Bernabò Brea, L., Militello, E. and La Piana, S., 1969. 'Mineo (Catania). La necropoli detta del Molino della Badia: nuove tombe in contrada Madonna del Piano'. *Notizie Scavi*: 210–76.

Bietti Sestieri, A.M., 1973. 'The metal industry of continental Italy, 13th–11th century BC, and its Aegean connections'. *Proceedings of the Prehistoric Society* 39: 383–424.

Bietti Sestieri 1986, 'Fibulae' – see Bietti Sestieri 1986.

Bietti Sestieri 1986 'Weapons and Tools' – see Bietti Sestieri 1986.

Bietti Sestieri, A.M. 1986. 'Italian swords and fibulae of the late Bronze and early Iron Ages'. In Swaddling 1986: 3–23.

Bietti Sestieri, A.M., 1997. 'Italy in Europe in the Early Iron Age'. *Proceedings of the Prehistoric Society* 63: 371–402.

Bietti Sestieri, A.M., 2004. 'Groups of Copper, Bronze and Iron Age metal artifacts from the Italian collections in the British Museum'. *Accordia Research Papers* 9, 2001–3: 23–43.

Bietti Sestieri, A.M. and De Santis, A. 2003. 'Il processo formativo della cultura laziale'. In *Atti della XXXV Riunione Scientifica dell'Istituto Italiano di Preistoria e Protostoria*, Lipari 2000. Florence: 745–63.

Bietti Sestieri, A.M. and De Santis, A., 2007. 'Il Lazio antico fra Età del Bronzo Finale e Prima Età del Ferro: l'organizzazione politico-territoriale in relazione con il processo di formazione urbana'. In *Atti della XL Riunione Scientifica dell'Istituto Italiano di Preistoria e Protostoria*, Roma 2005. Florence.

Bietti Sestieri, A.M. and Giardino C., 2003. 'Alcuni dati sull'industria metallurgica in Abruzzo'. In *Preistoria e protostoria dell'Abruzzo, Atti della XXXVI Riunione Scientifica dell'Istituto Italiano di Preistoria e Protostoria,* Chieti-Celano 2001. Florence: 411–30.

Bietti Sestieri, A.M., Formigli, E. and Pacini, A., 2003. 'Esperimenti di riproduzione di strumenti, ornamenti e armi dell'età del bronzo e del ferro provenienti dal territorio dell'Abruzzo'. In Bellintani and Moser 2003: 283–90.

Bietti Sestieri, A.M., Giardino, C., Gigante, G.E., Guida, G. and Ridolfi, S., 2003. 'Primi risultati delle indagini non invasive mediante EDXRF sul ripostiglio di S. Francesco di Bologna'. In C. D'Amico (ed.) *Atti del Secondo Congresso Nazionale di Archeometria,* Bologna 2002. Bologna: 669–82.

BM Guide 1904. A Guide to the Antiquities of the Bronze Age in the Department of British and Mediaeval Antiquities. Trustees of the British Museum, Oxford.

BM Guide 1908. British Museum, Department of Greek and Roman Antiquities, A Guide to the Exhibition Illustrating Greek and Roman Life. Trustees of the British Museum, London. All the illustrations in this Guide of objects included in this catalogue are repeated in the 2nd edn, *BM Guide 1920.* All references to the relevant illustrations are taken from *BM Guide 1920.*

BM Guide 1920. British Museum, Department of Greek and Roman Antiquities, A Guide to the Exhibition illustrating Greek and Roman Life. Trustees of the British Museum, London (2nd edn).

BM Guide 1920a. A Guide to the Antiquities of the Bronze Age in the Department of British and Mediaeval Antiquities. Trustees of the British Museum, Oxford (2nd edn).

BM Guide 1929. British Museum, Department of Greek and Roman Antiquities, A Guide to the Exhibition Illustrating Greek and Roman Life. Trustees of the British Museum, London (3rd edn). Only three illustrations in this Guide of objects included in this Catalogue appear in *BM Guide 1929.* References to the relevant illustrations are taken from *BM Guide 1920.*

Bologna 2000. Principi etruschi tra Mediterraneo ed Europa. Bologna, Museo Civico, 2000.

Bonghi Jovino, M. and Chiaromonte Trere, C. , 1997. *Tarquinia. Testimonianze archeologiche e ricostruzione storica. Scavi sistematici nell'abitato, campagne 1982–88.* Rome.

Boucher, S., 1970. *Bronzes grecs, hellénistiques et étrusques (sardes, ibériques et celtiques) des Musées de Lyon.* Collections des Musées de Lyon 9. Lyon.

Brailsford, J.W., 1953. *Later Prehistoric Antiquities of the British Isles.* Trustees of the British Museum, London.

Brizio, E., 1894. 'Verucchio, Spadarolo e Rimini'. *Notizie Scavi*: 292–309.

Brown, A.C., 1980. *Ancient Italy before the Romans.* Ashmolean Museum, Oxford.

Buffa, V., 1994. '1.6, Torre del Mordillo (Spezzano Albanese). 1.6.3 Necropoli'. In R. Peroni and F. Trucco (eds), *Enotri e Micenei* ll-*Altri siti della Sibaritide.* Taranto: 737–55.

Burn, L. (ed.), 1997. 'Sir William Hamilton, collector and connoisseur'. *Journal of the History of Collections* 9.2: 187–303.

Camporeale, G., 1967. *La Tomba del Duce.* Florence.

Camporeale, G., 1969. 'I commerci di Vetulonia in età orientalizzante'. *Studi e Materiali dell'Istituto di Etruscologia e Antichità Italiche dell'Università di Roma* 7. Florence.

Caneva, C., Giardino, C. and Guida, G., 2003. 'Interpretative limit evaluation in compositional studies of protohistoric bronzes'. In *Archaeometallurgy in Europe (Milan, Sept. 2003)*: 303–10.

Carancini, G.L., 1991–92. 'L'Italia centro-meridionale'. In 'L'età del bronzo in Italia nei secoli dal XVI al XIV a.C'. *Rassegna di Archeologia* 10: 235–54.

Carancini, G.L., 1993. 'Primi sviluppi della metallurgia nell'area medio-tirrenica nel quadro della protostoria peninsulare'. In *Vulcano a Mezzano. Insediamento e produzione artigianale nella media valle del Fiora durante l'età del bronzo.* Valentano: 125–55.

Carancini, G.L., 1999. 'La valle del Fiora a l'area metallurgica tosco–laziale dall' età del rame all' età del ferro'. In *Atti del convegno Ferrante rittatore Vonwiller e la Maremma, 1936–76.* Ischia di Castro: 29–42.

Carancini, G.L. and Peroni, R., 1999. *L'età del bronzo in Italia: per una cronologia della produzione metallurgica.* Ali&no, Perugia.

Cateni, G., 1997. 'Limone (Livorno)'. In A. Zanini (ed.), *Dal bronzo al ferro. Il II millennio a.C. nella Toscana centro-occidentale.* Pacini editore, Ospedaletto, Pisa: 206–18.

Catling, H.W., 1956. 'Bronze cut and thrust swords in the Eastern Mediterranean'. *Proceedings of the Prehistoric Society* 22: 102–25.

Catling, H.W., 1961. 'A new bronze sword from Cyprus'. *Antiquity* 35: 115–22.

Catling, H.W., 1968. 'Late Minoan vases and bronzes in Oxford'. *Annual of the British School of Archaeology at Athens* 63: 89–131.

Caygill, M. and Cherry, J. (eds), 1997. *A.W. Franks. Nineteenth-century Collecting and the British Museum.* British Museum Press, London.

Cazzella, A., 2000. 'Sicilia e Malta durante l'Età del Rame'. *Sicilia Archeologica* 33, fasc. 98: 87–96.

Cazzella, A. and Moscoloni, M., 1998. 'Coppa Nevigata'. In A. Cinquepalmi and F. Radina (eds), *Documenti dell'età del bronzo.* Fasano di Brindisi: 29–43.

Cazzella, A. and Silvestrini, M. , 2005. 'L'eneolitico delle Marche nel contesto degli sviluppi culturali dell'Italia centrale'. In *Atti della XXXVIII Riunione Scientifica dell'Istituto Italiano di Preistoria e Protostoria*, Portonovo 2003. Florence: 379–91.

Cerchiai, L., 2002. 'Le fibule da parata di Capua e Suessula'. In Pietropaolo 2002: 143–7.

Cerveteri–Sorbo 1972. I. Pohl, *The Iron Age necropolis of Sorbo at Cerveteri.* Stockholm.

Cline, E.H., 1994. *Sailing the wine-dark sea. International trade and the Late Bronze Age Aegean.* British Archaeological Reports. International Series 591. Tempus Reparatum, Oxford.

Close-Brooks, J., 1967. 'A Villanovan belt from Euboea'. *Bulletin of the Institute of Classical Studies* 14: 22–4.

Close-Brooks, J. and Coles, J.M. 1980. 'Tinned axes', *Antiquity*, 54, 228–9.

Colini, G.A., 1898. 'Il sepolcreto di Remedello Sotto nel bresciano e il periodo eneolitico in Italia'. *Bullettino di Paletnologia Italiana*: 24–7.

Colucci Pescatori, G., 1971. I. 'Bisaccia (Avellino). Materiale sporadico'. *Notizie Scavi*: 476–80.

Colucci Pescatori, G., 1971. II. 'Cairano (Avellino). Tombe dell'età del ferro'. *Notizie Scavi*: 481–537.

Comstock, M. and Vermeule, C., 1971. *Greek, Etruscan and Roman Bronzes in the Museum of Fine Arts, Boston.* Meriden, Connecticut.

Cook, B.F., 1985. The Townley Marbles. British Museum Press, London.

Cowell, M.R. 1998. 'Coin analysis by energy dispersive X-ray fluorescence spectrometry'. In W.A. Oddy and M.R. Cowell (eds), *Metallurgy in Numismatics*, vol. 4, Royal Numismatic Society, London: 448–60.

Craddock, P.T. 1976. 'The composition of the copper alloys used by the Greek, Etruscan and Roman civilisations. 1. The Greeks before the Archaic Period', *Journal of Archaeological Science* 3, 2: 93–113.

Craddock, P.T. 1977. 'The composition of the copper alloys used by the Greek, Etruscan and Roman civilisations. 2. The Archaic, Classical and Hellenistic Greeks'. *Journal of Archaeological Science* 4, 2: 103–23.

Craddock, P.T. 1979. 'Deliberate alloying in the Atlantic Bronze Age'. In M. Ryan (ed.) *The Origins of Metallurgy in Atlantic Europe.* The Stationery Office, Dublin, 369–85 + microfiche.

Craddock, P.T., 1986a. 'The metallurgy of Italic and Sardinian bronzes'. In Swaddling 1986: 143–50.

Craddock, P.T. 1986b. 'The metallurgy and composition of Etruscan bronze', *Studi Etruschi* 52: 211–71.

Craddock, P.T. and Burnett, A.M. 1998. 'The composition of Etruscan and Umbrian copper alloy coinage'. In W.A. Oddy and M.R. Cowell (eds), *Metallurgy in Numismatics*, vol. 4. Royal Numismatic Society, London: 262–75.

Craddock, P.T. and Meeks, N.D. 1987. 'Iron in ancient copper'. *Archaeometry* 29, 2: 187–204.

Cuma 1903. Pellegrini, G., 'Tombe greche arcaiche e tomba greco-sannitica a tholos della necropoli di Cuma'. *Monumenti Antichi dei Lincei* 13: cols. 201–94.

Cuma 1913. Gabrici, E., 'Cuma'. *Monumenti Antichi dei Lincei* 22: cols. 5–766.

D'Agostino, B., 1964. 'Oliveto Citra. Necropoli arcaica in località Turni'. *Notizie Scavi*: 40–99.

D'Agostino, B., 1970. 'Tombe della prima età del ferro a S. Marzano sul Sarno'. *Mélanges de l'Ecole Française de Rome* 82: 571–619.

Davies, O., 1935. *Roman Mines in Europe.* Oxford.

De Gregorio, A., 1917. *Iconografia delle collezioni preistoriche della Sicilia.* Palermo.

De la Genière, J., 1968. *Recherches sur L' Age du Fer en Italie Méridionale. Sala Consilina.* Bibliothèque de L'Institut Français de Naples. Deuxième série vol. 1. Publications du Centre Jean Berard I. Naples.

De la Genière, J., 1992. 'Greci e indigeni in Calabria'. *Atti e Memorie Società Magna Grecia*, s.III: 111–20.

Delpino, F., 1977. 'La prima età del ferro a Bisenzio. Aspetti della cultura villanoviana nell'Etruria meridionale interna'. *Memorie Accademia dei Lincei*, s. 8, vol. 21, fasc. 6: 453–93.

Delpino, F., 1997. 'Fra Gabbro e Colognole (Rosignano Marittimo, Livorno)'. In A. Zanini (ed.), *Dal bronzo al ferro. Il II millennio a.C. nella Toscana centro-occidentale.* Pacini editore, Ospedaletto, Pisa: 201–5.

D'Ercole, V., 1998. 'La necropolis dell'età del bronzo finale delle Paludi di Celano'. In V. D'Ercole and R. Cairoli (eds), *Archeologia in Abruzzo.* Arethusa, Tarquinia: 157–66.

d'Hancarville, Manuscript Catalogue of Hamilton Collection. The British Museum, Department of Greek and Roman Antiquities Library, 2 vols, 1778.

De Marinis, R.C., 1975. 'Ripostiglio dell'antica età del bronzo dal Lodigiano'. *Bollettino del Centro Camuno di Studi Preistorici* 12: 61–83.

De Marinis, R.C., 1992. 'La più antica metallurgia nell'Italia settentrionale'. In F. Höpfel, W. Platzer and K. Spindler (eds), *Der Mann im Eis*, Band 1. Bericht über das Internationale Symposium 1992, Innsbruck: 389–409.

De Marinis, R.C., 1998. 'The eneolithic cemetery of Remedello Sotto (Brescia) and the relative and absolute chronology of the Copper Age in northern Italy'. *Notizie Archeologiche Bergomensi* 5: 33–51.

De Marinis, R.C., 1999. 'Towards a Relative and Absolute Chronology of the Bronze Age in Northern Italy'. *Notizie Archeologiche Bergomensi* 7: 23–100.

De Marinis, R.C., 2001. 'Aspetti della metallurgia dell'antica età del bronzo in Toscana'. In *Atti della XXXIV Riunione Scientifica dell'Istituto Italiano di Preistoria e Protostoria,* Firenze 1999. Florence: 253–81.

De Marinis, R.C., 2005. 'Evolution et variation de la composition chimique des objects en métal aux ages du cuivre et du bronze ancien dans l'Italie septentrionale'. *Mémoire 37 de la Société Préhistorique française*: 249–64.

Deshayes, J., 1960. *Les outils de bronze de l'Indus au Danube (IVe au IIe millénaire).* Paris.

Di Stefano, G. and Giardino, C., 1994. 'Il ripostiglio di bronzi in contrada

Castelluccio sull'Irmino'. *Notizie Scavi*: 489–546.

Dizionari Terminologici 1980. *Dizionari Terminologici. Materiali dell'età del bronzo finale e della I età del ferro*. Istituto Centrale per il Catalogo e la Documentazione, Ministero BAC, Rome.

Dohan, E.H. 1942. *Italic Tomb-groups in the University Museum*. University of Pennsylvania Press, Philadelphia, London and Oxford.

Egg, M. 1992. 'Die Ausruestung des Toten'. In M. Egg, R. Goedecker-Ciolek, W. Groenman-van Waatering and K. Spindler (eds), *Die Gletschermumie vom ende der steinzeit aus dem Ötztaler Alpen*. Jahrbuch des Römisch-Germanischen Zentralmuseum Mainz 39.

Falconi Amorelli, M.T., 1969. 'Corredi di tre tombe rinvenute a Vulci nella necropoli di Mandriane di Cavalupo'. *Studi Etruschi* 37: 181–211.

Formigli, E. (ed.), 2003. *Fibulae, dall'età del bronzo all'alto Medioevo. Tecnica e tipologia*. Edizioni Polistampa, Florence.

Frasca, M., 1992. 'Tra Magna Grecia e Sicilia: Origine e Sopravvivenza delle coppie-amuleto a figura umana'. *Bolletino d'Arte* 76: 19–24.

Freidin, N., 1980. 'A bronze cult-wagon from Lezoux (Puy-de-Dome) in the Ashmolean Museum, Oxford'. *Antiquaries Journal* 60: 320–7.

Fugazzola Delpino, M.A.,1984. *La cultura villanoviana. Guida ai materiali della prima età del Ferro nel museo di Villa Giulia*. Rome.

Gambari, F.M., 1997. 'L'Italia nord-occidentale nell'età del bronzo media e recente'. In *Terramare* 1997: 441–4.

Garagnani, G.L., Imbeni,V. and Martini, C., 1997. 'Analisi chimiche e microstrutturali di manufatti in rame e bronzo dalle Terramare'. In *Terramare* 1997: 554–66.

Garrucci, R., 1867. 'Remarks on a bronze object found at Lucera' (translation by W.M. Wylie). *Archaeologia* 41/2: 275–82.

Gastaldi, P., 1979. 'Le necropoli protostoriche della Valle del Sarno: proposta per una suddivisione in fasi'. *Annali dell'Istituto Orientale di Napoli, Sez. Archeologia e Storia Antica* I: 13–55.

Gerhard, E., 1830. 'Sformate immagini di bronzo'. *Bullettino dell'Istituto di Corrispondenza Archeologica*: 11–6.

Gerhard, E., 1840. *Etruskische Spiegel*, vol. I. Berlin (reprint 1966, Rome).

Giardino, C., 1985. 'Il ripostiglio di Nemi'. *Documenta Albana*, serie II, n. 7: 7–15. Museo Civico Albano.

Giardino, C., 1994. 'Bronzi protostorici dalla Sibaritide conservati presso il British Museum'. In R. Peroni and F. Trucco (eds), *Enotri e Micenei nella Sibaritide*. Taranto, II: 779–82.

Giardino, C., 1995. *Il Mediterraneo occidentale fra XIV e VIII sec.a.C. Cerchie minerarie e metallurgiche. The West Mediterranean between the 14th and 8th Centuries BC. Mining and Metallurgical spheres*. British Archaeological Reports. International Series 612. Tempus Reparatum, Oxford.

Giardino, C., 2000. 'The beginning of metallurgy in Tyrrhenian south-central Italy: the Eneolithic facies of Gaudo'. In D. Ridgway, F.R. Serra Ridgway, M. Pearce, E. Herring, R.D. Whitehouse and J.B. Wilkins (eds), *Ancient Italy in its Mediterranean setting. Studies in Honour of Ellen Macnamara*. London: 49–65.

Giardino, C., 2001. 'Mediterraneo occidentale, medio Tirreno, Egeo: attività metallurgiche e traffici nella prima metà del II millennio'. In C. Giardino (ed.) *Culture marinare nel Mediterraneo centrale e occidentale fra il XVII e il XV secolo a.C.* Rome: 339–66.

Giardino, C. and Lo Schiavo, F. (eds), forthcoming. *I ripostigli sardi algheresi della tarda età nuragica*.

Gierow, P.G., 1966. *The Iron Age Culture of Latium*, I, *Classification and Analysis*. Gleerup, Lund.

Giuliani Pomes, M.V., 1954. 'Cronologia delle situle rinvenute in Etruria'. *Studi Etruschi* 23: 149–94.

Giumlia-Mair, A. 1998. 'Iron Age metal workshops in the eastern Alpine area'. In *Metallurgica Antiqua – In honour of Hans-Gert Bachmann and Robert Maddin*. Der Anschnitt, Beiheft 8. Bochum: 45–55.

Giumlia-Mair, A., 2003. 'Evoluzione e tecnica formale nella produzione di fibule e spilloni tra il IX e il IV sec. a.C. nell'area alpino-orientale'. In Formigli 2003: 49–58.

Greenwell, W., 1902. 'On some rare forms of bronze weapons and implements'. *Archaeologia* 58: 1–16.

Gregory, E. 1932. *Metallurgy*. Blackie, London: 232.

Hammond, N.G.L., 1967. *Epirus*. Oxford.

Hanfmann, G.M.A., 1936. *Altetruskische Plastik I*. Wurzburg.

Hanfmann, G.M.A., 1937. 'The Origin of Etruscan Sculpture'. *Critica d'Arte* 2: 158–66.

Harden, D.B., 1981. *Catalogue of Greek and Roman Glass in the British Museum*, vol. I. British Museum Publications, London.

Harding, A. F., 1973. 'Prehistoric bronzes in the Department of Prehistoric and Romano-British Antiquities'. *British Museum Quarterly* 37: 140–4.

Harding, A. F., 1975. 'Mycenaean Greece and Europe: the evidence of bronze tools and implements'. *Proceedings of the Prehistoric Society* 41: 183–202.

Hawkes, C.F.C., 1938. 'Sicilian bronze axe from near Hengistbury Head'. *Antiquity* 12: 225–8.

Haynes, S., 1985. *Etruscan Bronzes*. London.

Hencken, H., 1956. 'Carp's tongue swords in Spain, France and Italy'. *Zephyrus* 7: 125–78.

Hencken, H., 1968. *Tarquinia, Villanovans and early Etruscans*. Cambridge, Mass.

Hencken, H., 1971. *The Earliest European Helmets*. American School of Prehistoric Research, Peabody Museum, Harvard University Bulletin 28.

Hennig, H., 1995. 'Zur Frage der Datierung des Grabhügels 8 "Hexemberh" von Wehringen, Lkr. Augsburg, Bayerisch-Schwaben'. In *Trans-Europa, Festschrift M.Primas*. Bonn: 129–45.

Herrmann, H.V., 1984. 'Altitalisches und Etruskisches in Olympia'. *Annuario della Scuola Archeologica di Atene e delle Missioni Italiane in Oriente* 61: 271–94.

Hill, D.K., 1956. 'Other geometric objects in Baltimore'. *American Journal of Archaeology* 60:35–42.

Hill, S., *Catalogue of the Archives of Charles Townley in the British Museum*, British Museum Occasional Paper 138, London 2001.

Hook, D.R., 1998. 'Inductively coupled plasma atomic emission spectrometry and its rôle in numismatic studies'. In W.A. Oddy and M.R. Cowell (eds), *Metallurgy in Numismatics*, vol. 4, Royal Numismatic Society, London: 237–52.

Hook, D.R., 2003. 'The composition and technology of early copper-alloy metalwork from Italy'. *Proceedings of the Archaeometallurgy in Europe Conference*. Milan, (AIM), vol. 2: 57–66.

Hook, D.R., 2005. 'The composition and technology of Italian Bronze Age and Early Iron Age copper-alloy metalwork'. In H. Kars and E. Burke (eds), *Proceedings of the 33rd International Symposium on Archaeometry, April 2002, Amsterdam*. Vrije Universiteit, Amsterdam: 347–50.

Hook, D.R. and Craddock, P.T., 1996. 'The scientific analysis of the copper alloy lamps: aspects of Classical alloying practices'. In D. Bailey *Catalogue of the Lamps in the British Museum, vol. 4: Lamps of Metal and the Lampstands,* British Museum Press, London: 144–63.

Hook, D.R., Arribas Palau, A., Craddock, P.T., Molina, F. and Rothenberg, B. 1987. 'Copper and silver in Bronze Age Spain'. In W.H. Waldren and R.C. Kennard (eds), *Bell Beakers of the Western Mediterranean: Definition, Interpretation, Theory and new Site Data*. The Oxford International Conference, 1986, pt I. BAR International Series, Oxford: 147–72.

Hughes, M.J, Cowell, M.R and Craddock, P.T., 1976. 'Atomic absorption techniques in Archaeology'. *Archaeometry*, 18: 19–37.

Hull, M.R. and Hawkes, C.F.C., 1987. *Corpus of Ancient Brooches in Britain. Pre-Roman Bow Brooches*. British Archaeological Reports. British Series 168. Oxford.

Inventaria Archaeologica 1967. Peroni, R., *Il ripostiglio di Ardea. Ripostigli delle età dei Metalli, Italia, Fascicolo 4*. Sansoni, Florence.

Jacobsthal, P., 1944 (reprint 1949). *Early Celtic Art*. Oxford.

Jenkins, I. and Sloan, K., 1996. *Vases and Volcanoes. Sir William Hamilton and his Collection*. British Museum Press, London.

Johannowsky, W., 1983. 'Materiali di età arcaica dalla Campania'. *Monumenti Antichi della Magna Grecia 4*. Macchiaroli, Naples.

Johannowsky, W., 1994. 'Appunti sulla cultura di Capua nella prima eta di ferro'. In *La Presenza Etrusca nella Campania meridionale*. Atti delle Giornate di Studio Salerno-Pontecagnano 1990. Istituto Nazionale di Studi Etruschi e Italici. Biblioteca di Studi Etruschi. Florence, 28: 83–109.

Junghans, S., Sangmeister, E., and Schröder, M., 1960. *Studien zu den Anfängen der Metallurgie*. Metallanalysen kupferzeitlicher und frühbronzezeitlicher Bodefunde aus Europa, 1. Berlin.

Junghans, S., Sangmeister, E. , and Schröder, M., 1968 and 1974. 'Kupfer und Bronze in der frühen Metallzeit Europas', *Studien zu den Anfängen der Metallurgie*, band 2. Gebr Mann Verlag, Berlin.

Jurgeit, F., 1999. *Die etruskischen und italischen Bronzen sowie Gegenstände aus Eisen, Blie und Leder im Badischen Landesmuseum Karlsruhe*. Pisa-Rome.

Kemble, J.M., 1855. 'Sepulchral objects from Italy, Styria and Mecklenburgh'. *Archaeologia* 36: 349–69.

Kilian, K., 1966. 'Testimonianze di vita religiosa della prima età del ferro in Italia meridionale'. *Rendiconti Accademia Napoletana di Archeologia, Lettere e Belle Arti*, Naples, 41: 91–106.

Kilian, K., 1970. 'Früheisenzeitliche Funde aus der Südostnecropole von Sala Consilina. (Provinz Salerno)'. *Römische Mitteilungen, Erganzungsheft* 15.

Kilian, K., 1977a. 'Zwei italische Kammhelme aus Griechenland'. *Bulletin de Correspondence Hellénique*, suppl. 4: 429–42.

Kilian, K., 1977b. 'Das Kriegergrab aus Tarquinia'. *Jahrbuch des deutschen archäologischen Instituts* 92: 24–98.

Kinnes, I. A., Needham, S.P., Craddock, P.T. and Lang, J. 1979. 'Tin-plating in the Early Bronze Age: the Barton Stacey axe'. *Antiquity*, 53: 141–3.

Klemm, G., 1854. *Werkzeuge und Waffen*. Leipzig.

Kossack, G., 1950. 'Uber italische Cinturoni'. *Prähistorische Zeitschrift* 34/5, 1949/50: 132–47.

Lang, J. and Middleton, A.P. 2005. *Radiography of Cultural Material*. 2nd edn, Butterworth-Heinemann, Oxford.

La Rocca, E., 1978. 'Crateri di argilla figulina del Geometrico Recente a Vulci'. *Mélanges de l'Ecole Française de Rome* 90/2: 465–514.

Le Fèvre-Lehöerff, A., 1999. 'La fabrication des fibules en Italie centrale entre le xii et le viii siècle avant notre ère'. In M. Pernot and C. Rolley (eds), *Techniques antiques du bronze 2, méthodes d'étude-procédées de fabrication*. Centre de recherches sur les techniques gréco-romaines n. 15. Dijon: 45–78.

Lilliu, G., 1966. *Sculture della Sardegna nuragica*. Verona.

Loftus-Hills, G. and Solomon, M. 1967. 'Cobalt, nickel and selenium in sulphides as indicators of ore genesis'. *Mineralium Deposita*, 2: 226–42.

Lo Porto, F.G., 1969. 'Metaponto. Tombe a tumulo dell' età del ferro scoperte nel suo entroterra'. *Notizie Scavi*: 121–70.

Lo Schiavo, F., 1984. 'La Daunia e l'Adriatico'. *Atti del XIII Convegno di Studi Etruschi e Italici,* Manfredonia 1980. Florence: 213–47.

Lo Schiavo, F., 1988. 'Il ripostiglio di Chilivani (Ozieri, Sassari)'. *Quaderni della Soprintendenza Archeologica per le province di Cagliari e Oristano* 5: 77–90.

Lo Schiavo, F., 1996. 'Miniere e metallurgia in Sardegna: la ricerca archeologica dal presente al passato'. In Piola Caselli and Piana Agostinetti 1996: 187–206.

Lo Schiavo, F. 2003. 'Le fibule di bronzo dell'Italia meridionale e della Sicilia, dalle origini al vi sec. a.C. Materiali e tecnica'. In Formigli 2003: 19–39.

Lo Schiavo, F. (ed.), forthcoming. *Archeometallurgia in Sardegna dalle origini alla I Età del Ferro.*

Lo Schiavo, F. and Peroni, R., 1979. 'Il bronzo finale in Calabria'. In *Atti della XXI Riunione Scientifica dell'Istituto Italiano di Preistoria e Protostoria: L'Età del Bronzo Finale in Italia,* Firenze 1977. Florence: 551–69.

Lo Schiavo, F., Macnamara, E. and Vagnetti, L., 1985. 'Late Cypriot imports to Italy and their influence on local bronzework'. *Papers of the British School at Rome* 53: 1–71.

Lo Schiavo, F., Albanese Procelli, R.M. and Giumlia Mair, A., 2002. 'La produzione e la tecnologia metallurgica a Madonna del Piano (Mineo, Catania)'. In A. Giumlia Mair, (ed.), *I bronzi antichi: produzione e tecnologia*. Editions Monique Mergoil, Montagnac: 76–88.

Lubritto, C., *et al.* 2003, in press. 'Accelerator Mass Spectrometry dating of archaeological samples from Nola area (Naples, Campania)'. *Proceedings of the International Conference of Archaeometry, CMPCA, Bordeaux.*

MacGregor, A. 1985. *Bone, Antler, Ivory and Horn. The Technology of Skeletal Materials since the Roman Period*. Croom Helm, London.

Macnamara, E., 1970. 'A group of bronzes from Surbo, Italy: new evidence for Aegean contacts with Apulia during Mycenaean IIIB and C'. *Proceedings of the Prehistoric Society* 36: 241–60.

Macnamara, E., 1990. *The Etruscans*. British Museum Publications, London.

Macnamara, E., 2002. 'Some bronze typologies in Sardinia and Italy from 1200 to 700 BC. Their origin and development'. In *Etruria e Sardegna Centro-Settentrionale tra l'Età del Bronzo Finale e l'Arcaismo. Atti del XXI Convegno di Studi Etruschi ed Italici,* Sassari, Alghero, Oristano, Torralba. Florence: 151–74.

Macnamara, E., Ridgway, D. and Serra Ridgway, F.R., 1984. *The Bronze Hoard from S. Maria in Paulis, Sardinia*. British Museum Occasional Paper, no. 45, London.

Maggi, R. and Pearce, M., 2005. 'Mid fourth-millennium copper mining in Liguria, north-west Italy: the earliest known copper mines in Western Europe'. *Antiquity*: 79, no. 303: 66–77.

Marshall, F.H., 1911. *Catalogue of the Jewellery, Greek, Etruscan and Roman, in the Department of Antiquities, British Museum*. Trustees of the British Museum, Oxford.

Martinelli, M.C. (ed.), 2005. *Il villaggio dell'età del Bronzo medio di Portella a Salina nelle isole Eolie*. Origines, Istituto Italiano di Preistoria e Protostoria, Florence.

Maryon, H., 1938. 'Some prehistoric metalworkers' tools'. *Antiquaries Journal* 18: 243–50.

Marzatico, F., 2001. 'L'età del bronzo recente e finale'. In M. Lanzinger, F. Marzatico and M.L. Pedrotti, *Storia del Trentino, vol. I, La Preistoria e la Protostoria*. Il Mulino, Bologna: 367–416.

Marzocchella, A., 2004. 'Dal Bronzo Finale all'Età del Ferro: nuove testimonianze dalla Campania'. In *Atti della XXXVII Riunione Scientifica dell'Istituto Italiano di Preistoria e Protostoria,* Calabria 2002. Florence: 616–20.

Matthäus, H., 1980. 'Italien und Griechenland in der ausgehenden Bronzezeit'. *Jahrbuch des Deutschen archäologischen Instituts* 95: 109–39.

Maxwell-Hyslop, R., 1953. 'Bronze lugged axe or adze blades from Asia'. *Iraq* 15: 69–87.

McKerrell, H. and Tylecote, R.F., 1972. 'The working of copper-arsenic alloys in the Early Bronze Age and the effect on the determination of provenance'. *Proceedings of the Prehistoric Society*, 38: 209–18.

Meeks, N.D., 1993. 'Surface characterisation of tinned bronze, high-tin bronze, tinned iron and arsenical bronze'. In S.C. La Niece and P.T. Craddock (eds), *Metal Plating and Patination*, Butterworth-Heinemann, Oxford: 247–75.

Miller, E., 1973. *That Noble Cabinet. A History of the British Museum*. London.

Montelius, O., 1895–1910. *La Civilisation Primitive en Italie depuis l'introduction des métaux*, 5 vols. Stockholm.

Müller-Karpe, H., 1959. *Beiträge zur Chronologie der Urnenfelderzeit nördlich und südlich der Alpen*. Römisch-Germanische Forschungen 22. Berlin.

Müller-Karpe, H., 1962. *Zur Stadtwerdung Roms*. F.H. Kerle Verlag. Heidelberg.

Müller-Karpe, H., 1974. 'Das Grab 871 von Veii, Grotta Gramiccia'. *PBF* XX, 1: 89–97.

Muntoni, I., 1997. 'Madonna del Petto'. In A. Cinquepalmi and F. Radina (eds), *Documenti dell'età del bronzo*. Fasano di Brindisi: 57–66.

Needham, S. and Bowman, S., 2005. 'Flesh-hooks, technological complexity and the Atlantic Bronze Age feasting complex in Europe'. *European Journal of Archaeology* 8(2): 93–136.

Nijboer, A., 2005. 'La cronologia assoluta dell'Età del Ferro nel Mediterraneo, dibattito sui metodi e sui risultati'. In Bartoloni and Delpino 2005: 527–56.

Nijboer, A., Van der Plicht, J., Bietti Sestieri, A.M. and De Santis, A., 1999–2000. 'A high chronology for the Early Iron Age in central Italy'. *Palaeohistoria* 41–2: 163–76.

Northover, J.P. 2004. 'Analyse der Metallfunde aus Zug-Sumpf', (trans. S. Hämmerle). In I. Bauer, B. Rückstuhl and J. Speck, *Der Funde der Grabungen 1923–37: Zug Sumpf*. Zug: Kantonales Museum für Urgeschichte Zug, Bd 3/1, 102–43 and Bd 3/2 A1–A29.

O'Riordain, S.P., 1937. 'The halberd in Bronze Age Europe: a study of prehistoric origins, evolution, distribution and chronology'. *Archaeologia* 86: 195–321.

Orsi, P., 1905. 'Necropoli e stazioni sicule di transizione. Necropoli al Molino della Badia presso Grammichele'. *Bullettino di Paletnologia Italiana* 31: 96–133.

Ortiz, G., 1993. In *Art of the Italic Peoples from 3000 to 300 BC*. Swiss collections. Exhibition catalogue. Geneva and Paris: 293–94.

Osteria dell'Osa 1992. Bietti Sestieri, A.M. (ed.), *La necropoli laziale di Osteria dell'Osa*. Quasar, Rome.

Otto, H. and Witter, W., 1952. *Handbuch der ältesten vorgeschichtlichen Metallurgie in Mitteleuropa*. Verlag J. A. Bart, Leipzig.

Paribeni, R., 1928. 'Capodimonte. Ritrovamento di tombe arcaiche'. *Notizie Scavi*: 434–67.

Pasqui, A., 1888. 'Scavi della necropoli di Torre Mordillo nel comune di Spezzano Albanese'. *Notizie Scavi*: 244–68, 462–80.

PBF = *Prähistorische Bronzefunde*:

PBF III, 3. 2000. Tomedi, G., *Italische Panzerplatten und Panzerscheiben.*

PBF IV, 1. 1970. Bianco Peroni, V., *Le spade nell'Italia continentale.*

PBF IV, 12. 1993. Kilian-Dirlmeier, I., *Die Schwerter in Griechenland (ausserhalb der Peloponnes), Bulgarien und Albanien.*

PBF IV, 14. 1995. Harding, A., *Die Schwerter im ehemaligen Jugoslawien.*

PBF VI, 10. 1994. Bianco Peroni, V., *I pugnali nell'Italia continentale.*

PBF VII, 2. 1976. Bianco Peroni, V., *I coltelli nell'Italia continentale.*

PBF VIII, 2. 1979. Bianco Peroni, V., *I rasoi nell'Italia continentale.*

PBF VIII, 3. 1980. Jockenhoevel, A., *Die Rasiermesser in Westeuropa.*

PBF IX, 4. 1972. Abels, B-U., *Die Randleistbeile in Baden-Württemberg, dem Elsaß, der Franche-Comté und der Schweiz*.

PBF IX, 12. 1984. Carancini, G.L., *Le asce nell'Italia continentale II*.

PBF XI, 2. 1979. Kilian Dirlmeier, I., *Anhänger in Griechenland von der mykenischen bis zur spätgeometrischen Zeit*.

PBF XIII, 2. 1975. Carancini, G.L., *Gli spilloni nell'Italia continentale*.

PBF XIV, 5. 1976. von Eles Masi, P., *Le fibule dell'Italia settentrionale*.

PBF XIV, forthcoming. Lo Schiavo, F., *Le fibule dell'Italia meridionale e della Sicilia dall'età del bronzo recente al VI sec. a.C.*

PBF XVI, 1. 1969. von Hase, F-W., *Die Trensen der Fruheisenzeit in Italien*.

PBF XVII, 1. 1978. Woytowitsch, E., *Die Wagen der Bronze-und frühen Eisenzeit in Italien*.

PBF XX, 1. 1974. Müller-Karpe, H. (ed.), *Beiträge zur italienischen und griechischen Bronzefunden*.

Pearce, M., 1998. 'Reconstructing prehistoric metallurgical knowledge: the northern Italian Copper and Bronze ages'. *European Journal of Archaeology* 1, no. 1: 51–70.

Peroni, R., 1967. *Archeologia della Puglia preistorica*. Rome.

Peroni, R., 1971. *L'età del bronzo nella penisola italiana. 1. L'antica età del bronzo*. Hoepli, Florence.

Peroni, R., 1987. 'La Protostoria'. In Settis, S.(ed.), 1987: 67–136.

Peroni, R. and Vanzetti, A., 2005. 'Intorno alla cronologia della Prima Età del Ferro Italiana: da H. Müller-Karpe a Ch. Pare'. In Bartoloni and Delpino 2005: 81–90.

Peroni, R., Carancini, G.L., Bergonzi, G., Lo Schiavo, F. and von Eles, P., 1980. 'Per una definizione critica di facies locali. Nuovi strumenti metodologici'. *Archeologia*, Materiali e Problemi 1.

Petersen, E., 1897. 'Dreifuss von Lucera'. *Mitteilungen des Deutschen Archäologischen Instituts, Römische Abteilung*, 12: 3–26.

Petitti, P., Bondioli, L., Conti, A.M., Macchiarelli, R., Persiani, C. and Salvadei, L., 2002. 'La tomba 23 della necropoli della Selvicciola (Ischia di Castro, Viterbo): analisi archeologica e aspetti tafonomici e antropologici'. *Preistoria e Protostoria in Etruria* 5: 523–37.

Petrie, W.M., 1917. *Tools and Weapons*. London and Aylesbury.

Piceni 1999. *Piceni popolo d'Europa*. Exhibition catalogue. De Luca, Rome.

Pietropaolo, L., 2002. *Sformate Immagini di Bronzo. Il Carrello di Lucera tra VIII e VII secolo a.C.* Foggia.

Pincelli, R.and Morigi Govi, C., 1975. *La necropoli villanoviana di San Vitale*. Fonti per la storia di Bologna, Cataloghi I, Istituto per la Storia di Bologna.

Piola Caselli, F.P. and Piana Agostinetti, P. (eds) 1996. *La miniera, l'uomo e l'ambiente. Fonti e metodi a confronto per la storia dell'attività mineraria*. Cassino 1994. Florence.

Pithekoussai 1993. Buchner, G. and Ridgway, D., *Pithekoussai I. La necropoli: tombe 1–723, scavate dal 1952 al 1961*. Monumenti Antichi dei Lincei, serie monografica, vol. IV. G. Bretschneider, Rome.

Poggiani Keller, R., 2004. 'Aspetti del Bronzo Recente nella sequenza insediativa di Scarceta (Manciano, Grosseto)'. In D. Cocchi Genick (ed.), *L'età del bronzo recente in Italia*. Viareggio-Lucca: 469–74.

Poggiani Keller, R. and Raposso, B., 2004. 'Il sito di Parre (Bergamo) nel quadro della tarda età del bronzo della Lombardia prealpina'. In D. Cocchi Genick (ed.), *L'età del bronzo recente in Italia*. Viareggio-Lucca: 443–8.

Pontecagnano 1988. Gastaldi, P. and d'Agostino, B., *Pontecagnano II. La necropoli del Picentino. 1. Le tombe della Prima Età del Ferro*. Istituto Universitario Orientale, Naples.

Pontecagnano 1992. De Natale, S., *Pontecagnano II. La necropoli di S. Antonio, prop. ECI. 2. Tombe della Prima Età del Ferro*. Istituto Universitario Orientale, Naples.

Pontecagnano 2001. Cinquantaquattro, T., *Pontecagnano II.6. L'Agro Picentino e la necropoli in località Casella*. Istituto Universitario Orientale, Naples.

Ponzi Bonomi, L., 1972. 'Il Ripostiglio di Contigliano'. *Bullettino di Paletnologia Italiana* 79: 95–156.

Quattro Fontanili 1963. 'Veio (Isola Farnese). Scavi in una necropoli villanoviana in località "Quattro Fontanili"'. *Notizie Scavi*: 77–279.

Quattro Fontanili 1965. 'Veio (Isola Farnese). Continuazione degli scavi nella necropoli villanoviana in località "Quattro Fontanili"'. *Notizie Scavi*: 49–236.

Quattro Fontanili 1967. 'Veio (Isola Farnese). Continuazione degli scavi nella necropoli villanoviana in località "Quattro Fontanili"'. *Notizie Scavi*: 87–286.

Quattro Fontanili 1970. 'Veio (Isola Farnese). Continuazione degli scavi nella necropoli villanoviana in località "Quattro Fontanili"'. *Notizie Scavi*: 178–329.

Quattro Fontanili 1972. 'Veio (Isola Farnese). Continuazione degli scavi

nella necropoli villanoviana in località "Quattro Fontanili"'. *Notizie Scavi*: 195–384.

Quattro Fontanili 1975. 'Veio (Isola Farnese). Continuazione degli scavi nella necropoli villanoviana in località "Quattro Fontanili"'. *Notizie Scavi*: 63–184.

Quattro Fontanili 1976. 'Veio (Isola Farnese). Continuazione degli scavi nella necropoli villanoviana in località "Quattro Fontanili"'. *Notizie Scavi*: 149–220.

Quattro Fontanili 1986. J. Toms, 'The relative chronology of Quattro Fontanili'. *Annali dell'Istituto Universitario Orientale di Napoli, Sez. Archeologia e Storia Antica* 8: 41–97.

Rehren, Th. and Northover, J.P. 1991. 'Selenium and tellurium in ancient copper ingots'. In E. Pernicka and G.A. Wagner (eds), *Archaeometry '90*. Birkhäuser Verlag, Basle: 221–8.

Richardson, E.H., 1962. 'The recurrent geometric in the sculpture of central Italy and its bearing on the problem of the origin of the Etruscans'. *Memoirs of the American Academy at Rome* 27: 159–98.

Roes, A., 1933. *Greek Geometric Art. Its symbolism and its origin*. Haarlem and Oxford.

Roma 1976. Colonna G.(ed.), *Civiltà del Lazio Primitivo*. Roma, Palazzo delle Esposizioni. 1976. Multigrafica Editrice, Rome.

Rystedt, E., 1985. 'An unusual Etruscan vase from Chiusi'. *Opuscula Romana* 15: 97–104.

Salzani, L., 1994. 'Nogara. Rinvenimento di un ripostiglio di bronzi in località Pila del Brancon'. *Quaderni di Archeologia del Veneto* 10: 83–94.

Seidmann, G. 2007, 'Greville Chester? who was he?' In L. Gilmour (ed.), *Pagans and Christians – from Antiquity to the Middle Ages. Papers in honour of Martin Henig, presented on the occasion of his 65th birthday*, British Archaeological Reports. International Series S1610. Oxford: 171–2.

Serra Ridgway, F.R., 1983. 'Nuragic Bronzes in the British Museum'. In M.S. Balmuth (ed.), *Studies in Sardinian Archaeology, vol. II. Sardinia in the Mediterranean*: 85–101. Ann Arbor, Michigan.

Settis, S. (ed.), 1987. *Storia della Calabria Antica*. Rome and Reggio Calabria.

Skeates, R. and Whitehouse, R., 1994. *Radiocarbon Dating and Italian Prehistory*, London.

Sprenger, M. and Bartoloni, G., 1977. *Die Etrusker. Kunst und Geschichte*. Munich.

Stary, P.F., 1981. *Zur eisenzeitlichen Bewaffnung und Kampfesweise in Mittelitalien*. Marburgerstudien zur Vor- und Frühgeschichte 3, Mainz a. R.

Stary, P.F., 1986. 'Italische Helme des I Jahrtausends vor Christus'. In Swaddling 1986: 25–36.

Strøm, I., 1971. *Problems concerning the origin and early developments of the Etruscan Orientalizing style*. Odense University Press.

Strong, D.E., 1966. *Catalogue of the carved amber in the Department of Greek and Roman Antiquities*. British Museum Trustees, London.

Suessula 1878. 'Suessula'. *Notizie Scavi*: 393–406.

Sundwall, J., 1943. *Die alteren italischen Fibeln*. Berlin.

Swaddling, J. (ed.), 1986. *Italian Iron Age Artefacts in the British Museum*. Papers of the Sixth British Museum Classical Colloquium 1982. British Museum Press, London.

Taramelli, A., 1922. 'Ripostiglio di armi e strumenti di età nuragica rinvenuto in regione Chilivani'. *Notizie Scavi*: 287–93.

Terramare 1997. Bernabò Brea, M., Cardarelli, A. and Cremaschi, M.(eds), *Le Terramare. La più antica civiltà padana*. Electa, Milan.

Toms, J., 1994. *Some aspects of the Villanovan culture of south Etruria, with special reference to Tarquinia*. D.Phil. Thesis, Hertford College, Oxford.

Toms, J., 2000. 'The arch fibula in Early Iron Age Italy'. In D. Ridgway *et al.* (eds), *Ancient Italy in its Mediterranean Setting. Studies in Honour of Ellen Macnamara*. Accordia Specialist Studies in the Mediterranean, 4: 91–116.

Torre Galli 1999. Pacciarelli, M., *Torre Galli. La necropoli della prima età del ferro (scavi Paolo Orsi 1922–3)*. Rubbettino, Catanzaro.

Trampuž Orel, N. 1996. 'Spektrometricne raziskave depojskih najdb pozne bronaste dobe (Spectrometric Research of the Late Bronze Age Hoard Finds)'. In B. Terzan (ed.), *Depojske in posamezne kovinske najdbe bakrene in bronaste dobe na Sloenskem (Hoards and Individual Metal Finds from the Eneolithic and Bronze Ages in Slovenia)*, 2. Ljubljana: 165–242.

Turco, M., 2000. *La necropoli di Cassibile*. Cahiers du Centre J. Berard 21. Paris.

Turfa, J.M.,1982. 'The Etruscan and Italic Collection in Manchester Museum'. *Papers of the British School at Rome*, 50: 166–95.

Tylecote, R.F. 1985. 'The apparent tinning of bronze axes and other artefacts'. *Journal of the Historical Metallurgy Society*, 19(2): 169–75.

Tylecote, R.F., Balmuth, M.S. and Massoli-Novelli, R. 1983. 'Copper and bronze metallurgy in Sardinia'. *Journal of the Historical Metallurgy Society*, 17(1): 63–78.

Verucchio 1994. Forte, M. (ed.), *Il dono delle Eliadi. Ambre e oreficerie dei principi etruschi di Verucchio*. Verucchio (Rimini), Museo Civico Archeologico.

Vickers, M., 2002. 'The Lucera bronzes, the view from Oxford'. In Pietropaolo 2002: 67–76.

Villa Giulia 1980. Proietti, G., Bordenache Battaglia, G., Moretti, M.and Pallottino, M., *Il Museo Nazionale Etrusco di Villa Giulia*. Rome.

von Duhn, F., 1887. 'La necropoli di Suessula'. *Mitteilungen des Deutschen Archäologischen Instituts, Römische Abteilung*, 2: 237–75.

von Hase, F.W., 1979. *Zur Interpretation villanovazeitlicher und frühetruskischer Funde in Griechenland und der Ägais*. Kleine Schriften aus Vorgeschichtlichen Seminar Marburg. Heft 5.

von Hase, F.W., 1997. 'Présences étrusques et italiques dans les sanctuaires grecs (VIIIe–VIIe siècle a. J.C.)'. In *Les Etrusques, les plus religieux des hommes*. XIIe Rencontre de l'Ecole du Louvre, Paris: 293–323.

Walters, H.B., 1899. *Catalogue of the Bronzes, Greek, Roman and Etruscan, in the Department of Greek and Roman Antiquities, British Museum*. Trustees of the British Museum, London.

Walters, H.B., 1927–8. 'The Hall collection'. *British Museum Quarterly* 2: 85–7.

Warden, P.G., 1983. 'Bullae, Roman custom and Italic tradition'. *Opuscula Romana* 14: 69–73.

Webster, G., 2001. *Duos Nuraghes. A Bronze Age settlement in Sardinia*. British Archaeological Reports. International Series 949, vol. I. Oxford.

Wilson, D.W., 2002. *The British Museum. A History.* British Museum Press, London.

Wylie, W.M., 1867. Translator's note concluding Garrucci 1867. *Archaeologia* 41.2: 281–2.

Zancani Montuoro, P., 1983. 'Francavilla Marittima'. *Atti e Memorie della Società Magna Grecia*, n.s.: 21–3.

Zannoni, A., 1907. *La fonderia di Bologna scoperta e descritta dall'ingegnere e architetto Antonio Zannoni*. Bologna.

Concordances

Concordance A   PRB Registration and Catalogue Numbers

PRB Reg. no.	Cat. no.	PRB Reg. no.	Cat. no.	PRB Reg. no.	Cat. no.	PRB Reg. no.	Cat. no.
PRB Old Acquistion 98	45	PRB 1883.4-26.8	751	PRB WG1084.(1909)	496	PRB WG1157.(1909)	837
PRB Old Acquistion 101	824	PRB 1883.8-2.6	823	PRB WG1085.(1909)	99	PRB WG1158.(1909)	836
PRB Old Acquistion 102	23	PRB 1883.8-2.7	500	PRB WG1086.(1909)	100	PRB WG1159.(1909)	129
PRB Old Acquistion 103	67	PRB 1883.8-2.8	505	PRB WG1089.(1909)	181	PRB WG1166.(1909)	348
PRB Old Acquistion 104	65	PRB 1888.7-19.8	88	PRB WG1090.(1909)	172	PRB WG1262.(1909)	127
PRB Old Acquistion 135	511	PRB 1888.9-1.5	186	PRB WG1091.(1909)	163	PRB WG2256.(1909)	800
PRB (P) Old Acquistion 205	370	PRB 1889.2-1.1	164	PRB WG1092.(1909)	158	PRB WG2263.(1909)	482
PRB 1853.4-12.11	123	PRB 1889.2-1.2	7	PRB WG1093.(1909)	159	PRB 1909.3-18.1	799
PRB 1856.12-26.703	46	PRB 1889.2-1.3	177	PRB WG1094.(1909)	160	PRB 1911.4-1.1	574
PRB 1866.6-27.86	499	PRB 1889.11-1.159	78	PRB WG1095.(1909)	157	PRB 1916.6-5.177	756
PRB 1866.6-27.96	21	PRB 1890.7-18.51	89	PRB WG1096.(1909)	248	PRB 1916.6-5.178	397
PRB 1866.6-27.97	152	PRB 1891.4-18.1	93	PRB WG1097.(1909)	246	PRB 1916.6-5.179	2
PRB 1866.6-27.98	148	PRB 1891.5-14.65	757	PRB WG1098.(1909)	423	PRB 1916.6-5.180	134
PRB 1866.6-27.99	154	PRB 1894.7-27.7	188	PRB WG1099.(1909)	402	PRB 1916.6-5.184	624
PRB 1866.6-27.100	468	PRB Morel 1239.(1901)	498	PRB WG1100.(1909)	415	PRB 1916.6-5.186	361
PRB 1866.6-27.101	489	PRB Morel 2139.(1901)	211	PRB WG1101.(1909)	424	PRB 1916.6-5.187	363
PRB 1866.6-27.102	473	PRB WG264.(1909)	80	PRB WG1102.(1909)	416	PRB 1916.10-14.1	578
PRB 1866.6-27.103	484	PRB WG265.(1909)	120	PRB WG1103.(1909)	417	PRB 1918.10-5.1	755
PRB 1866.6-27.107	94	PRB WG266.(1909)	122	PRB WG1104.(1909)	418	PRB 1919.12-13.1	561
PRB 1866.6-27.108	167	PRB WG413.(1909)	101	PRB WG1105.(1909)	453	PRB 1922.11-10.1	226
PRB 1867.5-8.183	60	PRB WG1042.(1909)	146	PRB WG1106.(1909)	454	PRB 1925.10-17.3	436
PRB 1867.5-8.184	61	PRB WG1046.(1909)	465	PRB WG1107.(1909)	451	PRB 1927.11-14.14	107
PRB 1867.10-11.9	191	PRB WG1047.(1909)	5	PRB WG1108.(1909)	452	PRB 1935.10-18.1	8
PRB 1868.12-28.279	460	PRB WG1048.(1909)	6	PRB WG1109.(1909)	777	PRB 1935.10-18.2	26
PRB 1868.12-28.280	143	PRB WG1049.(1909)	47	PRB WG1110.(1909)	376	PRB 1935.10-18.3	37
PRB 1873.6-2.14	90	PRB WG1050.(1909)	48	PRB WG1112.(1909)	233	PRB 1935.10-18.4	28
PRB 1873.6-2.15	483	PRB WG1051.(1909)	49	PRB WG1113.(1909)	405	PRB 1935.10-18.5	74
PRB 1875.12-29.2	461	PRB WG1052.(1909)	50	PRB WG1114.(1909)	394	PRB 1935.10-18.6	24
PRB 1876.7-6.10	514	PRB WG1053.(1909)	51	PRB WG1115.(1909)	419	PRB 1935.10-18.7	34
PRB 1878.11-1.207	474	PRB WG1054.(1909)	19	PRB WG1116.(1909)	407	PRB 1935.10-18.8	31
PRB 1878.11-1.208	149	PRB WG1055.(1909)	30	PRB WG1118.(1909)	408	PRB 1935.10-18.9	29
PRB 1879.2-4.1A	358	PRB WG1056.(1909)	38	PRB WG1119.(1909)	404	PRB 1935.10-18.10	36
PRB 1880.5-1.29	193	PRB WG1057.(1909)	32	PRB WG1120.(1909)	238	PRB 1935.10-18.11	62
PRB 1880.8-2.28	520	PRB WG1058.(1909)	77	PRB WG1121.(1909)	228	PRB 1935.10-18.12	12
PRB 1880.8-2.29	265	PRB WG1059.(1909)	84	PRB WG1124.(1909)	435	PRB 1935.10-18.13	63
PRB 1880.8-2.30	195	PRB WG1060.(1909)	85	PRB WG1125.(1909)	438	PRB 1935.10-18.14	68
PRB 1880.8-2.31	196	PRB WG1061.(1909)	76	PRB WG1126.(1909)	439	PRB 1935.10-18.15	73
PRB 1880.8-2.32	262	PRB WG1062.(1909)	82	PRB WG1127.(1909)	398	PRB 1935.10-18.18	492
PRB 1880.8-2.33	260	PRB WG1063.(1909)	83	PRB WG1128.(1909)	399	PRB 1935.10-18.19	138
PRB 1880.8-2.34	197	PRB WG1064.(1909)	10	PRB WG1129.(1909)	781	PRB 1935.10-18.20	139
PRB 1880.8-2.35	266	PRB WG1065.(1909)	135	PRB WG1130.(1909)	778	PRB 1935.10-18.21	140
PRB 1880.8-2.38	18	PRB WG1066.(1909)	136	PRB WG1131.(1909)	779	PRB 1935.10-18.22	183
PRB 1880.8-2.39	176	PRB WG1067.(1909)	241	PRB WG1132.(1909)	780	PRB 1935.10-18.23	485
PRB 1880.8-2.40	40	PRB WG1068.(1909)	242	PRB WG1133.(1909)	743	PRB 1935.10-18.24	475
PRB 1880.8-2.41	27	PRB WG1069.(1909)	243	PRB WG1135.(1909)	42	PRB 1935.10-18.25	486
PRB 1880.8-2.42	406	PRB WG1070.(1909)	245	PRB WG1136.(1909)	457	PRB 1935.10-18.26	462
PRB 1880.8-2.43	178	PRB WG1071.(1909)	137	PRB WG1137.(1909)	459	PRB 1935.10-18.27	476
PRB 1880.8-2.44	502	PRB WG1072.(1909)	92	PRB WG1138.(1909)	458	PRB 1935.10-18.28	503
PRB 1880.8-2.46	144	PRB WG1073.(1909)	145	PRB WG1143.(1909)	219	PRB 1935.10-18.29	497
PRB 1880.8-2.47	162	PRB WG1074.(1909)	491	PRB WG1144.(1909)	224	PRB 1935.10-18.30	504
PRB 1880.8-2.48	81	PRB WG1075.(1909)	469	PRB WG1145.(1909)	750	PRB 1935.10-18.32	247
PRB 1880.12-14.1	14	PRB WG1076.(1909)	470	PRB WG1146.(1909)	517	PRB 1935.10-18.33	96
PRB 1883.4-26.1	4	PRB WG1077.(1909)	471	PRB WG1147.(1909)	244	PRB 1935.10-18.34	493
PRB 1883.4-26.2	72	PRB WG1078.(1909)	479	PRB WG1148.(1909)	41	PRB 1935.10-18.36	97
PRB 1883.4-26.3	422	PRB WG1079.(1909)	480	PRB WG1149.(1909)	79	PRB 1935.10-18.37	165
PRB 1883.4-26.4	71	PRB WG1080.(1909)	105	PRB WG1149A.(1909)	831	PRB 1935.10-18.38	173
PRB 1883.4-26.5	515	PRB WG1081.(1909)	252	PRB WG1150.(1909)	119	PRB 1935.10-18.39	171
PRB 1883.4-26.6	64	PRB WG1082.(1909)	253	PRB WG1151.(1909)	109	PRB 1935.10-18.40	161
PRB 1883.4-26.7	758	PRB WG1083.(1909)	506	PRB WG1152.(1909)	118	PRB 1935.10-18.40A	175

Concordance B   GR Registration and Catalogue Numbers

PRB Reg. no.	Cat. no.	PRB Reg. no.	Cat. no.	GR Reg. no	Cat. no.	GR Reg. no	Cat. no.
PRB 1935.10-18.41	1	PRB 1964.12-1.393	490	GR 1757.8-15.40A	207	GR 1814.7-4.237	646
PRB 1935.10-18.42	22	PRB 1964.12-1.394	86	GR 1772.3-3.1000	835	GR 1814.7-4.238	641
PRB 1935.10-18.43	20	PRB 1964.12-1.395	147	GR 1772.3-5.22	821	GR 1814.7-4.249	298
PRB 1935.10-18.44	481	PRB 1964.12-1.398	507	GR 1772.3-7.72	538	GR 1814.7-4.250	285
PRB 1935.10-18.45	174	PRB 1964.12-1.399	513	GR 1772.3-7.121	656	GR 1814.7-4.251	344
PRB 1937.5-8.1	25	PRB 1964.12-1.400	508	GR 1772.3-7.122	655	GR 1814.7-4.252	610
PRB 1937.11-9.1	95	PRB 1964.12-1.401	512	GR 1772.3-7.123	637	GR 1814.7-4.253	614
PRB 1944.7-2.5	580	PRB 1964.12-1.402	509	GR 1772.3-7.126	661	GR 1814.7-4.262	216
PRB 1944.7-2.7	215	PRB 1964.12-1.403	510	GR 1772.3-7.131	795	GR 1814.7-4.701	519
PRB 1964.12-1.200	15	PRB 1964.12-1.404	495	GR 1772.3-7.132	796	GR 1814.7-4.705	786
PRB 1964.12-1.201	17	PRB 1964.12-1.407	494	GR 1772.3-7.133	638	GR 1814.7-4.706	787
PRB 1964.12-1.202	16	PRB 1964.12-1.408	501	GR 1772.3-7.135	642	GR 1814.7-4.794	588
PRB 1964.12-1.203	827	PRB 1964.12-1.426	250	GR 1772.3-7.141	662	GR 1814.7-4.797	576
PRB 1964.12-1.204	57	PRB 1964.12-1.440	179	GR 1772.3-7.145	663	GR 1814.7-4.800	577
PRB 1964.12-1.205	55	PRB 1964.12-1.441	180	GR 1772.3-7.149	650	GR 1814.7-4.1010	752
PRB 1964.12-1.206	56	PRB 1964.12-1.459	826	GR 1772.3-7.151	651	GR 1814.7-4.1011	235
PRB 1964.12-1.207	52	PRB 1964.12-1.460	13	GR 1772.3-7.153	669	GR 1814.7-4.1055	806
PRB 1964.12-1.208	53	PRB 1964.12-1.510	282	GR 1772.3-7.156	659	GR 1814.7-4.1577	409
PRB 1964.12-1.209	58	PRB 1964.12-1.513	329	GR 1772.3-7.157	658	GR 1814.7-4.1579	672
PRB 1964.12-1.210	59	PRB 1964.12-1.514	43	GR 1772.3-7.162	664	GR 1814.7-4.1589	549
PRB 1964.12-1.211	54	PRB 1964.12-6.75	91	GR 1772.3-7.164	550	GR 1824.4-6.2	652
PRB 1964.12-1.212	251	PRB 1964.12-6.76	249	GR 1772.3-7.165	660	GR 1824.4-6.3	792
PRB 1964.12-1.213	156	PRB 1964.12-6.77	782	GR 1772.3-7.167	657	GR 1824.4-6.4	793
PRB 1964.12-1.214	66	PRB 1964.12-6.78	437	GR 1772.3-7.168	668	GR 1824.4-6.5	794
PRB 1964.12-1.215	11	PRB 1964.12-6.79	631	GR 1772.3-7.174	639	GR 1824.4-6.6	791
PRB 1964.12-1.216	33	PRB 1964.12-6.80	556	GR 1772.3-7.177	357	GR 1824.4-6.7	790
PRB 1964.12-1.217	393	PRB 1964.12-6.84	770	GR 1772.3-7.178	636	GR 1824.4-6.22	740
PRB 1964.12-1.218	456	PRB 1964.12-6.86	472	GR 1772.3-7.180	788	GR 1824.4-7.2	771
PRB 1964.12-1.219	455	PRB 1964.12-6.94	563	GR 1772.3-7.181	789	GR 1824.4-34.10	290
PRB 1964.12-1.220	466	PRB 1964.12-6.96	555	GR 1772.3-7.210	533	GR 1824.4-34.21	592
PRB 1964.12-1.223	153	PRB 1964.12-6.114	603	GR 1772.3-7.316	272	GR 1824.4-34.37	581
PRB 1964.12-1.224	87	PRB 1964.12-6.116A and B	746	GR 1772.3-9.3	599	GR 1824.4-34.38	595
PRB 1964.12-1.327	374	PRB 1964.12-6.117	279	GR 1772.3-9.5	600	GR 1824.4-34.41	324
PRB 1964.12-1.328	375	PRB(P) 1974.12-1.163	44	GR 1772.3-9.6	602	GR 1824.4-34.42	609
PRB 1964.12-1.329	414	PRB(P) 1974.12-1.264	121	GR 1772.3-9.9	601	GR 1824.4-34.43	217
PRB 1964.12-1.356	184	PRB(P) 1974.12-1.322	566	GR 1772.3-9.15	345	GR 1824.4-98.3	817
PRB 1964.12-1.357	69	PRB(P) 1974.12-1.323	299	GR 1772.3-9.21	586	GR 1824.4-98.4	818
PRB 1964.12-1.358	39	PRB(P) 1974.12-1.324	558	GR 1772.3-9.22	587	GR 1824.4-98.5	819
PRB 1964.12-1.363	70	PRB 2000.1-1.1	551	GR 1772.3-9.30	443	GR 1824.4-98.6	809
PRB 1964.12-1.364	75	PRB 2000.1-1.2	281	GR 1772.3-9.31	310	GR 1824.4-98.8	810
PRB 1964.12-1.371	3	PRB 2000.1-1.4	565	GR 1772.3-9.34	444	GR 1824.4-98.18	616
PRB 1964.12-1.374	9	PRB 2000.1-1.16	553	GR 1772.3-9.36	210	GR 1824.4-98.19	615
PRB 1964.12-1.377	825	PRB 2000.1-1.17	591	GR 1772.3-9.37	611	GR 1824.4-98.20	625
PRB 1964.12-1.382	488	PRB 2000.1-1.23	562	GR 1772.3-9.38	326	GR 1824.4-99.20	531
PRB 1964.12-1.383	142	PRB 2000.1-1.24	559	GR 1772.3-9.40	320	GR 1838.6-8.73	648
PRB 1964.12-1.384	141	PRB 2000.1-1.25	560	GR 1772.3-9.41	304	GR 1838.6-8.80	268
PRB 1964.12-1.385	155	PRB 2000.1-1.32	234	GR 1772.3-9.42	213	GR 1839.11-9.45	263
PRB 1964.12-1.386	487	PRB 2000.1-1.33	392	GR 1772.3-9.43	333	GR 1839.11-9.48A	221
PRB 1964.12-1.387	151	PRB 2000.1-1.34	400	GR 1772.3-9.44	288	GR 1839.11-9.48B	222
PRB 1964.12-1.388	463	PRB 2000.1-1.35	401	GR 1772.3-9.46	300	GR 1840.2-12.18	525
PRB 1964.12-1.389	477	PRB 2000.1-1.36	254	GR 1772.3-9.71	284	GR 1842.7-28.682	832
PRB 1964.12-1.391	464	PRB BM.23	297	GR 1772.3-9.72	286	GR 1842.7-28.705	187
PRB 1964.12-1.392	478	PRB no Registration number	150	GR 1772.3-9.77	584	GR 1842.7-30.1	223
				GR 1772.3-9.115	618	GR 1846.6-8.1	552
				GR 1772.3-9.116	630	GR 1847.8-6.140	192
				GR 1772.3-9.132	632	GR 1849.5-18.30A	367
				GR 1772.3-18.10	813	GR 1849.5-18.30B	368
				GR 1772.3-18.11	814	GR 1849.5-18.46	425
				GR 1772.3-18.12	784	GR 1849.5-18.47	754
				GR 1772.3-18.13	785	GR 1849.11-19.2	352
				GR 1772.3-18.15	816	GR 1850.1-17.57	115
				GR 1772.3-18.16	627	GR 1850.1-17.85	190
				GR 1772.3-18.17	349	GR 1853.2-18.3	388
				GR 1772.3-18.23	622	GR 1856.5-14.1	189
				GR 1772.3-18.24	815	GR 1856.12-26.618A	365
				GR 1814.7-4.230	647	GR 1856.12-26.618B	366
				GR 1814.7-4.231	653	GR 1856.12-26.619	362
				GR 1814.7-4.233	640	GR 1856.12-26.620	387
				GR 1814.7-4.234	643	GR 1856.12-26.696	534
				GR 1814.7-4.235A	449	GR 1856.12-26.704	227
				GR 1814.7-4.236	450	GR 1856.12-26.716	274

GR Reg. no	Cat. no.	GR Reg. no	Cat. no.	GR Reg. no	Cat. no.	GR Reg. no	Cat. no.
GR 1856.12-26.717	623	GR 1878.10-19.143	199	GR 1938.3-31.11	446	GR 1975.7-12.29	741
GR 1856.12-26.718	613	GR 1878.10-19.144	116	GR 1938.3-31.12	589	GR 1975.7-12.35	277
GR 1856.12-26.719	613	GR 1878.10-19.157	303	GR 1938.3-31.13	593	GR 1975.7-12.36	289
GR 1856.12-26.720	356	GR 1878.10-19.159	564	GR 1951.6-6.18	98	GR 1975.7-12.41	335
GR 1856.12-26.722	635	GR 1878.10-19.163	205	GR 1954.6-1.1	541	GR 1975.7-12.42	338
GR 1856.12-26.724	644	GR 1878.10-19.164	343	GR 1954.6-1.2	542	GR 1975.7-12.45	530
GR 1856.12-26.728	547	GR 1878.10-19.165	347	GR 1958.8-22.8	535	GR 1975.7-12.68	354
GR 1856.12-26.734	276	GR 1878.10-19.166	629	GR 1958.10-27.1	440	GR 1975.7-30.1	104
GR 1856.12-26.745	206	GR 1878.10-19.167	634	GR 1964.12-21.4	725	GR 1975.7-30.2	103
GR 1856.12-26.762	619	GR 1878.10-19.180	654	GR 1968.6-27.1	811	GR 1975.7-30.16	112
GR 1856.12-26.763	620	GR 1878.10-19.242	113	GR 1969.12-31.77	110	GR 1975.7-30.17	108
GR 1856.12-26.764	621	GR 1878.10-19.244	532	GR 1969.12-31.81	111	GR 1975.7-30.19	194
GR 1856.12-26.898	318	GR 1878.10-19.249	275	GR 1969.12-31.83	106	GR 1975.7-30.20	258
GR 1856.12-26.903	306	GR 1880.2-28.1	126	GR 1969.12-31.86	35	GR 1975.9-3.1	353
GR 1856.12-26.904	214	GR 1884.10-11.45	617	GR 1969.12-31.132	744	GR 1975.9-4.1	727
GR 1856.12-26.907	545	GR 1886.3-9.6	828	GR 1974.12-3.9	628	GR 1975.9-4.2	728
GR 1856.12-26.975	182	GR 1887.11-1.23	102	GR 1974.12-3.11	536	GR 1975.9-4.3	729
GR 1856.12-26.976	239	GR 1890.5-12.6	313	GR 1974.12-3.17	820	GR 1975.9-4.4	730
GR 1856.12-26.1038	607	GR 1890.5-12.7	311	GR 1975.5-18.1	125	GR 1975.9-4.5	731
GR 1856.12-26.1053	540	GR 1890.5-12.8	308	GR 1975.5-18.2A	748	GR 1975.9-4.6	732
GR 1856.12-26.1074	328	GR 1890.5-12.9	316	GR 1975.5-18.2B	749	GR 1975.9-4.7	733
GR 1856.12-26.1087	759	GR 1890.5-12.10	315	GR 1975.5-18.3	225	GR 1975.9-4.8	734
GR 1856.12-26.1088	257	GR 1890.5-12.13	323	GR 1975.5-18.4	360	GR 1975.9-4.9	735
GR 1857.10-13.2	804	GR 1890.9-21.18	803	GR 1975.5-18.5	364	GR 1975.9-4.10	736
GR 1859.2-16.152	377	GR 1890.9-21.19	808	GR 1975.5-18.6	369	GR 1975.9-4.11	737
GR 1859.2-16.153	386	GR 1905.1-15.1	575	GR 1975.5-18.7	745	GR 1975.9-4.12	724
GR 1859.2-16.167	351	GR 1908.11-20.27	543	GR 1975.5-18.8	518	GR 1975.9-4.13	738
GR 1865.7-20.48	585	GR 1909.6-21.1	830	GR 1975.6-5.78	441	GR 1975.9-4.14	711
GR 1865.7-20.51	261	GR 1909.6-22.1	572	GR 1975.6-5.79	442	GR 1975.9-4.15	712
GR 1865.7-20.53	764	GR 1910.4-20.2	302	GR 1975.6-5.80	131	GR 1975.9-4.16	713
GR 1865.7-20.54	395	GR 1910.10-15.2	218	GR 1975.6-5.81	130	GR 1975.9-4.17	693
GR 1865.7-20.105	467	GR 1910.10-15.3	606	GR 1975.6-5.82	240	GR 1975.9-4.18	714
GR 1865.7-22.9	373	GR 1912.11-25.51	822	GR 1975.6-5.84	132	GR 1975.9-4.19	715
GR 1865.7-22.11	760	GR 1912.12-18.1	544	GR 1975.6-5.85	128	GR 1975.9-4.20	706
GR 1865.11-18.153	321	GR 1915.12-28.1	322	GR 1975.6-5.86	133	GR 1975.9-4.21	707
GR 1867.5-8.142	200	GR 1916.6-1.6	301	GR 1975.6-27.1	229	GR 1975.9-4.22	694
GR 1867.5-8.143	833	GR 1916.6-1.7	571	GR 1975.6-27.2	421	GR 1975.9-4.23	695
GR 1867.5-8.161	597	GR 1916.6-1.8	568	GR 1975.6-27.3	379	GR 1975.9-4.24	708
GR 1867.5-8.169	204	GR 1916.6-1.16	378	GR 1975.6-27.4	420	GR 1975.9-4.25	709
GR 1867.5-8.171	293	GR 1916.6-1.17	403	GR 1975.6-27.5	384	GR 1975.9-4.26	710
GR 1867.5-8.172	278	GR 1916.6-1.18	236	GR 1975.6-27.7	412	GR 1975.9-4.27	696
GR 1867.5-8.181	314	GR 1916.6-1.19	426	GR 1975.6-27.9	767	GR 1975.9-4.28	720
GR 1867.5-8.185	772	GR 1916.6-1.20	117	GR 1975.6-27.11	413	GR 1975.9-4.29	722
GR 1867.5-8.186	410	GR 1916.6-1.21	389	GR 1975.6-27.12	427	GR 1975.9-4.30	723
GR 1867.5-8.188	774	GR 1916.6-1.22	834	GR 1975.6-27.14	231	GR 1975.9-4.31	721
GR 1867.5-8.189	775	GR 1916.6-1.29	220	GR 1975.6-27.15	761	GR 1975.9-4.32	697
GR 1867.5-8.190	773	GR 1920.11-18.2	579	GR 1975.6-27.16	232	GR 1975.9-4.33	716
GR 1867.5-8.212	797	GR 1920.11-18.3	567	GR 1975.6-27.17	411	GR 1975.9-4.34	717
GR 1867.5-8.213	798	GR 1920.11-18.4	296	GR 1975.6-27.18	433	GR 1975.9-4.35	698
GR 1867.5-8.216	829	GR 1920.11-18.5	295	GR 1975.6-27.19	428	GR 1975.9-4.36	699
GR 1867.5-8.217	829	GR 1920.11-18.6	291	GR 1975.6-27.20	429	GR 1975.9-4.37	700
GR 1867.5-8.382	264	GR 1920.11-18.16	594	GR 1975.6-27.21	430	GR 1975.9-4.38	685
GR 1872.6-4.684	447	GR 1920.11-18.17	596	GR 1975.6-27.22	753	GR 1975.9-4.39	686
GR 1872.6-4.685	448	GR 1920.11-18.18	604	GR 1975.6-27.23	431	GR 1975.9-4.40	687
GR 1872.6-4.687	355	GR 1920.11-18.21	340	GR 1975.6-27.24	396	GR 1975.9-4.41	688
GR 1872.6-4.722	341	GR 1922.4-13.39	280	GR 1975.6-27.25	390	GR 1975.9-4.42	689
GR 1872.6-4.722bis	325	GR 1927.11-15.36	529	GR 1975.6-27.26	380	GR 1975.9-4.43	690
GR 1872.6-4.911	309	GR 1928.1-17.2	812	GR 1975.6-27.27	768	GR 1975.9-4.44	671
GR 1872.6-4.912	605	GR 1930.4-22.1	317	GR 1975.6-27.28	385	GR 1975.9-4.45	673
GR 1872.6-4.913	312	GR 1935.8-23.3	124	GR 1975.6-27.29	432	GR 1975.9-4.46	691
GR 1872.6-4.1089	612	GR 1935.8-23.54	267	GR 1975.6-27.30	237	GR 1975.9-4.47	692
GR 1872.6-4.1090	342	GR 1935.8-23.55	523	GR 1975.6-27.31	381	GR 1975.9-4.48	677
GR 1872.10-8.4	807	GR 1935.8-23.56	521	GR 1975.6-27.32	769	GR 1975.9-4.49	678
GR 1873.8-20.229A	371	GR 1935.8-23.57	524	GR 1975.6-27.33	762	GR 1975.9-4.50	674
GR 1873.8-20.229B	372	GR 1935.8-23.58	528	GR 1975.6-27.34	230	GR 1975.9-4.51	675
GR 1873.8-20.231	765	GR 1935.8-23.59	270	GR 1975.6-27.36	434	GR 1975.9-4.52	679
GR 1873.8-20.237	255	GR 1935.8-23.65	742	GR 1975.6-27.38	776	GR 1975.9-4.53	680
GR 1873.8-20.238	766	GR 1935.8-23.66	726	GR 1975.6-27.39	382	GR 1975.9-4.54	681
GR 1875.3-13.8	522	GR 1935.8-23.68	201	GR 1975.6-27.41	383	GR 1975.9-4.55	682
GR 1876.9-2.1	573	GR 1938.3-31.1	346	GR 1975.6-27.42	391	GR 1975.9-4.56	683
GR 1876.11-7.1	327	GR 1938.3-31.2	626	GR 1975.7-2.2	783	GR 1975.9-4.57	684
GR 1878.10-19.139	114	GR 1938.3-31.8	336	GR 1975.7-3.1	805	GR 1975.9-4.58	718
GR 1878.10-19.140	198	GR 1938.3-31.10	445	GR 1975.7-10.1A & 1B	271	GR 1975.9-4.59	719

Concordance C: H.B. Walters, *Catalogue of the Bronzes in the British Museum*, 1899, and numbers in this Catalogue

GR Reg. no.	Cat. no.	Walters no.	Cat. no.
GR 1975.9-4.60	701	339	820
GR 1975.9-4.61	702	345	817
GR 1975.9-4.62	703	346	818
GR 1975.9-4.63	704	347	819
GR 1975.9-4.64	705	348	627
GR 1975.9-4.65	676	349	784
GR 1975.9-4.66	670	350	785
GR 1975.9-4.67	739	351	628
GR 1975.9-5.10	645	352	813
GR 1975.9-5.14	665	353	814
GR 1975.9-5.15	666	354	815
GR 1975.9-5.15bis	649	355	816
GR 1975.9-5.16	667	359	547
GR 1975.10-5.18	537	360	548
GR 1975.10-5.20	539	377	807
GR 1975.12-3.9	548	380	809
GR 1975.12-3.10	801	394	821
GR 1975.12-3.11	802	408	542
GR 1976.1-3.1	256	409	541
GR 1976.2-5.1	633	412	540
GR 1976.2-5.3	583	1929	613
GR 1976.2-5.4	554	1930	616
GR 1976.2-5.5	582	1931	617
GR 1976.2-5.6	287	1932	618
GR 1976.2-5.7	307	1933	614
GR 1976.2-5.8	212	1934	345
GR 1976.2-5.9	319	1935	612
GR 1976.2-5.10	305	1936	610
GR 1976.2-5.11	337	1937	611
GR 1976.2-5.12	331	1938	609
GR 1976.2-5.13	330	1939	341
GR 1976.2-5.14	339	1940	344
GR 1976.2-5.15	334	1941	342
GR 1976.2-5.16	332	1942	620
GR 1976.2-5.19	203	1943	619
GR 1976.2-6.1	569	1944	621
GR 1976.2-8.1	557	1945	622
GR 1976.2-8.2	598	1958	573
GR 1976.2-8.5	283	1962	583
GR 1976.2-8.6	292	1963	576
GR 1976.2-8.8	208	1964	577
GR 1976.3-1.5	608	1965	586
GR 1976.12-31.179	350	1967	588
GR 1976.12-31.232	185	1969	585
GR 1980.2-1.32	590	1970	554
GR 1982.3-2.63	546	1971	587
GR 1982.6-17.21	168	1972	569
GR 1982.6-17.22	166	1973	318
GR 1982.6-17.23	169	1974	599
GR 1982.6-17.25	170	1975	600
GR 1982.6-17.27	763	1976	602
GR 1982.6-17.56	259	1977	601
GR 1982.6-17.57	526	1982	592
GR 1982.6-17.58	269	1983	595
GR 1982.6-17.59	527	1992	290
GR 1982.6-17.61	209	1993	293
GR 1982.6-17.63	516	1994	582
GR 1991.12-18.21	570	1996	314
GR 1994.8-3.1	359	1997	288
GR 1994.8-3.2	747	1998	285
GR 1994.8-3.4	202	1999	207
GR 1994.8-3.9	273	2000	287
GR 2001.3-30.1	294		

Walters no.	Cat. no.	Walters no	Cat. no.
2001	298	2745	373
2002	284	2751	367
2003	206	2754	126
2007	310	2755	257
2008	306	2756	190
2009	307	2757	189
2010	210	2758	192
2011	313	2759	519
2012	311	2760	518
2013	308	2762	194
2014	316	2772	395
2015	315	2782	832
2016	312	2785	387
2017	443	2786	772
2018	212	2787	775
2019	214	2788	774
2020	213	2789	410
2021	216	2790	760
2022	319	2791	771
2023	320	2793	391
2024	305	2794	752
2025	325	2795	235
2026	324	2796	765
2027	326	2855	804
2028	323	2911	8
2035	337	2912	26
2036	331	2913	37
2040	333	2914	28
2041	330	2915	74
2042	339	2916	24
2043	334	2917	34
2044	332	2918	31
2046	605	2919	29
2053	327	2920	36
2064	217	2921	62
2065	203	2922	12
2066	204	2923	63
2420	261	2924	68
2421	263	2925	73
2422	522	2926	467
2423	525	2928	492
2707	125	2929	138
2708	221	2930	139
2708	222	2931	140
2709	748	2932	183
2709	749	2933	485
2710	368	2934	475
2711	386	2935	486
2712	383	2936	462
2713	425	2937	476
2714	754	2938	503
2715	388	2939	497
2735	362	2940	504
2736	225	2942	247
2737	360	2943	96
2738	364	2944	493
2739	223	2946	97
2742	365	2947	165
2742	366	2948	173
2743	227	2949	171
2744	371	2950	161
2744	372	2950	175

Typological Table

Cat no.	Pl. no.	Register no	Type	Cat no.	Pl. no.	Register no	Type
1	1	PRB 1935. 10-18. 41	Axes 1	61	14	PRB 1867. 5-8. 184	Daggers 3
2	1	PRB 1916. 6-5. 179	Axes 2	62	15	PRB 1935. 10-18. 11	Axes 14
3	1	PRB 1964. 12-1. 371 (286)	Axes 4	63	15	PRB 1935. 10-18. 13	Axes 14
4	1	PRB 1883. 4-26.1	Axes 4	64	15	PRB 1883.4-26.6	Axes 15
5	1	PRB WG 1047	Close to Axes 4	65	15	PRB Old Acquisition 104 (Registered OA 21 July 1939)	Axes 15
6	1	PRB WG 1048	Axes 4				
7	1	PRB 1889. 2-1.2	Axes 4	66	15	PRB 1964. 12-1. 214 (306)	Axes 18
8	2	PRB 1935. 10-18.1	Axes 5a	67	15	PRB Old Acquisition 103 (Registered OA 19 July 1939)	Axes 19
9	2	PRB 1964. 12-1. 374 (344)	Axes 5a				
10	2	PRB WG 1064	Axes 63	68	15	PRB 1935. 10-18. 14	Axes 19
11	2	PRB 1964. 12-1. 215 (299)	Axes 64	69	16	PRB 1964. 12-1. 357 (287)	Axes 20
12	2	PRB 1935. 10-18. 12	Axes 65	70	16	PRB 1964. 12-1. 363 (336)	Axes 20
13	2	PRB 1964. 12-1. 460 (346)	Axes unclassified	71	16	PRB 1883. 4-26. 4	Close to Axes 20
14	3	PRB 1880. 12-14. 1	Halberds 1	72	16	PRB 1883. 4-26.2	Axes 21
15	3	PRB 1964. 12-1. 200 (288)	Axes 3	73	16	PRB 1935. 10-18. 15	Axes 21
16	3	PRB 1964. 12-1. 202 (301)	Axes 3	74	16	PRB 1935. 10-18. 5	Axes 21
17	3	PRB 1964. 12-1. 201 (300)	Axes unclassified	75	17	PRB 1964. 12-1. 364 (337)	Axes 21
18	4	PRB 1880.8-2.38	Axes 6	76	17	PRB WG 1061	Axes 21
19	4	PRB WG 1054	Axes 7	77	17	PRB WG 1058	Axes 22
20	4	PRB 1935. 10-18. 43	Axes 7	78	17	PRB 1889.11-1.159	Axes 23
21	4	PRB 1866.6-27.96	Axes 8	79	18	PRB WG1149	Daggers 6
22	4	PRB 1935. 10-18. 42	Axes 8	80	18	PRB WG 264	Daggers 7
23	4	PRB Old Acquistion 102 (Registered OA 19 July 1939)	Axes 8	81	18	PRB 1880. 8-2. 48	Swords 1
				82	19	PRB WG 1062	Axes 16
24	4	PRB 1935. 10-18.6	Axes 8	83	19	PRB WG 1063	Axes 17
25	5	PRB 1937.5-8.1	Axes 9	84	19	PRB WG 1059	Axes 21
26	5	PRB 1935. 10-18. 2	Axes 10	85	19	PRB WG 1060	Axes 21
27	5	PRB 1880. 8-2. 41	Axes 10	86	20	PRB 1964. 12-1. 394 (339)	Axes 24
28	5	PRB 1935. 10-18. 4	Axes 10	87	20	PRB 1964. 12-1. 224 (307)	Axes 26
29	5	PRB 1935. 10-18. 9	Axes 10	88	20	PRB 1888.7-19.8	Axes 27
30	5	PRB WG 1055	Axes 10	89	20	PRB 1890.7-18.51	Axes 27
31	5	PRB 1935. 10-18.8	Axes 10	90	20	PRB 1873.6-2.14	Axes 28
32	6	PRB WG 1057	Axes 11	91	21	PRB 1964.12-6.75	Axes 28
33	6	PRB 1964. 12-1. 216 (289)	Axes 11	92	21	PRB WG 1072	Axes 28
34	6	PRB 1935. 10-18.7	Axes 11	93	21	PRB 1891.4-18.1	Axes 44
35	6	GR 1969. 12-31. 86	Axes 12	94	21	PRB 1866.6-27.107	Axes 44
36	6	PRB 1935. 10-18. 10	Axes 12	95	22	PRB 1937.11-9.1	Close to Axes 44
37	7	PRB 1935. 10-18.3	Axes 12	96	22	PRB 1935. 10-18. 33	Axes 45
38	7	PRB WG 1056	Axes 12	97	22	PRB 1935. 10-18. 36	Axes 45
39	7	PRB 1964. 12-1. 358 (294)	Axes 13	98	22	GR 1951.6-6. 18	Axes 45
40	7	PRB 1880. 8-2. 40	Axes 13	99	23	PRB WG 1085	Axes 53
41	8	PRB WG1148	Halberds 2	100	23	PRB WG 1086	Axes 53
42	8	PRB WG1135	Daggers 1	101	23	PRB WG 413	Needles 1
43	9	PRB 1964. 12-1. 514	Daggers 2	102	23	GR 1887. 11-1.23	Needles 1
44	10	PRB (P) 1974. 12-1. 163	Daggers 4	103	23	GR 1975. 7-30. 2	Chisels 1
45	10	PRB Old Acquisition 98 Registered OA 6 July 1939	Daggers 5	104	23	GR 1975. 7-30. 1	Chisels 1
				105	23	PRB WG 1080	Winged adzes 1
46	11	PRB 1856. 12-26.W.T.703	Daggers 5	106	24	GR 1969. 12-31.83	Razors 1
47	12	PRB WG 1049	Axes 5b	107	24	PRB 1927. 11-14. 14	Razors 1
48	12	PRB WG 1050	Axes 5b	108	24	GR 1975. 7-30. 17	Razors 1
49	12	PRB WG 1051	Axes 5b	109	24	PRB WG1151	Close to Razors 1
50	12	PRB WG 1052	Axes 6	110	24	GR 1969. 12-31.77	Razors 2
51	12	PRB WG 1053	Axes 7	111	24	GR 1969. 12-31.81	Razors 2
52	12	PRB 1964. 12-1. 207 (293)	Axes 12	112	24	GR 1975. 7-30. 16	Razors 2
53	12	PRB 1964. 12-1. 208 (295)	Axes 12	113	25	GR 1878. 10-19. 242	Pins 1
54	13	PRB 1964. 12-1. 211 (298)	Axes 12	114	25	GR 1878. 10-19. 139	Pins 2
55	13	PRB 1964. 12-1. 205 (291)	Axes 12	115	25	GR 1850. 1-17.57	Pins 3
56	13	PRB 1964. 12-1. 206 (292)	Axes 12	116	25	GR 1878. 10-19. 144	Pins 4
57	13	PRB 1964. 12-1. 204 (290)	Axes 12	117	25	GR 1916.6-1.20	Daggers 8
58	13	PRB 1964. 12-1. 209 (296)	Axes 12	118	25	PRB WG1152	Daggers 8
59	13	PRB 1964. 12-1. 210 (297)	Axes 12	119	25	PRB WG1150	Daggers 9
60	14	PRB 1867. 5-8. 183	Daggers 2	120	26	PRB WG265	Daggers 10

Cat no.	Pl. no.	Register no.	Type	Cat no.	Pl. no.	Register no.	Type
121	26	PRB (P)1974. 12-1. 264	Daggers 11	194	41	GR 1975. 7-30. 19	Knives 4
122	26	PRB WG266	Daggers 11	195	42	PRB 1880. 8-2. 30	Razors 3
123	26	PRB 1853. 4-12. 11	Daggers 11	196	42	PRB 1880. 8-2. 31	Razors 4
124	26	GR 1935. 8-23. 3	Daggers 12	197	42	PRB 1880. 8-2. 34	Razors 4
125	27	GR 1975. 5-18. 1	Swords 2	198	42	GR 1878. 10-19. 140	Pins 5
126	27	GR 1880. 2-28. 1	Swords 3	199	42	GR 1878. 10-19. 143	Pins 6
127	27	PRB WG1262	Swords 4	200	42	GR 1867. 5-8. 142	Pins 7
128	28	GR 1975. 6-5. 85	Arrowheads 1	201	42	GR 1935. 8-23. 68	Sheet disc 1
129	28	PRB WG1159	Arrowheads 1	202	43	GR 1994. 8-3. 4	Fibulae 1
130	28	GR 1975. 6-5. 81	Arrowheads 1, variant	203	43	GR 1976. 2-5. 19	Fibulae 2
131	28	GR 1975. 6-5. 80	Arrowheads 1, variant	204	43	GR 1867. 5-8. 169	Close to Fibulae 2
132	28	GR 1975. 6-5. 84	Arrowheads 2	205	43	GR 1878. 10-19. 163	Fibulae 3
133	28	GR 1975. 6-5. 86	Arrowheads 2	206	43	GR 1856. 12-26. 745	Fibulae 4
134	29	PRB 1916.6-5.180	Axes 29	207	43	GR 1757.8-15. 40A	Fibulae 5
135	29	PRB WG 1065	Axes 29	208	43	GR 1976. 2-8.8	Probably Fibulae 5
136	29	PRB WG 1066	Axes 29	209	43	GR 1982. 6-17.61	Fibulae 6
137	29	PRB WG 1071	Axes 29	210	44	GR 1772. 3-9. 36	Fibulae 16
138	29	PRB 1935. 10-18. 19	Axes 29	211	44	PRB Morel 2139	Fibulae 38
139	30	PRB 1935. 10-18. 20	Axes 29	212	44	GR 1976. 2-5.8	Fibulae 38
140	30	PRB 1935. 10-18. 21	Axes 29	213	44	GR 1772. 3-9. 42	Fibulae 38
141	30	PRB 1964. 12-1. 384 (382)	Axes 29	214	44	GR 1856. 12-26. 904	Fibulae 38
142	30	PRB 1964. 12-1. 383 (308)	Axes 29, variant	215	44	PRB 1944. 7-2. 7	Fibulae 38
143	30	PRB 1868.l2-28.280	Axes 30	216	44	GR 1814. 7-4. 262	Fibulae 39
144	31	PRB 1880. 8-2.46	Axes 31	217	44	GR 1824. 4-34. 43	Fibulae 42
145	31	PRB WG 1073	Axes 32	218	44	GR 1910. 10-15. 2	Fibulae 42
146	31	PRB WG 1042	Axes 33	219	45	PRB WG1143	Close to Swords 4
147	31	PRB 1964. 12-1. 395 (232)	Axes unclassified	220	45	GR 1916. 6-1. 29	Swords 5
148	32	PRB 1866.6-27.98	Axes 34	221	46	GR 1839. 11-9. 48 A	Swords 5
149	32	PRB 1878. 11-1.208	Axes 34	222	46	GR 1839. 11-9. 48 B	Probably Sheaths 1
150	32	PRB - no register number	Axes 34	223	46	GR 1842. 7-30. 1	Swords 5
151	32	PRB 1964. 12-1. 387 (377)	Axes 34	224	47	PRB WG1144	Swords 5
152	32	PRB 1866.6-27.97	Axes 34, variant	225	47	GR 1975. 5-18. 3	Swords 5
153	33	PRB 1964. 12-1. 223 (309)	Axes 35	226	48	PRB 1922. 11-10. 1	Close to Swords 5
154	33	PRB 1866.6-27.99	Axes 36	227	48	GR 1856. 12-26. 704	Swords 6
155	33	PRB 1964. 12-1. 385 (312)	Axes 36	228	49	PRB WG1121	Spearheads 1
156	33	PRB 1964. 12-1. 213 (314)	Axes 36	229	49	GR 1975. 6-27. 1	Spearheads 2
157	34	PRB WG 1095	Close to Axes 45	230	49	GR 1975. 6-27. 34	Spearheads 2
158	34	PRB WG 1092	Close to Axes 45	231	50	GR 1975. 6-27. 14	Spearheads 2
159	34	PRB WG 1093	Axes 46	232	50	GR 1975. 6-27. 16	Spearheads 2
160	34	PRB WG 1094	Axes 46	233	50	PRB WG1112	Spearheads 3
161	35	PRB 1935. 10-18. 40	Axes 47	234	50	PRB 2000.l- l.32	Spearheads 3
162	35	PRB 1880. 8-2.47	Axes 47	235	51	GR 1814. 7-4. 1011	Spearheads 3
163	35	PRB WG 1091	Axes 47	236	51	GR 1916. 6-1. 18	Spearheads 3
164	35	PRB 1889.2-1.1	Axes 47	237	51	GR 1975. 6-27. 30	Spearheads 3 variant
165	36	PRB 1935. 10-18. 37	Axes 47	238	51	PRB WG1120	Spearheads 17
166	36	GR 1982. 6-17. 22	Axes 47	239	51	GR 1856. 12-26. 976	Unclassified
167	36	PRB 1866.6-27.108	Axes 47	240	51	GR 1975. 6-5.82	Arrowheads 3
168	36	GR 1982. 6-17. 21	Axes 48	241	52	PRB WG 1067	Axes 25
169	37	GR 1982. 6-17. 23	Axes 48	242	52	PRB WG 1068	Close to Axes 30
170	37	GR 1982. 6-17. 25	Axes 48	243	52	PRB WG 1069	Close to Axes 30
171	37	PRB 1935. 10-18. 39	Axes 48	244	52	PRB WG1147	Knives 1
172	37	PRB WG 1090	Axes 49	245	53	PRB WG 1070	Axes 43
173	37	PRB 1935. 10-18. 38	Axes 49	246	53	PRB WG 1097	Axes 50
174	38	PRB 1935. 10-18. 45	Axes 49	247	53	PRB 1935. 10-18. 32	Axes 51
175	38	PRB 1935. 10-18. 40a	Axes 49	248	53	PRB WG 1096	Axes 51
176	38	PRB 1880. 8-2.39	Axes 66	249	53	PRB 1964.12-6.76	Axes 51
177	38	PRB 1889.2-1.3	Axes 67	250	54	PRB 1964. 12-1. 426 (371)	Axes 54
178	38	PRB 1880. 8-2.43	Axes 68	251	54	PRB 1964. 12-1. 212 (322)	Axes 56
179	39	PRB 1964. 12-1. 440 (187)	Axes 69	252	54	PRB WG 1081	Axes 60
180	39	PRB 1964. 12-1. 441	Axes 69	253	54	PRB WG 1082	Axes 60
181	39	PRB WG 1089	Axes 70	254	54	PRB 2000.1-1.36	Axes 60
182	40	GR 1856. 12-26. 975	Chisels 2	255	55	GR 1873. 8-20. 237	Spindles 1
183	40	PRB 1935. 10-18. 22	Winged adzes 1	256	55	GR 1976. 1-3. 1	Spindles 2
184	40	PRB 1964. 12-1. 356 (381)	Winged adzes 1	257	55	GR 1856. 12-26. 1088	Knives 5
185	40	GR 1976. 12-31. 232	Sicilian sock. tools 1	258	55	GR 1975. 7-30. 20	Knives 6
186	40	PRB 1888.9-1.5	Sicilian sock. tools 2	259	56	GR 1982. 6-17. 56	Razors 5
187	40	GR 1842. 7-28. 705	Hammers 1	260	56	PRB 1880. 8-2. 33	Razors 5
188	40	PRB 1894. 7-27. 7	Sickles 1	261	56	GR 1865. 7-20. 51	Razors 6
189	41	GR 1856. 5-14. 1	Knives 1	262	56	PRB 1880. 8-2. 32	Razors 6
190	41	GR 1850. 1-17.85	Knives 1	263	56	GR 1839. 11-9. 45	Razors 6
191	41	PRB 1867. 10-11.9	Knives 1	264	56	GR 1867. 5-8. 382	Razors 7
192	41	GR 1847. 8-6. 140	Knives 2	265	56	PRB 1880. 8-2. 29	Razors 8
193	41	PRB 1880. 5-1.29	Knives 3	266	57	PRB 1880. 8-2. 35	Razors 10

Cat no.	Pl. no.	Register no.	Type	Cat no.	Pl. no.	Register no.	Type
267	57	GR 1935.8-23.54	Razors 11	340	67	GR 1920.11-18.21	Fibulae 49
268	57	GR 1838.6-8.80	Razors 11	341	67	GR 1872.6-4.722	Fibulae 52
269	57	GR 1982.6-17.58	Razors 11	342	68	GR 1872.6-4.1090	Fibulae 52
270	57	GR 1935.8-23.59	Razors 12	343	68	GR 1878.10-19.164	Fibulae 52
271	57	GR 1975.7-10.1A and 1B	Razors 13	344	68	GR 1814.7-4.251	Fibulae 52
272	58	GR 1772.3-7.316	Pins 8	345	69	GR 1772.3-9.15	Fibulae 57
273	58	GR 1994.8-3.9	Hair-rings 1	346	69	GR 1938.3-31.1	Fibulae 57
274	58	GR 1856.12-26.716	Pendants 1	347	69	GR 1878.10-19.165	See Fibulae 56 or 57
275	58	GR 1878.10-19.249	Ornaments unclassified	348	69	PRB WG1166	Fibulae unclassified
276	58	GR 1856.12-26.734	Torques 1	349	69	GR 1772.3-18.17	Fibulae unclassified
277	58	GR 1975.7-12.35	Torques 1	350	69	GR 1976.12-31.179	Fibulae unclassified
278	59	GR 1867.5-8.172	Fibulae 7	351	70	GR 1859.2-16.167	Bracelets 2a
279	59	PRB 1964.12-6.117	Fibulae 7	352	70	GR 1849.11-19.2	Bracelets 2a
280	59	GR 1922.4-13.39	Fibulae 7	353	70	GR 1975.9-3.1	Bracelets 2a
281	59	PRB 2000.1-1.2	Fibulae 7	354	71	GR 1975.7-12.68	Close to Bracelets 2a
282	59	PRB 1964.12-1.510 (210)	Fibulae 7	355	71	GR 1872.6-4.687	Bracelets 2b
283	59	GR 1976.2-8.5	Fibulae 7	356	71	GR 1856.12-26.720	Bracelets 3a
284	59	GR 1772.3-9.71	Fibulae 8	357	71	GR 1772.3-7.177	Bracelets 3b
285	59	GR 1814.7-4.250	Fibulae 8	358	72	PRB 1879.2-4.1A	Swords 7
286	60	GR 1772.3-9.72	Fibulae 9	359	72	GR 1994.8-3.1	Sheaths 1
287	60	GR 1976.2-5.6	Fibulae 9	360	73	GR 1975.5-18.4	Swords 8a
288	60	GR 1772.3-9.44	Fibulae 9	361	73	PRB 1916.6-5.186	Swords 8a
289	60	GR 1975.7-12.36	Fibulae 10	362	73	GR 1856.12-26.619	Swords 8a
290	60	GR 1824.4-34.10	Fibulae 10	363	74	PRB 1916.6-5.187	Swords 8a
291	60	GR 1920.11-18.6	Fibulae 10	364	74	GR 1975.5-18.5	Probably Swords 8a
292	60	GR 1976.2-8.6	Fibulae 10	365	74	GR 1856.12-26.618A	Probably Swords 8a
293	61	GR 1867.5-8.171	Fibulae 11	366	74	GR 1856.12-26.618 B	Sheaths 3
294	61	GR 2001.3-30.1	Fibulae 11	367	75	GR 1849.5-18.30 A	Swords 8b
295	61	GR 1920.11-18.5	close to Fibulae 11	368	75	GR 1849.5-18.30 B	Sheaths 2
296	61	GR 1920.11-18.4	Fibulae 11	369	75	GR 1975.5-18.6	Swords 8b
297	61	PRB BM.23	Fibulae 11	370	76	PRB POA 205	Swords 12
298	61	GR 1814.7-4.249	Fibulae 12a	371	76	GR 1873.8-20.229 A	Swords 12
299	61	PRB (P) 1974.12-1.323	Fibulae 12a	372	76	GR 1873.8-20.229 B	Sheaths unclassified
300	61	GR 1772.3-9.46	Fibulae 12a	373	76	GR 1865.7-22.9	Sheaths 2
301	61	GR 1916.6-1.6	Fibulae 12a	374	77	PRB 1964.12-1.327 (324)	Spearheads 2
302	61	GR 1910.4-20.2	Fibulae 13	375	77	PRB 1964.12-1.328 (325)	Spearheads 2
303	61	GR 1878.10-19.157	Fibulae 14	376	77	PRB WG1110	Spearheads 2
304	62	GR 1772.3-9.41	Fibulae 17	377	77	GR 1859.2-16.152	Spearheads 2
305	62	GR 1976.2-5.10	Fibulae 17	378	77	GR 1916.6-1.16	Spearheads 2
306	62	GR 1856.12-26.903	Fibulae 17	379	78	GR 1975.6-27.3	Spearheads 2
307	62	GR 1976.2-5.7	Fibulae 17	380	78	GR 1975.6-27.26	Spearheads 2
308	62	GR 1890.5-12.8	Fibulae 17	381	78	GR 1975.6-27.31	Spearheads 2
309	62	GR 1872.6-4.911	Fibulae 17	382	79	GR 1975.6-27.39	Spearheads 2
310	62	GR 1772.3-9.31	Fibulae 17	383	79	GR 1975.6-27.41	Spearheads 2
311	62	GR 1890.5-12.7	Fibulae 17	384	80	GR 1975.6-27.5	Spearheads 3
312	62	GR 1872.6-4.913	Fibulae 17	385	80	GR 1975.6-27.28	Spearheads 3
313	63	GR 1890.5-12.6	Fibulae 18	386	80	GR 1859.2-16.153	Spearheads 3, variant
314	63	GR 1867.5-8.181	Fibulae 32	387	81	GR 1856.12-26.620	Spearheads 4
315	63	GR 1890.5-12.10	Fibulae 33	388	81	GR 1853.2-18.3	Spearheads 4
316	63	GR 1890.5-12.9	Fibulae 33	389	81	GR 1916.6-1.21	Spearheads 4, variant
317	63	GR 1930.4-22.1	Fibulae 36	390	82	GR 1975.6-27.25	Spearheads 4, variant
318	63	GR 1856.12-26.898	Fibulae 37	391	82	GR 1975.6-27.42	Spearheads 4, variant
319	64	GR 1976.2-5.9	Fibulae 39	392	83	PRB 2000.1-1.33	Spearheads 5
320	64	GR 1772.3-9.40	Fibulae 39	393	83	PRB 1964.12-1.217 (328)	Spearheads 5
321	64	GR 1865.11-18.153	Fibulae 39	394	84	PRB WG1114	Spearheads 5
322	64	GR 1915.12-28.1	Fibulae 39	395	84	GR 1865.7-20.54	Spearheads 5
323	64	GR 1890.5-12.13	Fibulae 40	396	84	GR 1975.6-27.24	Spearheads 5
324	64	GR 1824.4-34.41	Fibulae 41a	397	85	PRB 1916.6-5.178	Spearheads 6
325	64	GR 1872.6-4.722bis	Fibulae 41b	398	85	PRB WG1127	Spearheads 6, variant
326	65	GR 1772.3-9.38	Fibulae 43	399	85	PRB WG1128	Spear-butts 5
327	65	GR 1876.11-7.1	Fibulae 44	400	86	PRB 2000.1-1.34	Spearheads 8
328	65	GR 1856.12-26.1074	Fibulae 45	401	86	PRB 2000.1-1.35	Spearheads 8
329	66	PRB 1964.12-1.513	Fibulae 46	402	87	PRB WG1099	Spearheads 8
330	66	GR 1976.2-5.13	Fibulae 46	403	87	GR 1916.6-1.17	Spearheads 8
331	66	GR 1976.2-5.12	Fibulae 46	404	87	PRB WG1119	Spearheads 9
332	66	GR 1976.2-5.16	Fibulae 47	405	87	PRB WG1113	Spearheads 9
333	66	GR 1772.3-9.43	Fibulae 47	406	88	PRB 1880.8-2.42	Spearheads 10
334	66	GR 1976.2-5.15	Fibulae 47	407	88	PRB WG1116	Spearheads 10
335	66	GR 1975.7-12.41	Fibulae 47	408	88	PRB WG1118	Spearheads 10
336	66	GR 1938.3-31.8	Fibulae 47	409	88	GR 1814.7-4.1577	Spearheads 10
337	67	GR 1976.2-5.11	Fibulae 48	410	88	GR 1867.5-8.186	Spearheads 10
338	67	GR 1975.7-12.42	Fibulae 48	411	89	GR 1975.6-27.17	Spearheads 10
339	67	GR 1976.2-5.14	Fibulae 48	412	89	GR 1975.6-27.7	Spearheads 10, variant

Cat no.	Pl. no.	Register no.	Type	Cat no.	Pl. no.	Register no	Type
413	89	GR 1975.6-27.11	Spearheads 10, variant	486	109	PRB 1935.10-18.25	Axes 40
414	90	PRB 1964.12-1.329 (329)	Spearheads 11	487	110	PRB 1964.12-1.386 (311)	Axes 40
415	90	PRB WG1100	Spearheads 11	488	110	PRB 1964.12-1.382 (378)	Axes 40
416	90	PRB WG1102	Spearheads 11	489	110	PRB 1866.6-27.101	Axes 41
417	91	PRB WG1103	Spearheads 11	490	110	PRB 1964.12-1.393 (313)	Axes 41
418	91	PRB WG1104	Spearheads 11	491	111	PRB WG 1074	Axes 42
419	91	PRB WG1115	Spearheads 11	492	111	PRB 1935.10-18.18	Axes 42
420	91	GR 1975.6-27.4	Spearheads 11	493	111	PRB 1935.10-18.34	Axes 52
421	91	GR 1975.6-27.2	Spearheads 11	494	112	PRB 1964.12-1.407 (363)	Axes 55
422	92	PRB 1883.4-26.3	Spearheads 13	495	112	PRB 1964.12-1.404 (362)	Axes 56
423	92	PRB WG1098	Spearheads 13	496	112	PRB WG 1084	Axes 57
424	92	PRB WG1101	Spearheads 13	497	112	PRB 1935.10-18.29	Axes 57
425	93	GR 1849.5-18.46	Spearheads 13	498	113	PRB Morel.1239	Axes 58
426	93	GR 1916.6-1.19	Spearheads 13	499	113	PRB 1866.6-27.86	Axes 58
427	93	GR 1975.6-27.12	Spearheads 13	500	113	PRB 1883.8-2.7	Axes 58
428	93	GR 1975.6-27.19	Spearheads 13	501	113	PRB 1964.12-1.408 (310)	Axes 58
429	94	GR 1975.6-27.20	Spearheads 13	502	113	PRB 1880.8-2.44	Axes 59
430	94	GR 1975.6-27.21	Spearheads 13	503	113	PRB 1935.10-18.28	Close to Axes 60
431	95	GR 1975.6-27.23	Spearheads 13	504	113	PRB 1935.10-18.30	Close to Axes 60
432	95	GR 1975.6-27.29	Spearheads 13	505	114	PRB 1883.8-2.8	Axes 61
433	96	GR 1975.6-27.18	Spearheads 14	506	114	PRB WG 1083	Axes 61
434	96	GR 1975.6-27.36	Spearheads 14	507	114	PRB 1964.12-1.398 (316)	Axes 61
435	97	PRB WG1124	Spearheads 16	508	114	PRB 1964.12-1.400 (319)	Axes 61
436	97	PRB 1925.10-17.3	Spearheads 16	509	115	PRB 1964.12-1.402 (317)	Axes 62
437	97	PRB 1964.12-6.78	Spearheads 16	510	115	PRB 1964.12-1.403 (318)	Axes 62
438	98	PRB WG1125	Spearheads 16	511	115	PRB Old Acquisition 135 (Registered OA 21 August 1946)	Axes 62
439	98	PRB WG1126	Spear-butts 5				
440	98	GR 1958.10-27.1	Spear-butts 4	512	115	PRB 1964.12-1.401 (320)	Axes 62
441	98	GR 1975.6-5.78	Arrowheads 3	513	115	PRB 1964.12-1.399 (321)	Axes 62
442	98	GR 1975.6-5.79	Arrowheads 3	514	116	PRB 1876.7-6.10	Chisels 3
443	99	GR 1772.3-9.30	Fibulae 35	515	116	PRB 1883.4-26.5	Chisels 4
444	99	GR 1772.3-9.34	Fibulae 35	516	116	GR 1982.6-17.63	Knives 7
445	99	GR 1938.3-31.10	Fibulae 37	517	116	PRB WG1146	Knives 8
446	99	GR 1938.3-31.11	Fibulae 37	518	117	GR 1975.5-18.8	Knives 9
447	100	GR 1872.6-4.684	Bracelets 1	519	117	GR 1814.7-4.701	Knives 9
448	100	GR 1872.6-4.685	Bracelets 1	520	118	PRB 1880.8-2.28	Razors 9
449	100	GR 1814.7-4.235	Bracelets 1	521	118	GR 1935.8-23.56	Razors 14
450	100	GR 1814.7-4.236	Bracelets 1	522	118	GR 1875.3-13.8	Razors 14
451	101	PRB WG1107	Spearheads 2	523	118	GR 1935.8-23.55	Razors 14
452	101	PRB WG1108	Spearheads 2	524	119	GR 1935.8-23.57	Razors 15
453	101	PRB WG1105	Spearheads 6	525	119	GR 1840.2-12.18	Razors 16
454	101	PRB WG1106	Spearheads 6	526	119	GR 1982.6-17.57	Razors 16
455	102	PRB 1964.12-1.219 (326)	Spearheads 13	527	119	GR 1982.6-17.59	Razors 16
456	102	PRB 1964.12-1.218 (327)	Spearheads 14	528	119	GR 1935.8-23.58	Razors 16
457	103	PRB WG1136	Swords 8a	529	120	GR 1927.11-15.36	Pins 9
458	103	PRB WG1138	Spearheads 4	530	120	GR 1975.7-12.45	Pendants 2
459	103	PRB WG1137	Spearheads 5	531	120	GR 1824.4-99.20	Pendants 3
460	104	PRB 1868.12-28.279	Axes 37	532	120	GR 1878.10-19.244	Pendants 4
461	104	PRB 1875.12-29.2	Axes 37	533	120	GR 1772.3-7.210	Pendants 5
462	104	PRB 1935.10-18.26	Axes 37	534	120	GR 1856.12-26.696	Pendants 5
463	104	PRB 1964.12-1.388 (374)	Axes 37	535	120	GR 1958.8-22.8	Pendants 5, variant
464	104	PRB 1964.12-1.391 (375)	Axes 37	536	120	GR 1974.12-3.11	Pendants 6
465	105	PRB WG 1046	Axes 38	537	121	GR 1975.10-5.18	Pendants 7
466	105	PRB 1964.12-1.220 (315)	Close to Axes 38	538	121	GR 1772.3-7.72	Pendants 7
467	105	GR 1865.7-20.105	Axes 38	539	121	GR 1975.10-5.20	Pendants 7
468	105	PRB 1866.6-27.100	Axes 38	540	121	GR 1856.12-26.1053	Pendants 8
469	106	PRB WG 1075	Axes 39	541	121	GR 1954.6-1.1	Pendants 9
470	106	PRB WG 1076	Axes 39	542	121	GR 1954.6-1.2	Pendants 9
471	106	PRB WG 1077	Axes 39	543	122	GR 1908.11-20.27	Pendants 10
472	106	PRB 1964.12-6.86	Axes 39	544	122	GR 1912.12-18.1	Pendants 11
473	106	PRB 1866.6-27.102	Axes 39	545	122	GR 1856.12-26.907	Pendants 11
474	107	PRB 1878.11-1.207	Axes 39	546	122	GR 1982.3-2.63	Pendants 11
475	107	PRB 1935.10-18.24	Axes 39	547	123	GR 1856.12-26.728	Pendants 12
476	107	PRB 1935.10-18.27	Axes 39	548	123	GR 1975.12-3.9	Pendants 12
477	107	PRB 1964.12-1.389 (373)	Axes 39	549	123	GR 1814.7-4.1589	Belt clasp ring
478	107	PRB 1964.12-1.392 (376)	Axes 39	550	123	GR 1772.3-7.164	Torques 2
479	108	PRB WG 1078	Axes 40	551	124	PRB 2000.1-1.1	Fibulae 12b
480	108	PRB WG 1079	Axes 40	552	124	GR 1846.6-8.1	Fibulae 15
481	108	PRB 1935.10-18.44	Axes 40	553	124	PRB 2000.1-1.16	Fibulae 19
482	108	PRB WG 2263	Axes 40	554	124	GR 1976.2-5.4	Fibulae 19
483	109	PRB 1873.6-2.15	Axes 40	555	124	PRB 1964.12-6.96	Fibulae 19
484	109	PRB 1866.6-27.103	Axes 40	556	124	PRB 1964.12-6.80	Fibulae 19
485	109	PRB 1935.10-18.23	Axes 40	557	124	GR 1976.2-8.1	Fibulae 19

Cat no.	Pl. no.	Register no.	Type	Cat no.	Pl. no.	Register no.	Type
558	124	PRB (P) 1974. 12-1. 324	Fibulae 19	631	137	PRB 1964. 12-6. 79	Fibulae unclassified
559	124	PRB 2000.1-1. 24	Fibulae 19	632	137	GR 1772. 3-9. 132	Fibulae unclassified
560	125	PRB 2000.1-1.25	Fibulae 20	633	137	GR 1976. 2-5.1	Fibulae unclassified
561	125	PRB 1919. 12-13. 1	Fibulae 20	634	137	GR 1878. 10-19. 167	Fibulae unclassified
562	125	PRB 2000.1-1.23	Fibulae 21	635	138	GR 1856. 12-26. 722	Bracelets 2c
563	125	PRB 1964. 12-6. 94	Fibulae 21	636	138	GR 1772. 3-7. 178	Bracelets 2d
564	125	GR 1878. 10-19. 159	Fibulae 22	637	138	GR 1772. 3-7. 123	Bracelets 3a variant
565	125	PRB 2000.1-1.4	Fibulae 23	638	139	GR 1772. 3-7. 133	Bracelets 4
566	125	PRB (P) 1974. 12-1.322	Fibulae 23	639	139	GR 1772. 3-7. 174	Bracelets 4
567	125	GR 1920. 11-18. 3	Fibulae 23	640	139	GR 1814. 7-4. 233	Bracelets 4
568	126	GR 1916. 6-1.8	Fibulae 23	641	140	GR 1814. 7-4. 238	Bracelets 4
569	126	GR 1976. 2-6. 1	Fibulae 23	642	140	GR 1772. 3-7. 135	Bracelets 4
570	126	GR 1991. 12-18. 21	Fibulae 23	643	140	GR 1814. 7-4. 234	Bracelets 4
571	126	GR 1916. 6-1.7	Fibulae 23	644	140	GR 1856. 12-26. 724	Bracelets 4
572	126	GR 1909. 6-22. 1	Fibulae 24	645	141	GR 1975. 9-5. 10	Bracelets 5
573	126	GR 1876. 9-2. 1	Fibulae 24	646	141	GR 1814. 7-4. 237	Bracelets 5
574	127	PRB 1911. 4-1. 1	Fibulae 25	647	141	GR 1814. 7-4. 230	Bracelets 5
575	127	GR 1905. 1-15. 1	Fibulae 25	648	141	GR 1838. 6-8.73	Bracelets 5
576	127	GR 1814. 7-4. 797	Fibulae 25	649	141	GR 1975. 9-5. 15 bis	Bracelets 5 variant
577	127	GR 1814. 7-4. 800	Fibulae 25	650	142	GR 1772. 3-7. 149	Bracelets 6
578	127	PRB 1916. 10-14. 1	Fibulae 25	651	142	GR 1772. 3-7. 151	Bracelets 6
579	127	GR 1920. 11-18. 2	Fibulae 25	652	142	GR 1824. 4-6. 2	Bracelets 6
580	127	PRB 1944. 7-2. 5	Fibulae 25	653	142	GR 1814. 7-4. 231	Bracelets 7
581	128	GR 1824. 4-34. 37	Fibulae 26	654	142	GR 1878. 10-19. 180	Bracelets 7
582	128	GR 1976. 2-5. 5	Fibulae 27	655	143	GR 1772. 3-7. 122	Bracelets 8
583	128	GR 1976. 2-5. 3	Fibulae 27	656	143	GR 1772. 3-7. 121	Bracelets 8
584	128	GR 1772. 3-9.77	Fibulae 27	657	143	GR 1772. 3-7. 167	Bracelets 9a
585	128	GR 1865. 7-20. 48	Fibulae 27	658	143	GR 1772. 3-7. 157	Bracelets 9a
586	129	GR 1772. 3-9. 21	Fibulae 28	659	143	GR 1772. 3-7. 156	Bracelets 9a
587	129	GR 1772. 3-9. 22	Fibulae 28	660	143	GR 1772. 3-7. 165	Bracelets 9a
588	129	GR 1814. 7-4. 794	Fibulae 28	661	143	GR 1772. 3-7. 126	Bracelets 9b
589	129	GR 1938. 3-31. 12	Fibulae 28, variant	662	144	GR 1772. 3-7. 141	Bracelets 10a
590	129	GR 1980. 2-1. 32	Fibulae 28, variant	663	144	GR 1772. 3-7. 145	Bracelets 10a
591	129	PRB 2000.1-1.17	Fibulae 28, variant	664	144	GR 1772. 3-7. 162	Bracelets 10a
592	129	GR 1824. 4-34. 21	Fibulae 29	665	144	GR 1975. 9-5. 14	Bracelets 10a
593	129	GR 1938. 3-31. 13	Fibulae 29	666	145	GR 1975. 9-5. 15	Bracelets 10a
594	129	GR 1920. 11-18. 16	Fibulae 29	667	145	GR 1975. 9-5. 16	Bracelets 10b
595	129	GR 1824. 4-34. 38	Fibulae 29	668	145	GR 1772. 3-7. 168	Bracelets 11
596	129	GR 1920. 11-18. 17	Fibulae 29	669	145	GR 1772. 3-7. 153	Bracelets 11
597	129	GR 1867. 5-8. 161	Fibulae 29	670	146	GR 1975. 9-4.66	Bracelets 12a
598	130	GR 1976. 2-8. 2	Fibulae 30a	671	146	GR 1975. 9-4. 44	Bracelets 12a
599	130	GR 1772. 3-9. 3	Fibulae 30b	672	146	GR 1814. 7-4. 1579	Bracelets 12a
600	130	GR 1772. 3-9. 5	Fibulae 30b	673	146	GR 1975. 9-4. 45	Bracelets 12a
601	130	GR 1772. 3-9. 9	Fibulae 30b	674	146	GR 1975. 9-4. 50	Bracelets 12a
602	130	GR 1772. 3-9. 6	Fibulae 30b	675	146	GR 1975. 9-4. 51	Bracelets 12a
603	130	PRB 1964. 12-6. 114	Fibulae 34	676	146	GR 1975. 9-4.65	Bracelets 12a
604	131	GR 1920. 11-18. 18	Fibulae 50	677	147	GR 1975. 9-4. 48	Bracelets 12a
605	131	GR 1872. 6-4.912	Fibulae 51a	678	147	GR 1975. 9-4. 49	Bracelets 12a
606	131	GR 1910. 10-15. 3	Fibulae 51b	679	147	GR 1975. 9-4. 52	Bracelets 12a
607	131	GR 1856. 12-26. 1038	Fibulae 51b	680	147	GR 1975. 9-4. 53	Bracelets 12a
608	131	GR 1976. 3-1. 5	Fibulae 51b	681	147	GR 1975. 9-4. 54	Bracelets 12a
609	131	GR 1824. 4-34. 42	Fibulae 53a	682	147	GR 1975. 9-4. 55	Bracelets 12a
610	131	GR 1814. 7-4. 252	Fibulae 53b	683	147	GR 1975. 9-4. 56	Bracelets 12a
611	132	GR 1772. 3-9. 37	Fibulae 53b	684	147	GR 1975. 9-4. 57	Bracelets 12a
612	132	GR 1872. 6-4. 1089	Fibulae 54	685	147	GR 1975. 9-4. 38	Bracelets 12a
613	133	GR 1856. 12-26. 718-719	Fibulae 55	686	147	GR 1975. 9-4. 39	Bracelets 12a
614	133	GR 1814. 7-4. 253	Fibulae 55	687	147	GR 1975. 9-4. 40	Bracelets 12a
615	133	GR 1824. 4-98. 19	Probably Fibulae 55	688	147	GR 1975. 9-4. 41	Bracelets 12a
616	134	GR 1824. 4-98. 18	See Fibulae 55	689	147	GR 1975. 9-4. 42	Bracelets 12a
617	134	GR 1884. 10-11. 45	See Fibulae 55	690	147	GR 1975. 9-4. 43	Bracelets 12a
618	134	GR 1772. 3-9. 115	See Fibulae 55	691	147	GR 1975. 9-4. 46	Bracelets 12a
619	135	GR 1856. 12-26. 762	See Fibulae 55	692	147	GR 1975. 9-4. 47	Bracelets 12a
620	135	GR 1856. 12-26. 763	See Fibulae 55	693	148	GR 1975. 9-4. 17	Bracelets 12a
621	135	GR 1856. 12-26. 764	See Fibulae 55	694	148	GR 1975. 9-4. 22	Bracelets 12a
622	135	GR 1772. 3-18. 23	See Fibulae 55	695	148	GR 1975. 9-4. 23	Bracelets 12a
623	135	GR 1856. 12-26. 717	Fibulae 54 or 55	696	148	GR 1975. 9-4. 27	Bracelets 12a
624	136	PRB 1916. 6-5. 184	Fibulae 56	697	148	GR 1975. 9-4. 32	Bracelets 12a
625	136	GR 1824. 4-98. 20	Fibulae 56	698	148	GR 1975. 9-4. 35	Bracelets 12a
626	136	GR 1938. 3-31. 2	Fibulae 56	699	148	GR 1975. 9-4. 36	Bracelets 12a
627	136	GR 1772. 3-18. 16	Fibulae 58	700	148	GR 1975. 9-4. 37	Bracelets 12a
628	136	GR 1974. 12-3. 9	See Fibulae 58	701	148	GR 1975. 9-4. 60	Bracelets 12a
629	137	GR 1878. 10-19. 166	Fibulae unclassified	702	148	GR 1975. 9-4. 61	Bracelets 12a
630	137	GR 1772. 3-9. 116	Fibulae unclassified	703	148	GR 1975. 9-4. 62	Bracelets 12a

Cat no.	Pl. no.	Register no.	Type	Cat no.	Pl. no.	Register no.	Type
704	148	GR 1975. 9-4. 63	Bracelets 12a	772	165	GR 1867. 5-8. 185	Spearheads 15
705	148	GR 1975. 9-4. 64	Bracelets 12a	773	165	GR 1867. 5-8. 190	Spear-butts 4
706	149	GR 1975. 9-4. 20	Bracelets 12a	774	166	GR 1867. 5-8. 188	Spearheads 15
707	149	GR 1975. 9-4. 21	Bracelets 12a	775	166	GR 1867. 5-8. 189	Spearheads 15
708	149	GR 1975. 9-4. 24	Bracelets 12a	776	167	GR 1975. 6-27. 38	Spearheads 15
709	149	GR 1975. 9-4. 25	Bracelets 12a	777	167	PRB WG1109	Spearheads 15
710	149	GR 1975. 9-4. 26	Bracelets 12a	778	168	PRB WG 1130	Spear-butts 1
711	149	GR 1975. 9-4. 14	Bracelets 12a	779	168	PRB WG1131	Spear-butts 1
712	149	GR 1975. 9-4. 15	Bracelets 12a	780	168	PRB WG1132	Spear-butts 1
713	149	GR 1975. 9-4. 16	Bracelets 12a	781	168	PRB WG1129	Spear-butts 2
714	149	GR 1975. 9-4. 18	Bracelets 12a	782	168	PRB 1964. 12-6. 77	Spear-butts 3
715	149	GR 1975. 9-4. 19	Bracelets 12a	783	168	GR 1975. 7-2. 2	Spear-butts 3
716	150	GR 1975. 9-4. 33	Bracelets 12a	784	169	GR 1772. 3-18. 12	Fibulae 31
717	150	GR 1975. 9-4. 34	Bracelets 12a	785	169	GR 1772. 3-18. 13	Fibulae 31
718	150	GR 1975. 9-4. 58	Bracelets 12a	786	170	GR 1814. 7-4. 705	Bracelets 4
719	150	GR 1975. 9-4. 59	Bracelets 12a	787	170	GR 1814. 7-4. 706	Bracelets 4
720	150	GR 1975. 9-4. 28	Bracelets 12a	788	170	GR 1772. 3-7. 180	Bracelets 4
721	150	GR 1975. 9-4. 31	Bracelets 12a	789	170	GR 1772. 3-7.181	Bracelets 4
722	150	GR 1975. 9-4. 29	Bracelets 12a	790	171	GR 1824. 4-6. 7	Bracelets 5
723	150	GR 1975. 9-4. 30	Bracelets 12a	791	171	GR 1824. 4-6. 6	Bracelets 5
724	150	GR 1975. 9-4. 12	Bracelets 12a variant	792	171	GR 1824. 4-6. 3	Bracelets 5
725	151	GR 1964. 12-21. 4	Bracelets 12b	793	171	GR 1824. 4-6. 4	Bracelets 5
726	151	GR 1935. 8-23. 66	Bracelets 12b	794	171	GR 1824. 4-6. 5	Bracelets 5
727	151	GR 1975.9-4.1	Bracelets 12b	795	172	GR 1772. 3-7. 131	Bracelets 13a
728	151	GR l975.9-4.2	Bracelets l2b	796	172	GR 1772. 3-7. 132	Bracelets 13a
729	151	GR l975.9-4.3	Bracelets l2b	797	172	GR 1867. 5-8. 212	Bracelets 13c
730	151	GR l975.9-4.4	Bracelets 12b	798	172	GR 1867. 5-8. 213	Bracelets 13c
731	151	GR l975.9-4.5	Bracelets 12b	799	173	PRB 1909. 3-18.1	Spearheads 15
732	151	GR 1975.9-4.6	Bracelets 12b	800	173	PRB WG2256	Spearheads 15
733	152	GR l975.9-4.7	Bracelets 12b	801	174	GR 1975. 12-3. 10	Horse bit
734	152	GR 1975.9-4.8	Bracelets 12b	802	174	GR 1975. 12-3. 11	Horse bit
735	152	GR 1975.9-4.9	Bracelets 12b	803	174	GR 1890. 9-21. 18	Openwork disc
736	152	GR 1975.9-4. 10	Bracelets 12b	804	175	GR 1857. 10-13. 2	Belt plaque
737	152	GR 1975.9-4.11	Bracelets 12b	805	176	GR 1975. 7-3. 1	Belt plaque
738	152	GR 1975.9-4. 13	Bracelets 12c	806	176	GR 1814. 7-4. 1055	Belt plaque
739	152	GR 1975.9-4.67	Bracelets 12d	807	177	GR 1872. 10-8. 4	Openwork disc
740	153	GR 1824. 4-6. 22	Bracelets 13a	808	177	GR 1890. 9-21. 19	Armour disc
741	153	GR 1975. 7-12. 29	Bracelets 13b	809	178	GR 1824. 4-98. 6	Tube with finial
742	153	GR 1935. 8-23. 65	Bracelets 13d	810	178	GR 1824. 4-98. 8	Finial
743	154	PRB WG1133	Swords 9a	811	179-180	GR 1968. 6-27. 1	Villanovan helmet
744	154	GR 1969. 12-31. 132	Sheaths 3	812	181-182	GR 1928. 1-17. 2	Vessel & Lid
745	155	GR 1975. 5-18. 7	Swords 9b	813	183	GR 1772. 3-18. 10	Band with birds
746	155	PRB 1964. 12-6. 116a, b	Swords 9b	814	183	GR 1772. 3-18. 11	Band with birds
747	156	GR 1994. 8-3. 2	Sheaths 3	815	183	GR 1772. 3-18. 24	Band with birds
748	156	GR 1975. 5-18. 2 A	Swords 10	816	184	GR 1772. 3-18. 15	Band with birds
749	156	GR 1975. 5-18. 2 B	Sheaths 4	817	185-190	GR 1824. 4-98. 3	Pastiche
750	156	PRB WG1145	Swords 11	818	191-194	GR 1824. 4-98. 4	Pastiche
751	157	PRB 1883. 4-26. 8	Spearheads 2	819	195-196	GR 1824. 4-98. 5	Pastiche
752	157	GR 1814. 7-4. 1010	Spearheads 3	820	197	GR 1974. 12-3. 17	Figurine
753	157	GR 1975. 6-27. 22	Spearheads 3 variant	821	197	GR 1772. 3-5. 22	Figurine
754	158	GR 1849. 5-18. 47	Spearheads 4	822	197	GR 1912. 11-25. 51	Figurine
755	158	PRB 1918. 10-5. 1	Spearheads 4	823	198	PRB 1883. 8-2. 6	Axes unclassified
756	158	PRB 1916. 6-5. 177	Spearheads 4	824	198	PRB Old Acquistion 101 (Registered OA 19 July 1939)	Axes unclassified
757	159	PRB 1891. 5-14. 65	Spearheads 4				
758	159	PRB 1883. 4-26. 7	Spearheads 4 variant	825	198	PRB 1964. 12-1. 377 (305)	Tools unclassified
759	160	GR 1856. 12-26. 1087	Spearheads 6	826	198	PRB 1964. 12-1. 459 (345)	Chisels unclassified
760	160	GR 1865. 7-22. 11	Spearheads 6 variant	827	198	PRB 1964. 12-1. 203 (302)	Chisels unclassified
761	161	GR 1975. 6-27. 15	Spearheads 7	828	198	GR 1886. 3-9. 6	Bracelets unclassified
762	161	GR 1975. 6-27. 33	Spearheads 7	829	198	GR 1867. 5-8. 216, 217	Bracelets unclassified
763	161	GR 1982. 6-17. 27	Spearheads 7	830	199	GR 1909. 6-21. 1	Close to Swords 12
764	161	GR 1865. 7-20. 53	Spearheads 7	831	199	PRB WG1149a	Swords unclassified
765	162	GR 1873. 8-20. 231	Spearheads 7	832	200	GR 1842. 7-28. 682	Spearheads unclassified
766	162	GR 1873. 8-20. 238	Spear-butts 5	833	200	GR 1867. 5-8. 143	Spearheads unclassified
767	163	GR 1975. 6-27. 9	Spearheads 12	834	200	GR 1916. 6-1. 22	Spearheads unclassified
768	163	GR 1975. 6-27. 27	Spearheads 12	835	200	GR 1772. 3-3. 1000	Spearheads unclassified
769	164	GR 1975. 6-27. 32	Spearheads 12	836	200	PRB WG1158	Arrowheads unclassified
770	164	PRB 1964. 12-6. 84	Spearheads 12	837	200	PRB WG1157	Arrowheads unclassified
771	165	GR 1824. 4-7. 2	Spearheads 15				

Index of Types

Type	Cat. no.	Type	Cat. no.	Type	Cat. no.
Fibulae 42	217, 218	Pendants 1	274	Spear-butts 4	440, 773
Fibulae 43	326	Pendants 2	530	Spear-butts 5	399, 439, 766
Fibulae 44	327	Pendants 3	531	Spearheads 1	228
Fibulae 45	328	Pendants 4	532	Spearheads 2	229–232, 374–383, 451, 452, 751
Fibulae 46	329–331	Pendants 5	533, 534		
Fibulae 47	332–336	Pendants 5, variant	535	Spearheads 3	233–236, 384, 385, 752
Fibulae 48	337–339	Pendants 6	536	Spearheads 3, variant	237, 386, 753
Fibulae 49	340	Pendants 7	537–539	Spearheads 4	387, 388, 458, 754–757
Fibulae 50	604	Pendants 8	540	Spearheads 4, variant	389–391, 758
Fibulae 51a	605	Pendants 9	541, 542	Spearheads 5	392–396, 459
Fibulae 51b	606–608	Pendants 10	543	Spearheads 6	397, 453, 454, 759
Fibulae 52	341–344	Pendants 11	544–546	Spearheads 6, variant	398, 760
Fibulae 53a	609	Pendants 12	547, 548	Spearheads 7	761–765
Fibulae 53b	610, 611	Pins 1	113	Spearheads 8	400–403
Fibulae 54	612	Pins 2	114	Spearheads 9	404, 405
Fibulae 54 or 55	623	Pins 3	115	Spearheads 10	406–411
Fibulae 55	613, 614	Pins 4	116	Spearheads 10, variant	412, 413
Fibulae 55, probably	615	Pins 5	198	Spearheads 11	414–421
Fibulae 55, see	616–622	Pins 6	199	Spearheads 12	767–770
Fibulae 56	624–626	Pins 7	200	Spearheads 13	422–432, 455
Fibulae 56 or 57, see	347	Pins 8	272	Spearheads 14	433, 434, 456
Fibulae 57	345, 346	Pins 9	529	Spearheads 15	771, 772, 774–777, 799, 800
Fibulae 58	627	Razors 1	106–108		
Fibulae 58, see	628	Razors 1, close	109	Spearheads 16	435–438
Fibulae unclassified	348–350, 629–634	Razors 2	110–112	Spearheads 17	238
Figurine	820	Razors 3	195	Spearheads unclass	832–835
Figurine	821	Razors 4	196, 197	Spindles 1	255
Figurine	822	Razors 5	259, 260	Spindles 2	256
Finial	810	Razors 6	261–263	Swords 1	81
Finial, tube with	809	Razors 7	264	Swords 2	125
Hair-rings 1	273	Razors 8	265	Swords 3	126
Halberds 1	14	Razors 9	520	Swords 4	127
Halberds 2	41	Razors 10	266	Swords 4, close	219
Hammers 1	187	Razors 11	267–269	Swords 5	220, 221, 223–225
Helmet, Villanovan	811	Razors 12	270	Swords 5, close	226
Horse bits	801, 802	Razors 13	271	Swords 6	227
Knives 1	189–191, 244	Razors 14	521–523	Swords 7	358
Knives 2	192	Razors 15	524	Swords 8a	360–363, 457
Knives 3	193	Razors 16	525–528	Swords 8a, probably	364, 365
Knives 4	194	Sheaths 1	359	Swords 8b	367, 369
Knives 5	257	Sheaths 1, probably	222	Swords 9a	743
Knives 6	258	Sheaths 2	368, 373	Swords 9b	745, 746
Knives 7	516	Sheaths 3	366, 744, 747	Swords 10	748
Knives 8	517	Sheaths 4	749	Swords 11	750
Knives 9	518, 519	Sheaths unclassified	372	Swords 12	370, 371
Needles 1	101, 102	Sheet disc 1	201	Swords 12, close	830
Openwork disc	803	Sicilian sock. tools 1	185	Swords unclassified	831
Openwork disc	807	Sicilian sock. tools 2	186	Tools unclassified	825
Ornaments unclass	275	Sickles 1	188	Torques 1	276, 277
Pastiche	817	Spear-butts 1	778–780	Torques 2	550
Pastiche	818	Spear-butts 2	781	Unclassified	239
Pastiche	819	Spear-butts 3	782, 783	Vessel & Lid	812

Index of Provenances and Alleged Provenances

Figures in bold refer to catalogue numbers.

Abruzzo, **4,72,422**
  'Alba della Massa', probably Massa d'Albe
    (L'Aquila) **480**
  Albe (L'Aquila) **38**
  Complio (probably Campli, Teramo), **109**
  Magliano (L'Aquila), **79,160**
  'Massica' (probably Marsica, L'Aquila), **135,
    159,177,201,348,404,408,419,779**
  Popoli (Pescara), **394**
  Sulmona (L'Aquila), **451,452**
  Teramo, **119**
Acerra (Naples), Campania, **750**
Agrigento, Sicily, **47,48,49,50,51,423**
'Alba della Massa', probably Massa d'Albe
  (L'Aquila), Abruzzo, **480**
Albe (L'Aquila), Abruzzo, **38**
Albania, *See* Scutari
Anagni (Frosinone), Lazio, **32**
Ancona, Marche, **100**
Apulia,
  Bari, **387,453,454,498,755**
  Bovino, Capitanata (Foggia), **163,398, 399**
  Ruvo (Bari), **6,274,318,362,545,613,623**
Arezzo, Tuscany, **455,456,763**
Armento (Potenza), Basilicata, **227,356,365,
  366,635,644**
Athens, Greece, **35,259,261,585**
Austria, *See* Gorz, Kustenland
  Prettau, Tirol, **146**
  Steiermark, **121,299,558**
  Tirol, **566**
Bagni di Lucca, Tuscany, **40**
Bari, Apulia, **387,453,454,498,755**
Basilicata, *See* Armento (Potenza)
  Metaponto (Matera), **416**
  Potenza, **98,105**
Bazzano (Bologna), Emilia Romagna, **33**
Belgrade, Serbia, **279**
Bisignano (Cosenza), Calabria, **219**
Bologna, Emilia Romagna, **99,118,447,448,
  471,803**
Bolsena (Viterbo), Lazio, **780**
Bomarzo (Viterbo), Lazio, **799,800**
Bovino, Capitanata (Foggia), Apulia, **163,398,
  399**
Box, Wiltshire, England, **574**
Brescia, Lombardy, **19**
Cagliari, Sardinia, **181**
Calabria, **249,407,778,781**
  Bisignano (Cosenza), **219**
  Castrovillari (Cosenza), **157**
  Locri (Reggio Calabria), **742,743,744**
Calvatone (Cremona), Lombardy, **14**
Campania, **1,20,22,174,481,809,817,818**
  Acerra (Naples), **750**
  Capua (Caserta), **7,27,248,346,376,393,402,
    418,435,770,777**
  Caserta, **807**
  Cuma (Naples), **162,277,355,405,406,837**
  Naples, **2,137,220,358,359,361,363,397,
    403,417,424,426,500,515,617,747,756,823**
  Nola (Naples), **71,327**
  Paestum (Salerno), **341**

Pozzuoli (Naples), **10,91,164,233, 415** *See
  also* Cuma, **406**
Terra di Lavoro (Caserta), **626**
Torre Annunziata (Naples), **46,534,619,
  620,621**
Canino (Viterbo), Lazio, **136** *See also* Vulci
Capua (Caserta), Campania, **7,27,248,346,
  376,393,402,418,435,770,777**
Caserta, Campania, **807**
Cassino (Frosinone), Lazio, **457,458,459**
'Castiglion de Sago', Lake Como, Lombardy,
  241,242,243,244
Castiglione del Lago (Perugia), Umbria, **517**
Castro Giovanni (=Enna), Sicily, **178**
Castrovillari (Cosenza), Calabria, **157**
Chiusi (Siena), Tuscany, **521,524**
'Complio', probably Campli (Teramo), Abruzzo,
  109
'Corinth', Greece, **169**
Corneto (Tarquinia, Viterbo), Lazio, **5,30,836**
  See also Tarquinia
Croatia, *See* Osor, Island of Cres
Cuma (Naples), Campania, **162,277,355,405,
  406,837**
Dorset, England, **215,580**
Emilia Romagna
  Bazzano (Bologna), **33**
  Bologna, **99,118,447,448,471,803**
  Salso (Parma), **470**
England, **297**
  Box, Wiltshire, **574**
  Dorset, **215,580**
  'Foxcote', **90,483**
  Lakenheath, Suffolk, **107**
  Lewes, Sussex, **123**
  Reculver, Kent, **567**
  Southbourne, Dorset, **95**
  Taunton, Somerset, **578**
  York, **561**
Enna, Sicily, **176,178**
Etruria, Tuscany, or northern Lazio, **270,528**
Fiesole (Florence), Tuscany, **460**
Florence, Tuscany, **187,529**
'Fondi Lavoro', probably Fondi (Latina), Lazio,
  496
'Foxcote', England, **90,483**
France, **211**
  Tarascon, Provence, **461,482**
Friuli Venezia Giulia. *See* Gorizia
Frosinone, Lazio, **41,127**
Gela, Sicily, **530**
Germany, *See* "Rhineland"
Girgenti, *See* Agrigento, Sicily
Gorizia, Friuli Venezia Giulia, **603**
Gorz, Kustenland, Austria, *See* Gorizia
Greece, **143**
  Athens, **35,259,261,585**
  'Corinth', **169**
  Naxos, **124**
  Olympia, **395,467,764**
Grosseto, Maremma di Toscana, Tuscany, **502**
Hungary, *See* Poszory, Semlin
Italy, **42,44,87,138,139,140,153,336,445,446,
  589,593**
Kosice, Slovakia, **555**

Lake Como, *See* Castiglion de Sago
Lake Trasimeno (Perugia), Umbria, **129,166,
  491**
Lakenheath, Suffolk, England, **107**
Lazio,
  Anagni (Frosinone), **32**
  Bolsena (Viterbo), **780**
  Bomarzo (Viterbo), **799,800**
  Canino (Viterbo), **136**
  Cassino (Frosinone), **457,458,459**
  Corneto (Tarquinia, Viterbo), **5,30,836**
  'Fondi Lavoro', probably Fondi (Latina), **496**
  Frosinone, **41,127**
  Maremma, near Veii (Rome), **631**
  Nemi (Rome), **84,85**
  Poli (Rome), **76**
  Palestrina (Rome) *See* Praeneste
  Praeneste (Rome), **519,786,787**
  River Tiber, near Rome, **228**
  Rome, **18,236,245,253,269,308,311,313,315,
    316,323,832**
  Tarquinia (Viterbo), **726**
  Viterbo, **437**
  Vulci (Viterbo), **811**
Lewes, Sussex, England, **123**
Liguria
  Sarzana (La Spezia), **479**
Little St. Bernard (Aosta), Val d'Aosta, **835**
Locri (Reggio Calabria), Calabria, **742,743,744**
Lodi (Milan), Lombardy, **82,83**
Lombardy
  Brescia, **19**
  Calvatone (Cremona), **14**
  Castiglion de Sago, Lake Como, **517**
  Lodi (Milan), **82,83**
  River Ticino, near Milan, **145**
  Sesto Calende (Varese), **828**
Magliano (L'Aquila), Abruzzo, **79,160**
Magna Graecia, southern Italy, **165**
Marche
  Ancona, **100**
Maremma di Toscana' (Siena), Tuscany, **469**
Maremma, near Veii (Rome), Lazio, **631**
Massica' (probably Marsica, L'Aquila),
  Abruzzo, **135,159,177,201,348,404,408,
  419,779**
Metaponto (Matera), Basilicata, **416**
Mineo (Catania), Sicily, **172,246,438,439**
Naples, Campania, **2,137,220,358,359,361,363,
  397, 403,417,424,426,500,515,617,747,
  756,823**
Naxos, Greece, **124**
Nemi (Rome), Lazio, **84,85**
Nola (Naples), Campania, **71,327**
Olympia, Greece, **395,467,764**
Orvieto, Umbria, **506,556,575,782**
Osor, Island of Cres, Croatia, **81**
Paestum (Salerno), Campania, **341**
Palermo, Sicily, **77,93**
Palestrina (Rome), Lazio, *See* 'Praeneste'
Paternò (Catania), Sicily, **158,238**
Perugia, Umbria, **134,224,252,568,808,834**
Peschiera, Boccatura del Mincio (Verona),
  Veneto, **80,101,102,120,122**
Poli (Rome), Lazio, **76**

Index of Donors and Collectors

Map 1 Italian provenances and alleged provenances of the Copper Age artefacts indicated by their catalogue numbers. (© Fabio Parenti)

Map 2 Italian provenances and alleged provenances of the Early Bronze Age artefacts indicated by their catalogue numbers.
(© Fabio Parenti)

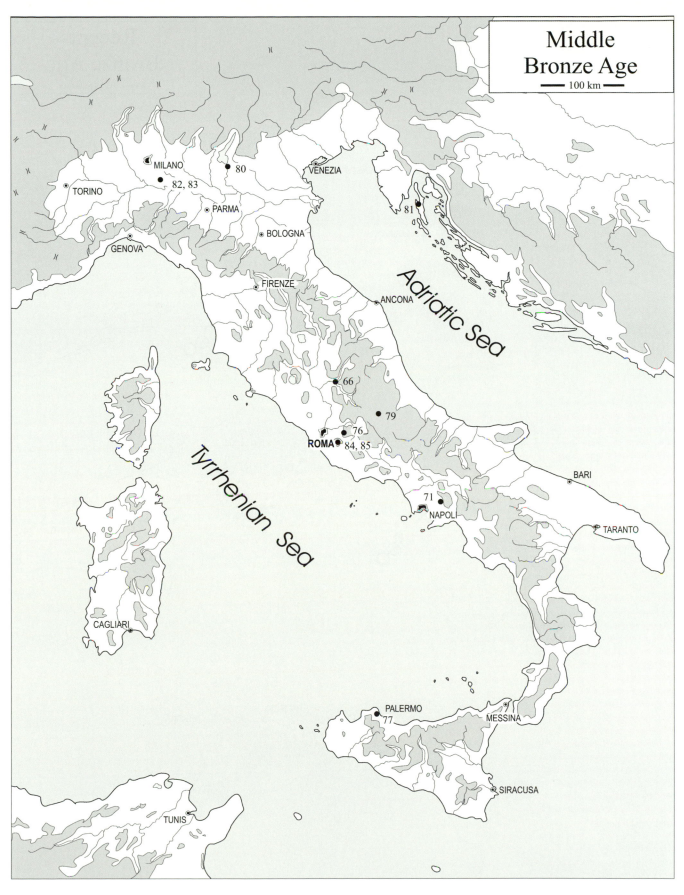

Map 3   Italian provenances and alleged provenances of the Middle Bronze Age artefacts indicated by their catalogue numbers. (© Fabio Parenti)

Map 4 Italian provenances and alleged provenances of the Recent Bronze Age artefacts indicated by their catalogue numbers.
(© Fabio Parenti)

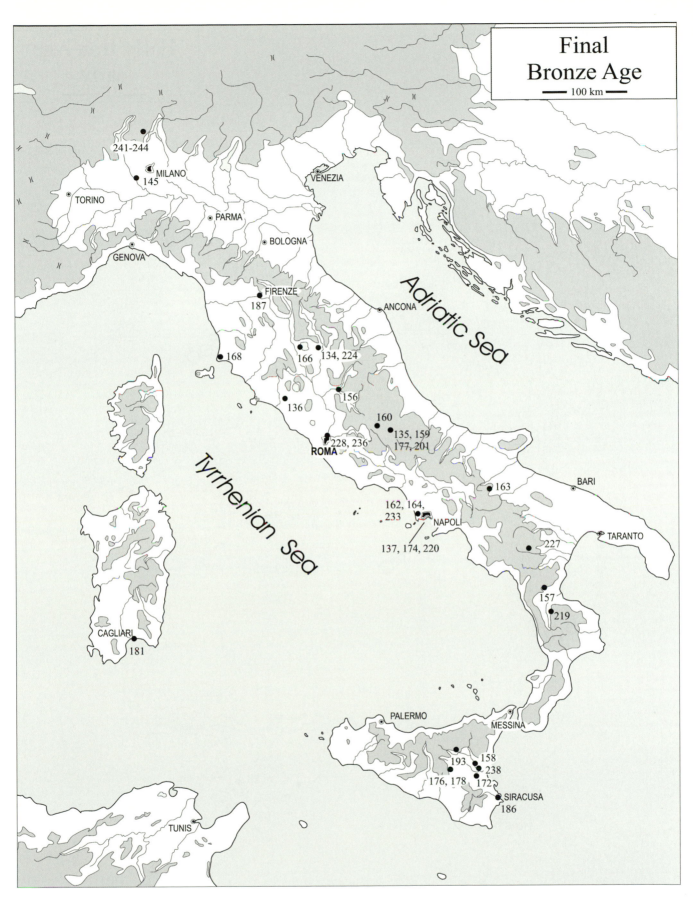

Map 5   Italian provenances and alleged provenances of the Final Bronze Age artefacts indicated by their catalogue numbers.
(© Fabio Parenti)

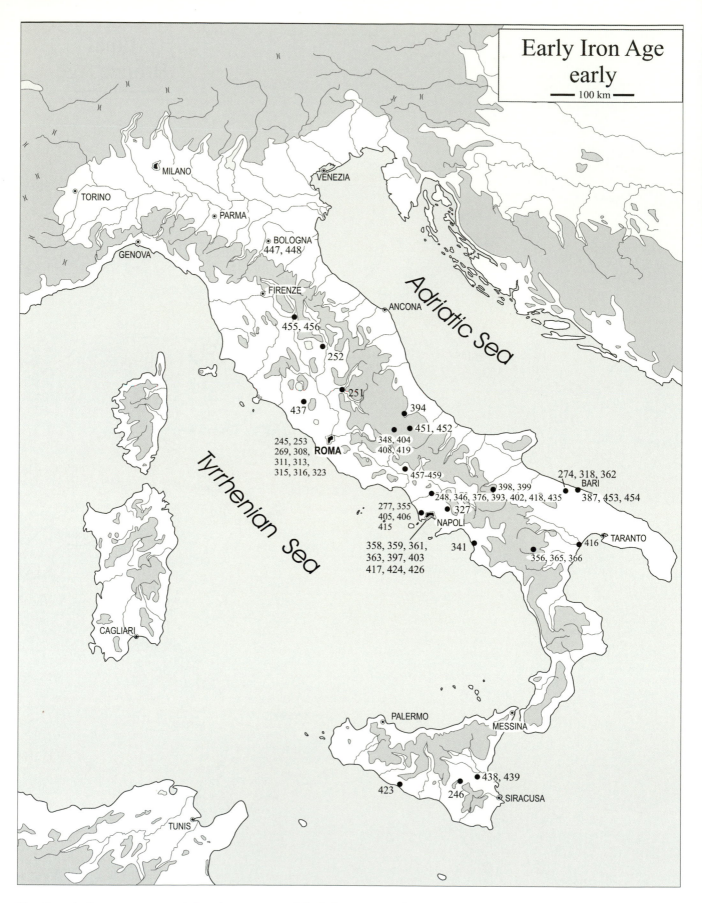

Map 6   Italian provenances and alleged provenances of the Early Iron Age, early, artefacts indicated by their catalogue numbers.
(© Fabio Parenti)

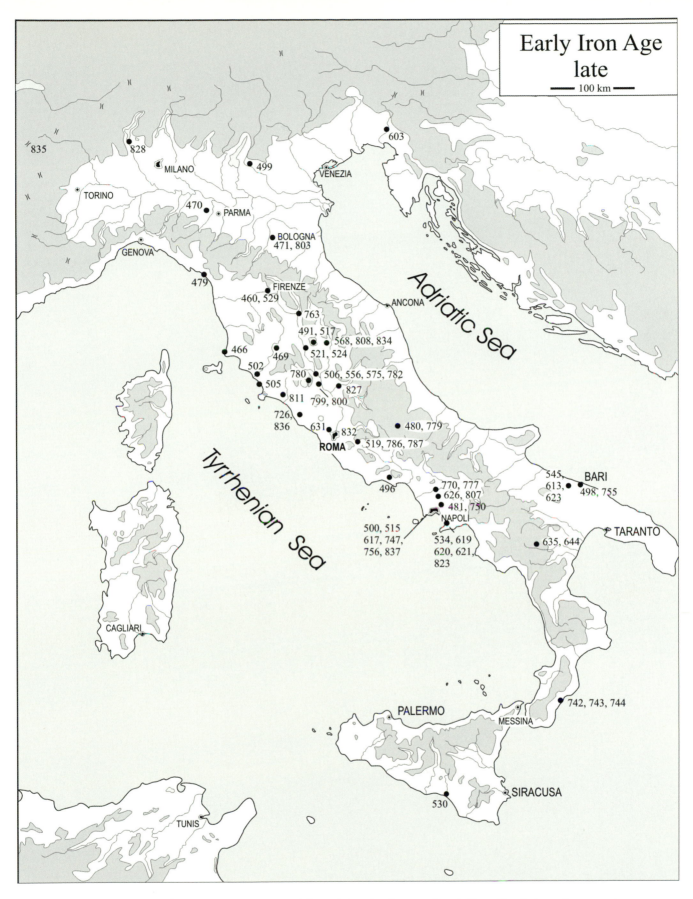

Map 7 — Italian provenances and alleged provenances of the Early Iron Age, late, artefacts indicated by their catalogue numbers.
(© Fabio Parenti)